Game Development and Simulation with Unreal Technology

T0138624

Game Development
and Simulation with
Unreal Technology

By
Alireza Tavakkoli

CRC Press
Taylor & Francis Group
Boca Raton London New York

CRC Press is an imprint of the
Taylor & Francis Group, an **informa** business

CRC Press
Taylor & Francis Group
6000 Broken Sound Parkway NW, Suite 300
Boca Raton, FL 33487-2742

Printed on acid-free paper
Version Date: 20181109

International Standard Book Number-13: 978-1-138-09219-8 (Paperback)
International Standard Book Number-13: 978-1-138-09220-4 (Hardback)

Library of Congress Cataloging-in-Publication Data

Names: Tavakkoli, Alireza, author.
Title: Game development and simulation with Unreal technology/Alireza Tavakkoli.
Description: Second edition. | Boca Raton : Taylor & Francis, CRC Press, 2018.|
Includes bibliographical references.
Identifiers: LCCN 2018023413| ISBN 9781138092198 (pbk. : alk. paper) |
ISBN 9781138092204 (hardback : alk. paper)
Subjects: LCSH: Computer games--Programming. | UnrealScript (Computer program language)
Classification: LCC QA76.76.C672 T38 2018 | DDC 794.8/1525--dc23
LC record available at https://lccn.loc.gov/2018023413

Visit the Taylor & Francis Web site at
http://www.taylorandfrancis.com

and the CRC Press Web site at
http://www.crcpress.com

Dedication

This book is dedicated to my family, whose unconditional love and support has helped me through my academic and professional endeavors.

Contents

SECTION I   Unreal Technology Basics: Introductory Development Techniques

SECTION II   Making Game Worlds Stand Out: Intermediate Development Concepts

SECTION III   Example Games: Advanced Game Development Concepts

Preface

U NREAL Engine is a complete suite of tools developed by Epic Games, Inc., for game development, simulation, and visualization. The Unreal technology has been one of the most widely used game engines in the game development industry, real-time film, and visualization, thanks to its powerful components including the graphics rendering engine, animation and physics engine, Cascade Particle System, and many more state-of-the-art technologies.

A HISTORY OF UNREAL TECHNOLOGY

Established in 1991, Epic Games, Inc., has been a pioneer in cutting-edge gaming technologies with their trademark Unreal Engine game engine. The Engine was used in Epic Games' blockbuster "Unreal" – released in 1998. Unreal had an incredible set of modular pieces sewn together behind the scenes of the Unreal game that made amazing computer generated graphics, vast outdoor environments, and even Artificial Intelligence possible.

Unreal technology also had another amazing component to it that gave gamers, who were interested in doing a little programming, a taste of what they can achieve by modifying existing games. UnrealScript, a programming language similar to C/C++, was the tool that gave mod makers the ability to interact with the engine and make their own gameplay.

In response to the great reception of the Unreal Engine, Epic Games launched the Unreal Developer Network (UDN). The UDN was a bustling online hub for Unreal Engine users, programmers, and developers, to find up-to-date information and documentation about different features of the game engine and step-by-step tutorials on utilizing this engine to create projects ranging from level design to multiplayer networked games.

By 2006, Epic Games created Unreal Engine 3, one of the most advanced game engines in the world, and the technology behind blockbuster games such as Gears of War (2006), Unreal Tournament III (2007), Gears of War 2 (2008), and of course Borderlands 2 (2012) and XCOM:Enemy Unknown (2012). Epic games also made the technology behind Unreal Engine 3 available to independent developers and students for free, in the form of Unreal Development Kit (UDK). UDK included all of the Unreal Engine 3's features and components except the engine source code in C++, which was only available to Unreal Engine 3 licensees. However, UDK developers still had access to the UnrealScript and were able to develop games and content similar to what was achievable by the full Unreal Engine 3.

UNREAL ENGINE 4

As game developers created fantastic games with the amazing and powerful Unreal Engine 3 and UDK, the good folks at Epic Games didn't stop. In April 2014, Epic Games released yet another masterpiece – the Unreal Engine 4 and the subject of this book. The engine is a complete suite of game development tools which enable game developers to create a variety of different games from 2D side scroller and mobile games to high-end visualization, films, and even simulation content.

Epic Games has also pioneered a drastically different licensing model for the Unreal Engine 4, which brings this amazing technology to all game developers, from top-notch studios to Indie developers, and even to students. The Unreal Engine 4 is licensed with a subscription model. Developers may obtain the license at an incredibly affordable monthly subscription of $19 + 5\%$ of gross revenue.[1] Moreover, Epic Game's commitment to support students and schools has made Unreal Engine 4 available to colleges and universities free of charge for academic and educational purposes and for providing students with free licenses.

The license gives access to all features of Unreal Engine 4, including the entire engine's source code in C++, UE4's community network, documentation, and the Unreal Marketplace. This new model of access as well as Epic's history of bringing developers together as a community will make Unreal Engine one of the most prevalent game development technologies for years to come.

WHAT IS COVERED IN THIS BOOK?

As the name suggests, this book is about Unreal technology and its use in developing games and other simulation content. The focus of this book is on the latest version of the Unreal Engine, Unreal Engine 4 (UE4). UE4 is comprised of several advanced tools and technologies. These technologies control many aspects of games; and because of their immense power may be utilized in other areas such as visualization, simulation, and even virtual reality.

UE4 includes an advanced graphic rendering engine which is built on a new shading/rendering model called Physically Based Shading. Other fascinating components of UE4 include the Cascade Particle Editing system, Physics and Animation engines, Artificial Intelligence, and much more. Because of the sheer number of the tools and components that make up the fabric of UE4, it is quite difficult to cover all of it in one book.

In this book, we will cover Unreal Engine components that are quite fundamental in game development and will learn about the following features in UE4:

Material Pipeline

UE4 has introduced a brand new material pipeline. The new materials in UE4 are called Physically Based Materials. This new rendering mechanism makes the cre-

---

[1]For information about details, please refer to the Unreal Engine 4's End User License Agreement (EULA) at Unreal Engine Website.

ation of materials in UE4 quite intuitive, since the traditional material features such as diffuse, specular, and ambient components are replaced by physical features such as base color, roughness, metallic, etc.

We will cover UE4's materials and material pipeline in two chapters:

Chapter 4: Introduces you to UE4's new material pipeline and covers a great portion of this new rendering tool. There are step-by-step tutorials designed to give you hands-on experience with creating materials in UE4 to achieve quite realistic imagery and great visuals.

Chapter 5: Gives you an introduction to more advanced tools and features in the UE4's new material pipeline, covering features such as new shading models, layered materials, and material instancing.

Blueprint Scripting System

Blueprint visual scripting tool is another brand new feature introduced in UE4. It combines the Kismet's[2] ease of use with the flexibility and power of UnrealScript.[3] There is more to the Blueprint Scripting tool than just combining the best of these two worlds! Blueprints are actually pieces of code, and as such are incredibly modular and powerful. Gone are the days of having to script each aspect of your game into an intertwined network of Kismet sequences and many lines of UnrealScript code. You can create blueprint assets from almost anything in UE4, and use them anywhere you wish in UE4, even in other UE4 projects!

In this book we will cover blueprints in two chapters:

Chapter 3: Introduces you to UE4's new Blueprint system and gives you an overview of what can be achieved with this powerful component of Unreal Engine 4. It has been said of the UE4 Blueprints that a group of artists can create a fully functional game without touching a single line of code. In fact Blueprints are so powerful that you can create multiplayer games with them without the need to program in the engine's native language (C++). This power is thanks to the fact that blueprints are essentially code, wrapped in efficient visual modules for non-programmers to implement logic.

Chapter 8: Gets you even deeper into programming with UE4 Blueprints, introducing concepts such as casting, blueprint communications, event dispatchers, and so on. This chapter guides you through building a game with a simple HUD system, Save/Load game features, and a scoreboard to keep track of players' highest scores.

---

[2]Kismet was the Visual Scripting tool in Unreal Engine 3.

[3]UnrealScript was a code-based scripting language for UE3.

CASCADE PARTICLE SYSTEMS

Although this component of UE4 seems to have gone through the least amount of change over the Cascade in Unreal Engine 3, it is as powerful as other UE4 components. You can create many amazing visual effects in Cascade including CPU particles, GPU-based particles, Mesh-based particles, and Beam and Ribbon particles. Cascade works quite closely with your other engine components including the Blueprint system and UE4 Materials to unleash its power in creating astonishing effects.

We cover the Cascade Particle system in one of the chapters in this book:

Chapter 6: Introduces you to UE4's Cascade Particle Editing system. In this chapter we cover the basics of creating particle effect in Cascade. Several step-by-step tutorials are designed to give you hands-on experience with particle systems and visual effects in Cascade. You will learn to create sparks, snow, rain, and fire. By combining these effects, you should be able to create many more complicated and astounding visual effects in Cascade.

Landscapes

Another new feature introduced in Unreal Engine 4, Landscapes are equivalent to Terrains in Unreal Engine 3. The new Landscape editing tool in Unreal Engine 4 is quite powerful and allows for layering materials into landscape layers to seamlessly blend different landscape features such as grass, sand, snow, rock, and so on. Moreover, landscape materials can be designed in the UE4's Material Editor to utilize fading, which in turn can work with the foliage instancing and clustering features of the landscape system. This enables the engine to efficiently and smoothly fade foliage actors in and out of view based on their distance to the camera for improved performance.

Another new feature in UE4's landscape system is the introduction of spline tools. Splines are two-dimensional actors that can represent linear features in your landscape such as rivers, roads, trails, etc. You can assign static meshes to the landscape splines to easily implement such linear features in your landscape. Moreover, landscape splines have the ability to interact with your landscape geometry to deform the shape of the landscape to their path. This feature will be a great timesaver when you are working with vast outdoor environments.

Landscapes and Landscape tools are covered in one of the chapters in this book:

Chapter 7: Introduces you to UE4's Landscapes and Landscape Editing system. In this chapter we cover all aspects of creating vast outdoor environments. Several step-by-step tutorials are designed to give you hands-on experience with Landscapes, starting from landscape creation and sculpting, to instancing and clustering, to landscape splines.

Project Templates

To showcase the power and flexibility of UE4, the engine comes with a large number of pre-built game templates for the developers to adopt. These templates include traditional games you would expect from Unreal Engine such as First Person Shooters and Third Person Shooters, to 2D mobile games, Side Scrollers, and even a Puzzle game template.

We will cover the project templates in one of the chapters in this book:

> **Chapter 1:** Introduces you to the game templates available in UE4. We will cover some of the most widely used ones and give you an overview of what features are built in, and how you can utilize these templates in your own games. It will save you a tremendous amount of time to start your game from one of the templates on which your game mechanics are built and work your way up to modifying the template to suit your needs.

HOW IS THE BOOK STRUCTURED?

The book is structured in three sections. Section 1 covers the basics of game development in Unreal Engine 4. Section 2 delves deeper into the tools and techniques available in UE4 for the creation of complex visual features. Finally, Section 3 presents more advanced features in UE4 and walks you through developing two games, a first person shooter with a basic HUD system and scoreboard, and a top-down shooter with enemy bots whose behavior is controlled by Artificial Intelligence.

SECTION I – UNREAL TECHNOLOGY BASICS: INTRODUCTORY DEVELOPMENT TECHNIQUES

We will start with giving you an overview of the UE4 project templates and the main features that each provides in Chapter 1. Chapter 2 will then present a quick tour of UE4 while going over different stages of level design, starting from the brush phase all the way to the polish phase – all done in UE4. We will start looking at the Unreal Engine Blueprint Visual Scripting tools in Chapter 3, while Chapter 4 will give you a thorough experience with the new Material pipeline in UE4.

SECTION II – MAKING GAME WORLDS STAND OUT: INTERMEDIATE DEVELOPMENT CONCEPTS

This section starts from where the previous section left off – i.e., Unreal Materials. Chapter 5 presents advanced topics in the new UE4 material pipeline, including layered materials, different shading models, and so on. These concepts will tie in when you are introduced to UE4's Cascade and Particle Systems in Chapter 6. Chapter 7 will complete your tour of visual components of UE4 by introducing you to the new Landscape tools. You will also learn to create advanced materials and other visual features such as water and post process effects in this chapter.

SECTION III – EXAMPLE GAMES: ADVANCED DEVELOPMENT CONCEPTS

Finally, the two chapters in this section complete your tour of Unreal Engine 4 in this book. Both of these chapters are designed to walk you through building your own games with UE4. Chapter 8 gives you an advanced coverage of Blueprint systems in UE4. In this chapter you will start off from a First Person Template project and build a game with a simple HUD system with the ability to keep track of your score, saving and loading games, and a scoreboard. All of these components will showcase the amazing power of UE4's blueprints and blueprint communications. In Chapter 9, on the other hand, you will build a top-down shooter game from scratch. You will learn how to utilize Blueprints to create your own game mode, player controller, character, enemy, and projectile classes. You will also learn how to incorporate a simple Artificial Intelligence in your game.

WHY IS THIS BOOK NECESSARY?

Epic Games, Inc., has made an incredibly powerful game engine. The team also has a great deal of documentation and tutorials online while the UE4's developers community has been producing a lot of content and tools ever since UE4 was released. Such vast amount of available online resources for such a new game engine has made it clear to me that a single resource would be quite helpful in giving a quick foothold to newcomers to the world of Unreal Engine. Moreover, such a resource will be a great asset for educators who wish to utilize the Unreal Engine 4 in their curriculum in level design and game engine technologies. It is my hope that this book will become a useful resource for UE4 educators, students, and developers.

COMPANION WEBSITE

The Unreal Engine 4 is quite a new game engine, having been released in April 2014. However, as of the writing of this book, even in less than a year, the engine is now up to UE4.6, with version 4.7 preview 8 available to subscribers. While writing this book, I tried to stay away from the features that were likely to go through major revisions. However, in order to provide the readers of this book with the most up-to-date resources, I am maintaining a companion website with tutorial changes, files and assets and even new tools and tutorials. Please feel free to visit the website at: http://www.RVRLAB.com/UE4Book/ for up-to-date information, files, and even additional tutorials that complement this book.

WHERE CAN I GET UNREAL ENGINE 4?

Getting an incredibly powerful game engine with the entire engine's source code has never been so easy and affordable. All you need to do is to go to the Unreal Engine's website at: https://www.unrealengine.com/, register an account, subscribe for a license, and download your copy of Unreal Engine. If you are a student you may be eligible to get a free subscription through your college or university. You can get access to the GitHub Student Developer Pack from the Unreal Education page at: `https://www.unrealengine.com/education`. If you are an educator or an administrator in an academic program who wishes to use Unreal Engine 4 in your curriculum or for research, you may visit the Unreal Education page to contact the Unreal Engine's Education team and register your school or program.

> Now, without further ado, let's get started with Unreal Engine 4.

Contributors

Andrew Morales: Andrew contributed to the development of chapter contents for Chapter 1: Unreal Project Templates, Chapter 3: Blueprints in Unreal Engine, and Chapter 8: Advanced Blueprint Concepts. He designed, developed, and tested the tutorials presented in these chapters.

Jeff Cavazos: Jeff designed the Top-Down game and its accompanying tutorials in Chapter 9.

Thomas Brantley: Thomas contributed to the first two tutorials of Chapter 4: Materials in Unreal Engine.

Isaac Elenbaas: Isaac contributed in updating the contents to the latest version of the Unreal Engine.

Acknowledgments

Epic Games has always played a significant role in the educational and academic arena. Unreal Engine's Educational portal and generously free academic licensing makes Unreal Engine an important tool for faculty to integrate the technology into the curriculum, and provides students with a powerful technology to learn game development. This book would not have been possible without Epic Game's support for education and their dedication to academia.

In this book there are several tutorials that are designed, implemented, and tested by my former and current students, Andrew Morales, Thomas Brantley, Jeff Cavazos, and Isaac Elenbaas. I would like to acknowledge the countless hours they have put into creating these enjoyable and educational hands-on activities.

Section I

Unreal Technology Basics: Introductory Development Techniques

1 Setting Up Unreal Project Templates

1.1 INTRODUCTION

IN this chapter we will go over a new, and unique, feature in Unreal Engine 4. Upon creating a new project in Unreal Engine 4, the engine gives us a choice of what template to use. Unreal Engine project templates will automatically create the basic functionality required for that template's gameplay. These templates will help rapidly prototype your gameplay.

For example, a first person template, will create the game mode, player controller and user input/interaction models, as well as setting up your first person camera and animation assets. The choice of templates are quite diverse, which gives game developers using Unreal Engine 4 the ability to design games from 2D side scrollers, to third person shooters, tabletop card games, even to racing games.

1.2 UNREAL PROJECT TYPES

There are two types of unreal game projects you can create, i.e., Blueprint and C++ Code. You do not need any additional developer tools to create and develop Blueprint projects. However, if you wish to use the C++ Code projects, you will need to have downloaded and built the Unreal Engine 4's source code. You will also need to have access to Microsoft Visual Studio 2013 (either the free express edition or other professional/ultimate editions).

Blueprint projects use the UE4's new visual scripting tools called Blueprints. In a sense, blueprint scripting is similar to the pervious versions of Unreal Engine (UE3 or UDK) visual scripting tool called Kismet. However, Blueprints are drastically more powerful than Kismet scripts. In fact, blueprints are so powerful that you can even create multiplayer games without having to write code in C++.

On the other hand, your Unreal Engine 4 subscription comes with full access to the entire engine's source code in C++. Having the source of the engine, developers can create C++ Code projects. Once you create a code project, you will be able to open your project in Microsoft Visual Studio 2013 to write your game functionality in C++. This will give you a tremendous amount of control and power over the design, development, and programming functionality of your project. You will also have the ability to debug your code in Unreal Editor, design your level and game assets in the editor and build and compile your game both in Visual Studio, and in certain scenarios in the Unreal Editor.

1.3 CREATING BLANK PROJECTS AND MIGRATING CONTENTS

In this section we will see how you can migrate contents from one project into another. One of the simplest ways to set up a project and fill it with content is to create a project template, include the Unreal Engine's starter contents in the project, and then migrate contents from another project into it.

TUTORIAL 1.1   Creating a Project and Migrating Contents

CREATE A BLANK PROJECT

FIGURE 1.1: Creating a New Project.

In this tutorial we will set up an empty project and migrate contents of the **Demo Room** from the Unreal Engine's `Example Contents` project into it.

The first thing to do is to create a project to which we will add the **Demo Room**. Launch the Unreal Editor and create a **Blank** project. Give your project a name such as "MyNewGameProject." Leave the **Include starter content** check box checked to have access to starter contents (see Figure 1.1).

After you have created this blank project, you will close the project and open the `Content Examples` projects. There is a folder in this project that contains the contents of a **Demo Room**.

MIGRATING CONTENT FROM UNREAL PROJECTS

In this section we will migrate the **Demo Room** contents from the **Content Example** project into our own project to be able to set up a nice environment to visualize the effects we create.

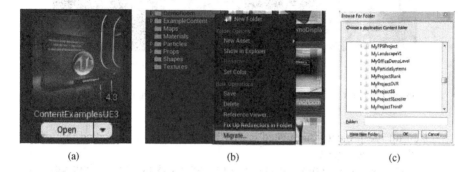

(a) (b) (c)

FIGURE 1.2: (a) Opening the Content Examples. (b) Migrating the Demo Room. (c) Choosing the Destination for Demo Room in Our MyParticleSystems Project.

1. If you haven't downloaded the **Content Examples** from the Unreal Marketplace, use the Unreal Engine Launcher to download the Content Examples. This item comes with your Unreal Engine 4 subscription and contains several useful maps and examples for you to explore and use in your projects free of charge.
2. Open the **Content Examples** project from the Unreal Engine Launcher (Figure 1.2(a)).
3. In the **Content Browser** of the **Content Examples** project, right-click on the Demo Room Folder, and choose **Migrate** (Figure 1.2(b)).
4. The `Asset Report` window pops open, informing you which assets within the Demo Room folder will be exported to a new location. These assets include Textures, Blueprints, Materials, Meshes, etc. Select **OK** to proceed.
5. From the windows explorer window that opens, navigate to the location of the "MyNewGameProject" project you created earlier in this tutorial (Figure 1.2(c)). Select the `Content` subfolder of your project. Depending on how your Unreal Engine is set up, this location should be in `My Documents/Unreal Projects/MyNewGameProject/Content` folder.
6. Close the Contents Example project.

SETTING UP YOUR DEMO ROOM

Now we will add a new map to our project to host a display room.

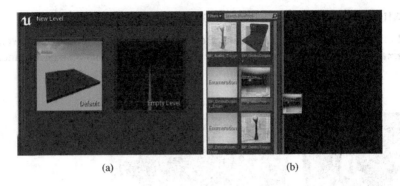

                (a)   (b)

FIGURE 1.3: (a) Creating an Empty Level. (b) Adding the Demo Room to the Level.

1. Open up the project you created earlier in page 4 (earlier, I called this project "MyNewGameProject").
2. Now, let's add a new empty level to this project. Click on **File->New Level** and choose `Empty Level` (Figure 1.3(a)).
3. Go to the **DemoRoom/BluePrint** folder by double clicking on **DemoRoom** folder and then on **BluePrint** folder.
4. Drag the **BP_DemoRoom** blueprint into your level (Figure 1.3(b)).
5. Wait for the Unreal Engine to compile the shaders and build the materials.
6. Click on **Build** from the Unreal toolbar to build the lighting (this may take a few minutes depending on your machine).

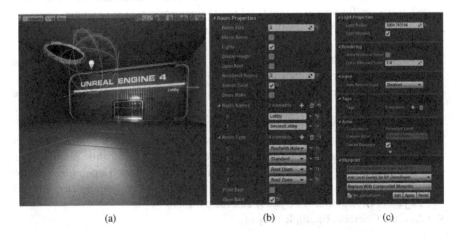

                (a)   (b)   (c)

FIGURE 1.4: (a) Demo Room. (b) Demo Room Properties. (c) Additional Room Properties.

7. Now that you have the **Demo Room** created, you can explore its options. We will be using this room throughout this book to deploy the contents and materials we create (Figure 1.4).

8. Table 1.1 explains how each room property value affects the **Demo Room**. Take your time to play with different settings to get familiar with the room.
9. Save your level in the Maps folder of your Unreal project and give it a name such as DisplayRoomLevel.

TABLE 1.1

Description of Basic Properties of the Demo Room Template.

Room Property	Type	Description
Room Size	Integer	Defines the number of sections in the room
Mirror Room	Boolean	If checked, mirrors the room along the cross section
Lights	Boolean	If unchecked, removes all lights from the room
Double Height	Boolean	If checked, increases the height of the room
Open Roof	Boolean	If unchecked, removes the roof from the room
Number of Rooms	Integer	Specifies the number of rooms in the environment
Switch Color	Boolean	Changes the room color template
Glass Walls	Boolean	Toggles the glass walls on and off
Front Door	Boolean	If checked, places a door mesh at the front of the room
Open Back	Boolean	If unchecked, removes the back wall of the room
Room Names	Element Array	You can add names to the room by pressing the (+) sign
Room Type†	Standard	This option is the standard room option
	Roof With Hole	This option places a vent hole at the section of roof
	Open Roof	This option removes the roof from the section of room

†: Pressing the (+) icon allows you to add Room Types to each section of the room. For example, for a room with size 4, you may press the (+) icon four times, and assign different room types to each section.

OVERVIEW AND SETTING UP A DISPLAY

Now that we have our level created and the Demo Room added to our level, we will set up a couple of display items to showcase our creations.

Just like the **Demo Room** object, the **Display Item** is a Blueprint. This means that this object is a class with meshes, components, and other properties, as well as functionalities that can be utilized to configure it and to make it interact with the world and players. Blueprints are very important components of the Unreal Engine 4. In fact, the concept of Blueprints is the major item introduced with the release of the Unreal Engine 4. We will dedicate two entire chapters to Blueprints in this book.

To create a display item, perform the following steps:

1. Now that we have the demo room set up, let's add a display. Navigate to the BluePrint folder of the DemoRoom folder of your project. Locate the **BP_DemoDisplay** blueprint into the demo room (Figure 1.5(a)).

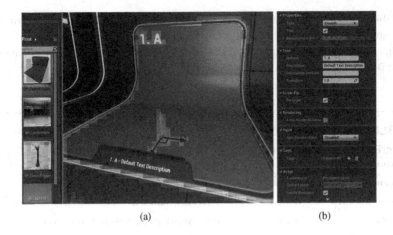

(a)   (b)

FIGURE 1.5: Adding A Demo Display Item to the Demo Room in the Map. (a) The Demo Display Item. (b) The Display Properties.

TABLE 1.2
Description of Display Item Properties.

Category	Property	Description/ Values
Properties	Type	Round, SquareL, RoomL, DescriptionOnly, SquareLFlatWall
	Text	If Checked, Toggles display item text description
	Back Color	Changes the color of the display item walls
Text	Number	This text will show as label of the display item
	Description	This text will show as the title of the display item
	Desc. 2nd Line	Subtitle of the display item
	Transform	Scales the title of the display item

2. Table 1.2 shows some of the important properties of the Display Item that can be configured within its details panel.
3. From the Properties of the Demo Display make the following changes:
    a. **Number: 1-A.**
    b. **Description: Pick up Item from Here...**
    c. **Type: Round**
4. Save your progress.

ADDING INTERACTIONS TO THE DEMO ROOM LEVEL

Now that we have the Display Item added, let's add a **Player Start** actor to the level. This is an Unreal Actor which makes the player initiate at its location whenever the level is run, e.g., when you press the **Play** button on the Unreal Editor toolbar or launch the game.

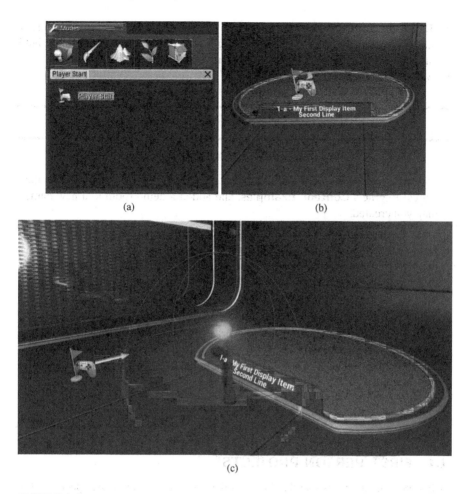

(a)

(b)

(c)

FIGURE 1.6: (a) Search for Player Start. (b) Actor Placed Properly. (c). Place Demo Trigger.

1. In the search box of the **Modes** panel (Figure 1.6(a)) type `Player Start`. This will search for the Player Start actor from the Unreal Engine classes. Note that this search is context-sensitive and after typing a few letters it will refine the search filters to narrow down the selections.
2. Drag a copy of the **Player Start** actor to create a `Player Start` object in the level (Figure 1.6(a)).
3. Use the **Move** and **Rotate** gizmos to place and orient the **Player Start** actor in front of the Display Item (Figure 1.6(b)). Notice that the blue arrow coming out of the Player Start actor is the direction the player will face when the game starts.
4. Now, you should still be in the `Blueprints` folder of the `Demo Room` in the content browser. Drag a copy of `BP_DemoTrigger` class in the level and place it between the **Player Start** actor and the **Demo Display** item (Figure 1.6(c)).

5. **Ready for Your Reward?** Go ahead! Play the level and see what getting close to, and walking away from, the **Demo Trigger** item does. It's not really fancy, but it should hopefully help you want to learn more about this engine.

6. Save your project and all the levels.

What Happened in TUTORIAL 1.1...

You just set up a blank project, migrated the **Demo Room** contents from the Unreal Engine's **Content Examples**, and added a demo room to a new game map you created.

Once the Demo Room blueprint was added to the scene, we populated it with Demo Trigger actors and a Player Start actor. Player Start actor will ensure that the player will spawn at a specific location and be oriented in a specific direction every time the game starts.

The Demo Trigger is a Blueprint object which contains interactions. It has a sphere of intersection which will trigger events if player's collision bounds overlap with it. By default, if a player is overlapping the trigger collision sphere, it will toggle the material of its button to a red material. Once the player steps away from the trigger so that their collision boundaries are not overlapping, the trigger button material toggles back to a green material.

Now it's your turn to do some more exercises with blank project templates and the demo room.

1.4 FIRST PERSON PROJECTS

A first person camera is one that is controlled from a first person perspective. Basically, the player experiences the game's world through the eyes of the character, and any input the game receives will control the character/camera directly.

In this section, we will go through and explain the contents of the first person blueprint as well as go over the basics of how it works.

TUTORIAL 1.2   Creating a Project Based on First Person Blueprint

CREATE AN FPS PROJECT

The first thing we need to do is to create a new project using the first person blueprint template. The templates are located in the same place where we created a blank project in a previous section. When the editor is launched, select New Project at the top and scroll down to Blueprint First Person. Type a

FIGURE 1.7: Creating a New Project Based on FPS Template.

name for the project at the bottom and select Create Project. Checking the box **Include starter content** will bring in the UE4 default assets that were talked about earlier (Figure 1.7).

Once the project is created, Unreal 4 will launch and will load the example map packaged with the template, shown in Figure 1.8(a). This is a simple map with walls and physics enabled boxes used to demonstrate the basics of the template.

If you click **Simulate** from the toolbar (or **Play in Viewport**, **Alt+P**), you will notice that you are in control of a first person character with blue arms and a gun that shoots balls. The functionality that the player gets in this sample comes entirely from the Unreal 4 blueprints.

What Happened in TUTORIAL 1.2...

Let's go ahead and take a look at the **MyCharacter** blueprint that we are controlling in this first person template. You can find it by clicking the **Blueprints** folder in the **Content Browser** pane in the lower left side of the Editor (this location is the default location of the **Content Browser**). If the **Content**

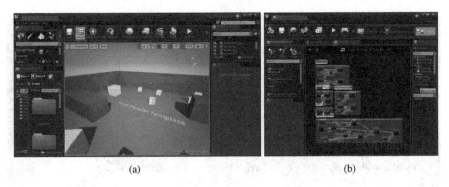

FIGURE 1.8: (a) A View of the Project Based on FPS Template in UE4. (b) The **My Character** Blueprint Network.

Browser pane is not in the lower left side, you can find it by clicking the Window tab in the top left corner and clicking **Content Browser** 1. Once you have found the **MyCharacter** blueprint, you can open it by double-clicking it or by right clicking and selecting **"Open in full editor."** This blueprint is shown in Figure 1.8(b).

Once the blueprint is open in the blueprint editor, we can start looking at the visual script as well as the actual components that make up the default first person character. In Figure 1.8(b), you can see the main event graph for the blueprint, as well as the My Blueprint pane on the left side. The My Blueprint pane will give you access to the Variables, Functions, and Events in the MyCharacter blueprint. The Event Graph contains all of our functionality for the character, including what to do when input is received either from a controller, or a keyboard, as well as the functionality to spawn the projectile when the gun is fired by the player.

If you click on the components tab, you will see the parts that make up the character. This character is made up of a camera, which the player is looking through in-game; a capsule, which is used for the collision; as well as some blue arms, hands, and a gun. The arms, hands, and gun are actually another asset called a skeletal mesh. This is a UE4 asset that contains skeleton components, meshes, and animations for those meshes. This asset is located in the Character folder and is named **HeroFPP**, but don't worry about messing with this asset for now.

This template takes in mouse input, as well as keyboard input to rotate the camera or to move the character in a certain direction when a button is pressed. The node **inputAxis MoveForward**, for example, is attached to Add Movement Input which moves the character in the direction of its own forward vector. Simply put, this input will move the character in the forward direction.

In order to specify what buttons or mouse movements are attached to certain input functionalities, we have to set them in the project settings. This is done for us by default for this particular template. We can view these settings by clicking

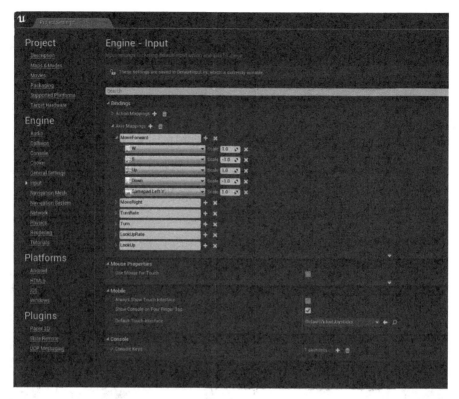

FIGURE 1.9: Input Axis and Action Mappings.

Edit in the top left corner of the editor, and finding Project Settings. This will bring up all the settings available to us for our particular project. Under Engine on the left side, find the Input section and click on it. This brings up all of our default input mapping.

As you can see, Pressing W, or the UP arrow will increase our movement in the positive direction. Pressing S or the DOWN arrow returns a negative value to move us in the negative direction relative to our camera. By calling it MoveForward, we insure we have a node with this name that we can access in the blueprint. You can go through the others to better understand where the input mapping comes from.

If you click on the components tab, you will see the parts that make up the character. This character is made up of a camera, which the player is looking through in-game; a capsule, which is used for the collision; as well as some blue arms, hands, and a gun. The arms, hands, and gun are actually part of another asset called a skeletal mesh. This is a UE4 asset that contains skeleton components, meshes, and animations for those meshes. This asset is located in the Character folder and is named HeroFPP.

You can view this asset but don't worry about completely understanding it for now.

1.5 THIRD PERSON

A third person camera refers to the camera style where you can fully see the character you are controlling. This is often called an over-the-shoulder camera as well. In the next Tutorial we will create a project using the third person template.

TUTORIAL 1.3　**Creating a Project Based on Third Person Blueprint**

CREATE A TPS PROJECT

FIGURE 1.10: Creating a New Third Person Project Template.

To create a new project using the third person template, you need to follow the same steps from the previous section. Launch Unreal 4 and click the **New Project** tab at the top of the window. Click the **Blueprint** tab and locate the **Third Person** icon.

If you want to include the starter content, make sure you leave the **Include Starter Content** setting to migrate the assets into your project. As before, leave the other settings on their default values for now. Give it a name and click Create Project (Figure 1.10).

Once the editor is launched, you will see the example map that is included with the third person blueprint. You should notice at this point that the map is

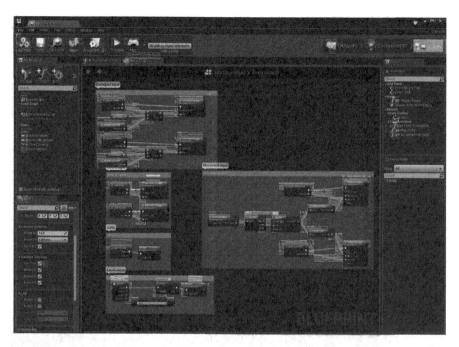

FIGURE 1.11: (a) A View of the Project Based on TPS Template in UE4. (b) The **My Character** Blueprint Network.

not the same as the first person map. There are no physics objects, just a small structure for you to test out the default character provided with this template. The character for the third person template is called **MyCharacter** and can be found by navigating the **Content Browser** to `Blueprints->MyCharacter`.

The event graph contains similar events to the first person template. The movement and input need some extra vector calculations due to the shifted origin of the character. We will explain this later.

What Happened in TUTORIAL 1.3...

At this point, we have successfully created and run a project using the third person template. Let's go through the **MyCharacter** blueprint to better understand the functionality of this template.

If you click on the Components tab, you will see the physical components that make up the `MyCharacter` blueprint (Figure 1.12).

The HeroTPP mesh is a bit more complex than the first person **HeroFPP** mesh. This is due to the fact that we can see the entire character in the camera frame, and it wouldn't make sense to see only a couple of floating arms.

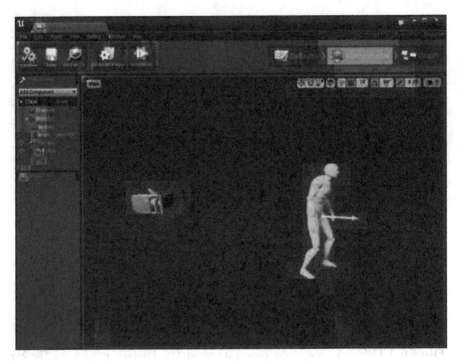

FIGURE 1.12: The Components of **HeroTPP** Blueprint.

The camera is also attached to a component called a **Spring Arm**. If you click on **CameraBoom** in the Components pane on the left side, you will see the details, as well as a red line that shows you the boom itself. The job of the **Camera Boom** (spring arm component) is to keep the camera at the maximum distance possible according to the parameters given. If the camera runs into a wall or another object, the boom will become smaller until it is no longer obstructed.

In the details pane under the Camera tab, you see a variable called **Target Arm Length**. This is the farthest length that we want the camera to be from the character. To further explain how this works, minimize the **MyCharacter** blueprint and click play in the main editor window. When you move the mouse around, the camera moves around the character at a constant distance of 300 units. However, if you use WASD to walk toward a wall or a structure and then try to move the camera around, the camera will move in toward the character as it is blocked by the wall, to prevent the camera from clipping through the wall or structure. This functionality is a very important part of the third person character and one of the main differences between this template and the first person template.

The other noticeable difference is in how the camera rotation happens. Instead of rotating the camera directly, what we want to do is rotate the camera around the character so that the character is always in frame. This is done with a simple setting in the Components section.

If you click on **CameraBoom** and scroll down to the **Camera Settings** section, you will notice that **Use Pawn Control Rotation** is selected. This means that we can rotate the pawn itself when the camera is rotated. This gives us more control of the camera while playing our game. We can rotate the camera boom without updating the character's position by dragging the mouse around. This is possible because **CameraBoom** is a child component of the **CapsuleComponent**. The Spring arm will rotate around the character so that we can keep the character on the screen at all times.

FIGURE 1.13: Creating a New Side Scroller Project Template.

1.6 SIDE SCROLLER

Next, we will talk about the side scroller template (Figure 1.13). A side scroller camera is a type of camera that moves left and right, and views the main character from the side. You don't have a 3D range of movement like you do with the third person camera, but you can make very interesting platforming games as well as action games with a side scrolling camera. In this section we will create a project using the side scroller template.

TUTORIAL 1.4   Creating a Project Based on Side Scroller Blueprint

FIGURE 1.14: A View of the Project Based on Side Scroller Template in UE4. (b) The **My Character** Blueprint network.

CREATE A SIDE SCROLLER PROJECT

To use the side scroller template, we first launch the engine and click the New Project tab. Click the **Blueprint** tab and find the **Side Scroller** template. Give it a name, and click **Create Project** in the lower right corner (Figure 1.14). Remember to leave the **Include starter content** selected to have the UE4 include starter contents into your project.

When the project is launched, you will see the example map that comes with the side scroller template. This map is designed as a platformer test map for you to use the default side scroller character. The map is fairly large, but the character is only able to traverse left and right from the starting position. If you click play, you will notice that movement is only possible on the Y and Z axis and not the X axis.

What Happened in TUTORIAL 1.4...

At this point, we have successfully created a project in UE4 using the side scroller blueprint template. Let's take a closer look at the **MyCharacter** blueprint of this template to better understand what makes it tick.

To view the logic that gives the character movement, we must again look at the **MyCharacter** blueprint. This can be accessed by locating the **Content Browser** in the lower left corner and clicking Blueprints-> MyCharacter. Once the MyCharacter blueprint is open, you will see a very simple event graph for the character (Figure 1.15).

In fact, this event graph only has 3 events in it: InputAxis->MoveRight, InputAction->Jump, and InputTouch. In order to move left, the character is

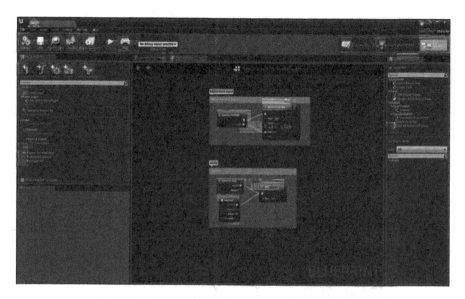

FIGURE 1.15: The **My Character** Blueprint Network.

technically moving in a negative direction relative to a right movement. This means we only need one event for the Y-axis movement. The jump event simply calls the Jump function when the **spacebar** is pressed.

If you click on the components tab in the top right corner, you will see the physical components that make up the side scroller character (Figure 1.16). This character is similar to the third person character except for the camera setup. In this case, the camera is raised slightly higher and is fixed on the character. This means that the camera position and rotation do not change when the character moves.

When the character moves in-game, the camera moves with it at a fixed rotation and distance. The camera is attached to a Spring Arm Component, which allows us to adjust the camera distance and angle relative to the character. For a side scroller, it is unlikely that the camera will collide with a wall and have to spring inward toward the character, but this is still accomplished by this component if need be.

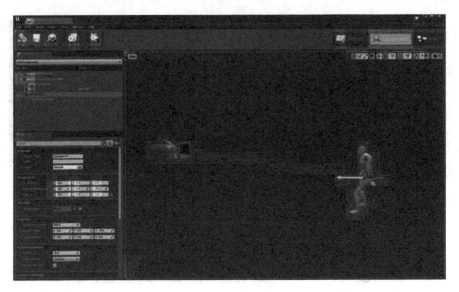

FIGURE 1.16: The Components of **HeroTPP** Side Scroller Blueprint.

1.7 TOP DOWN TEMPLATES

The next template we will go over is the top down template (Figure 1.17). A top down camera is basically described in its title. Your character or environment is viewed from above from a camera that generally has a fixed rotation (although this is not always the case) and a fixed angle. The UE4 top down template has a simple character/camera setup to get you started in the creation of a top down style game. In the next tutorial we will create a project using the top down blueprint template.

TUTORIAL 1.5   Creating a Project Based on Top Down Blueprint

To create a project using the top down blueprint template, simply select the template under the **New Project** tab in the **Unreal Project Browser** window. Select the **Blueprint** tab and find the **Top Down** template icon. Give it a name and select **Create Project**.

After you select Create Project, you will be greeted with the example map packaged in the top down template. Clicking play will allow you to jump into the game and take control of your top down character.

You may notice that the standard keys from the third person and first person templates ('W','A','S','D') don't actually control the character in the top down template. This character is controlled by mouse clicks. By clicking anywhere on the floor of the map, your character will automatically run to the location of the mouse click. Clicking again will change the character's path. By holding

FIGURE 1.17: A View of the Project Based on the Top Down Template in UE4.

the mouse button down, you can even have the path of the character update endlessly and your character will constantly follow the tip of the mouse cursor.

What Happened in TUTORIAL 1.5...

In this tutorial we simply created a project using the top down blueprint template. Let's take a look under the hood of this template to see what's actually going on.

If you followed along with the first person and third person tutorials, you might think that our character functionality will be located inside the **MyCharacter** blueprint. However, the top down template is actually quite a bit different.

The **Components** section for the top down **MyCharacter** blueprint should look similar to the **MyCharacter** blueprint from the third person template. The most noticeable difference is the placement of the camera. This particular camera is positioned to give us a top down view of the character that we will be controlling in the game. The camera is attached to a spring arm but in this case, to have a fixed rotation while the character is walking around in game (see Figure 1.18).

Of course, since the **MyCharacter** blueprint has no functionality in the event graph, we must be getting our movement logic from somewhere else. In this case,

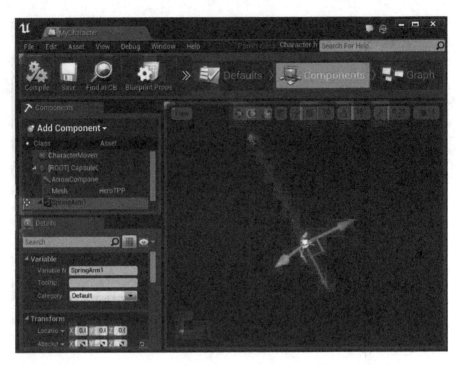

FIGURE 1.18: The Placement of Camera and Character Mesh in the Top Down Template.

we get our movement logic from a blueprint called **MyController**.

Before opening the **MyController** blueprint from the Content Browser, mouse over the icon to view some of its properties. These properties will tell you the path to the particular asset, as well as other useful information. In this case, we can note that the parent class for this blueprint is of type **PlayerController**. By using this as a parent class, we will inherit all the attributes that make up a **PlayerController** into our own class blueprint. In other words, **MyController** is the class blueprint that is giving our character the ability to move around in game.

When the **MyController** Blueprint is opened, go to the graph tab to view our character's functionality (see **Event Graph** tab in Figure 1.19). This may be a little complicated at first glance so let's go over it bit by bit.

The cluster of nodes in Figure 1.19 begins with an **Event Tick** – the red node on the upper left corner of the canvas. **Event Tick** is a function that will fire once every iteration of the core game loop. In every game with real-time graphics, there is a core game loop in which the graphics are rendered over and over again as long as the game is playing. This means the graphics on screen are updated constantly. The speed at which this occurs depends on many different things including the speed of the machine that is running the code. Just know that for every frame rendered on the screen, this event tick function will fire.

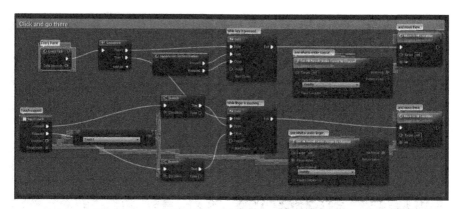

FIGURE 1.19: Controller Event Graph in the Top Down Template in UE4.

After the **Event Tick** is fired, we check for input from a mouse as well as input from a touchscreen, which is generally used for mobile platforms. This is done using a sequence gate. The first sequence must completely finish before the next sequence is called. We move from a sequence gate to another gate function that allows us to open and close the flow based on the input from the mouse.

What this allows us to do is, if the mouse button is pressed down, we can drag the mouse around and constantly update the location of the player. You can also simply click a location and have the character move toward that location. Either way, once the mouse button is released, the gate is closed and the last location sent through will be the character's current location.

Once we pass through the gate, we call a custom function called **Moveto-HitLocation** (see Figure 1.20). We can view this function by clicking it on the left side of the blueprint window, in the My Blueprint tab, under Functions. The **MovetoHitLocation** function will receive a **struct** called **Hit Result. Hit Re-sult** stores information about the current location of the mouse cursor.

The **MovetoHitLocation**'s job is to move the character to the location of the mouse cursor, at the time that the function was called. It also checks to see if the player clicked too close to the pawn to justify movement. This is based on a variable called **MinClickDistance** that was created for this purpose. If the current player location minus the new target location is less than the **MinClick-Distance**, then we do nothing. This enables us to ignore moving the character to locations too close to it.

If we have clicked on a location that is far enough away to warrant movement, then we will call a function called **SimpleMoveToLocation**. This function runs a path finding algorithm to move your character from the previous location to the new location without walking into walls or objects that might block the path.

Path finding algorithms use nodes to find an optimal path around objects. The nodes in this case come from a **Volume** called `NavMeshBoundsVolume1`. You can quickly find this by searching for it in the **Scene Outliner** window in the

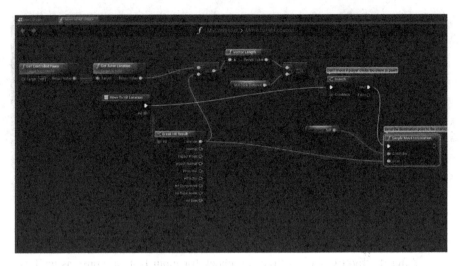

FIGURE 1.20: The Functionality that Moves a Character to a Mouse-Click Location in the Top Down Template.

top right of the main editor (see Figure 1.21). Don't worry too much about this now. Just know that in order for the **SimpleMoveToLocation** function to work properly, we need a **NavMeshBoundsVolume** in place.

1.8 SUMMARY

In this chapter we discussed Unreal Engine 4's project templates. There are two types of Unreal Projects you can create; Unreal Blueprint projects and Unreal Code projects. While blueprint projects utilize the new unreal blueprints as the visual scripting language, unreal code projects utilize C++ programming language. To compile and build code projects you will need to have Microsoft Visual Studio 2013.

Regardless of the project type (either code or blueprint), you will have access to a large number of templates to choose from for your project. These templates range from simple 2D side scroller template to racing (vehicle) templates. This gives developers using unreal engine a tremendous amount of power to rapidly create the basic gameplay dynamics they need for their project with a simple click of a button.

1.9 EXERCISES

Exercise 1. Creating a Customized Room
        a. Create a new map.
        b. Add a new **DemoRoom** to this map.
        c. Set the room up so that it will have the following properties:

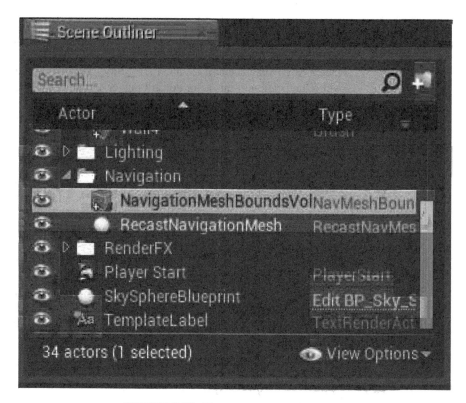

FIGURE 1.21: The Navigation Mesh Volume.

Property	Spec	Description
Room Size	3	An environment with three rooms
Room #1	Name	Lobby
Room #1	Sections	3 (one of each sections)
Room #2	Name	Lab
Room #2	Sections	3 (all sections with holes in room)
Room #3	Name	Yard
Room #3	Sections	All Open Roof

Exercise 2. Setting Up Displays for the Room

a. Bring one `demo display` item for each section in the room created in **Exercise 1.**

b. Give each `demo display` a name that reflects the room where it is located and a description of its purpose.

Exercise 3. Adding Player Start and a Sky Dome

a. Add a **Player Start** actor to the level.

      b. Place and orient the **Player Start** actor such that when the game is run, the player starts from the front of the first room, facing the back of the room.

      c. Place a Sky Dome actor (it is called **BP_Sky_Sphere**) to the level. The location of this actor doesn't matter, but you can drag and drop it anywhere in the map.

      d. Place a directional light to the level. The location of this light doesn't matter, but it would be nice to place it in the *outdoor* room (i.e., room #3).

Exercise 4. Extra Credit: Controlling the Sky Dome!

      a. Assign the **Directional Light** actor to the **Sky Dome** lighting controller. (Hint: Locate the **Sky_Sphere** actor, and use its **Directional Light Actor** property to pick a compatible actor from the scene for it.)

      b. Change the direction of the light and update the **Sky Dome**.(Hint: Use the **Refresh Material** property of the **Sky_Sphere** actor.)

      c. Do you notice any difference? Can you make the environment to be at night time?

2 A Premier on Level Design in Unreal Technology

2.1 INTRODUCTION AND OBJECTIVES

I︎N this chapter we will go through the basic stages of level design to create our first map in Unreal Engine 4. We will not assume any familiarity with any game engine or previous versions of the Unreal Engine. However, it is highly recommended that you go over the basic User Interface of the Unreal Engine 4 to get basic familiarity with the UI and simple object manipulations you can do in the main editor, such as translating, rotating, and scaling objects.

To build our first level, we will start by drawing out its geometry. We will utilize Binary Space Partitioning (BSP) brushes for this purpose. Once the geometry of our level is established, we will utilize materials to enhance its visual look. Next, we will go through our initial mesh pass. In this stage, we will add static meshes to our level. These meshes may be utilized as decorations in the level, as objects with which the player may interact, or even to replace parts of the geometry that are currently created by BSP brushes.

The next step is to create the lighting of our level. We can use directional lights, point light, spotlights, and skylights in this step. This is also the phase in which we can enhance the visual look of our level by adjusting the material/light interactions and shading computations.

Before wrapping up the chapter, we will establish some basic functionality in our level's blueprint. Blueprints are powerful scripting tools that are new to Unreal Engine 4. Each level has a unique Blueprint, called the Level Blueprint. This is where the level-based functionality resides. There is another kind of blueprint in UE4 called a Class Blueprint. The Class Blueprint is a very powerful tool by which you can create a complete encapsulated class with its own components, such as lights, static meshes, triggers, and functionality. We will use the Level Blueprint in this chapter to make sliding door meshes open and close when a player walks up to them or steps away from them.

In the final polish pass, we can introduce particle systems and visual effects to our level – although we will not cover this concept in this chapter.

2.2 ESTABLISHING THE GEOMETRY

One of the first stages of designing a level is to establish your level's geometry. In most cases, if you are using the Unreal Engine, you will accomplish this task by means of brush geometry. In this tutorial we will build the geometry of our level – a two-story building.

> To find updates to this tutorial and updated instructions about its implementation on other UE4 versions please visit the book's companion website at: `http://www.RVRLAB.com/UE4Book/`

TUTORIAL 2.1   Creating a Project and Including Starter Contents

FIGURE 2.1: Creating a Blank Project for Your First Level.

CREATING A FIRST PERSON PROJECT

In this tutorial we will set up an empty project and include the starter contents from the Unreal Engine into it. The first thing to do is to create a project to which we will add the starter content. Launch the Unreal Editor and create a **First Person** project. Give your project a name such as "LevelDesignProject." Leave the **Include starter content** included to have access to starter contents (see Figure 2.1).

1. Open the Unreal Launcher and select the version of the engine you would like to work with.
2. Once the Editor Opens, choose **New Project** (see Figure 2.1).

3. Select the **Blueprint** as your project type, and make sure that the **First Person** is selected.
4. Select your platform (Desktop/Console) and your graphics quality.
5. Make sure you include the starter content (see Figure 2.1).
6. Give your project a name and click **Create Project**.

CREATE A LEVEL WITHIN THE PROJECT

Once the editor opens up after you have created the project, you will see the example map created by Unreal Engine, with some geometry and an actor placed in the map. We will now create a new level and start populating our design process.

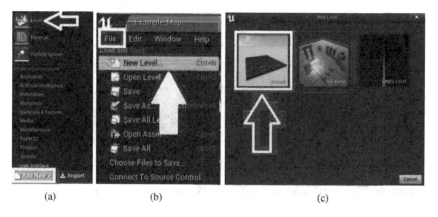

(a)   (b)   (c)

FIGURE 2.2: Adding a New Level to the Project: (a) Create a New Level, (b) Select the Default Level Option.

7. Create a New Level and give it an easy-to-remember name. You can do this by performing one of the following three tasks:
    - In the **Content Browser** Left-Click on the **Add New** icon and select **Level** option from the popup menu (see Figure 2.2(a)).
    - In the menu, find and click on **File▶Level**(see Figure 2.2(b)).
    - Press **Control+N** on your keyboard.
8. From the window, select the **Default Level** (see Figure 2.2(c)). This will create a default level, with a skysphere, light, ambient sound, and visual items.
9. The default level should look similar to Figure 2.3(a). This level contains several important actors that allow you to see a nice outdoor, daylight environment.

> **SkySphere:** This is the actor that displays the clouds and the daylight.
> **Light Source:** This is the light that makes the scene visible. This light is also used within the skysphere blueprint to make the time of day. If this light is rotated (or its direction changed) the skysphere will use

the light direction to render the sky with appropriate properties.

Atmospheric Fog: This actor enables the effect of having a small amount of fog in the scene, making more distant objects look a bit blurred.

Player Start: This actor is used to initiate the location of the player character when the game starts.

Floor Static Mesh: This is a static mesh. This actor is used as a ground for the player to stand on when the game starts. Without this actor, if you start the game, the player will fall indefinitely.

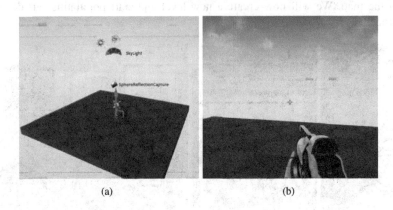

(a)   (b)

FIGURE 2.3: (a) Default Level Actors. (b) Playing the Level with First Person View.

10. You may play this level by either pressing CTRL+P on your keyboard, or by clicking on the play icon ▶ from the menu bar. Your play-in-editor should look similar to Figure 2.3(b). As you see in this figure, a player character mesh is used to render the player.

11. Save your level and progress so far by pressing Control+S or the Save icon in the menu bar. Give your level an easy-to-remember name. I called my level MyArchitectureLevel.

HIDING THE PLAYER MESH

Now that our map is created, and playable, it is time to make a slight modification to make it less distracting when we start the design process. If you play the map, you will notice that the game is in the first person mode. Moreover, you will be able to see the first person mesh of the player.

This is a nice feature when you are playing the game. When we add our level's geometry and details, we will switch back and forth between the editing and playing of the level to see what we have done. Having the player mesh occupy space when we play the level while in the design process, the mesh could get in the way and obscure our view.

Thankfully, the process of hiding the player mesh is fairly straightforward and simple. Follow the steps below to accomplish this task:

12. In the **Content Browser** find the `Blueprints` folder and open it. You can open a folder by `Double-clicking` it.

13. Open the `FirstPersonCharacter` blueprint by `Double-clicking` it.

14. Once the blueprint is open, you will notice that your blueprint editor is in the `Event Graph` mode. This is where the programming functionality of the blueprint resides. We want to access the components of our blueprint.

15. On the top of the blueprint editor, find and `Left-Click` on the **Viewport** tab (see Figure 2.4).

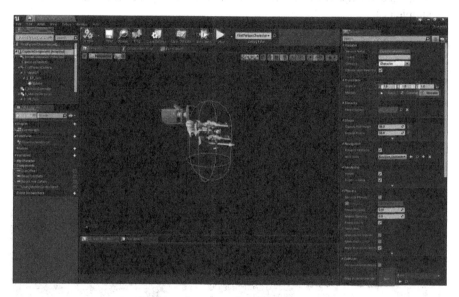

FIGURE 2.4: Hiding the Player Mesh.

16. In the `Viewport` mode, find and select (`Left-Click`) the player's mesh. It is called `Mesh2P`.

17. In the details rollout of the selected mesh, scroll down and find the **Rendering** section.

18. In the **Rendering** section, un-check the `Visible` checkboxes for both the Mesh2P and FP_Gun (see Figure 2.4). This will hide the character's mesh (the arms and the gun).

19. Compile the blueprint, by `Left-clicking` on the **Compile** button ▨ (see Figure 2.4).

20. Save the blueprint and close the blueprint editor.

21. Now if you play the level you will see that the first person mesh will not be rendered and your view will be freed up. However, the player functionality and the crosshair icon will still be in effect in the game. *You can still shoot projectiles by `Left-clicking` while in the play mode.*

REMOVING THE PLAYER START AND THE PLATFORM

With the player mesh hidden, we need to remove the player start actor. This actor is used to place the player when the game starts. Having the player start actor will be useful when we want the game to start. But again, since we will be switching between editing the level and playing it, this actor will force the start location every time we play the level.

Therefore, not having this actor will allow us to play the level from any location and helps with our design process. Removing the player start is a very simple task:

22. Find and **Left-Click** on the player start actor in the level to select it.
23. Remove the player start actor by pressing the **Del** button on the keyboard.
24. **Left-Click** on the platform and delete it as well.
25. Save your level and progress so far.

ESTABLISHING THE DEFAULT AND STARTUP LEVELS

Now that you have your basic level ready to build, we will need to establish our level as the default map for when the editor is started. This way, each time we open this project, we will be taken to this map.

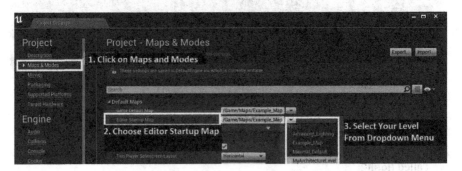

FIGURE 2.5: Setting Up the Editor Startup Map.

26. **Left-Click** on the **Settings** button from the toolbar and choose **Project Settings** from the menu.
27. Choose the **Maps & Modes**.
28. Click on the ▼ next to the **Editor Startup Map**.
29. Select your map from the drop-down list (see Figure 2.5).
30. Save your project.

What Happened in TUTORIAL 2.1...

You just set up a blank project, and included the starter content from the Unreal Engine to it.

Once the project was created you added a new level. You then made this level the default level to open upon the start of the editor. This helps you to come back to this level if you close the editor and restart the project at a later time.

In the next step of the process you made the player's mesh to be hidden when you run the level to decrease distractions and to help your design process.

We wanted to ensure that our level will be loaded up the next time we open the project in the Unreal Editor. To achieve this, we assigned the level as the editor startup map in our project's "Maps and Modes" section of the "Project Setting."

With our project created, and a relatively empty slate set up, we are ready to create the basic geometry of our level. In Tutorial 2.2 we will establish this geometry purely from Brushes. But before delving into how to build the basic geometry of your level, let's first take a more detailed look at geometry brush actors in UE4.

2.2.1 GEOMETRY BRUSH OVERVIEW

Geometry Brush is the most basic tool in Unreal Engine by which you can design a level. These brushed are used by level designers to add geometry to the level or to carve our geometry from already placed brushes within the level. In the latter stages of the level design process, the geometry built by brushes will be replaced by static meshes.

Still, the geometry brushes are the most basic tool for rapidly prototyping the level and objects within the level. Moreover, if you don't have easy access to 3D modeling tools such as Maya or 3ds Max, you can use these brushes to create rough 3D models and use in your level. While Static Meshes are now primarily used to populate levels with geometry, Geometry Brushes still have their place. Here we look at some of the typical uses of Geometry Brushes [16].

There are several stages in the workflow of developing a level, starting with blocking the level and establishing paths within the level, to play testing the flow and gameplay, all the way to the final "Polish" pass. Figure 2.6 shows these stages as a diagram.

The first step is to establish a rough sketch of the level and generate a mechanism by which basic paths may be developed for programmatic components of the gameplay. The geometry brushes are used in this phase to create the basic layout of the level. Once the basic geometry is established, static meshes and other static components of the game can be integrated into the level. The initial lighting pass is the next step, after static meshes are added to the level to replace the brush geometry. After the initial mesh and lighting pass, collisions and other performance factors are tested. Once all the remaining performance issues are taken care of, the final polish phase will complete the aesthetics of the game, by adding special effects and other audio visual elements.

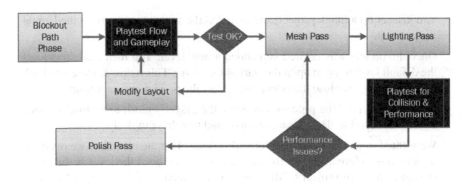

FIGURE 2.6: Stages of Level Design.

Brush geometry will be quite useful in two stages of the level design process. As explained above, in the initial phase of the process, the brushes are an important tool to establish the basic geometry of the level. Brushes are also quite important when the level designer needs a simple piece of geometry to use as a simple prop or a simple asset, or to fill a space while the artists are designing these assets to be utilized in the final product. Brushes give us a fast way for designing all this "filler geometry" in the Unreal Editor without the need to rely on a third-party 3D modeling tool.

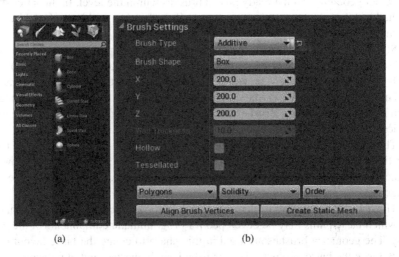

FIGURE 2.7: (a) Geometry Tab. (b) Brush Settings.

Creating Brushes

To create brushes you will use the **Geometry** tab in the **Place Mode** Panel (Figure 2.7(a)).

Brush Properties [16][1]

Brushes in Unreal Engine have certain properties. Some of these properties depend on the brush shape, while others are shared among different shapes. Figure 2.7(b) shows the basic properties of a Box Brush.

Brush Type: BSP brushes in UE4 have two types, Additive and Subtractive:
- **Brush Type Property**

> **Additive:** Sets the brush to Additive. An additive brush is like a filled-in object. For example, you use additive brushes to add objects such as walls, floors, ceilings, tables, etc., to the level.
>
> **Subtractive:** Set the brush to Subtractive. A subtractive brush is like a hollow, carved-out space. You can use this type of brush to carve out and remove space from the geometry, such as doors, windows, gaps, and openings previously created by additive brushes.

Advanced Properties: These properties are accessible by clicking on the ▼ icon in the details rollout of the brush.
- **Polygons**

> **Merge:** Merges together any planar faces on a brush.
> **Separate:** Reverses the effects of a merge.

- **Solidity**

> **Solid:** Sets the brush to Solid. Solid brushes block players and projectiles, can be both additive and subtractive, and create cuts in the surrounding BSP brushes.
>
> **Semi-Solid:** Sets the brush Semi-solid. Semi-solid brushes block players and projectiles, can only be additive, and do not create cuts in the surrounding BSP brushes.
>
> **Non-Solid:** Sets the brush to Non-solid. Non-solid brushes do not block players or projectiles, can only be additive, and do not create cuts in the surrounding BSP brushes.

---

[1] The contents of this section are adapted from the official UE4 online documentation found at: https://docs.unrealengine.com/latest/INT/.

- **Order**

> **To First:** Makes the selected brush the first to be calculated.
> **To Last:** Makes the selected brush the last to be calculated.

- **Align and Create Static Mesh Buttons**

> **Align Brush Vertices:** Snaps the brush vertices to the grid.
> **Create Static Mesh:** Creates a static mesh based on the selected
>   brush and allows for it to be saved at the given location.

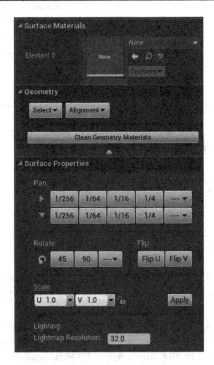

FIGURE 2.8: Brush Surface Properties.

Brush Surface Properties

If you select a Brush surface (use Ctrl + Shift + Left Click to select the surface and not the Brush), you will see the surface properties (Figure 2.8) in the Details rollout:

Geometry Category: This category contains several tools to help manage the geometry and materials on a brush.

- **Geometry Category Buttons**

> **Select:** Contains commands to help select brush surfaces.
>
> **Alignment:** Re-aligns the texture coordinates for surfaces based on desired settings.
>
> **Clean Geometry Materials:** Fixes the problem of lost materials on the surfaces of the brush.

Surface Properties: This category contains tools to help control the texture mapping of the materials applied to a surface.

- **Surface Property Categories**

> **Pan:** This button allows you to pan (move) the texture across the surface either horizontally or vertically.
>
> **Rotate:** This button rotates the texture on the surface.
>
> **Flip:** This button flips the texture on the surface either horizontally or vertically.
>
> **Scale:** This button resizes the texture mapping on a surface.

Lighting: This sections allows you to change the light-related properties of your brush surfaces.

- **Lighting Properties**

> **Lightmap Resolution:** This item allows for the adjustment of the shadows across a surface. Lower numbers represent tighter shadow resolution, with more accuracy but at the cost of lighting build time.

- **Lightmass Settings**

> **Use Two Sided Lighting:** If true, this surface will receive light on both the positive and negative side of each polygon.
>
> **Shadow Indirect Only:** If true, this surface will only create shadows from indirect lighting.
>
> **Diffuse Boost:** Scales the amount of influence diffuse color will have on indirect lighting.
>
> **Fully Occluded Samples Fraction:** Fraction of samples along this surface that must be occluded before it is considered to be occluded from indirect lighting calculations.

Now that we have covered the basics of brush geometry, let's start using these brushes to add geometry to our level.

To find updates to this tutorial and updated instructions about its implementation on other UE4 versions please visit the book's companion website at:
http://www.RVRLAB.com/UE4Book/

TUTORIAL 2.2   Establishing the Level's Geometry with Brushes

In this tutorial we will build the basic geometry of a two-story building.

We will need our level to be set up before we can proceed with the rest of
the tutorial. You may find instructions to set up your level in Tutorial 2.1
on page 28.

BUILDING THE OUTSIDE WALLS

The building that I have in mind for us to design is made of three modules –
North and South wings connected to a Central Lobby. So let's go ahead and
build these modules. But first we need a ground floor!

1. If you have closed the project, open it up. Since in the previous tutorial we set our
   map as the default startup map for the editor, it should open up. Otherwise, find
   the map in the **Content Browser** and open it.
2. In the **World Outliner** in the upper right corner of the Unreal Editor click on New
   Folder next to the search bar.
3. Name this folder Level Geometry.
4. To place a ground we will add an additive Box brush to the level. From the **Place**
   mode in the upper left corner of the editor, find the **BSP** tab.
5. Locate the Box brush from the **BSP** mode and drag it into the level. Assign the
   following properties to this Box brush:

> **Brush Name:** Ground
> **Brush Type:** Additive
> **Brush Shape:** Box
> **X:** 5000
> **Y:** 5000
> **Z:** 20

6. Drag the Ground brush you just created in the **World Outliner** and move it to the
   Level Geometry Folder. Alternatively, you can Right-Click on the brush in
   the **World Outliner**, move your mouse over the Move to Folder option from
   the popup menu, and select the Level Geometry folder.
7. Locate the Box brush from the **BSP** mode and drag it into the level. Assign the
   following properties to this Box brush:

Brush Name: SouthWing
Brush Type: Additive
Brush Shape: Box
X: 3000
Y: 1200
Z: 1800
Hollow: Checked.
Wall Thickness: 20

8. You want to make sure that this building is aligned with the ground. To do so, drag the brush along its Z-axis up until it is well above the ground. Then press the End button on your keyboard. This should snap this brush to the ground level.

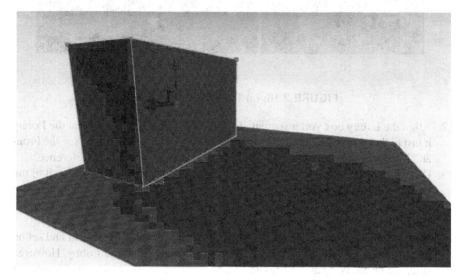

FIGURE 2.9: The South Wing Placed in the Level.

9. You might need to move the **South Wing** brush around to place it on the side of the **Ground** brush, like the image shown in Figure 2.9.
10. Drag the **SouthWing** brush you just created in the **World Outliner** and move it to the **Level Geometry Folder**. Alternatively, you can **Right-Click** on the brush in the **World Outliner**, move your mouse over the **Move to Folder** option from the popup menu, and select the **Level Geometry** folder.
11. Place another **Box** brush from the **BSP** mode into the level. Assign the following properties to this Box brush:

Brush Name: Lobby
Brush Type: Additive
Brush Shape: Box

X: 2000
Y: 1500
Z: 1500
Hollow: Checked.
Wall Thickness: 20

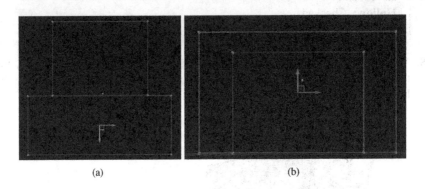

(a)   (b)

FIGURE 2.10: (a) Top View. (b) Front View.

12. Align the `Lobby` box you just created with the `SouthWing` box, so that the Lobby it just to the north of the South Wing, with walls touching each other. See the Front and Top view shown in Figure 2.10(a) and Figure 2.10(b) for your reference.

13. Drag the `Lobby` brush you just created in the **World Outliner** and move it to the `Level Geometry Folder`. Alternatively, you can `Right-Click` on the brush in the **World Outliner**, move your mouse over the `Move to Folder` option from the popup menu, and select the `Level Geometry` folder.

14. Next, we will create the North Wing. We could add another box brush and set its properties, much like what we did for the South Wing and the Lobby. However, since the North Wing and the South Wing are similar in size and type of brush, we will simply copy the South Wing to Create the North Wing. To do this, perform the following actions:

    a. Go to the top viewport, by either clicking `Alt+J` or by selecting the **Top** form the viewport selection tab on the upper right corner of the editor window.

    b. `Left-Click` on the `SouthWing` brush wireframe to select it.

    c. Hold down the `Alt` key on the keyboard and drag the `Green` axis of the translate gizmo to create a copy of the `SouthWing` brush and place it on the opposite side of the `Lobby` brush.

    d. Change the name of this copy from `southWing_2` to **NorthWing**.

15. Notice that by doing this, we escaped from having to create a brush, setting up its values, and then attempting to align it with the rest of the geometry on all 3 axes. Moreover, the brush will also be automatically located in the `Level Geometry` folder.

16. Save your map. Now the exterior of your building should look similar to Figure 2.11.

FIGURE 2.11: The Exterior of the Building.

THE INTERIOR: LOCKING A LIGHT ACTOR TO VIEWPORT

Now that the three sections of our building are created, we can add some basic geometry to its interior. You can scroll in, or use **WASD** keys on the keyboard while holding the **Right Mouse Button** to navigate in the level, much like playing a game.

17. Navigate inside the **Lobby** of the building.
18. If looking around in the interior of the building you notice that some of the walls are quite dark you fix this problem as follows, otherwise proceed to the next section.
19. Hold down the key **L** on your keyboard and **Double-Click** somewhere in the editor.
20. This will place a **Point Light** in the level (see Figure 2.12(a)).
21. Select the **Point Light** and make the following changes to its properties in the Details rollout:

> **Light Name:** PointLight3
> **Expand Light Section by Clicking on the ▼**
> **Intensity:** 10
> **Attenuation Radius:** 4000
> **Use Inverse Square Falloff:** Un-check

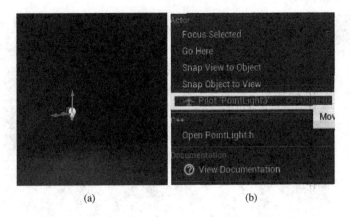

(a)   (b)

FIGURE 2.12: (a) Placing a Light Source. (b) Locking the Viewport to Light Source.

22. This will create a light for you with its values set in such a way that the light will fall off very gradually so that you can see dark corners.
23. With the Light Source still selected, **Right-Click** the light source from the **World Outliner**.
24. From the pop-up menu, select the **Pilot PointLight** (see Figure 2.12(b)).
25. This will lock the light to your viewport. From this point on, when you move around in the viewport, you will have this light source attached to your location, as if you had a bright headlight. You should also see a pilot 🔲 on the upper left corner of the perspective viewport. You may use these icons to eject from the Pilot mode.
26. Save your level.

THE INTERIOR: PLACING STAIRS

Now we are ready to add the interior geometry. We will first place stairs and the second and third floors of our building in the South and North Wings.

27. Navigate inside of the **Lobby**.
28. To place a staircase we will add an additive Linear Stair Brush to the level. From the **Place** mode in the upper left corner of the editor, find the **BSP** tab.
29. Locate the **Linear Stair** brush from the **BSP** mode and drag it into the level. Assign the following properties to this box brush:

> **Brush Name:** WestStairLv1
> **Brush Type:** Additive
> **Brush Shape:** Linear Stair
> **Step Length:** 30
> **Step Height:** 20
> **Step Width:** 200

Num Steps: 15

30. Drag the WestStairsLv1 up along its Z-axis. Then press the **End** key on your keyboard to snap it to the floor.
31. Drag the WestStairsLv1 brush you just created in the **World Out-liner** and move it to the Level Geometry Folder. Alternatively, you can Right-Click on the brush in the **World Outliner**, move your mouse over the Move to Folder option from the pop up menu, and select the **Level Geometry** folder.

FIGURE 2.13: Aligning Landing and Stairs.

32. Locate the Box brush from the **BSP** mode and drag it into the level. Assign the following properties to this box brush:

Brush Name: LandingLvl1
Brush Type: Additive
Brush Shape: Box
X: 200
Y: 200
Z: 20

33. Align the LandingLv1 with the WestStairsLv1 so that it will be just on top of the last step and completely aligned with the width of the stairs (see Figure 2.13).
34. Drag the LandingLv1 brush you just created in the **World Outliner** and move it to the Level Geometry Folder. Alternatively, you can Right-Click on the brush in the **World Outliner**, move your mouse over the Move to Folder option from the pop up menu, and select the **Level Geometry** folder.

35. Select the `WestStairsLv1` brush, hold the `Alt` key on your keyboard and drag one of the horizontal axes of the gizmo to make a duplicate of this brush.

36. Rename this duplicate to `EastStairsLv1`.

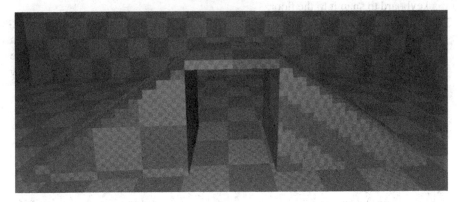

FIGURE 2.14: Aligning Landing and Both Stairs on the Ground Floor.

37. Rotate and align the `EastStairsLv1` with the other side of the `LandingLv1` brush (see Figure 2.14).

38. You might want to double-check your alignments in the Top (`Alt+J`), Front (`Alt+H`), and Side (`Alt+K`) viewports for accuracy and then switch back to the Perspective viewport (`Alt+G`). *In order to be able to move in the Top, Front, and Side viewports, you should unlock the light. Alternatively, you may move the light in those viewports to pan your view.*

39. Place another `Linear Stair` brush from the **BSP** mode and into the level. Assign the following properties to this Box brush:

> **Brush Name:** SouthStairLv1
> **Brush Type:** Additive
> **Brush Shape:** Linear Stair
> **Step Length:** 30
> **Step Height:** 20
> **Step Width:** 200
> **Num Steps:** 15

40. Rotate and move the `SouthStairsLv1` to align it with the `LandingLv1` brush, such that its first step is completely aligned with the top of the landing brush (see Figure 2.15).

41. Drag the `SouthStairsLv1` brush you just created in the **World Outliner** and move it to the `Level Geometry Folder`. Alternatively, you can `Right-Click` on the brush in the **World Outliner**, move your mouse over the `Move to Folder` option from the pop up menu, and select the `Level Geometry` folder.

FIGURE 2.15: Aligning Landing and the South Stairs.

42. Next we will have to align the stairs with the South Wing of our building. To do this perform the following steps:
    a. Select the stair brushes in this order: `SouthStairsLv1`, `WestStairsLv1`, `EastStairsLv1`, and `LandingLv1`. This will give you the translation gizmo in such a way that you will be able to easily move all the selected brushes around.
    b. Move the selected brushes on the horizontal axes until the South Stairs are completely aligned with the Wall of the South Wing (see Figure 2.16).

THE INTERIOR: PLACING FLOORS

With our stairs created and aligned with the walls, it is now time to create the floor for the second level of our building. To do this we will create additive Box brushes and align them with the top of the stairs. The process may be a bit tricky, since the South Wing floor is going to be in the South Wing, while the stairs are in the Lobby. To make this task easier, move the floor such that it will cut into the Lobby, align it with the stairs, and then move it back all the way into the South Wing.

43. Place a **Box** brush from the **BSP** mode into the level. Assign the following properties to this Box brush:

> **Brush Name:** SouthWingFloorLv2
> **Brush Type:** Additive
> **Brush Shape:** Box
> **X:** 2980
> **Y:** 1180

FIGURE 2.16: Aligning the Stairs with Walls.

Z: 20
Hollow: Un-Checked

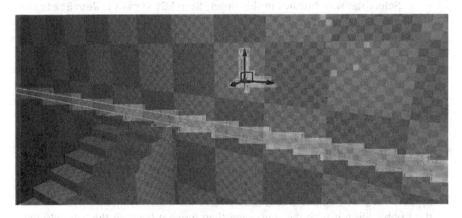

FIGURE 2.17: Aligning the Stairs with the Second Floor.

44. Align the `SouthWingFloorLv2` brush with the top of the stairs as shown in Figure 2.17.
45. Drag the `SouthWingFloorLv2` brush you just created in the **World Outliner** and move it to the `Level Geometry Folder`. Alternatively, you can `Right-Click` on the brush in the **World Outliner**, move your mouse over the `Move to Folder` option from the popup menu, and select the `Level Geometry` folder.
46. With the `SouthWingFloorLv2` brush selected, hold the `Alt` key on your keyboard and move the brush to create a duplicate copy of it.

47. Rename the duplicate floor brush to `NorthWingFloorLv2`.
48. Move the `NorthWingFloorLv2` brush to the North Wing of the building on the opposite side of the stairs. Align the `NorthWingFloorLv2` so that it fits in the North Wing and does not stick out from the walls.

THE INTERIOR: PLACING ELEVATOR AND WALKWAYS

In this step, we will add an elevator box to the Lobby and walkways between the South Wing and the North Wing of our building.

49. Place a `Box` brush from the **BSP** mode into the level. Assign the following properties to this Box brush:

> **Brush Name:** ElevatorBox
> **Brush Type:** Additive
> **Brush Shape:** Box
> **X:** 400
> **Y:** 300
> **Z:** 1200
> **Hollow:** Checked
> **Wall Thickness:** 20

50. Drag the `ElevatorBox` brush along its Z-axis and press the **End** key on your keyboard to snap it to the floor of the lobby.
51. Align the `ElevatorBox` brush with the north-side wall of the Lobby (see Figure 2.18).
52. In the **World Outliner** move the `ElevatorBox` to the **Level Geometry Folder**. Alternatively, you can **Right-Click** on the brush in the **World Outliner**, move your mouse over the **Move to Folder** option from the popup menu, and select the **Level Geometry** folder.
53. Place another `Box` brush from the **BSP** mode into the level. Assign the following properties to this box brush:

> **Brush Name:** NorthSideWalkway
> **Brush Type:** Additive
> **Brush Shape:** Box
> **X:** 1980
> **Y:** 600
> **Z:** 20
> **Hollow:** Un-Checked

54. Align the `NorthSideWalkway` brush with the north-side wall of the Lobby (see Figure 2.18).
55. In the **World Outliner** move the `NorthSideWalkway` to the **Level Geometry Folder**. Alternatively, you can **Right-Click** on the brush in the **World Outliner**, move your mouse over the **Move to Folder** option from the popup menu, and select the **Level Geometry** folder.

FIGURE 2.18: Aligning the Elevator and Walkways.

56. Place another Box brush from the **BSP** mode into the level. Assign the following properties to this box brush:

> **Brush Name:** WestSideWalkway
> **Brush Type:** Additive
> **Brush Shape:** Box
> **X:** 300
> **Y:** 880
> **Z:** 20
> **Hollow:** Un-Checked

57. Align the WestSideWalkway brush with the NorthSideWalkway and the south wall of the Lobby (see Figure 2.19).
58. In the **World Outliner** move the WestSideWalkway to the Level Geometry Folder. Alternatively, you can Right-Click on the brush in the **World Outliner**, move your mouse over the Move to Folder option from the popup menu, and select the Level Geometry folder.
59. Select the WestSideWalkway, hold the Alt key on your keyboard, and move the gizmo. This will make a duplicate of this brush.
60. Rename this duplicate brush to EastSideWalkway.
61. Move the EastSideWalkway to the opposite side of the building. Leave a gap between the EastSideWalkway and the east wall of the lobby.

FIGURE 2.19: Complete Interior View from the Lobby.

62. Figure 2.19 shows a complete interior view of the building from the second floor of the lobby.

SUBTRACTING GEOMETRY: CUTTING HOLES FOR DOORS

Now that our basic geometry for the Lobby, North Wing, and the South Wing is established, we need to be able to walk in and out of these sections. To cut geometry from BSP brushed, we will use Subtractive brushes.

63. Place a Box brush from the **BSP** mode into the level. Assign the following properties to this Box brush:

> **Brush Name:** WestDoorCutOut
> **Brush Type:** Subtractive
> **Brush Shape:** Box
> **X:** 100
> **Y:** 600
> **Z:** 500
> **Hollow:** Un-Checked

64. Align the WestDoorCutOut brush with the west-side wall of the Lobby (see Figure 2.20).

65. In the **World Outliner** move the WestDoorCutOut to the **Level Geometry Folder**. Alternatively, you can **Right-Click** on the brush in the **World Outliner**, move your mouse over the **Move to Folder** option from the popup menu, and select the **Level Geometry** folder.

FIGURE 2.20: The West Door Cut Out as Viewed from the Lobby.

66. With the `WestDoorCutOut` brush selected, hold the `Alt+Shift` keys on your keyboard and move the brush gizmo towards the east side of the lobby. You will notice that this action will create a duplicate of the selected brush and your camera will move with it.

67. Keep dragging the duplicate brush until it is placed in the opposite side of the lobby to cut out a whole in the east-side wall of the lobby.

68. Rename this duplicate subtractive brush to `EastDoorCutOut`.

69. Place a **Box** brush from the **BSP** mode into the level. Assign the following properties to this Box brush:

> **Brush Name:** SouthWingCutOutEast
> **Brush Type:** Subtractive
> **Brush Shape:** Box
> **X:** 200
> **Y:** 100
> **Z:** 300
> **Hollow:** Un-Checked

70. Align the `SouthWingCutOutEast` brush with the south wall of the Lobby on the second floor along the `EastSideWalkway` (see Figure 2.21).

71. In the **World Outliner** move the `SouthWingCutOutEast` to the **Level Geometry Folder**. Alternatively, you can **Right-Click** on the brush in the **World Outliner**, move your mouse over the **Move to Folder** option from the popup menu, and select the **Level Geometry** folder.

72. With the `SouthWingCutOutEast` brush selected, hold the `Alt+Shift` keys on your keyboard and move the brush gizmo towards the west side of the lobby. You will notice that this action will create a duplicate of the selected brush and your

FIGURE 2.21: The Door Cut Out on the Second Floor to South Wing.

camera will move with it.

73. Keep dragging the duplicate brush until it is placed at the top of the stairs.

74. Rename this duplicate subtractive brush to `StairsDoorCutOut`.

75. Select the `SouthWingCutOutEast` brush, hold the `Alt+Shift` keys on your keyboard and move the brush gizmo towards the west side of the lobby. You will notice that this action will create a duplicate of the selected brush and your camera will move with it.

76. Keep dragging the duplicate brush until it is placed at the `WestSideWalkWay`.

77. Rename this duplicate subtractive brush to `SouthWingCutOutWest`.

78. Select the `SouthWingCutOutEast` brush, hold the `Alt+Shift` keys on your keyboard and move the brush gizmo towards the north side of the lobby. You will notice that this action will create a duplicate of the selected brush and your camera will move with it.

79. Keep dragging the duplicate brush until it is placed at the north wall of the Lobby, opposite the location of the original brush you are duplicating.

80. Rename this duplicate subtractive brush to `NorthWingCutOutEast`.

81. Select the `SouthWingCutOutWest` brush, hold the `Alt+Shift` keys on your keyboard, and move the brush gizmo towards the north side of the lobby. You will notice that this action will create a duplicate of the selected brush and your camera will move with it.

82. Keep dragging the duplicate brush until it is placed at the north wall of the lobby, opposite the location of the original brush you are duplicating.

83. Rename this duplicate subtractive brush to `NorthWingCutOutWest`.

84. Select the `StairsDoorCutOut` brush, hold the `Alt+Shift` keys on your keyboard and move the brush gizmo towards the north side of the lobby. You will notice that this action will create a duplicate of the selected brush and your camera will move with it.
85. Keep dragging the duplicate brush until it is placed at the elevator. Place the brush such that it is centered at the front wall of the elevator.
86. Rename this duplicate subtractive brush to `ElevatorDoorCutOutFloor2`.
87. Select the `ElevatorDoorCutOutFloor2` brush, hold the `Alt+Shift` keys on your keyboard and move the brush gizmo down towards the first floor of the lobby. You will notice that this action will create a duplicate of the selected brush and your camera will move with it.
88. Keep dragging the duplicate brush until it is placed on the first floor. Place the brush such that it is centered at the front wall of the elevator.
89. Rename this duplicate subtractive brush to `ElevatorDoorCutOutFloor1`.
90. Place a `Box` brush from the **BSP** mode into the level inside of the elevator. Assign the following properties to this Box brush:

> **Brush Name:** ElevatorFloorCutOut
> **Brush Type:** Subtractive
> **Brush Shape:** Box
> **X:** 380
> **Y:** 280
> **Z:** 100
> **Hollow:** Un-Checked

91. Place this brush inside the elevator on the second floor to create an opening. This will ensure that when you place an elevator mesh, it will be able to move through the elevator stall up and down without colliding with the second floor walkway.
92. Select `SouthWingCutOutEast`, `SouthWingCutOutWest`, `NorthWingCutOutEast`, and `NorthWingCutOutWest` brushes by holding the `Control` key on your keyboard and clicking on them in the **World Outliner**.
93. Hold the `Alt+Shift` keys on your keyboard and move the brush gizmo down towards the first floor of the lobby. You will notice that this action will create a duplicate of the selected brush and your camera will move with it.
94. Keep dragging the duplicate brush until the door cutout duplicates are placed on the first floor.
95. Save your level and progress.

SUBTRACTING GEOMETRY: CUTTING HOLES FOR WINDOWS

Let's add some windows to our building. To do this we will start out on the west side of the building, place our windows with the subtractive brushes, and then copy the brushes to the east side of the building.

FIGURE 2.22: The Final Look from the West Side after the Brush Geometry Pass.

96. Place a `Box` brush from the **BSP** mode into the level. Assign the following properties to this box brush:

> **Brush Name:** NorthWindowFloor1_1
> **Brush Type:** Subtractive
> **Brush Shape:** Box
> **X:** 100
> **Y:** 80
> **Z:** 140
> **Hollow:** Un-Checked

97. Align the `NorthWindowFloor1_1` brush with the west-side wall of the North Wing.
98. In the **World Outliner** move the `NorthWindowFloor1_1` to the **Level Geometry Folder**. Alternatively, you can `Right-Click` on the brush in the **World Outliner**, move your mouse over the **Move to Folder** option from the popup menu, and select the **Level Geometry** folder.
99. With the `NorthWindowFloor1_1` brush selected, hold the **Alt+Shift** keys on your keyboard and move the brush gizmo to create a duplicate of the selected brush and your camera will move with it.

100. Keep dragging the duplicate brush until it is placed in the opposite side of the North Wing to cut out a hole in the second window.
101. Rename this duplicate subtractive brush to `NorthWindowFloor1_2`.
102. Select the `NorthWindowFloor1_1` brush, hold the `Alt+Shift` keys on your keyboard and move the brush gizmo to create a duplicate of the selected brush while your camera will move with it.
103. Keep dragging the duplicate brush until it is placed between the two windows.
104. Rename this duplicate subtractive brush to `NorthWindowFloor1_3`.
105. Hold the `Control` key on your keyboard and select the `NorthWindowFloor1_1`, `NorthWindowFloor1_2`, and `NorthWindowFloor1_3`.
106. Hold the `Alt+Shift` keys on your keyboard and move the brush gizmo upwards to create a duplicate of the selected brushes while your camera will move with it.
107. Keep dragging the duplicate brushes upwards until they are placed somewhere on the second floor.
108. With `NorthWindowFloor1_1`, `NorthWindowFloor1_2`, and `NorthWindowFloor1_3` still selected, hold the `Alt+Shift` keys on your keyboard and move the brush gizmo upwards to create a duplicate of the selected brushes while your camera moves with it.
109. Place these duplicates on the upper sections of the second floor in the North Wing.
110. Select all of the window cut out brushes by holding the `Control` key on your keyboard and clicking on them in the **World Outliner**.
111. With the 9 brushes selected, hold the `Alt+Shift` and create 9 duplicates.
112. Drag these 9 duplicates on the east side of the North Wing.
113. Select all of the 18 window cut out brushes by holding the `Control` key on your keyboard and clicking on them in the **World Outliner**.
114. With the 18 brushes selected, hold the `Alt+Shift` and create 18 duplicates.
115. Drag these 18 duplicates to the west and east sides of the South Wing.
116. The view of your building should look similar to Figure 2.22 from the west.
117. Save your level and progress.

What Happened in TUTORIAL 2.2...

In this tutorial we added geometry to our level by placing Binary Space Partitioning brushes. We used two different types of brushes for this purpose. We added geometry to our level by means of additive brushes. To place openings in our geometry for doors and windows we used subtractive brushes.

The majority of the work in this tutorial was repetitive, and requires fine alignment of different pieces of geometry. So there wasn't much complicated issues or steps to discuss in detail. We also learned how to use a folder in the **World Outliner** to organize our assets – in this particular instance our BSP geometry.

2.3   IMPROVING THE LEVEL AESTHETICS WITH MATERIALS

With our BSP geometry created, it is now time to give our level a better look. To do this we will utilize materials. Although designing and created incredibly realistic materials is one of the greatest features of Unreal Engine 4, we will not go over the material creation in this chapter.

> To learn about materials in Unreal Engine 4, please check out Chapter 4–
> Materials In Unreal Engine and Chapter 5– Advanced Material Concepts.

We have a couple of chapters dedicated to materials and material creation later on. For now, we will use the materials that are included in the starter content to add to the look of our level. We will use the brushes' surface properties to make simple modifications to panning, rotation, and tiling of our material's textures on the surfaces and avoid directly modifying the materials in the UE4's **Material Editor**.

In the next tutorial we will apply some materials to our level brush geometry.

> To find updates to this tutorial and updated instructions about its implemen-
> tation on other UE4 versions please visit the book's companion website at:
> http://www.RVRLAB.com/UE4Book/

TUTORIAL 2.3   Enhancing the Level with Materials

First, we will have to create a special visual actor in the level, called, **Sphere Reflection Capture**. Since some of the materials we will use in this level have metallic properties, this actor will enable the light interaction on these materials to take place naturally. If your level doesn't have a **Sphere Reflection Capture**, follow the steps below to add one to the scene.

PLACING A REFLECTION CAPTURE ACTOR

1. Make sure you are in the `Place` mode in the **Modes** tab. Alternatively, press `Shift+1` on your keyboard to switch to this mode.
2. Click on the **Visual** tab.
3. Scroll down and locate the **Sphere Reflection Capture**.
4. Drag a **Sphere Reflection Capture** actor into the level and place it in front of the elevator on the lobby, just above the Stair landings.

APPLYING GROUND MATERIALS

Now, with the sphere reflection actor placed in the level, it's time for us to apply materials to our brushes. The first material we will apply to our brush geometry will be the ground.

FIGURE 2.23: Applying Materials to the Ground Geometry.

5. **Left-Click** on the **Ground** brush in the editor to select it. Alternatively, you can select this brush by clicking on its name in the **World Outliner**.
6. Locate a folder called **Materials** in the **Starter Content** folder in the **Content Browser**.
7. Open the **Materials** folder and locate the **M_Rock_Marble_Polished**.
8. **Left-Click** on the **M_Rock_Marble_Polished** material once to have it selected in the **Content Browser**.
9. In the **Geometry** section of the Details rollout of the **Ground** brush, click on the **Apply Material** button.
10. Select the **Apply Material: M_Rock_Marble_Polished** to apply this material to the brush surface you have selected (see Figure 2.23).

APPLYING THE STAIR MATERIALS

The next material we will apply to our brush geometry will be the stairs materials. We will use a metallic material for our stairs.

11. **Left-Click** on the **WestStairsLv1** brush in the editor to select it. Alternatively, you can select this brush by clicking on its name in the **World Outliner**.
12. This will select one of the faces (surfaces) of this brush. We will need to select all of the brush surfaces to apply our material. To do so, click on the **Select** Button on the **Geometry** section of this brush's Details rollout.
13. From the menu, select the **Select Matching Brush**. This will select the entire brush for us to which we will apply the material.
14. Locate a folder called **Materials** in the **Starter Content** folder in the **Content Browser**.
15. Open the **Materials** folder and locate the **M_Rock_Marble_Polished**.

16. `Left-Click` on the `M_Rock_Marble_Polished` material once to have it selected in the **Content Browser**.

17. In the `Geometry` section of the Details rollout of the `WestStairlsLv1` brush, click on the **Use Selected Asset** ![button icon] button.

18. This will apply the material to the brush surface you have selected.

19. Perform steps 11–18 for the `EastStairsLv1`, `SouthStairsLv1`, and `LandingLv1`, to apply materials to the whole staircase.

FIGURE 2.24: The Wall Materials Applied to the Brush Geometry.

APPLYING WALL MATERIALS

Now let's apply the interior and exterior wall materials. We will first select all of the walls in our building and apply the interior material to them. Then we will select the exterior walls and apply a brick material to those walls only.

20. Select one of the walls; it doesn't matter if it is an interior wall of an exterior one.

21. Click on the **Select** button in the `Geometry` section of the Details rollout, and choose **Select All Adjacent Wall Surfaces** to select all of the adjacent walls. You may alternatively select all adjacent wall surfaces by pressing the `Shift+W` keys on your keyboard.

22. With all of the walls selected, locate the **M_Basic_Wall** material from the **Starter Content ▶ Materials** folder.

23. Click on **Apply Material** button in the `Geometry` section of the Details rollout and choose `Apply Material: M_Basic_Wall`.

24. With the material applied to the wall, we will now go and apply a brick material to the exterior walls individually.
25. Go outside of the building, and choose each exterior wall individually.
26. With each wall selected, find the `M_Brick_Clay_New` material and apply it to the wall by taking the following actions:
    a. Select the wall surface.
    b. Select the material in the **Content Browser**.
    c. Press the `Shift` key and `Left-Click` on the selected surface to apply the material to it, or
    d. Drag the material from the **Content Browser** onto the selected surface to apply the material to it.
27. Perform steps 26a–26d for the remaining exterior walls.
28. Your level should look similar to Figure 2.24.
29. Save your progress so far.

FIGURE 2.25: The Floor and Ceiling Materials Applied to the Brush Geometry.

APPLYING FLOOR AND CEILING MATERIALS

Now let's apply the floor and ceiling materials. We will use different materials for this purpose: tiles for the lobby, wood for the north and South Wing floors on the first floor, a carpet-like materials for the floors on the second story, and a couple of metallic material for the ceilings of our building and for the walkways.

30. Navigate to the inside of the lobby and select the lobby floor.
31. With the lobby floor selected, find and select the `M_Ceramic_tile_Checker` material from the `Material` folder of the `Starter Content` in the **Content Browser**.

32. Apply the material to the selected floor surface. *Remember, you can drag the material on the surface, shift+click on the surface, or apply it by pressing the Apply Material button.*
33. Locate the `Surface Properties` section in the Details rollout.
34. Locate the `Scale:` tab.
35. Click on the `Lock` icon in the `Scale` tab.
36. Type in the value 2 in `U` or `V`, and then press apply to increase the floor tile sizes.
37. Navigate to the North Wing and select its floor on the ground level.
38. With the North Wing floor selected locate the `M_Wood_Floor_Walnut_Polished` material and apply it to the floor.
39. Locate the `Surface Properties` section in the Details rollout.
40. Make modifications to the `Scale Pan` and `Rotate` options to make the material align the way you desire.
41. Apply the `M_Wood_Floor_Walnut_Polished` material to the floor of the South Wing on the ground level, similar to what you did for the North Wing.
42. Apply the `M_Tech_Hex_Tile` material to the ceilings of the North and South Wings. Make modifications to the `Scale Pan` and `Rotate` options to make the material align and scale the way you desire.
43. Apply the `M_Metal_Steel` material to all interior surfaces of the Elevator brush.
44. Apply the `M_Metal_Steel` material to the bottom surfaces of the `WestWalkway`, `EastWalkway`, and `NorthSideWalkway`.
45. Navigate to the second level and apply the following materials:
    a. Apply `M_Tech_Checker_Dot` material to the floors of the `NorthWing`, `SouthWing`, `WestWalkway`, `EastWalkway`, and `NorthSideWalkway`. Make any necessary modifications to `Scale`, `Pan`, and `Rotate` options.
    b. Apply `M_Tech_Hex_Tile` material to the ceilings of the `NorthWing`, `SouthWing`, `Lobby`, and make any necessary modifications to `Scale`, `Pan`, and `Rotate` options.
46. Figure 2.25 shows a view of the interior of our building with the materials applied.
47. Save your progress.

What Happened in TUTORIAL 2.3...

In this tutorial we added some materials to our brush geometry. There are several ways by which we can add materials to our brush surfaces. We can click on a surface and then select a material from the **Content Browser** and press the Apply Material button, or simply drag a material from the **Content Browser** onto the surface in the main editor.

Sometimes we might need to apply the same material to several surfaces, such as the entire brush, all of the walls or floors in an area, etc. We saw how the Select button helps us select several brushes that have certain relationships with each other, such as being walls, being co-planar, belonging to the same brush, etc.

2.4   REFINING THE GEOMETRY AND ADDING MESHES

Great! The baseline level geometry is created and some materials are applied to the brushes to give our level a nice look. In the production pipeline the art team would have finished some props in the form of static meshes for us by this time. With these meshes to populate the level we can add more realism, and at a later stage dynamism to our level.

In the next tutorial we will start integrating some static meshes from the **Starter Contents** to populate the level. We will place some door frames and window frames in our level. We will also use glass meshes and door meshes to fit inside the door frames and window frames. Another concept we will learn in this tutorial is to group meshes together so that we can place and duplicate them more easily.

> To find updates to this tutorial and updated instructions about its implementation on other UE4 versions please visit the book's companion website at: `http://www.RVRLAB.com/UE4Book/`

TUTORIAL 2.4   Enhancing the Level's Geometry with Meshes

In this tutorial we will populate our level with some static mesh actors from the Starter Contents we added to the project when it was created.

LOBBY ENTRANCE DOORS

Let's first add the entrance doors to our lobby. We will first place a door frame over the opening in the West (or East) side of the lobby and resize it so that it fits the opening. Then we will add two glass doors, and a door handle to each glass door.

In a later tutorial we will add functionality to the glass doors to open when the player walks up to them and close when the player steps away.

1. Navigate to the West side of the building in the main editor.
2. Locate and open the **Props** folder in the **Starter Content** folder in the **Content Browser**.
3. Find the **SM_DoorFrame** static mesh in the **Props** folder.
4. Drag the **SM_DoorFrame** static mesh onto the level in the main editor (see Figure 2.26(a)).
5. Rename this actor to **WestDoorFrame** and make the following changes to its **Scale** in the **Transform** section of its Details rollout:

> **Mesh Name:** WestDoorFrame
> **Scale X:** 3
> **Scale Y:** 6
> **Scale Z:** 2.5

6. Position the `WestDoorFrame` mesh so that it fits on the west entrance of the Lobby. You might want to check out the placement of the mesh from both inside and outside to make sure its placement is all right (see Figure 2.26(b)).

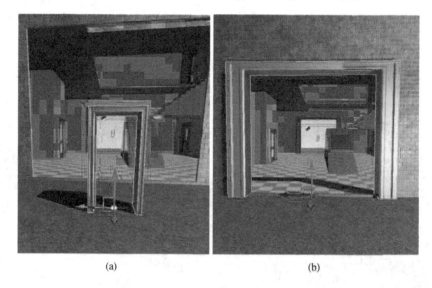

(a)   (b)

FIGURE 2.26: (a) Original Door Frame Mesh. (b) Door Frame Scaled Up and Placed.

7. Find the `SM_GlassWindow` static mesh in the **Props** folder.
8. Drag the `SM_GlassWindow` static mesh onto the level in the main editor.
9. Make the following changes to its `Scale` in the `Transform` section of this mesh's Details rollout:

> **Mesh Name:** WestDoor1
> **Scale X:** 1.0
> **Scale Y:** 2.8
> **Scale Z:** 2.5

10. Position the `WestDoor1` mesh so that it fits on the left half of the door frame. You might want to check out the placement of the mesh from both inside and outside to make sure its placement is all right and exactly in the middle of the door frame.
11. Find the `SM_PillarFrame300` static mesh in the **Props** folder.
12. Drag the `SM_PillarFrame300` static mesh onto the level in the main editor on top of the glass door mesh.
13. Make the following changes to its `Scale` in the `Transform` section of this mesh's Details rollout:

> **Mesh Name:** WestDoor1Handle
> **Scale X:** 0.1

FIGURE 2.27: The Placement of the Door Handle.

Scale Y: 0.2
Scale Z: 0.05

14. Position the `WestDoor1Handle` mesh so that it fits on the right side inner edge of the glass door, where a sliding door handle would usually be. You might want to check out the placement of the mesh from both inside and outside to make sure its placement is all right and exactly in the middle of the glass door (see Figure 2.27).

15. We will now parent the door handle to the door, so that it will be moved with the door when the door opens. To do this perform the following steps:

    a. Find the `WestDoor1Handle` in the **World Outliner**.

    b. `Right-Click` on the `WestDoor1Handle` in the **World Outliner** and choose the `Attach To` option from the menu.

    c. Find and select the `WestDoor1` from the list. This will attach the door handle to the door.

    d. You can alternatively drag the `WestDoor1Handle` in the **World Outliner** onto the `WestDoor1` in the **World Outliner** to parent it.

16. This will complete the placement of one of the glass doors in the door frame.

FIGURE 2.28: The West Door Complete.

17. Add the second sliding glass door and its handle in the door frame by taking similar steps you took in step 7– step 16.
18. Rename the second glass door and its handle WestDoor2 and WestDoor2Handle, respectively.
19. This will complete the placement of the entrance on the west side of the lobby. Your entrance should look similar to Figure 2.28.
20. Hold the Control key on your keyboard and Left-Click on the WestDoor1, WestDoor2, and WestDoorFrame to select all of the door related meshes. Notice that since we have parented the door handles to the doors, selecting the door will also select the handle.
21. With all of the door meshes selected, hold Alt+Shift and drag a copy of the door meshes onto the east side entrance of the lobby.
22. Replace the word West with East in the name of each duplicate copy.

ADDING INTERIOR DOORS

With our lobby entrances placed, let's focus on the interior of our building. We will add interior doors inside of our building in the next few steps. The process is similar to what we did for the entrance doors. We place a door frame mesh and then add the door mesh itself. We will then parent the door mesh with the door frame mesh, so that we can easily replicate it for the rest of the level.

1. Navigate to the inside of the lobby in the main editor.
2. Locate and open the **Props** folder in the **Starter Content** folder in the **Content Browser**.
3. Find the **SM_DoorFrame** static mesh in the **Props** folder.
4. Drag the **SM_DoorFrame** static mesh onto the level in the main editor (see Figure 2.29(a)).
5. Rename this actor to a name like **FirstFloorDoorFrame1** and make the following changes to its **Scale** in the **Transform** section of its Details rollout:

> **Mesh Name:** FirstFloorDoorFrame1
> **Scale X:** 1.0
> **Scale Y:** 2.0
> **Scale Z:** 1.5

6. Position the **FirstFloorDoorFrame1** mesh so that it fits on the entrance of one of the rooms between the lobby and the north (or south) wing. You might want to check out the placement of the mesh from both inside and outside to make sure its placement is all right (see Figure 2.29(b)).

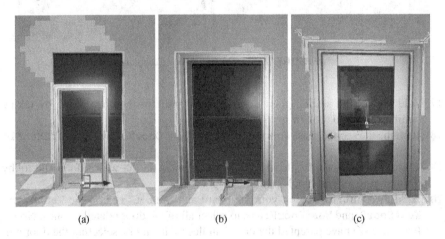

(a)   (b)   (c)

FIGURE 2.29: (a) Original Door Frame Mesh. (b) Door Frame Scaled Up and Placed. (c) Door Positioned Inside Door Frame.

7. Find the **SM_Door** static mesh in the **Props** folder.
8. Drag the **SM_Door** static mesh onto the level in the main editor.
9. Rename this actor to a name like **FirstFloorDoor1** and make the following changes to its **Scale** in the **Transform** section of its Details rollout:

> **Mesh Name:** FirstFloorDoor1
> **Scale X:** 1.5
> **Scale Y:** 2.0

> **Scale Z:** 1.5

10. Position the `FirstFloorDoor1` mesh so that it fits in the door frame. You might want to check out the placement of the mesh from both inside and outside to make sure its placement is all right (see Figure 2.29(c)).
11. Parent the door to the door frame. Within the **World Outliner** you may drag the door onto the door frame actor to parent them, or `Right-Click` on the door and choose `Attach To` and select the door frame from the list of actors.
12. Select both the door and door frame mesh. You may hold the `Control` key and `Left-Click` on each mesh to select both, or select them from the **World Outliner**.
13. With both meshes selected, press `Control+G` on your keyboard to group the two static meshes together. This will group the two meshes together, so that selecting one will automatically select both. This will make it much easier to replicate these actors in the scene.
14. Select the grouped door/door frame static meshes.
15. Hold `Alt+Shift` and drag the left (or right) horizontal axis of the translate gizmo to make a copy of these meshes.
16. Place the copy inside of the interior openings between the lobby and the wing (north/south).
17. Repeat Steps 15–16 for other door openings on the first floor.
18. Repeat Steps 15–16 for other door openings on the second floor.
19. Repeat Steps 15–16 for elevator door openings on the first and second floor.
20. Save your level and progress.

ADDING WINDOWS

Let's now focus on adding the windows to our building. The process will be similar to the process of adding doors. Each window is made of a window frame mesh and a glass mesh. Both of these meshes are available from the Starter Content we included in the project at its creation time. Similar to placing the door meshes, we will first place the window frame, add the glass mesh to it, and group the two meshes. We will then copy this group for each window opening in our geometry.

1. Navigate to the outside of the building on the west or east side of the north wing or the South Wing in the main editor.
2. Locate and open the `Props` folder in the `Starter Content` folder in the **Content Browser**.
3. Find the `SM_WindowFrame` static mesh in the `Props` folder.
4. Drag the `SM_WindowFrame` static mesh onto the wall in the main editor (see Figure 2.30(a)).
5. Rename this actor to a name like `WindowFrame1` and make the following changes to its `Scale` in the `Transform` section of its Details rollout:

> **Mesh Name:** WindowFrame1
> **Scale X:** 1.0
> **Scale Y:** 1.0
> **Scale Z:** 1.0

6. Position the `WindowFrame1` mesh so that it fits inside one of the window openings in the north (or south) wing. You might want to check out the placement of the mesh from both inside and outside to make sure its placement is all right (see Figure 2.30(b)).

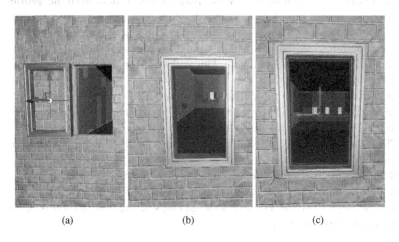

(a)   (b)   (c)

FIGURE 2.30: (a) Original Window Frame Mesh. (b) Window Frame Mesh Placed. (c) Window Glass Positioned Inside Window Frame and Grouped.

7. Find the `SM_GlassWindow` static mesh in the `Props` folder.
8. Drag the `SM_GlassWindow` static mesh onto the level in the main editor.
9. Make the following changes to its `Scale` in the `Transform` section of this mesh's Details rollout:

> **Mesh Name:** WindowGlass1
> **Scale X:** 1.0
> **Scale Y:** 0.75
> **Scale Z:** 0.6

10. Position the `WindowGlass1` mesh so that it fits on the window frame. You might want to check out the placement of the mesh from both inside and outside to make sure its placement is all right and exactly in the middle of the window frame.
11. Parent the window glass mesh to the window frame. Within the **World Outliner** you may drag the window glass onto the window frame actor to parent them, or `Right-Click` on the door and choose `Attach To` and select the window frame from the list of actors.

12. Select both glass and window frame meshes. Hold the `Control` key and `Left-Click` on each mesh to select both, or select them from the **World Out-liner**.
13. With both meshes selected, press `Control+G` on your keyboard to group the two static meshes together. This will group the two meshes together, so that selecting one will automatically select both. This will make is much easier to replicate these actors in the scene.
14. Select the grouped window glass/window frame static meshes.
15. Hold `Alt+Shift` and drag the left (or right) horizontal axis of the translate gizmo to make a copy of these meshes.
16. Place the copy inside of the window openings of the wing (north/south).
17. Repeat Steps 15–16 for the remaining windows on both side of each wing.
18. Save your level and progress.

What Happened in TUTORIAL 2.4...

In this tutorial we added some static meshes to our level. We used the static meshes available from the Starter Content to add some doors and windows to our level. We learned to group static meshes for convenient selection and manipulation purposes. We also learned how to parent static meshes to one another.

So far we have created our geometry with BSP brushes and some static meshes. In order for us to see around in the level, especially the interior of the building, while we were adding geometry, we created a point light and locked our viewport to the light in step 24 of Tutorial 2.2 on page 42.

In the next tutorial we will place some static lights in the level. After we place these lights and make modifications to their properties to suit our need, we will remove our point light and build the lighting.

> If you build lighting before you have placed lights in the level, the majority of your level will look dark. To get the un-lit version of the level back, click on the ▼ next to the **Build** button on the menu bar, and choose `Build Geometry`. This should make the lighting neutral for you to proceed with the design process.

2.5 REFINING THE LEVEL WITH LIGHTING

After the initial mesh pass (in which you will populate the level with your initial meshes) it is time to have your lighting established. This stage of the process will involve placing lights into the level and adjusting lighting parameters, building the lighting, and working on the light/material interactions to get the visuals of your level right.

In the next tutorial we will populate our level with some light actors.

To find updates to this tutorial and updated instructions about its implementation on other UE4 versions please visit the book's companion website at: http://www.RVRLAB.com/UE4Book/

TUTORIAL 2.5   Establishing the Level's Lighting

We will make the lights static so that they will not affect the run-time performance of the level.

ADDING YOUR FIRST LIGHT

1. Navigate to the inside of the lobby.
2. Click on the **Lights** tab in the **Place** mode under the **Modes** in the upper left corner of the main editor. *Alternatively, you can press* Shift+1 *to go to the* **Place** *tab.*
3. Drag a Point Light into the level. *Alternatively, you can hold the L key on your keyboard and* Left-Click *in the level to place a Point Light.*
4. If the Point Light is not selected, Left-Click on its icon to select it.
5. In the Details rollout of the Point Light change its properties to the following:

Mobility: Static
Intensity: 5000
Attenuation Radius: 1000
Source Radius: 10
Source Length: 100
Affects World: Checked
Cast Shadow: Checked
Use Inverse Squared Falloff: Checked

6. Place the light under one of the Walkways, centered with the Lobby door (see Figure 2.31(a)).
7. Make a copy of this light (by Alt-dragging) and place it on the left side of the walkway close to the wall (see Figure 2.31(b)).
8. Make another copy of this light (by Alt-dragging) and place it on the right side close to the other end of the walkway close to the wall.
9. Hold the Control key on your keyboard and Left-Click on the three lights to select them.
10. Press Control+G to group these lights together.
11. With the group of lights still selected Shift+Alt drag to make a copy of the group.

12. Keep dragging the lights to place them under the other walkway at the opposite end of the lobby (see Figure 2.31(c)).

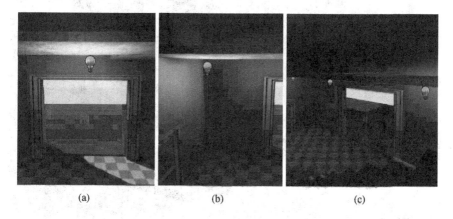

(a)   (b)   (c)

FIGURE 2.31: (a) Placing the First Light. (b) Placement of the Duplicate Light. (c) The Three lights on the First Floor Duplicated and Placed at the Opposite Walkway.

13. With the duplicated three lights selected, hold the `Control` key on your keyboard and `Left-Click` on the first three lights to add them to the selection.
14. With the group of lights selected `Shift+Alt` drag upwards to make a copy of the group.
15. Keep dragging the duplicate lights upwards to place them below the ceiling of the lobby.
16. Perform Steps 2–15 to add lights to each floor of the North and the South Wing, until you get a lighting condition that suits your taste.
17. Build the lighting of your level, by clicking on the **Build** button ![icon] in the toolbar located at the top of the main editor viewport.
18. Feel free to adjust the light locations, add or remove lights, and rebuild the lighting until you get the desired lighting conditions.
19. Save your level when you are satisfied with the lighting of your level.
20. A view of the level lobby, while played with the lighting built, is shown in Figure 2.32.

What Happened in TUTORIAL 2.5...

In this tutorial we added some basic lights to our level. We used static lights so as to not affect the runtime performance of our level. We learned to group lights much in the same way we grouped static meshes in order to conveniently place them in the level.

FIGURE 2.32: The Level Lighting Build.

2.6 ADDING FUNCTIONALITY

So far we have been placing static items in our level, whether they were brush geometry, static meshes for the doors and windows, or the lighting of the level. One important feature is missing, functionality! In the next tutorial we will implement a simple functionality into the lobby entrance doors – i.e., the ability for the doors to detect the player and open when the player gets close and close when he/she walks away from the door.

In Unreal Engine 4, our programming tool is called Blueprint Editor. There are two types of Blueprints, the **Level Blueprint** and the **Class Blueprint**. In the next tutorial we will use the Level Blueprint for our programming to implement a sliding door functionality. Later on in this book we dedicate two chapters to programming blueprints.

> To find updates to this tutorial and updated instructions about its implementation on other UE4 versions please visit the book's companion website at: http://www.RVRLAB.com/UE4Book/

TUTORIAL 2.6   Enhancing the Level's Geometry with Meshes

In this tutorial we will learn how to use the level blueprint to add some functionality to our level, such as having the lobby doors slide open when a player walks up to them and close when the player steps away.

LOBBY ENTRANCE DOORS TRIGGERS

Let's first add a trigger volume to our level so that we can trigger an event when something happens in the level (e.g., when a player overlaps with the trigger volume).

1. Navigate to the west side of the building in the main editor.
2. Click on the **Basic** tab in the **Place** mode under the Modes in the upper left corner of the main editor. *Alternatively, you can press Shift+1 to go to the **Place** tab.*
3. Drag a Box Trigger into the level.
4. If the Box Trigger is not selected, Left-Click on its icon to select it.

FIGURE 2.33: The Trigger Volume for the Entrance of the Lobby.

5. In the Details rollout of the Box Trigger, change its properties to the following:

Mobility: Static
Box Trigger Name: WestTriggerBox
Box Extent X: 300
Box Extent Y: 300
Box Extent Z: 250

6. Move and place the `Box Trigger` so that it is placed and centered at the middle of the Lobby entrance door.
7. You want to have the box stick out of the door frame on both the inside and outside of the door so that it gives enough space for the player to activate the sliding doors (see Figure 2.33).
8. With the `WestTriggerBox` selected hold the `Alt+Shift` and drag a copy of the trigger box onto the east entrance of the lobby.
9. Rename the duplicate Trigger Box to `EastTriggerBox`.

OPENING THE LEVEL BLUEPRINT

With the trigger box created, we are now ready to start programming the sliding door functionality.

10. On the main editor toolbar locate the **Blueprints** button ▓.
11. `Left-Click` on the ▼ next to the **Blueprints** button and from the popup menu select the `Open Level Blueprint` option.
12. This will open up the Level Blueprint in the Blueprint Editor.

ADDING TIMELINES

With the Level Blueprint open in the Blueprint Editor, you will see the Event Graph empty. This is where you program your level blueprint. The first task we will perform is to create a timeline. A timeline is basically a curve that we can utilize to control any dynamic aspect of the game controlled by a time-dependent function. Since the sliding door functionality can be represented as the translation of the glass doors over a period of time, this functionality is perfectly suitable to be implemented by a timeline.

13. `Right-Click` somewhere on the Event Graph in the Blueprint Editor.
14. Type `Timeline` in the search bar of the popup menu.
15. Select the `Add Timeline` option.
16. This will create a timeline in your level blueprint (see Figure 2.34(a)).
17. Rename this timeline to `WestDoorTimeline`.
18. `Double-Click` on the timeline to open it up in the curve editor.
19. Check the checkbox `Use Last Keyframe?` for the `WestDoorTimeline`.
20. `Left-Click` on the New Variable Icon + icon to add a **Vector Track** to your timeline (see Figure 2.34(b)).
21. Rename the **Vector Track** to `WestDoorwayTrack`.

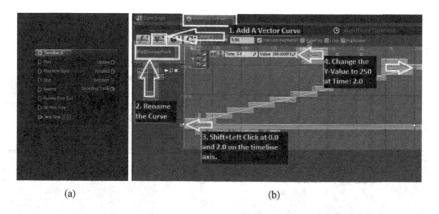

(a)   (b)

FIGURE 2.34: (a) Create a Timeline. (b) Create a Vector Track for Sliding Doors in the Curve Editor.

22. Hold the `Shift` key on your keyboard and `Left-Click` on the track at time 0.0 to add a key in that location along the timeline.
23. Hold the `Shift` key on your keyboard and `Left-Click` on the track at time 2.0 to add another key in that location along the timeline.
24. We would like to have the doors slide along their Y-axes. We will lock the X- and Z- axes. To do so, `Left-Click` on the lock icon next to the X- and Z- axes.
25. With the X- and Z- axes locked, we can now enter values in our Y component of the vector track. We would like the door to slide about 250 units along its Y- axis.
26. `Left-Click` on the key (the diamond shape) at time 2.0 and type the value of 250 in the **Value** box on the upper left corner of the curve editor (see Figure 2.34(b)).
27. If the key frame snaps out of the view, you can rescale the curve editor by clicking on the ↕ in the upper left corner of the editor .
28. Repeat Steps 13–27 to create another timeline and Vector track for the East Door. Name this timeline `EastDoorTimeline` and its corresponding Vector track `EastDoorwayTrack`.

ESTABLISHING INITIAL DOOR LOCATIONS

Now that we have our timelines and vector tracks for the locations of sliding doors ready, it is time to start programming. In this step, we will establish the initial locations of the four sliding glass doors and store these values in variables. Remember that we have two sliding doors for the west entrance and two for the east entrance to the lobby.

29. `Left-Click` on the new **Variable** (⁺V icon) under the **My Blueprint** tab to create a new variable in your level blueprint.
30. Rename this variable to `WestDoor1Location`.
31. In the `WestDoor1Location` variable's Details rollout, click on the **Variable Type** drop-down list and choose **Vector** (see Figure 2.35(a)).

32. Create three additional variables of type **Vector** and rename them to WestDoor2Location, EastDoor1Location, and EastDoor2Location.

33. Your My Blueprint tab should look similar to Figure 2.35(b).

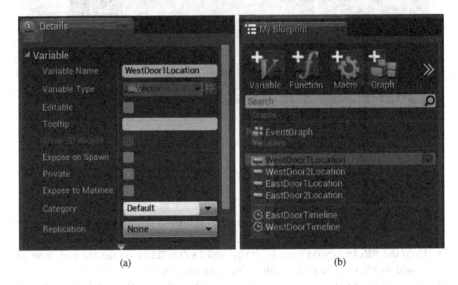

      (a)   (b)

FIGURE 2.35: (a) Variable Details Rollout. (b) Four Variables Created to Hold the Glass Doors Initial Locations.

34. Go back to the main editor by either minimizing the Blueprint Editor or moving it out of the way, temporarily.

35. In the main editor Left-Click on the WestDoor1 glass door mesh to select it.

36. With the WestDoor1 selected, go back to the Blueprint Editor.

37. Right-Click on the Event Graph.

38. From the menu select the **Create Reference to WestDoor1** (see Figure 2.36(a)).

39. Right-Click above the WestDoor1 reference on the Event Graph.

40. Type **Event Begin Play** in the search bar and place the **Event Begin Play** event trigger above the WestDoor1 reference.

41. Drag a wire out from the WestDoor1. This will open up the popup menu again.

42. Uncheck the **Context Sensitive** checkbox and type **Get Actor Location** in the search bar.

43. Place the **Get Actor Location** node to the right of the WestDoor1 actor referent (see Figure 2.36(b)).

44. Drag the WestDoor1Location variable you created earlier onto the Event Graph to the right of the **Get Actor Location** node and choose **Set** from the menu. This will place a Setter for the WestDoor1Location variable.

45. Make the following connections (see Figure 2.36(c)):

Get Actor Location Return Value output ↔ WestDoor1Location input.
Event Begin Play exec (white) output ↔ Set exec (white) input.

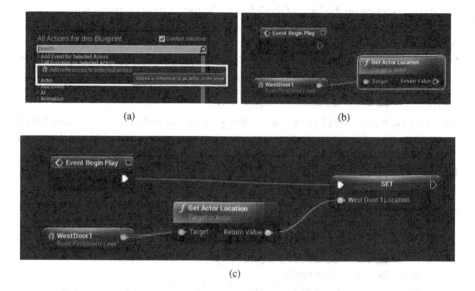

(a)   (b)

(c)

FIGURE 2.36: (a) Placing a Reference to an Actor in the Event Graph. (b) Getting the Actor's Location. (c) Storing the Initial Location of the Door.

46. Go back to the main editor by either minimizing the Blueprint Editor or moving it out of the way, temporarily.
47. In the main editor **Left-Click** on the **WestDoor2** glass door mesh to select it.
48. With the **WestDoor2** selected, go back to the Blueprint Editor.
49. **Right-Click** on the Event Graph below the **Get Actor Location**.
50. From the menu select the **Add Reference to WestDoor2**.
51. Drag a wire out from the **WestDoor2**. This will open up the popup menu again.
52. Make sure the **Context Sensitive** checkbox is unchecked and type **Get Actor Location** in the search bar.
53. Place the **Get Actor Location** node to the right of the **WestDoor2** actor reference.
54. Drag the **WestDoor2Location** variable you created earlier onto the Event Graph to the right of the **Get Actor Location** node and choose **Set** from the menu. This will place a Setter for the **WestDoor2Location** variable.
55. Make the following connections:

Get Actor Location Return Value output ↔ WestDoor2Location input.
1st Set exec (white) output ↔ 2nd Set exec (white) input.

56. Go back to the main editor by either minimizing the Blueprint Editor or moving it out of the way, temporarily.
57. In the main editor **Left-Click** on the **EastDoor1** glass door mesh to select it.
58. With the **EastDoor1** selected, go back to the Blueprint Editor.
59. **Right-Click** on the Event Graph below the **Get Actor Location**.
60. From the menu select the **Add Reference to EastDoor1**.
61. Drag a wire out from the **EastDoor1**. This will open up the popup menu again.
62. Make sure the **Context Sensitive** checkbox is unchecked and type **Get Actor Location** in the search bar.
63. Place the **Get Actor Location** node to the right of the **EastDoor1** actor referent.
64. Drag the **EastDoor1Location** variable you created earlier onto the Event Graph to the right of the **Get Actor Location** node and choose **Set** from the menu. This will place a Setter for the **EastDoor1Location** variable.
65. Make the following connections:

> Get Actor Location Return Value output $\leftrightarrow$ EastDoor1Location input.
> 2nd Set exec (white) output $\leftrightarrow$ 3rd Set exec (white) input.

66. Go back to the main editor by either minimizing the Blueprint Editor or moving it out of the way, temporarily.
67. In the main editor **Left-Click** on the **EastDoor2** glass door mesh to select it.
68. With the **EastDoor2** selected, go back to the Blueprint Editor.
69. **Right-Click** on the Event Graph below the **Get Actor Location**.
70. From the menu select the **Add Reference to EastDoor2**.
71. Drag a wire out from the **EastDoor2**. This will open up the popup menu again.
72. Make sure the **Context Sensitive** checkbox is unchecked and type **Get Actor Location** in the search bar.
73. Place the **Get Actor Location** node to the right of the **EastDoor2** actor referent.
74. Drag the **EastDoor2Location** variable you created earlier onto the Event Graph to the right of the **Get Actor Location** node and choose **Set** from the menu. This will place a Setter for the **EastDoor2Location** variable.
75. Make the following connections:

> Get Actor Location Return Value output $\leftrightarrow$ EastDoor2Location input.
> 3rd Set exec (white) output $\leftrightarrow$ 4th Set exec (white) input.

76. Your network for setting the four doors initial location should look similar to Figure 2.37.
77. Marquee drag around all of the graph for setting the four door locations and press the **C** key on your keyboard to create a comment section for this network. Name the section **Set Doors Initial Locations**.

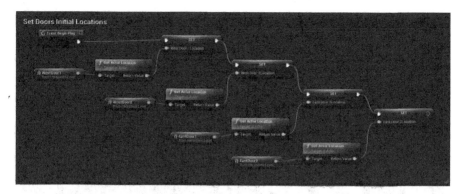

FIGURE 2.37: The Complete Network for Setting Door Locations.

PROGRAMMING WITH THE TIMELINE

Now with our sliding glass doors' initial location established in their respective variables, we are ready to program the doors in such a way that when a player walks up to them they slide open.

In order to do this, we will use a begin overlap and end overlap events for each trigger. On begin overlap (which happens when a player enters the trigger box) we will play the timeline. On end overlap event (which happens when the player leaves the trigger box) we reverse the timeline.

Remember that we created a vector track in our timeline. We will use the values of this vector track to add from the location of one of the doors to update its location along the timeline's timing. This will slide the door out. For the other door, we wish to slide it in the opposite direction. To achieve this, we will subtract the second door's location from the vector track of the timeline to slide the door to the opposite direction.

78. Go back to the main editor by either minimizing the Blueprint Editor or moving it out of the way, temporarily.
79. In the main editor `Left-Click` on the `WestDoor1` glass door mesh to select it.
80. Change the `Mobility` of the mesh to `Movable`, if it is static.
81. Change the `Mobility` of the other three glass door meshes and their handles to `Movable` as well.
82. In the main editor `Left-Click` on the `WestTriggerBox` glass door mesh to select it.
83. With the `WestTriggerBox` selected, scroll to the **Collision** section of its Details rollout.
84. `Left-Click` on the `Collision Preset` and from the dropdown list select `Custom`.
85. Set the `Collision Responses` of everything to `Ignore` except for the **Pawn**.
86. Set the `Collision Responses` of the **Pawn** to `Overlap` (see Figure 2.38(a)).
87. With the `WestTriggerBox` still selected in the main editor, open the Blueprint

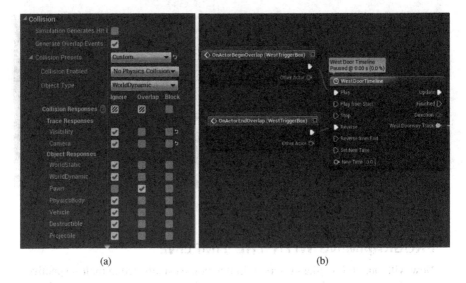

(a)   (b)

FIGURE 2.38: (a) Only Pawn's Collision Is Set to Overlap. (b) Play and Reverse the Timeline on Begin Overlap and End Overlap Events.

Editor.

88. **Right-Click** on the Event Graph to the left of the **WestDoorTimeline** and type **Actor Begin Overlap** in the search box.

89. Select and place the **OnActorBeginOverlap** event to the left of the **WestDoorTimeline**.

90. Connect the exec(white) output of the **OnActorBeginOverlap** event to the **Play** input of the **WestDoorTimeline**.

91. **Right-Click** on the Event Graph below the **AOnctorBeginOverlap** and type **Actor End Overlap** in the search box.

92. Select and place the **OnActorEndOverlap** event to the left of the **WestDoorTimeline**.

93. Connect the exec(white) output of the **OnActorEndOverlap** event to the **Reverse** input of the **WestDoorTimeline**.

94. Your network should look similar to Figure 2.38(b) so far.

95. Go back to the main editor by either minimizing the Blueprint Editor or moving it out of the way, temporarily.

96. In the main editor **Left-Click** on the **EastTriggerBox** glass door mesh to select it.

97. With the **EastTriggerBox** selected, scroll to the **Collision** section of its Details rollout.

98. **Left-Click** on the **Collision Preset** and from the dropdown list select **Custom**.

99. Set the **Collision Responses** of everything to **Ignore** except for the **Pawn**.

100. Set the **Collision Responses** of the **Pawn** to **Overlap**.

101. With the **EastTriggerBox** still selected in the main editor, open the Blueprint

Editor.

102. **Right-Click** on the Event Graph to the left of the `EastDoorTimeline` and type `Actor Begin Overlap` in the search box.

103. Select and place the `OnActorBeginOverlap` event to the left of the `EastDoorTimeline`.

104. Connect the exec(white) output of the `OnActorBeginOverlap` event to the `Play` input of the `EastDoorTimeline`.

105. **Right-Click** on the Event Graph below of the `OnActorBeginOverlap` and type `Actor End Overlap` in the search box.

106. Select and place the `OnActorEndOverlap` event to the left of the `EastDoorTimeline`.

107. Connect the exec(white) output of the `OnActorEndOverlap` event to the `Reverse` input of the `EastDoorTimeline`.

108. Compile your blueprint to save your progress so far.

UPDATING DOOR LOCATIONS FROM THE TIMELINE

109. Find the `WestDoor1` reference (the blue node) in the graph editor from the `Set Doors Initial Locations` section we created in Step 38 on page 74.

110. Duplicate this reference by either pressing `Control+W` on your keyboard or copying and pasting it.

111. Place the duplicate reference to `WestDoor1` slightly above and to the right of the `WestTimeline`.

112. Drag a wire out from this `WestDoor1` reference and check the `Context Sensitive` checkbox.

113. Type `Set Actor Location` in the search bar and place the `Set Actor Location` to the right of the `WestDoor1` reference.

114. Drag a copy of the `WestDoor1Location` variable onto the event graph from the `My Blueprint` tab to the left.

115. Select `Get` from the popup menu.

116. Place the `WestDoor1Location` getter node below the `WestDoor1` reference.

117. Drag a wire out from the `WestDoor1Location` getter node and type − in the search bar.

118. Place a `Vector-Vector` expression. This should connect the output of the `WestDoor1Location` getter node to the **A** input of the − expression.

119. Make the following connections (see Figure 2.39):

> Update of WestDoorTimeline ↔ exec(white) input of Set Location
> WestDoorWay Track of WestDoorTimeline ↔ B input of −
> Output of − ↔ New Location input of Set Location

120. Drag a copy of the `WestDoor2Location` variable onto the event graph from the `My Blueprint` tab to the left.

121. Select `Get` from the popup menu.

122. Place the `WestDoor2Location` getter node below the − (subtract) expression.

123. Drag a wire out from the `WestDoor2Location` and type + in the search bar.

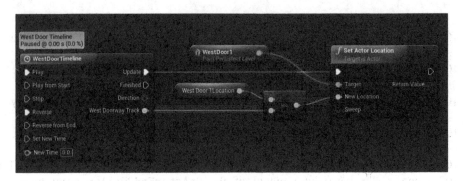

FIGURE 2.39: Updating West Door 1 Location.

124. Place a `Vector+Vector` node below the `Set Actor Location` node.
125. Drag a wire from the `WestDoorway Track` to the B input of the + node.
126. Find the `WestDoor2` reference (the blue node) in the graph editor from the `Set Doors Initial Locations` section.
127. Duplicate this reference by either pressing `Control+W` on your keyboard or copying and pasting it.
128. Place the duplicate reference to `WestDoor2` slightly below the first `Set Actor Location` expression.
129. Drag a wire out from this `WestDoor2` reference and make sure that the `Context Sensitive` checkbox is checked.
130. Type `Set Actor Location` in the search bar and place the `Set Actor Location` to the right of the `WestDoor2` reference.
131. Connect the output of the + expression to the `New Location` input of the `Set Actor Location` of the `WestDoor2`.
132. Connect the exec(white) output of the `Set Actor Location` of the first door to the exec(white) input of the `Set Actor Location` of the `WestDoor2`.
133. Marquee drag around all of the graph for updating the two west door locations and press the `C` key on your keyboard to create a comment section for this network. Name the section to `Update West Door Location`.
134. Your network should look similar to Figure 2.40.
135. Compile your blueprint and save your level and progress.
136. Close or minimize the blueprint editor.
137. Play the level by pressing `Control+P` or the Play button in the main editor.
138. Walk up to the West entrance of the lobby to check out and see if the doors open properly.
139. If the doors opened the wrong way, swap the − expression and + expression places in the calculations network. This may be due to your naming of the doors in a different order than what we have done in this chapter.
140. Perform Steps 109–139 for the East Doors to create the network that updates their location from the `EastDoorTimeline`.

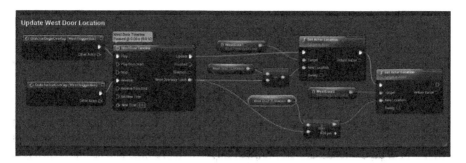

FIGURE 2.40: Updating Both West Door Locations.

MAKING THE PLAYER MESH VISIBLE

Now that your level is ready and the functionality for the lobby doors have created in the level blueprint, it's time to put the player mesh back in the game.

141. In the **Content Browser** find and open the **Blueprints**.
142. Open the **MyCharacter** blueprint by double-clicking on it.
143. Click on the **Components** tab on the upper right corner of the Blueprint Editor.
144. Select the **Mesh1P** mesh.
145. Locate the **Rendering** section of the **Mesh1P** Details rollout.
146. Check the **Visible** checkbox. This will make the first person mesh visible.
147. Compile and save the **MyCharacter** blueprint.
148. Close the Blueprint Editor.
149. Save all of your progress from the **File ▶ Save All**.
150. Play the level and enjoy your first functional map.

What Happened in TUTORIAL 2.6...

In this tutorial we added some basic functionality to our level. We placed trigger volumes inside our level where the lobby entrance doors were located. We then utilized these trigger volumes to program our level blueprint to perform certain actions when a player steps inside of the trigger volumes and when he/she steps outside of the volume.

We also learned about a very important and handy feature in the new Unreal Engine 4's programming toolbox, called Timelines. We learned how to utilize this feature to animate dynamic aspects of the gameplay, such as movable actors, controlling colors and lights, etc. We used Timelines to slide the doors of the entrance to the lobby open and closed.

In previous Unreal Engine releases such as Unreal Engine 3 and Unreal Development Kit, we had to use Matinee and Kismet to animate objects or control dynamic features in the level. The new Timeline feature saves us a tremendous amount of work to perform these tasks, all of which can now be simply programmed in Unreal Engine Blueprints.

2.7 SUMMARY

This chapter has introduced you to the process of level design. You also got your first overview of many concepts used throughout the different stages of game creation. It would be a great idea to go over the tutorials one more time and see how different pieces fell in place to create a functional shell for a simple game.

We learned about the brush geometry and how we can utilize these powerful tools to sketch out our level. We learned how to improve the visual look of our level by utilizing materials and lighting. We also got to include static meshes as well as movable static mesh objects into our level to decorate and create functionality. Finally, we added some very basic functionality to our level by programming the level blueprint.

Throughout the rest of this book we will delve into several aspects of Unreal Engine 4 that we utilized in the creation of this level. We will present details about UE4's materials, blueprint scripting system, and particle effects. We will also discuss other concepts that we didn't get to use in this level, such as terrains and landscapes.

2.8 EXERCISES

Exercise 1. In Tutorial 2.1 we created a new level based on the **Default** template. The **Default** level comes in with a few actors already placed in the level. Create a new level based on the **Blank** level template and add the basic actors we need to be able to proceed with the rest of the tutorials we covered in this chapter.

Exercise 2. In the first few steps of Tutorial 2.2 we created the basic outline geometry of our level. If you check out the exterior of our building as shown in Figure 2.41(a), you'll notice that the roofs are flat. Make the building roofs slanted similar to Figure 2.41(b). Perform the following tasks:

    a. Add a roof box to the top of each section of the building with a height of 64.

    b. Use the **Geometry Editing** mode (**shift+5**) to split the top edges of each roof box.

    c. Drag the new edge upwards to make the roof slanted similar to Figure 2.41(b).

    d. Can you make the roof look similar to Figure 2.42?

Exercise 3. Place some props in the building such as tables, chairs, etc.

Exercise 4. Section the North and South Wings of the building so that they each have multiple rooms.

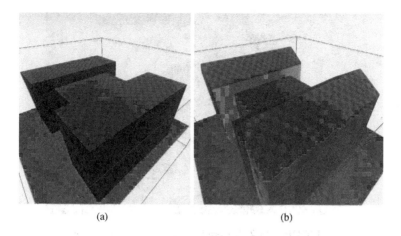

(a)   (b)

FIGURE 2.41: Different Types of Roofs for the Building.

Exercise 5. Use the concepts of adding functionality by blueprint scripting you learned in Tutorial 2.6 to make some of the interior doors open and close. Notice that we don't want these doors to slide open/close. We wish these doors to rotate as they open and close.

Exercise 6. Create an Elevator Car for the level.

Exercise 7. Make the Elevator go up when the player steps inside from the first floor, and down when the player steps inside from the second floor.

FIGURE 2.42: Decorating the Roof of the Building

3 Unreal Visual Scripting with Blueprints

3.1 INTRODUCTION TO UNREAL BLUEPRINTS

T HE blueprint system introduced in Unreal Engine 4 is an excellent way to hash out the functionality of your project without having to write everything out in code. The visual scripting that blueprints offer is a powerful tool for programmers and artists alike. From opening and closing doors, to complex path finding algorithms, everything in your game can be programmed entirely with blueprints.

In this chapter, we will go over several examples that dive into the visual scripting abilities that blueprints offer. These tutorials will build upon each other and therefore, it is important to complete the first tutorial, before moving on to the next.

3.2 A TOUR OF UNREAL BLUEPRINT EDITOR

The blueprint editor is the central location where you will be building your class blueprints and Level blueprints. The editor allows us to create visual scripts in the event graph that function like code to perform specific tasks. It also allows us to use the Components view to customize the physical assets that make up our blueprints. During the blueprint template overviews, we observed how these are used to create a character that can be moved by user input, but blueprints can be used for anything. From turning lights on and off to complex Artificial Intelligence algorithms.

3.2.1 GRAPH EDITOR

The Graph Editor panel is the heart of the Blueprint system. It is here that you will create the networks of nodes and wires that will define your scripted behavior. Nodes can quickly be selected by clicking on them and repositioned via dragging [22]. Table 3.1 presents the controls you can use to work within the graph editor[1]:

3.3 TYPES OF BLUEPRINTS

Unreal Engine 4 enables us to use visual scripting to perform a number of tasks including, level design, game logic programming, or encapsulating objects and classes. All of these tasks are available through the new visual scripting toolkit in Unreal Engine 4, called Blueprint scripting.

---

[1] The contents of this section are adapted from the official UE4 online documentation found at: https://docs.unrealengine.com/latest/INT/.

TABLE 3.1

Graph Editor Controls

Right-Click +Drag:	Pans the Graph	
Mouse Scroll:	Zooms the Graph	
Right-Click:	Brings up Context Menu	
Left-Click on a Node:	Selects the Node	
Left-Click +Drag:	Empty Space:	Selects the Nodes inside the marquee select box
	On a Node:	Moves the Node
	Pin to Pin:	Wires the pins together
	Pin to Space:	Brings up context menu showing only relevant nodes. Wires the original pin to a compatible pin on the created node
Ctrl+Left-Click +Drag:	Empty Space:	Toggles selection of nodes inside the select box
	Pin to Pin:	Moves wires from origin pin to the destination pin
Shft+Left-Click +Drag:	Adds the Nodes inside the marquee select box to the current selection	

There are different types of blueprints we can utilize in our games: Level blueprints, Class Blueprints, and Data-Only Blueprints. Each of these blueprint types has its own unique features that make it suitable for certain things.

3.3.1 LEVEL BLUEPRINTS

A Level blueprint is a specialized type of Blueprint that acts as a level-wide global event graph. Events pertaining to the level as a whole, or specific instances of Actors within the level, are used to fire off sequences of actions in the form of function calls or flow control operations [33].

The previous versions of Unreal Engine such as UDK or UE3 used a visual scripting tool called Kismet. In a sense, UE4's Level blueprints are similar to Kismet in previous versions of the Unreal Engine.

On of the important aspects of Level blueprints is their ability to provide control mechanisms for level streaming and Matinee. Moreover, you can utilize Level blueprints to bind events to Actors placed in the level and communicate information from class blueprints to the Level blueprint for updating certain game features, such as when a player levels up.

Each map has a Level blueprint by default that can be edited within Unreal Editor. However, new Level blueprints cannot be created through the editor interface [33].

For the first few tutorials in this chapter, we will create a project using the first person blueprint template. To create this project, we will select the **New Project** tab and find the **First Person** icon under the **Blueprint** tab. We will include **Starter Content**. Finally, we will give the new project a name such as **BlueprintTutorial01**.

3.3.2 CLASS BLUEPRINT

A Class Blueprint, often shortened to Blueprint, is an asset that allows content creators to easily add functionality on top of existing gameplay classes [4]. One of the benefits of these blueprints is the fact that you can create them visually, instead of by typing code. These assets are then saved in a content package and will be available through **Content Browser**. In other words, class blueprints are similar to new class or type of Actor which can then be placed into maps as instances.

3.3.3 DATA-ONLY BLUEPRINTS

A Data-Only Blueprint is a Class Blueprint that contains only the code (in the form of node graphs), variables, and components inherited from its parent [4]. These allow those inherited properties to be tweaked and modified, but no new elements can be added. These are essentially a replacement for archetypes and can be used to allow designers to tweak properties or set items with variations [4].

> We discussed the about the First Person Template Project in the Blueprint Template section from Chapter 1– Setting Up Unreal Project Templates. If you want to know how the first person template is working you can refer back to this chapter.

> To find updates to this tutorial and updated instructions about its implementation on other UE4 versions please visit the book's companion website at: http://www.RVRLAB.com/UE4Book/

TUTORIAL 3.1   Creating a Project and Including Starter Contents

CREATING A BLANK PROJECT

In this tutorial we will set up an empty project and include the starter contents from the Unreal Engine into it. We will first create a project to which we will add the starter content.

1. Open the Unreal Launcher and select the version of the engine you would like to work with.
2. Once the Unreal Launcher opens, choose **New Project** (see Figure 3.1).
3. Select the **Blueprint** as your project type, and make sure that the **First Person** is selected.
4. Select your platform (Desktop/Console) and your graphics quality.
5. Make sure you include the starter content (see Figure 3.1).
6. Give your project a name and click **Create Project**.

FIGURE 3.1: Creating a Blank Project.

PLAYING THE LEVEL

Now that our new project is created, we can begin exploring the Blueprint editor.

7. At this point, go ahead and press Play at the top of the editor. You can alternatively press `Alt+P` to play the level.
8. Move around in the level and get a feel for the `WASD` movement.
9. Press the `Escape` key to end the gameplay.

OPENING THE BLUEPRINT EDITOR

We will now open the Blueprint Editor and start learning a bit more detail about its sections and how it works on the Level blueprint. We will go over the differences between Level blueprints and Class Blueprints later in this chapter.

10. At the top of the editor window, you will notice an icon that says **Blueprints**.
11. `Left-Click` on the Blueprints button to open the popup menu.
12. `Left-Click` on the `Open Level blueprint` option in order to open and view the Level blueprint.
13. After opening the Level blueprint, you will be greeted with the `Event Graph` for our current level (see Figure 3.2). In this case, the Event Graph is the central location for all level specific events. As you can imagine, on a large level, this

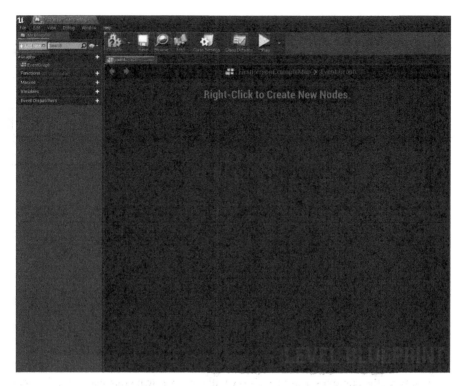

FIGURE 3.2: Blueprint Editor and Its Components.

graph can get cluttered. If it gets too cluttered, you can always create another event graph simply for organizational purposes.

14. To create a new Event Graph,**Left-Click** on **Graph** on the left side in the My **Blueprint** window. *Note: If you can't see the My Blueprints, click the arrows to bring up hidden options that don't fully fit on the screen.*

15. For our purposes, a single event graph should be enough. Just know that this option is available to you if you need it for a larger project. Notice that **Variables**, **Functions**, **Macros**, etc., are among other things that can also be added to your blueprint via the **My Blueprint window**. These things will be discussed in future sections.

What Happened in TUTORIAL 3.1...

You just set up a blank project, and included the starter content from the Unreal Engine to it.

Once the project was created you opened up the Level blueprint. This opens up the Blueprint Editor. You learned about the Event Graph and other items available for you to program your level.

To find updates to this tutorial and updated instructions about its implementation on other UE4 versions please visit the book's companion website at: http://www.RVRLAB.com/UE4Book/

TUTORIAL 3.2   Creating New Nodes

As you might have noticed, the empty Event Graph is displaying the message Right-Click to Create New Nodes, so let's do just that.

CREATING A NEW NODE

We will create a node called Event Begin Play. This node is called one time when the level is first opened. This event is useful for initializing default values for the level or running a sequence at the start of the level, before anything else takes place. For our game, let's display a message to the player on the screen.

1. Right-Click on the event graph and the search popup menu opens up.
2. Type Event Begin Play in the search bar (see Figure 3.3(a)). Notice that, as you type, the context sensitive window will narrow down your search for the item you are looking for.
3. Place the Event Begin Play node on the Event Graph (see Figure 3.3(b)).

(a)   (b)

FIGURE 3.3: (a) Searching for Event Begin Play. (b) The Event Begin Play Node.

4. The next node we need is called Print String which will print text on the screen, or print text to a log file. This is generally used for debugging purposes. There are multiple ways to add this node to the Event Graph at this point.
5. The best, and easiest, way is to click the right arrow on the Event Begin Play node, and then drag and release in an empty area on the Event Graph. This will

bring up the same context sensitive window as before, but this time, because it is context sensitive, it will only give us options that could work off of the Event Begin Play node. This helps narrow down our search when we are looking for a node that we might not know the name of.

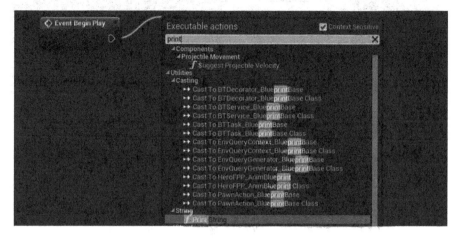

FIGURE 3.4: Adding Print String Node to the Event Graph.

6. In the search bar on the context sensitive window, type **Print**. *Because we know we want to print text to the screen, this will show options that are related to printing. The Executable Actions window shows us the closest options available to us based on what we typed. In this case we can use this predictive text to find the Print String node.*

7. Select the **Print String** node to place it in the Event Graph. This will auto-matically connect the **Print String** node to the **Event Begin Play** node (see Figure 3.4).

8. Compile and Save the Level blueprint.

9. At this point, if you press **Play** button in either the Blueprint Editor window or the main UE4 level editor, the default text "Hello" will display in the upper left corner of the main level viewport (see Figure 3.5).

What Happened in TUTORIAL 3.2...

In this tutorial, we have successfully created two nodes that worked together to print the word "Hello" on the screen. The purpose of this exercise was to demonstrate the simplicity of creating nodes and linking them together.

The logic of your game will obviously be more intricate and complex, but the way you implement this logic is just as simple as placing nodes the way we have just done. The blueprint system is designed to reduce the difficulty of

FIGURE 3.5: When the Level Starts, It prints Hello on the Screen.

implementing game logic. It also allows artists and programmers the freedom of being able to work together in a much more efficient way.

3.4   VARIABLES, FUNCTIONS, AND EVENTS

When creating blueprints, it is often necessary to utilize Variables, Functions, and Events to solve problems and complete tasks. In the previous tutorials, we utilized an event called **Event Begin Play** and a function called **Print String** but we didn't really explain what these are or what their similarities/differences are. In this section, these will be properly explained to avoid confusion in future sections. Figure 3.6

FIGURE 3.6: A Simple Network of Events/Actions.

starts with an event called **Start Game**. This event calls a node that sets the value of a variable **DeltaTime** to 0.0. Lastly, a function called **Setup Level** is called.

3.4.1   EVENTS

Events are nodes that can be placed in the event graph that will fire whenever a specific event has occurred. The engine listens for these events in such a way as to avoid an extreme amount of computing power and when the event in question happens, the event node fires and runs the code branching off of it.

This can be used to check for many different things such as taking damage or dying, seeing if an object has been destroyed or if an objective has been completed in a level. This list goes on endlessly, however using too many listeners, especially on mobile platforms, it can be quite computationally expensive. Just keep that in mind on larger projects to avoid having hundreds or thousands of unnecessary event listeners in the main game loop.

3.4.2 FUNCTIONS

Functions are also nodes that you place in the event graph but they are quite different from events. Functions are run as they are called in a logic tree and cannot be fired as an event listener is fired. In our Tutorial 3.2, we have the function **Print String** being called in a logic tree that originates with an event being fired. The print string function can be placed in the event graph by itself but it will never do anything unless it is called upon by an event.

Functions can be designed to do just about anything. They can simply print text to the screen or they can perform complex AI calculations. Because of this, the computational power needed to run a function entirely depends on the logic contained inside the function. We can make our own local functions that exist only within the blueprint from which they were created to simplify code and improve readability. We can also use functions to fire events located in other blueprints.

3.4.3 VARIABLES

Variables are used in many different ways throughout the blueprint system, just as they are used in programming. Variables simply store a particular type of data to a name that can be written to or read from to perform all kinds of different tasks. For example, a float variable would store a floating point number (a number with a decimal point) such as 200.0. This can be used to store a player's health value so that the game can keep track of how much life the player has left, or it could be used in a complex calculation to determine how much damage needs to be dealt to an enemy. Variables can also store static meshes, materials, lights, or even other blueprints. In this chapter, we will often use functions that have variable inputs and outputs of different types.

3.5 CLASS BLUEPRINTS VS. LEVEL BLUEPRINTS

Now that we are somewhat familiar with the blueprint editor, we can now define the differences between class blueprints and Level blueprints. A Level blueprint is unique to the current UE4 level, and it is similar to the old style UDK kismet system, which had a tendency to become cluttered. Level blueprints can be useful for small sequences that are 100% unique and level specific.

In most cases however, it is better to use a class blueprint. Class blueprints are a unique feature newly introduced in Unreal Engine 4. A Class blueprint can contain the functionality of an encapsulated module with its own components, events, functions, and variables. Therefore, a Class blueprint has the potential to be reused throughout the level, or even across several levels, when needed.

This important property of Class blueprints saves space and can improve computational efficiency. Class blueprints can also save us from having to rescript the exact same sequences over and over as they are needed throughout a level. Only place script in the Level blueprint that is unique to the level, such as a cut scene or a boss fight.

Programmers, who are familiar with object-oriented programming, will recognize the term Class blueprint as a blueprint from which objects are created. This is exactly what a Class blueprint is. It directly ties into the concepts of classes and objects in programming languages such as Java and c++.

You create a class once as a template that can be used multiple times and in many different ways. Think back to Tutorial 3.3.3(b) where we placed two nodes in the Level blueprint in order to display text at the start of the level. What if we wanted this functionality in every level that we created? We would have to place these two nodes in every level's Level blueprint. Instead of doing it this way, let's implement the same simple functionality with a Class blueprint.

> To find updates to this tutorial and updated instructions about its implementation on other UE4 versions please visit the book's companion website at: http://www.RVRLAB.com/UE4Book/

TUTORIAL 3.3   Creating New Class Blueprints to Display Text

In this tutorial we will create a Class blueprint that is responsible for printing a text on the screen. The first thing we need to do is create the Class blueprint that we will be designing.

CREATING A CLASS BLUEPRINT

Since we already have a folder structure in place (because we selected the first person template for our project), we can place a new blueprint inside the Blueprints folder.

1. Find the `Blueprints` folder by navigating to it inside the **Content Browser** (lower left corner by default).
2. Once inside the `Blueprint` folder, you can create a new **Blueprint** in a couple different ways:
   a. You can click on the **Add New** button in the upper left corner of the **Content Browser** and select `Blueprint Class`. When you're prompted to select which type of Blueprint you want to create, choose **Actor** and give it the name `DisplayText`.
   b. You can also create a Blueprint by `right-clicking` a blank area in the **Content Browser** and selecting **Blueprint Class**.

3. After adding the Class blueprint either way, you should end up with a Blueprint called `DisplayText` in your **Content Browser** (see Figure 3.7).

FIGURE 3.7: A Class blueprint Created in the **Content Browser**.

PROGRAMMING THE CLASS BLUEPRINT

Next, we shall open this new Class blueprint in the Blueprint Editor to program its functionality within its Event Graph.

4. `Double-Click` on this newly created blueprint to open it in the Blueprint Editor.
5. This time, you may notice, it opens to the **Components** tab. Level blueprints don't have a components tab because any components of the level will simply be placed inside the level itself. The Defaults tab is also reserved for Class blueprints for the same reason.
6. `Left-Click` on the **Event Graph** tab in the upper right corner of the Blueprint editor to reveal the blank EventGraph of our new `DisplayText` Blueprint. Here is where we will place our nodes to display our string value, as we did in the previous tutorial.
7. Have the `Event Being Play` call the `Print String` function. *Note: You could also copy and paste these two nodes from the Level blueprint into the DisplayText blueprint if you wish* (see Figure 3.8).
8. After you do this, make sure you click **Compile** and **Save** to ensure that your Blueprint's nodes have been Compiled into code properly.
9. If there is an error, this icon will change and you will need to fix the problems with your nodes before you can continue. This is the same as debugging code that won't compile and run. In our case, everything should be working properly.

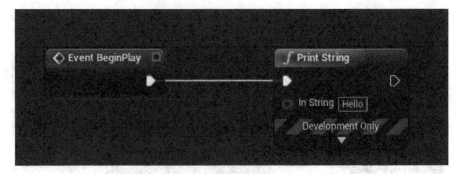

FIGURE 3.8: Programming the Print String Functionality in the Class blueprint.

PLACING CLASS BLUEPRINTS

In order for our blueprint to run, it must be placed into the level. The simplest way to place a Class blueprint in the level is to drag and drop it from the **Content Browser** onto the level viewport.

10. Drag and drop the `DisplayText` Blueprint from the **Content Browser** into the level somewhere.
11. At this time it is not important where it ends up in the level as there are not visual components, physics, audio, or other special components in our Blueprint.
12. We need to remove the nodes from the **Level blueprint** to ensure that we are only using the Class blueprint we created to display the text.
13. Open the Level blueprint.
14. Marquee drag around the `Event Begin Play` node and the `Print String` function to select them.
15. Press the **DEL** key to remove the network.
16. Compile and Save your Level blueprint.
17. After this is done, press **Play** in either the blueprint editor or the level editor to play the level.
18. As soon as the level starts, you should be able to see the word "Hello" in the top left corner of the main level viewport.

What Happened in TUTORIAL 3.3...

We have successfully created our own custom Blueprint in order to simply display text on the screen. This Class blueprint can be used as many times, in as many levels, as we want.

Using a Class blueprint is as simple as placing an actor based on the blueprint inside the level. You can place a Class blueprint by easily dragging it from the **Content Browser** on the level. If your blueprint class doesn't have any visible component it will not be visible in the level. In order to select such a Class blueprint you should find it in the list of actors within the **Scene Outliner**.

3.6   CONSTRUCTION SCRIPT

Before we move on, let's go over an important item that separates Class blueprints from Level blueprints – i.e., the **Construction Script**. The Construction Script runs following the Components list when an instance of a Class blueprint is created [8].

If you closed the `DisplayText` Blueprint editor, reopen it by finding it in the Content Browser. Once it's open, click the Graph button to view the Event Graph. Here, you will find another tab labeled **Construction Script**. If you do not see this tab, you can find it on the left side in the My Blueprint pane.

The purpose of the **Construction Script** is simple. Anything branching off of the **Construction Script** node will be run when the blueprint is created in the level. This allows us to initialize values for our Blueprints before they are run, and then simply have them created as the Blueprint is created in-game.

For example, we can set default health values and mana values for an enemy that hasn't been created in-game yet. When the enemy spawns, the construction script is called before anything else, and runs whatever nodes are attached to it. The most important thing to know about this script is that it will be run upon the creation of the Blueprint before any other part (even before Event Begin Play nodes). If you need to initialize values for your blueprint, this is a good place to do so.

Construction Scripts can be extremely powerful. Actions like performing traces into the world, or initial settings of meshes and materials may be performed in constructions scripts to achieve context-specific setup. For instance, a light Blueprint could determine what type of ground it is placed upon and choose the correct mesh to use from a set of meshes or a fence Blueprint could perform traces extending out in each direction to determine how long a fence is needed to span the distance [8].

3.7   COMPONENTS MODE

In Components Mode, you can add components to your Blueprint, manage the details of existing components, and arrange components. The list of components in Components Mode is hierarchical.

3.7.1   COMPONENTS

The Components pane allows components to be added to the Blueprint upon creation [6]. This provides a way for the level designers to add various components to a blueprint such as, collision volumes, static meshes, lights, etc. The components added in the Components list can also be assigned to instance variables providing access to them in the graphs of this or other Blueprints.

To add a component you can simply select the type of components you wish to add, and then press the **Add Component** button. You can also drag and drop the component from the **Content Browser** onto the gray area under the components list. You can parent components to one another by simply dragging and dropping the child component onto the parent.

To rename a component or an instanced variable you can simply `Left-Click` on the name of the component and press F2 and type in the new name. Components can also be renamed and transformed from their Details Rollout.

3.7.2   COMPONENTS EVENTS AND FUNCTIONS

Depending on the type of component, you are able to quickly add events and/or functions based on them within the Event Graph. For instance, a Box Component can have an Overlap event for when another Actor (such as a Pawn) passes into it, or a Point Light Component can have a Set Brightness function created for it. Any events or functions created in this manner are specific to that particular function, and do not have to be tested to verify which component is involved [6].

> To find updates to this tutorial and updated instructions about its implementation on other UE4 versions please visit the book's companion website at: `http://www.RVRLAB.com/UE4Book/`

TUTORIAL 3.4   Modifying the Default Character Blueprint

For this tutorial, we will be adding functionality to the default character blueprint that comes with the first person blueprint template we created. The blueprint in question is called **MyCharacter** and can be located inside the Blueprints folder of the Content browser.

MODIFYING MY CHARACTER BLUEPRINT

This blueprint is where the functionalities of the first person character are programmed.

1. Locate the `Blueprints` folder in the **Content Browser**.
2. Locate and open the `FirstPersonCharacter` blueprint by double-clicking on it.
3. Once it is open we can see the blueprint editor window. We will be adding a few nodes in the Event Graph to allow our character to have a flashlight. We will also need to add the directional light component to the Blueprint's Components section.
4. With the `FirstPersonCharacter` blueprint open in the Blueprint Editor, `Left-Click` on the **Viewport** tab.

ADDING THE SEARCH LIGHT

The first thing we need to do is to add a directional light to our character. We want this light attached to the **Capsule Component** of our blueprint so that

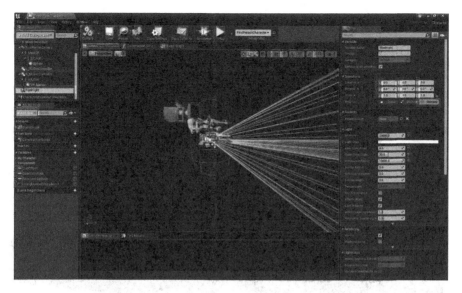

FIGURE 3.9: Adding the Flashlight to MyCharacter Blueprint.

the light moves with the character properly and any adjustment we make to the light will be made with the **Capsule Component** as the origin.

5. In the `Viewport` tab `Double-Click` on the **Capsule Component** to select it.
6. With the **Capsule Component** selected in the Components window, select `Add Component` at the top and add a `Spot Light` in one of the following ways:
   a. Find **Spot Light** on the list.
   b. Typing in the search bar `Spot Light` to narrow the list down and make it easier to find.
7. Add the **Spot Light** to your components. You should end up with a spot light in the middle of the main capsule component (see Figure 3.9).
8. Rename this light to **Flashlight** just in case other lights are used in the future.
9. After all is done, `Left-Click` on Compile in the top left corner to make sure the blueprint compiles properly with no errors.

ADJUSTING THE FLASHLIGHT

Now we need to make adjustments to our light, so that it looks and feels more like a flashlight.

10. First, lower the `Outer Cone Angle` to 30 (in the Details rollout under the **Light** section).
11. Also increase the Inner Cone Angle to 4.
12. We can also raise the intensity to 20000 so that we have a brighter light.
13. Increase the Attenuation Radius to 10000 to effectively increase the distance that the light will reach.

14. Make sure you compile after this is done, and we can test our new light in-game.

ADDING A ROOF TO THE LEVEL

To make the test level dark, we need to add a roof and enclose the entire area.

FIGURE 3.10: Adding the Roof to the Level.

15. To add a roof quickly and easily, `Left-Click` on the ground to select the floor mesh.
16. Press and hold the `Alt` key, and drag the `Z-axis` arrow upward to duplicate the floor mesh.
17. Keep dragging the duplicate mesh until it is sitting on top of the level. This will create a copy of the mesh and drag the new one to the new location (see Figure 3.10).

REBUILDING THE LIGHTING

At this point, if you press play, you will notice that the room is still lit. This means we must rebuild the lighting of the level, in order to render the new enclosed room properly.

18. `Left-Click` on the **Build** button at the top of the editor window to rebuild the scene. Note that if you have the lighting quality set high, it could take a very long time to build. You can lower the lighting quality to Preview by clicking the down arrow (▼) next to the Build button.
19. Find the **Lighting Quality** and select the desired setting.
20. Once the level is rebuilt, you can press the **Play** button (or press `Alt+P`) to see the effect of your new flashlight in-game (see Figure 3.11).

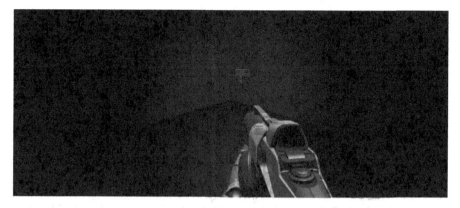

FIGURE 3.11: Flashlight Effect.

What Happened in TUTORIAL 3.4...

We have successfully created a flashlight and attached it to the default character blueprint that comes with the First Person template. We also modified the level to give us a dark (and somewhat creepy) environment to test our new flashlight in. In the following tutorials, we will be creating lights to add to this room so that it isn't pitch black. For now let's review what we learned.

Adding a light component to a blueprint is quite simple. We attached a spot light to the Capsule Component and modified its settings to give the desired effect. There are a lot more settings to go over with lights than will be explained in this chapter, but you are encouraged to play with these settings to see what happens when certain things are changed. Try changing the color of the light for example. This setting can be found in Details window under the Light tab.

Next, we want to allow the player to turn the light on and off. This is a simple task that can be accomplished with the event graph in the MyCharacter Blueprint.

To find updates to this tutorial and updated instructions about its implementation on other UE4 versions please visit the book's companion website at: http://www.RVRLAB.com/UE4Book/

TUTORIAL 3.5   Modifying the Default Character Blueprint

In this tutorial we will enable the player to interact with their flashlight to turn it on and off. We will open the MyCharacter Blueprint and navigate to the Event

Graph by clicking the **Graph** tab in the top right corner. This is where all the logic for the character takes place. But before we can program our actions, we will have to map them to user inputs.

USER INPUTS AND ACTION MAPPING

We need to tell the engine what button we want to press to perform the task of turning the flashlight on and off. This is done by action mapping – i.e., mapping a keyboard button press to a particular action in the editor settings.

1. If **Project Settings** is not currently open, **Left-Click** on **Edit** at the top of the window.
2. From the popup window select **Project Settings**.
3. In the **Project Setting** window, under the Engine tab on the left side, select **Input** to bring up the engines input settings.
4. Under the **Bindings tab**, click the arrow next to the **Action Mappings** tab to expand it. You should see **Jump** and **Fire** as our only two actions so far.
5. To add a new one, click the **+** icon to the right of **Action Mappings**.
6. Name this new action **Flashlight** and expand it to give us our key options. We can actually map multiple keys to a single action if we wanted to, but for now we will simply map the **Tab** button to the **Flashlight**.
7. Click the dropdown list that says **None** and type **Tab** to find the button (see Figure 3.12(a)).
8. Once the **Tab** button is added to the list of actions for **Flashlight**, you can close the window.

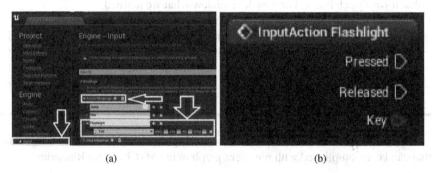

(a)   (b)

FIGURE 3.12: Action Mappings for Flashlight.

PROGRAMMING THE FLASHLIGHT ACTION

We have now mapped the Tab button to the input action **Flashlight**. We will now work in the Graph Editor to program our flashlight on/off actions.

9. Return to the **MyCharacter** event graph.

10. **Right-Click** in an empty space and start typing **flashlight** to find the input action we just created. It should appear under action events. Select it to place it in the graph (see Figure 3.12(b)).
11. For this functionality, we will only be using the **Pressed** option. Now we just need to connect our input to the light that our character is holding.
12. On the left side in the **My Blueprint** window, you can find the **Flashlight** component. Click on this component so that it is selected and we can reference it in the event graph.
13. With the component selected, drag off from the **Pressed** output of the **Flashlight** action on the graph editor and release to the right of our **Input Action** node.
14. Type **Toggle** in the search bar to search for the functionality that allows us to toggle the light on and off by pressing this button. So without knowing the exact node we are looking for, we can type the word Toggle into the search bar.
15. At the top, we see the option **Toggle Visibility (Flashlight)**. This is exactly what we want. Select this option to place the node in the event graph (see Figure 3.13).
16. To make sure our new nodes are compiled, make sure you always hit the **Compile** button in the top left corner after making changes.

FIGURE 3.13: Toggling Flashlight On and Off.

17. At this point, if you go to the main editor window and press **Play**, the flashlight will turn on and off as many times as we press the **Tab** button.
18. This is the functionality we desired for our flashlight. Before we finish, let's add a comment to the Event Graph to avoid confusion in the future.
    a. Marquee drag around both nodes we have just created and press the **C** button on your keyboard.

b. A comment box will automatically be created. Give this box the name **Flashlight** and press **Enter**. This comment box can be resized and moved as needed.

POINTING THE FLASHLIGHT

Now, the last thing we need to happen is to rotate the light with the mouse input. This will allow us to use the mouse movements to have our flashlight rotate with the camera. We accomplish this by using the nodes, **InputAxis Turn** and **InputAxis LookUp** to change the rotation of the light. These nodes are already generated as a part of the first person template and tied to mouse movements.

19. On the Event Graph locate and move the **Movement Input** comment window and all the nodes it contains to the right so that we have a bit of space next to the **Mouse Input** comment box.
20. Place the **Flashlight** comment box you created in Step 18b just to the right of the **Mouse Input** comment box, so that we can easily get to the **InputAxis** nodes it contains. If this is a bit confusing, use Figure 3.14 as a reference to rearrange your event graph.

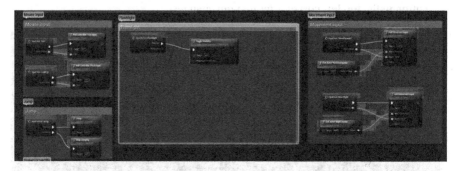

FIGURE 3.14: Rearranging the Networks in the Event Graph for My Character.

21. We rearranged the graph in this way because we cannot create copies of the InputAxis nodes and the result would be wires running across other nodes which would create confusion. Keep this in mind when you are creating more complex logic trees in your event graph as they can become unreadable quite easily.
22. Now we need to add another function to the **Flashlight** comment box. Select the **Flashlight** component from the list on the left side of the blueprint editor.
23. **Right-Click** somewhere inside of the **Flashlight** comment box and search for **Set World Rotation (Flashlight)**.
24. Place this node below the **Toggle Visibility** function.
25. Drag a wire out to the left from the **New Rotation** input variable in the **Set World Rotation** function and search for **Get Control Rotation**, to set the rotation of our flashlight to the control rotation of the pawn. This will set the rotation of the flashlight to be the same as the rotation of the pawn, whenever this function is called.

26. To make sure this function is called every time the mouse input is updated, we will utilize the existing Mouse input logic. Connect the exec (white) output of both functions **Add Controller Yaw Input** and **Add Controller Pitch Input** functions in the `Mouse input` comment box to the exec (white) input of the `Set World Rotation` function we just created.

27. Your network should look similar to Figure 3.15.

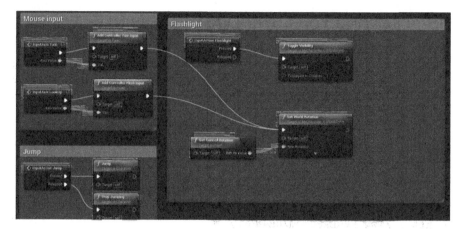

FIGURE 3.15: Complete Network to Move the Flashlight Around.

28. Once your event graph is set up properly, compile and save the blueprint. We have now completed our flashlight and we can run it in game to see the results.

29. If you play the level you will notice that now the flashlight should move up and down with the camera rotation and turn on and off when you press the `Tab` key.

What Happened in TUTORIAL 3.5...

We have completed our flashlight functionality by adding the ability to turn the light on and off. In the future, we can expand on this functionality in order to have the light turn off automatically, to disable the input for a short period in case of a cut scene in the game, or perhaps a scripted sequence where the flashlight runs out of power. Feel free to play around with the nodes to have the light do different things. Increase the brightness of the flashlight by increasing the intensity, or change the color from the same light settings.

Notice the target on the Toggle Visibility node is **Self. Self**, in this case, is referring to the blueprint that we are working on, which is the MyCharacter blueprint. It is possible to target other objects to toggle their in-game visibility, which is why this option is given. For instance, we can turn a lamp on and off or pick up an item which would disappear from your view and be stored in your inventory.

There are other ways we could have implemented this flashlight but the way that I chose was quick, simple, and efficient. The flashlight rotation is only updated when the rotation actually changes. For example, if we had used an event tick to update the rotation, it would be updated at a much higher rate, but it would also be much more inefficient.

3.8 CREATING YOUR OWN CLASS BLUEPRINTS

In this section, we will go over techniques that will aid you whenever you need to create a Class blueprint for your game. Just simply creating a Class blueprint and throwing our assets into it is not always going to save you time and energy in the long run. Making a well thought out modular blueprint will allow it to be used in as many instances as possible.

To start out, we will create a light that we can place throughout the level to light up our enclosed area. If you did not create the enclosed area, please follow the Tutorial 3.4 from earlier in this chapter before continuing forward.

> To find updates to this tutorial and updated instructions about its implementation on other UE4 versions please visit the book's companion website at: http://www.RVRLAB.com/UE4Book/

TUTORIAL 3.6   Creating Wall Light Using Class blueprints

As we mentioned earlier, designing a proper Class blueprint, that is well thought out could be a tremendous help in the long run. This is because Class blueprints can be reused over and over again in the level when needed. They can also be reused in different levels and even projects.

CREATING YOUR CLASS BLUEPRINT

The first thing we need to do is actually create our blueprint.

1. Navigate to the Blueprints folder in the **Content Browser**.
2. Left-Click on the **Create** button and select Blueprint.
3. The type of blueprint that we are creating will be of type Actor. Select this option at the top of the Pick Parent Class window.
4. Name the blueprint WallLamp.
5. Once you have your blueprint created, go ahead and open it to launch the Blueprint Editor.

ADDING BLUEPRINT COMPONENTS: THE WALL LAMP

Our lamp will contain a light component and a mesh component. We will borrow the mesh from the starter content by navigating to the Starter

Content folder in the content browser and further navigating to the Props folder.

> If you do not see the **Starter Content** folder, you did not include the starter content with your project when you created it. You will have to import the **Starter Content** manually. To do so, find a project that has the **Starter Content** folder, copy, and paste it in the **Contents** folder of your project.

6. Locate the **Starter Content** folder and open it.
7. Locate and open the **Props** folder.
8. Locate a static mesh in the **Props** folder called SM_Lamp_Wall.
9. There are a couple of ways to move this mesh into the **Components** section of our blueprint.
   a. The easiest way is to click and drag the item from the **Content Browser** into the **Components** list in the blueprint editor. If you are using a single monitor, this might be tricky.
   b. You can also click on the asset in the **Content Browser** and with the asset still selected, click the **Add Component** button in the **Components** section in the blueprint editor and select the asset near the top of the list.
10. Once you added the SM_Lamp_Wall, the asset should appear in the main viewport in your blueprint editor (see Figure 3.16).
11. Give the asset the name Lamp Wall Mesh.
12. Compile and save the blueprint.

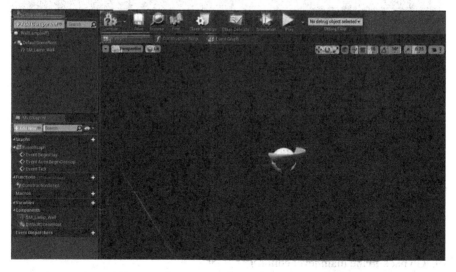

FIGURE 3.16: Lamp Wall Mesh Added to Blueprint Components.

ADDING BLUEPRINT COMPONENTS: THE LIGHT

So far, we have added a mesh to give a visual representation of our light source, so now we need to add the light itself.

13. `Left-Click` on the **Add Component** button and search for a `Point Light`. A point light is simply a light with a single source that emits outward in all directions.
14. When the light appears in the blueprint, you will notice that it is a bit off center of the inside of the lamp itself.
15. Move the light using the translate gizmo arrows so that it is inside the yellow light cover of the mesh. Use Figure 3.17 as reference.
16. Rename the light to `Main Light Source`.

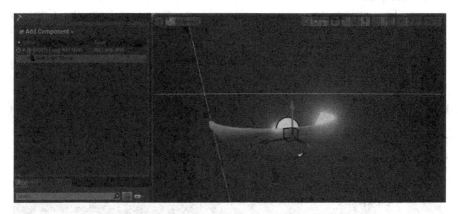

FIGURE 3.17: Main Light Added to Blueprint Components.

17. Change the light's **Mobility** to `Static` in the `Transform Section` of the Details rollout. This tells the engine that this light will be baked into the scene before the game is run. Dynamic lights are very computationally expensive but static lights are not.
18. Compile and save the blueprint.

PLACING THE BLUEPRINT IN THE LEVEL

Before we continue on, let's place our new blueprint in our level to see how it looks. We will have to set the viewport lighting to ignore the light calculations so that we can see in the dark level.

19. Go back to the main level editor.
20. Set the **View Mode** (on top of the viewport) to `Unlit`. This will make it easier to place objects in the level due to it having no lights yet.
21. To place the `WallLamp` blueprint we have created into the level, simply `Left-Click` on it and drag it into the main viewport.
22. Place the lamp against the back wall.

23. Getting the lamp in the correct position on a wall can be tricky so be patient and take your time with it. If it doesn't look good you can always move it.
    a. To make this easier, arrange your viewport so that you have a side, front, top, and perspective view.
    b. If you only have one viewport showing, click the icon in the top right corner of the viewport to restore the viewport to a $1/4^{th}$ view.
    c. Utilize the other viewports to line up the light against a wall, rotating the blueprint if necessary.
    d. If you can't get it to line up perfectly, you can change the grid snap setting to a lower value (try 5 or 1) by clicking the number next to the grid snap icon ⌗ at the top of the viewport.

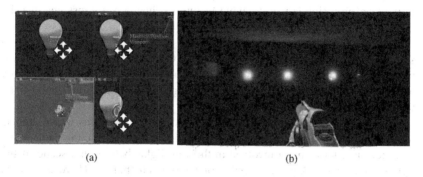

(a)   (b)

FIGURE 3.18: Wall Lamp Blueprint Placed in the Level.

24. The result should look similar to Figure 3.18(a).
25. You can quickly place multiple copies of the same blueprint into the level by performing one of the following actions:
    a. You can copy and paste the lamp blueprint
    b. Hold the **Alt** key and move the translate arrows.
26. Go ahead and place four **WallLamp** blueprints on one of the large walls.
27. Once this is done, build the level. To do this **Left-Click** on the **Build** button on the toolbar.
28. Save the level and all assets in the **Content Browser**.
29. Play the game to see your lights in-game.

ADJUSTING THE LIGHT BRIGHTNESS

The lights appear to be working at this point but they are a little dim (see Figure 3.18(b)). This is no problem because, even though we have placed four lights in this scene, we only used a single blueprint source. We can simply edit the settings in this blueprint to change the brightness of all four lights.

30. Open the **WallLamp** blueprint. **Double-Click** on the **WallLamp** blueprint in the **Content Browser** to open it up.
31. Select the **Main Light Source** from the components window.

32. In the Details rollout, find the **Light** section and increase the `Intensity` to 12,000.
33. Compile and save the blueprint.
34. Return to the main level editor.
35. Build the scene again and click play. The brightness of all the lights has increased.

What Happened in TUTORIAL 3.6...

We have successfully created a Class blueprint from scratch and placed it in the main level. We have learned how blueprints can be edited once they are placed in the level in a simple way to avoid having to change every instance that the blueprint is used.

What we have created is a simple example of how a blueprint can be used to simplify the level design. If we had not used a Class blueprint, we would have to place all the meshes and lights individually and modify their values individually as well. This takes much more time even though we only have four lights on the wall at the moment.

When we end up with hundreds of lights in a large level, this would dramatically increase the amount of tedious work needed to complete the game. Note that there is a lot of math involved in the way lights behave in a scene. If the lighting does not look perfect, don't worry too much about it. There are dozens of factors involved in making lighting look realistic in a scene that we won't be going over in this chapter.

3.9   USER INPUT AND INTERACTION

The `WallLamp` blueprint that we created in the previous tutorial was our first attempt at creating a blueprint from scratch. The `WallLamp` serves its purpose but what if we wanted to interact with it?

The primary means of setting up user interactions in Unreal Engine 4 is by means of **Action Mapping** and **Axis Mapping**. These concepts are quite important as they will bind user interactions to events, which then will fire when such interaction occurs in-game. The engine will look for the interactions as a part of the game loop, and will automatically detect and fire appropriate events bound to the occurring interaction.

Action and Axis Mappings provide a mechanism to conveniently map keys and axes to input behaviors by inserting a layer of indirection between the input behavior and the keys that invoke it. Action Mappings are for key presses and releases, while Axis Mappings allow for inputs that have a continuous range [23].

3.9.1   ACTION MAPPINGS

Action Mappings map a discrete button or key to a "friendly name" that will later be bound to event-driven behavior. The end effect is that pressing (and/or releasing) a key, mouse button, or keypad button directly triggers some game behavior [24].

3.9.2 AXIS MAPPINGS

These mappings map keyboard, controller, or mouse inputs to a "friendly name" that will later be bound to continuous game behavior, such as movement. The inputs mapped in Axis Mappings are continuously polled, even if they are just reporting that their input value is currently zero. This allows for smooth transitions in movement or other game behavior, rather than the discrete game events triggered by inputs in Action Mappings [24].

We should make a habit of mapping our game's input in the project settings. This will make it much easier to change settings later if you decide to use a different key, as the key will be mapped to the action/axis and bound to the interactions and event. Therefore, if later in the process we decide to make changes to the keys or input modes, we will only need to change the mappings and not the entire game network.

We can add design elements to our blueprint that will allow us to interact with them. In the following tutorial, we will add the functionality to open and close a door as the user wishes. For this tutorial we will create a new blank project and utilize the starter content to create a door blueprint that opens and closes on player input.

To find updates to this tutorial and updated instructions about its implementation on other UE4 versions please visit the book's companion website at: http://www.RVRLAB.com/UE4Book/

TUTORIAL 3.7   Creating an Interactive Door Blueprint

In this tutorial we will create an interactive door. The door will be capable of detecting when a player walks close to it. It will be able to also open and close when the player presses a key when standing close to the door.

CREATING A BLANK PROJECT

In this tutorial we will set up an empty project and include the starter contents from the Unreal Engine into it. The first thing to do is to create a project to which we will add the starter content. We will give the project a name such as **BlueprintTutorial02**. Leave the **Include Starter Content** selected to have access to starter contents (see Figure 3.19).

1. Open the Unreal Launcher and select the version of the engine you would like to work with. The following tutorial is created with Unreal Engine 4.18.
2. Once the Editor Opens, choose **New Project** (see Figure 3.19).
3. Select the **Blueprint** as your project type, and make sure that the **Blank** is selected.
4. Select your platform (Desktop/Console) and your graphics quality.
5. Make sure you include the starter content (see Figure 3.19).
6. Give your project a name and click **Create Project**.

FIGURE 3.19: Creating a Blank Project.

LOADING THE STARTER MAP

Once you have the project created and launched, you will be greeted with the default map. The starter content brings in this map that we can add things to so we are not starting completely from scratch.

7. Navigate to `File ▶ Open Level`.
8. `Left-Click` on the `Game ▶ Starter Content` folder. Then `Left-Click` on the `Game ▶ Map` folder. There should be a level called `StarterMap`.
9. Load the `Starter Map` level so that we can use it to help create our door blueprint (see Figure 3.20).

FIGURE 3.20: Starter Map.

WORKING IN THE STARTER MAP

If you press **Play**, you will notice that you are able to freely fly around the level (see Figure 3.21). This level does not have a built-in character class like the First Person template.

For now, we don't need one. This level shows off a variety of UE4 assets including basic materials, advanced materials, particle effects, audio, physics objects, and more. This is an excellent level to use as a reference when you are stuck on something UE4 specific.

FIGURE 3.21: Starter Map Playing.

10. Stop the gameplay.
11. Fly inside the little room in the center of the level so you can see the table and chairs clearly. They are currently in our way for now.
12. Select both chairs, the table, and the glass statue on top of the table. *Note: Hold the Control key to select multiple actors.*
13. Drag the chairs, table, and glass statue outside the room using the transform tool (see Figure 3.21).
14. Now that we have these assets out of the way, we can see the empty doorway in the room. This is where we will place our door blueprint.
15. Navigate to the **Blueprints** folder in the **Content Browser** and create a new Actor blueprint called **Blueprint_Door**.
16. Once this is created, go to the **Components** tab so we can add our mesh.
17. Select **Add Component**.
18. Find the **Static Mesh**, select it, and name it **Door**. This will place a static mesh component into our blueprint but we still need to select which mesh we actually want to render.
19. The starter content we included has a mesh called **SM_Door** that will be perfect. To add it, perform the following tasks:
    a. Select the **Door** mesh component from the components list and find **Static Mesh** section in its Details rollout.
    b. **Left-Click** on the down arrow (▼) on the drop-down list that reads **None**.

c. From the menu search for **SM_Door** to add it (see Figure 3.22(a)).

(a)   (b)

FIGURE 3.22: Door Mesh Component Added to Blueprint and the Level.

20. Once the door mesh is placed inside the blueprint, we can drag our **Blueprint_Door** asset into the scene and place it in the door frame.
21. The mesh is designed to fit this frame, so it shouldn't need resizing. Figure 3.22(b) shows the door placement in the level.

CREATING A TIMELINE

Now the tricky part begins. We want to control the movement of our door so that it will rotate open and close. This is effectively an animation sequence by which the rotation of a static mesh (which should be set as movable by default) is controlled over time. In previous versions of the Unreal Engine such as UE3, or UDK, this kind of operation was done with Matinee. However, Unreal Engine 4 introduced a very important concept to Blueprint scripting called a timeline. A timeline is a curve that can control several dynamic aspects of the gameplay through blueprint sequences.

22. If your **Blueprint_Door** blueprint is closed, open it up.
23. Go to the Event Graph.
24. **Right-Click** somewhere on the Event Graph.
25. From the menu that opens up, type **timeline** to search for a timeline node.
26. **Left-Click** on the **Add Timeline** at the bottom of the list to create a timeline in your event graph.
27. Once you place the timeline in the event graph, name it **Door Movement** and press enter.
28. **Double-Click** on the timeline to open the timeline editor in a new tab.
29. In the timeline editor tab, click the Float track icon (f^+) in the top left corner to add a new float track to the timeline.
30. On the left side give it the name such as **Door Movement**. The length of the track will determine how long our movement will take to complete from beginning to end.

31. At the top, change the default length of 5 to 2 so that the door does not take quite as long to open/close.
32. Next, `Right-Click` on the track and select **Add Key** to place a key on the track.
33. You can drag this key into place but it is easiest to type the values directly with the key selected:
    a. Set the time to 0
    b. Set the value to 0
34. The first key will be our starting key.
35. Add another key in the same manor but this time:
    a. Set the time to 2.0
    b. Set the value to 1.0
36. The result should look similar to Figure 3.23.

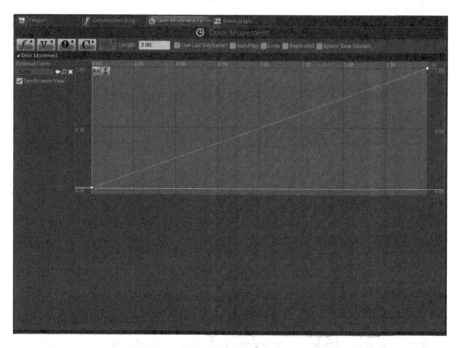

FIGURE 3.23: The Door Movement Track.

PROGRAMMING THE TIMELINE

We have created a timeline, called `Door Movement`, that will increase its float value linearly from 0 to 1, over 2 seconds. We can use this to adjust the rotation of the door from 0 to 90 over the same period.

37. To use the timeline to rotate the door, first return to the Event Graph by clicking the **Graph** tab in the upper left corner of the viewport.
38. `Left-Click` on the `Door` component on left to select it.

39. Drag a wire off from **Update** exec output on the timeline.
40. Search for the `Set World Rotation` function.
41. Place the `Set World Rotation` node in the graph.
42. Now we want to rotate the door from 0 to –90 degrees so that it opens inward from where we place it.
43. To do this, drag off from the **Door Movement** float output of the timeline and search for the `float × float` math function.
44. Type –90 for the second float value.
45. Next, drag off from the output of the × function and search for a node called **Make Rotator**. This will create a Rotator object using three float values. The only axis we are rotating on is the **Yaw**.
46. Disconnect from **Pitch** by `Alt+Left-Click` on the pin.
47. Reconnect to **Yaw**.
48. Drag the **Return Value** pin of the **Make Rot** node to the **New Rotation** input of the `Set World Rotation` function. This will complete our logic (see Figure 3.24).

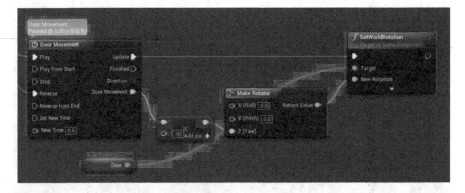

FIGURE 3.24: Timeline Used to Rotate Door.

ACTION MAPPING AND INTERACTING WITH TIMELINE

In order to make this logic fire, we must create an event that allows us to press a button to perform this action. For now, we will use the "F" key on the keyboard as the default interact button.

49. Go back to the main editor.
50. Navigate to **Edit ▶ Project Settings**.
51. `Left-Click` on `Input` on the left side under **Engine**.
52. Add an `Action Mapping` under the **Bindings** tab.
53. Name the action mapping to `Interact`.
54. Finally, search for the "F" key under **Keyboard** and select it (see Figure 3.25).
55. Return to our `Blueprint_Door`. If it is closed, open it up from the **Content Browser**.

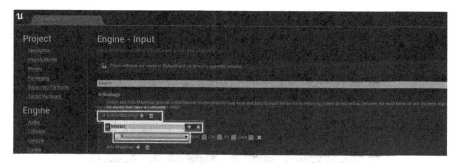

FIGURE 3.25: Door Action Mapping Called Interact.

56. Add the new event **InputAction Interact** to the left of the timeline. To do this perform the following task:
    a. **Right-Click** to the left of the timeline, and search for **InputAction Interact**.
57. Drag off a wire from the **Pressed** pin and search for a **FlipFlop** node. This node is a logic gate that will switch from **A** to **B** every time it is called. You can think of it as a toggle switch.
58. Connect the **A** output of the **FlipFlop** to the **Play** input of the timeline.
59. Connect the **B** output of the **FlipFlop** to the **Reverse** input of the timeline.
60. This will let us open and close the door. Your network should look similar to Figure 3.26.

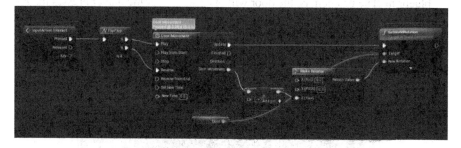

FIGURE 3.26: Door Action Mapping Network.

61. In order to get input to work in a blueprint, you must actually enable input on the blueprint itself. To do this perform the following tasks:
    a. For now, add an **Event Begin Play** event. To do this **Right-Click** on the Event Graph above the timeline and search for **Event Begin Play**.
    b. From the exec (white) output of the event drag a wire and search for function called **Enable Input**.
    c. You will need to get the player controller for this function. Drag off a wire from the **Player Controller** pin and search for **Get Player Controller**.

    d. This function will return the default player controller. The nodes should look like Figure 3.27.

FIGURE 3.27: Enabling Input upon Begin Play.

62. Compile and Save your blueprint.

USING TRIGGERS

At this point, we can play the game and press the "F" key to open and close the door. If your door is not moving at this point, there might be an issue with the timeline. Double check to make sure the timeline is constructed correctly and that the node structure matches Figures 3.26 and 3.27.

Even though our door is opening and closing, we have not yet finished our blueprint. The problem is, the door will open whenever the player presses the F key from anywhere in the level. We don't want to be able to just open and close a door from anywhere in the game world.

The current logic doesn't make much sense. We need to narrow down the area in which we are able to interact with the door, to the area just around the door. This can be achieved by using a trigger box.

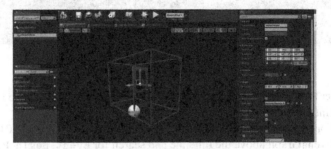

FIGURE 3.28: Setting Up the Trigger Box.

63. Return to the `Blueprint_Door` blueprint. If the blueprint editor is closed, open it up by double-clicking on the `Blueprint_Door` asset in the **Content Browser**.

64. Go to the blueprint's **Components** tab.
65. `Left-Click` on the **Add Components**, add a Box, and give it the name `Interact Volume`.
66. Set the box's location to 0, 0, 0.
67. Set the box's scale to 5.0, 2.7, 3.4.
68. This will create the space that the character must be in to open or close the door (see Figure 3.28).
69. Return to the Event Graph by clicking on the **graph** tab on the upper right corner.
70. Select the `Interact Volume` from the components list on the left side.
71. `Right-Click` in an empty space above the previous nodes, and search for **Event Component Actor Begin Overlap**.
72. This event is called when a component overlaps the target (in this case the Interact Volume we created). The event will return the object that overlaps the box so we can make sure it is the player object.
73. Drag off a wire from the `Other Actor` output pin of the `Event Component Begin Overlap`.
74. Type `==` in the search box to place the Equal (object) math function.
75. The object we need to compare to is the default player pawn. You can get this by performing the following tasks:
    a. `Left-Click` on the `Open Object` pin
    b. Drag a wire to the left
    c. Search for and place the `Get Player Pawn` node.
76. Next, we need a flow control node called a **Branch** statement. Perform the following tasks:
    a. Drag off a wire from the exec (white) output pin of the `OnComponent BeginOverlap` event.
    b. Type and Search for **Branch** to place this node.
    c. The **Branch** node will check a Boolean value and branch off to true or false depending on the value of the Boolean.
    d. Connect the Boolean (red) output of the `==` to the `Condition` input pin of the branch statement.
    e. Disconnect the exec (white) input of the `Enable Input` node from the `Event Begin Play`. You can do this by holding the `Alt` key and `Left-Clicking` on the connection.
    f. Marquee drag around the `Enable Input` and the `Get Player Controller` nodes to select them both.
    g. Move the `Enable Input` and the `Get Player Controller` nodes to the right of the **Branch** node.
    h. Connect the `True` output pin of the **Branch** node to the Enable Input function (see Figure 3.29).
77. This will enable the input on our door blueprint only if we intersect the volume, to guarantee that we cannot interact with the door unless we are in close proximity.
78. Next, we need to disable input when we leave the volume. The logic is very similar except we will need an `OnComponentEndOverlap` event and a `Disable Input` function. To do this perform the following tasks:

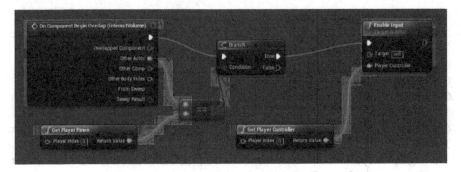

FIGURE 3.29: Enable Input when Overlap Trigger Box.

a. Marquee drag around the network you created for triggering the enable input with the trigger volume to select the network.

b. Duplicate the network by pressing `Control+W` keys on your keyboard.

c. Place the duplicate network above the original one.

d. Select the `On Component Begin Overlap` node from the duplicate network and delete it by pressing the `Del` key.

e. `Left-Click` on the `Interact Volume` in the components list (located to the left of the event graph) to select it.

f. With the `Interact Volume` selected, `Right-Click` on the graph editor in place of the `On Component Begin Overlap` node you just removed.

g. Search for and place an `On Component End Overlap` node.

h. Connect the exec (white) output pin of the `On Component End Overlap` node to the exec(white) input of the duplicate `Branch`.

i. Connect the `Other Actor` output of the `On Component End Overlap` node to the now-disconnected blue input pin of the `==` node.

j. `Left-Click` on the duplicate `Enable Input` node, then delete it by pressing the `Del` key.

k. Drag a wire off from the exec (white) output of the `Branch` node and search for and place a `Disable Input` input node.

l. Connect the `Player Controller` input pin of the `Disable Input` input node to the now-disconnected `Get Player Controller` node.

79. Your disable input network should now look similar to Figure 3.30.

80. Compile and Save your blueprint.

81. If your blueprint has any errors and didn't compile double check all your nodes and their connections and make sure that you followed the instructions above.

82. If you now play the level, you will notice that you may no longer open and close the door from a distance.

83. Fly over close to the door and press the F key on your keyboard. This should rotate the door open and closed.

84. Once you get sufficiently away from the door, pressing the F key will no longer interact with the door, since the input is now disabled.

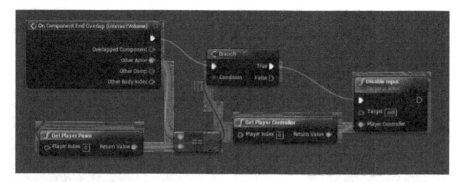

FIGURE 3.30: Enable Input when Overlap Trigger Box.

COMMENTING YOUR NETWORKS

When you work with blueprint scripting editor, you will add nodes, make connections and implement your game/interaction logic in intricate networks. This can make the network quite confusing. To avoid confusion, you should always comment sections of your network and give them representative names. Comments also make the arrangement of your entire blueprint graph easier by allowing you to move chunks of networks by dragging their comment box.

85. Marquee drag around your part of the network that is responsible for enabling and disabling the input by trigger events.
86. With the network selected, press the C key on your keyboard, type in a name such as **Enable/Disable Input** and press **Enter** on your keyboard. This will wrap a comment box around this section of the network.
87. Marquee drag around the section of the network that toggled the door open/closed by updating the door rotation from the timeline.
88. Comment this section as **Close/Open** door.
89. Your network and comments should look similar to Figure 3.31).
90. Compile and Save your blueprint.

What Happened in TUTORIAL 3.7...

We constructed a simple blueprint for a door that can be placed in many different locations throughout the game. If we were to place the door in the level multiple times, everything would function as expected. Opening one door will not open all doors, and we can resize the door and even add design elements to the blueprint to replace the mesh and keep the functionality. This cuts down on the implementation process tremendously.

Note that you should always comment on your blueprint nodes to simplify the logic for you in the future, or for someone else who might be working on a

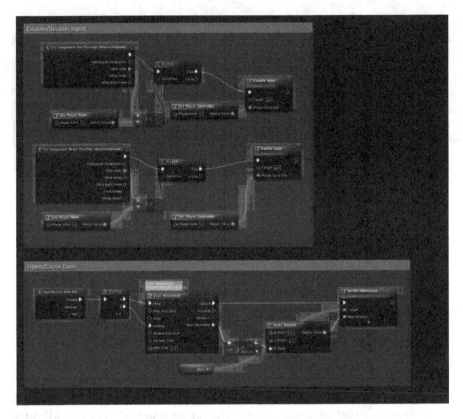

FIGURE 3.31: Commenting the Network.

project with you. To leave a comment on a node, simply `Right-Click` the node and add the comment at the bottom, or press the C key. When your blueprints get larger and more complex, this will help with debugging problems.

3.10 SUMMARY

In this chapter, we introduced the basics of working with blueprints. The blueprint editor gives you access to the visual scripting as well as the physical components that make up the blueprint. Class blueprints are used to create modular sequences that will be used many times. Level blueprints should only be used for blueprint-script that will only be used on that particular level.

Functions, variables, and events are used, just as they are in programming, to create blueprints that have good readability and efficiency. Functions are called by other nodes in blueprint-scripts and events are constantly listening for a specific trigger before it is fired and the code is executed. Many different types of blueprints exist. Although, only a couple types were touched on in this chapter. Other types of blueprints will be discussed and utilized in Chapter 8–Advanced Blueprint Concepts.

3.11   EXERCISES

Exercise 1. In Tutorial 3.3 implement the following items and functionalities:
   a. Create a collision box in the blueprint component.
   b. Make the blueprint print a string on the string indicating a player has entered the box.
   c. Make the blueprint print a string on the screen indicating a player has exited the box.
   d. Now add a **Text Render** component in the blueprint and make it show whether a player is entering the box or leaving it.
Exercise 2. In Tutorial 3.5 make the player be able to adjust the height of the flashlight by pressing the + key to increase the height, and the – key to decrease the height.
Exercise 3. In Tutorial 3.6 make the following modifications to the wall light blueprint.
   a. Each light should be toggled by the player when he presses the L on the keyboard.
   b. Each light must be only toggled when the player is within a box around it. *Note: The player should not be able to toggle the lights on/off if he/she is standing far away.*
   c. Add a **Text Render** component to keep track of how many times the light has been toggled (on/off).
Exercise 4. Make the following modifications to Tutorial 3.7:
   a. Make the interactive door a Class blueprint.
   b. Make a sliding door with two doors sliding the opposite way:
      i. The door should have a door frame (from starter content).
      ii. The door should have two glass door meshes (from starter content).
      iii. The door should have a collision box.
      iv. The collision box should only detect player's overlap.
      v. The door should use one (1) timeline to open both sliding glass doors.
      vi. The door should open when the player enters the collision box and close when the player exits collision doors.
      vii. The door should have a **Text Render** that shows the number of times it has been opened.

4 Materials in Unreal Engine

4.1 INTRODUCTION

IN order to achieve the beauty and realism that Unreal Engine 4 has to offer, it is necessary for you to master creating materials. Do you want to create hyperrealistic scenes that are so highly detailed that the player feels as if they're actually inside the game? Need to make stunning animated explosions that let forth a visual shockwave? Perhaps you need to create simple cartoon-like cell-shaded characters sailing across a vast ocean. Each of these will require materials.

When it comes to achieving the stunning visual potential that Unreal Engine 4 has to offer, the **Material Editor** is perhaps the most important engine component. The **Material Editor** allows the user to create and edit materials that drive the visual elements in a game or simulation and control the final visual look of all static meshes, characters, environments, particle effects, and more. In this chapter we will explore what materials are, what they're made of, and how to start making your own materials in the Unreal Engine 4 **Material Editor**.

FIGURE 4.1: A Simple Mesh Object with no Material (*left*) and with a Material (*right*).

4.2 WHAT IS A MATERIAL?

Depending on your familiarity with game engines, you may or may not know what a material is, exactly. To put it simply, materials are a kind of "paint" which is applied to the surfaces of objects within a digital environment. If an object lacks a material in Unreal Engine 4, it becomes simply a 3-dimensional low poly mesh with no visible details. Once a material is applied, the object becomes more recognizable. A flat

125

mesh can become a mirror, concrete, wood flooring, or even metal grating. Moreover, materials may give objects effects such as splotches, stains, cracks, rust, or anything you can think to apply to them to achieve the desired look.

This basic analogy does not accurately convey what materials are and what they are capable of, however, as it is an oversimplification of the concept. Applying paint to a surface controls the color of that surface, whereas a material can control the color, shininess, reflectivity, roughness, metallic aspects, and much more. They can make an object gleam in light, look dirty or tarnished, or give minute details to a character model such as stubble or scarring. See Figure 4.1 for an example of an object with (*left*), and without (*right*), a material.

For now, it is easiest to think of materials as a visual overlay for an object. However, once you understand and become more comfortable with materials, how they work, and how to create them, it will become easier instead to think of materials as substantial, just as much a part of the object as the mesh. For the time being, we will keep a basic understanding of materials as an overlay in order to keep the concept simple.

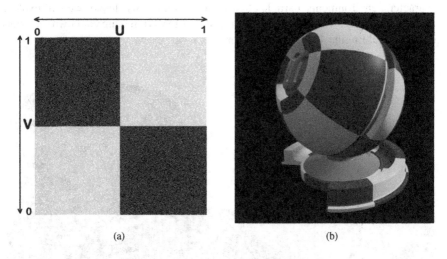

(a)   (b)

FIGURE 4.2: (a) UV space is a coordinate system that runs from 0 to 1, beginning in the lower left corner. Each vertex of a surface has values that correspond to the coordinates of a texture that is applied to a surface. (b) An example of how the UVs of an object affect how the texture is applied to the surface of that object.

4.2.1 MATERIALS VS. TEXTURES

A simple mistake made by newcomers to game design is the confusion between materials and textures. Although they are closely related and are often associated, there are a few key differences between the two. Textures are simply two-dimensional images consisting of pixels that make up what you can see, whereas materials are a combination of different elements, oftentimes including one or more textures. While you will inevitably use both materials and textures, it is important to remember that they are not the same. When materials are created, textures are utilized to give the material color, transparency, depth, and other effects – see Figure 4.2.

4.2.2 TEXTURE COORDINATES (UVS)

When applying materials to the surface of objects, there must be some method by which Unreal Engine 4 determines where to render each pixel relative to the surface of the object. This is achieved through use of texture coordinates, or, more commonly, UVs. Figure 4.2(a) shows how a texture is applied to a surface.

UVs get their name from the variables used to map two-dimensional images to three-dimensional objects, U and V, which run horizontally and vertically along the coordinate space of an object. Every three-dimensional surface necessarily has its own set of UV coordinates. These coordinates are set in a 3D modeling application such as 3D Studio Max or Maya and can be manipulated using the **Material Expressions** within the Unreal Engine's **Material Editor** to create unique effects. See Figure 4.2(b) for a visual example of a static mesh UV.

FIGURE 4.3: Material Editor in Unreal Engine 4.

4.3 UNREAL MATERIAL EDITOR

The **Material Editor** in Unreal Engine 4 is where all materials used by the engine are created and edited. Figure 4.3 shows the **Material Editor** in Unreal Engine 4. By default, the **Material Editor** has several different subdivided areas that are used to facilitate the material creation process.

TABLE 4.1

Items in the Toolbar of the Unreal Engine's Material Editor. Blow is a list of tools in Figure 4.4(a) from left to right.

Tool	Description
Save	Saves the material and applies changes to all instances of the material in the editor.
Find in CB	Displays the material in the Content Browser.
Apply	Applies all changes made to the material in the editor.
Search	Searches the Material Expressions for a desired result.
Home	Snaps the view of the Graph Canvas back to the Node.
Clean Up	Removes any unused Material Expressions.
Connectors	Shows or hides unused Connectors.
Live Preview	When enabled, allows the Preview Window to live update.
Live Nodes	When enabled, allows the Connectors to live update.
Live Update	When enabled, allows the Nodes on the Graph to live update.
Stats	Shows the material's stats.
Release Stats	Shows the material's stats in Release.
Built-in Stats	Shows the material's stats within the Engine.
Mobile Stats	Shows the material's stats when run on a mobile device.

4.3.1   THE TOOLBAR

Located at the top of the **Material Editor** view, the **Toolbar** (shown in Figure 4.4(a)) contains a few useful tools that can be utilized to navigate and preview your materials. Table 4.1 presents a list of options included in the **Toolbar** with a short description of what each tool will do.

4.3.2   PREVIEW WINDOW

The **Preview Window** (Figure 4.4(b)) shows a preview of the final material applied to the user's choice of polygon. The available polygon options are a `Cylinder`, `Sphere`, `Plane`, or `Cube`. To preview the look of a material on an actual mesh, you may select the mesh from the Content Browser and use the `Teapot` to preview the look in the **Preview Window**. The preview window also has options to toggle a grid on or off, and to live update the window.

The bottom right corner of the **Preview Window** shows an `XYZ` coordinate display to help orient the user. The **Preview Window** is designed to give a solid idea of what the material will look like in the Editor and once deployed in-game.

4.3.3   GRAPH CANVAS

The Graph Canvas is where all materials are designed. You will design the network that will drive every aspect of your material on this canvas. It contains all material **Expressions** that are utilized to create the material, and shows how they interact with each other through the use of connectors (Figure 4.4(c)). The vast majority of work

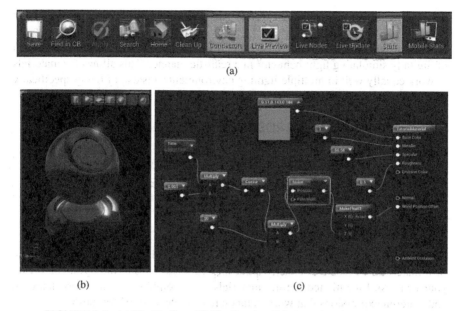

FIGURE 4.4: (a) The Toolbar. (b) The Preview Window. (b) The Graph Canvas.

will be done using this window, so it is important for you to familiarize yourself with navigating about the canvas.

4.3.4 DETAILS PANEL

The properties of the Material and all Material Expressions are displayed in this window. The Details Menu will change depending on what is selected. To select a Material Expression, simply click on its respective node. Each Material Expression, as well as the Material Node, contains its own set of unique properties, which will be explained later in the chapter.

4.3.5 EXPRESSIONS PALETTE

The Expressions Palette is a list of every Material Expression available for use in creating a material. The list of expressions is separated into a few different categories, both of which are arranged in alphabetical order. These expressions can also be accessed by right-clicking on the Graph Canvas. We will explore Material Expressions in greater detail later in this chapter.

4.4 PHYSICALLY BASED MATERIALS IN UNREAL ENGINE 4

When reading or hearing about Unreal Engine 4, you may have heard the term "Physically Based Rendering" or "Physically Based Materials," and may wonder what these terms mean. To put it simply, physically based materials are materials that are based off of physical objects in the real world. This concept was revealed in SIGGRAPH 2013 [54].

Unreal Engine 4 is a unique game engine in this regard, as it takes the approach of digitally simulating light behavior in a realistic manner. This allows for materials to work equally well in multiple lighting environments, instead of being specifically designed for specific environments.

CROSS-REFERENCE

This model of material and light interaction is new to Unreal Engine 4. To learn more about the Physically Based Materials, please see Section 5.6 of Chapter 5– Advanced Material Concepts In Unreal Engine.

4.5 ANATOMY OF AN UNREAL ENGINE 4 MATERIAL

Now that you understand what materials are, we can delve further into the concept of a material and discover exactly what they're made of, and how you can create your own. As I mentioned before, materials are a combination of colors, textures, and material expressions that work in tandem to create a "skin" for meshes.

As we progress through the chapter and particularly in this section, you will discover how these pieces will come together to make unique materials. Not only are you going to learn more and more about materials, but will actually create materials – from very simple to quite realistic materials – so as to learn how materials are constructed and work in Unreal Engine 4.

A material has three primary components: a Node, Channels, and Expressions. Figure 4.5 shows how these three components interact to form a material.

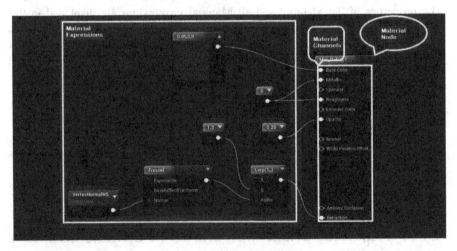

FIGURE 4.5: A Diagram Illustrating the Relationship between Material Nodes, Channels, and Expressions.

4.5.1 MATERIAL NODES

A Node is the base object of a material in Unreal Engine 4. Material Nodes have many properties that can be adjusted to change the overall behavior of the material. These properties can be found in the Details menu inside the Material Editor.

By default, all new materials in Unreal Engine 4 are set to be **Opaque** and **Lit**. An **Opaque** setting means that the material is completely non-transparent. The **Lit** options mean that the material will, by default, interact with scene lighting. These settings can be changed, however, to make the material semitransparent, masked, or even have the object not react to environmental lighting.

4.5.2 MATERIAL CHANNELS

While the properties of the `Material Node` are important, the most important component within the Material Node is the set of inputs that can be seen in the **Graph Canvas** view. These inputs are called the **Material Channels**.

Material Channels are basically the connections between the **Material Node** and the material's network of **Expressions**. Effectively the **Material Channels** serve what the material receives to drive each of its aspects and complete the instructions about how to render the material.

Different expressions can be plugged into the various **Material Channels**, with each resulting in a unique final material. Here we will discuss the different **Material Channels**, what they do, and how their use will affect the final look of your materials.

FIGURE 4.6: Materials with different Base Colors. Notice how the light behaves the same way for each material. The Base Color Channel does not affect the behavior of light on the surface of the material.

Base Color Channel

The **Base Color Channel**, known as the Diffuse channel in previous installments of Unreal Engine, is simply a color or texture that is painted on the surface of an object. In other words, it is the set of pixels of a texture directly mapped to the UV coordinates of a mesh. Changing the Base Color will do nothing but map different color pixels to the mesh, and thus only change its base appearance.

Figure 4.6 shows how different values for the **Base Color** channel change the look of an object on which the material is applied. The left two meshes have a base color in the form of a `Constant3Vector`, meaning that the value of the color is in the form of an RGB value. The leftmost color is white (with R:1.0, G:1.0, B:1.0) while the mesh object from the left has a red color (with R:1.0, G:0.0, B:0.0) applied to its **Base Color** channel. To the next two meshes the **Base Color** channel is controlled by a `Texture Sample` expression, effectively applying a texture map to drive the base color of the surface of each mesh.

FIGURE 4.7: Materials with the same Base Color but different Metallic values. Notice how the light behaves differently for each material. The Metallic value affects the behavior of light on the surface of the material, with higher values making the material look more metallic – or shiny. The meshes from left to right have materials with the metallic value of 0.0, 0.5, 1.0, and a checkerboard texture sample, respectively.

Metallic Channel

The **Metallic Channel** determines the *metal-ness* of the whole, or sections of, a material. The value for this channel can range from 0.0 to 1.0. The value of 0 renders the material completely non-metallic (plastic, wood, fabric, etc.). Setting this channel to the value of 1.0 makes the material completely metallic.

This channel can be controlled either by a single scalar value or a texture. If you use a single scalar value for this channel, the value will be applied to the entire surface of the mesh. Using a texture to feed into the **Metallic** channel will apply the texture on the surface, and each location on the surface determines its metallic property from the value of the corresponding texture location.

Figure 4.7 shows how different value on the **Metallic** channel changes the look of a mesh with otherwise the same Base Color value. The mesh to the left uses a material with **Metallic** value of 0.0. Notice how the color of this mesh looks almost like a matte paint. The second object's Metallic value is 0.5, making the object look like plastic. The third object (from left) has a full metallic value of 1.0, looking like red metal.

Finally, the **Metallic** channel of the last object (rightmost) is driven from a checkerboard pattern from a texture. Notice how the material looks like metal for those surfaces corresponding to the white checkerboard squares (values of 1.0) while the areas corresponding to the black squares look like cloth or matte paint.

FIGURE 4.8: Materials with the same Base Color but different Specular values. Notice how the light behaves differently for each material. The Specular value affects the behavior of highlight on the surface of the material, with higher values making the material look more shiny and have a brighter highlight. The meshes from left to right have materials with the specular value of 0.0, 0.5, 1.0, and a checkerboard texture sample, respectively.

Specular Channel

The **Specular Channel** controls how the material interacts with lighting. The **Specular Channel** accepts a scalar value between 0.0 and 1.0. A value of 1.0 denotes complete interaction with environment lighting and making the material shiny (or with a bright highlight on from the reflection angle of the light source to the material).

A value of 0.0 denotes absolutely no highlights on the surface of a material. This controls one aspect of the shininess of a material. Unlike previous installments of Unreal Engine, however, the **Specular Channel** works in tandem with the **Roughness Channel** (described next) to create a shiny, reflective material, or a complete diffusive surface.

Figure 4.8 shows how different values on the **Specular** channel change the look of a mesh with otherwise the same Base Color value. In this figure, the object on the left has a material with a Specular value of 0.0. Notice the lack of highlight on its red surface. The second object from the left has a medium specular value (0.5), and the third object's specular value is high (1.0). Notice, how more focused the highlight on the object with the high specular value is compared to the one with a medium value of specularity.

Finally, the material on the rightmost object has its specular channel calculated from a checkerboard texture sample. Notice how the texture sample is used to apply different specular values to different locations of the object. This example shows that texture samples can be utilized to control the specular values across an entire mesh.

One thing that you notice by comparing Figure 4.8 and Figure 4.7, is that the effect of the **Specular** channel is much more subtle than that of the **Metallic** channel.

Roughness Channel

The **Roughness Channel** controls how light is scattered when it hits the material. This, in turn, adjusts the overall reflectivity of the material. The value for roughness

FIGURE 4.9: Materials with the same Base Color but different Roughness values. Notice how the light reflects differently for each material. The Roughness value affects the smoothness on the surface of the material, with lower values making the material look more smooth and glossy, while higher roughness values make the material look rugged and rough. The meshes from left to right have materials with the roughness value of 0.0, 0.5, 1.0, and a checkerboard texture sample, respectively.

ranges from 0 to 1. A low value for **Roughness** will result in a higher polish with 0 being completely polished and smooth, whereas a high value for **Roughness** results in low reflectivity with 1 being completely non-reflective and coarse.

Much like specular and metallic channels, this channel can either use a single scalar value or a texture. If supplied with a single scalar value, the value will be applied throughout the material. Supplying this channel with a texture sample will take the roughness values from the texture map and apply it to its respective location on the mesh on which the material is applied. Note that we may connect only one of the scalar channels (R, G, B, or Alpha) of a texture sample to the **Roughness** channel of a material node.

Figure 4.9 shows how different values on the **Roughness** channel change the look of a mesh with otherwise the same Base Color value. In this figure, the object on the left has a material with a Roughness value of 0.0. Notice the smoothness of the material as the light reflects off of this material on almost a perfect reflection angle. The second object from the left, has a medium roughness value (0.5), and the third object's roughness value is high (1.0). Notice, how more rough and rugged the object with the high roughness value is compared to the one with a medium value of roughness.

Finally, the material on the rightmost object has its roughness channel calculated from a checkerboard texture sample. Notice how the texture sample is used to apply different roughness values to different locations of the object. This example shows that texture samples can be utilized to control the roughness values across an entire mesh.

Emissive Color

The Emissive Color channel (formerly known simply as Emissive) allows you to do one of two things. The first, more traditional use of Emissive, is the ability to create glow effects on a material. The second is to display colors independent of lighting

FIGURE 4.10: Materials with the same Base Color but different Emissive values. Notice how the light reflects differently for each material. The Emissive value affects the glow (or bloom) on the surface of the material, with lower values (i.e., values less than 1.0 for each RGB value) making the materials look like they glow with the emissive color, while higher emissive values (RGB greater than 1.0) make the material look like the color blooms. The meshes from left to right have materials with the emissive value of (R:0.0, G:0.0, B:0.2), (R:0.0, G:0.0, B:1.0), (R:0.0, G:0.0, G:20.0), and (R:0.0, G:0.0, G:50.0), respectively.

effects. The second method becomes very useful when you want to create a game for a mobile platform or a two-dimensional gaming environment that does not have advanced lighting. Values from 0 to 1 in the Emissive Color Channel will cause the emission of color, and values beyond 1 cause a "bloom" effect, where the color will bleed over into surrounding pixels, creating a simulated glow (see Figure 4.10).

Figure 4.10 shows how different RGB values on the **Emissive** channel change the look of a mesh with otherwise the same Base Color value. In this figure, the object on the left has a material with an **Emissive Color** value of (R:0.0, G:0.0, B:1.0). Notice the very subtle glow of the material emitting out of this mesh. The second object from the left, has the **Emissive Color** value of (R:0.0, G:0.0, B:0.2). Notice how this material glow perfectly, much like a light.

The third object's **Emissive Color** value is high (R:0.0, G:0.0, G:20.0). Notice the bloom of the blue color out of the mesh and into the scene. Finally, the material on the rightmost object has its emissive color channel ramped up to an incredibly high value of (R:0.0, G:0.0, G:50.0). This high value of the emissive color actually affects the color of the neighboring pixels in the scene, as if the light overshadows them.

There is one important fact to keep in mind when working with materials with emissive colors. The emissive color is not an actual light and will not cast any shadows. So if you wanted to approach a realistic simulation of actual lighting, you should place lights inside of (or around) objects that you want to emit light into the scene and cast shadows on other objects.

Opacity

The opacity channel uses a single scalar value between 0.0 and 1.0 to control how transparent or opaque a material is. A value of 0.0 will result in the material be-

FIGURE 4.11: Materials with the same Base Color but different Opacity values. Notice how the transparency is different for each material. The Opacity value affects how opaque the surface of the material is, with lower values making the material look more translucent or see-through, while higher opacity values make the material look less see-through. The meshes from left to right have materials with the opacity value of 0.0, 0.5, 1.0, and a checkerboard texture sample, respectively.

ing completely transparent, while a value of 1.0 will result in the material being completely opaque. Values between 0.0 and 1.0 will result in varying degrees of transparency.

Much like specular, roughness, and metallic channels, the opacity channel also can use either a single scalar value or a texture. If supplied with a single scalar value, the value will be applied throughout the material. Supplying this channel with a texture sample will take the opacity value from the texture map and apply it to its respective location on the mesh on which the material is applied. Note that we may connect only one of the scalar channels (R, G, B, or Alpha) of a texture sample to the **Opacity** channel of a material node.

Figure 4.11 shows how different values on the **Opacity** channel change the look of a mesh with otherwise the same Base Color value. In this figure, the object on the left has a material with an Opacity value of 0.0. Notice how see-through the material looks as the light passes through the mesh like glass. The second object from the left, has a medium opacity value (0.5), and the third object's opacity value is high (1.0). Notice, how more opaque the object with the high opacity value is compared to the one with a medium value of opacity.

Finally, the material on the rightmost object has its opacity channel calculated from a checkerboard texture sample. Notice how the texture sample is used to apply different opacity values to different locations on the object. This example shows that texture samples can be utilized to control the opacity across an entire mesh.

There is one important fact to keep in mind if you wish to use the **Opacity Channel**. This channel is only available when the **Material Node**'s Blend Mode is `Translucent` or `Additive`. Moreover, since we have to change the material's blend mode, the way the material will process lighting will be different than the usual materials we have discussed so far. We will discuss these issues further later in the chapter.

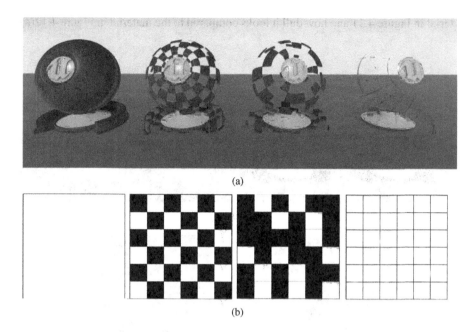

(a)

(b)

FIGURE 4.12: (a) Materials with the same Base Color but different Opacity Masks. (b) The textures from which the opacity mask is supplied to the materials.

Opacity Mask

This channel is a more resource-friendly version of the Opacity Channel. The main difference between the two channels is that the Opacity Mask Channel only has two values, either 0 or 1 –off or on. This is used specifically to mask specific pixels to be transparent inexpensively, and still allow the rest of the material to process lighting.

Figure 4.12(a) shows how different values on the **Opacity Mask** channel change the look of a mesh with otherwise the same Base Color value. In this figure, the objects from left have a material with an Opacity Mask supplied from the textures in the corresponding location from 4.12(b). Notice how you can turn the see-throughness of the material on and off by supplying black-and-white textures into the opacity mask channel.

I would like to bring your attention to how the lighting of the material has been calculated in the usual way with the scene lighting. The object on the left in Figure 4.12(a) is completely opaque as its mask uses the value of 1.0 throughout the material supplied from the texture on the left in Figure 4.12(b).

Now check out the third material from the left in Figure 4.11. This material is using the value of 1.0 throughout the mesh as supplied to its **Opacity** channel. However, since the **Opacity** channel is only available for materials with the blend mode of either `Translucent` or `Additive`, this material does not interact with the scene lighting in the usual way. You can notice the effect by checking out the look of the material in Figure 4.11 and how dull it looks compared to the material in Figure 4.12(a).

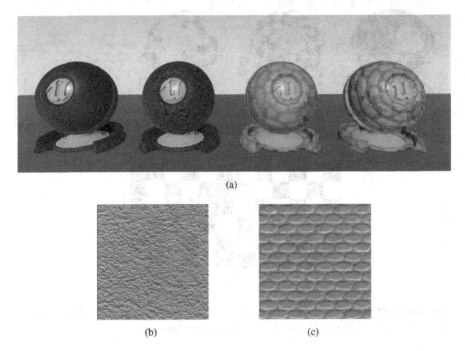

FIGURE 4.13: (a) Materials with the same Base Color without Normal Maps (*left*) and with Normal maps (*right*). (b) A noise normal map applied to the second material from the left. (c) Brick normal map applied to the right-most materials.

Normal Channel

The **Normal Channel** uses vectors to manipulate the way light is reflected off a material. This is done by perturbing, or altering, the "normal" vector at points on the surface of an object at which light hits the surface. This, in other words, is the facing direction of pixels on the surface of the object.

In order to use the **Normal Channel** to modify the normal vectors on the surface of objects, we should use a texture known as a `Normal Map`. The use of the **Normal Channel** via normal maps allows for much greater detail on objects without having a complicated geometry or the burden of increasing polygon count. Normal maps are usually created in 3D modeling programs such as ZBrush or 2D programs such as Gimp or Photoshop.

Figure 4.13(a) shows a pair of materials applied an a pair of models. The left model, in each pair, dose not have a Normal map applied to its **Normal** channel, while the model on the right has its **Normal** channel fed a normal map texture. In the first pair of objects, the normal map is a noise map. In the second pair, the normal map is calculated from the Base Color texture map to create the bulging of bricks and the crevices between bricks. Notice the tremendous amount of realism added to the object without incurring any additional geometry (or poly-count).

FIGURE 4.14: Materials with the same base color, but different World Position Offset values. The leftmost object is a mesh with a material with no position offset applied to its World Position Offset channel. The second mesh from the left has the value of (R:0.0, B:0.0,G:10.0) supplied to its World Position Offset channel. As you can see, this vector value will push all of the mesh's vertices on which the material is applied 10.0 units along the z-direction (upward). The third mesh from the left has a value of (R:-50, G:0.0, B:0.0) applied to its World Position Offset channel. The mesh vertices are pushed −50 units along the x-direction, pushing the mesh away from the viewer. Finally, the last mesh has its World Position Offset channel controlled by a texture sample. Notice the deformation applied to the geometry without the need to change the geometry of the mesh.

World Position Offset

The **World Position Offset Channel** is a very new, and quite interesting addition to the programming functionalities of Unreal Engine materials. This channel actually allows vertices of an object to be manipulated by the material. This gives you the ability to modify objects' geometry by moving or animating the mesh vertices without the need to create a skeletal mesh and incorporating rigging.

This opens the door to a host of very interesting possibilities. Suppose that you wanted to have chains moving in a dungeon without the need to establish Inverse Kinematics and rigging the model. Or to have a wooden box set aflame to deform as it burns. All this can be accomplished at no cost to the geometry. It is important to note that, to my knowledge, no other game engine supports such an interesting feature and interaction between the material of a mesh and its geometry.

Like the **Base Color** channel, the **World Position Offset** channel can take up a Constant3vector or a **Texture Sample** as input. If supplied with a Constant3Vector, the RGB values of the input will be applied to the XYZ directions of displacement, respectively, throughout the mesh. This will affect all of the vertices of the mesh on which the material is applied with the same amount of displacement. To have more control over the localities on the mesh, we can supply a texture through a **Texture Sample** input. If a texture is supplied to the **World Po-**

sition Offset channel, the effect of displacement will be calculated from the texture and applied to appropriate vertices and location on the mesh.

Figure 4.14 shows how different values of the **World Position Offset** channel affect the geometry of a mesh directly from the material. In this figure, the object on the left has a material with no **World Position Offset**. The material applied to the second object from the left has a `Constant3Vector` with values of (R:0.0, G:0.0, B:10.0) applied to its **World Position Offset** channel.

FIGURE 4.15: Materials with the Same Base Color and Normal Maps (*left*) and with World Displacement (*right*).

Notice that the RGB values affect the mesh's vertices along the XYZ coordinates respectively. Therefore, all vertices of this mesh are pushed 10.0 units upwards (i.e., along the positive value of the z-axis). It is important to note that using the **World Position Offset** may result in the object to expand beyond its bounds. However, the renderer still uses the original bounds of the object. This may result in parts of the object getting culled or in shadowing problems.

World Displacement

The **World Displacement Channel** works similarly to the **World Position Offset**, but utilizes tessellation vertices rather than the object's vertices to offset the material. This channel can be utilized to make objects have true depth, rather than the simulated depth achieved by using a normal map alone.

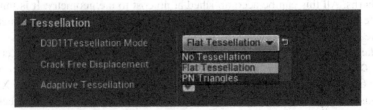

FIGURE 4.16: A Tessellation Has to Be Selected for the World Displacement Channel to Function.

Figure 4.15 shows two pairs of objects with the same Base Color and Normal maps, with (*the right object*) and without (*the left object*) **World Displacement**. Notice how much more rugged the object to the right (with **World Displacement**) is compared to the object which only has its normal channel.

It is important to note that the rendered will still use the original bounds of the object, even when the object's vertices are placed outside of the original bounds as a result of applying the **World Displacement** to expand the object. This may result in parts of the object being culled or getting shadowing errors.

One important fact to note is that, this channel can only function if `Tessellation` is activated. Figure 4.16 shows how you can set the `Tessellation` property of a material node to something other than `NONE` to activate the **World Displacement** channel.

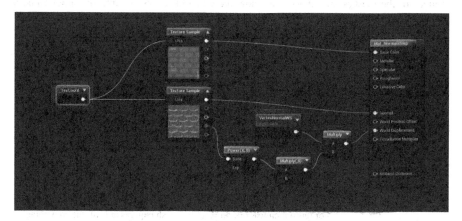

FIGURE 4.17: The Network Generating the World Displacement Values for the Rightmost Mesh in Figure 4.15.

Figure 4.17 shows the network that draws the **World Displacement** channel of the right-most material shown in Figure 4.15. Basically, the network takes the perpendicular value of the normal map, magnifies it and applies it to the normal value drawn from a mesh vertex in the `World Space`. The resulting calculation is then applied to the **World Displacement** channel of the material. The end effect of this operation is to push the vertices that lay in the crevices down, while pulling the rest of the vertices on the mesh outwards, giving some real geometric depth to the object.

Tessellation Multiplier

The **Tessellation Multiplier** Channel controls the amount of tessellation on the surface of an object. This will allow for details to be added or removed from the geometry. This channel is only enabled when `Tessellation` is activated (see Figure 4.16).

Tessellation is a DX11 feature and requires hardware that supports DX11. The main functionality of tessellation is to split triangles into smaller triangles at runtime.

FIGURE 4.18: The effects of different values for the Tessellation Multiplier Channel. Wireframes of the meshes are rendered to show the effect. The Tessellation Multiplier value is increased from left to right.

TABLE 4.2

Tessellation Settings

Tessellation Setting	Description
None	No Tessellation Applied. **Tessellation Multiplier** and **World Displacement** channels will be disabled.
Flat	This setting splits up triangles on each polygonal face of the surface. To create new surface details you may use the `World Position` of the new vertices by using the **Normal** map and the **World Displacement** channels.
PN Triangles	This setting smooths the object by utilizing the mesh's smoothing group. For this option to work properly the mesh requires at least one smoothing group. Much like the `Flat` option, the world displacement and normal maps may be used to displace the newly tessellated vertices to create much more detail on the surface.

This will have the benefit of increasing the surface detail of a mesh. However, effects that require the use of tessellation can be very slow to render and should be used only if such realism is required.

Figure 4.18 shows the effect of the **Tessellation Multiplier** channel on the wireframe of the shown objects. The value of this channel is increased from left to right in the figure. Notice how much more complicated the details on the rightmost object (with a higher Tessellation Multiplier) is compared to the leftmost object (with much lower values for the Tessellation Multiplier channel). By using both the **Tessellation Multiplier** channel and the **World Displacement** channel you can create very complicated geometry directly from your materials.

There are three Tessellation settings, as shown in Table 4.2. The table presents a detailed description of each `Tessellation option` available on the **Details** Panel of the material node in Unreal Engine's material editor.

FIGURE 4.19: The effects of Subsurface Color channel on materials. From left: the first material uses the **Lit** shading model and no subsurface color is active. The material on the second mesh has the **Subsurface** shading model with nothing applied to its **Subsurface Color** channel. The third material has a red color (R:0.2, G:0.0, B:0.0) applied to its subsurface channel with the same Base Color as the first material. The last material only has the red subsurface color (as in the third material) but no Base Color.

Subsurface Color

The **Subsurface Color** Channel allows you to add a color or texture that shifts the color of the material as light passes through the surface. This effect is similar to "mother of pearl," as you will see different colors depending on how you are looking at the material. Note that this channel is only available when using a `Subsurface` shading model (see Figure 4.20).

The subsurface shading model simulates the effect of subsurface scattering, a phenomenon in which the light penetrates the surface of an object and diffuses through it. Objects such as ice, wax, and skin present this effect most visibly. To simulate this effect, the subsurface color allows the light to pass through the material and diffuse the subsurface color of the material in the lighting calculations.

Figure 4.21 shows the effect of subsurface scatter on a material without the subsurface channel (*left*) and with the subsurface channel (*right*). Notice how solid the object to the left looks, as its lighting is calculated by the `Lit` shading model. This does not allow for the light to penetrate the object, and all light rays that hit the surface of the object reflect back or get absorbed by the object. The object to the right uses the `Subsurface` shading model. As such, some of the light penetrates the object and scatters below the surface, reflecting back the subsurface color of the object. Notice how wax-like the object with subsurface scatter looks.

Clear Coat

The **Clear Coat Channel** is used to simulate a material that has a thin translucent layer over the surface of the material, much like a clear coat over the surface of acrylic paint. This can be used to achieve an acrylic or lacquer effect on the top of the material. In order to use this material channel, the material shading model should

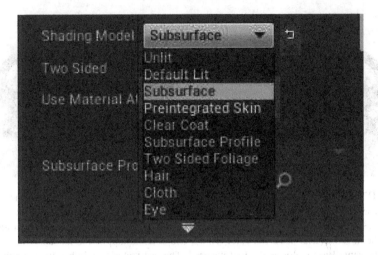

FIGURE 4.20: Subsurface Color channel is available when the material's `Shading Model` is set to subsurface.

be set to `Clear Coat` shading model.

The **Clear Coat Shading Model** simulates the effect of multilayer materials with a thin translucent layer of film over the surface of the material. This model can be used on both metal and non-metal materials. You can use the `Clear Coat` channel with the **Clear Coat Roughness** channel to simulate many multilayered materials and effects.

You must use either the value of 0 or 1 for the **Clear Coat** channel. The amount of 0 acts like a standard material without a clear coat applied to it. The value of 1 allows a full clear coat to be applied to the material via its **Clear Coat Roughness** channel. This option is useful for masking as well. You may apply a `Constant` scalar value or a black-and-white texture map to this channel.

Figure 4.22 shows the effect of this channel and the `Clear Coat Shading Model` on the look of the material. The leftmost mesh in the figure uses the standard shading model. The second mesh from the left uses a material with the `Clear Coat Shading Model` and a value of 1 applied to its **Clear Coat** channel. In the third material (from left) a checker board texture with values switching between 0 and 1 is applied to the **Clear Coat** channel. Notice how some parts of the material look shiny while others look matte colored. Finally, the last material (from left) uses a value other than 0 or 1 applied to its **Clear Coat** channel. Notice the undesirable effect when a value other than a masking value of 0 or 1 is used for the **Clear Coat** channel.

Clear Coat Roughness

The **Clear Coat Roughness** channel works in tandem with the **Clear Coat** channel, and controls the reflectivity of the clear coat layer. We can use this channel to control

FIGURE 4.21: A Closeup view of effects of the subsurface shading model.

FIGURE 4.22: The effects of different values for the Clear Coat Channel on materials with the same Base Color. From left, the first material uses the standard shading model, while others use the Clear Coat shading model. The second material has a value of 1 applied to its **Clear Coat** channel. The third material uses a checker board texture map to supply its **Clear Coat** channel. The forth material uses values other than 0 or 1 as input to its **Clear Coat** channel.

the shininess of the clear coat applied to a material when its **Clear Coat** is set to 1. Note that this channel only controls the reflectivity of the layer on top of the base material layer. The reflectivity of the base material layer is still controlled by the Roughness channel.

According to the Unreal Engine's official documentation the approximation of this channel is valid for small values. If very rough clear coat channels are applied, the calculations may not be accurate compared to their real-world counterparts.

Ambient Occlusion

The **Ambient Occlusion** channel handles detailed self shadowing that usually appears in the crevices of objects, such as scratches, notches, or imperfections on the surface of the object. Much like the **Normal Channel**, the **Ambient Occlusion**

Channel is controlled by an ambient occlusion map, which is usually created in a 3D modeling program.

(a)

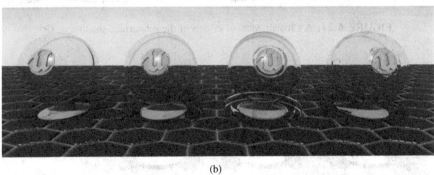

(b)

FIGURE 4.23: The effects of different values for the Refraction Channel on materials with 0.25 Opacity value. From left, the first material uses the value 1.0 for its Refraction channel. The second material has a medium value of 1.3 applied to its **Refraction** channel. The Refraction value for the third material is relatively high (1.75). The fourth material uses a checker board texture map (ranging from 1.0 to 1.5) to supply its **Refraction** channel. (a) In these materials the values are directly plugged in the **Refraction** Channel. (b) In these materials a Fresnel expression is used to calculate the refraction values depending on the normal to the surface.

Refraction

The **Refraction** Channel uses a texture or a value to simulate the refraction of light that happens when images or light pass through a translucent object like water or glass. This channel is useful when creating realistic effects, such as distortion when looking through a glass of water.

It should be noted that it is best to use this channel with the help of a **Fresnel** (pronounced fr·eh·nel) expression. We connect the output of the **Fresnel** expression to the `Alpha` channel of a **Lerp** (Linear Interpolate) expression to choose refraction values between 1.0 and the Refraction Index of the material we are simulating.

This effect can be seen in Figure 4.23. We have applied a refraction value directly to the materials' **Refraction** channel in Figure 4.23(a), while Figure 4.23(b) uses a **Fresnel** expression to apply the surface normal vector to interpolate a refraction value between 1.0 and the surface's `Refraction Index`. Notice that since our object is round, applying the `Refraction Index` directly to its **Refraction** channel may result in the object treated as a solid object filled with the material with the refractive index(see Figure 4.23(a)).

In Figure 4.23 the leftmost material has a refraction index of 1.0, while the refraction indices in the second and third materials are 1.3 and 1.75, respectively. The material on the right has a texture value supplying its **Refraction** channel. This texture ranges between the values of 1.0 and 2.0.

TABLE 4.3

Common Indices of Refraction

Material	Air	Ice	Water	Glass	Diamond	Silicon
Refraction Index	1.0	1.31	1.33	1.52	2.42	3.48

CROSS-REFERENCE

More details about the mathematical models of refraction and reflection may be found in Section 5.13 on page 287.

4.5.3   MATERIAL SHADING MODELS

As we mentioned earlier, the difference between a material and a paint color is in the fact that not only does the material represent the paint color of an object, but it also includes a complex mathematical calculation of how light interacts with the surface on which the material is applied. This light interaction with the surface is implemented in the materials **Shading Model** in Unreal Engine 4.

A material's Shading Model controls (or determines) how different components of light interaction (e.g., various inputs in Unreal Engine) should be combined to create the final color value that will be rendered on the surface of an object. There are six shading models available in Unreal Engine, and Table 4.4 shows a brief description of each model.

CROSS-REFERENCE

The available shading models in Unreal Engine 4 provide for a tremendous amount of power in designing and simulating realistic materials. To learn more about Unreal's Shading Models please check out Section 5.2 on page 261.

TABLE 4.4

Description of Shading Models in Unreal Engine 4 [39].

Shading Model	Description
Unlit	The Material is defined by the Emissive and Opacity inputs only. It does not respond to light.
Default Lit	The default shading model. Perfect for most solid objects.
Subsurface	Used for subsurface scattering materials, such as wax and ice. Activates the Subsurface Color input.
Preintegrated Skin	Used for materials similar to human skin. Activates the Subsurface Color input.
Clear Coat	Used for materials that have a translucent coating on top like clear coat car paint or lacquer. Activates the Clear Coat and Clear Coat Roughness inputs.
Subsurface Profile	Used for materials similar to human skin. Requires the use of a Subsurface Profile in order to work correctly.

4.5.4   MATERIAL DOMAIN

To set the usage of a material, we can use the **Material Domain** setting. This will enable the engine to perform any additional instructions needed for materials that have certain usage, such as `Decals`. It is important, therefore, to designate the usage of the materials by selecting the appropriate option in this setting. Table 4.5 shows a brief description of each model.

TABLE 4.5

Description of Material Domains in Unreal Engine 4 [39].

Domain	Description
Surface	This setting defines the Material as something that will be used on an object's surface; think metal, plastic, skin, or any physical surface. As such this is the setting that you will use most of the time.
Deferred Decal	When making a **Decal Material**, you will use this setting.
Light Function	Used when creating a Material for use with a Light Function.
Post Process	Used if the Material will be used as a Post Process Material.

CROSS-REFERENCE

To learn more about Section **Decal Materials** please See section 5.11 on page 286 of Chapter 5–Advanced Material Concepts in Unreal Engine.

CROSS-REFERENCE

To learn more about **Post Process** materials please check out Section 5.12 on page 287 of Chapter 5–Advanced Material Concepts in Unreal Engine.

TABLE 4.6

Description of material Blend Modes in Unreal Engine 4 [39].

Mode	Description
Opaque	Sets the Final color = Source color. This means that the Material will draw on top of the background. This blend mode is compatible with lighting.
Masked	Sets the Final color = Source color if **OpacityMask> OpacityMaskClip- Value,** otherwise the pixel is discarded. This blend mode is compatible with lighting.
Translucent	Sets the Final color = Source color Opacity + Dest. color (1 - Opacity). This blend mode is **NOT** compatible with dynamic lighting.
Additive	Sets the Final color = Source color + Dest. color. This blend mode is **NOT** compatible with dynamic lighting.
Modulate	Sets the Final color = Source color × Dest. color. This blend mode is **NOT** compatible with dynamic lighting, or fog, unless this is a decal material.

4.5.5 MATERIAL BLEND MODE

Blend Modes specify how the result of the calculation of current material on a particular surface is blended with the results of other calculations that are already drawn on that location. The end result of any calculation that describes the colors at each pixel is stored in the frame buffer.

The blend mode of a material tells the engine how to include the results of the material calculations for each pixel with the destination color already in the frame buffer. Unreal Engine has five available **Blend Modes**. Table 4.6 shows a brief description of each model.

CROSS-REFERENCE

To learn more about **Material Blend Modes** please check out section 5.3 on page 263.

Now that we have covered some basics of what materials are in UE4 and got a quick overview of the **Material Editor** in Unreal Engine 4, let's try make a couple of basic materials. In the next few tutorials we will go over the creation of a number of materials based on the physically based shading models. But first, in Tutorial 4.1 we will set up our project and migrate some assets to be able to showcase our work.

To find updates to this tutorial and updated instructions about its implementation on other UE4 versions please visit the book's companion website at: http://www.RVRLAB.com/UE4Book/

TUTORIAL 4.1   Creating a Project and Migrating Contents

FIGURE 4.24: Creating a Blank Project for Material Tutorials.

CREATE A BLANK PROJECT

In this tutorial we will set up an empty project and migrate the contents of the **Demo Room** from the Unreal Engine's **Example Contents** project into it. The first thing to do is to create a project to which we will add the **Demo Room**. We will select the **Include starter content** to have access to starter contents (see Figure 4.24).

1. Open the Unreal Launcher and select the version of the engine you would like to work with.
2. Once the Launcher Opens, choose **New Project** (see Figure 4.24).
3. Select the **Blueprint** as your project type, and make sure that the **Blank** is selected.
4. Select your platform (Desktop/Console) and your graphics quality.

5. Make sure you include the starter content (see Figure 4.24).
6. Give your project a name and click **Create Project**.

   After you create this blank project, you will close the project and open the
   Content Examples projects. There is a folder in this project that contains the
   contents of a **Demo Room**.

MIGRATING CONTENT FROM UNREAL PROJECTS

In this section we will migrate the **Demo Room** contents from the **Content
Example** project into our own project to be able to set up a nice environment
to visualize the effects we create.

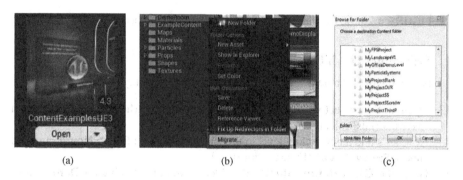

(a)   (b)   (c)

FIGURE 4.25: (a) Opening the Content Examples. (b) Migrating the Demo Room. (c) Choosing the Destination for Demo Room in Our MyMaterialsProject Project.

7. If you haven't downloaded the **Content Examples** from the Unreal Marketplace,
   use the Unreal Engine Launcher to download the Content Examples. This item
   comes with your Unreal Engine 4 subscription and contains several useful maps
   and examples for you to explore and use in your projects free of charge.
8. Open the **Content Examples** project from the Unreal Engine Launcher (Figure 4.25(a)).
9. In the Content Browser of the **Content Examples** project, Right-Click on the
   Demo Room Folder, and choose **Migrate** (Figure 4.25(b)).
10. The Asset Report window pops open, informing you which assets within the
    Demo Room folder will be exported to a new location. These assets include, Textures, Blueprints, Materials, Meshes, etc. Select **OK** to proceed.
11. From the explorer window that opens, navigate to the location of the
    MyMaterialsProject project you created earlier in this tutorial (Figure 4.25(c)).
    Select the Content subfolder of your project. Depending on how your Unreal Engine is set up, this location should be in My Documents/Unreal
    Projects/MyMaterialsProject/Content folder.
12. Close the Contents Example project.

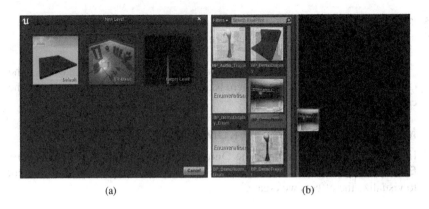

(a)   (b)

FIGURE 4.26: (a) Creating an Empty Level. (b) Adding the Demo Room to the Level.

SETTING UP YOUR DEMO ROOM

Now we will add a new map to our project to host a display room.

13. Open up the project you created earlier on page 150 (earlier, I called this project "MyMaterialsProject").

14. Now, let's add a new empty level to this project. Click on **File->New Level** and choose `Empty Level` (Figure 4.26(a)).

15. Go to the **DemoRoom/BluePrint** folder by double clicking on **DemoRoom** folder and then on **BluePrint** folder.

16. Drag the **BP_DemoRoom** blueprint into your level (Figure 4.26(b)).

17. Wait for the Unreal Engine to compile the shaders and build the materials.

18. Click on **Build** ![icon] from the Unreal toolbar to build the lighting (this may take a few minutes depending on your machine).

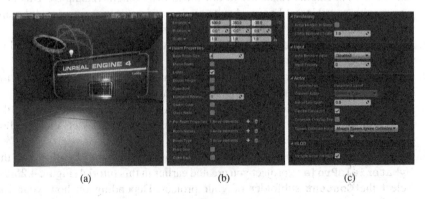

(a)   (b)   (c)

FIGURE 4.27: (a) Demo Room. (b) Demo Room Properties. (c) Additional Room Properties.

19. Now that you have the **Demo Room** created, you can explore its options. We will be using this room throughout this book to deploy the contents and materials

we create.

20. The list below explains how each room property value affects the **Demo Room**. Take time to play with different settings to get familiar with the room.

21. Save your level in the `Maps` folder of your Unreal project and give it a name such as `DisplayRoomLevel`.

OVERVIEW AND SETTING UP A DISPLAY

Now that we have our level created and the Demo Room added to our level, we will set up a couple of display items to showcase our creations.

CROSS-REFERENCE

To learn about Blueprints in UE4 checkout chapter 3– Blueprints, and chapter 8– Advanced Blueprint Concepts.

Just like the **Demo Room** object, the **Display Item** is a `Blueprint`. This means that this object is a class with meshes, components, and other properties, as well as functionalities that can be utilized to configure it and to make it interact with the world and players. Blueprints are very important components of the Unreal Engine 4. In fact, the concept of Blueprints is the major item introduced with the release of the Unreal Engine 4.

To create a display item, perform the following steps:

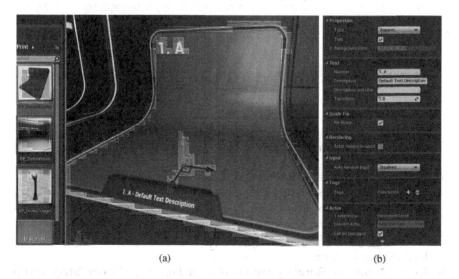

(a)   (b)

FIGURE 4.28: Adding a Demo Display Item to the Demo Room in the Map: (a) The Demo Display Item. (b) The Display Properties.

22. Now that we have the demo room set up, let's add a display. Navigate to

TABLE 4.7

Description of Display Item Properties.

Category	Property	Description/ Values
	Type	Round, SquareL, RoomL, DescriptionOnly, SquareLFlatWall
Properties	Text	If Checked, Toggles Display Item Text Description
	Back Color	Changes the Color of the Display Item Walls
	Number	This Text Will Show as Label of the Display Item
Text	Description	This Text Will Show as the Title of the Display Item
	Desc. 2nd Line	Sub Title of the Display Item
	Transform	Scales the Title of the Display Item

the **BluePrint** folder of the **DemoRoom** folder of your project. Locate the **BP_DemoDisplay** blueprint and drag it into the demo room (Figure 4.28(a)).

23. Table 4.7 shows some of the important properties of the Display Item that can be configured within its details panel.

24. From the Properties of the Demo Display make the following changes:

Number: 1-M.
Description: Basic Materials ...
Type: Round

25. Save your progress.

ADDING INTERACTIONS TO THE DEMO ROOM LEVEL

Now that we have the Display Item added, let's add a **Player Start** actor to the level. This is an Unreal Actor which makes the player initiate at its location whenever the level is run, e.g., when you press the **Play** button on the Unreal Editor toolbar or launch the game.

26. In the search box of the **Modes** panel (Figure 4.29(a)) type **Player Start**. This will search for the Player Start actor from the Unreal Engine classes. Note that this search is context-sensitive and after typing a few letters it will refine the search filters to narrow down the selections.

27. Drag a copy of the **Player Start** actor to create a **Player Start** object in the level (Figure 4.29(a)).

28. Use the **Move** and **Rotate** gizmos to place and orient the **Player Start** actor in front of the Display Item (Figure 4.29(b)). Notice that the blue arrow coming out of the Player Start actor is the direction the player will face when the game starts.

29. Now, you should still be in the **Blueprints** folder of the **Demo Room** in the content browser. Drag a copy of **BP_DemoTrigger** class in the level and place it between the **Player Start** actor and the **Demo Display** item (Figure 4.29(c)).

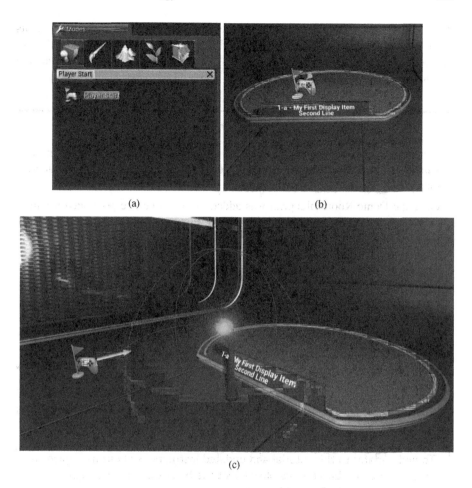

FIGURE 4.29: (a) Search for Player Start. (b) Actor Placed. (c). Place Demo Trigger.

30. From the Properties of the Demo Display make the following changes to the Display Item to a **Square-L** shape:

> **Number:** 1-M.
> **Description:** Basic Materials ...
> **Type:** Square-L

31. **Ready for Your Reward?** Go ahead! Play the level and see what getting close to, and walking away from, the **Demo Trigger** item does. It's not really fancy, but you should hopefully want to learn more about this engine.
32. Save your project and all the levels.

In this tutorial we simply created a new project, migrated the **Demo Room** contents from the **Content Examples** of the Unreal Engine 4 marketplace. We did this, so that in the rest of this chapter we could place our creations in a nicely lit environment for demonstrations.

What Happened in TUTORIAL 4.1...

You just set up a blank project, migrated the **Demo Room** contents from the Unreal Engine's **Content Examples**, and added a demo room to a new game map you created.

Once the Demo Room blueprint was added to the scene, we populated it with Demo Trigger actors and a Player Start actor. Player Start actor will ensure that the player will spawn at a specific location and be oriented in a specific direction every time the game starts.

The Demo Trigger is a Blueprint object which contains interactions. It has a sphere of intersection which will trigger events if player's collision bounds overlap with it. By default, if a player is overlapping the trigger collision sphere, it will toggle the material of its button to a green material. Once the player steps away from the trigger so that their collision boundaries are not overlapping, the trigger button material toggles back to a red material.

Now that your demo room is set up, it's time to create some basic materials and place them in the Display Item. We will next create a material based on a texture and start adding some realism and depth to it by utilizing normal maps.

To find updates to this tutorial and updated instructions about its implementation on other UE4 versions please visit the book's companion website at: http://www.RVRLAB.com/UE4Book/

TUTORIAL 4.2   Your First Unreal Material

In this tutorial we will set up our first material in Unreal Engine 4. The first thing to do is to create a project to which we add the particle system. The initial setup of this tutorial should resemble the image shown in Figure 4.30.

NOTE

We will need the demo room to be set up before we can proceed with the rest of the tutorial. You may find instructions to set up your demo room in Tutorial 4.1 on page 150.

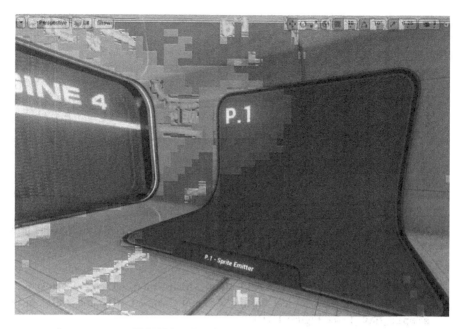

FIGURE 4.30: Room and Display Setup.

SETTING UP THE LEVEL

To have a uniform level that we can work with, you may perform one of the following options to start the work:

1. If you haven't created the demo room, perform the tasks in Tutorial 4.1 on page 150 to create a project which includes a **Demo Room**, a **Player Start**, and a **Demo Display** item as shown in Figure 4.30.

CREATING AND ORGANIZING ASSETS

Now that we have our level available, we will organize all of our materials we create in the content browser.

2. In the content browser, create a folder called `MyMaterials`.
3. `Double-Click` the `MyMaterials` folder you just created, and create a folder within it called `SimpleMaterials`. This is the folder where we will put our first material we are going to create.

CREATING THE `SIMPLE_MAT_X` MATERIAL

There are three ways to create a new material in Unreal Engine 4, one of which requires importing textures. We will look at two of the simpler ways of creating materials now.

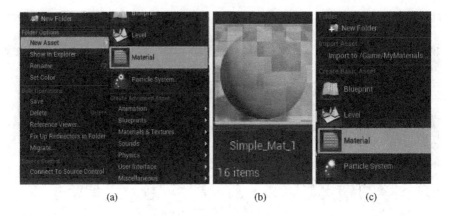

(a)   (b)   (c)

FIGURE 4.31: (a) New Material Window (b) Renaming the Material (c) You can also Right-Click to create a new material.

4. In the Content Browser, choose **Add New->Material** (see Figure 4.31(a)).
5. You will see a new object in the Content Browser. Rename this object simple_mat_1 (see Figure 4.31(b)).
6. We can now re-create the material with the second method for material creation (see Figure 4.31(c)).
7. Right-Click on the empty Content Browser and select Material under Basic Assets. Rename the material to simple_mat_2.
8. Right-Click on the material in the Content Browser and select Edit. This opens the Material Editor. From here you can see the Material Node in the center of the screen. You can also see that the Material Node has a series of inputs. These are the Material Channels, which we will discuss in the next section. Close the Material Editor by closing the tab labeled simple_mat_1 at the top of the screen.

SAVING THE MATERIAL

We will now need to save the game's package. There are two ways to do this:

9. The first is to Right-Click on the Game folder inside of the Content Browser, and click Save from the Context menu.
10. The other is to click **File-> Save All...**(Ctrl+Shift+S). Since we have already created and named our project, Unreal Engine 4 will simply save the new content as it appears in the Content Browser.

EDITING THE MATERIAL

Now we will edit our material.

11. Open the **Material Editor** by either double-clicking the material inside of the content browser, or right-clicking it and selecting **Edit**.

12. The first step to creating a new material is to add a base color or texture. Perform the following tasks to add a texture.

   a. You must utilize a material expression called **TextureSample**. There are four different ways in total to add a texture sample into the **Graph Editor**:

      i. The first is to `Right-Click` the graph and either select TextureSample in the Texture subcategory of the drop-down menu, or you may search for TextureSample in the search bar.

      ii. The second way is to find the TextureSample expression in the Palette on the right side of the screen and drag-and-drop it onto the graph.

      iii. The third way is to hold down the T key on the keyboard and left-click on the graph.

      iv. The final way to create a TextureSample expression is to drag-and-drop the desired texture from the Content Browser directly onto the graph in the Material Editor.

   b. For now, we will use the `Right-Click` method. If you haven't already created the **Texture Sample**, `Right-Click` on the graph and search for **TextureSample**. This adds an empty texture expression onto the graph editor.

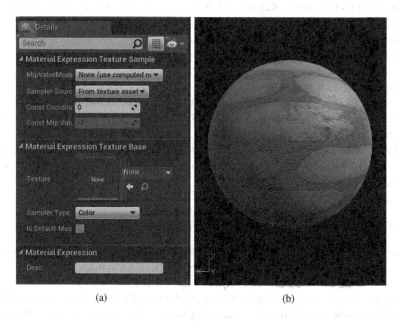

(a)   (b)

FIGURE 4.32: (a) Details Panel. (b) Brick Texture Assigned.

13. Click to select the new **TextureSample** expression that you just created. You will notice the **Details** Panel on the left-hand side of the screen has changed to reflect that you have selected this expression.

14. In the **Details** Panel, you will notice that there is a box labeled Texture (see Figure 4.32(a)). We will need to give the expression a texture to reference.

15. Go into the Content Browser and select `T_Brick_Hewn_Stone_D` texture.
16. Return to the Material Editor and select the arrow next to the box labeled Texture. This will give the **TextureSample** expression a texture to reference.
17. Connect the white connector on the right side of the **TextureSample** expression (i.e., its output channel) by clicking on it and dragging your mouse over to the **BaseColor** channel of the Material Node box. Notice how the Preview Window on the left side of the editor changes to reflect your modifications. Your material should look like the one in Figure 4.32(b).
18. Save the material and close the material editor.

ADDING THE NORMAL MAP

Notice that your material doesn't interact with the lighting in any interesting way. It simply looks bland. It looks just like a flat image transposed onto a three-dimensional object. Adding a normal map will add additional normal vectors on the surface of the object to allow for light interactions with the surface of your material to make the material much more interesting.

19. In the content browser, `Right-Click` on the material you have created so far and select **Duplicate**. This will create a duplicate of your material. We will use this duplicate material to add the normal map.
20. Select the duplicate material you created in the above step. Press **F2** and rename the material to `Mat_Simple_Normal`.
21. `Double-Click` this material to open it in the Material Editor.
22. `Right-Click` on the graph and add another **TextureSample** parameter. From the Content Browser, select `T_Brick_Hewn_Stone_N` and set it as the texture to reference, just like you did in step 13.
23. Connect the new **TextureSample** with the normal map to the **Normal** input channel of the Material Node. Notice how the preview window reflects these changes (see Figure 4.33(b)).
24. Save the material and close the material editor.

MODIFYING THE NORMAL TO ADD MORE DEPTH

Your material already looks a lot better, but it is possible to add some more depth of detail to it by editing the vectors of your normal map.

25. In the content browser, `Right-Click` on the `Mat_Simple_Normal` material and select **Duplicate**. This will create a duplicate of your material. We will use this duplicate material to add the normal map.
26. Select the duplicate material you created in the above step. Press **F2** and rename the material to `Mat_Enhanced_Normal`.
27. `Double-Click` the `Mat_Enhanced_Normal` material to open it in the Material Editor.
28. Create a **Constant3Vector** by either right-clicking on the graph editor and searching for it, or holding the key 3 on your keyboard and clicking on the graph.

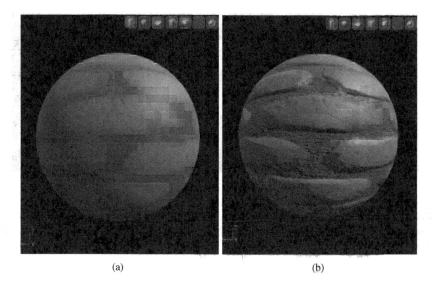

(a)   (b)

FIGURE 4.33: The material without a Normal Map (a) vs. the same material with the Normal Map applied (b).

29. In the **Details** Panel, expand the **Constant** section if it is not already expanded by clicking on the small triangle next to it.
30. You will see three floating point numbers labeled R, G, and B. Edit the value of B to 1.0. This changes the **Constant3Vector** to be pure blue.
31. Add another **Constant3Vector** below the first one.
32. Change the R and G values to 1.0. Leave the B value at 0.0. This will change the **Constant3Vector** to yellow.
33. Time to edit the depth of the normal map. Add a **Constant** below the second **Constant3Vector**, you created above, by either right-clicking on the graph editor and searching for it, or by holding the key 1 on your keyboard and clicking on the graph.
34. Change the value of the **Constant** to 2.0 in the **Details** Panel.
35. Create a **Multiply** expression by right-clicking the graph and searching for it. *Note:* You can also add a **Multiply** expression by holding the key M on your keyboard and clicking on the graph.
36. Connect the **Constant** output to the B input of the **Multiply** expression.
37. Connect the yellow **Constant3Vector** output to the A input of the **Multiply** expression. This will increase the intensity of the **Normal Map**.
38. Create an **Add** expression further to the right by right-clicking the graph and searching for it. *Note:* You can also add an **Add** expression by holding the key A on your keyboard and clicking on the graph.
39. Connect the Blue **Constant3Vector** output to the A input of the **Add** expression,

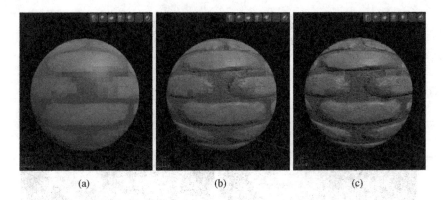

(a)   (b)   (c)

FIGURE 4.34: The material without a Normal Map (a) vs. the same material with the Normal Map applied (b) and the material with the enhanced Normal Map as designed by the network in steps 28–43.

and the **Multiply** output to the B input. This adds the two vectors together to complete the normal map.

40. Now create another **Multiply** expression to the right of both the original **Texture-Sample** containing the normal map, and the new **Add** expression you created above. Connect the normal map's **TextureSample** output to the A input of the **Multiply** expression, and the **Add** output to the B input of this **Multiply** expression.

41. Finally, create a **Normalize** expression to the right of the newest **Multiply** expression. To do this **Right-Click** on the graph editor and search for **Normalize**.

42. Connect the output of the **Multiply** to the input of **Normalize**. The reason this is necessary is that a normal vector must have a magnitude of 1. By normalizing, it brings the magnitude down to 1, and thus ensures that no undesirable lighting artifacts occur.

43. Connect the **Normalize** output to the **Normal** input channel of the Material Node. Notice the new changes on the material; the bricks appear to have slightly more depth than before. This method can be utilized if a normal map doesn't have enough depth (see Figure 4.34(a)–4.34(c)).

COMMENTING THE NETWORK

44. Highlight the 8 expressions that make up your new normal map network by marquee selecting them (**Left-Click** and drag around the network).

45. **Right-Click** on the selection on the graph canvas.

46. Click **Create Comment from Selection** and name the selection **Normal Network**. It is always good practice to keep your material expressions organized by category. Your comment should look like Figure 4.35.

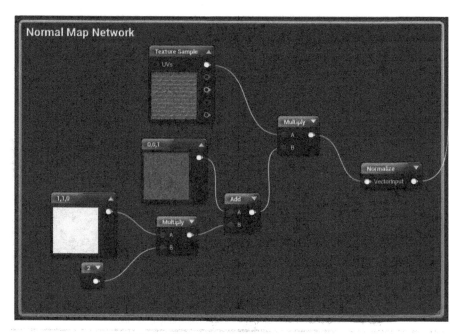

FIGURE 4.35: Normal Map Network Is Commented.

APPLYING MATERIALS IN THE DEMO ROOM

47. In the content browser, look for a folder called **Props** and open it.
48. In the **Props** folder look for and find a mesh called **SM_MatPreviewMesh_02** and drag it into the Display Item you have already placed in the Demo Room.
49. Rotate, scale, and position the mesh so that it faces outwards from the Display Item.
50. **Alt-Drag** the mesh to create two copies of it on the Display Item (see Figure 4.36). You can alternatively copy and paste the mesh in the editor on the Display Item.
51. In the Demo Room select the left mesh in the **Demo Display** you created earlier. Drag the **Mat_Simple** material to its **Element 0** material slot.
52. In the Demo Room select the middle mesh in the **Demo Display** you created above. Drag the **Mat_Simple_Normal** material to its **Element 0** material slot.
53. In the Demo Room select the right mesh in the **Demo Display** you created above. Drag the **Mat_Enhanced_Normal** material to its **Element 0** material slot.
54. Build the lighting ▨ and play the level by pressing **Alt+P** or clicking on the Player icon ▶.
55. Your material progressions should look like Figure 4.36.
56. Save all your materials and your level so far.

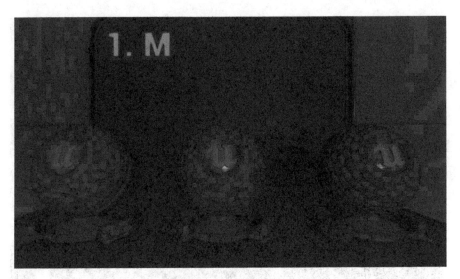

FIGURE 4.36: Tutorial 4.2 material progression.

What Happened in TUTORIAL 4.2...

You just created your first material in Unreal Engine 4. In the first step, you opened (or created) a simple demo environment to deploy the effect. Next, we took some simple steps to create the first basic material.

SETTING UP THE LEVEL

In this step we simply created a level with a Demo Room and Display Item blueprints and a Player Start. If you have completed Tutorial 4.1 you skip this step.

CREATING AND ORGANIZING ASSETS

In this step, we simply created a folder called MyMaterials for organizational purposes. We will place all of the materials we create in this chapter into this folder.

CREATE A SIMPLE MATERIAL

This section was a simply hands-on experience with how we can create new materials in Unreal Engine 4. We saw two different ways to create new materials in the **Content Browser**. We also opened the new material in the Unreal Engine's **Material Editor**.

EDITING THE MATERIAL

This section walked us through editing our newly created material in the Unreal Engine's **Material Editor**. We wanted to create a Brick material. To do this we created a **Texture Sample** expression and assigned a diffuse brick texture to it. We usually use diffuse texture to simulate the color of the material. Diffuse textures are simple bitmaps (or images) that look like the material we need to make.

We saw three different ways to create **Texture Sample** expressions. You can `Right-Click` on the graph editor and search form them in the search box. You can also find the expression from the `Palette` and drag it onto the graph editor. Finally, you can use the shortcut (hold the `T` key and `Left-Click` on the graph editor) to place the expression.

Once a **Texture Sample** expression is placed on the graph editor, you should assign a texture to it from the **Content Browser**. To do this you can go to the **Details** Panel of the expression, open the drop-down list next to the `Texture` section and assign the texture. Alternatively, you can select a texture from the **Content Browser**, and then click on the `Left-Arrow` ◀ in the `Texture` section to assign the selected texture from the **Content Browser**. You may also drag and drop a texture from the **Content Browser** onto the `Texture` section.

To create the look of the brick material, we simply connected the RGB (white) output channel of the **Texture Sample** expression to the `Base Color` channel of our material node.

ADDING THE NORMAL MAP

Normal maps are bitmap (or images) that, for each pixel, contain a 3D vector representing the pixel's normal vector. A normal vector is a vector that points out of a surface and is perpendicular to the surface. In computer graphics, normal maps are intensively used to create a 3D look on otherwise flat surfaces without the need to add any complex geometry.

The lighting calculation will take into account three vectors, the viewer vector (also known as the camera vector), the light vector (also known as the incident vector), and the normal vector to calculate the amount of light that is scattered on a surface and reaches the viewer's eyes.

If we don't apply a normal map to our material, all of the pixels on the surface on which the material will be applied will have the same direction for their normal. Therefore, the light will reflect out uniformly on the surface and will make it look flat. Applying a normal map to a material will assign different normal vectors to different locations on the surface. This will make the light rays that hit different locations on the surface reflect with different angles. The end result is that the surface with normal maps will look 3D, even if its geometry is perfectly flat. You can see the difference in Figure 4.33(a) (without normals) and Figure 4.33(b) (with normals applied).

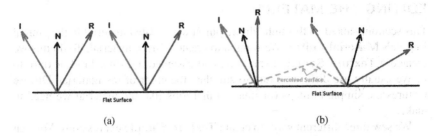

(a)   (b)

FIGURE 4.37: (a) Reflection on a regular flat surface. (b) Reflection on a flat surface with modified normals. The dashed-line shows the perceived surface after normal modifications. Notice how the surface would look bumpy.

MODIFYING THE NORMAL TO ADD MORE DEPTH

Figure 4.37(a) shows a flat surface with its normal vectors unchanged. The black arrows labeled N are the normal vectors, the red arrows labeled I are the light vectors, and the blue arrows labeled R are the reflection vectors. Figure 4.37(b) shows the same flat surface after its normals are modified – i.e., they point in different directions.

In both Figure 4.37(a) and Figure 4.37(b), the light vectors are the same to indicate that the direction of light hasn't changed. Notice that with changes in the normal directions, the reflection vectors change. This will create the illusion that the surface is not flat, but rather follows the green dashed line. Notice after the normals are modified, the surface seems to actually have a bump, and therefore looks 3D.

We used the notion that when normal vectors actually point towards a different direction than the perpendicular direction to a surface, they make the surface look bumpy. Therefore, if we use the normals from normal map and skew them even more, we will make the illusion of depth even more magnified. To this end we took the normal map, and multiplied its Red and Green channels by two, keeping its Blue channel unchanged.

The Red, Green, and Blue channels represent the X, Y, and Z axis. Therefore, the Blue channel of a the normal map actually represents the perpendicular direction to the surface (its Z-axis). This means that the Red and Green channels of a normal map are the tangent directions. Multiplying these directions will skew the normal map further away from the perpendicular direction. As a result this effect will add more depth to the surface, is obvious from the comparisons between Figure 4.34(a), Figure 4.34(b), and Figure 4.34(c).

APPLYING MATERIALS IN THE DEMO ROOM

In the final step of this tutorial we applied our three materials, `Mat_Simple`, `Mat_Simple_Normal`, and `Mat_Simple_NormalMoreDepth` to the three preview mesh props in the level.

In Tutorial 4.2, we worked with the most primary material channels, the `Base Color` channel and the `Normal` channel. The base color channel is responsible for the color and texture of our material. It is the paint applied to the surface and nothing more. The normal channel on the other hand had a bit more of an interesting role.

As we discussed in the `What Happened ...` section above, the normal map actually applies the normal vectors when the light reflection from a surface is calculated. This is what makes our material look 3D. We actually used the normal texture for our material in a network to even give more depth to our material than is supplied in the normal texture. This made the imperfections and cracks in our material a bit more magnified!

We will learn about other material channels and their use in giving a certain look in the next couple of tutorials. We will use the roughness channel to give a little dampness to our material and enhance its look with the metallic channel in Tutorial 4.3.

> To find updates to this tutorial and updated instructions about its implementation on other UE4 versions please visit the book's companion website at:
> `http://www.RVRLAB.com/UE4Book/`

TUTORIAL 4.3   Enhancing the Material's Look

Now that our material has a normal map to give it some depth, let's enhance its look. We will create a couple of networks to feed the **Roughness** and the **Metallic** channels of our material.

In the new Unreal Engine's material model, called Physically Based Materials, the reflection and shininess of a material are encoded within the **Metallic** and **Roughness** channels.

ADDING MOISTURE WITH ROUGHNESS CHANNEL

For an even more realistic look to our material, it is best to add a **Roughness** channel. Adding this channel will give our brick wall the appearance of being slightly wet or glossy in certain areas.

1. Add a **TextureSample** expression and set the Texture value to be `T_Brick_Hewn_Stone_M`.
2. Create two **Constant** expressions above the new **TextureSample**. Set the first to 0.7 and the second to 0.2.
3. Create a **LinearInterpolate** (Lerp) expression by right clicking on the graph editor and searching for it. Place it to the right of the **TextureSample** and the two **Constant** expressions and make the following connections:

> **Constant with value 0.7** ↔ Input A of the **Lerp** expression.
> **Constant with value 0.2** ↔ Input B of the **Lerp** expression.

> **TextureSample Red Output** ↔ Input `Alpha` of the **Lerp** expression.
> **Lerp Output** ↔ `Roughness` channel of the Material Node.

4. Comment the 4 expressions you just created and call this section `Moisture Network` (see Figure 4.38(a)).
5. The preview window will reflect these changes. Notice how the material has a glossier look. If you rotate the preview mesh, you can see how drastically the light interaction changes (see Figure 4.38(b)).
6. Save your material so far.

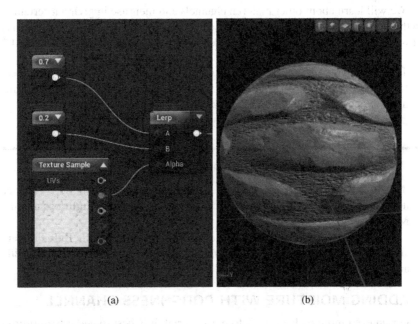

(a)   (b)

FIGURE 4.38: (a) The network that simulates the moisture on the brick wall. (b) The brick wall now looks shiny in some areas with moisture.

ADDING GLOSSINESS WITH METALLIC CHANNEL

Now we will make our material to look a bit reflective on the areas where it is moist by adding a **Metallic** channel. Adding this channel will give our brick wall the appearance of being slightly reflective where it's wet in certain areas.

7. Add a **TextureSample** expression and set the Texture value to be `T_BrickWall_M`. *Note: If you have already added this texture in step 1, you may skip to the next step.*
8. Create two **Constant** expressions above the new **TextureSample**. Set the first to 0.7 and the second to 0.2.

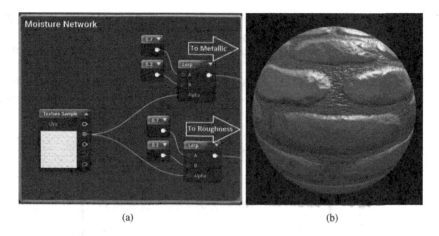

(a)   (b)

FIGURE 4.39: (a) The network that simulates the moisture reflections on the brick wall. (b) The brick wall now looks slightly reflective in some areas with moisture.

9. Create a **LinearInterpolate** (Lerp) expression by right clicking on the graph editor and searching for it. Place it to the right of the **TextureSample** and the two **Constant** expressions.

> **Constant with value 0.7** ↔ Input **A** of the **Lerp** expression.
> **Constant with value 0.2** ↔ Input **B** of the **Lerp** expression.
> **TextureSample Red** ↔ Input **Alpha** of the **Lerp** expression.
> **Lerp Output** ↔ **Metallic** channel of the Material Node.

10. Comment the 4 expressions you just created (or rearrange your Moisture comment section) and call this section **Moisture Network** (see Figure 4.39(a)).
11. The preview window will reflect these changes. Notice how the material has a glossier look. If you rotate the preview mesh, you can see how drastically the light interaction changes (see Figure 4.39(b)).

APPLYING MATERIALS IN THE DEMO ROOM

12. In the content browser, look for a folder inside the **Demo Room** folder called **Blueprints** and open it.
13. Drag a copy of **Display Item** onto the level and place it to the right of the first **Display Item**. Change its properties to the following:

> **Number:** 2-M.
> **Description:** Basic Materials Enhanced...
> **Type:** Square-L

14. In the content browser, look for a folder called **Props** and open it.

15. In the **Props** folder look for and find a mesh called **SM_MatPreviewMesh_02** and drag it into the Display Item you have already placed in the Demo Room.
16. Rotate, scale, and position the mesh so that it faces outwards from the Display Item.
17. **Alt-Drag** the mesh to create two copies of it on the Display Item (see Figure 4.36). You can alternatively copy and paste the mesh in the editor on the Display Item.

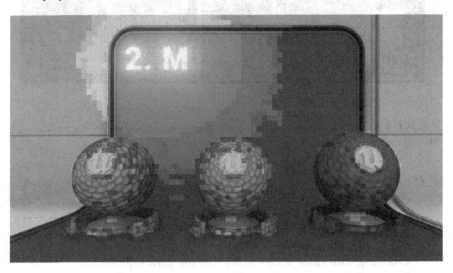

FIGURE 4.40: Tutorial 4.3 material progression so far.

18. In the Demo Room select the left mesh in the **Demo Display** you created earlier. Drag the Mat_Enhanced_Normal material to its **Element 0** material slot.
19. In the Demo Room select the middle mesh in the **Demo Display** you created above. Drag the Mat_EnhancedV1 material to its **Element 0** material slot.
20. In the Demo Room select the right mesh in the **Demo Display** you created above. Drag the Mat_EnhancedV2 material to its **Element 0** material slot.
21. Build the lighting and play the level by pressing **Alt+P**.
22. Your material progressions should look like Figure 4.40.
23. Save all your materials and your level so far.

MODIFYING MATERIALS AND PLACING SPOTLIGHTS

If you have noticed, adding the metallic channel to make the material look moist has changed the material and made it look a bit darker. You may have further noticed that the three materials (the normal mapped, the material with added roughness, and the one with added metallic value) don't really look different. It is because we don't have direct light shining on them, e.g., the sun shining to brighten the moist areas of the surface. We will fix these issues next.

24. First, let's brighten up the last material (i.e., the Mat_Simple_EnhancedV2).

FIGURE 4.41: Adding Spotlights to the Demo Room.

25. **Double-Click** on the `Mat_Simple_EnhancedV2` material to open it in the content browser:

a. **Right-Click** between the **TextureSample** and the **Base Color** of the material node and add a `Multiply` expression.

b. Connect the white output channel of the Base Color **TextureSample** to the **A** input channel of the **Multiply** expression.

c. Type the value of 2.0 in the **B** channel of the **Multiply** expression.

d. Connect the output of the **Multiply** expression to the **Base Color** channel of the material node.

26. This will brighten up the material to make its color similar to its counterparts.

27. Now let's bring some spotlights into the room and place them in front of the props in our demo display item.

a. Back in the main editor click on **Lights** in the **Modes** tab (top-left corner of the editor).

b. Drag a spotlight into the demo room and place it in front of the left mesh (see Figure 4.41).

c. Rotate the light so that it faces the mesh (you need to press the **E** key on your keyboard to activate the rotate gizmo, rotate the light, and press the **W** key to get the translate gizmo back) (see Figure 4.41).

d. In the **Details** Panel of the spotlight, go to the **Light** section and change the **Intensity** to 100.

e. Also in the **Light** section find and un-check the **Cast Shadows** checkbox.

f. **Alt-Drag** the spotlight icon to create two copies of the spotlight and place them in front of the other props (see Figure 4.36). You can alternatively copy and paste the mesh in the editor on the Display Item.

28. Build the lighting and play the level by pressing **Alt+P**.

FIGURE 4.42: Tutorial 4.3 material progression.

29. Your material progressions should look like Figure 4.42. You might need to adjust the location and rotation of the lights to see the difference on your materials and objects.
30. Save all your materials and your level so far.

We are making great progress, even with simple steps. We just simulated the effect of moisture and its reflectiveness (although slightly) on our material. We placed the progression of our materials on a Display Item in the demo room. Let's go over some details about how our material has been enhanced over the course of this tutorial.

What Happened in TUTORIAL 4.3...

You just modified our material to give it a more natural look. We used the Metallic and Roughness channels of our material node to make certain parts of our material look more moist and glossy than some other parts. We also placed some spotlights in the scene to see the effects more easily.

ADDING MOISTURE WITH ROUGHNESS CHANNEL

Linear Interpolation is a type of blend between two values or textures using an Alpha value. An alpha value of 0.0 will result in 100% input A, whereas a value of 1.0 will result in 100% input B. All values between 0.0 and 1.0 will blend the two values or textures accordingly.

FIGURE 4.43: The Red channel of `T_Brick_Hewn_Stone_M`.

Let's take a look at the red channel of the `T_Brick_Hewn_Stone_M` texture shown in Figure 4.43. A quick look at this texture reveals that we have darker areas where the bricks are located. Suppose that we wanted the bricks to retain more moisture than the grout between them.

By connecting the Red channel of this texture sample to the alpha of the **Lerp** expression, we make the roughness values of our material range from 0.7 to 0.2 depending on how much red color the **TextureSample** has in it on each pixel. Doing so makes the roughness values for the bricks more than the grout, as the roughness will go from 0.2 (on the grout) to 0.7 (on the bricks). This network makes the bricks less polished than the grout and look more moist.

ADDING GLOSSINESS WITH METALLIC CHANNEL

We created the same network as the one for the **Roughness** channel of our material for the **Metallic** channel. Since the moist areas are a bit glossy we want the network to be similar to the roughness channel network. We used a **Lerp** expression to interpolate between a metallic value of 0.7 on the brick to 0.2 on the grout. The effect looks pretty neat!

APPLYING MATERIALS IN THE DEMO ROOM

In order to compare the results of our work in the past two tutorials, we created three preview mesh props on a new display item. We applied our depth modified material to the leftmost prop, our moist material with the roughness channel to the middle prop, and the moist and metallic material to the rightmost prop.

We noticed that our material that incorporated a metallic channel looks a bit dim. We simply multiplied its Base Color by 2, to make it look more comparable to the other materials we have created.

We finally placed three spotlights in the scene to shine some light on our three materials to see the differences more easily.

Now that we have our material looking pretty impressive, we are going to step into one of the newest features of Unreal Engine 4 in regards to materials. As mentioned earlier in this chapter, Unreal Engine 4 allows for materials to actually change the geometry. This can be done in two ways: 1) by manipulating the **World Position Offset** channel; 2) utilizing the **Tessellation Multiplier** and **World Displacement** channels.

We will use the **World Displacement** channel in the following tutorial to add more depth to the material via this channel.

> To find updates to this tutorial and updated instructions about its implementation on other UE4 versions please visit the book's companion website at: http://www.RVRLAB.com/UE4Book/

TUTORIAL 4.4   Adding More Depth via Displacement

Thus far, your focus has been on adding a type of simulated depth to your brick wall material by manipulating the way light interacts with it. However, Unreal Engine 4 has the ability to change the actual geometry of the mesh using the **World Displacement** channel. When you utilize this channel, the material actually modifies the polygons of the object in order to create real depth.

CREATING THE WORLD DISPLACEMENT NETWORK

Let's now add some more depth to our material to make it actually look 3D.

1. In the content browser, open the folder where you have been creating your materials so far.
2. `Right-Click` on the last material you created (the `Mat_Simple_EnhancedV2` and choose duplicate.
3. This will make a duplicate copy of your material with all expressions carried over.
4. `Right-Click` on this Duplicate material (or press the **F2** key) to rename it to something like `Mat_Advanced_WD`.
5. Select the material node and in the **Details** Panel scroll down to the section called **Tessellation**.
6. In the **Tessellation** section change the **D3D11TessellationMode** to Flat Tessellation (see Figure 4.44(a)). This will activate your materials tessella-

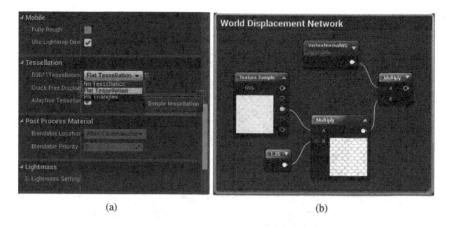

(a)   (b)

FIGURE 4.44: (a) You need to change the D3D11Tessellation Mode for this network to work. (b) The network that uses a texture map to modify the mesh vertices' geometry.

tion to be processed by DirectX 11. (*Note: This mode is only available if your hardware supports DirectX 11.*)

7. Add a **TextureSample** expression (by holding the **T** key on your keyboard and clicking on the graph editor) to the graph.

8. Change this **TextureSample**'s texture to T_Brick_Hewn_Stone_M.

9. Add a Constant below this **TextureSample** and set its value to 1.25.

10. To the right of these two expressions, create a **Multiply** expression.

11. Connect the Green output channel of the **TextureSample** expression to the **A** input of the **Multiply** expression.

12. Connect the output channel of the **Constant** expression to the **B** input of the **Multiply** expression.

13. Add a **VertexNormalWS** expression above the **TextureSample** expression. To do this, Right-Click above the **TextureSample** and type VertexNormalWS in the search box. This expression will output a normal vector for each vertex of a mesh so that your material can modify it to apply the geometry change to your mesh.

14. Create another **Multiply** expression to the right of the **VertexNormalWS** and **TextureSample**.

15. Connect the **VertexNormalWS** output to the input **A** of the **Multiply** expression.

16. Connect the output channel of the first **Multiply** expression to the input **B** of the **Multiply** expression (see Figure 4.44(b)).

17. This combination of expressions will modify the amount that the vertices are offset. The lighter areas of the texture will move the vertices of the object in the positive direction (outward), and the darker areas will move them in the negative direction (inward), creating actual depth.

18. Connect output of the last **Multiply** expression to the now activated **World Displacement** channel of your material node.

19. Save your material so far.

FIGURE 4.45: Tutorial 4.4 material progression.

APPLYING MATERIALS IN THE DEMO ROOM

Now we will place the last of each of the materials we created in each section side-by-side in the Demo Room to showcase our progress.

20. In the content browser, look for a folder inside the **Demo Room** folder called **Blueprints** and open it.
21. Drag a copy of **Display Item** onto the level and place it to the right of the second `Display Item`. Change its properties to the following:

> **Number:** 3-M.
> **Description:** Basic Materials Comparisons. . .
> **Type:** Square-L.

22. In the content browser, look for a folder called **Props** and open it.
23. In the **Props** folder look for and find a mesh called **SM_MatPreviewMesh_02** and drag it into the Display Item you have already placed in the Demo Room.
24. Rotate, scale, and position the mesh so that it faces outwards from the Display Item.
25. `Alt-Drag` the mesh to create two copies of it on the Display Item (see Figure 4.36). You can alternatively copy and paste the mesh in the editor on the Display Item.
26. Now let's bring some spotlights into the room and place them in front of the props in our demo display item:

a. In the **Modes** tab (top-left corner of the editor) click on **Lights** section.

b. Drag a spotlight into the demo room and place it in front of the left mesh (see Figure 4.41).

c. Rotate the light so that it faces the mesh (you need to press the E key on your keyboard to activate the rotate gizmo, rotate the light, and press the W key to get the translate gizmo back) (see Figure 4.41).

d. In the **Details** Panel of the spotlight, go to the Light section and change the Intensity to 100.

e. Also in the **Light** section find and un-check the **Cast Shadows** checkbox.

f. Alt-Drag the spotlight to create two copies of the spotlight and place them in front of the other props (see Figure 4.36). You can alternatively copy and paste the mesh in the editor on the Display Item.

27. Select the left mesh in the **Demo Display** you created earlier . Drag the Mat_Enhanced_Normal material to its **Element 0** material slot.

28. Select the middle mesh in the **Demo Display** you created above. Drag the Mat_Simple_EnhancedV2 material to its **Element 0** material slot.

29. Select the right mesh in the **Demo Display** you created above. Drag the Mat_Advanced_WD material to its **Element 0** material slot.

30. Build the lighting and play the level by pressing Alt+P.

31. Your material progressions should look like Figure 4.45. You might need to adjust the location and rotation of the lights to see the difference on your materials and objects.

32. Save all your materials and your level so far.

What Happened in TUTORIAL 4.4...

You just got a taste of one of the newest features of materials in Unreal Engine 4, the world displacement channel. This channel is actually quite powerful. It is a link between a material and the geometry on which it is applied. Not only will you have control over the light interactions with your object, but you will also have control of its geometry with the world displacement.

Remember from our discussion of the normal maps and the way the normal channel controls the reflection of light on a surface to simulate depth, when it is not there. There are two ways to have a material affect the geometry. The first is through the world position offset channel of the material, and the second is through the world displacement channel and tessellation multiplier.

In this tutorial we worked with the world displacement channel to pull some vertices outwards and push others in, to create real depth.

CREATING THE WORLD DISPLACEMENT NETWORK

The first thing to remember about the world displacement in UE4, is that this feature is only available if the hardware supports DX11. If your hardware doesn't support DX11, you cannot use the Tessellation features that enable the world displacement. In such cases, you still can use the world position offset channel of your material to affect geometry.

To enable the world displacement, we first selected the material node and under its details rollout, changed the Tessellation mode to `D3D11 Tessellation Mode`. Once the Tessellation mode is set to anything other than `None`, your material node's `World Displacement` and `Tessellation Multiplier` channels will become activated.

Both the `World Displacement` and `Tessellation Multiplier` channels work with the geometry's vertices. As such, we usually use a **Vertex Normal WS** expression in the network that will be used to supply these channels. The **Vertex Normal WS** will give us the normal vector of each vertex in the world space.

Remember the normal vector is the vector perpendicular to the surface at any given location. Therefore, having the normal vector at each vertex, we can push and pull it with the `World Displacement` channel. This is exactly what we did in our network. We used the green channel of the `T_Brick_Hewn_Stone_M` texture. This channel has larger values for the brick locations and lower values for the grout location. We then multiplied the output of this channel by the **Vertex Normal WS** to pull the object's vertices. Since the brick values are more than the grout values, the vertices located on the bricks are pulled out more than those on the group. This will make our object have real depth compared to what is possible with only the normal channel.

In the previous series of tutorials, we started by working with a simple material off of a texture map, and worked our way towards making this material look very realistic. In fact, you just created your first advanced material using Unreal Material Editor! We populated our demo room with these materials to showcase your progress and the power of Unreal Engine.

It is highly recommended that you play around with some of the values of the expressions to see how they are affected. Try increasing or decreasing the values of the **World Displacement** constant or adding a constant value to the `Tessellation Multiplier` channel. There is no limit to what you can do with the Material Editor in Unreal Engine 4!

4.6 MATERIAL EXPRESSIONS IN UNREAL 4

The third, and most important, component of a material is the collection of **Material Expressions** that make up the material itself. Material Expressions are the building blocks of materials. To those readers who are mathematically inclined, the material expressions are like terms in the mathematical equations that govern each aspect of a material.

Each of the many Material Expressions in Unreal Engine 4 are used to give specific effects to a material, such as adding a texture, adding scalar or vector values,

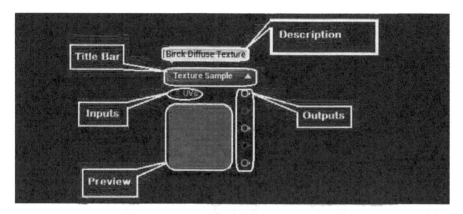

FIGURE 4.46: Material Expression Components.

panning materials over time, or modifying the UV coordinates of the material. By using combinations of simple **Material Expressions**, it is possible to create elaborate textures that can make an object come to life.

Figure 4.46 shows a Texture Sample material expression with its components. Each material expression has these five components: Description, Title Bar, Inputs, Outputs, and Preview. Descriptions of each of these components are presented below:

Description: All material expressions have a common property called **Desc** in their Details rollout. The text provided for this property will be shown in the Material Editor to show short notes about the functionality of the expression. You may enter any text in the Description section.

Title Bar: This components displays the name or any important information about the material expression.

Inputs: These are links that can be connected to the output channels of other expressions to carry input values into the expression.

Outputs: These are links that provide the output values of the material expression's calculations to other expressions or to the input channels of a material node.

Preview: A small window that shows how the value of the expression looks. It basically is a 2D bitmap of the values of the expression. If the expression is a constant, the preview will show black or white, or a shade of gray depending on the value. If the expression is a vector, then this preview will be a color associated with the RGB values of the expression. You may expand or collapse the expression by clicking on the `Triangle` icon on the Tool Bar of the Material Expression. This window updates if the real-time update is enabled, or can be updated manually by pressing `space-bar` on the keyboard.

TABLE 4.8

Frequently Used Categories of Material Expressions.

Most Commonly Used Material Expressions	
TextureSample2D	Scalar Parameter
VectorParameter	VertexColor
LinearInterpolate	Fresnel
Mathematical Material Expressions	
Abs	Floor
Add	Frac
Ceil	Multiply
Cosine	OneMinus
CrossProduct	Power
Divide	Sine
DotProduct	Subtract
Texture Coordinate Material Expressions	
TextureCoordinate	Panner
Rotator	Time

4.6.1 PARAMETER VS. NON-PARAMETER EXPRESSIONS

Certain material expressions are parameters while others are not. A parameter makes the value of the expression exposed to the run-time component of the engine to allow for it to be modified. One of the most basic ways of using material parameters is to create a **Material Instance** from the base material. The parameters in the material instance will be available at level-design in the editor or at run-time to modify and dynamically change.

To change the values of a parameter in a material expression, you must use its **Parameter Name**. The parameter name will be available to the run-time engine to programmatically alter its value as well. For this reason it is important to set a meaningful **Parameter Name** for each Parameter Expression in a material. If there are multiple material parameters with the same Parameter Name, the engine will assume them to be the same parameter. Changing the value of one of these duplicate parameters will change the values of all of its duplicates. You may also assign a `Default` value to the Material Parameters at creation of the parameters.

4.6.2 COMMONLY USED MATERIAL EXPRESSIONS

Table 4.8 lists a breakdown of some commonly used materials expressions. We will discuss the functions of some useful and commonly used **Material Expressions** below [36]. A more comprehensive list and descriptions of functionalities may be found on the Unreal Engine documentation website.[1]

---

[1] https://docs.unrealengine.com/latest/INT/Engine/Rendering/Materials/ExpressionReference/index.html

CROSS-REFERENCE

More details about the Material Expressions may be found in Appendix A.

4.6.2.1 Constant Expressions

Constant expressions[2] can be of the form of a single-valued, multi-valued (e.g., Vectors), or dynamically changing items, but are generally fixed and do not change once their values are set in the editor. However, certain constant expressions (such as **Time** and **Particle Color**) are available for the engine to control and update their values [7].

Constant: This expression outputs a single floating-point value – i.e., a real-valued number. Its output can be connected to the input of any other expression. For example if it is connected to an expression that needs a `3Vector` value, the engine will cast its output into a `3Vector` value automatically. A description of the properties of a Constant expression are listed below:
- **Properties**
    - **R:** Specifies the float value of the expression output.

Constant2Vector: This expression outputs two floating-point values. Its output can be considered as a 2-dimensional vector. This expression's properties include:
- **Properties**
    - **R:** Specifies the first float value of the expression output.
    - **G:** Specifies the second float value of the expression output.

Constant3Vector: This expression outputs three floating-point values. Its output can be considered a 3-dimensional vector. You can use this expression to specify a color (RGB values) or a point in 3D space (XYZ) values. The X, Y, and Z values in space correspond to the values R, G, and B, respectively.
- **Properties**
    - **R:** Specifies the first float value of the expression output.
    - **G:** Specifies the second float value of the expression output.
    - **B:** Specifies the third float value of the expression output.

Constant4Vector: This expression outputs four floating-point values. Its output can be considered a 4-dimensional vector. You can use this expression to specify a color-alpha (RGBA values) or a point in the 4D homogenous space (XYZW) values. The X, Y, Z, and W values in space correspond to the values R, G, B, and A, respectively. This expression properties include:

---

[2] The contents of this section are adapted from the official UE4 online documentation found at: `https://docs.unrealengine.com/latest/INT/`.

- **Properties**
  - **R:** Specified the first float value of the expression output.
  - **G:** Specified the second float value of the expression output.
  - **B:** Specified the third float value of the expression output.
  - **A:** Specified the fourth float value of the expression output.

> **NOTE**
>
> If you need to separate the output channels into its R, G, B, or A components you must use a **Component Mask** expression. For more information on **Component Mask** on page 186.

Time: This expression is used to add the passage of time to the material's calculations. There are a number of different ways that this expression will be useful. For example using it as the input to a **Panner** or **Rotator** expression to move a texture map on the surface of a mesh. Or you can use this expression as the input of a **Sine** or **Cosine** expression to create a dynamically changing value between -1.0 and +1.0. The **Time** expression properties include:

- **Properties**
  Ignore Pause: If this property is set to **True**, the time will continue to pass even after the game is paused.

Vertex Color: This expression is useful to access the material that will be rendered on a module of sprite particle emitters.

4.6.2.2 Mathematical Expressions

Mathematical expressions[3] in Unreal Engine's materials allow us to combine values from other expressions, variables, and objects in the game and create values that are useful for our calculations of all aspects of a material. These expressions are basically mathematical functions – they take some input values and combine these inputs to generate resulting values [40].

---

[3] The contents of this section are adapted from the official UE4 online documentation found at: https://docs.unrealengine.com/latest/INT/.

Abs: This expression takes a value (positive or negative) and drops the sign and returns the absolute value of the input it receives. In mathematical terms, the absolute value of a number x is calculated according to the following equation:

$$\text{ABS}(x) = |x| = \begin{cases} x & x \geq 0 \\ -x & x < 0 \end{cases} \tag{4.1}$$

Examples: **Abs** of −3.4 is 3.4 and **Abs** of 4.32 is 4.32. We write this mathematically as $|-3.4| = 3.4$ and $|4.32| = 4.32$, respectively.

Example Usage: The **Abs** expression is commonly used on the result of a **Dot Product** to take the sign of the value out and use the actual number, regardless of whether it is positive or negative (see Figure 4.47)). In this example, we are using the Dot Product to calculate the angle between the reflection vector and the camera vector. The brighter color represents when the two vectors align.

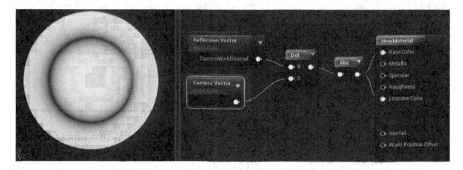

FIGURE 4.47: Abs Expression Example.

Add: This expression takes its two input values (A and B) and returns the summation of the two values. The addition operation is performed on a per-channel basis. In other words, if you add to Constant3Vectors, the result will be a Constant3Vector in which the R, G, and B components are the sum of the two input R, G, and B channels, respectively.

Mathematically speaking, Let **X** and **Y** be two N-channel vectors. Then the **Add** expression of these two values will be:

$$\text{ADD}(\mathbf{X}, \mathbf{Y}) = \mathbf{X} + \mathbf{Y} = [x_1 + y_1, x_2 + y_2, \cdots, x_N + y_N] \tag{4.2}$$

- **Properties**
    - **Const A:** Take the value to add to. Only used if the A input channel is not connected.
    - **Const B:** Take the value to be added to. Only used if the B input channel is not connected.
- **Inputs**

A: Take the value to add to.

B: Take the value to be added.

Example Usage: You can connect the output channels of two **Texture Sample** expressions to the A and B inputs of an **Add** expression to create a combination of the two textures. *Note: If the result of the Add expression on two Texture Samples is used as base color it brightens the material* (see Figure 4.48).

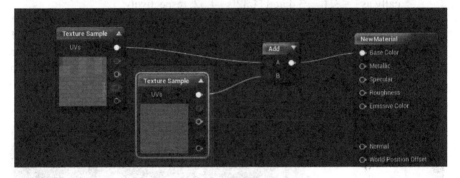

FIGURE 4.48: Add Expression Example.

Append Vector: This operation, as the name suggests, takes in two inputs and creates a vector from these two inputs by appending the B input channel value to the end of the A input channel value. For example, if you use two Constant expressions c_1 and c_2 and connect them to the A and B input channels of the **Append Vector** expression, the output will be a 2-channel vector with c_1 being the first component, and c_2 being the second component.

- **Inputs**

  A: Take the value to be appended to.

  B: Take the value to be appended.

Example Usage: To create an RGB color from three Constant values r, g, and b you may use two **Append Vector** expressions, connect the r and g to the A, and B, channel of the first expression. Then connect the result of the first expression to the A channel, and the value b to the B channel of the second expression (see Figure 4.49).

Ceil: This operation, as the name suggests, takes in one input and returns its ceiling value – i.e., rounds the input up to the next integer number. If the input to this expression is a vector, then the expression outputs the ceiling on a per-channel basis.

Example: The ceiling of 3.4 is 4, and the ceiling of 3.9 is also 4.

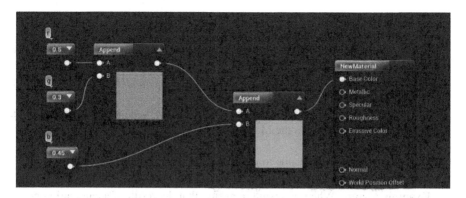

FIGURE 4.49: Append Vector Example.

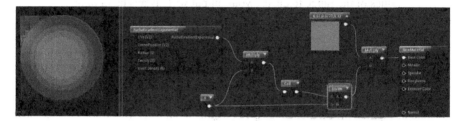

FIGURE 4.50: Ceiling Expression Example.

Example Usage: You can multiply a vector or constant by some constant K, then take the ceiling of the result and divide it by the same K to create bands with varying colors (see Figure 4.50). In this example we use a Radial Gradient Exponential expression to create values that range from 0 to 1. We then use the Ceiling expression to create the concentric bands that are supplied to the Base Color of the material. To make the bands parallel lines instead of concentric circles, you may use a Linear Gradient instead of the Radial Gradient Exponential expression.

Clamp: This expression takes one input channel, one MIN input, and one MAX input, and returns a clamped output from the input value. If the input value is less than MIN, the output will return MIN. If the input value is greater than MAX, the output returns MAX. Otherwise, the expression returns the input value unchanged.

Mathematically, let x be the input value, and MAX and MIN be the maximum and minimum clamp input values, the output o will be calculated according to the following equation:

$$\text{CLAMP}(x, MIN, MAX) = \begin{cases} MAX & x \geq MAX \\ x & MIN < x < MAX \\ MIN & x \leq MIN \end{cases} \qquad (4.3)$$

- **Properties**

  Clamp Mode: Selects the type of clamp. `CMODE_Clamp` will clamp both ends of the range. `CMODE_ClampMin` and `CMODE_ClampMax` will only clamp their respective ends of the range.

  Min Default: Takes in the value to use as the minimum when clamping. Only used when the Min input is unused.

  Max Default: Takes in the value to use as the maximum when clamping. Only used when the Max input is unused.

- **Inputs**

  Min: Takes in the value to use as the minimum when clamping.

  Max: Takes in the value to use as the maximum when clamping.

Example Usage: When you want to ensure that the result of a calculation never falls outside of a certain range, you can use the minimum and maximum values of the range to ensure your output will always be in range.

Component Mask: This expression allows you to select a specific subset of channels (R, G, B, and/or A) from the expression's input to pass through to the expression's outputs. The current channels selected to be passed through are displayed in the title bar of the expression. In case of the expressions that are more than one-dimensional, if the channel is not available an error will occur if you check that channel to be passed through. A description of the properties of a Constant expression is listed below:

- **Properties**

  R: If checked, the Red (or first) component of the vector will be masked and available to pass through from input to output.

  G: If checked, the Green (or second) component of the vector will be masked and available to pass through from input to output.

  B: If checked, the Blue (or third) component of the vector will be masked and available to pass through from input to output.

  A: If checked, the Alpha (or fourth) component of the vector will be masked and available to pass through from input to output.

Example: If you have an RGB Constant3Vector of (1.2, 3.2, 5.3, 1.0) as the input to this expression and check the R and A boxes, the output will be (1.2, 1.0).

Cosine: This expression calculates and returns the cosine of its input value. Note that the input value is always in radians (and not in degrees). By connecting the output channel of a **Time** expression to this expression you will be able to create a waveform that oscillates between −1.0 and +1.0 over time.

- **Properties**

  Period: Specifies the period of the resulting wave form. Larger values result in slower oscillations while smaller values result in faster oscillations.

Example Usage: To create a pulsating material, connect the **Time** expression to the input of a **Cosine** expression and plug the output channel of the cosine to the `Emissive Color` channel of the material node.

Divide: This expression takes its two input values and returns the division of the first value by the second value. The division operation is performed on a per-channel basis. Mathematically speaking, Let **X** and **Y** be two N-channel vectors. Then the **Divide** expression of these two values will be:

$$\text{DIVIDE}(\mathbf{X}, \mathbf{Y}) = \frac{\mathbf{X}}{\mathbf{Y}} = \left[\frac{x_1}{y_1}, \frac{x_2}{y_2}, \cdots, \frac{x_N}{y_N} \right] \tag{4.4}$$

- **Properties**
  Const A: Take the value to be divided. Only used if the A input channel is not connected.
  Const B: Take the value to divide by. Only used if the B input channel is not connected.
- **Inputs**
  A: Take the value to be divided, the dividend.
  B: Take the value to divide by, the divisor.

Example Usage: You can connect the output channels of one **Texture Sample** expression to the A and a Constant value to the B input of a **Divide** expression to make the texture look dimmer. *Note: The constant value must be greater than 1.0 to make the texture dimmer. If the constant value is less than 1.0, the texture will look brighter.*

Dot Product: This expression takes two vectors as input and returns a scalar value that is equal to the dot product of the two input vectors. Mathematically speaking, the dot product will create a scalar that is proportional to the Cosine of the angle between the two input vectors.

Let **X** and **Y** be two vectors. The dot product of these two vectors is calculated according to the following equation:

$$\mathbf{X} \odot \mathbf{Y} = |\mathbf{X}| \cdot |\mathbf{Y}| \cdot \cos(\theta) \tag{4.5}$$

where θ is the angle between vectors **X** and **Y**.
- **Inputs**
  A: Takes in a value or vector of any length as the first vector.
  B: Takes in a value or vector of any length as the second vector.

Example Usage: Use the cross product of two vectors to find the angle between them. If the vectors are parallel the value will be close to +1 or −1. If the vectors are perpendicular the value will be 0. Otherwise the value will range between −1 and +1.

Floor: This operation, as the name suggests, takes in one input and returns its floor value – i.e., rounds the input down to the previous integer number. If the input to this expression is a vector, then the expression outputs the floor value on a per-channel basis.

Example: The floor of 3.4 is 3, and the floor of (3.9, 5.4) is (3, 5).

Example Usage: You can multiply a vector or constant by some constant K, then take the ceiling of the result and divide it by the same constant K to create bands with varying colors. Similar to what we did for the Ceiling on page 184.

If: This expression, compares two scalar floating point input values, and three condition values. Then it passes through one of the three values from its input condition channels based on which condition is true on the two input scalar values.

FIGURE 4.51: If Expression Example.

- **Inputs**
  A: Takes in a scalar floating point value as the first input.
  B: Takes in a scalar floating point value as the second input.
  A<B: Takes in a value to output if the A is less than B.
  A==B: Takes in a value to output if the A is equal to B.
  A>B: Takes in a value to output if the A is greater than B.

Example Usage: You can connect a Texture Sample to the A input and a scalar value Th (as the threshold) to the B channel, then connect three different Constant3Vectors to the A<B, A=B, and A>B to create a tri-color map based on the input texture and the threshold value (see Figure 4.51).

Linear Interpolate (Lerp): This expression blends between two input value(s) based on a third input value used as a mask. This can be thought of as a mask to define transitions between two textures, like a layer mask in Photoshop.

The intensity of the mask Alpha channel determines the ratio of color to take from the two input values. If Alpha is 0.0/white, the first input is used. If Alpha is 1.0/black, the second input is used. If Alpha is gray (somewhere between 0.0 and 1.0), the output is a blend between the two inputs.

Mathematically speaking, let A be the first input, B be the second input, and $0 \leq \alpha \leq 1$ be the mask input. The output O will be calculated according to the following equation:

$$O = (1 - \alpha) \times A + \alpha \times B \qquad (4.6)$$

Keep in mind that the blend happens per channel. So, if Alpha is an RGB color, Alpha's red channel value defines the blend between A and B's red channels independently of Alpha's green channel, which defines the blend between A and B's green channels.

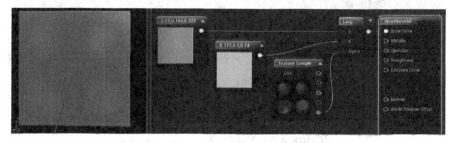

FIGURE 4.52: Linear Interpolate (Lerp) Expression Example.

- **Properties**
  Const A: The value mapped to black (0.0). Only used if the A input is unconnected.
  Const B: The value mapped to white (1.0). Only used if the A input is unconnected.
  Const Alpha: Takes in the value to use as the mask alpha. Only used if the Alpha input is unconnected.
- **Inputs**
  A: Takes in the value(s) mapped to black (0.0).
  B: Takes in the value(s) mapped to white (1.0).
  Alpha: Takes in the value to use as the mask alpha.
- **Example Usage:** You can connect two Constant3Vector RGB colors to the inputs A and B and the alpha channel of a Texture Sample to the Alpha input channel of the Lerp expression to Interpolate the values between two colors. Connecting the output channel of the Lerp to the Base color channel of a material node will have the result shown in color (see Figure 4.52).

Multiply: This expression takes its two input values (A and B) and returns the multiplication of the first value by the second value. The multiply operation is performed on a per-channel basis. Mathematically speaking, Let $\mathbf{X}$ and $\mathbf{Y}$ be two N-channel vectors. Then the **Multiply** expression of these two values will be:

$$\mathrm{MULTIPLY}(\mathbf{X}, \mathbf{Y}) = [x_1 \times y_1, x_2 \times y_2, \cdots, x_N \times y_N] \qquad (4.7)$$

- **Properties**

  Const A: Take the value to be multiplied. Only used if the A input channel is not connected.

  Const B: Take the value to multiply to. Only used if the B input channel is not connected.

- **Inputs**

  A: Take the first value to multiply, multiplicand.

  B: Take the second value to multiply, the multiplier.

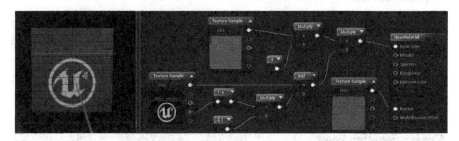

FIGURE 4.53: Multiply Expression Example.

Example Usage: You can connect the output channels of two **Texture Sample** expressions to the A and B inputs of a **Multiply** expression to make the texture affect each other (see Figure 4.53). *Note: If the input texture RGB values are less than one, the resulting texture will look much dimmer. You may need to multiply the result by a constant value greater than 1 to compensate.*

Normalize: This expression performs a very important operation on vectors called normalization. The Normalize expression takes in a vector as input and normalizes it and returns the normalized vector. Mathematically speaking, the normalization operation will make the length of the vector equal to unit length (i.e., 1).

Unreal Engine uses L-2 lengths– the square root of the sum of squares of each element in the vector.

Let $\mathbf{X} = [x_1, x_2, \cdots, x_N]$ be an N-dimensional vector, the L-2 norm (or length) of $\mathbf{X}$ is calculated according to the following equations:

$$|\mathbf{X}| = \sqrt{\sum_{i=1}^{N} x_i^2} \tag{4.8}$$

Then the normalized vector $\hat{\mathbf{X}}$ is calculated by dividing $\mathbf{X}$ by its L-2 norm:

$$\hat{\mathbf{X}} = \frac{\mathbf{X}}{|\mathbf{X}|} \tag{4.9}$$

Notice that after normalization the length (L-2 norm) of the normalized vector will be equal to 1.

Example Usage: When using the **Cross Product** expression to find the perpendicular vector to a plane of two input vectors, you can normalize the result to get a unit vector. This may be helpful in deciding to apply a World Position Offset with exact measurements.

NOTE

There is no need to normalize a vector that is being connected to the Normal channel of a material.

One Minus: This expression, as the name suggests, takes an input and returns an output value that is exactly equal to 1 minus the input value. Like other basic arithmetic expressions in Unreal Engine 4, this expression performs its operation on a per-channel basis. For example if the input is a 3Vector with R, G, and B values, the output of the **One Minus** will be a 3Vector with values of 1-R, 1-G, and 1-B.

Mathematically, let $\mathbf{X} = [x_1, x_2, \cdots, x_N]$ be an N-dimensional vector. The result of the **One Minus** expression on $\mathbf{X}$ will be:

$$\text{ONEMINUS}(\mathbf{X}) = \mathbf{1} - \mathbf{X} = [1 - x_1, 1 - x_2, \cdots, 1 - x_N] \qquad (4.10)$$

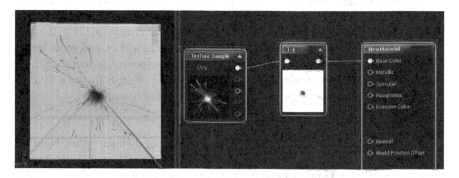

FIGURE 4.54: One Minus Expression Example.

Example: OneMinus value of 0.1 is 0.9 and OneMinus value of $(1.3, 0.4, -0.7)$ is $(-0.3, 0.6, 1.7)$.

Example Usage: You can use this expression to invert the colors of a texture map, much like negative photography (see Figure 4.54).

Power: This expression takes two input values, the **Base** and the **Exp**. The output will be equal to the **Base** raised to the **Exp** power. This operation multiplies the value of **Base**, **Exp** times, by itself.

Mathematically, let $\mathbf{X} = [x_1, x_2, \cdots, x_N]$ be an N-dimensional vector and p be a constant. The result of the **Power** expression on $\mathbf{X}$ as Base and p as Exp will be:

$$\text{POWER}(\mathbf{X}, p) = \left[x_1^p, x_2^p, \cdots, x_N^p \right] \qquad (4.11)$$

- **Properties**
  Const Exponent: Takes in the exponent value. Used only if the Exp input is unused.
- **Inputs**
  Base: Takes in the base value.
  Exp: Takes in the exponent value.

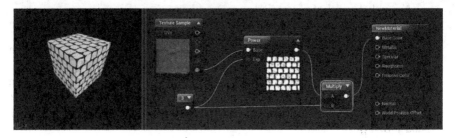

FIGURE 4.55: Power Expression Example.

Example: Power of 0.1 as base and 2 as exp is 0.01 and Power of (0.9,0.5,0.1) as base and 3 as exp is (0.729,0.125,0.001).

Example Usage: You can use this expression as a kind of contrast adjuster. Looking at the example above, notice that raising 0.9 to the power of 3 still gives a relatively high value of 0.729, while raising a small value of 0.1 to the same power makes it much smaller (0.001). If you feed a black and white texture map as base of the Power expression and an exponent greater than 1, the result will have more contrast (see Figure 4.55). We usually use a Multiply expression after the power to brighten up the texture map.

Sine: This expression calculates and returns the sine of its input value. Note that the input value is always in radians (and not in degrees). By connecting the output channel of a **Time** expression to this expression you will be able to create a waveform that oscillates between −1.0 and +1.0 over time.

- **Properties**
  Period: Specifies the period of the resulting wave form. Larger values result in slower oscillations while smaller values result in faster oscillations.

Example Usage: To create a pulsating material, connect the **Time** expression to the input of a **Sine** expression and plug the output channel of the Sine to the `Emissive Color` channel of the material node.

Subtract: This expression takes its two input values (A and B), subtracts the second input (B) from first input (A), and returns the subtraction value. The Subtract operation is performed on a per-channel basis. In other words, if you Subtract two Constant3Vectors, the result will be a Constant3Vector in which the R, G, and B components are the subtraction of the two input R, G, and B channels, respectively.

Mathematically speaking, Let **X** and **Y** be two N-channel vectors. Then the **Add** expression of these two values will be:

$$\text{SUBTRACT}(\mathbf{X}, \mathbf{Y}) = \mathbf{X} - \mathbf{Y} = [x_1 - y_1, x_2 - y_2, \cdots, x_N - y_N] \qquad (4.12)$$

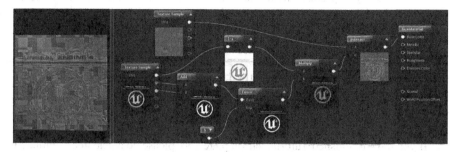

FIGURE 4.56: Subtract Expression Example.

- **Properties**

    Const A: Take the value to subtract from. Only used if the A input channel is not connected.

    Const B: Take the value to be subtracted. Only used if the B input channel is not connected.

- **Inputs**

    A: Take the value to subtract from.

    B: Take the value to be subtracted.

Example Usage: You can connect the output channels of two **Texture Sample** expressions to the A and B inputs of a **Subtract** expression to create a combination of the two textures. *Note: If the result of the Subtract expression on two Texture Samples is used as base color, it darkens the material* (see Figure 4.56).

With this overview of the mathematical material expressions in UE4, it's now time to get some hands-on experience with these expressions. In Tutorial 4.5 we will create a burning wood material by utilizing the concepts we have learned so far. This work will deliver three materials, a static pine-wood material as our base material, another static version of the pine-wood material with the burn marks, and finally a dynamic and time-varying material in which the embers glow and fade periodically.

To find updates to this tutorial and updated instructions about its implementation on other UE4 versions please visit the book's companion website at:

http://www.RVRLAB.com/UE4Book/

TUTORIAL 4.5   Materials with Time Varying Effects I: Burning Wood

So far the materials we have created in Tutorials 4.2 – 4.4 have been static.

BEFORE YOU PROCEED

Before you proceed with this Tutorial, and you haven't finished Tutorial 4.1 on page 150, please go ahead and complete it. In order to view the effects we will create in this Tutorial we need the Demo Room to have been included in our project.

ORGANIZING ASSETS AND PLACING THE DISPLAY ITEM

We will place a Display Item in the Demo Room and place three meshes on it, so that we can demonstrate our creations later.

5. If you haven't finished Tutorial 4.1 on page 150, please go ahead and complete it. We will need the Demo Room to have been included in our project.
6. In the content browser, look for a folder inside the **Demo Room** folder called **Blueprints** and open it.
7. Drag a copy of **Display Item** onto the level and place it along a wall. Change its properties to the following:

> **Number:** 4-M.
> **Description:** Time Varying Materials. . .
> **Type:** Square-L

8. In the content browser, look for a folder called **Props** and open it.
9. In the **Props** folder look for and find a mesh called **SM_MatPreviewMesh_02** and drag it into the Display Item you have already placed in the Demo Room.
10. Rotate, scale, and position the mesh so that it faces outwards from the Display Item.
11. **Alt-Drag** the mesh to create two copies of it on the Display Item (see Figure 4.36 on page 164). You can alternatively copy and paste the mesh in the editor on the Display Item.
12. Save your level so far.

CREATING THE BASE MATERIAL

We now have a display item and three meshes in the level to demonstrate our progress as we go along in this tutorial.

13. In the **Content Browser**, find your materials folder you have created in earlier tutorials. If you don't have one, **Right-Click** on the **Game** folder, create a new folder and call it **MyMaterials**.

14. Double-Click on the MyMaterials folder to open it up.
15. Create a **New Material** in this folder and call it M_Static.
16. Double-Click on the newly created M_Static material to open it in the Material Editor.
17. In the Material Editor, Left-Click to the left of the Base Color and place a **Texture Sample** expression. Make the following changes to this **Texture Sample** expression in its **Details** Panel:

> **Texture:** Apply the texture "T_Wood_Pine_D".
> **Description:** Type-in the text "Pine Diffuse".

18. Below the Pine Diffuse texture Left-Click and place a **Texture Sample** expression. Make the following changes to this **Texture Sample** expression in its **Details** Panel:

> **Texture:** Apply the texture "T_Wood_Pine_N".
> **Description:** Type-in the text "Pine Normal".

19. Connect the RGB (white) output channel of the Pine Diffuse texture sample expression to the Base Color channel of the material node.
20. Connect the RGB (white) output channel of the Pine Normal texture sample expression to the Normal channel of the material node.

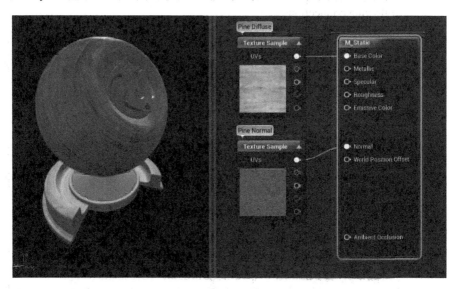

FIGURE 4.57: The static base material and its network.

21. Save your material. Your material should look similar to Figure 4.57 so far. *NOTE: In the simulation viewport I have applied the prop mesh to what see the final look will be when applied to the same prop mesh in the level.*

Great! Our base material is created. The material doesn't really look fancy; it's pine wood, basically.

BURNT WOOD WITH EMBER EFFECTS

Now imagine if this material belonged to a surface which was burnt. What if there were still ember residues on this material? We will now start working on making it happen.

22. We don't want to make any changes to our Base Material (we called it M_Static) as we will use it in the level for comparison later. So let's first duplicate it and work the next steps on the duplicated material.
23. In the **Content Browser**, Right-Click on the material M_Static and choose **Duplicate**.
24. Rename the duplicate Material to M_Static_Burnt.
25. Double-Click on the M_Static_Burnt material to open it in the material editor. It should be identical to your M_Static material you have so far.
26. We will now establish an after-burn effect on this material. Feel free to rearrange your texture sample expressions to give yourself some room in the graph editor.
27. The first step is to bring in a flame texture. To do so, perform the following tasks:
    a. Move the **Pine Normal** texture to the left to give yourself some room to work.
    b. Place an **Add** expression to the right of the **Pine Normal** and make the following connections:

> **Add A Channel** ↔ **Red** channel of **Pine Normal**.
> **Add B Channel** ↔ **Green** channel of **Pine Normal**.

    c. Below the Add, Right-Click and place a **Texture Sample** expression. Make the following changes to this texture sample expression in its **Details** Panel:

> **Texture:** Apply the texture "T_Fire_Tiled_D".
> **Description:** Type-in the text "Fire Diffuse".

    d. Place a **Multiply** expression to the right of the Flame Diffuse texture sample you just created and make the following connections:

> **Multiply A Channel** ↔ **Add** output.
> **Multiply B Channel** ↔ **Flame Diffuse** RGB channel.

    e. Place a **Constant** expression (press the 1 key and Left-Click) below the **Multiply** expression you just created and make the following changes to its details rollout:

> **Value:** 5.
> **Description:** Flame Intensity.

f. Place another **Multiply** expression (press the M key and Left-Click) to the right of the first **Multiply** expression.

g. Make the following connections:

> **Output of First Multiply** ↔ A channel of second multiply.
> **Flame Intensity** ↔ B channel of second multiply.

h. Below the second **Multiply** expression create another **Constant** expression and make the following changes to its details rollout:

> **Value:** 3.
> **Description:** Flame Focus.

i. Place a **Power** expression to the right of the second **Multiply** expression and make the following connections:

> **Output of Second Multiply** ↔ Base channel of the **Power** expression.
> **Flame Focus** ↔ Exp channel of **Power** expression.
> **Output of Power** ↔ Emissive Color channel of the material node.

28. Now we will make the material's Base Color a little darker to give the burnt feel to it.

29. Place another **Constant** expression above the Pine Diffuse texture sample expression and make the following changes in its details rollout:

> **Value:** 0.95.
> **Description:** Burn.

30. Place a third **Multiply** expression to the right of the **Burn** expression and make the following connections:

> **Burn Output** ↔ A channel of the **Multiply** expression.
> **RGB Output of Pine Diffuse** ↔ B channel of **Multiply** expression.
> **Output of Multiply** ↔ Base Color channel of the material node.

31. Save your material. The material and its network should look similar to Figure 4.58. Notice the slivers of flame placed on the surface of the material.

So far so good! We now have a material which also has some burn-marks on it. But it all looks static. Ember residues don't stay put on a surface, do they? Let's fix this problem next.

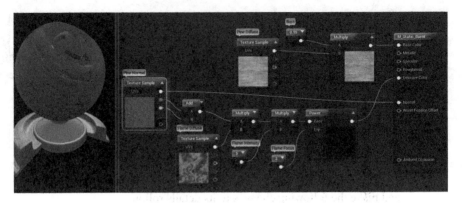

FIGURE 4.58: The static burnt material and its network.

EMBERS DYNAMIC BURN EFFECT

In the next few steps we will create a duplicate of our material. We will build dynamic Ember Burn effects in the duplicated material.

32. We don't want to make any changes to our Burnt Material (we called it M_Static_Burnt) as we will use it in the level for comparison later. So let's first duplicate it and work the next steps on the duplicated material.

33. In the **Content Browser**, **Right-Click** on the material M_Static_Burnt and choose **Duplicate**.

34. Rename the duplicate Material to M_Dynamic_Burnt.

35. **Double-Click** on the M_Dynamic_Burnt material to open it in the material editor. It should be identical to your M_Static_Burnt material you have so far.

36. We will now establish dynamic after-burn effects on this material. Feel free to rearrange your texture sample expressions to give yourself some room in the graph editor.

37. Place a **Time** expression below the **Flame Intensity** Constant expression.

38. Place a **Cosine** expression to the right of the **Time** expression.

39. In the details of the **Cosine** expression, type a value of 4 for its **Period**.

40. Connect the **Time** expression to the **Cosine** expression.

41. Place another **Constant** expression below the **Cosine** expression and make the following changes in its details rollout:

Value: 3.0.
Description: Flame Bias.

42. Place an **Add** expression to the right of the **Cosine** and the **Flame Bias** expressions, and make the following connections:

> **Cosine Output** ↔ A channel of the **Add** expression.
> **Flame Bias output** ↔ B channel of **Add** expression.

43. Place another **Constant** expression below the **Add** expression and make the following changes to its details rollout:

> **Value:** 0.5.
> **Description:** Flame Multiplier.

44. Place a **Multiply** expression to the right of the **Add** and the **Flame Multiplier** expressions, and make the following connections:

> **Add Output** ↔ A channel of the **Multiply** expression.
> **Flame Multiplier Output** ↔ B channel of **Multiply** expression.
> **Desc of the Multiply expression:** Type-in Flame Time

45. Find the **Multiply** expression that is connected to the **Base** channel of the **Power** expression.
46. Disconnect the **Multiply** and the **Power** expressions. *Note: Holding the* Alt *key while you* Left-Click *on a connection will remove it.*
47. Place a **Multiply** expression between the first **Multiply** and the **Power** expressions you just disconnected and make the following connections:

> **Left Multiply Output** ↔ A channel of the new **Multiply** expression.
> **Flame Time Output** ↔ B channel of the new **Multiply** expression.
> **The New Multiply Output** ↔ Base channel of the **Power** expression.

48. Your network and material should look similar to Figure 4.59. Now this material has come to life! Notice how the after-burn colors fade and intensify over time to simulate the effects of a gentle blow on the burnt surface of the wood.
49. Save your material.

APPLYING MATERIALS TO THE PROPS

Now with our three materials (M_Static, M_Static_Burnt, and M_Dynamic_Burnt) created, we can apply them on the props we placed in the display item of the demo room.

50. Left-Click on the leftmost object to select it.
51. Go to your MyMaterials folder in which you created the three materials.
52. Find the M_Static material and select it.
53. Drag the M_Static material into the Element 0 of the **Materials** section of the Details rollout of the static mesh actor selected in the scene.
54. Left-Click on the middle object to select it.

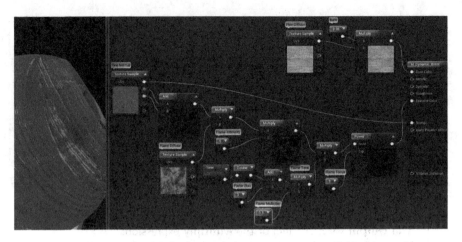

FIGURE 4.59: The dynamic burnt material and its network.

55. Go to your **MyMaterials** folder in which you created the three materials.
56. Find the **M_Static_Burnt** material and select it.
57. Drag the **M_Static_Burnt** material into the **Element** 0 of the **Materials** section of the Details rollout of the static mesh actor selected in the scene.
58. **Left-Click** on the rightmost object to select it.
59. Go to your **MyMaterials** folder in which you created the three materials.
60. Find the **M_Dynamic_Burnt** material and select it.
61. Drag the **M_Dynamic_Burnt** material into the **Element** 0 of the **Materials** section of the Details rollout of the static mesh actor selected in the scene.
62. Your scene and the materials applied to static mesh actors within it should look similar to Figure 4.60.

What Happened in TUTORIAL 4.5...

In this tutorial we created a simple static material based on a pine wood texture and made it dynamically show burn marks, in a number of successive steps.

ORGANIZING ASSETS AND PLACING THE DISPLAY ITEM

Just like other tutorials in this chapter, the first task is to create a display item in our level to showcase our work. Once the display item was set up, we placed three Preview Mesh props onto it (see Figure 4.60).

CREATING THE BASE MATERIAL

With the preview meshes in the level, our job is now to create our material. To see the progression of our work we broke the task into three steps. At the end of

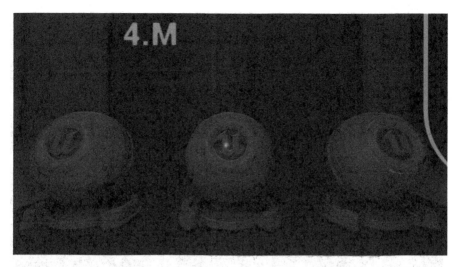

FIGURE 4.60: The three materials from left: M_Static, M_Static_Burnt, and M_Dynamic_Burnt applied to the props.

each step we would have finished one stage of our material.

So the first step was to create our pine wood material, a simple static material. This task is incredibly easy. All we needed to do was to create two **Texture Sample** expressions and apply the diffuse texture and normal texture of the pine wood to them. After the textures were assigned, we connected the output of the diffuse texture to the **Base Color** channel and the output of the normal texture to the **Normal** channel of our material node. This will effectively set up the mesh on which the material will be applied to look like it is made of pine wood.

BURNT WOOD WITH EMBER EFFECTS

What we have done so far is to create a base material with two textures (diffuse and normal). To create our second phase material, we duplicated the first material and renamed it. This will keep our textures in the duplicated material and allow us to build up from there.

I was looking for a look similar to what you see in Figure 4.61. The effect I wanted to achieve was the look of some small burning areas mostly aligned with the crevices in the wood. So, let's see how we can achieve this.

If you remember the discussion we had about the Normal maps, we talked about how normal maps make a material look 3D. Usually we see the minor depths in a material, such as crevices, cracks, dimples, etc., on areas where there are edges (or cuts). In other words, the irregularities that are present in the normal map (as normal vectors for vertices on the surface of an object) should align with edges on the surface. Let's take a look and validate our hypothesis.

Figure 4.62(a) shows the Pine Wood normal map in RGB. Each pixel in this image represents a 3D vector normal to the surface at which the pixel would

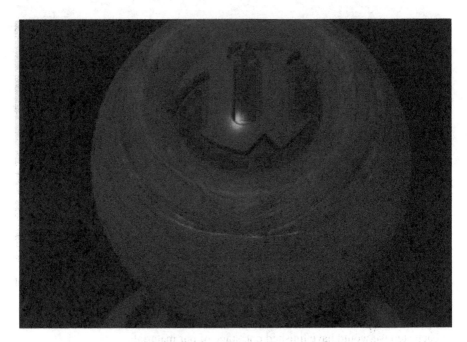

FIGURE 4.61: The static burnt pine wood.

be located. The R, G, and B channels in normal map represent the X, Y, and Z coordinates respectively. Looking at Figure 4.62(b) and Figure 4.62(c), we can clearly see that the R channel of the normal map represents vertical edges in our material and the G channel represents the horizontal edges.

So clearly, in order to align embers in the crevices of my pine wood material, we must use a combination of the red and green channels of our normal map texture. In this tutorial, I opted for the simplest of combinations, i.e., addition. So we added the R with the G channel of our normal map (see Figure 4.63(a)).

As Figure 4.63(a) shows, adding the R and G channels of the normal map creates a texture that is bright in the crevices and dark on flat surfaces. This is perfect for our cause. Our next task is to make the embers have a fiery look and feel to them. Thankfully, the starter contents in Unreal Engine 4 has a flame texture (shown in Figure 4.63(b)). We simply take the red and green channel additions of our normal map with the flame texture to produce fire-colored embers aligned with the crevices of our wood material (see Figure 4.63(c)).

We are almost done. We could have simply applied the results of Figure 4.63(c) to the **Emissive Color** channel of our material to produce the ember effects. However, if you try that you will see that the fire looks a little unrealistic. It will show in other areas as well. I wanted to achieve a much more focused look.

This is when the **Power** expression comes in handy. When you have a texture and want to make it look more sharp and focused, you can use the **Power**

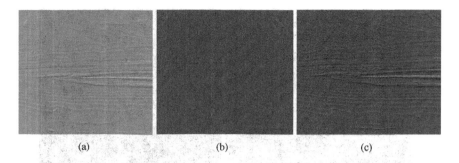

FIGURE 4.62: (a) RGB Output of the Pine Wood Normal Map. (b) The Red Channel of the Normal Map. (c) The Green Channel of the Normal Map.

expression. The **Exp** channel of the power expression is a value by which the base is raised. Using higher values for **Exp** will make the effect more focused and increases the effect's fall-off (see Figure 4.63(d)).

With this network set up, we applied the output of the **Power** expression to the **Emissive Channel** of our material node to make the embers glow from within the cracks and crevices of the pine wood material.

EMBERS DYNAMIC BURN EFFECT

The burning of the wood should not look static. As the air blows across a piece of burning wood, the embers' intensity changes, giving the burning look. Our material does have the color aligned nicely where the embers are, but it doesn't change. Our next task was to make the change happen.

We can achieve this by utilizing a **Time** expression. This expression changes as time goes by. But we want to also simulate an oscillation. We want the embers' flame intensity (color) to increase and decrease as time goes by. To achieve this effect we used a **Cosine** expression. So if we feed the **Time** expression to the **Cosine** expression, the output will oscillate between −1.0 to +1.0 (as shown in Figure 4.64).

So this network of **Time** and **Cosine** gives me the oscillating input I am looking for, but we have a problem. The output of **Cosine** goes from −1 to +1. If we multiply this value by our ember colors, we will get negative values for the **Emissive Color** channel.

Although not illegal, connecting negative values to the **Emissive Color** channel would make the ember color become black and not show on the material. This will give the look that the fire is extinguished. When time passes and the value is positive, the return of embers would make our material not realistic.

To resolve this problem, I targeted the output of my time/cosine network to oscillate between 1 and 2 instead of −1 and +1. A simple mathematical calculation will be all that is needed. We add the result of our **Cosine** expression to a value (I called it **Flame Bias**) and then multiply the result by another value (I called this one **Flame Multiplier**).

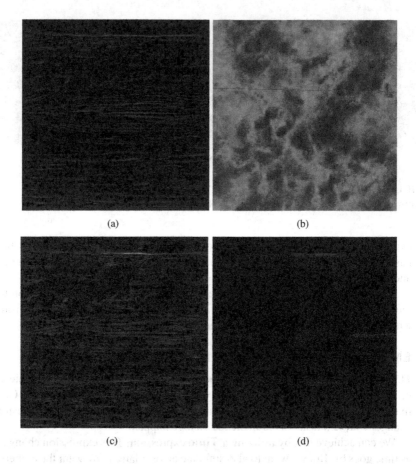

FIGURE 4.63: (a) R and G Channels Added. (b) The Flame Texture. (c) Flame Texture Multiplied by the R+G Channels. (d) The Final Ember Look.

Putting different values in the **Flame Bias** and **Flame Multiplier** would make the result range between a maximum and a minimum value. For those mathematically inclined, I am going to perform the calculations to find the values of **Flame Bias** and **Flame Multiplier** for a certain Maximum and Min oscillation range below.

Let t be time, x stand for the **Flame Bias**, and y for **Flame Multiplier**. We are adding the **Flame Bias** to the Cosine results and multiply it by the **Flame Multiplier**. Therefore, the equation that we have for our oscillation is in the form of:

$$O = (x + \cos(t)) \times y \qquad (4.13)$$

Let min and max be the minimum and maximum oscillation range. So when $\cos(t) = -1$ we want the result to be $O = $ min, and when $\cos(t) = +1$ the result

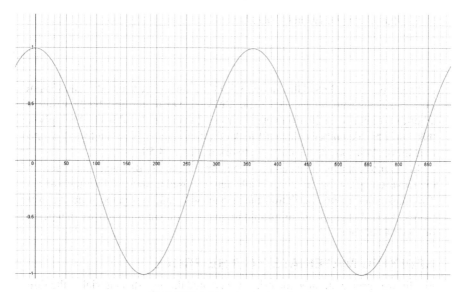

FIGURE 4.64: The Cosine Graph.

to be $O = $ max. We will have the following equations:

$$\min = (x - 1) \times y \qquad (4.14)$$

and

$$\max = (x + 1) \times y \qquad (4.15)$$

If we divide equation (4.14) by equation 4.15 we will get:

$$\frac{\min}{\max} = \frac{(x+1) \times y}{(x+1) \times y} = \frac{x-1}{x+1} \qquad (4.16)$$

Solving equation (4.16) for x will result in:

$$x = \frac{\max + \min}{\max - \min} \qquad (4.17)$$

Substituting the value of x from equation (4.17) into either one of equations (4.14) or (4.15) will lead the following value for y:

$$y = \frac{\max - \min}{2} \qquad (4.18)$$

As you see, it was very easy to find values to adjust the range of oscillation we get from our **Cosine** network. I wanted the network to oscillate between 1 and 2 (instead of -1 and +1). So in this case, I have max $= 2$ and min $= 1$.

Given max $= 2$ and min $= 1$, from equation (4.17) I know that:

$$x = \frac{\max + \min}{\max - \min} = \frac{2+1}{2-1} = 3 \qquad (4.19)$$

Similarly, from equation (4.18) I have:

$$y = \frac{max - min}{2} = \frac{2-1}{2} = 0.5 \qquad (4.20)$$

From the above, I used the value of 3.0 for `Flame Bias` to add to the **Cosine**. Then I used the value of 0.5 for `Flame Multiplier` to multiply by the resulting addition to get my oscillation network to go from 1 to 2 and back. Multiplying this result by the ember color will make the final ember burn the look I wanted to achieve. You can see the entire network in Figure 4.59.

In order to control the speed of oscillation we can use the `Period` property of the **Cosine** expression. In our example here we used a value of 4 for the `Period`. This makes an entire oscillation take about 4 seconds in game time. In other words, the embers go from minimum intensity to maximum intensity in a period of about 4 seconds.

APPLYING MATERIALS TO THE PROPS

Finally we applied all three materials we created through this tutorial to the three props in the level to see our progression side-by-side.

4.6.2.3　Coordinate Expressions

These expressions[4] utilize the 2D or 3D coordinate systems in the World Space or Texture Coordinates to enable interactions between these coordinate spaces and certain aspects of the materials [9].

You can create effect such as geographically color-coding the geometry, changing the tiling of texture maps on the geometry, and even creating dynamic materials.

Panner: This expression creates UV coordinates that are panned by the speed. The **Panner** has three input channels: Coordinate, Speed, and Time, and four properties as described below:
- **Properties**
  SpeedX: Specifies the U coordinate to use as the center of rotation.
  SpeedY: Specifies the V coordinate to use as the center of rotation.
  Const Coordinate : Only used if the Coordinate input is not connected.
  Fractional Part : Only outputs the fractional part of the Panner output for greater precision.
- **Inputs**
  Coordinate: Takes the base UV texture coordinates to modify by the expression.

---

[4] The contents of this section are adapted from the official UE4 online documentation found at: https://docs.unrealengine.com/latest/INT/.

Time: Takes in the value used to determine the current translation of texture as determined by its speed along the U and V directions of the texture coordinates. This is usually connected to the output of a **Time** expression or a network based on the **Time** Expression. However, you may use a parameter for this input and dynamically control the value of the parameter through Matinee or Blueprint sequences.

Speed: It is a Vector2D speed scale.

Usage Example: To move the texture on a surface you usually connect the output of a **Time** expression or a network based on the **Time** Expression to the Time channel of the **Panner** expression. However, you may use a parameter for this input and dynamically control the value of the parameter through Matinee or Blueprint sequences. You then connect the output of this expression to the UVs input channel of a **Texture Sample** expression to move the texture across the surface on which the material will be applied.

Rotator: This expression creates UV coordinates that are rotated by the speed. The **Rotator** has two input channels: Coordinate and Time, and three properties as described below:

- **Properties**

  CenterX: Specifies the U coordinate to use as the center of rotation.

  CenterY: Specifies the V coordinate to use as the center of rotation.

  Speed: Specifies the speed to rotate the coordinate. Positive values are clockwise and negative values are counter clockwise.

  Const Coordinate : Only used if the Coordinate input is not connected.

- **Inputs**

  Coordinate: Takes the base UV texture coordinates to modify by the expression.

  Time: Takes in the value used to determine the current rotation position. This is usually connected to the output of a **Time** expression or a network based on the **Time** Expression. However, you may use a parameter for this input and dynamically control the value of the parameter through Matinee or Blueprint sequences.

Usage Example: To rotate the texture on a surface you usually connect the output of a **Time** expression or a network based on the **Time** Expression to the Time channel of the **Rotator** expression. However, you may use a parameter for this input and dynamically control the value of the parameter through Matinee or Blueprint sequences. You then connect the output of this expression to the UVs input channel of a **Texture Sample** expression to rotate the texture.

Texture Coordinate: This expressions allows for the manipulation of the UV coordinates of Texture Sample Expressions by outputting a 2-channel vector value.

You can use this expression in conjunction with other Coordinate expressions such as **Panner** or **Rotator** expressions to change the tiling, dynamically modify texture spaces, or operate on the UVs of a mesh.

- **Properties**

  Coordinate Index: Specifies the UV Channel to use.

  UTiling: Specifies the amount of tiling in the U direction.

  VTiling: Specifies the amount of tiling in the U direction.

  Un Mirror U: If set to `True`, undoes any mirroring in the U direction.

  Un Mirror v: If set to `True`, undoes any mirroring in the V direction.

Example Usage 1: To access the second UV channel of a mesh, you can create a **Texture Coordinate** and set its `Coordinate Index` to 1 – 0 is the first channel, 1 is the second, 2 is the third, and so on. connect the output of the expression to the UVs input channel of a **Texture Sample** expression.

Example Usage 2: You can apply different values to the UTiling and VTiling values of this expression and connect its output to the UVs input channel of a **Texture Sample** expression to change the tiling of its texture. Values grater than 1 will make the texture smaller, while values smaller than 1 will make the texture expand along the U, V, or both directions.

Vertext Normal WS: This expression outputs the world space vertex normal. It can only be used in material inputs that are executed in the vertex shader. An example of such material is one that is using its **World Position Offset** channel.

Usage: One example for this expression usage is to manipulate the size of an object through the **World Position Offset** or the **World Displacement** channels. This expression supplied the normal vector of each vertex in the world space. By multiplying this the output of this expression by a value you will be able to push or pull the geometry inwards or outwards along its normal vector at each vertex, thereby changing the geometry from the material.

This overview of the coordinate expressions in Unreal Engine 4 should have presented a convincing case in proving their power and versatility. In the next hands-on work, Tutorial 4.6, we will learn how to utilize these expressions in creating astonishing effects with no need for affecting the geometry.

To find updates to this tutorial and updated instructions about its implementation on other UE4 versions please visit the book's companion website at: `http://www.RVRLAB.com/UE4Book/`

TUTORIAL 4.6   Materials with Time Varying Effects II: Moving Tiles

In this tutorial we will learn how to use coordinate expression to create dynamic effects in our materials.

BEFORE YOU PROCEED

Before you proceed with this Tutorial, and you haven't finished Tutorial 4.1 on page 150, please go ahead and complete it. In order to view the effects we will create in this Tutorial we need the Demo Room to have been included in our project.

ORGANIZING ASSETS AND PLACING THE DISPLAY ITEM

We will place a Display Item in the Demo Room and place three meshes on it, so that we could demonstrate our creations later.

5. If you haven't finished Tutorial 4.1 on page 150, please go ahead and complete it. We will need the Demo Room to have been included in our project.
6. In the content browser, look for a folder inside the **Demo Room** folder called **Blueprints** and open it.
7. Drag a copy of **Display Item** onto the level and place it to along a wall. Change its properties to the following:

Number: 5-M.
Description: Dynamic Materials. . .
Type: Square-L

8. In the content browser, look for a folder called **Props** and open it.
9. In the **Props** folder look for and find the **SM_MatPreviewMesh_02** mesh and drag it into the Display Item you have already placed in the Demo Room.
10. Rotate, scale, and position the mesh so that it faces outwards from the Display Item.
11. `Alt-Drag` the mesh to create two copies of it on the Display Item (see Figure 4.36 on page 164). You can alternatively copy and paste the mesh in the editor on the Display Item.
12. Save your level so far.

CREATING THE BASE MATERIAL'S DIFFUSE NETWORK

Great! We now have a display item and three meshes in the level to demonstrate our progress as we go along in this tutorial.

13. In the **Content Browser**, find your materials folder you have created in earlier tutorials. If you don't have one, `Right-Click` on the `Game` folder, create a new folder and call it `MyMaterials`.
14. `Double-Click` on the `MyMaterials` folder to open it up.
15. Create a **New Material** in this folder and call it `M_Panels_Static`.
16. `Double-Click` on the newly created `M_Panels_Static` material to open in in the Material Editor.

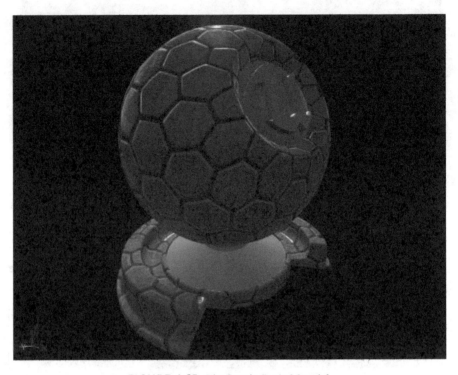

FIGURE 4.65: The Panels Static Material.

17. The base material we will create now for our **M_Panels_Static** will be a little more complicated than the one we created for the base material in Tutorial 4.5. Figure 4.65 shows the final look of our **M_Panels_Static**. Notice the hexagonal tiles, and the grout between them. We will use four textures for this look, a diffuse steel texture and its normal map texture, and a hexagonal mask texture and its normal map texture.

18. In the Material Editor, **Left-Click** to the left of the **Base Color** and place a **Texture Sample** expression. Make the following changes to this **Texture Sample** expression in its **Details** Panel:

> **Texture:** Apply the texture "T_Metal_Steel_D".
> **Description:** Type-in the text "Steel Diffuse".

19. Below the **Steel Diffuse** texture **Left-Click** and place another **Texture Sample** expression. Make the following changes to this **Texture Sample** expression in its **Details** Panel:

Texture: Apply the texture "T_Tech_Hex_Tile_M".
Description: Type-in the text "Hex Tile Mask".

20. Place a **Multiply** expression to the right of the two texture samples and make the following connections:

- **Steel Diffuse** (white) output ↔ A channel of **Multiply**.
- **Hex Tile Mask** Red output ↔ B channel of **Multiply**.
- **Multiply** output ↔ `Base Color` channel of material node.

21. Place a **Lerp** expression below the **Multiply** expression and make the following connections:

- **Hex Tile Mask** Green output ↔ `Alpha` channel of **Lerp**.
- **Lerp** output↔ `Metallic` channel of material node.

22. Place another **Lerp** expression below the first **Letp** expression and make the following connections:

- **Hex Tile Mask** Green output ↔ `Alpha` channel of the second **Lerp**.
- **Lerp** output↔ `Roughness` channel of material node.

23. Comment this network (the two textures samples, two lerps, and the multiply) as `Tiles Diffuse Network`.

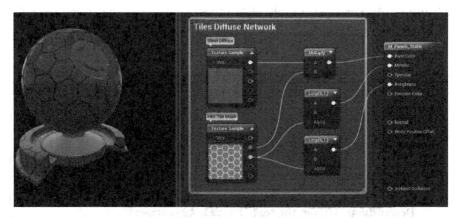

FIGURE 4.66: The static panels diffuse color, metallic, and roughness network.

24. Save your material. Your material should look similar to Figure 4.66 so far. *NOTE: In the simulation viewport I have applied the prop mesh to see how the final look will be when applied to the same prob mesh in the level..*

Our base material's diffuse network is created. It is responsible for creating the tiled look of our material with completely different material looks, one for the tiles, and one for the grout between the tiles. This is the power of masking in Unreal Engine 4. We used the green channel of the tile mask to create the two completely different look within one relatively simple network.

CREATING THE BASE MATERIAL'S NORMAL NETWORK

Now let's create the normal network of our material. I will use two normal map textures for this purpose. I will combine the Steel normal map as the fine grains, and the Hex Tile's normal map to create the spaces between steel tiles.

25. In the Material Editor, **Left-Click** far to the left of the **Normal** channel and place a **Texture Sample** expression. Make the following changes to this **Texture Sample** expression in its **Details** Panel:

> **Texture:** Apply the texture "T_Metal_Steel_N".
> **Description:** Type-in the text "Steel Normal".

26. Below the **Steel Diffuse** texture **Left-Click** and place another **Texture Sample** expression. Make the following changes to this **Texture Sample** expression in its **Details** Panel:

> **Texture:** Apply the texture "T_Tech_Hex_Tile_N".
> **Description:** Type-in the text "Hex Tile Normal".

27. Place a **Add** expression to the right of the two texture samples and make the following connections:

> • **Steel Normal** RGB (white) output ↔ A channel of **Add**.
> • **Hex Tile Normal** RGB (white) output ↔ B channel of **Add**.

28. Place a **Const3Vector** below the **Add** expression and make the following changes to its details rollout:

> **R:** 2.0
> **G:** 2.0
> **B:** 1.0
> **Description:** Type-in the text "Normal Adjustment".

29. Place a **Multiply** expression to the right of the **Normal Adjustment** and the **Add** expressions and make the following connections:

> • **Add** output ↔ A channel of **Multiply**.
> • **Normal Adjustment** output↔ B channel of **Multiply**.

30. Place **Normalize** expression to the right of the **Multiply** expression and make the following connections:

> • **Multiply** output ↔ Input channel of **Normalize**.
> • **Normalize** output↔ Normal channel of material node.

31. Comment this network (the two textures samples, the vector, add, multiply and the normalize) as `Tiles Normal Network`.

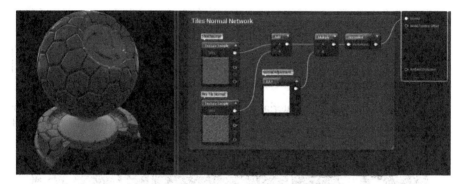

FIGURE 4.67: The static panels normal network.

32. Save your material. Your material should look similar to Figure 4.67 so far. *NOTE: In the simulation viewport I have applied the prop mesh to see how the final look will be when applied to the same prob mesh in the level..*

CREATE THE DYNAMIC MATERIAL

So far our material is static. It has a very interesting texture and look, but that's about it. Now we will make our material to move. This is achieved by means of a texture panner expression. Perform the following tasks to create the dynamic material.

33. We don't want to make any changes to our Base Material (we called it `M_Panels_Static`) as we will use it in the level for comparison later. So let's first duplicate it and work the next steps on the duplicated material.

34. In the **Content Browser**, `Right-Click` on the material `M_Panels_Static` and choose **Duplicate**.

35. Rename the duplicate Material to `M_Panels_Dynamic`.

36. `Double-Click` on the `M_Panels_Dynamic` material to open it in the material editor. It should be identical to your `M_Panels_Static` material you have so far.

37. We will now establish movement on our texture. We would like to achieve this without the need to make any changes to our geometry.
38. The task of moving our texture can be accomplished in one step:
39. Place a **Panner** to the left of both the `Tiles Normal Network` and the `Tiles Diffuse Network` sections you created in the previous two steps.
40. Make the following change to your **Panner**'s details rollout:

> **SpeedX:** 0.1
> **SpeedY:** 0.0
> **Desc:** Tiles Movement.

41. Make the following connections:

> - **Panner** Output ↔ UVs channel of **Steel Diffuse**.
> - **Panner** Output ↔ UVs channel of **Hex Tile Mask**.
> - **Panner** Output ↔ UVs channel of **Steel Normal**.
> - **Panner** Output ↔ UVs channel of **Hex Tile Normal**.

42. Save your material. The material network panner connection should look similar to Figure 4.68(c). Notice the metal tiles seem rotate around the object's center and around its main axes (Figure 4.68(a) and Figure 4.68(b)).

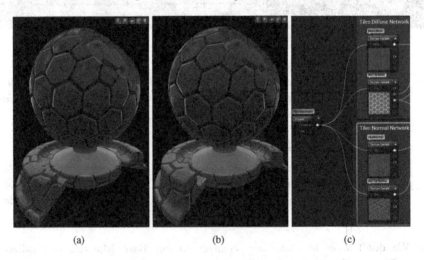

(a)   (b)   (c)

FIGURE 4.68: The static panels normal network.

CREATE PULSATION IN THE MATERIAL

We have made our material to rotate around its mesh's major axis by means of panning its texture. Notice that we used a panner instead of a rotator, since our texture coordinate is wrapped around a round object. Therefore, panning will give us the feeling of rotation on the object.

The material has become more interesting, but we can make it even look more out of worldly by making the grout pulsate with between different colors. We'll do this next.

43. We don't want to make any changes to our original materials. We will use all of the successions of our materials in the level for comparison later. So let's first duplicate the material and work the next steps on the duplicated one.

44. In the **Content Browser**, Right-Click on the material M_Panels_Dynamic and choose **Duplicate**.

45. Rename the duplicate Material to M_Panels_Dynamic_Flames.

46. Double-Click on the M_Panels_Dynamic_Flames material to open it in the material editor. It should be identical to your M_Panels_Dynamic material you have so far.

47. We will now establish pulsation on our texture.

48. The task of making the pulsation in our texture can be accomplished in a few steps. We will bring in a flame texture, use a network with a **Sine** expression to pulsate between 0 and 1, and use this pulsation value to linearly interpolate between two colors to place into the Emissive Color channel of our material. So, let's do it:

49. Before we do anything, let's rearrange our **Tiles Diffuse Network** and **Tiles Normal Networks** to give ourselves some room to work.

50. Move the **Tiles Diffuse Network** up in the graph editor.

51. Move the **Tiles Normal Network** down in the graph editor.

52. Place a **Texture Sample** expression in the space you created between **Tiles Diffuse Network** and **Tiles Normal Networks** and make the following changes to its details rollout:

> **Texture:** T_Fire_Tiled_D
> **Desc:** Fire Texture

53. Place a **Time** expression below the Fire Texture you just created.

54. Place a **Sine** expression to the right of the **Time** expression and connect the output of the **Time** expression to the input of the **Sine** expression.

55. Make the following change to the **Sine** expression in its details rollout:

> **Period:** 10.0

56. Place a **OneMinus** expression above the **Sine** expression and make the following connection:

> • **Panner** output ↔ **Fire Texture** UVs channel.
> • **Fire Texture** RGB (white) output ↔ **OneMinus** input channel.

57. Place a **Multiply** to the right of the **OneMinus** expression and make the following changes to its details rollout:

> **Description:** Ice Multiply

58. Place another **Multiply** just above the first one (the one named **Ice Multiply**) and make the following changes to its details rollout:

> **Description:** Fire Multiply

59. Make the following connections:

> - **Fire Texture** RGB (white) output ↔ B channel of **Fire Multiply**.
> - **OneMinus** output ↔ B channel of **Ice Multiply**.
> - **Hex Tile Mask**'s Green channel ↔ A channel of **Fire Multiply**.
> - **Hex Tile Mask**'s Green channel ↔ A channel of **Ice Multiply**.

60. Place a **ConstantBiasScale** expression below the two **Multiply** expression and make sure its properties in its default rollout are as follows:

> **Bias:** 1.0
> **Scale:** 0.5

61. Place a **Lerp** expression to the right of the two **Multiply** and the **ConstantBiasScale** expression and make the following connections:

> - **Fire Multiply** output ↔ A channel of **Lerp**.
> - **Ice Multiply** output ↔ B channel of **Lerp**.
> - **ConstantBiasScale** output ↔ Alpha channel of **Lerp**.
> - **Lerp** output channel ↔ Emissive Color channel of the material.

62. Comment this network as Tiles Emissive Network.
63. Save your material. The material network connection should look similar to Figure 4.69(a). Notice the metal tiles seem rotate around the object's center and around its main axes (Figure 4.69(b) and Figure 4.69(c)).

APPLYING MATERIALS TO THE PROPS

Now with our three materials (M_Panels_Static, M_Panels_Dynamic, and M_Panels_Dynamic_Flames) created, we can apply them on the props we placed in the display item of the demo room. But first, we need a light close by to where the props are located, so we could see the effect a little more clearly.

64. Left-Click on the leftmost object to select it.
65. Go to your MyMaterials folder in which you created the three materials.
66. Find the M_Panels_Static material and select it.

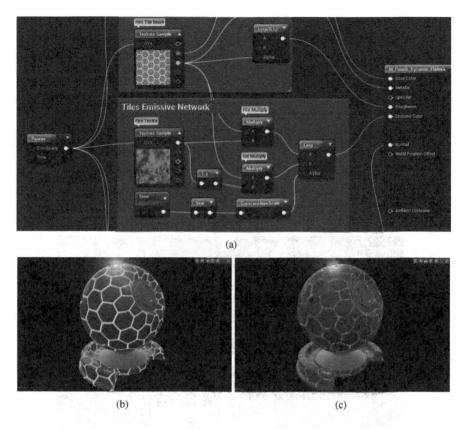

FIGURE 4.69: The dynamic panels with pulsation network and material.

67. Drag the `M_Panels_Static` material into the **Element 0** of the **Materials** section of the Details rollout of the static mesh actor selected in the scene.
68. **Left-Click** on the middle object to select it.
69. Go to your `MyMaterials` folder in which you created the three materials.
70. Find the `M_Panels_Dynamic` material and select it.
71. Drag the `M_Panels_Dynamic` material into the **Element 0** of the **Materials** section of the Details rollout of the static mesh actor selected in the scene.
72. **Left-Click** on the rightmost object to select it.
73. Go to your `MyMaterials` folder in which you created the three materials.
74. Find the `M_Panels_Dynamic_Flames` material and select it.
75. Drag the `M_Panels_Dynamic_Flames` material into the **Element 0** of the **Materials** section of the Details rollout of the static mesh actor selected in the scene.
76. Your scene and the materials applied to static mesh actors within it should look similar to Figure 4.70.

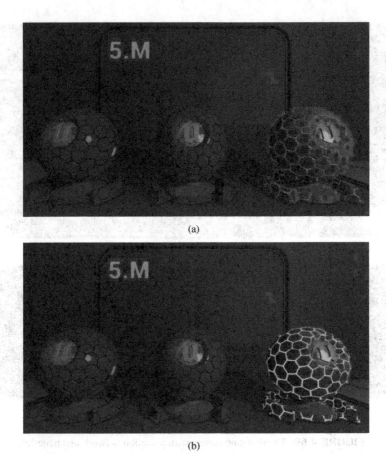

(a)

(b)

FIGURE 4.70: The three materials from left: M_Panels_Static, M_Panels_Dynamic, and M_Panels_Dynamic_Flames applied to the props.

Making textures move along our material was quite easy! All we needed was a coordinate expression called **Panner**. A **Panner** expression will modify our texture UV coordinates by moving them at a constant speed of (SpeedX,SpeedY).

However, we must be careful to apply this **Panner** coordinate expression to the UVs channel of all of the texture expressions we are using in our material. Otherwise, you will see parts of the material's look stay static while others move.

To create the pulsation look we also used a dynamic effect. This time, we used a **Sine** expression with its input connected to a **Time** expression in a **Lerp** network to pick the emissive color of our grout to range from flame to ice.

What Happened in TUTORIAL 4.6...

In this tutorial, we created three materials, a simple but static Steel Tile material, a dynamic version of it that seems to rotate on the surface of the object to which it will be applied, and a time varying version that makes the grout oscillate between ice cold, to fiery hot.

ORGANIZING ASSETS AND PLACING THE DISPLAY ITEM

Like all other tutorials in this chapter so far, we started with creating a display item and organizing our materials into our own material folder.

CREATING THE BASE MATERIAL'S DIFFUSE NETWORK

For this material's base network, I wanted to show you how we can use masking in conjunction with the idea of **Physically Based Materials** in Unreal Engine 4 to simplify our material networks. To do so, we used two different sets of textures.

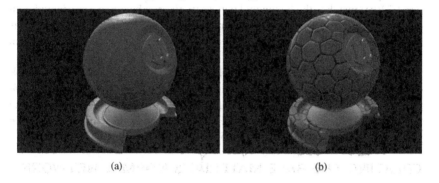

(a)   (b)

FIGURE 4.71: Steel material with and without masking

The first set was our usual color and normal textures for the base material. We used a steel diffuse texture for the color and a steel normal texture for its normal. However, simply applying these two textures to our **Base Color** and **Normal** channels would not result in a tiled look that we wanted to achieve.

Figure 4.71 shows what will happen if we don't use a mask to create the tiles' look. The material in Figure 4.71(a) is simply using a diffuse and normal steel texture. Using a tile mask, we could augment the material to look much more sophisticated as shown in Figure 4.71(b). So how exactly did we achieve the look in Figure 4.71(b)?

A closer inspection of a texture from the Starter Contents called **T_Tech_Hex_Tile_M** (Figure 4.72) reveals a very interesting pattern. We can use these patterns as masks to achieve our desired look on the material.

Multiplying the red channel of the **T_Tech_Hex_Tile_M** texture (shown in Figure 4.72(a)) with any color (or texture) will result in a hexagonal tiled pattern. Each hexagonal tile will have a brighter version of the multiplied color (or texture) and the boundaries between tiles a darker color.

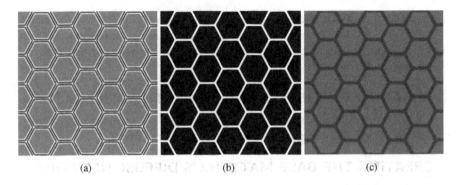

FIGURE 4.72: (a) The Red Channel, (b) The Green Channel, and (c) The Blue Channel

The green channel of the **T_Tech_Hex_Tile_M** texture (shown in Figure 4.72(b)) matches the hexagonal pattern, with each hexagon represented with the black color, and the areas between hexagons with a white color. Using this channel as a selector (or switch) between a metallic/non-metallic and between rough/glossy features will result in the desired look of our materials.

We wanted the tiles to be non-metallic while the grout to have a metallic look. To achieve this effect, we used two linear interpolation (**Lerp**) expressions. We connected the green channel of our mast texture to the **Alpha** channel of the **Lerp** expressions to interpolate between the values of 0 and 1 for the **Metallic** and **Roughness** channels of our material.

CREATING THE BASE MATERIAL'S NORMAL NETWORK

To give some three-dimensionality to our material, we are using the normal channel. We have two normal textures to use for this material. The base material is of steel. Therefore, we used a normal map for a steel material to give the over-all look of the small pores you would usually see on steel. We also have the material sectioned into hexagonal tiles. We used the normal map associated with the hexagonal tiles to created the 3D feel of our tiled material. We combined these two textures by simply adding them to each other.

To achieve more depth, we also adjusted the normal map a little. If you remember from our discussion of normal maps from a previous tutorial, each pixel in the normal map represents a three dimensional vector, perpendicular to the surface at the location of the pixel. The R, G, and B, values of the normal map pixels represent the X, Y, and Z values of the normal vector.

The Z-value represents the length of the vector perpendicular to the surface, if the surface were a flat plane. The larger the Z-value is in comparison to the X and Y values, the more flat the surface will look like. In order to magnify the 3D look of our material we can multiply each channel of the normal map with a value. If the Red and Green channels of normal map are multiplied with values larger than the value multiplied by the Blue channel, the resulting vector will emphasize the 3D-ness of the surface. To achieve this, we multiplied the (R,G,B) channels of the normal map by (2,2,1). Since normal vectors must have a length of 1, we normalized the result.

CREATE THE DYNAMIC MATERIAL

With our static steel panel material created, we can now focus on make the material dynamic. Unreal Engine's **Coordinate** material expressions are those with the ability to interact with the coordinates of a material's texture or geometry. We can make our material dynamic in two different manners, either by changing its geometry or by manipulating the way in which its texture is applied to its geometry.

In this tutorial we opted to work with the texture to achieve the dynamic look. We modified the texture tiling of our material by panning it across the surface on which it will be applied. A **Panner** expression is the perfect tool for this purpose. The **Panner** expression takes in as input a `SpeedX` and a `SpeedY` value. The `SpeedX` specified the speed of panning the U-channel of the texture coordinate, while the `SpeedY` controls the panning speed of the V-channel.

We used `SpeedX=0.1` and `SpeedY=0` to pan our texture on the surface of the object along its U-channel. Connecting the output of the **Panner** coordinate expression to the `UVs` channels of all of our texture sample expressions will make the material move across the object's surface. Since our object is a round object (we used the preview mesh of the UE4's starter content), the end result looks like the object is rotating along its major axes.

CREATE PULSATION IN THE MATERIAL

To make our material look a bit more interesting we made the grout between tiles to pulsate between a fire and and ice color/texture. The idea was pretty straightforward, much like the pulsation in Tutorial 4.5.

The pulsation network will be connected to the `Emissive Color` channel of our material, and its texture comes from the `T_Flame_Tile_D` texture. We used the original texture as the fire and subtract it from 1 (1-the original texture) for the ice. To confine the pulsation to just the grout, we multiply the ice and fire textures with the green channel of our `T_Tech_Hex_Tile_M` mask texture. Doing so will make the ice and color become non-zero only in the grout area and zero on the tiles (see Figure 4.72(b)).

To pulsate between ice and fire, we linearly interpolated between them. Therefore, we connected the fire network to the **A** channel and the ice network to the B channel of a **Lerp** expression. The `Alpha` channel of the **Lerp** is responsible for smoothly transitioning between the two. We used a network based on a **Sine** expression to oscillate between the values of 0 and 1 for the `Alpha` channel of the **Lerp**. To see how we scaled and biased the output values of the sine expression, checkout the calculations in equation (4.13)–(4.18) on page 204.

APPLYING MATERIALS TO THE PROPS

The final task in this tutorial was to apply the materials to the props in the level. The process was similar to all the other tutorials in this chapter. We simply selected each prop, and applied the material to its `Element[0]` in its **Materials** section of its details rollout.

4.6.2.4 Depth Expressions

These expressions[5] utilize the frame buffer to calculate the depth. This depth is then used to create seamless transitions within the scene [12].

Depth Fade: This expression can be used to remove the artifacts that appear as objects intersect each other, especially when translucent objects intersect with opaque objects.
- **Properties**
  Fade Distance Property: World Space distance over which the fade should take place. This is used if the FadeDistance Input is not connected.
- **Inputs**
  Opacity Input: Takes in the existing opacity for the object prior to the depth fade.
  Fade Distance Input: World Space distance over which the fade should take place.

Pixel Depth: This expression generates as output the distance of each pixel from camera at render-time. This is very useful to utilize to generate special effects such as murkiness in the water as the depth increases.
  Example Usage: Scene depth can be used in a network if connected to the alpha channel of a **Lerp** expression to interpolate between two color based the distance of pixels on the object from camera to darken long hallways.

Scene Depth: This expression generates as output the existing scene depth. This is similar to **PixelDepth**, except that **PixelDepth** can sample the depth only at the pixel currently being drawn, whereas **SceneDepth** samples depth at any location.
- **Inputs**
  UVs Input: Takes in the UV texture coordinates used to determine how to sample the depth texture.
  Example Usage: Scene depth can be used in a network if connected to the alpha channel of a **Lerp** expression to interpolate between two color based the distance of all locations in the scene. *Note: Only translucent materials may utilize the* **Scene Depth** *expression.*

---

[5] The contents of this section are adapted from the official UE4 online documentation found at: `https://docs.unrealengine.com/latest/INT/`.

ADVANCED TOPIC:

Scene Depth expression returns a raw depth value. This value is an integer value in the range of 0 to $2^{24} - 1$. To normalize this value to a linger range of 0 to 1 use the following equations:

$$Depth_{norm} = \frac{1 - MAXZ}{SceneDepth + MAXZ} \qquad (4.21)$$

where $Depth_{norm}$ is the normalized depth value between 0 and 1, and $MAXZ = 2^{24} - 1 = 16777215$ is the maximum perceivable depth.

4.6.2.5 Font Expressions

The Font category of Material Expressions deals with creating font materials to be displayed using a TextRender component within Unreal Engine 4 [15].

Font Sample: This expression allows you to sample font textures from a font resource into a two-dimensional texture. The Alpha channel of the font should contain the fount outline value. Only valid Font pages are allowed to be specified. This expression has two properties: Font and Font Texture Page.
- **Properties**
  Font: Holds the default font asset (from the Content Browser) to be held within the expression.
  Font Texture Page: The current font texture page to be used as a part of the texture.

Font Sample Parameter: This expression provides a way to create a font-based parameter using a material instance constant. This allows easy switching between different fonts without having to use many different font materials. This expression has four properties:
- **Properties**
  Parameter Name: Specified the name used to identify the parameter in the material instance through code or blueprint sequence.
  Group: Provides a way to organize parameter names into groups, or categories, within a Material Instance Constant. All parameters within a material that have the same Group property name will be listed underneath that category in the instance.
  Font: Hold the default font asset (from the content browser) to be held within the expression.
  Font Texture Page: The current font texture page to be used as a part of the texture.

4.6.2.6 Parameter Expressions

This section[6] presents an overview of Parameter Expressions [42]. These are expressions that can be reference in Materials, Textures, Blueprints, etc. You can think of these expression as variables in a programming language. Much like variables, you may use the name of these parameters to reference them and make modifications to their values.

CROSS-REFERENCE

To learn more about the Parameter Expressions and their use in conjunction with material instances check out Section 5.4 of Chapter 5– Advanced Material Concepts.

Font Sampler Parameter: This expression provides a way to expose a font-based parameter in a material instance constant, making it easy to use different fonts in different instances. The alpha channel of the font will contain the font outline value. Only valid font pages are allowed to be specified.
- **Properties**
  Parameter Name: Specifies the name used to identify the parameter in instance of the material and through code.
  Group: Provides a way to organize parameter names into groups, or categories, within a **Material Instance Constant**. All parameters within a material that have the same Group property name will be listed underneath that category in the instance.
  Font: Holds the default font asset (from the Content Browser) to be held within the expression.
  Font Texture Page: The current font texture page to be used as a part of the texture.

Scalar Parameter: This parameter expression is the equivalent to a Constant expression in that it stores a single float value and returns this value. However, like all other parameters in Unreal Engine, it can be referenced and its values changed in an instance of the material at run-time, by level designers, or by the other engine components such as Cascade and Matinee.
- **Properties**
  Parameter Name: Specifies the name used to identify the parameter in instance of the material and through code.

---

[6] The contents of this section are adapted from the official UE4 online documentation found at: https://docs.unrealengine.com/latest/INT/.

Group: Provides a way to organize parameter names into groups, or categories, within a `Material Instance Constant`. All parameters within a material that have the same Group property name will be listed underneath that category in the instance.

Default Value: Specifies the initial value that the parameter takes on.

Vector Parameter: This parameter expression is the equivalent to a Constant4Vector expression in that it stores a four values (RGBA) and returns these values. However, like all other parameters in Unreal Engine, it can be referenced and its values changed in an instance of the material at run-time, by level designers, or by the other engine components such as Cascade and Matinee.

- **Properties**

    Parameter Name: Specifies the name used to identify the parameter in instance of the material and through code.

    Group: Provides a way to organize parameter names into groups, or categories, within a `Material Instance Constant`. All parameters within a material that have the same Group property name will be listed underneath that category in the instance.

    Default Value R: Specifies the initial value of the first, or red, channel that the parameter takes on.

    Default Value G: Specifies the initial value of the second, or green, channel that the parameter takes on.

    Default Value B : Specifies the initial value of the third, or blue, channel that the parameter takes on.

    Default Value A: Specifies the initial value of the fourth, or alpha, channel that the parameter takes on.

Texture Sample Parameter2D: This parameter expression is the equivalent to a Texture Sample expression in that it stores a texture map and returns these values. However, like all other parameters in Unreal Engine, it can be referenced and its values changed in an instance of the material at run-time, by level designers, or by the other engine components such as Cascade and Matinee.

- **Properties**

    Parameter Name: Specifies the name used to identify the parameter in instance of the material and through code.

    Group: Provides a way to organize parameter names into groups, or categories, within a `Material Instance Constant`. All parameters within a material that have the same Group property name will be listed underneath that category in the instance.

    Blend: Blends together each frame of the SubUV sprite layout, rather than instantly "popping" from one frame to the next.

    Texture: Specifies the texture sampled by the expression.

Sampler Type: The data type that will be sampled and output from the node.

Mip Value Mode: Applies a noise value to the texture that affects the look and performance.

- **Inputs**

  UVs: Takes in UV texture coordinates to use for the texture. If no values are input, the texture coordinates of the mesh are used.

- **Outputs**

  RGB: Outputs the three-channel RGB vector value of the color.

  R: Outputs the red channel value of the color.

  G: Outputs the green channel value of the color.

  B: Outputs the blue channel value of the color.

  A: Outputs the alpha channel vector value of the color.

Texture Sample Parameter Cube: This parameter expression is the equivalent to a Texture Sample expression in that it stores a texture map and returns these values except that it only accepts cubemaps. Moreover, like all other parameters in Unreal Engine, it can be referenced and its values changed in an instance of the material at run-time, by level designers, or by the other engine components such as Cascade and Matinee.

- **Properties**

  Parameter Name: Specifies the name used to identify the parameter in instance of the material and through code.

  Group: Provides a way to organize parameter names into groups, or categories, within a `Material Instance Constant`. All parameters within a material that have the same Group property name will be listed underneath that category in the instance.

  Blend: Blends together each frame of the SubUV sprite layout, rather than instantly "popping" from one frame to the next.

  Texture: Specifies the texture sampled by the expression.

  Sampler Type: The type of data that will be sampled and output from the node.

  Mip Value Mode: Applies a noise value to the texture that affects the look and performance.

- **Inputs**

  UVs: Takes in UV texture coordinates to use for the texture. If no values are input to the UVs, the texture coordinates of the mesh the material is applied to are used.

- **Outputs**

  RGB: Outputs the three-channel RGB vector value of the color.

  R: Outputs the red channel value of the color.

  G: Outputs the green channel value of the color.

  B: Outputs the blue channel value of the color.

  A: Outputs the alpha channel vector value of the color.

Texture Sample Parameter Movie: This parameter expression is the equivalent to a Texture Sample expression in that it stores a texture map and returns these values except that it only accepts movie textures. The movie textures must in the Bink video format. Moreover, like all other parameters in Unreal Engine, it can be referenced and its values changed in an instance of the material at run-time, by level designers, or by the other engine components such as Cascade and Matinee.

- **Properties**

    Parameter Name: Specifies the name used to identify the parameter in instance of the material and through code.

    Group: Provides a way to organize parameter names into groups, or categories, within a `Material Instance Constant`. All parameters within a material that have the same Group property name will be listed underneath that category in the instance.

    Blend: Blends together each frame of the SubUV sprite layout, rather than instantly "popping" from one frame to the next.

    Texture: Specifies the texture sampled by the expression.

    Sampler Type: The type of data that will be sampled and output from the node.

    Mip Value Mode: Applies a noise value to the texture that affects the look and performance.

- **Inputs**

    UVs: Takes in UV texture coordinates to use for the texture. If no values are input to the UVs, the texture coordinates of the mesh the material is applied to are used.

- **Outputs**

    RGB: Outputs the three-channel RGB vector value of the color.

    R: Outputs the red channel value of the color.

    G: Outputs the green channel value of the color.

    B: Outputs the blue channel value of the color.

    A: Outputs the alpha channel vector value of the color.

4.6.2.7   Particle Expressions

These expressions[7] act as a bridge between the Material Editor and Cascade Particle System Editor [43]. This link allows for a dynamic interaction between material components and those of per-particle based particle systems. Expressions in this category include Particle Color, Particle Direction, Particle Radius, Particle Size, Dynamic Parameter, Particle MacroUV, and so on. Here we will explain a few of more commonly used Particle Expressions and leave a comprehensive reference to A.

---

[7] The contents of this section are adapted from the official UE4 online documentation found at: https://docs.unrealengine.com/latest/INT/.

CROSS-REFERENCE

To learn more about these expressions and their use in managing particle properties such as particle colors in **Cascade** editor checkout Chapter 6-Visual Effects In Unreal Engine.

CROSS-REFERENCE

To learn more about the Particle Expressions and their use in conjunction with particle emitters check out Section 5.4 of Chapter 5– Advanced Material Concepts.

Particle Color: This expression creates a link between each particle in a particle-based data defined in Unreal Engine's **Cascade** particle editor system. This will allow you to expose the particle colors for particles defined in the **Cascade** editor and use the color values in **Cascade** to change the particle colors.
  • **RGBA:** Outputs the combined RGB vector value of a particle color.
  • **R:** Specified the Red color channel value of particle color.
  • **G:** Specified the Green color channel value of particle color.
  • **B:** Specified the Blue color channel value of particle color.
  • **A:** Specified the Alpha channel value of particle color.

4.6.2.8 Texture Expressions

These expressions allow you to read a texture map or other bitmaps and use their values according to UV texture coordinates to wrap the material on a 3D piece of geometry [48].

Font Sample: This expression allows you to sample the texture pages from a font resource as regular 2D textures. The alpha channel of the font will contain the font outline value. Only valid font pages are allowed to be specified.
  • **Properties**
    Font: This property holds the font asset from the **Content Browser**.
    Font Texture Page: This property holds the current font texture page to be used as a part of the texture.

Font Sample Parameter: This expression provides a way to create a font-based parameter using a material instance constant. This allows easy switching between different fonts without having to use many different font materials. This expression has four properties:

* **Properties**

    Parameter Name: Specified the name used to identify the parameter in the material instance through code or blueprint sequence.

    Group: Provides a way to organize parameter names into groups, or categories, within a Material Instance Constant. All parameters within a material that have the same Group property name will be listed underneath that category in the instance.

    Font: Hold the default font asset (from the content browser) to be held within the expression.

    Font Texture Page: The current font texture page to be used as a part of the texture.

Scene Color: This expression outputs the existing scene color.

* **Inputs**

    Offset Fraction: This input takes a 2D vector to offset the scene color in screen space.

Sprite Texture Sample: This expression automatically pipes a rendered sprite's texture into a Texture Parameter called `Sprite Texture` in the material. Useful for working with sprites in Paper 2D. Sprite instances pass their color as a vertex color.

* **Properties**

    Texture: Specifies the texture sampled by the expression.

    Sampler Type: This is the type of data to be sampled from the expression.

    Mip Value Mode: Applies a noise value to the texture.

* **Inputs**

    UVs: This input takes a UV Texture Coordinate to use for the texture.

* **Outputs**

    RGB: Outputs the three-channel RGB vector value of the color.

    R: Outputs the red channel of the color.

    G: Outputs the green channel of the color.

    B: Outputs the blue channel of the color.

    A: Outputs the Alpha channel of the color.

Texture Object: This expression is used to provide a default texture for a texture function input within a function. This node does not actually sample the texture, so it must be used in conjunction with a **Texture Sample** expression.

* **Properties**

    Texture: Specifies the texture sampled by the expression.

    Sampler Type: This is the type of data to be sampled from the node.

Texture Sample: This expression outputs the color value(s) from a texture. This texture can be a regular Texture2D (including normal maps), a cubemap, or a movie texture.

- **Properties**

  Texture: Specifies the texture sampled by the expression. To select a texture, you might first `Left-Click` on it in the **Content Browser**. When the texture is selected in the **Content Browser**, click on the **Left Arrow** in the **Details** Panel of this expression in the **Material Editor** to apply the texture.

  Sampler Type: This is the type of data to be sampled from the expression.

  Mip Value Mode: Applies a noise value to the texture.

- **Inputs**

  UVs: This input takes a UV Texture Coordinate to use for the texture.

- **Outputs**

  RGB: Outputs the three-channel RGB vector value of the color.

  R: Outputs the red channel of the color.

  G: Outputs the green channel of the color.

  B: Outputs the blue channel of the color.

  A: Outputs the Alpha channel of the color.

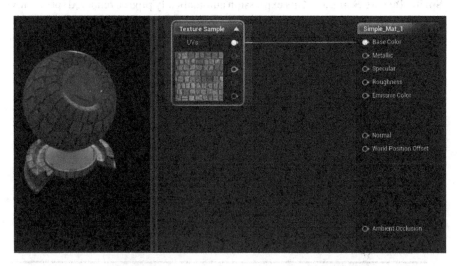

FIGURE 4.73: Texture Sample Expression Example.

Example Usage: You can assign a texture from the **Content Browser** to this expression and supply its output channels to the appropriate material node channels, e.g. Connect RGB channel to the `Base Color` (see Figure 4.73).

Shortcut: To place a **Texture Sample** expression, press the **T** key on the keyboard and `Left-Click` on the graph editor.

Particle SubUV: This expression can be used to render sub-images of a texture map to use in particle systems. Similar to flipbook (one of sprite editing features of the Unreal Engine 4) this expression allows for texture animation manipulation, but it exposes the textures to the Cascade Particle System editor.

- **Properties**

  Blend: Blends together each frame of the Sub UV sprite layout, rather than instantly "popping" from one frame to another.

  Texture: Specifies the texture sampled by the expression.

  Sampler Type: The type of data that will be sampled and output from the node.

  Mip Value Mode: Applies a noise value to the texture that affects the look and performance.

- **Inputs**

  UVs: Takes in UV texture coordinates to use for the texture. If no values are input to the UVs, the texture coordinates of the mesh the material is applied to are used.

- **Outputs**

  RGB: Outputs the three-channel RGB vector value of the color.

  R: Outputs the red channel value of the color.

  G: Outputs the green channel value of the color.

  B: Outputs the blue channel value of the color.

  A: Outputs the alpha channel vector value of the color.

Texture Object Parameter: This parameter expression defines a texture parameter and outputs the texture object, used in materials that call a function with texture inputs. This node does not actually sample the texture, so it must be used in conjunction with a **Texture Sample** expression.

- **Properties**

  Parameter Name: Specifies the name used to identify the parameter in instance of the material and through code.

  Group: Provides a way to organize parameter names into groups, or categories, within a `Material Instance Constant`. All parameters within a material that have the same Group property name will be listed underneath that category in the instance.

  Texture: Specifies the texture sampled by the expression.

  Sampler Type: The type of data that will be sampled and output from the node.

  Mip Value Mode: Applies a noise value to the texture that affects the look and performance.

Usage: This expression is used with **Material Functions**.

Texture Sample Parameter2D: This parameter expression is the equivalent to a Texture Sample expression in that it stores a texture map and returns these values.

However, like all other parameters in Unreal Engine, it can be referenced and its values change in an instance of the material at run-time, by level designers, or by the other engine components such as Cascade and Matinee.

- **Properties**

  Parameter Name: Specifies the name used to identify the parameter in instance of the material and through code.

  Group: Provides a way to organize parameter names into groups, or categories, within a `Material Instance Constant`. All parameters within a material that have the same Group property name will be listed underneath that category in the instance.

  Blend: Blends together each frame of the SubUV sprite layout, rather than instantly "popping" from one frame to the next.

  Texture: Specifies the texture sampled by the expression.

  Sampler Type: The type of data that will be sampled and output from the node.

  Mip Value Mode: Applies a noise value to the texture that affects the look and performance.

- **Inputs**

  UVs: Takes in UV texture coordinates to use for the texture. If no values are input to the UVs, the texture coordinates of the mesh the material is applied to are used.

- **Outputs**

  RGB: Outputs the three-channel RGB vector value of the color.

  R: Outputs the red channel value of the color.

  G: Outputs the green channel value of the color.

  B: Outputs the blue channel value of the color.

  A: Outputs the alpha channel vector value of the color.

Texture Sample Parameter Sub UV: This parameter expression is the equivalent to a Texture Sample Parameter SubUV expression, in that it is used to store Sub UVs of a sprite sheet or texture bitmaps for particle systems usage. However, like all other parameters in Unreal Engine, it can be referenced and its values change in an instance of the material at run-time, by level designers, or by the other engine components such as Cascade and Matinee.

- **Properties**

  Parameter Name: Specifies the name used to identify the parameter in instance of the material and through code.

  Group: Provides a way to organize parameter names into groups, or categories, within a `Material Instance Constant`. All parameters within a material that have the same Group property name will be listed underneath that category in the instance.

  Blend: Blends together each frame of the SubUV sprite layout, rather than instantly "popping" from one frame to the next.

  Texture: Specifies the texture sampled by the expression.

Sampler Type: The type of data that will be sampled and output from the node.

Mip Value Mode: Applies a noise value to the texture that affects the look and performance.

- **Inputs**

  UVs: Takes in UV texture coordinates to use for the texture. If no values are input to the UVs, the texture coordinates of the mesh the material is applied to are used.

- **Outputs**

  RGB: Outputs the three-channel RGB vector value of the color.

  R: Outputs the red channel value of the color.

  G: Outputs the green channel value of the color.

  B: Outputs the blue channel value of the color.

  A: Outputs the alpha channel vector value of the color.

Texture Sample Parameter Cube: This parameter expression is the equivalent to a Texture Sample expression in that it stores a texture map and returns these values except that it only accepts cubemaps. Moreover, like all other parameters in Unreal Engine, it can be referenced and its values change in an instance of the material at run-time, by level designers, or by the other engine components such as Cascade and Matinee.

- **Properties**

  Parameter Name: Specifies the name used to identify the parameter in instance of the material and through code.

  Group: Provides a way to organize parameter names into groups, or categories, within a `Material Instance Constant`. All parameters within a material that have the same Group property name will be listed underneath that category in the instance.

  Blend: Blends together each frame of the SubUV sprite layout, rather than instantly "popping" from one frame to the next.

  Texture: Specifies the texture sampled by the expression.

  Sampler Type: The type of data that will be sampled and output from the node.

  Mip Value Mode: Applies a noise value to the texture that affects the look and performance.

- **Inputs**

  UVs: Takes in UV texture coordinates to use for the texture. If no values are input to the UVs, the texture coordinates of the mesh the material is applied to are used.

- **Outputs**

  RGB: Outputs the three-channel RGB vector value of the color.

  R: Outputs the red channel value of the color.

  G: Outputs the green channel value of the color.

  B: Outputs the blue channel value of the color.

  A: Outputs the alpha channel vector value of the color.

4.6.2.9 Utility Expressions

These expressions[8] allow you to perform some utility functions in unreal engine in support of material and rendering functionalities. A comprehensive list of these functions may be found in the Appendix A, or online at Unreal Engine Documentation Pages [51].

Black Body: This expression simulates the effects of black body radiation in a material. The user may provide an input parameter temperature in Kelvin and connect the resulting outputs to the `Base Color` and `Emissive Color` channels of the material node for physically accurate results.

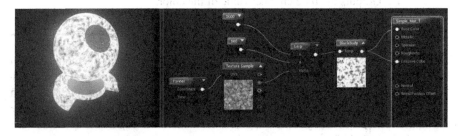

FIGURE 4.74: Black Body Expression Example.

Example Usage: You can connect the `Temp` input channel of this expression to a network that statically or dynamically derives the temperature in kelvin of a material (such as lava, stars, etc.). Feed the output result of this expression to the `Base Color` and the `Emissive Color` channels of the material to achieve physically realistic results. Figure 4.74 shows a network that moves a noise texture coordinates, while the noise texture samples temperatures ranging between 500°K (cold) to 5000°K (hot) on a surface of a radiating object.

Bump Offset: This expression is the Unreal Engine 4 term for what is commonly known as 'parallax mapping'. The **Bump Offset** expression allows a material to give the illusion of depth without the need for additional geometry. Materials with bump offset use a grayscale heightmap to give depth information. The brighter the value in the heightmap, the more 'popped out' the material will be; these areas will parallax (shift) as a camera moves across the surface. Darker areas in the heightmap are 'further away' and will shift the least.

• **Properties**

---

[8] The contents of this section are adapted from the official UE4 online documentation found at: `https://docs.unrealengine.com/latest/INT/`.

Height Ratio: Multiplier for the depth taken from the `heightmap`. The larger the value, the more extreme the depth will be. Typical values range from 0.02 to 0.1.

Reference Plane: This value specifies the approximate height in texture space to apply the effect. A value of 0 will appear to distort the texture completely off the surface, whereas a value of 0.5 (the default) means that some of the surface will pop off while some areas will be sunken in.

- **Inputs**

Coordinates: This input takes in base texture coordinates to be modified by the expression.

Height: This input takes in the texture (or a value) to be used as the heightmap.

Height Ratio Input: This input is the multiplier for the depth taken from the heightmap. The larger the value, the more extreme the depth will be. Typical values range from 0.02 to 0.1. If used, this input supersedes any value in the Height Ratio property.

Constant Bias Scale: This expression takes an input value, adds a bias value to it, and then multiplies it by a scaling factor outputting the result. The mathematical equation for this expression is as follows:

$$\mathrm{CBS}(\mathbf{X}, \mathbf{B}, s) = (\mathbf{X} + \mathbf{B}) \times s \qquad (4.22)$$

where $\mathbf{X}$ is the input vector, $\mathbf{B}$ is the bias vector, and s is the scaling factor. In this equation $\times$ stands for element-by-element multiplication.

- **Properties**

Bias: This value specifies the bias to be added to the input.

Scale: This value specifies the multiplier for the bias result.

Example: To convert input data from [-1,1] to [0,1] you would use a bias of 1.0 and a scale of 0.5. This is a common use when we are taking the Sine or Cosine values that range between -1 to 1 and would like to supply it for an Alpha value in **Lerp** expressions that range between 0 to 1.

Depth Fade: This expression is used to hide unsightly seams that take place when translucent objects intersect with opaque ones.

- **Properties**

Fade Distance: This value is the world space distance over which the fade should take place. This is used if the **Fade Distance** input is unconnected.

- **Inputs**

Opacity: This input takes in the existing opacity for the object prior to the depth fade.

Fade Distance: This input takes in the world space distance over which the fade should take place.

Example Usage: This expression can be used as to augment the `Opacity` channel of a translucent material. When the object with this material intersects another object, the results of this expression will create a nice blur and fade effect at the intersection site.

Depth of Field Function: This expression is designed to give artists control over what happens to a Material when it is being blurred by Depth of Field. It outputs a value between 0-1 such that 0 represents "in focus" and 1 represents "completely blurred." This is useful for interpolating between sharp and blurry versions of a texture, for instance. The Depth input allows for the existing results from the scene's Depth of Field calculations to be overridden by other calculations.

> **NOTE**
>
> For this expression to work, the material needs to be exposed to a
> **Post Process Volume** with Depth of Field settings.

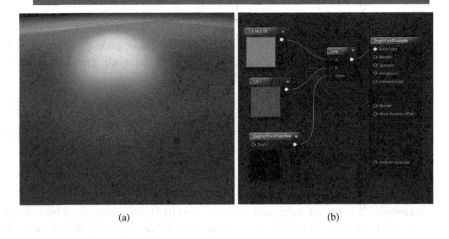

(a)   (b)

FIGURE 4.75: Depth of Field Function. (a) View of a Material with DoF and within a DoF Post Process Volume. (b) DoF Network that blends material between Blue and Red.

Example Usage: This expression can be used as the alpha channel of a Linear Interpolate expression to blend between different colors, or textures when exposed to a Depth of Field volume (see Figure 4.75(b)). The network in Figure 4.75(b) blends between a blue and a red color based on Depth of Field. The results are shown in Figure 4.75(a).

Desaturation: This expression converts the colors of its input to softer shades based on a certain percentage. Let **X** be the original color, **L** be the `Luminance Factor` and f be the `Fraction` value, then the desaturated color **D** will be calculated according to the following equation:

$$D = (1 - f) \times (X \odot L) + f \times X \qquad (4.23)$$

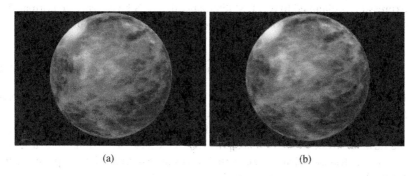

(a)   (b)

FIGURE 4.76: Results of Desaturation: (a) The original texture. (b) The desaturated texture with Luminance Factor of (R:0.33,G:0.59,B:0.11) and 20% Fraction

- **Properties**
  Luminance Factors: This property specifies the amount of each channel's contribution to the desaturated color.
- **Inputs**
  Fraction: This input value specifies the amount of desaturation to apply to the input color, or texture. An amount of 0 is used for no desaturation (full original color), or an amount of 1 is used for full desaturation (no colors, only gray scale).

Example Usage: Use this expression to soften the colors of high contrast colored textures. You can control how much of the red, green or blue colors of the original texture to keep based on the Luminance Factor you can specify. Figure 4.76(a) shows an original texture applied to the Base Color and the Emissive Color channels of a material. Figure 4.76(b) shows the same texture applied to the Base Color and Emissive Color channels after being desaturated with the Luminance Factor of (R:0.33, G:0.51, B:0.11) and 20% Fraction.

Distance: This expression calculates the Euclidean distance between two vectors. These vectors could represent colors, positions, etc. The expression can take on vectors with any number of dimensions.

- **Inputs**
  A: The first input vector of any dimension.
  B: The second input vector of any dimension.

Fresnel: This expression calculates the amount of fall off based on the dot product of the surface normal and the viewer vector. In other words, if the viewer is directly looking at a surface the output value is 0. When the viewer is looking at the surface perpendicularly, the fresnel will output a value of 1. The result of this expression is clamped to [0,1]. Mathematically, let $\mathbf{N}$ be the surface normal, $\mathbf{V}$ be the camera vector, and p be the exponent value, the **Fresnel** output is calculated according to the following equation:

$$\text{FRES}(\mathbf{N}, \mathbf{V}, p) = (1 - \mathbf{N} \odot \mathbf{V})^{p} \tag{4.24}$$

In UE4, the **Fresnel** expression also takes into account a `Base Reflection Fraction` value, b. This value augments the result of the Normal and Camera vector dot product to account for the fraction of the light specular reflection on the surface. A value of 0 for b is equivalent to the above equation, while a value of 1 for `Base Reflection Fraction` disables the **Fresnel**. The complete equation for the **Fresnel** expression is as follows:

$$\text{FRES}(\mathbf{N}, \mathbf{V}, p, b) = [1 - ((1 - b) \times (\mathbf{N} \odot \mathbf{V}))]^{p} \tag{4.25}$$

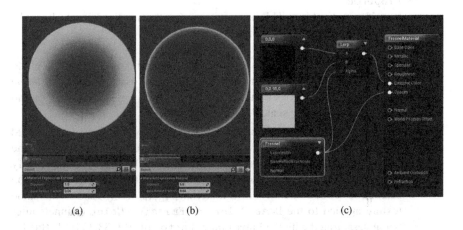

| (a) | (b) | (c) |

FIGURE 4.77: Results of Fresnel Expression: (a) The Fresnel with an exponent of 1. (b) The Fresnel result with an exponent of 5. (c) The Fresnel network for (a) and (b).

- **Properties**
    - **Exponent:** This property specifies how quickly the result fall off. The value p in equations (4.24) and (4.25). Larger values make the result fall off more quickly and have tighter boundaries.
    - **Base Reflection Fraction:** This property specifies the amount of specular reflection if viewed straight on. A value of 1 disables the **Fresnel** expression.
- **Inputs**

Exponent In: This input specifies the fall of values. It will replace the `Exponent` property if connected.

Base Reflection Fraction: This input specifies the fraction of specular reflection if viewed straight on. It will replace the `Base Reflection Fraction` property if connected.

Normal: This input takes in a 3-D vector as the Surface Normal. If you have used a normal map in the material, you can connect this input to a **Vertex Normal WS** expression to account for the normal map of the object. If this input is not connected, the engine will use the Tangent normal of the mesh.

Example Usage: Use this expression to simulate proper and physically accurate reflection/refraction of reflective and translucent objects. This expression is widely used to simulate water, glass, and other reflective and refractive surfaces. Figure 4.77(a) and Figure 4.77(b) show two materials with a Fresnel expression with exponent values of 1 and 5, respectively, controlling the `Emissive Color` and `Opacity` channels. Figure 4.77(c) shows the network responsible for this effect.

Noise: This expression creates a procedural noise field. With the many properties of this expression you can control how the noise field is generated to suit your application.

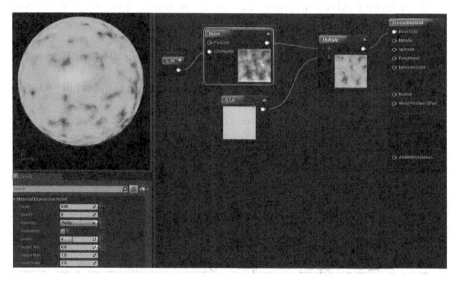

FIGURE 4.78: A Noise Expression Example.

- **Properties**
  Scale: This property controls the over all size of the noise cells. Lower numbers make the noise larger.

Quality: This property controls the trade off between quality and performance. A value of 0 is fast, but with lower quality.

Function: This property controls the type of noise. There are three options, `Simplex`, `Perlin`, and `Gradient`.

Turbulence: This property controls whether to calculate multiple levels of noise in iterations.

Levels: This property specifies the different levels of noise to combine. Used when Turbulence is checked.

Output Min: The minimum value of noise output.

Output Max: The maximum value of noise output.

Level Scale: This property controls the scale of individual levels when Turbulence is active and checked.

- **Inputs**

  Position: This input controls the adjustment of the texture size with a 3D vector.

  Filter Width: This input controls how much blur to be applied to the noise texture.

Example Usage: You can connect this expression to a texture or color to add some randomness to the look of your material (see Figure 4.78).

Rotate about Axis: This expression rotates a three-channel vector input about a given rotation axis and a pivot point. It is very helpful for animating objects using the **World Position Offset** channel of the material node.

- **Inputs**

  Normalized Rotation Axis: This input is the normalized rotation vector about which to rotate the object.

  Rotation Angle: This input is the angle of rotation. 1 equals full 360° rotation.

  Pivot Point: This is the three channel vector used as the pivot point for rotation.

  Position: This is a 3D vector representing the position of the object. The **Absolute World Position** expression is automatically created to be connected to this expression to calculate the location of the object to be rotated.

Example Usage: You can connect this expression to the `World Position Offset` channel of the material node to rotate the object on which the material is applied.

Sphere Mask: This expression outputs a mask value based on a distance calculation. If one input is the position of a point and the other input is the center of a sphere with some radius, the mask value is 0 outside and 1 inside with some transition area. This works on one, two, three, and four component vectors.

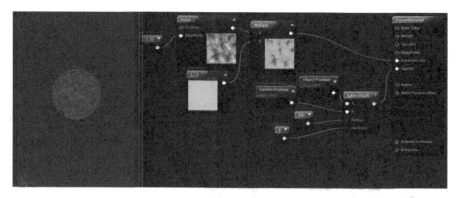

FIGURE 4.79: The Sphere Mask Expression Example. In this example the sphere will fade away as its distance from the camera increases.

- **Properties**
  Attenuation Radius: This value specifies the radius for the distance calcu-
  lation.
  Hardness Percent: This value specifies the transition area size.
- **Inputs**
  A: This input takes in the position of the point to check.
  B: This input takes in the center of the sphere.

Example Usage: You can connect this expression to control the opacity channel
of a material, when the object becomes farther than a certain distance from
the camera, it will fade away and finally disappear (see Figure 4.79).

To find updates to this tutorial and updated instructions about its implementation on other UE4 versions please visit the book's companion website at:
http://www.RVRLAB.com/UE4Book/

**TUTORIAL 4.7   Materials with Time Varying Effects III: Black Body
Radiation**

In this tutorial we will learn how to use a couple of **Utility** expression to simulate physically realistic dynamic effects in our materials.

BEFORE YOU PROCEED

Before you proceed with this Tutorial, and you haven't finished
Tutorial 4.1 on page 150, please go ahead and complete it. In
order to view the effects we will create in this Tutorial we need
the Demo Room to have been included in our project.

ORGANIZING ASSETS AND PLACING THE DISPLAY ITEM

We will place a Display Item in the Demo Room and place three meshes on it, so that we could demonstrate our creations later.

5. If you haven't finished Tutorial 4.1 on page 150, please go ahead and complete it. We will need the Demo Room to have been included in our project.
6. In the content browser, look for a folder inside the **Demo Room** folder called **Blueprints** and open it.
7. Drag a copy of **Display Item** onto the level and place it to along a wall. Change its properties to the following:

Number: 6-M.
Description: Black Body Materials. . .
Type: Square-L

8. In the content browser, look for a folder called **Props** and open it.
9. In the **Props** folder look for and find a mesh called **SM_MatPreviewMesh_02** and drag it into the Display Item you have already placed in the Demo Room.
10. Rotate, scale, and position the mesh so that it faces outwards from the Display Item.
11. **Alt-Drag** the mesh to create two copies of it on the Display Item (see Figure 4.36 on page 164). You can alternatively copy and paste the mesh in the editor on the Display Item.
12. Save your level so far.

CREATING THE BASE MATERIAL'S DIFFUSE NETWORK

We now have a display item and three meshes in the level to demonstrate our progress as we go along in this tutorial.

13. In the **Content Browser**, find your materials folder you have created in earlier tutorials. If you don't have one, **Right-Click** on the **Game** folder, create a new folder and call it **MyMaterials**.
14. **Double-Click** on the **MyMaterials** folder to open it up.
15. Create a **New Material** in this folder and call it **M_BlackBody_Static**.
16. **Double-Click** on the newly created **M_BlackBody_Static** material to open in in the Material Editor.
17. The base material we will create now for our **M_BlackBody_Static** will use a utility expression called **Black Body**. This expression is used to simulate the amount (and color) of light radiated from a hot surface at a particular temperature.
18. In the Material Editor, **Left-Click** to the left of the **Base Color** and place a **Black Body** expression. Make the following changes to this **Texture Sample** expression in its **Details** Panel:

Description: Type-in the text "Body Radiation".

19. Place a **Constant** expression to the left of the Body Radiation (hold 1 and Left-Click). Make the following changes to this expression in its **Details** Panel:

Value: 1000.
Desc: Temp1.

20. Make the following connections:

- **Temp1** output ↔ **Body Radiation** Input.
- **Body Radiation** output ↔ Base Color channel of material node.
- **Body Radiation** output ↔ Emissive Color channel of material node.

21. Your material network and its simulation preview should look like Figure 4.80(a).
22. Save your material.

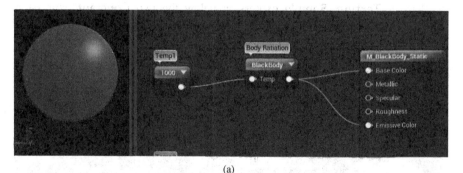

(a)

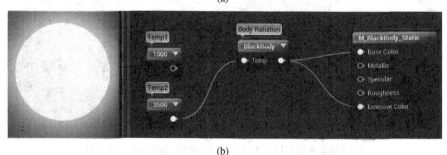

(b)

FIGURE 4.80: The Black Body Radiation at (a) 1000° Kelvin and (b) 3500° Kelvin .

23. Place another **Constant** expression below the first one (hold 1 and Left-Click). Make the following changes to this expression in its **Details** Panel:

> **Value:** 3500.
> **Desc:** Temp2.

24. If you connect the output of the **Temp2** to the input of the **Body Radiation** your material will glow with a bright yellow-white color (see Figure 4.80(b)).

    We now have two temperatures in our network (1000°K and 3500°K) for our black body. Next, we will set up a network to interpolate between these two values as if the body is made of a combination of hot/cool materials, just like the surface of a star.

25. Place a **Lerp** expression between the two **Constant** expressions and the **Black Body** expression and make the following connections:

> • **Temp1** output ↔ **Lerp** A channel.
> • **Temp2** output ↔ **Lerp** B channel.
> • **Lerp** output ↔ **Body Radiation** input channel.

26. Place a **Texture Sample** expression below the two **Constant** expressions (Temp1 and Temp2) and make the following changes in its details rollout:
    Texture: T_Perlin_Noise_M.
    Desc: Body Composition.
27. Make the following connections:

> • **Body Composition** Red output ↔ Alpha channel of **Lerp**.

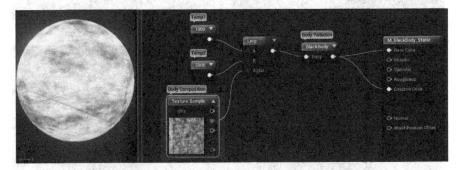

FIGURE 4.81: The blackbody material static interpolations.

28. Save your material. Your material should look similar to Figure 4.81 so far.

    Our base material's diffuse network is created. It is responsible for creating the black body radiation on the surface to which it will be applied.

CREATING THE DYNAMIC PATTERN

Now that we have our base material, it's time to make a duplicate so that we can keep our original material. We will then created a network based on dynamic **Coordinate** expressions to make the new copy of our material dynamic.

29. We don't want to make any changes to our Base Material (we called it M_BlackBody_Static) as we will use it in the level for comparison later. So let's first duplicate it and work the next steps on the duplicated material.
30. In the **Content Browser**, Right-Click on the material M_BlackBody_Static and choose **Duplicate**.
31. Rename the duplicate Material to M_BlackBody_Dynamic.
32. Double-Click on the M_BlackBody_Dynamic material to open it in the material editor. It should be identical to your M_Panels_Static material you have so far.
33. We will now establish movement and tiling on our texture. We would like to achieve this without the need to make any changes to our geometry.
34. Disconnect the **Body Composition** texture expression (the black and white noise texture) from the Alpha channel of the **Lerp** expression. *NOTE: To disconnect a link press* Alt *key and* Left-Click *on the either end of the connection.*
35. Move the texture to the left (about half a page's length) so that we can build our network in the free space.
36. Rename the texture sample to Macro Compostion1.
37. Place a **Panner** to the left of the **Macro Composition1** and set the following properties in its details rollout:

> **SpeedX:** -0.005
> **SpeedY:** -0.005
> **Desc:** MacroPan1.

38. Place a **TexCoord** expression the the left of the **MacroPan1** and set the following properties in its details rollout:

> **Coordinate Index:** 0
> **UTiling:** 0.1
> **VTiling:** 0.1
> **Desc:** MacroTexture1.

39. Make the following connections:

> • **MacroTexture1** Output ↔ Coordinates channel of **MacroPan1**.
> • **MacroPan1** Output ↔ UVs channel of **Macro Composition1**.

40. Your Coordinate Modification network should look similar to Figure 4.82.
41. Marque select (Left-Click and drag the mouse to select) the three expressions, **MacroTexture1, MacroPan1,** and **Macro Composition1**.

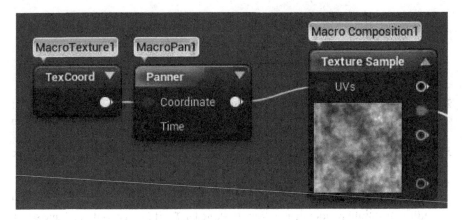

FIGURE 4.82: Coordinate modification network.

42. With these expression selected, duplicate them by pressing `Control+W`.
43. Make the following changes in the duplicate of **MacroTexture1** details rollout:

Coordinate Index: 0
UTiling: 1.0
VTiling: 1.0
Desc: `MicroTexture1`.

44. Make the following changes in the duplicate of **MacroPan1** details rollout:

SpeedX: 0.02
SpeedY: 0.02
Desc: `MicroPan1`.

45. Make the following change to the `Desc` of the duplicate of **Macro Composition1**:

Desc: `Micro Composition1`.

46. Marque select (`Left-Click` and drag the mouse to select) the three expressions, **MicroTexture1**, **MicroPan1**, and **Micro Compositionn1**.
47. With these expressions selected, duplicate them by pressing `Control+W`.
48. Make the following changes in the duplicate of **MicroTexture1** details rollout:

Coordinate Index: 0
UTiling: 0.8
VTiling: 0.8

> **Desc:** `MicroTexture2`.

49. Make the following changes in the duplicate of **MicroPan1** details rollout:

> **SpeedX:** -0.02
> **SpeedY:** 0.02
> **Desc:** `MicroPan2`.

50. Make the following change to the `Desc` of the duplicate of **Micro Composition1**:

> **Desc:** `Micro Composition2`.

51. Marque select (`Left-Click` and drag the mouse to select) the three expressions, **MicroTexture2**, **MicroPan2**, and **Micro Compositionn2**.
52. With these expression selected, duplicate them by pressing `Control+W`.
53. Make the following changes in the duplicate of **MicroTexture2** details rollout:

> **Coordinate Index:** 0
> **UTiling:** 0.2
> **VTiling:** 0.2
> **Desc:** `MacroTexture2`.

54. Make the following changes in the duplicate of **MicroPan2** details rollout:

> **SpeedX:** 0.01
> **SpeedY:** -0.01
> **Desc:** `MacroPan2`.

55. Make the following change to the `Desc` of the duplicate of **Micro Composition2**:

> **Desc:** `Macro Composition2`.

56. Place a **Subtract** expression to the right of both the **MacroComposition1** and **Micro Composition1** make the following changes in its details rollout:

> **Desc:** `MicMacSub1`

57. Make the following connections:

> - **Macro Composition1** R Output ↔ A channel of **MicMacSub1**.
> - **Micro Composition1** R Output ↔ B channel of **MicMacSub1**.

58. Place an **Abs** expression to the right of **MicMacSub1** and make the following changes in its details rollout:

> **Desc:** MicMacAbs1

59. Make the following connections:

> - **MicMacSub1** output ↔ Input channel of **MicMacAbs1**.

60. Place an **Add** expression to below **MicMacSub1** and make the following changes in its details rollout:

> **Desc:** MicMacAdd1

61. Make the following connections:

> - **Macro Composition1** Output ↔ A channel of **MicMacAdd1**.
> - **Micro Composition2** Output ↔ B channel of **MicMacAdd1**.

62. Place an **Add** expression below **MicMacAdd1** and make the following changes in its details rollout:

> **Desc:** MicMacAdd2

63. Make the following connections:

> - **Micro Composition1** Output ↔ A channel of **MicMacAdd2**.
> - **Macro Composition2** Output ↔ B channel of **MicMacAdd2**.

64. Place a **Subtract** expression below the **MicMacAdd2** and make the following changes in its details rollout:

> **Desc:** MicMacSub2

65. Make the following connections:

> - **Micro Composition2** Output ↔ A channel of **MicMacSub2**.
> - **Macro Composition2** Output ↔ B channel of **MicMacSub2**.

66. Place an **Abs** expression to the right of **MicMacSub2** and make the following changes in its details rollout:

> **Desc:** `MicMacAbs2`

67. Make the following connections:

> • **MicMacSub2** output ↔ `Input` channel of **MicMacAbs2**.

68. Place an **Add** expression to the right of **MicMacSub1** and make the following changes in its details rollout:

> **Desc:** `AbsAdd`

69. Make the following connections:

> • **MicMacAbs1** Output ↔ A channel of **AbsAdd**.
> • **MicMacAbs2** Output ↔ B channel of **AbsAdd**.

70. Place an **Add** expression below **AbsAdd** and make the following changes in its details rollout:

> **Desc:** `MicMacAdd3`

71. Make the following connections:

> • **MicMacAdd1** Output ↔ A channel of **MicMacAdd3**.
> • **MicMacAdd2** Output ↔ B channel of **MicMacAdd3**.

72. Place an **Add** expression to the right of **AbsAdd** and make the following changes in its details rollout:

> **Desc:** `TotalTextures`

73. Make the following connections:

> • **AbsAdd** Output ↔ A channel of **TotalTextures**.
> • **MicMacAdd3** Output ↔ B channel of **TotalTextures**.

74. Place a **Constant** expression below **TotalTextures** and make the following changes in its details rollout:

> **Value:** 5
> **Desc:** `AlphaScaling`

75. Place a **Divide** expression to the right of **TotalTextures** and make the following changes in its details rollout:

Desc: Composition

76. Make the following connections:

- **TotalTextures** Output ↔ **A** channel of **Composition**.
- **AphaScaling** Output ↔ **B** channel of **Composition**.
- **Composition** Output ↔ **Alpha** channel of **Lerp**.

77. Save your material. The material network coordinate connections should look similar to Figure 4.83.

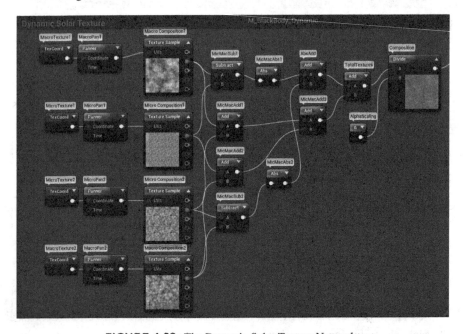

FIGURE 4.83: The Dynamic Solar Texture Network.

Now your material should look like hot plasma filling and swirling inside the preview mesh.

CREATING THE FLICKERING EFFECT

Now that we have our dynamic material, let's make a duplicate so that we can keep our original material. We will then create a network based on the dynamic **Coordinate** expressions and vertex normals to make the new copy of our material look like it's really hot.

78. In the **Content Browser**, Right-Click on the material M_BlackBody_Dynamic and choose **Duplicate**.

79. Rename the duplicate Material to M_BlackBody_Dynamic_Pulsing.
80. Double-Click on the M_BlackBody_Dynamic_Pulsing material to open it in the material editor. It should be identical to the M_BlackBody_Dynamic material you have so far.
81. Left-Click on the material node. In the details rollout, make the following changes to the **Tessellation** section:

> **D3D11 Tessellation:** Flat Tessellation

82. We will now establish the deformations on our hot material. We would like to achieve this by changing the geometry.
83. Move the texture to the Dynamic Solar Texture section of the material to the left a little so that we can build our network in the free space.
84. Place a **Subtract** expression to the right of the **Composition** expression.
85. Place a **Constant** expression to the left of B channel of the **Subtract** you just placed. Make the following changes in the **Constant** expression's details rollout:

> **Value:** 0.5
> **Desc:** WS Bias

86. Make the following connections:

> • **Composition** Output ↔ A channel of **Subtract**.
> • **WS Bias** Output ↔ B channel of **Subtract**.

87. Place a **Multiply** expression to the right of the **Subtract** expression.
88. Place a **Constant** expression below the **Subtract** and make the following changes in the **Constant** expression's details rollout:

> **Value:** 4
> **Desc:** WS Scale

89. Make the following connections:

> • **Subtract** Output ↔ A channel of **Multiply**.
> • **WS Scale** Output ↔ B channel of **Multiply**.

90. Place another **Multiply** expression to the right of the first **Multiply** expression.
91. Place a **Vertex Normal WS** expression below the first **Multiply** expression.
92. Make the following connections:

> - The first **Multiply** Output ↔ A channel of the second **Multiply**.
> - **Vertex Normal WS** Output ↔ B channel of the second **Multiply**.
> - The second **Multiply** Output ↔ `World Displacement` channel of the material node.

93. Marquee select these 6 expressions and comment this section as `World Displacement Shimmering`.
94. Save your material. Your network for changing world displacement should look similar to Figure 4.84.

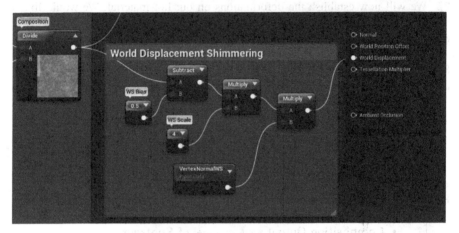

FIGURE 4.84: The Dynamic Solar World Displacement Network.

NOTE

If your platform doesn't support DX11, you can not use Tessellation and World Displacement. In this case connect the result of your `World Displacement Shimmering` network to the `World Position Offset` channel of your material node.

We have created three successions of our black body radiation material. The first iteration of our material was a simple static material based on a black body radiation simulation. In the second iteration we made the material dynamic by tiling and panning of our textures. Finally, we utilized the Vertex Normals of our geometry in World Space to push and pull the vertices based on the temperature of the black body at a given location.

Now let's place our materials in the scene in our Demo Room level:

APPLYING MATERIALS TO THE PROPS

Now with our three materials (`M_BlackBody_Static`, `M_BlackBody_Dynamic`, and `M_BlackBody_Dynamic_Pulsing`) created, we can apply them on the props we placed in the display item of the demo room.

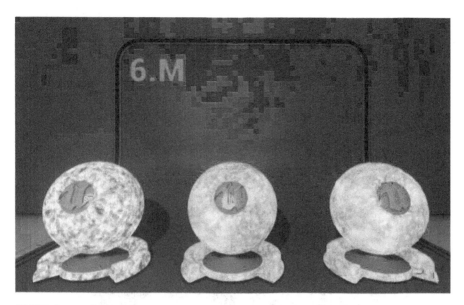

FIGURE 4.85: The three materials from left: `M_BlackBody_Static`, `M_BlackBody_Dynamic`, and `M_BlackBody_Dynamic_Pulsing` applied to the props.

95. **Left-Click** on the leftmost object to select it.
96. Go to your **MyMaterials** folder in which you created the three materials.
97. Find the **M_BlackBody_Static** material and select it.
98. Drag the **M_BlackBody_Static** material into the **Element 0** of the **Materials** section of the Details rollout of the static mesh actor selected in the scene.
99. **Left-Click** on the middle object to select it.
100. Go to your **MyMaterials** folder in which you created the three materials.
101. Find the **M_BlackBody_Dynamic** material and select it.
102. Drag the **M_BlackBody_Dynamic** material into the **Element 0** of the **Materials** section of the Details rollout of the static mesh actor selected in the scene.
103. **Left-Click** on the rightmost object to select it.
104. Go to your **MyMaterials** folder in which you created the three materials.
105. Find the **M_BlackBody_Dynamic_Pulsing** material and select it.
106. Drag the **M_BlackBody_Dynamic_Pulsing** material into the **Element 0** of the **Materials** section of the Details rollout of the selected static mesh actor.
107. Your scene should look similar to Figure 4.85.

Fantastic! We accomplished a lot in this Tutorial by working with a few techniques we have learned in this chapter. Now let's go over what happened in this tutorial and talk a little more in depth about tiling and texture coordinate manipulation.

What Happened in TUTORIAL 4.7...

In this tutorial, we created three materials, a simple but static material simulating Black Body radiation, a dynamic version of it to represent movements that occur due to convection, and a geometry deforming version that affects the vertices of an object on which it is applied based on the temperature they represent.

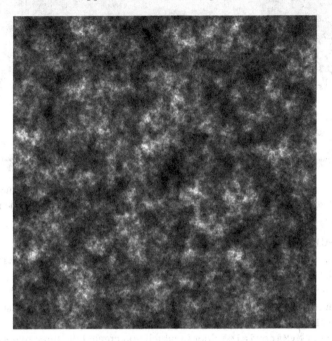

FIGURE 4.86: Perlin Noise.

ORGANIZING ASSETS AND PLACING THE DISPLAY ITEM

Like all other tutorials in this chapter so far, we started with creating a display item and organizing our materials into our own material folder.

CREATING THE BASE MATERIAL'S DIFFUSE AND EMISSIVE NETWORK

This was where we created the color of our material. We used a **Black Body** expression to take in a temperature and show the color associated with that temperature according to the black body radiation laws. We connected the radiation amount to both the **Base Color** and the **Emissive Color** channels of our material.

The look I was going for was that of a star surface, made of hot plasma-like materials of varying temperature. To get this look, I utilized a noise texture shown in Figure 4.86. In this texture, darker areas represent values close to 0 and brighter ones are associated to values close to 1. We connect one of the red, green, or blue channels of this texture (I chose the red channel) to the Alpha channel of a Linear Interpolate expression, we can feed a range of temperatures into our **Black Body** expression input channel to simulate a star-like radiation look.

CREATING THE DYNAMIC PATTERN

In this section we created the dynamic tiling and panning of our texture to allow for a much more elaborate look for the black body radiation. To create this sophisticated look, I used four versions of the Perlin noise texture, each with a different UV tiling as follows:

Texture Name	(UTiling, VTiling)	(SpeedX,SpeedY)
Micro Texture 1	(1.0,1.0)	(0.02,0.02)
Micro Texture 2	(0.8, 0.8)	(-0.02,0.02)
Macro Texture 1	(0.1, 0.1)	(-0.005,-0.005)
Macro Texture 2	(0.2, 0.2)	(0.01,-0.01)

After the tiling and panning of each of the four textures, we used them in the following equation to create the complex convection pattern for our black body:

$$\alpha = \frac{|Mac_1 - Mic_1| + |Mic_2 - Mac_2| + (Mac_1 + Mic_2) + (Mic_1 + Mac_2)}{5} \quad (4.26)$$

where α is the output of our calculation and is connected to the `Alpha` channel of the linear interpolation expression.

CREATING THE FLICKERING EFFECT

To create a complicated shimmering effect we actually manipulated the geometry on which our material is applied via the `World Displacement` channel. To do so, we first changed our material's **DX11Tessellation Mode** to `Flat Tessellation`. This gives us access to the `World Displacement` channel.

We took each vertex's normal channel and pushed/pulled it according to the amount of `Alpha` we calculated in equation (4.26). By doing this operation, we pull the vertices associated with the hot gasses in the star outwards, while pulling cooler vertices inwards. The final look of our materials and the progression of our work is actually quite nice and shown in Figure 4.85.

4.6.2.10 Vector Expressions

These expressions[9] are all in the form of Vectors (multi-dimensional entities in Unreal Engine 4). We have covered some of these expressions above. A comprehensive

---

[9] The contents of this section are adapted from the official UE4 online documentation found at: `https://docs.unrealengine.com/latest/INT/`.

list of these expressions may be found in Appendix A, or online at Unreal Engine Documentation Pages [52].

The **Vector** expressions not covered so far include the following:

Camera Vector: This expression outputs a three-channel vector value representing the direction of the camera with respect to the surface, in other words, the direction from the pixel to the camera. We can think of this vector as the Viewer vector as well.

    Example Usage: Camera Vector is often used to fake environment maps by connecting the **Camera Vector** to a **Component Mask** and use the x and y channels of the **Camera Vector** as texture coordinates.

Object Bounds: This expression outputs the size of the object in each axis.

    Example Usage: You can use the X, Y, and Z values of this expression as the R, G, and B colors of an object to change its color based on its size and shape.

Reflection Vector: This expression outputs a three-channel vector value representing the direction of the reflection with respect to the surface.

    Example Usage: Much like **Camera Vector**, the **Reflection Vector** is often used to fake environment maps by connecting the **Camera Vector** to a **Component Mask** and use the x and y channels of the **Reflection Vector** as texture coordinates.

4.7   SUMMARY

In this chapter we worked with materials and the material editor in Unreal Engine 4. Materials are much more complex than just the paint applied to a surface. They encode within themselves the way light interacts with and reflects from a surface in Unreal Engine.

A list of commonly used material expressions were discussed with example usages of most commonly used expression. We also learned about the concept of physically based material, a newly introduced concept revealed in SIGGRAPH 2013 [54] and how the shading model in UE4 makes use of two new material channels (`Metallic` and `Roughness`) to simulate physically realistic materials efficiently.

We first learned about the features and functionalities of the engine's rendering component. We then went through a series of Tutorials aimed to help us learn how to create materials in the material editor, how to build up our material from a simpler version of itself and create complicated visual simulations of the real-world materials in Unreal Engine 4.

We learned to create simple materials based on textures. We used normal maps to add more depth and realism to our materials. We learned how we can procedurally adjust normal maps to create more details and depth. An important and newly intro-duced functionality in UE4 to physically change the geometry of an object via the `World Displacement` and `Tessellation Multiplier` channels was introduced to us in one of the Tutorials in this chapter.

We also learned how to created dynamic materials by utilizing **Coordinate** ex-pressions. Time-based mathematical calculations can also provide time-dependent features into our materials' functionalities. We used time-based networks in our ma-terials for time varying looks and features.

4.8 EXERCISES

Exercise 1. Create the materials shown in Figure 4.6.
Exercise 2. Create the materials shown in Figure 4.7.
Exercise 3. Create the materials shown in Figure 4.8.
Exercise 4. Create the materials shown in Figure 4.9.
Exercise 5. Create the materials shown in Figure 4.10.
Exercise 6. Create the materials shown in Figure 4.11.
Exercise 7. Create the materials shown in Figure 4.12(a).
Exercise 8. Create the materials shown in Figure 4.13(a).
Exercise 9. Create the materials shown in Figure 4.14.
Exercise 10. Create the materials shown in Figure 4.15.
Exercise 11. Create the materials shown in Figure 4.19.
Exercise 12. Create the materials shown in Figure 4.22.
Exercise 13. Create the materials shown in Figure 4.23(a).
Exercise 14. Create the materials shown in Figure 4.23(b).
Exercise 15. In Tutorial 4.6 what happens if the **Panner** expression is not connected to the **UVs** channel of the **Texture expression** with the Flame tex-ture? Explain.

Section II

*Making Game Worlds Stand Out:
Intermediate Development
Concepts*

5 Advanced Material Concepts in Unreal Engine

5.1 INTRODUCTION

UNREAL Engine's rendering engine is a powerful tool that can be utilized to create incredible materials. In this chapter we will go over some of the more advanced concepts in designing physically based materials in Unreal Engine 4. I am taking a slightly different approach in this chapter than the other chapters in this book.

Instead of going over scenarios in step-by-step tutorials, I will cover the material concepts in this chapter at a very high level. This will give you a good overview of these concepts and their applications. You can then utilize these concepts in combination with those we learned in Chapter 4– Materials in Unreal Engine, to design very complicated, and amazingly realistic materials.

In this chapter, the advanced material concepts and models and their effects on light-material interactions are adopted from official Unreal Engine 4's documentation. Citations to appropriate documentation pages are provided for your reference, if you wish to investigate these concepts further.

5.2 MORE ABOUT UNREAL ENGINE'S SHADING MODELS

The **Shading Model**[1] controls how an incoming light ray will be reflected from the surface on which the material is applied. In other words, the shading model is responsible for computing how the input channels of the material make up its final look. As of version 4.6, Unreal Engine supports 10 shading models: `Default Lit`, `Unlit`, `Subsurface`, `Preintegrated Skin`, `Clear Coat`, `Subsurface Profile`, `Two-sided Foliage`, `Hair`, `Cloth`, and `Eye`.

Most users generally use the `Default Lit` shading model for standard materials. The other five models are intended for use in generating very realistic results on special kinds of surfaces, such as simulating light penetration of a surface, materials with two layers (a base layer and a clear coat layer), and so on.

The following list presents the shading model used in Unreal Engine 4, as of the release of Unreal Engine 4.6 [49].

5.2.1 DEFAULT LIT

The **Default Lit** shading model is the most widely used shading model in designing materials in Unreal Engine. This model simulates direct and indirect light-

---

[1] The contents of this section are adapted from the official UE4 online documentation found at: `https://docs.unrealengine.com/latest/INT/`.

ing. For reflections, this model uses the material's specularity. When using the **Default Lit** shading model, you will have the choice of several material inputs including, `Base Color, Metallic, Specular, Roughness, Emissive Color, Normal, World Position Offset`, and `Ambient Occlusion`.

5.2.2 UNLIT

The **Unlit** shading model, as the name suggests, does not interact with the lighting. Instead, this shading model uses the `Emissive Color` channel to output the color of the object. This is a very useful model for simulating special effects such as fire or glowing objects. However, you must recognize that materials using the **Unlit** shading models, despite their own glow, do not cast any light into the scene. As such, there will be no shadows or illumination cast into the scene from materials based on this shading model. If you wish to have light into the scene, you must place a light source with its color set to be close to the color of the material, separately.

The `Unlit` sharing model makes use of two channels – the `Emissive Color` and the `World Position Offset`.

5.2.3 SUBSURFACE

The **Subsurface** shading model simulates the subsurface scatter effects. When light hits an object in the real world, it penetrates the surface of the object and interacts with the material beneath the surface. For objects such as skin, wax and candle materials, and crystal like surfaces, the light that penetrates the surface diffuses through the surface and will be partially reflected back to the outside of the object. This shading model relies on the `Subsurface Color` input channel of the material as the light that will glow under the surface of the object (see Figure 5.1).

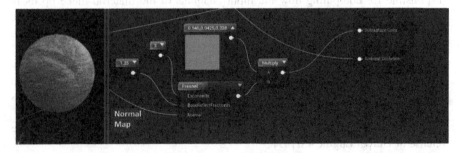

FIGURE 5.1: A Subsurface Scatter Network to Simulate a Crystal Rock.

The materials with `Subsurface` shading model utilize all of the input channels used in the `Default Lit` model with the addition of the `Subsurface Color` and `Opacity` channels.

5.2.4   PREINTEGRATED SKIN

The **Preintegrated Skin** shading model is similar to the **Subsurface** model in that it allows the light to penetrate the surface of the object, diffuse inside the object and reflect around the incident point. However, this model is optimized for lower-performance cost on skin rendering for human characters. This shading model uses the same channels as the ones used in the **Subsurface** shading model.

5.2.5   CLEAR COAT

The **Clear Coat** shading model simulates the effect of a multilayer material with a translucent material covering the base material. This model utilizes the `Clear Coat`, `Clear Coat Roughness`, and `Opacity` channels in addition to all the other channels used in the **Default Lit** shading model.

5.2.6   SUBSURFACE PROFILE

The **Subsurface Profile** shading model is an incredibly accurate model for rendering of human skin and is based on the work by Jorge Jimenez [53], [50]. This model utilizes an asset called `Subsurface Profile`. The `Subsurface Profile` stores information about the scattering of light under the surface of the skin.

There are three items of importance in a subsurface profile that affect the final look of the material. The `Scatter Radius` dictates how far inside the object the light can scatter. The `Subsurface Color` specifies the color of the subsurface, while the `Falloff Color` indicates the color of the light once it has exited the surface [50].

In order to use the **Subsurface Profile** shading model you must specify this model under the Details tab of your material node. Then you should apply a `Subsurface Profile` from the **Content Browser** to the material in its Details tab. You can create a `Subsurface Profile` by `Right-Click`ing in the **Content Browser** and selecting the `Subsurface Profile` asset from the menu.

Another important feature with the **Subsurface Profile** shading model is its ability to interpolate from the material's `Opacity` channel between a regular material and one with full subsurface scattering activated (see Figure 5.2).

5.3   MATERIAL BLEND MODES

In Unreal Engine, blend modes describe how the output of the current material is going to blend over the current location of the background in the fragment shader. This will effectively determine how the engine combines the current value from the frame buffer with the value of the rendered material in that location.

The following description of blend modes is adapted from the official Unreal Engine 4 documentations [35]:

FIGURE 5.2: Subsurface Profiles Can Be Masked by Opacity Channel.

5.3.1 OPAQUE BLEND MODE

The Opaque Blend Mode is easily the most straightforward, and probably the one you will use most often. It defines a surface through which light neither passes nor penetrates. This is perfect for most plastics, metals, stone, and the larger percentage of other surface types.

5.3.2 MASKED BLEND MODE

Masked Blend Mode is used for objects in which you will need to selectively control visibility in a binary (on/off) fashion. For example, consider a material that simulates a chain link fence or grate. You will have some areas that look solid while others are invisible. Such materials are perfect for the Masked Blend Mode.

5.3.3 TRANSLUCENT BLEND MODE

This Blend Mode works by taking in an opacity value or texture and applying it to the surface such that black areas are completely transparent, white areas are completely opaque, and the varying shades of gradation between result in corresponding transparency levels. This means that with a gray opacity texture, you can have objects that appear to be translucent, letting only some of the background through.

5.3.4 ADDITIVE BLEND MODE

The Additive Blend Mode simply takes the pixels of the material and adds them to the pixels of the background. This is very similar to the Linear Dodge (Add) Blend

Mode in Photoshop. This means that there is no darkening; since all pixel values are added together, blacks will just render as transparent. This Blend Mode is useful for various special effects such as fire, steam, or holograms.

5.3.5 MODULATE BLEND MODE

The Modulate Blend Mode simply multiplies the value of the material against the pixels of the background. The behavior is very similar to the Multiply Blend Mode in Photoshop.

5.4 MORE ADVANCED MATERIAL EXPRESSIONS

In this section[2] we will discuss the functions of some of the more advanced **Material Expressions** [36]. A more comprehensive list and descriptions of functionalities may be found on the Unreal Engine documentation website.[3]

> **CROSS-REFERENCE**
>
> More details about the Material Expressions may be found in Appendix A.

> **CROSS-REFERENCE**
>
> Some of more commonly used **Parameter Expressions** are discussed in Chapter 4, Section 4.6.2.

5.4.1 PARAMETER EXPRESSIONS

This section presents an overview of Parameter Expressions [42]. These are expressions that can be referenced in Materials, Textures, Blueprints, etc. You can think of these expression as variables in a programming language. Much like variables, you may use the name of these parameters to reference them and make modifications to their values.

Font Sampler Parameter: This expression provides a way to expose a font-based parameter in a material instance constant, making it easy to use different fonts in different instances. The alpha channel of the font will contain the font outline value. Only valid font pages are allowed to be specified.

---

[2] The contents of this section are adapted from the official UE4 online documentation found at: https://docs.unrealengine.com/latest/INT/.

[3] https://docs.unrealengine.com/latest/INT/Engine/Rendering/Materials/ExpressionReference/index.html

- **Properties**

   Parameter Name: Specifies the name used to identify the parameter in instance of the material and through code.

   Group: Provides a way to organize parameter names into groups, or categories, within a `Material Instance Constant`. All parameters within a material that have the same Group property name will be listed underneath that category in the instance.

   Font: Holds the default font asset (from the Content Browser) to be held within the expression.

   Font Texture Page: The current font texture page to be used as a part of the texture.

Scalar Parameter: This parameter expression is equivalent to a Constant expression in that it stores a single float value and returns this value. However, like all other parameters in Unreal Engine, it can be referenced and its values changed in an instance of the material at run-time, by level designers, or by the other engine components such as Cascade and Matinee.

- **Properties**

   Parameter Name: Specifies the name used to identify the parameter in instance of the material and through code.

   Group: Provides a way to organize parameter names into groups, or categories, within a `Material Instance Constant`. All parameters within a material that have the same Group property name will be listed underneath that category in the instance.

   Default Value: Specifies the initial value that the parameter takes on.

Vector Parameter: This parameter expression is equivalent to Constant4Vector expression in that it stores a four values (RGBA) and returns these values. However, like all other parameters in Unreal Engine, it can be referenced and its values changed in an instance of the material at run-time, by level designers, or by the other engine components such as Cascade and Matinee.

- **Properties**

   Parameter Name: Specifies the name used to identify the parameter in instance of the material and through code.

   Group: Provides a way to organize parameter names into groups, or categories, within a `Material Instance Constant`. All parameters within a material that have the same Group property name will be listed underneath that category in the instance.

   Default Value R: Specifies the initial value of the first, or red, channel that the parameter takes on.

   Default Value G: Specifies the initial value of the second, or green, channel that the parameter takes on.

Default Value B : Specifies the initial value of the third, or blue, channel that the parameter takes on.

Default Value A: Specifies the initial value of the fourth, or alpha, channel that the parameter takes on.

Texture Sample Parameter2D: This parameter expression is equivalent to a Texture Sample expression in that it stores a texture map and returns these values. However, like all other parameters in Unreal Engine, it can be referenced and its values changed in an instance of the material at run-time, by level designers, or by the other engine components such as Cascade and Matinee.

- **Properties**

    Parameter Name: Specifies the name used to identify the parameter in instance of the material and through code.

    Group: Provides a way to organize parameter names into groups, or categories, within a `Material Instance Constant`. All parameters within a material that have the same Group property name will be listed underneath that category in the instance.

    Blend: Blends together each frame of the SubUV sprite layout, rather than instantly "popping" from one frame to the next.

    Texture: Specifies the texture sampled by the expression.

    Sampler Type: The type of data that will be sampled and output from the node.

    Mip Value Mode: Applies a noise value to the texture that affects the look and performance.

- **Inputs**

    UVs: Takes in UV texture coordinates to use for the texture. If no values are input to the UVs, the texture coordinates of the mesh the material is applied to are used.

- **Outputs**

    RGB: Outputs the three-channel RGB vector value of the color.

    R: Outputs the red channel value of the color.

    G: Outputs the green channel value of the color.

    B: Outputs the blue channel value of the color.

    A: Outputs the alpha channel vector value of the color.

Texture Sample Parameter Cube: This parameter expression is equivalent to a Texture Sample expression in that it stores a texture map and returns these values except that it only accepts cubemaps. Moreover, like all other parameters in Unreal Engine, it can be referenced and its values changed in an instance of the material at run-time, by level designers, or by the other engine components such as Cascade and Matinee.

- **Properties**

  Parameter Name: Specifies the name used to identify the parameter in instance of the material and through code.

  Group: Provides a way to organize parameter names into groups, or categories, within a `Material Instance Constant`. All parameters within a material that have the same Group property name will be listed underneath that category in the instance.

  Blend: Blends together each frame of the SubUV sprite layout, rather than instantly "popping" from one frame to the next.

  Texture: Specifies the texture sampled by the expression.

  Sampler Type: The type of data that will be sampled and output from the node.

  Mip Value Mode: Applies a noise value to the texture that affects the look and performance.

- **Inputs**

  UVs: Takes in UV texture coordinates to use for the texture. If no values are input to the UVs, the texture coordinates of the mesh the material is applied to are used.

- **Outputs**

  RGB: Outputs the three-channel RGB vector value of the color.

  R: Outputs the red channel value of the color.

  G: Outputs the green channel value of the color.

  B: Outputs the blue channel value of the color.

  A: Outputs the alpha channel vector value of the color.

Texture Sample Parameter Movie: This parameter expression is equivalent to a Texture Sample expression in that it stores a texture map and returns these values except that it only accepts movie textures. The movie textures must be in the Bink video format. Moreover, like all other parameters in Unreal Engine, it can be referenced and its values changed in an instance of the material at run-time, by level designers, or by the other engine components such as Cascade and Matinee.

- **Properties**

  Parameter Name: Specifies the name used to identify the parameter in instance of the material and through code.

  Group: Provides a way to organize parameter names into groups, or categories, within a `Material Instance Constant`. All parameters within a material that have the same Group property name will be listed underneath that category in the instance.

  Blend: Blends together each frame of the SubUV sprite layout, rather than instantly "popping" from one frame to the next.

  Texture: Specifies the texture sampled by the expression.

  Sampler Type: The type of data that will be sampled and output from the node.

Mip Value Mode: Applies a noise value to the texture that affects the look and performance.

- **Inputs**
  UVs: Takes in UV texture coordinates to use for the texture. If no values are input to the UVs, the texture coordinates of the mesh the material is applied to are used.
- **Outputs**
  RGB: Outputs the three-channel RGB vector value of the color.
  R: Outputs the red channel value of the color.
  G: Outputs the green channel value of the color.
  B: Outputs the blue channel value of the color.
  A: Outputs the alpha channel vector value of the color.

Collection Parameters: This expression is used to act as a reference to access a Parameter Collection Asset. These will be a group of assets that may be reused by many different assets such a materials, blueprints, etc.

You can think of these collections as a generic or bundling of scalar and vector parameters that can be referenced in any material. These collections may be used to get global data and apply them to many materials at once. Moreover, these collections are very handy in driving per-level effects via blueprints, such as moisture amount, damage amount, etc.

Dynamic Parameter: This expression gives you a mechanism to pass up to four values in a material used for a particle system. Cascade particle editor will give access to this parameter via the **Parameter Dynamic** module to use these values in any manner in the particle system.

- **Properties**
  Param Names: An array of names to be used as parameters. These values will determine the text on the output of the expression in the Material Editor and will be used to interact with the **Parameter Dynamic** module in the Cascade Particle Editor.
- **Inputs**
  Param1: Outputs the value of the first parameter in the `Param Names` property. Based on the value in `Param Names` property the value of this output can change.
  Param2: Outputs the value of the second parameter in the `Param Names` property. Based on the value in `Param Names` property the value of this output can change.
  Param3: Outputs the value of the third parameter in the `Param Names` property. Based on the value in `Param Names` property the value of this output can change.

Param4: Outputs the value of the fourth parameter in the `Param Names` property. Based on the value in `Param Names` property the value of this output can change.

Texture Sample Parameter SubUV: This parameter expression is equivalent to a Particle SubUV expression in that it stores sub images of a texture for application to a particle. However, like all other parameters in Unreal Engine, it can be referenced and its values changed in an instance of the material at run-time, by level designers, or by the other engine components such as Cascade and Matinee.

- **Properties**
  Parameter Name: Specifies the name used to identify the parameter in instance of the material and through code.
  Group: Provides a way to organize parameter names into groups, or categories, within a `Material Instance Constant`. All parameters within a material that have the same Group property name will be listed underneath that category in the instance.
  Texture: Specifies the texture sampled by the expression.
  Sampler Type: The type of data that will be sampled and output from the node.
  Mip Value Mode: Applies a noise value to the texture that affects the look and performance.
- **Inputs**
  UVs: Takes in UV texture coordinates to use for the texture. If no values are input to the UVs, the texture coordinates of the mesh the material is applied to are used.
- **Outputs**
  RGB: Outputs the three-channel RGB vector value of the color.
  R: Outputs the red channel value of the color.
  G: Outputs the green channel value of the color.
  B: Outputs the blue channel value of the color.
  A: Outputs the alpha channel vector value of the color.

CROSS-REFERENCE

To learn more about visual effects through Particle Systems and the Cascade Particle Editor checkout Chapter 6. Section 6.3 on page 292 to learn about the Cascade Particle System Editor in detail.

5.4.2 PARTICLE EXPRESSIONS

These expressions[4] act as a bridge between the Material Editor and Cascade Particle System Editor. This link allows for a dynamic interaction between material compo-

---

[4] The contents of this section are adapted from the official UE4 online documentation found at: https://docs.unrealengine.com/latest/INT/.

nents and those of per-particle based particle systems. Expressions in this category include Particle Color, Particle Direction, Particle Radius, Particle Size, Dynamic Parameter, Particle MacroUV, and so on [43]. Here we will explain a few of the more commonly used Particle Expressions and leave a comprehensive reference to A.

Particle Color: This expression must be a part of the network that is plugged into the appropriate channel (e.g., Emissive Color). The expression creates a link between the Unreal renderer and the particle systems and makes it possible to control any per-particle data within Cascade.

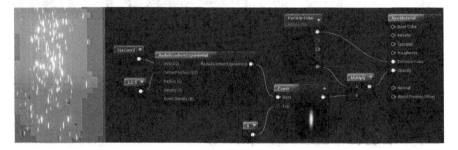

FIGURE 5.3: Particle Color Expression Example.

- **Outputs**
  RGBA: Outputs the RGBA vector data.
  R: Outputs the red channel data.
  G: Outputs the green channel data.
  B: Outputs the blue channel data.
  A: Outputs the alpha channel data.
- **Example Usage:** Connecting the RGBA output channel of this expression to the Emissive Color and a network driving from its alpha channel to the opacity channel of a material will expose the color of the material to the particle system. You can then manipulate the color, alpha, color over life, and alpha over life of each particle in an emitter from **Initial Color** and **Color Over Life** modules in the cascade editor (see Figure 5.3).

Particle Direction: This expression creates a link between the Unreal renderer and the particle systems and makes it possible to control the color of any per-particle data from the location of each particle in the world. This expression must be a part of the network that is plugged into the appropriate material channel (e.g., Emissive Color).
  Example Usage: Connecting the RGBA output channel of this expression through a network to the Emissive Color channel of a material will expose the rotation of each particle to the emissive color of the material. You can then manipulate the orientation of each particle in an emitter to change the emissive color of their material (see Figure 5.4).

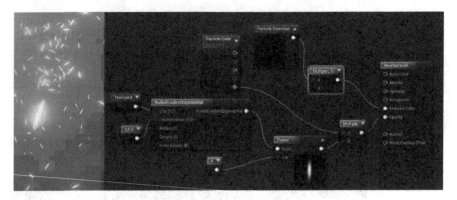

FIGURE 5.4: Particle Rotation Expression Example.

Particle Macro UV: This expression outputs UV texture coordinates that can be used to map any 2D texture onto the entire particle system in a continuous way. This will make the texture appear seamless across particles. The UVs will be centered around the `MacroUVPosition` with the `MacroUVRadius`. The `MacroUVPosition` and the `MacroUVRadius` can be found under the **Macro UV** section of the **Details** rollout of the **Required** emitter module.

The **Particle Macro UV** expression is useful for mapping continuous noise onto particles to break up the pattern introduced by mapping a texture onto each particle with normal texture coordinates. *Note: As of Unreal Engine 4.5, this expression is not compatible with GPU particle systems.*

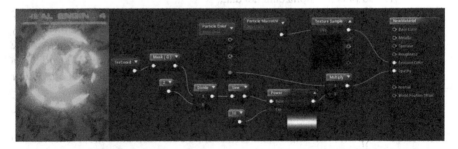

FIGURE 5.5: Particle Macro UV Expression Example.

Example Usage: Create a **Particle Macro UV** expression and connect its output channel to the UVs input channel of a **Texture Sample** expression. Set the texture of this **Texture Sample** expression to the texture you would like to map as the backdrop of your particle effect. Connecting the RGBA output channel of the **Texture Sample** expression to the Emissive Color channel of the material will create the effect shown in Figure 5.5.

Particle World Position WS: This expression exposes each particle's position in the world space coordinate to the material. You may use the output of this expression in a network to drive various aspects of particles' material. *Note: This expression works on a per-particle basis.*

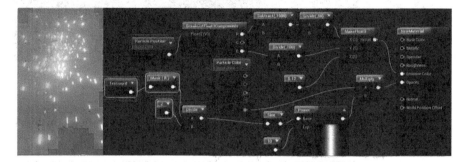

FIGURE 5.6: Particle Position Expression Example.

Example Usage: Create a **Particle World Position** expression and connect its output channel to a network that creates a 3Vector representing a color based on the position of each particle in the world space. Connecting the result of this network to the Emissive Color channel of a material node will create particles whose color will change based on their position in the world space as shown in Figure 5.6.

One important note to keep in mind, is that this expression will return the actual world space position of each particle in the material editor. As a result if the emitter is moved in the world, this will impact the position of spawned particles. This should be compensated for in a network within the material editor to avoid undesirable effects.

Particle Radius: This expression exposes each particle's radius to the material. You may use the output of this expression in a network to drive various aspects of particles' material. *Note: This expression works on a per-particle basis.*

Example Usage: Create a **Particle Radius** expression and connect its output channel to an **If** expression to pick between two colors based on the radius of each particle. Connecting the result of this network to the Emissive Color channel of a material node will create particles whose color will change based on their radius as shown in Figure 5.7.

Particle Relative Time: This expression exposes each particle's relative time (i.e., a particle's age as a number between 0 and 1) to the material. You may use the out-

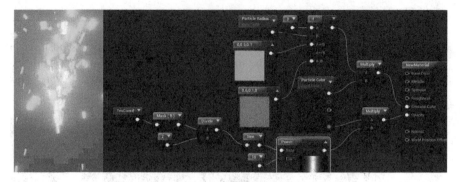

FIGURE 5.7: Particle Radius Expression Example.

put of this expression in a network to drive various aspects of particles' material. *Note: This expression works on a per-particle basis.*

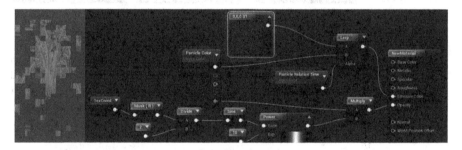

FIGURE 5.8: Particle Relative Time Expression Example.

Example Usage: Create a **Particle Relative Time** expression and connect its output channel to the alpha channel of a **Lerp** expression to pick between two colors based on the relative age of each particle. Connecting the result of this network to the Emissive Color channel of a material node will create particles whose color will change as they age (see Figure 5.8).

Particle Size: This expression exposes each particle's X and Y size (i.e., a particle's height and width) to the material. You may use the output of this expression in a network to drive various aspects of particles' material. *Note: This expression works on a per-particle basis.*

Example Usage: Use the X or Y components of the output channel of a **Particle Size** with an opacity texture and the emissive color network of the material. Connecting the result of this network to the Emissive and Opacity channels of a material node will create particles that will fade as their sizes shrink or get more opaque as well as glow more as their sizes increase (see Figure 5.9).

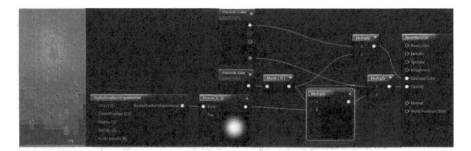

FIGURE 5.9: Particle Size Expression Example.

Particle Speed: This expression exposes each particle's speed to the material. You may use the output of this expression in a network to drive various aspects of particles' material. *Note: This expression works on a per-particle basis.*

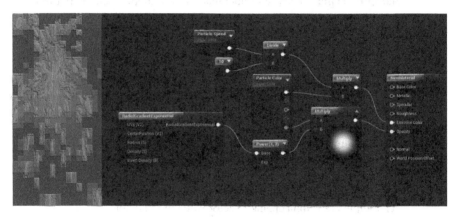

FIGURE 5.10: Particle Speed Expression Example.

Example Usage: Use the output channel of a **Particle Speed** to drive the opacity texture or the emissive color networks of a material. Connecting the result of these networks to the Emissive or Opacity channels of a material node will create particles that will fade as they slow down, or get more opaque and glow more as their speeds increase (see Figure 5.10).

Particle Sub UV: This expression can be used to render sub-images of a texture map to use in particle systems. It is similar to flipbook (one of the sprite editing features of the Unreal Engine 4) in that it allows for texture animation manipulation, but it exposes the textures to the Cascade Particle System editor.

- **Properties**
  Blend: Blends together each frame of the Sub UV sprite layout, rather than instantly "popping" from one frame to another.

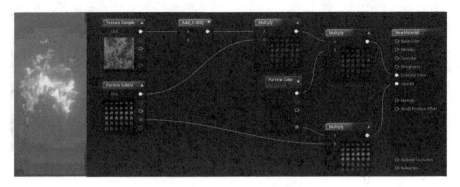

FIGURE 5.11: Particle Sub UV Expression Example.

Texture: Specifies the texture sampled by the expression.

Sampler Type: The type of data that will be sampled and output from the node.

Mip Value Mode: Applies a noise value to the texture that affects the look and performance.

- **Inputs**

  UVs: Takes in UV texture coordinates to use for the texture. If no values are input to the UVs, the texture coordinates of the mesh the material is applied to are used.

- **Outputs**

  RGB: Outputs the three-channel RGB vector value of the color.

  R: Outputs the red channel value of the color.

  G: Outputs the green channel value of the color.

  B: Outputs the blue channel value of the color.

  A: Outputs the alpha channel vector value of the color.

IMPORTANT NOTE

In order for the particle system to use the Sub UVs properly, you need to add a Sub UV Index Module to the particle emitter. Then add a curve to the distribution of this module to sample from the Sub UVs in the texture map.

Example Usage: Set the Texture of a **Particle SubUVs** to a texture map with Sub UVs. Use the output channel this expression to drive the opacity texture or the emissive color networks of a material. Connecting the result of these networks to the Emissive and Opacity channels of a material node will create particles that will use the Sub UVs of the input texture (see Figure 5.11).

CROSS-REFERENCE

To learn more about visual effects through Particle Systems and creating a Fire particle system checkout Tutorial 6.5 on page 337.

5.5 BLENDS

The Blends category defines all Material Expressions that are used to blend two colors or textures functions together. Each Blend expression has two inputs: the Base input, which is the original texture to be blended, and the Blend input, which is the texture that is to be combined with the original texture in a way denoted by the type of Material Expression used.[5]

Blend_ColorBurn: Blends the textures so that the darker the Blend color is, the more of that color will be used in the final result. If the Blend color is white, there will be no change.

Blend_ColorDodge: Lightens the result by inverting the Base input and dividing it by the Blend.

Blend_Darken: Chooses the darker value for each pixel from the Base and Blend colors. White does not produce a change.

Blend_Difference: Creates an inversion-style effect by subtracting the Base from the Blend and then outputting the absolute value of the result.

Blend_Exclusion: Halves both the Base and Blend textures, combines them, and does a partial inversion on the result.

Blend_HardLight: Either screens or multiplies the Base and Blend together. It does a comparison on the Blend color so that wherever the Blend is brighter than 50% gray, the Base and Blend will be combined via a URBBlend_Screen operation. If the Blend is darker than 50% gray, the Base will be multiplied by the Blend, as it is with the **Blend_Multiply** function.

Blend_Lighten: Compares each pixel of the Base and Blend colors and returns the brighter result.

Blend_LinearBurn: Adds the Base color to the Blend color and then subtracts 1 from the result.

Blend_LinearDodge: Adds the Base color to the Blend color.

Blend_LinearLight: A linear version of Blend_Overlay, providing harsher results.

Blend_OverLay: Either screens or multiplies the Base and Blend together.

Blend_PinLight: Either lightens or darkens the Base and Blend together.

Blend_Screen: Lightens the Base by the Blend color by inverting both colors, multiplying them together, and inverting the result.

---

[5] The contents of this section are adapted from the official UE4 online documentation found at: https://docs.unrealengine.com/latest/INT/.

Blend_SoftLight: A softer version of Blend_Overlay. Uses the same method, but softens the contrast so that the result is less harsh.

5.6 PHYSICALLY BASED MATERIALS IN UNREAL ENGINE 4

Unreal Engine 4 takes a very different approach in material rendering. In this model, the look of the material is achieved by approximating the interaction between the light and the material to create more accurate and natural behavior.

In previous versions of Unreal Engine, as well as many other graphics rendering engines, the effects of the light/material interactions are calculated by taking three light components, Diffuse, Specular, and Ambient to derive the equations that approximate the light/material interactions on the surface of the object.

In-depth and technical information about the physically based shading model in Unreal Engine 4 may be found in the 2013 SIGGRAPH course [55] presentation by Brian Karis [54]. In this shading model the Bidirectional Reflectance Distribution Function (BRDF) components are approximated in such a way as to utilize more natural input channels such as Color, Metallic, Roughness, etc., rather than Diffuse, Specular, and Ambient inputs. Moreover, this approach will enable us to design and utilize material layering in a much more efficient and simple manner without the need to create a complicated material network.

To utilize the physically based shading model in Unreal Engine 4 to create natural looking materials (and even non-realistic materials) you will make use of three basic channels as described above – i.e., the Base Color, Metallic, and Roughness. The Base Color defines the overall color of your material and is a Vector3 (a three-dimensional vector).

The Roughness controls how rough/coarse the material surface is, impacting how the light will scatter outwards from the incidence location. A smooth material reflects light more perfectly around the reflection vector, whereas a rough surface scatters the light along many directions around the reflection vector. The Metallic channel simulates how metal-like the surface of your material is. To simulate completely metallic surfaces you will use a value of 1 for this channel, while for complete non-metals you may use the value of 0. You may also use a value between 0 and 1 for a material that is hybrid.

In addition to these three channels, the physically based material in Unreal Engine 4 will also allow you to utilize the Specular channel as well. In most cases, we will not use this channel. However, you may find a Specular value between 0 and 1 to be useful to create a reasonable specular high-light for non-metallic surfaces (i.e., those in which the Metallic channel's value is set to 0). For very detailed normal maps this value will be useful to allow for the renderer to create small-scale shadowing, and is represented as a Cavity feature [54].

Physically-Based Shading Values for Natural Materials

As discussed above, Unreal Engine 4 utilizes this new shading model to simplify the material creation by approximating the BRDF more naturally. Below, some reference values are presented for natural materials for you to use on the official Unreal Engine Documentations [46].

- **Non-Metal Base Color Intensities**
  Charcoal: 0.02
  Fresh Asphalt: 0.02
  Worn Asphalt: 0.08
  Bare Soil: 0.13
  Green Grass: 0.21
  Desert Sand: 0.36
  Fresh Concrete: 0.51
  Ocean Ice: 0.56
  Fresh Snow: 0.81
- **Metal Base Color RGB Values**
  Iron: (0.560, 0.570, 0.580)
  Silver: (0.972, 0.960, 0.915)
  Aluminum: (0.913, 0.921, 0.925)
  Gold: (1.000, 0.766, 0.336)
  Copper: (0.955, 0.637, 0.538)
  Chromium: (0.550, 0.556, 0.554)
  Nickel: (0.660, 0.609, 0.526)
  Titanium: (0.542, 0.497, 0.449)
  Cobalt: (0.662, 0.655, 0.634)
  Platinum: (0.672, 0.637, 0.585)
- **Specular Values**
  Glass: 0.5
  Plastic: 0.5
  Quartz: 0.57
  Ice: 0.224
  Water: 0.225
  Milk: 0.277
  Skin: 0.35

5.7 MATERIAL FUNCTIONS IN UNREAL ENGINE 4

Material Functions[6] are snippets of material graphs that can be saved in packages and reused across multiple materials. They allow complex networks to be saved and quickly reused [38]. Best of all, edits to a single function are propagated throughout all networks which use it. So, if you need to make a fix or change how a function works, you will not have to make further edits to the many materials which may be using that function.

---

[6] The contents of this section are adapted from the official UE4 online documentation found at: https://docs.unrealengine.com/latest/INT/.

The benefit of utilizing material functions is the fact that you can combine a complex network into one channel. You can then drag and drop the material function asset into your material network graph in the **Material Editor** to use its attributes. You can also make a call to a material function by placing a `Material Function Call` on the graph in the **Material Editor**. Then you can assign a material function to the `Material Function Call` from its Details Panel, much like you assign a texture.

To create a material function, simply `Right-Click` on an empty area in the **Content Browser** and from the window that pops up choose `Materials & Textures` ▶ `Material Function` ■. There are several material function related expressions available for you to use. The lists below describe the frequently used material function expressions [37].

CROSS-REFERENCE

More details about the Material Expressions may be found in Appendix A.

FUNCTION INPUT

This expression can only be placed in a material function, where it defines one of the function's inputs.

- **Properties**
  Input Name: The input's name, which will be displayed on Material Function Call expressions that use the material function containing the input.
  Description: A description of the input, which will be displayed as a tooltip when the connector for this output on a Material Function Call expression is hovered over with the mouse.
  Input Type: The type of data this input expects. Data passed to this input will be cast to this type, throwing a compiler error if the cast fails because the data is not compatible.
  Preview Value: The value to use as a preview for this input when editing the material function containing it.
  Use Preview Value As Default: If `enabled`, the Preview Value will be used as the default value for this input if no data is passed in.
  Set Priority: Specifies the priority for this output to use when determining the order of the outputs to be displayed on a Material Function Call expression.

MATERIAL FUNCTION CALL

This expression allows you to use an external **Material Function** from another material or function. The external function's input and output nodes become inputs and outputs of the function call node. If a **Material Function** is selected in the

Content Browser when placing one of these expressions, it will automatically be assigned.

- **Properties**
  Material Function: Specifies the Material Function to be used.

Shortcut: To place this expression in the graph editor, hold the F key on your keyboard and left-click on the graph editor.

FUNCTION OUTPUT

This expression can only be placed in a material function, where it defines one of the function's outputs.

- **Properties**
  Output Name: The output's name, which will be displayed on Material Function Call expressions that use the material function containing the output.
  Description: A description of the output, which will be displayed as a tooltip when the connector for this output on a Material Function Call expression is hovered over with the mouse.
  Set Priority: Specifies the priority for this output to use when determining the order of the outputs to be displayed on a Material Function Call expression.

STATIC BOOL

This expression is used to provide a default bool value for a static bool function input within a function. This node does not switch between anything, so it must be used in conjunction with a StaticSwitch node.

- **Properties**
  Value: The value of the bool, True (checked) or False.

STATIC SWITCH

This expression works like a StaticSwitchParameter, except that it only implements the switch and does not create a parameter.

- **Properties**
  Default Value: The default boolean value of the parameter that determines which input is active, True (checked) or False.
- **Inputs**

True: The input that is used when the Value of the switch is `True`.
False: The input that is used when the Value of the switch is `False`.
Value: Takes in a **bool** value that determines which input is active.

TEXTURE OBJECT

This expression is used to provide a default texture for a texture function input within a function. This node does not actually sample the texture, so it must be used in conjunction with a **Texture Sample** expression.

- **Properties**
  Texture: The texture from the Content Browser that will be applied to this node.
  Sampler Type: The type of data that will be output from the node.

5.8   MATERIAL ATTRIBUTES EXPRESSIONS

Material Attribute expressions[7] are ideal for use in Layered Materials [34]. There are two such expressions as of the release of Unreal Engine 4.6. The **Break Material Attributes** and the **Make Material Attributes** expressions.

BREAK MATERIAL ATTRIBUTES

The **Break Material Attributes** expression is ideal when using a Layered Material – a feature of the Material Functions system. When using a Material Layer Function within a Material, you may want to use only one aspect of the layer. For example, you may have a Material Layer that defines a nice looking generic Material, such as steel.

You may want to use only the Roughness and Base Color attributes from that layer in your final Material, rather than using the whole thing. In such cases, you can use a Break Material Attributes node to split up all of the incoming attributes of the Material Layer, and then just plug in the ones you want. This also allows for complex blending of various Material Attributes.

MAKE MATERIAL ATTRIBUTES

The **Make Material Attributes** node does exactly the opposite of the Break Material Attributes node. Instead of splitting attributes apart, this brings them together. This is useful when creating your own Material Layer functions, as you will have access to all of the standard attributes for your output. This can also be used for

---

[7] The contents of this section are adapted from the official UE4 online documentation found at: `https://docs.unrealengine.com/latest/INT/`.

complex Material setups in which you want to define more than one type of Material and blend them together, all within one Material.

NOTE

In order to have access to a `Material Attributes` channel of a material to connect to a **Make Material Attributes** expression, make sure that the **Use Material Attributes** checkbox is set to *true* in the **Details** rollout of the Material.

5.9   LAYERED MATERIALS

With the availability of Material Functions, and Material Attribute Expressions in Unreal Engine 4, a brand new feature has been made possible. This feature is called **Layered Materials**. In the following, a quick overview of Layered Materials is adapted from the Unreal Engine 4 official documentations [32].

Layered materials are essentially an extension of Material Functions. We can use material functions to implement complex mathematical calculations that may be encapsulated within the function and then reused when needed. Therefore, you may define all of the features of an entire material within a material function. For example, you can implement the networks that drive the `Base Color`, `Metallic`, `Opacity`, `Normal`, and other features of a material entirely within one material function.

Combining the capability of material functions in encompassing your material channels' networks with the **Make Attribute** and **Break Attribute** expressions, you can combine all of the material channels' networks into one output material. As a result, Unreal Engine 4's **Material Layer Blend** functions allow us to combine multiple materials (as defined within their own respective material functions) together to create a multilayer material.

The key benefit of creating multilayer materials (also called Layered Materials) in Unreal Engine 4 is the fact that Layered Materials allow for modular creation of your materials which would otherwise require complicated networks to achieve the same result. Moreover, this feature will effectively simulate natural multi material objects and will allow for more intuitive design of your materials.

For example, if you have a chair with multiple materials on it, you can create each of those materials and use the `Make Attribute` expression to encapsulate each of these materials within their respective material function. You can then use the **Material Layer Blend** in your final Layered Material's graph to blend each of its individual materials into one final material.

Figure 5.12 shows an example of a material that is designed based on two independently created materials, a Rock material and a Brick Material. Each of the original materials, the rock and the brick, have been independently created and made into a material function, e.g., `RockMatFunction` and `BrickMaterialFunction` shown in Figure 5.12. The two material functions are then used as the inputs to the `Base` and `Top` material layers in the `MatLayerBlend_Standard` expression. The `Alpha` channel of the blend expression is connected to a checkerboard texture that ranges between 0 and 1 to blend between the two layers. The `Blended Material` output of the blend expression is a **Material Attribute**. It is connected to the `Material Attribute` channel of the final material.

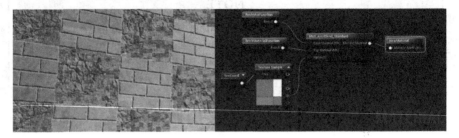

FIGURE 5.12: Layered Materials.

NOTE

In order to use the `Material Attribute` channel of the material node, check the box **Use Material Attribute** in the material node's Details Panel.

5.9.1 MATERIAL LAYER BLEND TYPES

The **Material Layer Blend**[8] expressions are quite diverse and each represents a specific blend type. The material layer blend types allow you to control the way you wish the material layers to be blended with each other, such as overriding specific material features. The list below is adapted from the Unreal Engine 4's official documentation [32].

MatLayerBlend_AO: Blends an ambient occlusion (AO) map over the surface to remove reflection.

MatLayerBlend_BaseColorOverride: Allows the Base Color to be replaced.

MatLayerBlend_BreakBaseColor: Outputs the Base Color from an incoming Material Layer.

MatLayerBlend_BreakNormal: Outputs the Normal from an incoming Material Layer.

---

[8] The contents of this section are adapted from the official UE4 online documentation found at: https://docs.unrealengine.com/latest/INT/.

MatLayerBlend_Decal: Blends a decal sheet over the Material using the 2nd UV channel.

MatLayerBlend_Decal_UV3: Blends a decal sheet over the Material Layer using the 2nd UV channel.

MatLayerBlend_Emissive: Blends an Emissive texture over the Material Layer.

MatLayerBlend_GlobalNormal: Blends a Normal texture over the Material Layer.

MatLayerBlend_LightmassReplace: Replaces the Base Color in Lightmass, allowing for changes to indirect lighting results.

MatLayerBlend_ModulateRoughness: Multiplies the Material Layer's Roughness by an incoming texture. Useful for a "greasy" look.

MatLayerBlend_NormalBlend: Blends a Normal texture across the surface, but by way of a mask texture, allowing for control of where the normal will appear.

MatLayerBlend_NormalFlatten: Diminishes the effect of the Normal map.

MatLayerBlend_RoughnessOverride: Replaces the Roughness texture of a Material Layer.

MatLayerBlend_Simple: Provides a simple linear interpolation (Lerp) blending solution for 2 Material Layers. Does not blend Normal; instead, retains Normal of the Base Material.

MatLayerBlend_Stain: Blends the Top Material over the Base Material as a stain, meaning that only the Base Color and Roughness values from the Top Material are used.

MatLayerBlend_Standard: Blends all attributes of two Material Layers.

MatLayerBlend_Tint: Allows for tinting of a Material Layer by inputting a tint color and a mask to control the tint's location. Useful for making partial color changes.

MatLayerBlend_TintAllChannels: Similar to Tint, but also affects Specular. This is a very special case function; generally, you will not need it.

MatLayerBlend_TopNormal: Blends all attributes of both Materials but only uses the Normal of the Top Material.

5.10 MATERIAL INSTANCES AND DYNAMIC MATERIAL MODIFICATIONS

Instanced Materials refer to materials in which specific features are represented as parameters in the base material. These parameters are in turn available within the **Material Instance Editor** for editing without the need to recompile the base material. This is a very important feature for in-game and dynamic modification of the instanced materials. This ability to change instanced materials allows for modifying the material while in gameplay in response to in-game events.

In order to instance a material and change its properties in the instanced materials, you need to represent such features as parameters. A **Material Parameter** expression, as we discussed earlier in this chapter is a data node that contains the default values given to it in the **Material Editor**. However, you may refer to the parameter in-game, at level design, or in the **Material Instance Editor** by the parameter's name.

Unreal Engine 4 allows for two types of material instances, Constant and Dynamic. A Constant material instance is calculated once, prior to the gameplay. You may not change its parameters' values in-game. Although these types of material instances are fixed and cannot be modified in-game, they still give you the performance advantage since they do not require compilation.

A Dynamic material instance (Material Instance Dynamic–MID) is a material instance which can be changed in-game at runtime. Therefore, you will be able to create a blueprint script or C++ code to make changes to its parameters' values. For example, you can create a Material Instance Dynamic in blueprint scripts by using a `Create Dynamic Material Instance` blueprint expression. You can then use the `Set <...> Parameter Value` expressions to make changes to the Material Instance parameters.

5.11 DECALS

Unreal Engine 4 allows you to define your material domains when you create the material in the **Material Editor**. **Deferred Decal** blend mode is one of the four available blend modes along with `Surface`, `Light Function`, and `Post Process`.

5.11.1 DECAL BLEND MODE

As the name suggests, this defines the Blend Mode that will be used when the Material Domain property is set to Deferred Decal and cannot be changed until the Material Domain is set accordingly. It contains different Blend Modes than those available to surfaces. Table 5.1 shows a description of different **Decal Blend Modes** available.

Deferred decals offer better performance since they write and work with the **GBuffer** instead of calculating the lighting [11]. This has the benefit of increased performance in the presence of multiple light sources as well as the ability to manipulate a screen space mask to create otherwise complicated effects, such as liquid stains, etc.

TABLE 5.1

Description of Decal Blend Modes in Unreal Engine 4 [11].

Mode	Description
Translucent	This will cause the decal to blend Base Color, Metallic, Specular, Roughness, Emissive color, Opacity, and Normal. With this you can blend in an entirely separate material, such as a wavy water puddle, complete with normal map-based muddy building around it.
Stain	Only blends Base Color and Opacity. Useful for decals that only change color, such as dry spray paint on a wall.
Normal	Only blends Normal and Opacity. This is useful for adding cracks to a surface.
Emissive	Only blends the Emissive and Opacity channels. Nice for making things glow that did not originally.
DBuffer_[Channel]	These allow you control over individual channels.

5.12 POST PROCESS MATERIALS

Post process materials are a by-product of the composition graph and may be created and assigned to the **Post Process Volume** to create interesting features. However, they should be used sparingly as many of the features such as bloom, depth of field, etc., are already implemented within the **Post Process Volume** efficiently.

5.13 REFRACTION AND REFLECTION

TABLE 5.2

Common Indices of Refraction

Material	Air	Ice	Water	Glass	Diamond	Silicon
Refraction Index	1.0	1.31	1.33	1.52	2.42	3.48

Table 5.2 shows a list of common solids and liquids with their refraction indices. In optics the index of refraction is a number that describes how the light propagates through a translucent object. This value in its simplest form is dependent on the ratio between the speed of light in vacuum c and the speed of light as it passes through the material v:

$$n = \frac{c}{v} \tag{5.1}$$

Figure 5.13 shows what happens to the direction of a light ray when it passes from a medium with refractive index of n_1 and enters another medium with refractive index of n_2. Let θ_i be the **Angle of Incidence**, θ_r is the **Angle of Refraction**, and n_1 and n_2 be the two medium's **Refractive Indices**, respectively, then:

$$n_1 \times \sin(\theta_i) = n_2 \times \sin(\theta_r) \tag{5.2}$$

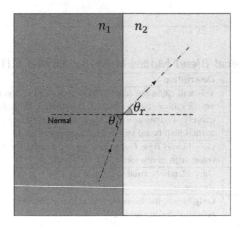

FIGURE 5.13: Refraction of light rays passing from a Mediums with Refractive Index n_1 through a medium with a Refractive Index of n_2.

5.14 SUMMARY

In this chapter, some of the more advanced material concepts were covered. These concepts are quite useful to enhance the realism of materials developed by the Unreal Engine 4. We covered the shading models available in Unreal Engine that help you design glowing materials, subsurface scattering effects, and multilayered materials.

We deviated from our ordinary coverage of the Unreal Engine 4 in this chapter, in that we didn't directly go through step-by-step tutorials. By this time, especially after covering the materials in depth, you should be able to extrapolate steps required to build advanced material concepts into the materials we designed in Chapter 4– Materials in Unreal Engine.

6 Visual Effects and Cascade in Unreal Engine

6.1 INTRODUCTION TO VISUAL EFFECTS AND PARTICLE SYSTEMS TERMINOLOGIES

IN Unreal Engine 4, a special engine component, called the Cascade Particle System Editor, is responsible for producing and simulating particle systems. At the very basic form, particles can be thought of as points in the 3D space with certain properties that govern their interactions with one another and the world surrounding them. The Cascade Particle System Editor allows level designers to control and set the particle system up and define all aspects of its governing rules, such as the shape of each particle, spawn rates, colors, lighting interactions, to name a few.

Before delving into the Cascade Particle System Editor and utilizing it to develop amazing visual effects, we will first cover fundamental terminologies and the taxonomy of the particle systems in Unreal Engine 4. Understanding these terminologies will help us get a fundamental grasp of the anatomy of particle systems in Unreal Technology.

6.2 ANATOMY OF VISUAL EFFECTS

In order for impressive visual effects to work in real-time we need to establish a system comprising several components. At the very least, we need a Particle Emitter, Particle Data Modules, Particle Material and Rendering System, and the Particles. In this section we will get an introduction to each of the important components in Unreal Engine 4's Particle and Visual Effects system.

6.2.1 PARTICLES

Let's first start with the particles themselves. A particle is basically a point in space whose initial and lifetime attributes include, but are not limited to, its location, color, geometry, etc. These attributes can be governed and controlled by a particle system. Unreal Engine uses such particle systems to calculate the spawning of each individual particle in the map to generate visual effects, such as clouds and dust, fire and sparks, and many more fantastic effects. It is very important for level designers and programmers to think about the effect they are trying to achieve in terms of each individual particle, and the way these particles interact with the world to achieve the best effect with the least computational expenditures imposed on the CPU or GPU to generate the effect.

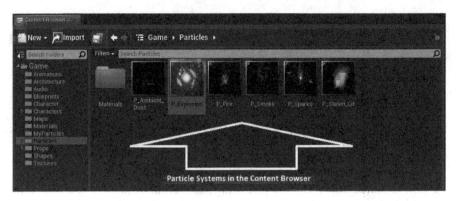

FIGURE 6.1: Particle Systems reside in, and can be accessed from, the content browser.

6.2.2   PARTICLE SYSTEM

The Particle System is the asset that resides in the level. This is the asset that level designers create to define the particle effect and all the rules that govern this effect. Figure 6.1 shows a view of the content browser and a few particle systems within it. Double clicking on a particle system will open it in the Unreal's Cascade Particle System Editor.

6.2.3   EMITTER ACTOR

This is the actor, or the object that resides in the map (the scene). The Emitter Actor holds the reference to your particle system and is responsible for emitting the particles that are governed under the rules of the Particle System it references. Figure 6.2 shows an emitter actor placed in the map, generating the bullet-like particles.

6.2.4   EMITTER

An Emitter is within the Cascade Particle System Editor. This term refers to the individual effect which Cascade utilizes to define the Particle System. It is important to note that a single visual effect may be defined by a number of individual emitters. For example, an explosion effect could be defined by several emitters within Cascade, one for the smoke effect, one for the lighting of the explosion, one for the pieces of shrapnel thrown out by the explosion, and so on. Figure 6.3 shows an example of a visual effect particle system made of five individual Emitters. Each individual Emitter controls one aspect of the particle system.

6.2.5   MODULE

A module is the component of an emitter that controls and defines a single aspect of the emitter. For example, if we want to control the initial color of each particle that is spawned by the particle system, we can use the **Initial Color** module of the emitter.

FIGURE 6.2: Particles are generated by a Particle System. An Emitter Actor is the actor placed in the map responsible for generating particles.

In Figure 6.3, rectangular sections under each emitter are the emitter's modules. The **Required** module and the **Spawn** module are present in all emitters and cannot be removed from the emitter (notice the different colors of these modules in Figure 6.3). All other modules may be added, removed, copied, or moved between emitters as necessary.

Module Categories

The many modules that can be added to an emitter are broken up into categories to clarify their contribution to the effect. Table 6.1 presents a description of the module categories available as of the release of Unreal Engine 4.3 [45].

Type Data Modules

This is a special kind of module, i.e., only one of this kind of module is allowed per emitter. Level designers can utilize this module to create a specialized emitter. These modules include **AnimTrail, GPU Sprite, Beam, Mesh,** and **Ribbon** type data which will specialize the emitter. We will cover these items later on in this chapter.

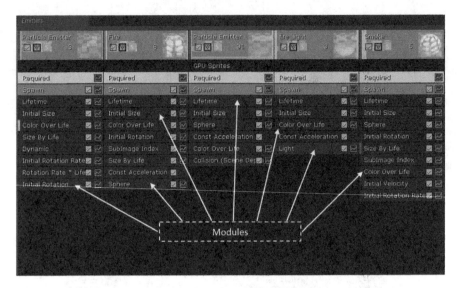

FIGURE 6.3: Emitters in the Cascade Particle System Editor. Notice that the effect is created by 5 individual emitters. Each emitter is composed of several modules that control every aspect of its rules.

6.2.6 PARTICLE SYSTEM COMPONENT

A Particle System Component is a blueprint system that instigates a Particle System. This is the fundamental component that uses a Particle System as the template of the system that it programmatically utilizes.

6.2.7 DISTRIBUTIONS

Distributions are a very important component of the unreal engine by which the engine determines a way that a value, either a scalar value or a vector value, changes over time. Appendix B covers this topic in great detail.

6.3 UNREAL CASCADE PARTICLE SYSTEM EDITOR

Figure 6.4 shows a snapshot of the Cascade Particle System Editor with the Cascade toolbar shown at the top of the figure. The following describes these important tools:

Restart Sim: This item allows you to restart simulations of the effect in the Cascade Viewport.

Restart Level: This item is used to make the effect changes applied to the Emitter Actor in the map.

Thumbnail: This tool allows you to capture a snapshot of the simulated effect to use as the thumbnail icon image for the Particle System in the Content Browser.

TABLE 6.1

Description of Module Categories in Cascade [45].

Category	Description
Acceleration	Modules governing how particle acceleration may be affected by forces.
Attraction	Modules which attract particles to various points in space.
Camera	Modules controlling how to move particles in camera space, allowing the user to make them seem closer or farther away from the camera.
Collision	Modules controlling how collisions between particles and geometry are handled.
Color	Modules which affect the color of particles.
Event	Modules which control the triggering of particle events, which can in turn cause a variety of in-game responses.
Kill	Modules governing particle deletion.
Lifetime	Modules which control how long particles should live.
Light	Modules governing particle lights.
Location	Modules controlling particle spawn locations relative to the emitter Actor location.
Material	Modules which control the material applied to the particles themselves.
Orbit	Modules which allow for screen-space orbital behavior.
Orientation	Modules that allow for a rotational axis of the particles to be locked.
Parameter	Modules which can be parameterized and controlled via external sources.
Rotation	Modules that control the rotation of particles.
RotationRate	Modules governing changes in rotation speed, such as spin.
Size	Modules controlling the scale of particles.
Spawn	Modules for adding specialized particle spawn rates.
SubUV	Modules which allow for animated sprite sheets to be displayed on a particle.
Velocity	Modules which control the velocity of each particle.

Boundaries: This tool toggles the effect boundaries in the viewport.

Origin Axis: This tool toggles the axis on/off in the simulation viewport.

LOD Tools: These tools are used to create, modify, and interact with Levels of Detail (LOD) for the particle effect. LODs are used to modify different complexities associated with the effect when viewed at different distances, for example.

Figure 6.4-(A) shows Cascade Viewport showing a preview of the overall effect. Figure 6.4-(B) shows the emitters section of the Cascade Editor. Properties of an emitter's selected module are shown in Figure 6.4-(C) while Figure 6.4-(D) shows the curve editor of the selected item within the module's properties section.

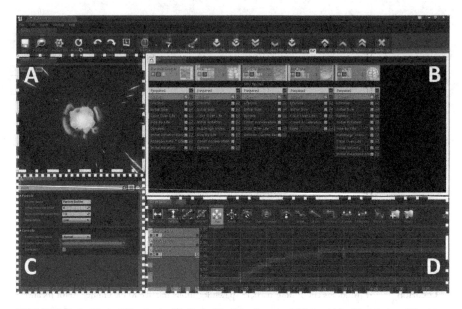

FIGURE 6.4: Unreal Engine's Cascade Particle System Editor. (A)- Simulation Viewport. (B)- Emitters List. (C)- Details Panel. (D)- Curve Editor.

6.3.1 SIMULATION VIEWPORT

Figure 6.5(a) shows a view of the Cascade editor. A simulation of the effect created by the engine can be previewed in this window. The preview allows the designer to see a closeup of the effect. Several options are available under the **View** tab.

    View Overlays allows you to see the **Particle Count, Particle Event Count**, as well as **Particle Times**, and **Particle Memory**. The **View Modes** allow you to choose between several options to view the effect, including **Wireframe, Unlit, Lit**, and **Shadow Complexity**.

    There are additional toggles available under the **View** tab to interact with the particle effect. One of the most useful options is the **Motion** checkbox. Checking this box moves the effect on a circular path whose radius may be changed by clicking on the **Motion Radius**.

6.3.2 EMITTERS LIST

Figure 6.4-(B) shows the list of all Emitters that contribute to the final effect generated by the particle system. By right-clicking in the black area in the Emitters list panel, you can add a new sprite emitter to the effect. Each emitter will occupy its own column in this panel.

    In order to interact with the emitters in the list you can right-click on the name of the emitters and choose from the options that appear in the pop-up menu, such as renaming, deleting, duplicating, or adding modules to the emitter (see Figure 6.5(b)).

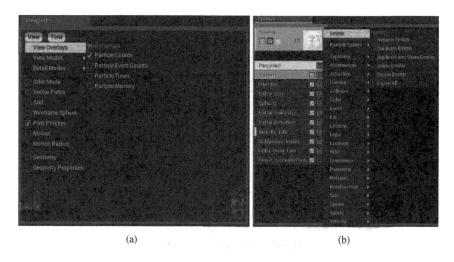

(a)   (b)

FIGURE 6.5: (a) The Simulation Viewport. (b) Interacting with Emitters.

6.3.3 DETAILS PANEL

Details about the properties of the particle system, and/or any emitter module selected within the emitters list appears under this panel. It is important to note that if
a module is selected, its properties will appear in the details panel.

However, to see the general properties of the entire particle system, you should
left-click on the blank area of the emitters list to de-select modules. This will change
the details panel to show the properties of the particle system itself (see Figure 6.6).

6.3.4 CURVE EDITOR

This section of the Cascade, shown in Figure 6.4-(D), gives you the ability to modify
the graph data governing the selected modules. You can add points on the curves.
The curve editor is covered in depth in Appendix C.

6.4 PARTICLE SPECIFIC MATERIALS SETUP

One of the first tasks in setting up a particle system is to establish its materials. In the
Required module of each emitter in the particle system, there is a section to assign
to the emitter its material.

In order to create a particle specific material you just simply create a material
and open it in the **Material Editor**. Once your material is open in the **Material
Editor** you will have to change its **Blend Mode** and **Shading Model** modes. You
should not use opaque material as particle materials. Therefore, the first thing to do
to create a particle specific material is to change its **Blend Mode** to **Translucent**.
This will allow the Cascade Particle Editor to manage the opacity of each particle
through **Alpha** values in color modules.

FIGURE 6.6: The Details Panel.

The particle specific materials must also have their **Shading Model** to be assigned as **Unlit**. Doing so will allow us to use the **Particle Color** expression to create a link between the particle material and its emitter. The network that creates the color of each particle will then be supplied to the `Emissive Color` channel. Similarly, the network that works on the `Alpha` channel of the **Particle Color** expression will supply the `Opacity` channel of the material node.

6.4.1 PARTICLE EXPRESSIONS

These expressions act as a bridge between the Material Editor and Cascade Particle System Editor [43]. This link allows for a dynamic interaction between material components and those of per-particle based particle systems. Expressions in this category include Particle Color, Particle Direction, Particle Radius, Particle Size, Dynamic Parameter, Particle MacroUV, and so on. A comprehensive reference to particle material expressions is presented in Appendix A.

CROSS-REFERENCE

To learn more about the Particle Expressions and their use in conjunction with particle emitters check out Section 5.4 of Chapter 5 (Advanced Materials).

6.5 CPU-BASED SPRITE EMITTERS

Perhaps one of the most basic Particle Emitters is one that uses a specific set of materials to generate sprites as particles. Then, based on certain rules that govern the spawning, location, velocity, color, and other aspects of these sprites, the particle emitter produces and emits these sprites.

At its core, a sprite is a 2-dimensional image that is always oriented to directly face the camera. Therefore, these sprites that a sprite emitter generates are going to be visible by the player, no matter where from he/she is looking at the particles.

> To find updates to this tutorial and updated instructions about its implementation on other UE4 versions please visit the book's companion website at: http://www.RVRLAB.com/UE4Book/

TUTORIAL 6.1 Creating a Project and Migrating Contents

FIGURE 6.7: Creating a Blank Project for Particle Tutorials.

CREATE A BLANK PROJECT

In this tutorial we will set up an empty project and migrate the contents of the **Demo Room** from the Unreal Engine's **Example Contents** project into it. The first thing to do is to create a project to which we will add the **Demo Room**. Launch the Unreal Editor and create a **Blank** project. Give your project a name such as "MyParticleEffectsProject." Select the **Include starter content** to have access to starter contents (see Figure 6.7).

1. Open the Unreal Launcher and select the version of the engine you would like to work with.
2. Once the Unreal Launcher Opens, choose **New Project** (see Figure 6.7).
3. Select the **Blueprint** as your project type, and make sure that **Blank** is selected.
4. Select your platform (Desktop/Console) and your graphics quality.
5. Make sure you include the starter content (see Figure 6.7).
6. Give your project a name and click **Create Project**.

After you create this blank project, you will close the project and open the `Content Examples` projects. There is a folder in this project that contains the contents of a **Demo Room**.

MIGRATING CONTENT FROM UNREAL PROJECTS

In this section we will migrate the **Demo Room** contents from the **Content Example** project into our own project to be able to set up a nice environment to visualize the effects we create.

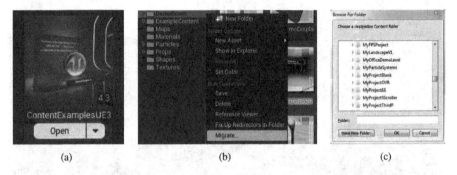

    (a)   (b)   (c)

FIGURE 6.8: (a) Opening the Content Examples. (b) Migrating the Demo Room. (c) Choosing the destination for Demo Room in our MyParticleEffectsProject project.

7. If you haven't downloaded the **Content Examples** from the Unreal Marketplace, use the Unreal Engine Launcher to download the Content Examples. This item comes with your Unreal Engine 4 subscription and contains several useful maps and examples for you to explore and use in your projects free of charge.
8. Open the **Content Examples** project from the Unreal Engine Launcher (Figure 6.8(a)).
9. In the Content Browser of the **Content Examples** project, right-click on the Demo Room Folder, and choose **Migrate** (Figure 6.8(b)).
10. The `Asset Report` window pops open, informing you which assets within the Demo Room folder will be exported to a new location. These assets include, Textures, Blueprints, Materials, Meshes, etc. Select **OK** to proceed.

11. From the windows explorer window that opens, navigate to the location of the "MyParticleEffectsProject" project you created earlier in this tutorial (Figure 6.8(c)). Select the `Content` subfolder of your project. Depending on how your Unreal Engine is set up, this location should be in `My Documents/Unreal Projects/MyMaterialsProject/Content` folder.

12. This will migrate the assets for a demo room into your blank project. We will use these assets to create our own effects.

13. Close the Contents Example project.

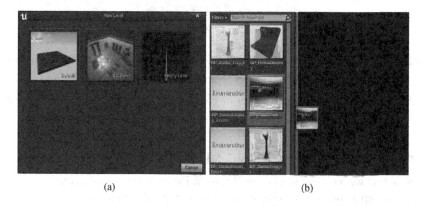

(a)   (b)

FIGURE 6.9: (a) Creating an Empty Level. (b) Adding the Demo Room to the Level.

SETTING UP YOUR DEMO ROOM

Now we will add a new map to our project to host a display room.

14. Open up the project you created earlier on page 297 (earlier, I called this project "MyParticleEffectsProject").

15. `Double-Click` on the **Game** folder to select it.

16. Now, let's add a new empty level to this project. Click on **File ▶ New Level** and choose `Empty Level` (Figure 6.9(a)).

17. Go to the **DemoRoom/BluePrint** folder by double clicking on **DemoRoom** folder and then on **BluePrint** folder.

18. Drag the **BP_DemoRoom** blueprint into your level (Figure 6.9(b)).

19. Wait for the Unreal Engine to compile the shaders and build the materials.

20. Click on **Build** from the Unreal toolbar to build the lighting (this may take a few minutes depending on your machine).

21. Now that you have the **Demo Room** created, you can explore its options. We will be using this room throughout this book to deploy the contents and materials we create.

22. Table 6.2 explains how each room property value affects the **Demo Room**. Take your time to play with different settings to get familiar with the room.

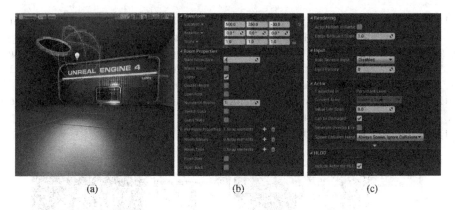

FIGURE 6.10: (a) Demo Room. (b) Demo Room Properties. (c) Additional Room Properties.

23. Save your level in the **Maps** folder of your Unreal project and give it a name such as `DisplayRoomLevel`.

OVERVIEW AND SETTING UP A DISPLAY

Now that we have our level created and the Demo Room added to our level, we will set up a couple of display items to showcase our creations.

CROSS-REFERENCE

To learn about Blueprints in UE4 checkout Chapter 3– Visual Scripting with Blueprints, and Chapter 8– Advanced Blueprint Concepts.

Just like the **Demo Room** object, the **Display Item** is a `Blueprint`. This means that this object is a class with meshes, components, and other properties, as well as functionalities that can be utilized to configure it and to make it interact with the world and players. Blueprints are very important components of the Unreal Engine 4. In fact, the concept of Blueprints is the major item introduced with the release of the Unreal Engine 4.

To create a display item, perform the following steps:

24. Now that we have the demo room set up, let's add a display. Navigate to the `BluePrint` folder of the `DemoRoom` folder of your project. Locate the **BP_DemoDisplay** blueprint into the demo room (Figure 6.11(a)).

25. From the Properties of the Demo Display make the following changes:

Number: `1-P`.
Description: `Basic Particles ...`
Type: `Round`

26. Save your progress.

TABLE 6.2

Description of Basic Properties of the Demo Room Template.

Room Property	Type	Description
Room Size	Integer	Defines the number of sections in the room
Mirror Room	Boolean	If checked, mirrors the room along the cross section
Lights	Boolean	If unchecked, removes all lights from the room
Double Height	Boolean	If checked, increases the height of the room
Open Roof	Boolean	If unchecked, removes the roof from the room
Number of Rooms	Integer	Specifies the number of rooms in the environment
Switch Color	Boolean	Changes the room color template
Glass Walls	Boolean	Toggles the glass walls on and off
Front Door	Boolean	If checked, places a door mesh at the front of the room
Open Back	Boolean	If unchecked, removes the back wall of the room
Room Names	Element Array	You can add names to the room by pressing the (+) sign
Room Type†	Standard	This option is the standard room option
	Roof with Hole	This option places a vent hole at the section of roof
	Open Roof	This option removes the roof from the section of room

†: Pressing the (+) icon allows you to add Room Types to each section of the room. For example, for a room with size 4, you may press the (+) icon four times, and assign different room types to each section.

ADDING INTERACTIONS TO THE DEMO ROOM LEVEL

Now that we have the Display Item added, let's add a **Player Start** actor to the level. This is an Unreal Actor which makes the player initiate at its location whenever the level is run, e.g., when you press the **Play** button on the Unreal Editor toolbar or launch the game.

27. In the search box of the **Modes** panel (Figure 6.12(a)) type `Player Start`. This will search for the Player Start actor from the Unreal Engine classes. Note that this search is context-sensitive and after typing a few letters it will refine the search filters to narrow down the selections.
28. Drag a copy of the **Player Start** actor to create a `Player Start` object in the level (Figure 6.12(a)).
29. Use the **Move** and **Rotate** gizmos to place and orient the **Player Start** actor in front of the Display Item (Figure 6.12(b)). Notice that the blue arrow coming out of the Player Start actor is the direction the player will face when the game starts.
30. Now, you should still be in the `Blueprints` folder of the `Demo Room` in the content browser. Drag a copy of `BP_DemoTrigger` class in the level and place it between the **Player Start** actor and the **Demo Display** item (Figure 6.12(c)).
31. From the Properties of the Demo Display make the following change: the Display Item to a `Square-L` shape:

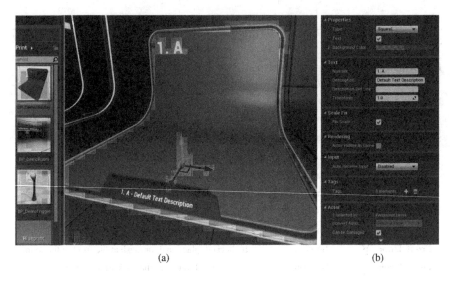

(a)　　　　　　　　　　　　　　　　(b)

FIGURE 6.11: Adding a Demo Display Item to the Demo Room in the Map. (a) The Demo Display Item. (b) The Display Properties.

> **Number:** P.1
> **Description:** Sprite Emitter...
> **Type: Square-L**

32. **Ready for Your Reward?** Go ahead! Play the level and see what getting close to, and walking away from, the **Demo Trigger** item does. It's not really fancy, but it should hopefully help you want to learn more about this engine.
33. Save your project and all the levels.

What Happened in TUTORIAL 6.1...

You just set up a blank project, migrated the **Demo Room** contents from the Unreal Engine's **Content Examples**, and added a demo room to a new game map you created.

Once the Demo Room blueprint is added to the scene, we populated it with Demo Trigger actors and a Player Start actor. The Player Start actor will ensure that the player will spawn at a specific location and be oriented in a specific direction every time the game starts.

The Demo Trigger is a Blueprint object which contains interactions. It has a sphere of intersection which will trigger events if players collision bounds overlap with it. By default, if a player is overlapping the trigger collision sphere, it

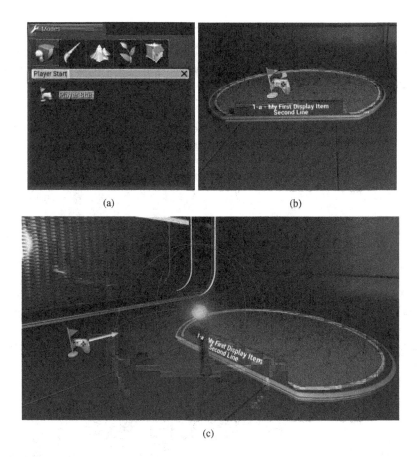

FIGURE 6.12: (a) Search for Player Start. (b) Actor Placed. (c). Place Demo Trigger.

will toggle its button's material to a red material. Once the player steps away from the trigger so that their collision boundaries are not overlapping, the trigger button material toggles back to a green material.

Now that your demo room is set up, it's time to start our journey into the UE4 particle system. We will next create our first particle system, a sprite emitter, to get some hands-on experience with CASCADE and particle effects in UE4.

To find updates to this tutorial and updated instructions about its implementation on other UE4 versions please visit the book's companion website at: http://www.RVRLAB.com/UE4Book/

TUTORIAL 6.2 Your First Particle System

In this tutorial we will set up our first particle system. The first thing to do is to create a project to which we add the particle system. The initial setup of this tutorial should resemble the image shown in Figure 6.13.

> **NOTE**
>
> We will need the demo room to be set up before we can proceed with the rest of the tutorial. You may find instructions to set up your demo room in Tutorial 6.1 on page 297.

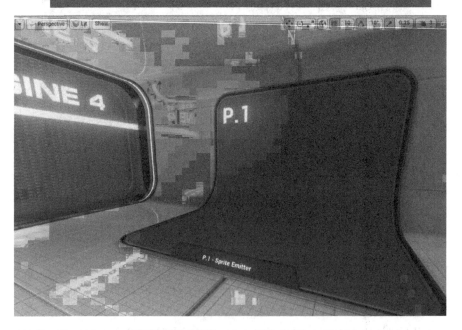

FIGURE 6.13: Room and Display Setup.

SETTING UP THE LEVEL

To have a uniform level that we can work with, you may perform one of the following options to start the work:

1. If you haven't created the demo room, perform the tasks in Tutorial 6.1 on page 297 to create a project which includes a **Demo Room**, a **Player Start**, and a **Demo Display** item as shown in Figure 6.13.

ORGANIZING ASSETS

Now that we have our level available, we will organize the particle systems we create in the content browser.

2. In the content browser, create a folder called **MyParticles**.
3. Double-Click the **My Particles** folder you just created, and create a folder within it called **Sprites**. This is the folder where we will put the sprite emitter we are going to create.
4. In the **Sprites** folder you just created, create a new material and call it **Mat_Sparks**.
5. In the **Sprites** folder you just created, create a new particle system and call it **P_Sparks**.

CREATING SPRITES' MATERIAL

6. The first step in creating this material is to set up its shading and basic properties. We would like the material to look like what is shown in Figure 6.14(a). To do so, double click on the **Mat_Sparks** material to open it up in the Unreal Material Editor. Set the following properties:

Blend Mode	Translucent
Shading Model	Unlit

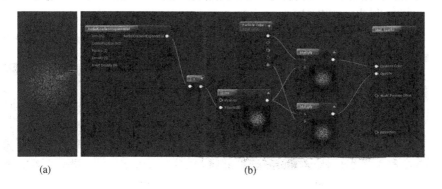

(a)   (b)

FIGURE 6.14: (a) Sprite Emitter Material Look. (b) Sprite Emitter Material Network.

7. To create a material network like the one shown in Figure 6.14(b) perform the following tasks:
   a. Right-click to the left of the material expression and type **Radial Gradient** to place a **Radial Gradient Exponential** expression.
   b. Place a **1-x** expression by holding the letter **O** key and clicking somewhere to the right of the Radial Gradient Expression. Connect the output of the Radial Gradient expression to the input of **1-x**.
   c. Place a **Noise** expression to the right of **1-x** expression. Connect the output of **1-x** to the **FilterWidth** input of the **Noise** expression.
   d. Place a **Particle Color** node above the **Noise** expression.
   e. Create two **Multiply** expressions to the right of both the **Noise** and **Particle Color** nodes.

   f. Connect the output of the **Noise** expression to the B input of both **Multiply** expressions.

   g. Connect the A input of one of the **Multiply** expressions to the color output of the **Particle Color** expression (its topmost node). Connect the output of this **Multiply** expression to the **Emissive Color** channel of the **Material** Expression.

   h. Connect the A input of the remaining **Multiply** expression to the alpha output of the **Particle Color** expression (its bottommost node). Connect the output of this **Multiply** expression to the **Opacity** channel of the **Material** Expression.

8. Your material is now set up. Save the Mat_Sparks material and close the Unreal Material Editor.

SETTING UP THE SPRITE EMITTER

Double-click on the **P_Sparks** particle system you created in the last section to open it in Cascade Particle Editor.

9. In the Emitters panel of the Cascade Editor, remove all modules from your Particle Emitter. Only the **Required** and the **Spawn** should be left (Figure 6.15(a)). We will build this emitter as we go on.

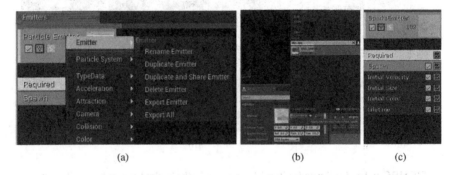

(a)   (b)   (c)

FIGURE 6.15: (a) Sprite Emitter Required Modules and Renaming the Sprite Emitter. (b) Applying a Material to the Emitter. (c) Additional Modules Added to the Emitter.

10. Right-click on the name of the emitter in the **Emitters** panel, choose **Emitter** and then **Rename Emitter**. Type in **SparksEmitter** in the name textbox and press enter.

11. Now we are going to apply our **Mat_Sparks** we created in the previous section to our emitter. Click on the **Required** module of the emitter, in the Emitter Panel (Figure 6.15(b)) click on the drop-down list next to **Material** and type in Mat_Sparks (or any name you gave your particle material in the previous step). Once you have found the material, click on it to assign it to the emitter. Alternatively, you can drag and drop the material from Content Browser to the material section of the Emitter panel. You shouldn't see any difference at this stage.

12. To be able to have a visible effect we need to set up at least three Initial Modules and a Lifetime Module. Right-click in the gray area under the SparksEmitter and select to add the following modules to your emitter (Figure 6.15(c)):

   a. **Color ► Initial Color**: Expand `Start Color` and `Distribution` properties and use values from Figure 6.16(a).
   b. **Size ► Initial Size**: Expand `Start Size` and `Distribution` properties and use values from Figure 6.16(b).
   c. **Velocity ► Initial Velocity**: Expand `Start Velocity` and `Distribution` properties and use values from Figure 6.16(c).
   d. **Lifetime ► Lifetime**: Expand `Lifetime` and `Distribution` properties and use values from Figure 6.16(d).

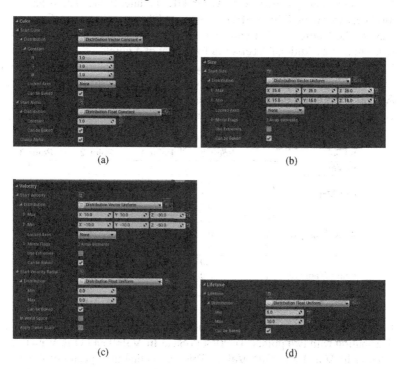

FIGURE 6.16: (a) Initial Color. (b) Initial Size. (c) Initial Velocity. (d) Lifetime.

13. At this stage of the work you should be able to see the performance of your particle emitter in the simulation preview window.
14. Save your progress.

OVER TIME PROPERTIES

In order to make our sprites change some of their attributes, we can use the `Over Life` modules. In this phase of this tutorial, we will first make a copy of our sprite emitter, and then make some of its emitted particles' attributes vary over the life of each particle.

15. In the content browser of your project, right-click on the **P_Sprites** particle system and choose the `Duplicate` option from the pop-up menu. This will create a copy of your original particle system.
16. Give the new copy of your particle system a name such as `P_VariableSprites`.
17. Double-click on this new particle system to open it up in the Cascade Editor.
18. In the Cascade Editor, `Right-Click` in the gray area in the particle emitter module (under the existing modules) to add a **Color Over Life** module to the emitter. (Note: This module is under the **Color** category.)
19. Click on this newly added **Color Over Life** module. In the Details panel of this module, expand the **Distribution** section, and then the **Constant Curve** section.
20. Next to the **Points** section you should have **2 Elements**. Click on the + sign twice to add 2 additional `Elements` for a total of 4 points.
21. Expand the **Points** section of the Details panel of the **Color Over Life** module.
22. Expand each of the points **0** - **3**. For each point you will see **In Val**, **Out Val**, **Arrival Tangent**, **Leave Tangent**, and **Interp Mode**.
23. Use the table below to enter these values into the parameters of each point:

Value		Point 0	Point 1	Point 2	Point 3
In Val		0	0.4	0.6	1.0
	X	2.0	0.1	2.0	0.0
Out Val	Y	0.5	0.6	1.0	0.0
	Z	0.1	2.0	0.5	0.0
	X	0.0	0.0	10	0.0
Arrive Tangent	Y	0.0	0.0	8.0	0.0
	Z	0.0	0.5	-4.0	0.0
	X	0.0	0.0	10.0	0.0
Leave Tangent	Y	0.0	0.0	8.0	0.0
	Z	0.0	0.5	-4.0	0.0
Interp Mode		Curve Auto	CurveAuto	CurveAuto	CurveAuto

24. Leave the **Alpha Over Life** values unchanged. Basically, this parameter is also a distribution with two points: The first point at **In Val**=0 and **Out Val**=1, and the other at **In Val**=1 and **Out Val**=0. This means that the opacity of this material goes from 1 to 0 over its lifetime, meaning each particle starts out as fully opaque (visible) and fades away over its lifetime (i.e., becoming fully translucent or see through).
25. Save your work.
26. Drag your sprite particle emitter from the content browser onto the level and place it somewhere on the Demo Display item on the map and enjoy the view!

What Happened in TUTORIAL 6.2...

You just set up your first visual effects using a simple sprite emitter. In the first step, you opened (or created) a simple demo environment to deploy the effect. Next, we set up the particle material.

SPRITE'S MATERIAL

The particle material is just like a regular material. However, instead of a color parameter or constant value, we used a `Particle Color` node to drive the color of our particle system's sprites from the color modules of the emitter. This node has the benefit of exposing the color of the sprites within the Color Modules of the Emitter to which this material is applied. This way, we can control the initial color and color over life of sprites within the Emitter module.

The material expression network is shown in Figure 6.14(b). To make the material translucent, we set the `Shading Model` of the material to Unlit, and its `Blend Mode` to translucent. Since the shading model for the material is set to Unlit, we can program the shading of the material via its **Emissive Color** channel. The output of any expression we plug into this node, will drive the shading of the material. To make the material become see through, we drive the **Opacity** channel of the material. So let's see how we achieved this:

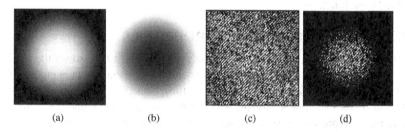

(a)   (b)   (c)   (d)

FIGURE 6.17: (a) Radial Gradient Exponential Expression Output. (b) One Minus Radial Exponential Value. (c) The Noise Expression. (d) Multiplying the Noise by (1-Radial Gradient).

- **Material's Emissive Color:** The effect that we are trying to achieve requires the material's color to be fully visible at the center of the particles and fade away as we get closer to their boundaries. To achieve this, we can use a function (i.e., a `Material Expression` node) that has a disk shape, – i.e., it goes from 1 to 0 by distance from the center (Figure 6.17(a)).

  Unreal Material Editor has a material expression called **Radial Gradient Exponential**. It simulates a circle in 2D with full value (equal to 1) at the center, dropping its value to 0 as the distance grows from the center.

  We could just multiply the output of the `Radial Gradient Exponential` expression with the Particle Color *RGB* values and assign it to the emissive channel of our sprite material. Our material would look like Figure 6.17(a). However, we would like to achieve a more fuzzy look (Figure 6.17(d)).

  To achieve this effect, we will use a **Noise** expression. The output of a regular noise expression looks like Figure 6.17(c). If we calculate the value of one minus the output of the **Radial Gradient Exponential** we get values shown in Figure 6.17(b). Using 1-Radial Gradient as the bandwidth of the **Noise** expression will give us the results we seek (Figure 6.17(d)). The full equation of the emissive color from network created in Figure 6.14(b) is calculated by:

$$EM_{rgb} = PCol_{rgb} \times \mathcal{N}\left(1 - (RBF(\cdot))\right) \tag{6.1}$$

where EM_{rgb} is the *RGB* color that the material emits, $PCol_{rgb}$ is the *RGB* color of each particle, $RBF(\cdot)$ is the Radial Gradient Exponential Expression, and $\mathcal{N}$ is the Noise function.

- **Material's Opacity:** The opacity channel of the material uses the same calculations as the emissive color, except the final step. We multiply the output of the noise expression by the Alpha channel of the **Particle Color** modules to calculate opacity (Figure 6.14(b)). see below:

$$\alpha = PCol_{\alpha} \times \mathcal{N}\left(1 - (RBF(\cdot))\right) \tag{6.2}$$

where α is the Opacity channel of the material, $PCol_{\alpha}$ is the Alpha value of each particle color, $RBF(\cdot)$ is the Radial Gradient Exponential Expression, and $\mathcal{N}$ is the Noise function.

INITIAL SPRITE EMITTER PROPERTIES

After setting up and assigning the Sprite's materials, it's time to set the particle system up. As we discussed earlier in this chapter, a visual effect is made of one or more Particle Emitters. Each emitter, in turn, is made of two or more modules. If you remember, the **Required** and **Spawn** modules are mandatory modules and must be present in each emitter. For most other modules, you can add it as an initial control module, or an over time module.

For this particular sprite emitter, we added four modules, three initial modules, and one lifetime module.

- **Initial Color:** We set the RGB values of the initial color to be $(1,1,1)$. Therefore, all of our particles will have a white color when they spawn.
- **Lifetime:** The lifetime module controls the minimum and maximum possible lifetime of each emitted sprite. We set the minimum value of the lifetime distribution to be 5, and maximum to be 10. With these values, each emitted sprite is assigned a lifetime of 5 to 10 seconds. The particle dies after its lifetime expires.
- **Initial Size:** We assigned an initial size between $(15,15,15)$ and $(25,25,25)$ to each spawned particle through this module. This should give a nice randomness to the shapes of the spawned sprites.
- **Initial Velocity:** To create more randomness for our visual effect, we use another distribution for the initial velocity of our particles. When a particle is about to spawn, Unreal will pick its initial velocity between the minimum and maximum values we set up for it. Since velocity is a vector in 3 dimensions – i.e., x, y, and z– we set two vectors for initial velocity. In this example we set the minimum speed

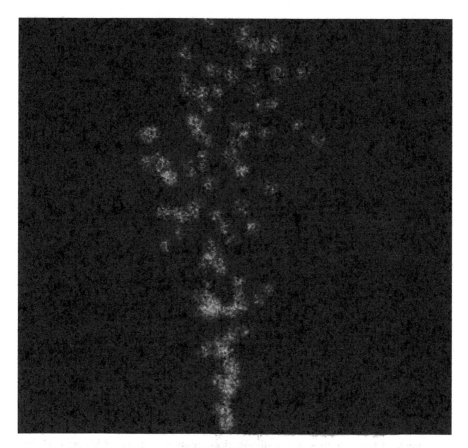

FIGURE 6.18: Sparks.

that a particle can be spawned with to be $[-10, -10, 30]^T$ and the maximum speed with which a particle can start to be $[10, 10, 50]^T$.

Notice that the speed along the z-axis is positive and ranges between 30 and 50. This ensures that all particles will be shot up from the location of the Emitter Actor that is placed in the map. The variations in the x- and the y- axes of the initial speed make the particles travel randomly in a fountain-like trajectory (Figure 6.18).

OVER LIFE PROPERTIES

For the majority of the modules you can set `Over Life` properties. You can control the way these properties change over the lifetime of a particle. This is usually done by working with the distribution of their attributes from the **Details** panel (Figure 6.19(a)) or their curve within the **Curve Editor** (Figure 6.20).

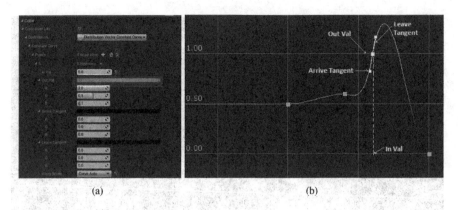

FIGURE 6.19: (a) Details Panel. (b) Distribution Point Values Explained.

WORKING WITH DISTRIBUTIONS

One of the ways to control the changes of attributes over the life of a particle is by means of distributions. Distributions are covered in great detail in Appendix B. However, we will go over the **Color Over Life** distribution here to see what happened in this tutorial.

If you look at the `Details` panel of your **Color Over Life** module, you will notice that its distribution is a **VectorConstantCurve**. This means that the values of the **Color Over Life** follow a Vector Curve, and at any given time in the lifetime of a particle, this value is a vector. This curve is controlled by a number of points. You can see these points in the `Details` panel of the module. In fact, we have 4 control points in our example.

Each of the attributes of the distribution points are shown in Figure 6.19(b). The **In Val** of a point is its location along the time axis (horizontal axis) of the curve. The **Out Val** is the value of each point along the vertical axis of the curve. For Vector Curves (as in the case of **Color Over Life** distribution) the **Out Val** is composed of three values, x, y, and z – for red, green, and blue color channels. The same is true for the **Arrival Tangent** and **Leave Tangent** properties.

For **FloatConstantCurve** distributions (as in the case of **Alpha Over Life**) the **Out Val, Arrival Tangent**, and **Leave Tangent** attributes are scalar values (i.e., they each only need one value).

In this tutorial, we controlled the color of each particle to start with an orange color ($[2.0, 0.5, 0.1]$) at time 0. At time 0.4 (about 40% of a particle's lifetime) we set the color to a blue color ($[0.1, 0.6, 2.0]$). We then set the particle color at time 0.6 (about 60% of its lifetime) back to a light yellow ($[2.0, 1.0, 0.5]$) and finally to black at time 1.0 (or at full lifetime). By this, each particle starts with an orange color when it is emitted from the emitter actor into the scene. Its color then changes over time to blue, yellow, and all the way to black over its lifetime.

If you look at the **Alpha Over Time** attribute of the `Color Over Time` module, you'll see that we have two points, one at the start ($t = 0$) and one at the end ($t = 1$) of the particle's lifetime. Remember from the previous section, we used the particle color's alpha value to drive the opacity of the sprite's materials. According to this distribution, the alpha channel of each particle is equal to 1 at the start point, and goes to 0 at the end point of this distribution. Therefore our particles start fully opaque and over time their materials become more and more translucent as they age. Right before the end of their lifetimes, the particles become fully see through and therefore fade away from being visible. This will create a vaporizing visual effect.

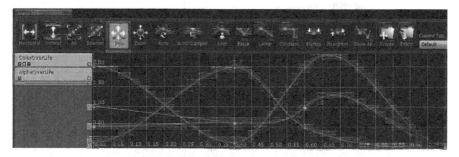

FIGURE 6.20: Curves in Curve Editor

WORKING WITH CURVES:

If you prefer to work with curves instead of numbers, you can access the Over Life module's distribution within the curve editor. To open each module's distribution in the curve editor, click on the square "graph" icon that is at the rightmost edge of the module. This will open the distribution in the curve editor. In our example, when you click on the graph icon of the **Color Over Life** you will see the ColorOverLife (this curve has three graphs for red, green, and blue color channels) and the AlphaOverLife graphs (this curve has a scalar curve).

To add a point to the curve, you can hold down the control key and left-click on the curve. By right-clicking on each point (points look like small rectangles on the curve) you may select the set time, set value, set color, or delete options to change the points (Figure 6.20).

You've created your very first visual effect using a sprite emitter to enhance the look of any level. This effect creates a smokey look. Now, let's see if we can create another kind of effect using the same kind of emitter. How about some rain!

To find updates to this tutorial and updated instructions about its implementation on other UE4 versions please visit the book's companion website at: http://www.RVRLAB.com/UE4Book/

TUTORIAL 6.3　Simulating Rain

In this tutorial we will set up another sprite emitter to simulate the effect of rain. Like all other tutorials, the first thing to do is to create a project to which we add the particle system. The initial setup of this tutorial should resemble the image shown in Figure 6.21.

FIGURE 6.21: Rain Demo Display.

> **NOTE**
>
> We will need the demo room to be set up before we can proceed with the rest of the tutorial. You may find instructions to set up your demo room in Tutorial 6.1 on page 297.

SETTING UP THE LEVEL

To have a uniform level that we can work with, you may perform one of the following options to start the work:

1. If you haven't created the demo room, perform the tasks in Tutorial 6.1 on page 297 to create a project which includes a **Demo Room**, a **Player Start**, and a **Demo Display** item as shown in Figure 6.13.

2. In the content browser, look for a folder inside the **Demo Room** folder called **Blueprints** and open it.
3. Drag a copy of **Display Item** onto the level and place it along a wall. Change its properties to the following:

> **Number:** P-2.
> **Description:** Rain Emitter . . .
> **Type:** Square-L

4. Save your level so far.

ORGANIZING ASSETS

Now that we have our level available, we will organize the particle systems we create in the content browser.

5. If you are following from Tutorial 6.2, then you should have a folder called MyParticles. Otherwise, in the content browser, create a folder called MyParticles.
6. If you don't have the Sprites folder, create a folder and call it Sprites. This is the folder where we will put the sprite emitter we are going to create.
7. In the Sprites folder you just created, create a new material and call it Mat_Rain.
8. In the Sprites folder you just created, create a new particle system and call it P_Rain.

CREATING THE RAIN MATERIAL

9. The first step in creating this material is to set up its shading and basic properties. We would like the material to look like what is shown in Figure 6.14(a). To do so, double click on the **Mat_Rain** material to open it up in the Unreal Material Editor. Set the following properties:

Blend Mode	Translucent
Shading Model	Unlit

10. To create a material network like the one shown in Figure 6.22(b) perform the following tasks:
    a. Right-click to the left of the material expression and type Radial Gradient to place a **Radial Gradient Exponential** expression.
    b. Place a **Particle Color** node above the **Radial Gradient** expression.
    c. Create two **Multiply** expressions to the right of both the **Radial Gradient** and **Particle Color** nodes.
    d. Connect the output of the **Radial Gradient** expression to the B input of both **Multiply** expressions.

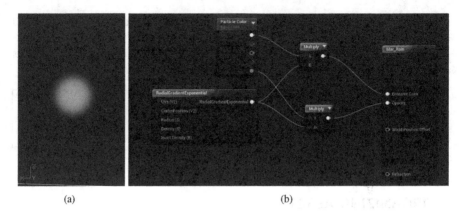

(a)   (b)

FIGURE 6.22: (a) Rain Emitter Material Look. (b) Rain Emitter Material Network.

      e. Connect the **A** input of one of the **Multiply** expressions to the `color` output of the **Particle Color** expression (its topmost node). Connect the output of this **Multiply** expression to the **Emissive Color** channel of the **Material** Expression.

      f. Connect the **A** input of the remaining **Multiply** expression to the `alpha` output of the **Particle Color** expression (its bottommost node). Connect the output of this **Multiply** expression to the **Opacity** channel of the **Material** Expression.

11. Your material is now set up. Save the `Mat_Sparks` material and close the Unreal Material Editor.

SETTING UP THE RAIN EMITTER

Double-click on the **P_Rain** particle system you created in the last section to open it in Cascade Particle Editor.

12. In the Emitters panel of the Cascade Editor, remove all modules from your Particle Emitter. Only the `Required` and the `Spawn` should be left (Figure 6.15(a)). We will build this emitter as we go on.

13. Right-click on the name of the emitter in the `Emitters` panel, choose `Emitter` and then `Rename Emitter`. Type in `RainEmitter` in the name textbox and press enter.

14. Now we are going to apply our **Mat_Rain** we created in the previous section to our emitter. Click on the **Required** module of the emitter, in the Emitter Panel (Figure 6.15(b)) click on the drop-down list next to **Material** and type in `Mat_Rain` (or whatever name you gave your particle material in the previous step).

15. To be able to have a visible effect we need to set up at least three Initial Modules, and a Lifetime Module. Right-click in the gray area under the `RainEmitter` emitter and select to add the following modules to your emitter (Figure 6.15(c)):

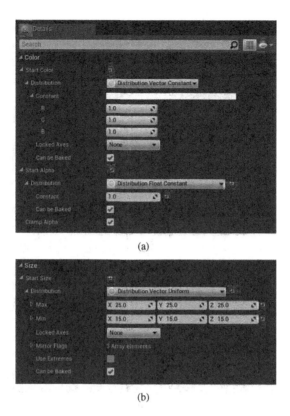

(a)

(b)

FIGURE 6.23: (a) Initial Color. (b) Initial Size.

a. **Color ▶ Initial Color**: Expand `Start Color` and `Distribution` properties and use values from Figure 6.23(a).
b. **Size ▶ Initial Size**: Expand `Start Size` and `Distribution` properties
   and use values from Figure 6.23(b).
c. **Velocity ▶ Initial Velocity**: Expand `Start Velocity` and `Distribution`
   properties and use values from Figure 6.24(a).
d. **Lifetime ▶ Lifetime**: Expand `Lifetime` and `Distribution` properties
   and use values from Figure 6.24(b).
16. At this stage of the work you should be able to see the performance of your par-
    ticle emitter in the simulation preview window – Figure 6.25(a). However, this is
    not quite the right effect for rain. Rain droplets should be generated over a large
    area not from a single point. We will do exactly this, in the next step.
17. Save your progress.

SETTING UP THE RAIN PLANE

If you have closed the Cascade Particle Editor, double-click on the **P_Rain**
particle system in the content browser to open it in the editor. Now we will set

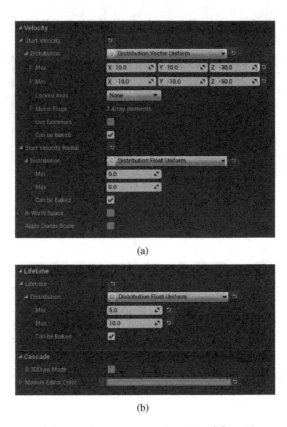

(a)

(b)

FIGURE 6.24: (a) Initial Velocity. (b) Lifetime.

up the distribution for the spawning of the rain particles, so that they will spawn from a plane instead of a single point.

18. Right-click under the last emitter module (it should be the **Lifetime** module), and choose the **Location ▶ Initial Location** module to add it to your particle emitter.

19. In the **Initial Location** module details panel, expand the **Start Location**, and the **Distribution** sections. Enter the value of **300** for the **Max**, and **-300** for the **Min** values for both **X** and **Y** components of the **Distribution**.

$$\textbf{Min} = [\text{X:-300, Y:-300, Z:0}] \qquad \textbf{Max} = [\text{X:300, Y:300, Z:0}]$$

20. This will make the particle emitter spawn rain droplets over a plane that spans from $(-300, -300, 0)$ to $(300, 300, 0)$ in space – Figure 6.25(b).

21. Place the **P_Rain** emitter actor in the level, by dragging a copy of it from the content browser onto the demo display item. Position the emitter actor at the center, and towards the top of the demo display item in the level – Figure 6.25(c).

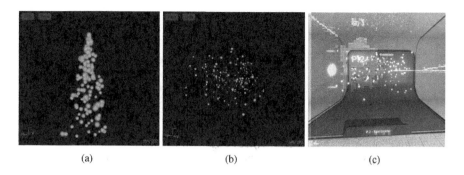

(a)   (b)   (c)

FIGURE 6.25: (a) The Rain Emitter spewing droplets from one point. (b) The Rain Emitter spawning rain droplets over a 2-dimensional plane. (c) Rain Emitter Actor shown in the level.

22. Save your progress so far. This particle emitter has certain aspects of simulating rain, but it looks far from over. In particular, we would like to have the rain drop at an angle (as if there was some wind affecting the rain). Moreover, the droplets of rain are perfectly spherical. We would like the rain droplets to be elongated to simulate the effect of the drag force of the atmosphere on them.

SIMULATING WIND AND ATMOSPHERIC DRAG FORCE

Double-click on the **P_Rain** particle system you created in the last section to open it in Cascade Particle Editor.

23. The first thing to do, to simulate the effect of the atmospheric drag force on the rain particles, is to change the **Screen Alignment** of the particles in the `Required` emitter module.
24. Click on the `Required` module and in its details panel change its `Screen Alignment` to **PSA_Velocity**.
25. Right-click under the last emitter module (it should be the `Initial Location` module), and choose the `Size ▶ Size By Speed` module to add it to your particle emitter.
26. Click on the `Size By Speed` module. In this module's details panel, make the following changes:

SpeedScale $= [X : 1.0, Y : 3.0]$ **MaxScale** $= [X : 1.0, Y : 3.0]$

27. As shown in Figure 6.26(a) the particles are too big to be rain droplets. This is because we are scaling the initial size of the particles up along the Y-axis of their velocity path. Let's make the following changes to the `Start Size ▶ Distribution` of the `Initial Size` module of the emitter – see results in Figure 6.26(b):

Max $= [X : 10.0, Y : 10.0, Z : 10.0]$ **Min** $= [X : 5.0, Y : 5.0, Z : 5.0]$

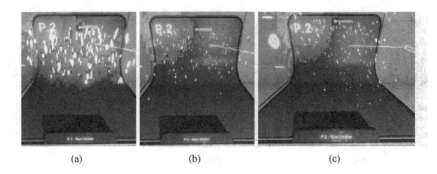

(a)   (b)   (c)

FIGURE 6.26: (a) The rain droplets are scaled along their speed path. (b) The rain droplet sizes after changing their initial size. (c) Rain Emitter Actor shown in the level. (c) Rain particles affected by gravity and wind forces.

28. One thing about this rain effect that's still not quite right is the way they drop to the ground. We have used an `Initial Velocity` module to give the particles a start speed. As each rain droplet has some mass, they are affected by a number of forces. Two of these forces are the earth's gravity, and the wind. To simulate these forces, we will add an **Acceleration** module to the emitter.

29. Make the following changes to the `Acceleration` ▶ `Distribution` parameters in the details panel of the `Acceleration` Module:

$$\mathbf{Max} = [X : 60.0, Y : 0.0, Z : -98.0] \qquad \mathbf{Min} = [X : 60.0, Y : 0.0, Z : -98.0]$$

30. You will notice that after adding the acceleration module and applying the forces to our particles, they tend to speed up as time goes by. This will make them exit our field of view, and therefore a few of the rain particles are now visible. We need to increase the number of these particles being spawned.

31. Click on the `Spawn` module of the emitter and change the constant value of its `Spawn` ▶ `Rate` ▶ `Distribution` to 90.0:

$$\mathbf{Constant} = 90.0$$

32. Save your progress and the level. Rain particles should now look like Figure 6.26(c).

What Happened in TUTORIAL 6.3...

In this tutorial you set up a visual effects system to simulate rain using a simple sprite emitter.

SPRITE MATERIAL

The particle material is just like a regular material. However, instead of a color parameter or constant value, we used a `Particle Color` node to drive the color of our particle system's sprites from the color modules of the emitter. This node has the benefit of exposing the color of the sprites within the Color Modules of the Emitter to which this material is applied. This way, we can control the initial color and color over life of sprites within the Emitter module.

The material expression network is shown in Figure 6.22(b). To make the material translucent, we set the `Shading Model` of the material to Unlit, and its `Blend Mode` to translucent. Since the shading model for the material is set to Unlit, we can program the shading of the material via its **Emissive Color** channel. The output of any expression we plug into this node will drive the shading of the material. So let's see how we achieved this:

- **Rain Material's Emissive Color:** The effect that we are trying to achieve requires the material's color to be fully visible at the center of the particles and fade away as we get closer to their boundaries. To achieve this, we can use a function (i.e., a `Material Expression` node) that has a disk shape, – i.e., it goes from 1 to 0 by distance from the center as shown in Figure 6.17(a).
  Unreal Material Editor has a material expression called **Radial Gradient Exponential**. It simulates a circle in 2D with full value (equal to 1) at the center, dropping its value to 0 as the distance grows from the center.
  We could just multiply the output of the `Radial Gradient Exponential` expression with the Particle Color *RGB* values and assign it to the emissive channel of our sprite material. Our material would look like Figure 6.17(a).
- **Material's Opacity:** The opacity channel of the material uses the same calculations as the emissive color. We multiply the output of the Alpha channel of the `Particle Color` module with the output of the `Radial Gradient Exponential` expression to calculate opacity – see Figure 6.22(b).

RAIN INITIAL PARAMETERS

After setting up and assigning the Rain Sprite's material, it's time to set the particle system up. As we discussed earlier in this chapter, a visual effect is made of one or more Particle Emitters. Each emitter, in turn, is made of two or more modules. If you remember, the **Required** and **Spawn** modules are mandatory modules and must be present in each emitter. For most other modules, you can add it as an initial control module, or an over time module.

For this Rain sprite emitter, we added five initial modules, four initial modules, and one lifetime module.

- **Initial Color:** We set the RGB values of the initial color to be $(1, 1, 1)$. Therefore, all of our particles will have a white color when they spawn.
- **Lifetime:** The lifetime module controls the minimum and maximum possible lifetime of each emitted sprite. We set the minimum value of the lifetime distribution

to be 5, and maximum to be 10. With these values, each emitted sprite is assigned a lifetime of 5 to 10 seconds. The particle dies after its lifetime expires.

- **Initial Size:** We assigned an initial size between $(15, 15, 15)$ and $(25, 25, 25)$ to each spawned particle through this module. This should give a nice randomness to the shapes of the spawned sprites.

- **Initial Velocity:** To create more randomness for the look of our visual effect, we use another distribution for the initial velocity of our particles. When a particle is about to spawn, Unreal will pick its initial velocity between the minimum and maximum values we set up for it. Since velocity is a vector in 3 dimension – i.e., x, y, and z– we set two vectors for initial velocity. In this example we set the minimum speed of a rain droplet to be between $[-10, -10, -50]$ and $[10, 10, -30]$. Notice that since the rain drops, we give negative values to the **Z** component of the min and max speed vectors.

  The variations in the x- and the y- axes of the initial speed make the particles travel in a random trajectory – see Figure 6.25(a).

- **Initial Location:** The problem so far with the particle system for rain is that it looks like rain droplets are all being generated from one point in space – Figure 6.25(a). However, real rain drops over a region and we can simulate this by creating an `Initial Location` module within our rain particle emitter. As shown in Figure 6.27(a) the initial location module basically allows the emitter to draw the spawn location of each particle from the volume enclosed within the `Start Location` distribution.

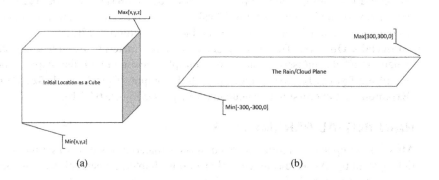

(a) (b)

FIGURE 6.27: (a) Particles will be spawned somewhere within the `Initial Location` rectangular cube. (b) In our example the clouds are assumed to be located at a plane.

In our tutorial, we assumed that the clouds are located over an area spanning a 600×600 rectangle. We set the minimum values of the `Start Location` distribution to $[-300, -300, 0]$ and its maximum value to $[300, 300, 0]$ – Figure 6.27(b).

SETTING UP FORCES AFFECTING RAIN DROPLETS

After setting up our rain particle system to spawn rain drops from a plane, we need to make the effect look realistic. The first part of this realistic effect is to simulate the elasticity of rain particles. As rain droplets fall they are subject to the air which puts a drag force on them. This force makes the droplets stretch along their falling path. Thankfully we can achieve this effect relatively easily, and with little computational cost to our CPU.

The emitter we are using is a sprite emitter. As such, each particle is basically a 2D bitmap (also called a sprite). The `Required` module of a sprite emitter has a component called **Screen Alignment**. This component controls how each sprite is aligned with respect to the world and the viewer camera.

TABLE 6.3

Screen Alignment in the Required Module of Emitters Controls How Each Sprite is Aligned.

Screen Alignment Option	Description
PSA Facing Camera Position	Sprites face the camera position but do not depend on the camera rotation. Produces more stable particles under camera rotation.
PSA Square	Only allows for uniform scaling of particles via SizeX for particles facing the camera.
PSA Rectangle	Allows for non-uniform scaling of particles via SizeX and SizeY for particles facing camera.
PSA Velocity	This method orients particles along the direction they are moving and the camera. Allows for non-uniform scaling of particles.
PSA Type Specific	This method uses the alignment method indicated in the Type Data module.
PSA Away From Center	This method uses the alignment method to face away from camera center.
PSA Facing Camera	This method uses the alignment method to face towards the camera.

Table 6.3 describes how each `Screen Alignment` type may affect the orientation and scaling of particle sprites. The default mode is **PSA Square**, which orients the sprites towards the camera and uses a uniform scale for their size. Since we are simulating rain drops, which are liquid, we need to use a non-uniform scaling factor as well as add the ability to orient the droplets along their motion path. We do this by changing the `Screen Alignment` of the `Required` module of the emitter to **PSA Velocity** in step 24.

Now that we have selected the appropriate `Screen Alignment`, we need to scale the rain drops non-uniformly by their speed. To do this we added a `Size by Speed` module to our emitter in step 26. We scaled each rain sprite along the major axis of its motion by choosing the value of 3.0 for the **Y** component of both its `Max Scale` and `Speed Scale` properties. This makes each particle grow to up to three times its initial size along its newly oriented Y-axis as it speeds up.

Since our newly added `Size by Speed` increases the size of the particles as they speed up, we changed the initial size of each rain drop by changing the minimum and maximum values of the distribution in the `Initial Size` module in step 27.

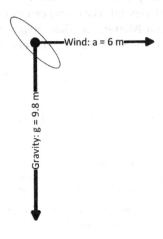

FIGURE 6.28: Forces applied to rain drops.

The final touch for our rain effect is to simulate the effects of the wind and gravitational forces on each rain drop. For simplicity, we assumed that the wind is a horizontal force along the X-axis of the world coordinate system. The gravitational force pulls the rain drops down along the vertical Z-axis of the world coordinate system.

According to Newton's second law of motion there is a direct relationship between an object's acceleration and the amount of force applied to it. In our example of the rain effect, we applied these two forces to each rain droplet, i.e., a horizontal wind force and a vertical gravitational force.

Let the earth's gravitational accelerations be 9.8 and the acceleration generated by the wind force be 6.0 applied to each raindrop as shown in Figure 6.28. To simulate these forces we added an `Acceleration` module to our emitter in step 29.

Since the gravitational force pulls the rain drops down, we used negative values for the **Z** component of the `Acceleration` distribution. Assuming that the wind is a horizontal force, we used a positive value for the **X** component and zero for the **Y** component of the `Acceleration` distribution in step 29.

6.6 GPU-BASED SPRITE EMITTERS

In Section 6.5 you created two special effects using CPU-based sprite particle emitters. CPU Sprite Emitters are quite powerful in generating many kinds of special effects. However, there is a computational limit that affects CPU-based particle systems.

At the core of a particle system lies the computation that is applied to each spawned particle. Therefore, if we spawn 10 particles, this computation is applied 10 times. If we spawn 100 particles, the computation needs to run 100 times. What happens if we need 10,000 particles? The particle emitter needs to apply the computation we define through its emitter'(s) modules 10,000 times.

As you can imagine, this will be a problem for a CPU-based particle system. Although the same computation is needed for all particle systems, a CPU has only a small number of core processing units that can run this computation in parallel. What's worse is the fact that running these 10,000 particles is not the only thing that our CPU must handle. There's your game logic, your operating system processes, and many other computational items that your CPU has to accommodate. This is why there is a maximum number of particles that can be active at any given time for a CPU-based particle system, so as to not drastically impact the program's performance.

This is where GPU Particle Systems will be quite handy. When you need to create a very complicated effect which requires a very large number of particles, a GPU Particle System will be the appropriate choice for a Particle Emitter.

6.6.1 GPU VS. CPU PARTICLES

There are a number of differences between a CPU-based particle system and a GPU-based one. The main difference between the two is the maximum number of particles that each system can handle. In the following sections other major differences between GPU and CPU particle systems are outlined.

Vector Fields

Another major difference between these two systems is the ability of GPU-based particle systems to utilize Vector Fields. A Vector Field in Unreal Engine is an environment in which every point is affected by a three-dimensional force vector. For example, if you want to simulate the effect of wind blowing the particles in a wind tube, you can create a vector field that simulates the amount of drag that a particle is subject to, at a given point in the tube.

There are several ways to create vector fields. You may use Autodesk Maya or 3ds Max, or other third-party software to create vector fields and import them into Unreal Engine 4.

Scene Depth Collision

GPU particles can utilize the GPU's depth buffer (also known as the z-Buffer) to calculate their collisions. This will be a handy effect that is available with very small computational cost to a GPU-based emitter.

Emitter Bounding Box

GPU-based particles must have their bounding box established to operate properly. Forgetting to create a proper bounding box for GPU particles will result in unpleasant disruptions in the GPU-based particle emitter's functionality. For example, a GPU particle system without a bounding box will stop emitting particles if its emitter actor exits the view frustum in the level.

In the next tutorial we will create a particle system to simulate the effect of a blizzard. We will use a GPU-based particle system for this tutorial so that we can generate many particles in the scene. In the exercises, you will be asked to create a vector field and apply it to your particle system to simulate wind forces applied to your snow storm.

> To find updates to this tutorial and updated instructions about its implementation on other UE4 versions please visit the book's companion website at:
> http://www.RVRLAB.com/UE4Book/

TUTORIAL 6.4   Simulating A Blizzard

In this tutorial we will set up another sprite emitter to simulate the effect of a raging blizzard. Like all other tutorials, the first thing to do is to create a project to which we add the particle system. The initial setup of this tutorial should resemble the image shown in Figure 6.29.

> **NOTE**
>
> We will need the demo room to be set up before we can proceed with the rest of the tutorial. You may find instructions to set up your demo room in Tutorial 6.1 on page 297.

SETTING UP THE LEVEL

To have a uniform level that we can work with, you may perform one of the following options to start the work:

1. If you haven't created the demo room, perform the tasks in Tutorial 6.1 on page 297 to create a project which includes a **Demo Room**, a **Player Start**, and a **Demo Display** item as shown in Figure 6.13.
2. In the content browser, look for a folder inside the **Demo Room** folder called **Blueprints** and open it.
3. Drag a copy of **Display Item** onto the level and place it along a wall. Change its properties to the following:

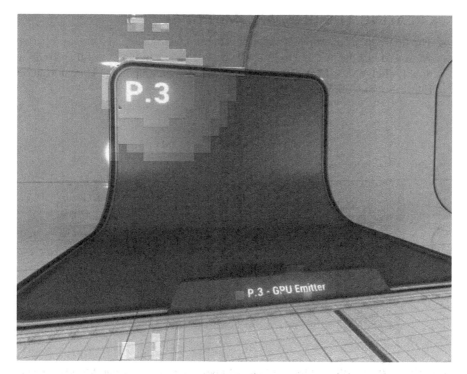

FIGURE 6.29: Blizzard Demo Display.

Number: P-3.
Description: GPU Emitter ...
Type: Square-L

4. Save your level so far.

ORGANIZING ASSETS

Now that we have our level available, we will organize the particle systems we create in the content browser.

5. If you are following from Tutorial 6.2, then you should have a folder called **MyParticles**. Otherwise, in the content browser, create a folder called **MyParticles**.

6. If you don't have the **Sprites** folder, create a folder and call it **Sprites**. This is the folder where we will put the sprite emitter we are going to create.

7. In the **Sprites** folder you just created, create a new material and call it **Mat_Blizzard**.

8. In the **Sprites** folder you just created, create a new particle system and call it **P_Blizzard**.

CREATING THE BLIZZARD MATERIAL

9. The first step in creating this material is to set up its shading and basic properties. We would like the material to look like what is shown in Figure 6.14(a). To do so, double click on the **Mat_Blizzard** material to open it up in the Unreal Material Editor. Set the following properties:

Blend Mode	Translucent
Shading Model	Unlit

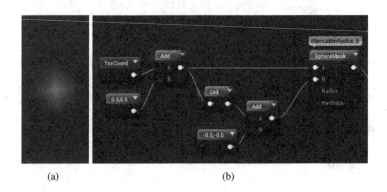

(a)   (b)

FIGURE 6.30: (a) Blizzard Emitter Material Look. (b) Blizzard Emitter Material Network Spikes.

10. To create a material network like the one shown in Figure 6.30(a) perform the following tasks:
    a. Right-click to the left of the material expression and type **Radial Gradient** to place a **Radial Gradient Exponential** expression.
    b. Pan the graph canvas for about three quarters of a page to the left of the **Radial Gradient** expression.
    c. Place a **TexCoord** expression on the graph.
    d. Place a **Constant2Vector** on the graph by holding the 2 key and **Left-clicking** just below the **TexCoord** expression.
    e. Type 0.5 in both R and G channels of this expression.
    f. Place an **Add** expression to the right of the **TexCoord** and the **Const2Vector**.
    g. Connect the output of the **TexCoord** to the A and the **Const2Vector** to the B input channel of the **Add** expression (see Figure 6.30(b)).
    h. Place a **Ceil** expression to the right of the **Add** expression.
    i. Place another **Constant2Vector** below the **Ceil**.
    j. Type the value of –0.5 in both the A and B channels of the **Const2Vector** expression.
    k. Place another **Add** expression to the right of the **Ceil** and the second **Const2Vector**.

l. Connect the output of the `Ceil` to the `A` and the second `Const2Vector` to the `B` input channel of the `Add` expression.

m. Place a `SphereMask` expression to the right of the second `Add` expression (see Figure 6.30(b)).

n. Connect the output of the first `Add` expression to the `A` input of the `SphereMask`.

o. Connect the output of the second `Add` expression to the `B` input of the `SphereMask`.

p. Place a `OneMinus` expression to the right of the `SphereMask` and connect the output of the `SphereMask` to its input.

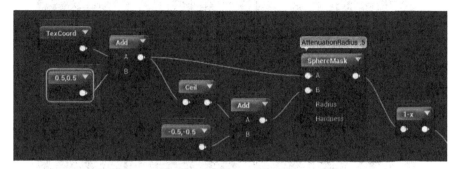

FIGURE 6.31: Blizzard Material Setup Continued.

q. Your network should look similar to Figure 6.31 so far.

r. Place a `Constant` expression below the `OneMinus` expression and type the value of 2 in its `R` channel.

s. Place a `Power` expression to the right of the `OneMinus` and the `Constant` expression.

t. Connect the `OneMinus` expression to the `Base` input of the `Power` expression.

u. Connect the `Constant` expression to the `Exp` input of the `Power` expression.

v. Place a `Multiply` expression to the right of both `Power` and the `RadialGradient` expressions.

w. Connect the output of the `power` to the `A` input of this `Multiply` expression.

x. Connect the output of the `RadialGradient` to the `B` input of this `Multiply` expression.

y. Connect the output of the **Radial Gradient** expression to the `B` input of this **Multiply** expression.

11. We will not create the Particle Color of our particle system:

a. Place a **Particle Color** node below the **Radial Gradient** expression.

b. Create two **Multiply** expressions to the right of both the first **Multiply** and **Particle Color** nodes.

c. Connect the output of the `Multiply` expression from step 10v to the `A` input of both of these new **Multiply** expressions.

d. Connect the RGB output of the `Particle Color` to the `B` input of the second `Multiply` expression.

e. Connect the **A** output of the `Particle Color` to the **B** input of the third `Multiply` expression.

f. Connect the output of the second **Multiply** expression to the **Emissive Color** channel of the **Material** Expression.

g. Connect the output of the third **Multiply** expression to the **Opacity** channel of the **Material** Expression.

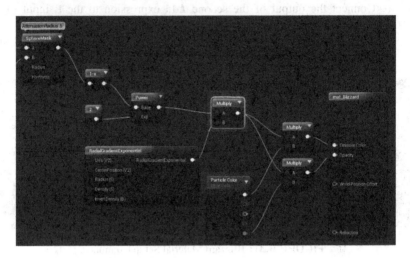

FIGURE 6.32: Blizzard Emitter Material Particle Color Network.

12. Your network should look similar to Figure 6.32.

13. Your material is now set up. Save the `Mat_Blizzard` material and close the Unreal Material Editor.

SETTING UP THE BLIZZARD EMITTER

Double-click on the **P_Blizzard** particle system you created in the last section to open it in Cascade Particle Editor.

14. In the Emitters panel of the Cascade Editor, remove all modules from your Particle Emitter. Only the `Required` and the `Spawn` should be left (Figure 6.15(a)). We will build this emitter as we go on.

15. Right-click on the name of the emitter in the **Emitters** panel, choose **Emitter** and then `Rename Emitter`. Type in `BlizzardEmitter` in the name textbox and press enter.

16. Right-click on the name of the emitter in the **Emitters** panel, go to `TypeData`, and then choose `New GPU Sprites`. This will convert the type of the sprite emitter to a GPU Particle System.

17. Now we are going to apply our **Mat_Blizzard** we created in the previous section to our emitter. Click on the **Required** module of the emitter, in the Emitter Panel (Figure 6.15(b)) click on the drop-down list next to **Material** and type in

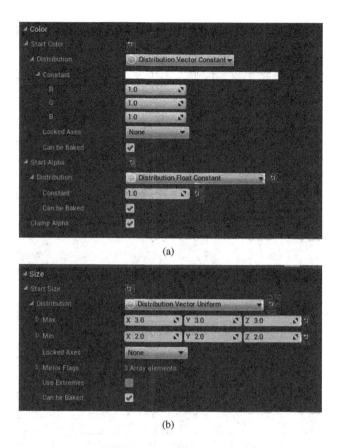

FIGURE 6.33: (a) Initial Color. (b) Initial Size.

Mat_Blizzard (or whatever name you gave your particle material in the previous step).

18. To be able to have a visible effect we need to set up at least three Initial Modules, and a Lifetime Module. Right-click in the gray area under the BlizzardEmitter emitter and select to add the following modules to your emitter (Figure 6.15(c)):

   a. **Color ▶ Initial Color**: Expand Start Color and Distribution properties and use values from Figure 6.33(a).

   b. **Size ▶ Initial Size**: Expand Start Size and Distribution properties and use values from Figure 6.33(b).

   c. **Velocity ▶ Initial Velocity**: Expand Start Velocity and Distribution properties and use values from Figure 6.34(a).

   d. **Lifetime ▶ Lifetime**: Expand Lifetime and Distribution properties and use values from Figure 6.34(b).

19. At this stage of the work you should be able to see the performance of your particle emitter in the simulation preview window – Figure 6.35(a). However, this is

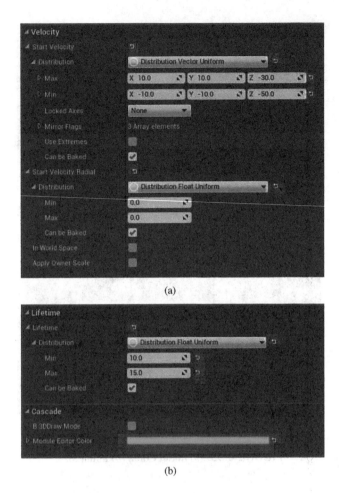

FIGURE 6.34: (a) Initial Velocity. (b) Lifetime.

not quite the right effect for snow. Snowflakes should be generated over a large area not from a single point. We will do exactly this in the next step.

20. Save your progress.

SETTING UP THE SNOW PLANE

If you have closed the Cascade Particle Editor, double-click on the **P_Blizzard** particle system in the content browser to open it in the editor. Now we will set up the distribution for the spawning of the rain particles, so that they will spawn from a plane instead of a single point.

21. Right-click under the last emitter module (it should be the `Lifetime` module), and choose the `Location` ▶ `Initial Location` module to add it to your particle emitter.

22. In the **Initial Location** module details panel, expand the `Start Location` and the `Distribution` sections. Enter the value of 300 for the `Max`, and –300 for the `Min` values for both **X** and **Y** components of the `Distribution`.

$$\textbf{Min} = [\text{X:-300, Y:-300, Z:0}] \qquad \textbf{Max} = [\text{X:300, Y:300, Z:0}]$$

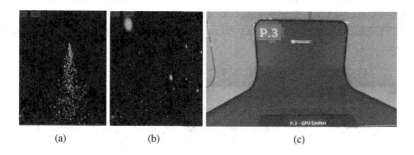

(a)   (b)   (c)

FIGURE 6.35: (a) The Blizzard Emitter spewing droplets from one point. (b) The Blizzard Emitter spawning snow droplets over a 2 dimensional plane. (c) Blizzard Emitter Actor shown in the level.

23. This will make the particle emitter spawn snowflakes over a plane that spans from $(-300, -300, 0)$ to $(300, 300, 0)$ in space – Figure 6.35(b).
24. Place the **P_Blizzard** emitter actor in the level by dragging a copy of it from the content browser onto the demo display item. Position the emitter actor at the center, and towards the top of the demo display item in the level – Figure 6.35(c).
25. Save your progress so far. This particle emitter has certain aspects of simulating snow, but it looks far from over. In particular, we would like to have the snow drop at an angle (as if there was some wind affecting the snow). Moreover, the droplets of snow are perfectly spherical. We would like the snow droplets to be elongated to simulate the effect of the drag force of the atmosphere on them.

SIMULATING WIND

Double-click on the **P_Blizzard** particle system you created in the last section to open it in Cascade Particle Editor.

26. The first thing to do, to simulate the effect of the atmospheric drag force on the snow particles, is to change the **Screen Alignment** of the particles in the `Required` emitter module.
27. Click on the `Required` module and in its details panel, change its `Screen Alignment` to **PSA_Velocity**.
28. Right-click under the last emitter module (it should be the `Initial Location` module), and choose the `Size ► Size By Speed` module to add it to your particle emitter.

29. Click on the `Size By Speed` module. In this module's details panel, make the following changes:

$$\textbf{SpeedScale} = [X:1.0, Y:2.0] \qquad \textbf{MaxScale} = [X:1.0, Y:2.0]$$

30. As shown in Figure 6.36(a) the particles are too big to be snowflakes. This is because we are scaling the initial size of the particles up along the Y-axis of their velocity path. Let's make the following changes to the `Start Size ▶ Distribution` of the `Initial Size` module of the emitter – see results in Figure 6.36(b):

$$\textbf{Max} = [X:5.0, Y:5.0, Z:5.0] \qquad \textbf{Min} = [X:3.0, Y:3.0, Z:3.0]$$

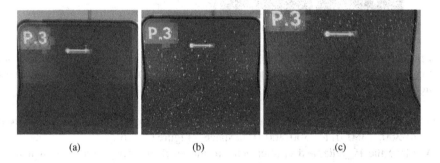

(a)   (b)   (c)

FIGURE 6.36: (a) The snow droplets are scaled along their speed path. (b) The snow droplets sizes after changing their initial size. (c) Blizzard Emitter Actor shown in the level. (c) Snow particles affected by gravity and wind forces.

31. One thing about this snow effect that's still not quite right is the way they drop to the ground. We have used an `Initial Velocity` module to give the particles a start speed. As all snowflakes have some mass, they are affected by a number of forces. Two of these forces are the earth's gravity, and the wind. To simulate these forces, we will add an **Acceleration** module to the emitter.

32. Make the following changes to the `Acceleration ▶ Const` parameters in the details panel of the `Acceleration` Module:

$$\textbf{Max} = [X:60.0, Y:0.0, Z:-98.0]$$

33. You will notice that after adding the acceleration module and applying the forces to our particles, they tend to speed up as time goes by. This will make them exit our field of view, and therefore a few of the snow particles are now visible. We need to increase the number of these particles being spawned.

34. Click on the `Spawn` module of the emitter and change the constant value of its `Spawn ▶ Rate ▶ Distribution` to 1500.0:

$$\textbf{Constant} = 1500.0$$

35. Save your progress and the level. Rain particles should now look like Figure 6.36(c).

Fantastic! Our blizzard effect is now complete. Let's take a look at the similarities and differences between the CPU-based rain effect and the GPU-based blizzard effect.

What Happened in TUTORIAL 6.4...

In this tutorial you set up a visual effects system to simulate a blizzard using a GPU sprite emitter.

The particle material for this system is just like a regular material. However, instead of a color parameter or constant value, we used a `Particle Color` node to drive the color of our particle system's sprites from the color modules of the emitter. This node has the benefit of exposing the color of the sprites within the Color Modules of the Emitter to which this material is applied. This way, we can control the initial color and color over life of sprites within the Emitter module.

To make the material translucent, we set the `Shading Model` of the material to Unlit, and its `Blend Mode` to translucent. Since the shading model for the material is set to Unlit, we can program the shading of the material via its **Emissive Color** channel. The output of any expression we plug into this node, will drive the shading of the material.

The material and particle setup was quite similar to the CPU-based particles. The only major difference is that the blizzard effect is a GPU-based particle system. Therefore, when we applied the acceleration module, we can only choose a constant acceleration for it. However, we can now spawn a lot more particles. In fact, we spawned 1500 snow particles, compared to a mere 90 for the rain emitter. Moreover, we will be able to apply Vector Fields to our GPU-based particle system to simulate a complex snow storm. An exercise will ask you to apply a vector field to this particle system to simulate a snow storm.

6.7   WORKING WITH SUB UVS

So far in our particle systems we have used textures or expressions to establish the look of the material. But this look stayed the same as each particle is created. We changed colors, sizes, alpha values, and so on, but the look (texture) of our particles was fixed at the time of their creation.

In the next Tutorial, we will create a fire effect. The difference between the look of flames and that of a raindrop, or a snowflake, is that flames change their shape. This look is easily created by employing sub images in your particle system. To be able to utilize sub images to change the look (texture) of a particle as it is created and ages, we need to take a few steps.

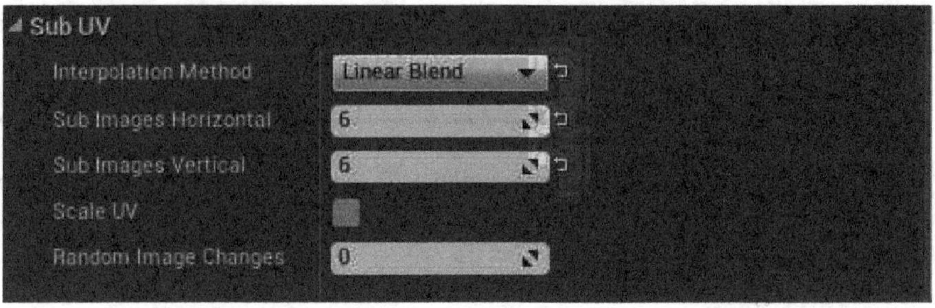

FIGURE 6.37: Particle Emitter Sub UV Properties.

The first step involves allowing the particle emitter to utilize **SUB UVs**. When you select an emitter in the Cascade Particle Editor, you will be able to modify its **Sub UV** properties in its Details rollout shown in Figure 6.37. In the **Sub UV** section you will see the `Interpolation Mode`, `Sub Images Horizontal`, `Sub Images Vertical`, `Scale UV`, and `Random Image Changes`.

Interpolation Mode: This sets the interpolation method the emitter uses to determine how to change sub images. The available options are as follows:
- `None`: This option does not apply Sub UV modules in the emitter.
- `Linear`: This option transitions between sub images in a given order without any blending between successive sub images.
- `Linear_Blend`: This option transitions between sub images in a given order and blends successive sub images as the emitter transitions from one sub image to the next.
- `Random`: This option transitions randomly between sub images without any blending between successive sub images.
- `Random_Blend`: This option transitions randomly between sub images and blends sub images as it transitions from one to the next.

Sub Images Horizontal: Number of horizontal sub images in the texture applied in the particle material.

Sub Images Vertical: Number of vertical sub images in the texture applied in the particle material.

Scale UV: This option specifies whether to scale the UVs, if the original model wasn't set up with sub UVs.

Random Image Changes: This option specifies the number of times to change a random sub image over the lifetime of a particle.

The second step in utilizing sub UVs and sub images in a particle system is to make its material draw from a texture composed of an array of images. The number of horizontal and vertical sub-textures in the texture we will use in the material should be equal to the **Sub Images Horizontal** and **Sub Images Vertical** num-

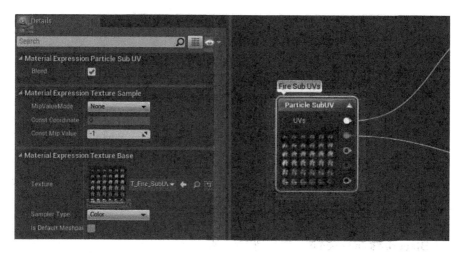

FIGURE 6.38: Particle SubUV Expression and Its Properties.

bers in the **Sub UV** section of the particle emitter's **Required** module. Once we have such a texture, in the **Material Editor** we will place a **Particle SubUV** material expression and assign the texture to it (see Figure 6.38).

Finally, with the particle material set up to accept sub images and the emitter set up to use horizontal and vertical sub images in order (or randomly), we will have to tell the emitter how to change the sub images over the lifetime of a particle. In order to do this, we will use a **SubImage Index** module. The **SubImage Index** module contains a SubImage Index distribution. This distribution will tell your emitter how to pick the sub images from the particle material. The simplest way to set this module up, is to make its distribution a `Float Constant Curve` distribution. Then, make the first point have the **In Val=0** and **Out Val=0**. Make the second point have **In Val=1** and **Out Val=**$U \times V - 1$. Where U is the number of horizontal sub images and V is the number of vertical sub images in your texture. Doing so will make a particle apply the upper-left texture sub image when it is spawned and go through the sub images one-by-one through the bottom-right texture sub image.

To find updates to this tutorial and updated instructions about its implementation on other UE4 versions please visit the book's companion website at: `http://www.RVRLAB.com/UE4Book/`

TUTORIAL 6.5   Simulating A Fire

In this tutorial we will set up another sprite emitter to simulate a fire effect. Like all other tutorials, the first thing to do is to create a project to which we add the particle system. The initial setup of this tutorial should resemble the image shown in Figure 6.29.

> **NOTE**
>
> We will need the demo room to be set up before we can proceed with the rest of the tutorial. You may find instructions to set up your demo room in Tutorial 6.1 on page 297.

SETTING UP THE LEVEL

To have a uniform level that we can work with, you may perform one of the following options to start the work:

1. If you haven't created the demo room, perform the tasks in Tutorial 6.1 on page 297 to create a project which includes a **Demo Room**, a **Player Start**, and a **Demo Display** item as shown in Figure 6.13.
2. In the content browser, look for a folder inside the **Demo Room** folder called **Blueprints** and open it.
3. Drag a copy of **Display Item** onto the level and place it along a wall. Change its properties to the following:

> **Number:** P-4.
> **Description:** Fire Emitter . . .
> **Type:** Square-L

4. Save your level so far.

ORGANIZING ASSETS

Now that we have our level available, we will organize the particle systems we create in the content browser.

5. If you are following from Tutorial 6.2, then you should have a folder called `MyParticles`. Otherwise, in the content browser, create a folder called `MyParticles`.
6. `Double-Click` on the `MyParticles` folder to open it up.
7. If you don't have the `Sprites` folder, create a folder and call it `Sprites`. This is the folder where we will put the sprite emitter we are going to create.
8. In the `Sprites` folder you just created, create a new material and call it `Mat_Fire`.
9. In the `Sprites` folder you just created, create a new particle system and call it `P_Fire`.

CREATING THE FIRE MATERIAL

10. The first step in creating this material is to set up its shading and basic properties. We would like the material to look like what is shown in Figure 6.14(a). To do so, double click on the **Mat_Fire** material to open it up in the Unreal Material Editor. Set the following properties:

Blend Mode: Translucent
Shading Model: Unlit

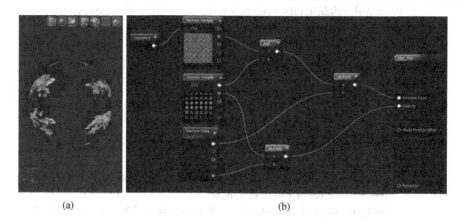

      (a)   (b)

FIGURE 6.39: (a) Fire Emitter Material Look. (b) Fire Emitter Material Network.

11. To create a material network like the one shown in Figure 6.39(a) perform the following tasks:
    a. Left-Click on the graph editor to the left of your material node to place a **Texture Coordinate** expression.
    b. Make the following changes to your texture coordinate:

    VTiling: 6
    UTiling: 6
    Desc: SubUVTilings

    c. Place a **Texture Sample** expression to the right of the SubUVTiling coordinate you just created. *NOTE: Hold down the **T** key and Left-Click to place the **Texture Sample** expression.*
    d. Make the following changes to the **Texture Sample** expression properties in its Details rollout (*Hint: To assign a texture click on the drop-down list and type the texture name*):

    Texture: T_Fire_Tiled_D
    Desc: Fire Texture

    e. Place a **Particle SubUV** expression blow the Fire Texture expression you just created. *NOTE: To do this Right-Click on the graph and type the name of the expression in the search bar.*
    f. Make the following changes to the **Particle SubUV** expression properties in its Details rollout:

> **Texture:** T_Fire_SubUV
> **Desc:** Fire Sub UVs

g. Place a **Particle Color** node below the Fire Sub UVs expression.

h. Place an **Add** expression to the right of both the Fire Texture and the Fire Sub UVs expressions and make the following connections:

> **Red channel of Fire Texture** → A channel of the **Add**
> **RGB (white) of Fire Sub UVs** → B channel of the **Add**

i. Place a **Multiply** expression to the right of both the **Add** expressions and make the following connections:

> **Output channel of ADD** → A channel of the **Multiply**
> **RGBA (white) of Particle Color** → B channel of the **Multiply**
> **Output channel of Multiply** → Emissive Color channel of the material node

j. Create another **Multiply** expression to the right of both the **Fire Sub UVs** and **Particle Color** expressions and make the following connections:

> **R channel of Fire Sub UVs**→ A channel of the **Multiply**
> **Alpha channel of Particle Color** → B channel of the **Multiply**
> **Output channel of Multiply** → Opacity channel of the material node

12. Your material is now set up. Save the Mat_Fire material and close the Unreal Material Editor.

SETTING UP THE FIRE EMITTER

Double-Click on the **P_Fire** particle system you created in the previous section to open it up in the Cascade Particle Editor.

13. In the Emitters Panel of the Cascade Particle Editor, click on the **Required** module to open it up in the Details rollout.

a. Make the following changes to the **Emitter** section Details rollout:

> **Material:** Mat_Fire
> **Screen Alignment:** PSA Velocity

b. Make the following changes to the **Sub UV** section Details rollout:

> **Interpolation Mode:** `Linear Blend`
> **Sub Images Horizontal:** 6
> **Sub Images Vertical:** 6

14. In the Emitters Panel of the Cascade Particle Editor, click on the **Spawn** module to open it up in the `Details` rollout.
    a. We will next change the **Spawn** section of `Details` rollout.
    b. Expand the **Rate** values and make the following changes:

> **Distribution:** `Float Constant`
> **Constant:** `5.0`

c. Expand the **Rate Scale** values and make the following changes:

> **Distribution:** `Float Constant`
> **Constant:** `1.0`

d. We will next change the **Burst** section of `Details` rollout.
e. Expand the **Burst Scale** values and make the following changes:

> **Distribution:** `Float Constant`
> **Constant:** `1.0`

15. In the Emitters Panel of the Cascade Particle Editor, click on the **Lifetime** module to open it up in the `Details` rollout.
    a. We will next change the **Lifetime** section of `Details` rollout.
    b. Expand the **Lifetime** values and make the following changes:

> **Distribution:** `Float Uniform`
> **Min:** `0.7`
> **Max:** `1.0`

16. In the Emitters Panel of the Cascade Particle Editor, click on the **Initial Size** module to open it up in the `Details` rollout.
    a. We will next change the **Size** section of `Details` rollout.
    b. Expand the **Start Size** values and make the following changes:

> **Distribution:** `Vector Uniform`
> **Max:** `X:60.0, Y:90.0, Z:0.0`
> **Min:** `X:40.0, Y:70.0, Z:0.0`

17. In the Emitters Panel of the Cascade Particle Editor, click on the **Initial Velocity** module to open it up in the `Details` rollout.
    a. We will next change the **Velocity** section of `Details` rollout.
    b. Expand the **Start Velocity** values and make the following changes:

> **Distribution:** `Vector Uniform`
> **Max:** `X:0.0, Y:0.0, Z:60.0`
> **Min:** `X:0.0, Y:0.0, Z:40.0`

   c. Expand the **Start Velocity Radial** values and make the following changes:

> **Distribution:** `Float Uniform`
> **Min:** `0.0`
> **Max:** `0.0`

18. In the Emitters Panel of the Cascade Particle Editor, click on the **Color Over Life** module to open it up in the `Details` rollout.

   a. We will next change the **Color** section of `Details` rollout.

   b. Expand the **Color Over Life** values and make the following changes:

> **Distribution:** `Vector Constant Curve`

     i. Expand the **Constant Curve**

    ii. Expand **Points**.

   iii. Make the following changes to **Point[0]**:

> **In Val:** `0.0`
> **Out Val:** `X:20.0, Y:5.0, Z:1.0`
> **Arrival Tangent:** `X:0.0, Y:0.0, Z:0.0`
> **Leave Tangent:** `X:0.0, Y:0.0, Z:0.0`
> **Interp Mode:** `Linear`

   iv. Make the following changes to **Point[1]**:

> **In Val:** `1.0`
> **Out Val:** `X:7.0, Y:1.0, Z:0.0`
> **Arrival Tangent:** `X:0.0, Y:0.0, Z:0.0`
> **Leave Tangent:** `X:0.0, Y:0.0, Z:0.0`
> **Interp Mode:** `Linear`

   c. Expand the **Alpha Over Life** values and make the following changes:

> **Distribution:** `Float Constant Curve`

     i. Expand the **Constant Curve**

    ii. Click on the **+** sign next to `Points` to add an element. You should have 3 elements.

   iii. Expand **Points**.

   iv. Make the following changes to **Point[0]**:

In Val: 0.0
Out Val: 0.0
Arrival Tangent: 0.0
Leave Tangent: 0.0
Interp Mode: Linear

v. Make the following changes to **Point[1]**:

In Val: 0.2
Out Val: 4.0
Arrival Tangent: 0.0
Leave Tangent: 0.0
Interp Mode: Linear

vi. Make the following changes to **Point[2]**:

In Val: 1.0
Out Val: 0.0
Arrival Tangent: 0.0
Leave Tangent: 0.0
Interp Mode: Linear

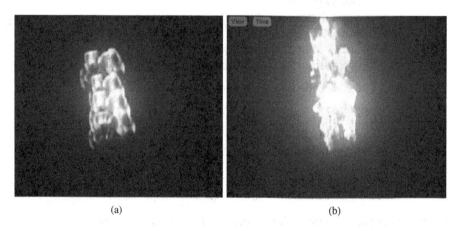

(a)   (b)

FIGURE 6.40: (a) Fire Emitter without Sub UV Indexing. (b) Fire Emitter with Sub UV Indexing.

At this stage your Fire emitter should look similar to Figure 6.40(a). However, we would like to have an effect similar to what is shown in Figure 6.40(b). At this point, each particle will use the first sub image of the material to apply and keep that image throughout its lifetime. We would like to make the particles change their shape by picking a different sub image from their material as they age.

We have already set up our particle system to utilize sub UV images in step 13b on page 340 when we set up the **Required** module of our emitter. Next, we will add a **SubImage Index** module to our emitter and make it select a different sub image for each particle as they age.

19. Right-Click on the gray area in your **Particle Emitter** below the Color Over Life module.
20. From the menu select **SubUV ▶ SubImage Index**.
21. In the Emitters Panel of the Cascade Particle Editor, click on the **SubImage Index** module you just created to open it up in the Details rollout.
     a. We will next change the **Sub UV** section Details rollout.
     b. Expand the **Sub Image Index** values and make the following changes:

> **Distribution:** Float Constant Curve

        i. Expand the **Constant Curve**
      ii. Expand **Points**.
     iii. Make the following changes to **Point[0]**:

> **In Val:** 0.0
> **Out Val:** 0.0
> **Arrival Tangent:** 0.0
> **Leave Tangent:** 0.0
> **Interp Mode:** Linear

     iv. Make the following changes to **Point[1]**:

> **In Val:** 1.0
> **Out Val:** 35.0
> **Arrival Tangent:** 0.0
> **Leave Tangent:** 0.0
> **Interp Mode:** Linear

22. Now your particle emitter should look similar to Figure 6.40(b).
23. Save your particle system.

PLACING THE EFFECT IN THE LEVEL

Now let's place the emitter actor based on our fire effect in the level.

24. Back in the main editor, find the Starter Content folder in the **Content Browser** and open it.

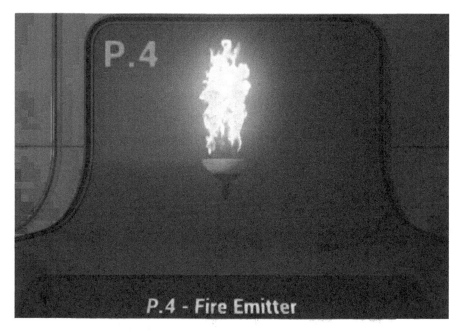

FIGURE 6.41: Fire Effect Placed in the Display Item.

25. Open the `Props` folder within the `Starter Content` folder.
26. Drag a copy of the **SM_Lamp_Wall** mesh into the **Display Item** in the level.
27. Place the mesh somewhat in the middle of the display item and at almost chest height.
28. In the **Content Browser** find your particle folder. *I have called my particle folder MyParticles.*
29. Open the `Sprites` folder from the `MyParticles` folder. This is where we created the **P_Fire** particle system.
30. Align the particle emitter actor with the `SM_Lamp_Wall` mesh so that the fire is coming out of the sconce. Your level should look similar to Figure 6.41.
31. Save your level and play it to check out the look of your particle system. Feel free to move the sconce and the particle emitter to get a desirable look.

ADDING LIGHT TO PARTICLES

Our particle system looks quite impressive so far in simulating the effects of a torch. However, it is not quite right. The color of the fire is merely set through the `Emissive Color` channel of the particle material. Although it looks like fire, it will not emit true light in the scene. We will next place a rock behind the torch to see why not having a light isn't quite right and then we will fix the problem.

32. Find the **Starter Content ▶ Props** folder in the **Content Browser** and open

it up.

33. Drag a copy of the static mesh **SM_Rock** onto the display item.

34. Arrange the rock behind the sconce so that it looks like the torch is held against the rock (see Figure 6.42(a)).

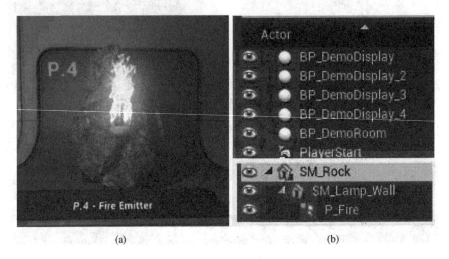

(a)   (b)

FIGURE 6.42: (a) Torch Placed in Front of a Rock. (b) Fire, Torch, and Rock Grouped.

35. Next we will group the Fire particle system, the lamp static mesh, and the rock static mesh so that we can move them together. To do this we will first parent the fire to the lamp mesh (fire to be the child of lamp), and parent the lamp to the rock. The relationship we would like to achieve is similar to Figure 6.42(b).

36. There are two ways to group items in the **Scene Outliner** (the upper-right corner of the main editor). The first way is to **Right-Click** on the child actor and then choose **Attach To**. Then, from the drop-down menu choose the actor that you want to be the parent. The second way to group actors is to drag the child actor in the **Scene Outliner** on top be the parent actor in the **Scene Outliner**.

37. Using one of the above two methods, parent the **P_Fire** effect to the **SM_Lamp_Wall**.

38. Next, parent the **SM_Lamp_Wall** to **SM_Rock** (see Figure 6.42(b)).

39. Make sure that all of these actors are selected.

40. Now that we have the items grouped, let's move them to the left. To do this, select the **SM_Rock** actor and move it to the left edge of the display item. Notice that the rock, torch, and fire will move together now that they are grouped. If this doesn't happen you need to re-do your grouping.

41. Now that you have moved the first group out of the way, we will duplicate the three actors. To do this hold the **Control** key and **Left-Click** on the particle emitter actor, the lamp mesh and the rock mesh to select the three items together.

42. With the three actors selected, hold the **Alt** key and translate (along the horizontal translate widget) to make a copy of these three actors.

FIGURE 6.43: Fire, Torch, and Rock Duplicated.

43. Your duplicated actors on the display item should look similar to Figure 6.43.
44. We will now duplicate our fire effect in the **Content Browser** and add a light module to it.
45. Find your particles folder in which you created the **P_Fire** effect in the **Content Browser** and open it up.
46. `Right-Click` on the **P_Fire** effect and choose `Duplicate` option from the popup menu.
47. Rename the duplicate particle system to something like P_Fire_Light.
48. `Double-Click` on the **P_Fire_Light** particle system in the **Content Browser** to open it in the Cascade Particle Editor.
49. `Right-Click` on the gray area in your **Particle Emitter** below the SubImage Index module.
50. From the menu select **Light ▶ Light**.
51. In the Emitters Panel of the Cascade Particle Editor, click on the **Light** module you just created to open it up in the Details rollout.
    a. Make the following changes to the **Light** section Details rollout:

    > **Use Inverse Squared Falloff:** Checked.
    > **Affect Translucency:** Un–Checked.
    > **Preview Light Radius:** Un–Checked.

    i. Expand the **Color Scale Over Life**

   ii. Expand **Distribution**.

  iii. Make the following changes to **Distribution**:

> **Distribution:** Vector Constant
> **Constant:** X:1.0, Y:1.0, Z:0.5
> **Locked Axes:** None

   iv. Expand the **Color Brightness Over Life**

    v. Expand **Distribution**.

   vi. Make the following changes to **Distribution**:

> **Distribution:** Float Uniform
> **Min:** 5.0
> **Max:** 10.0

  vii. Expand the **Radius Scale**

 viii. Expand **Distribution**.

   ix. Make the following changes to **Distribution**:

> **Distribution:** Float Constant
> **Constant:** 500.0

    x. Expand the **Light Exponent**

   xi. Expand **Distribution**.

  xii. Make the following changes to **Distribution**:

> **Distribution:** Float Constant
> **Constant:** 2.0

  b. Save your **P_Fire_Light** particle system and close (or minimize) the Cascade Particle Editor.

  c. Now in the main editor, we will apply this particle system to the duplicated particle emitter actor in the level. To do this perform the following actions:

     i. Left-Click on the duplicate emitter actor (the one on the right) in the level in main editor.

    ii. Navigate to your particles folder where you created the **P_Fire** and **P_Fire_Light** particle systems.

   iii. Assign the **P_Fire_Light** particle system to the Particles ▶ Template of the selected particle emitter actor in its details rollout. You may drag the **P_Fire_Light** onto the Template. Alternatively, you may Left-Click on the drop-down list next to the Template and choose **P_Fire_Light** from the list.

   iv. Now you should notice that the fire effect on the right casts shadows, reflections, and also flickers. Something that looks much more realistic (see Figure 6.44).

FIGURE 6.44: Fire With Light Effect.

52. Now your particle emitter should look similar to Figure 6.40(b).
53. Save the level and your progress.

Fantastic! We just created a really nice looking fire effect and applied it to a torch in our level. We worked on some modules that we were already familiar with and learned about some new particle modules as well, such as the **SubImage Index** and the **Light** modules. Let's see some details about what we did in this tutorial to set up this fire effect.

What Happened in TUTORIAL 6.5...

In this tutorial you set up a visual effects system to simulate a fire. We encountered and used a new emitter module which utilizes the sub images of a texture. This module and the technique are quite useful in creating effects such as fire, smoke, clouds, etc.

FIRE MATERIAL

As discussed above, the fire effect utilizes the `Sub Image Index` module to interpolate the look of the flame material between a number of sub images. In order for our emitter to successfully utilize this module, the particle material will have to handle the effect as well.

So, how exactly can we make the particle material compatible with the `Sub Image Index` module? The process is easy. Let's first look at a simple material which is made of just one texture. We use a texture sample to create the look of our material. Now, if we want our material to handle sub images, all we need to have is a texture which is divided in such as way that each sub image of the texture looks like a complete texture itself.

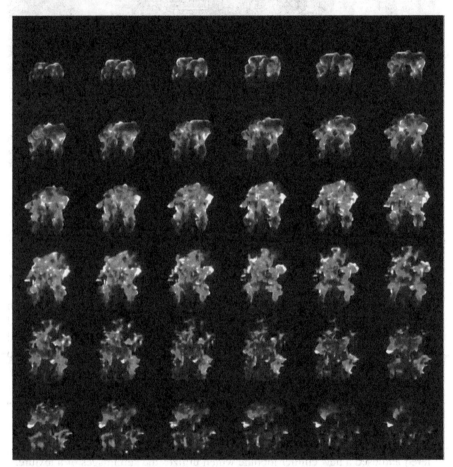

FIGURE 6.45: The Fire Sub Image Texture.

In order to accommodate this, we used a Flame texture that is composed of 36 smaller textures. If you open it up in the Unreal Texture Editor, it looks similar to Figure 6.45. As you can see in this image, the Flame texture is made of 6 rows and 6 columns of what a snapshot of a flame might look like. We used this texture in the creation of our fire particle material as shown in Figure 6.39(b).

In order for our fire to also have an orange fiery color, we used a flame texture. Since our original fire texture has 6 rows and 6 columns of sub images, we connected the fire texture to a **Texture Coordinate** expression and used the value of 6 for both **VTiling** and **UTiling**. This made the Fire texture look like an array of 6×6 sub images. We then multiplied this Fire Texture with our Flames texture to colorize the material.

SETTING UP THE FIRE EMITTER

With our Fire Particle Material created, we can now establish our emitter. We added our Fire material to the **Material** of our particle system and made its **Screen Alignment** become based on the velocity. This will stretch the particles as they speed up to make the effect more natural.

The next task was to make the particle system able to utilize our material's sub images. In order to do so we changed the **Interpolation Mode** of the **Sub UV** section of our particle system to **Linear Blend** and its **Sub Images Horizontal** and **Sub Images Vertical** to 6. This will make our particle system able to split the material into an array of 6×6 sub materials, and blend from one to another linearly.

We also need to make appropriate changes to the **Spawn**, and **Burst** sections of our particle emitter. Next, we added a **Lifetime** module to our emitter and made each particle last between 0.7 and 1.0 seconds. After setting the lifetime of each particle, we added an **Initial Size** module in which we assigned a random size to each emitted particle that ranges between [40,70,0] and [60,90,0].

Next, we gave our particles a speed value between 40 and 60 along their Z-axis by using a **Vector Uniform** distribution. We also made some modifications to the color and opacity of our particles. We want our particles' colors to start with a very bright glow ([20,5,1]), but for the glow to fade as the fire particles age ([7,1,0]). We made proper adjustments to the **Alpha Over Life** of our particle's **Color Over Life** module to make them transparent as they age, as well.

However, our effect isn't complete yet. The problem in our effect so far is that, despite setting its **Sub UV** values, the effect still uses just 1 out of the 6×6 sub images for each emitter particle. To make the effect be able to go over each sub image, we need a **Sub Image Index** module to be added to the emitter.

This module can be programmed in such a way that during the lifetime of each particle, it selects one of the 6×6 sub images as it ages. Once the **Sub Image Index** module is added to our emitter, we made it use a **Float Constant Curve**. This curve starts at the value of 0 (at time=0), and goes linearly to a value of 35 over the lifetime of our particles (time=1). Therefore, the particle emitter starts with sub image 0 and assigns it to each emitted particle, and as the particle ages, the image will change to 1, 2, …, and finally to 35, at the end of the particle's lifetime.

ADDING LIGHT TO PARTICLES

Once the particle emitter is placed in the level, and especially if it is placed close to a surface, you will soon realize that the emitter doesn't cast light into the level, despite its bright glow of fire. To make this effect even more realistic we added a

Light module to our emitter. We made proper modifications and adjustments to the light module for each emitted particle to cast a fiery light into the scene.

6.8　PARTICLE TYPE DATA MODULES

FIGURE 6.46: Assigning a Type Data to an Emitter.

So far we have used the CPU-based and GPU-based particles. The default data type of an emitter is a **Sprite** emitter. We referred to these emitters as CPU-based emitters. We have also worked with GPU-based emitters whose data type is **GPUS-prites**.

In order to select a data type for an emitter, simply `Right-Click` on the emitter. Move to the **Type Data** tab from the popup menu and choose the appropriate Type Data for your emitter (see Figure 6.46). If a non-sprite type data is assigned to a particle emitter and you wish to remove it, simply right-click on the type data and choose `Delete Module`.

In this section[1] we will go over different particle **Type Data** and discuss their specialty and applications [44].

6.8.1　GPU SPRITES TYPE DATA

The **GPU Sprite**[2] type data module supports simulating particles on the GPU. Traditional CPU systems allow for thousands of particles in a frame. GPU simulation

---

[1] The contents of this section are adapted from the official UE4 online documentation found at: https://docs.unrealengine.com/latest/INT/.

[2] The contents of this section are adapted from the official UE4 online documentation found at: https://docs.unrealengine.com/latest/INT/.

allows for hundreds of thousands of particles to be simulated and rendered efficiently [44].

GPU particles do not support all of the features available to traditional CPU particles, but they offer greater efficiency as well as a few unique features. Emission of particles still happens on the CPU to determine where, when, and how many particles to spawn. The CPU may also assign initial attributes such as size and velocity using methods available to traditional CPU particles [19].

We have already worked with **GPU Sprites** type data in Tutorial 6.4 on page 326 when we created a Blizzard effect. In the following we will discuss more details about this type of data and how it will be beneficial to create interesting visual effects.

The **GPU Sprites** type data has the following properties [19]:

Beam

Camera Motion Blur Amount: How much to stretch sprites based on camera's motion blur.

Attributes

The **GPU Sprites** type data does not support all of the modules and emitter attributes. The following are available attributes for GPU particles [20]:

Initial Location:
- Determined at spawn time.
- Supports most methods available to CPU particles

Initial Velocity:
- Determined at spawn time.
- May inherit velocity from the spawn source.

Acceleration:
- Constant for all particles across the lifetime of the emitter.

Drag:
- Initial drag coefficient is determined at spawn time and may vary per-particle.
- May be scaled over the life of the particle by a curve. The curve is shared among all particles.

Lifetime:
- Determined at spawn time and may vary per-particle.

Color:
- Initial color determined at spawn time. This color is the same for all particles.
- May be scaled over life by a curve. The curve is shared among all particles.

Size:
- Initial size is determined at spawn time and may vary per-particle.
- May be scaled over life by a curve. The curve is shared among all particles.

Rotation:
- Determined at spawn time and may vary per-particle.

Rotation Rate:
- Determined at spawn time and may vary per-particle.

Sub Image Index:
- The sub image index varies over the life of a particle as defined by a curve.
- The curve is shared among all particles.

GPU Particles Motion [17]

Particle motion is governed by simple Newtonian dynamics. At each time step, a particle's position and velocity are integrated forward based on its current position, current velocity, a constant acceleration, and force due to drag.

GPU particles also support orbit, though the details differ from those provided for traditional CPU particles. Conceptually, the particle moves as if the sprite is orbiting around the actual location of the particle offset by a varying amount. Orbit can be used to add additional detail motion to particles.

Vector Fields [21]

The most interesting feature of GPU particles, aside from their efficiency, is vector fields. A vector field is a uniform grid of vectors that influences the motion of particles. Vector fields are placed in the world as Actors (Global Vector Field) and can be translated, rotated, and scaled like any other Actor. They are dynamic and may be moved at any time. A field may also be placed within Cascade (Local Vector Field), limiting its influence to the emitter with which it is associated. When a particle enters the bounds of the vector field, its motion will be influenced by it and when a particle leaves the bounds, the influence of the field will fade out.

By default, vector fields impart a force on particles within them. Vector fields also have a "tightness" parameter. This parameter controls how directly particles follow the vectors in the field. When tightness is set to 1, particles read their velocity directly from the field and thus follow the field exactly.

Static vector fields are those in which the grid of vectors never change. These fields can be exported from Maya and imported as a volume texture. Static fields are very cheap and can be used to add interesting motion to particles, especially by animating the motion of the field itself.

Additionally, vector fields may be reconstructed from a 2D image. In this case, an image much like a normal map can be imported and used to reconstruct a volume texture by extruding or revolving it around a volume. A static vector field may be added on top of this reconstruction to introduce some noise and randomness. Further, the 2D images may be animated by storing individual frames in an atlas texture. Doing so allows you to perform a fluid simulation offline and reconstruct the motion in real-time at very little cost.

Performance of GPU Particles [18]

The CPU cost of GPU particles is dominated by the spawning of particles. Because particles are spawned on the CPU using the same methods as traditional CPU particles, the performance characteristics are similar.

The GPU cost of particles is primarily determined by the number of particles. Few features add additional cost to GPU particles above the fixed cost that already exists. The majority of the GPU cost can be attributed to sorting and rendering. Sorting is optional and should be enabled only when required for a particular emitter. Rendering is often dominated by fill rate. Reducing the size of particles, the number of instructions on a particle's material, and the total number of particles can all help. In some cases when the particles are very small, rendering is dominated by vertex cost, in which case reducing the number of particles is the only way to reduce cost.

6.8.2 BEAM TYPE DATA

The Beam[3] type data module indicates that the emitter should output beams [44]. This will make the emitter connect particles between a source point and a target point. This will create a stream between the two points.

For example, you may choose the source to be the emitter actor and the target point to be the player actor. This will make a stream of particles between the location of the emitter and the player to create effects such as lighting hitting the actor.

The Beam type data has the following properties according to the Unreal Engine 4 official documentation [2]:

Beam

> **Beam Method:** This property allows for setting the method for generating the beam:
> - **PEM2M_Distance:** Emit the beam along the X-axis of the emitter.
> - **PEM2M_Target:** Emit the beam from source to a supplied target.
> - **PEM2M_Branch:** Unused.
>
> **Texture Tile:** The number of times a texture is to be tiled along the beam.

---

[3] The contents of this section are adapted from the official UE4 online documentation found at: https://docs.unrealengine.com/latest/INT/.

Texture Tile Distance: The distance along the beam that represents one tile of the texture.

Sheets: The number of sheets to render along the beam.

Max Beam Count: The maximum number of live beams the emitter can have.

Speed: The speed at which the beam moves from the source to the target. A value of 0 will make the beam jump intravenously from the source to the target.

Interpolation Points: This number will allow the beam to use tangents along its path from the source to the target. Negative values will make the beam a straight line. Positive non-zero values will make the beam utilize as many tangents as the specified number to create curvatures along the path.

Always On: If set to *true*, will make beam always have live particles.

Up Vector Step Size: The approach to use for determining the up-vector of the beam:

- **0** The up-vector should be calculated at every point in the beam.
- **1** The up-vector should be calculated at the start of the beam and then used for all other points.
- **2** The up-vector should be calculated at every N-point. *Currently unsupported.*

Distance

Distance: This float distribution provides the distance along the X-axis the beam should travel when the Beam Method is set to **PEB2M_Distance**.

Taper

Taper Method: How the beam is tapered along its length. Can be one of the following values:

- **PEBTM_None** No tapering is applied to the beam.
- **PEBTM_Full** Taper the beam relative to source moving to target, regardless of current beam length.
- **PEBTM_Partial** Currently unused.

Taper Factor: A distribution supplying the amount to taper the beam. When using a constant curve, a time value of 0.0 represents the taper at the source of the beam, while a time value of 1.0 is the target.

Taper Scale: The amount of scaling for the taper.

Rendering

> **Render Geometry:** If set to *true*, the actual geometry of the beam will be rendered. Usually used, as otherwise the beam trail will not be visible.
>
> **Render Direct Line:** If set to *true*, a direct line will be rendered. Used for debugging in Cascade Particle Editor.
>
> **Render Lines:** If set to *true*, lines will be rendered along each segment of the beam. Used for debugging in Cascade Particle Editor.
>
> **Render Tessellation:** If set to *true*, a tessellated path will be rendered along the beam. Used for debugging in Cascade Particle Editor.

6.8.3   MESH TYPE DATA

The Mesh[4] type data module indicates that the emitter should use static mesh instances as each particle [44]. For example, you may choose a static mesh to be used and create effects such as a firing machine gun, shrapnel, or debris.

The Mesh type data has the following properties according to the Unreal Engine 4 official documentation [41]:

Mesh

> **Mesh:** This property is the Static Mesh that is rendered at the position of the emitter's particles.
>
> **Mesh Alignment:** The alignment to use when rendering the mesh. The `Screen Alignment` property of the **Required Module** *MUST* be set to `PSA_TypeSpecific` for this property to have any effect. The following options are provided:
>
> - **PSMA_MeshFaceCameraWithRoll:** Face the camera allowing for rotation around the mesh-to-camera vector (amount provided by the standard particle sprite rotation).
> - **PSMA_MeshFaceCameraWithSpin:** Face the camera allowing for the mesh to rotate about the tangential axis.
> - **PSMA_MeshFaceCameraWithLockedAxis:** Face the camera while maintaining the up vector as the locked direction.
>
> **Override Material:** If true, the meshes will be rendered using the material from the emitter (assigned in the **RequiredModule**) rather than those applied to the Static Mesh model. Use this over the Mesh Material module unless you have multiple UV channels on your mesh you need to assign material to, or you need to parameterize the material assignment for code.

---

[4] The contents of this section are adapted from the official UE4 online documentation found at: `https://docs.unrealengine.com/latest/INT/`.

Orientation

Pitch, Roll, Yaw: The 'pre' rotation pitch, roll, yaw (in degrees) to apply to the Static Mesh used.

Axis Lock Option: The axis to lock the mesh on:

- **XAxisFacing_NoUp:** The mesh's local X-axis faces the camera, while no attempt is made to face the other axes up or down.
- **XAxisFacing_ZUp:** The mesh's local X-axis faces the camera, while the mesh's local Z-axis will attempt to face up (towards the world positive Z-axis).
- **XAxisFacing_NegativeAUp:** The mesh's local X-axis faces the camera, while the mesh's local Z-axis will attempt to face down (towards the world negative Z-axis).
- **XAxisFacing_YUp:** The mesh's local X-axis faces the camera, while the mesh's local Y-axis will attempt to face up (towards the world positive Z-axis).
- **XAxisFacing_NegativeYUp:** The mesh's local X-axis faces the camera, while the mesh's local Y-axis will attempt to face down (towards the world negative Z-axis).
- **LockedAxis_ZAxisFacing:** The mesh's local X-axis is locked on the Axis Lock Option axis, while the mesh's local Z-axis is rotated to face towards camera.
- **LockedAxis_NegativeZAxisFacing:** The mesh's local X-axis is locked on the Axis Lock Option axis, while the mesh's local Z-axis is rotated to face away from camera.
- **LockedAxis_YAxisFacing:** The mesh's local X-axis is locked on the Axis Lock Option axis, while the mesh's local Y-axis is rotated to face towards camera.
- **LockedAxis_NegativeYAxisFacing:** The mesh's local X-axis is locked on the Axis Lock Option axis, while the mesh's local Y-axis is rotated to face away from camera.
- **VelocityAligned_ZAxisFacing:** The mesh's local X-axis aligned to the velocity, while the mesh's local Z-axis is rotated to face towards camera.
- **VelocityAligned_NegativeZAxisFacing:** The mesh's local X-axis aligned to the velocity, while the mesh's local Z-axis is rotated to face away from camera.
- **VelocityAligned_YAxisFacing:** The mesh's local X-axis aligned to the velocity, while the mesh's local Y-axis is rotated to face towards camera.
- **VelocityAligned_NegativeYAxisFacing:** The mesh's local X-axis aligned to the velocity, while the mesh's local Y-axis is rotated to face away from camera.

Camera Facing

Camera Facing Option: Determines how the mesh is oriented when the Camera Facing option is enabled. The following options are provided:

- **XAxisFacing_NoUp:** The mesh's local X-axis faces the camera, while no attempt is made to face the other axes up or down.
- **XAxisFacing_ZUp:** The mesh's local X-axis faces the camera, while the mesh's local Z-axis will attempt to face up (towards the world positive Z-axis).
- **XAxisFacing_NegativeAUp:** The mesh's local X-axis faces the camera, while the mesh's local Z-axis will attempt to face down (towards the world negative Z-axis).
- **XAxisFacing_YUp:** The mesh's local X-axis faces the camera, while the mesh's local Y-axis will attempt to face up (towards the world positive Z-axis).
- **XAxisFacing_NegativeYUp:** The mesh's local X-axis faces the camera, while the mesh's local Y-axis will attempt to face down (towards the world negative Z-axis).
- **LockedAxis_ZAxisFacing:** The mesh's local X-axis is locked on the Axis Lock Option axis, while the mesh's local Z-axis is rotated to face towards camera.
- **LockedAxis_NegativeZAxisFacing:** The mesh's local X-axis is locked on the Axis Lock Option axis, while the mesh's local Z-axis is rotated to face away from camera.
- **LockedAxis_YAxisFacing:** The mesh's local X-axis is locked on the Axis Lock Option axis, while the mesh's local Y-axis is rotated to face towards camera.
- **LockedAxis_NegativeYAxisFacing:** The mesh's local X-axis is locked on the Axis Lock Option axis, while the mesh's local Y-axis is rotated to face away from camera.
- **VelocityAligned_ZAxisFacing:** The mesh's local X-axis aligned to the velocity, while the mesh's local Z-axis is rotated to face towards camera.
- **VelocityAligned_NegativeZAxisFacing:** The mesh's local X-axis aligned to the velocity, while the mesh's local Z-axis is rotated to face away from camera.
- **VelocityAligned_YAxisFacing:** The mesh's local X-axis aligned to the velocity, while the mesh's local Y-axis is rotated to face towards camera.
- **VelocityAligned_NegativeYAxisFacing:** The mesh's local X-axis aligned to the velocity, while the mesh's local Y-axis is rotated to face away from camera.

Camera Facing: If set to *true*, then the X-axis of the mesh will always point towards the camera. When set, Axis Lock Option as well as all other locked axis/screen alignment settings are ignored.

Apply Particle Rotation as Spin: If set to *true*, the 'sprite' particle rotation is applied to the mesh about the orientation axis (the direction mesh is pointing). Otherwise, the 'sprite' particle rotation is applied to the mesh about the camera facing axis.

Face Camera Direction Rather than Position: If set to *true*, all camera facing options will point the mesh against the camera's view direction rather than pointing at the camera's location.

6.8.4   RIBBON TYPE DATA

The Ribbon[5] type data module indicates that the emitter should output trails – connecting particles to form ribbons. Particles are connected in the order of their birth. Therefore, the more erratic the initial velocity pattern of the particles, the more chaotic the ribbon [44].

The Ribbon type data module has the following properties according to the Unreal Engine 4 official documentation [47]:

Trail

Sheet Per Trail: The number of sheets, rotated around the length of the trail, to render for the trail.

Max Trail Count: The number of live trails allowed.

Max Particle In Trail Count: The maximum number of particles that the trail may contain at any one time.

Dead Trails On Deactivate: If set to *true*, trails are marked dead when the Particle System is deactivated. This means the trails will still render, but no new particles will be spawned, even if the Particle System is re-activated.

Dead Trails on Source Loss: If set to *true*, the trail is marked dead when the source of the trail is 'lost,' i.e., the source particle dies.

Clip Source Segment: If set to *true*, the trail will not be joined to the source position.

Enable Previous Tangent Recalculation: If set to *true*, the previous tangent will be recalculated each time a new particle is spawned.

Tangent Recalculation Every Frame: If set to *true*, all tangents are recalculated every frame to allow velocity/acceleration to be applied.

---

[5] The contents of this section are adapted from the official UE4 online documentation found at: https://docs.unrealengine.com/latest/INT/.

Spawn Initial Particle: If set to *true*, the ribbon will spawn a particle when it first starts moving.

Render Axis: The 'render' axis for the trail (what axis the trail is stretched out on). The following options are provided:

- **Trails_CameraUp:** Traditional camera-facing trail.
- **Trails_SourceUp:** Use the up axis of the source for each spawned particle.
- **Trails_WorldUp:** Use the world up axis.

Spawn

Tangent Spawning Scalar: The tangent scalar for spawning. Angles between tangent A and B are mapped to $[0.0 \cdots 1.0]$. This is then multiplied by Tangent Spawning Scalar to give the number of particles to spawn.

Rendering

Render Geometry: If set to *true*, the trail geometry will be rendered. This should typically be enabled as the trail is not visible otherwise.

Render Spawn Points: If set to *true*, stars are rendered in the location of each spawned particle point along the trail. Used for debugging in Cascade.

Render Tangents: If set to *true*, the tangent at each spawned particle point along the trail is rendered using a line. Used for debugging in Cascade.

Render Tessellation: If set to *true*, the tessellated path between each spawned particle is rendered. Used for debugging in Cascade.

Tiling Distance: The (estimated) covered distance to tile the 2nd UV set at. If 0.0, a second UV set will not be passed in.

Distance Tessellation Step Size: The distance between tessellation points for the trail. This is used to determine how many tessellation points the trail has, and thus how smooth the trail is. The exact calculation is:

$$TessellationPoints = \frac{Distance\ between\ Particles}{DistanceTessellationStepSize} \quad (6.3)$$

Enable Tangent Diff Interp Scale: If this flag is enabled, the system will scale the number of interpolated vertices based on the difference in the tangents of neighboring particles. Each pair of neighboring particles will compute the following CheckTangent value:

```
              if Checktangent <0.5
           Scale Distance Tessellation Step Size.
```

This will map so that from parallel to orthogonal (0 to 90 degrees) will scale from 0 to 1. Anything greater than 90 degrees will clamp at a scale of 1.

Tangent Tessellation Scalar: The tangent scalar for tessellation. Angles between tangent A and B are mapped to 0 to 1. This is then multiplied by this value to give the number of points to tessellate.

6.9   SUMMARY

In this chapter we learned about Particle Systems in Unreal Engine 4.0. The Unreal Engine uses a special component called Cascade Particle System Editor to manage and utilize particle effects. We learned about the Cascade interface and different tools available to us for creating particle systems with this component.

We first learned about the anatomy of a particle system in Unreal Engine 4, and about the different modules that should work together to create a given effect. We also discussed different types of particle systems that Cascade can create from simple CPU based particles to GPU particles, Beam particles, Mesh particles, and Ribbon particles.

We got some hands-on experience with Cascade in creating several interesting particle effects including, sparks, rain, snow storm, and fire. We worked with several modules that created the special features we wanted to achieve in each of the particle systems we created.

When it comes to the power of Unreal Engine and its Cascade Particle Editor System, there is little limit in what you can create. If you can imagine a visual effect requiring particles, chances are you can create it with Cascade.

6.10   EXERCISES

Now it's your turn to do some more exercises with blank project templates and the demo room.

Exercise 1. Create the rightmost emitter in Figure 6.47 using textures.
- a. Instead of the **Radial Gradient Exponential** material expression node that we used, use a spherical gradient texture in your sprite emitter material.
- b. Separate the Emissive Color texture from the Opacity texture to get more control over the particle materials and translucency.

Exercise 2. Create an explosive wide emitter, the second from right in Figure 6.47.
- a. Make changes to the initial velocity module to expand the cone over which the particles are spread.

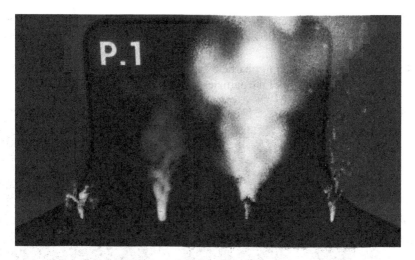

FIGURE 6.47: Sprite Emitter Exercise.

    b. Make changes over time to the size of the particles so they be-
come large and then shrink in size.

Exercise 3. Create a smoke emitter, the second from left in Figure 6.47.

    a. Make the color of the particles resemble burning of sodium.

    b. Particles should start with a bright white, turn ember, then intense
red, and fade with dark smoke.

Exercise 4. Extra Credit: Sparks with Mass (the leftmost emitter in Figure 6.47)!

    a. Give your particles some weight, such that they fall off to the
ground.

Exercise 5. Change the rain particle emitter of Tutorial 6.3 such that:

    a. The rain material uses a see through glassy texture.

    b. The rain is affected by two-dimensional wind force.

    c. Make the raindrops bounce back when they hit the ground.
HINT: Add a **Collision** module to your emitter. Use its `Damping
Factor` and `Max Collision` distributions to achieve the desired
effect. If your particles don't collide you might need to set up the
Bounds of the emitter by clicking on its button on the `toolbar`.

    d. Increase the volume in which the rain falls. In the tutorial above
you had a plane of size 600. Increase this size by a factor of 4.
You will notice that the number of spawned particles is too small
to visibly cover this large area.

    e. Increase the number of spawned particles to cover the area you
created for the rain in part d. Can you see the limit at which the
CPU sprites are spawned? Can you explain why particles don't
spawn more than that certain limit?

Exercise 6. Create a Vector Field in a software of your choice. Import this Vector Field to the Blizzard effect you create in Tutorial 6.4 to simulate a snow storm.

Exercise 7. Duplicate the fire particle system you designed in Tutorial 6.5 twice. Rename one of the particles systems to **P_Fire_Ember**.

FIGURE 6.48: Fire Effect Exercise.

    a. Open the **P_Fire_Ember** in the Cascade Particle Editor.

    b. Add a **GPU Emitter** to this particle system and make it spawn circular materials that look like embers produced by the Fire. Your final Effect should look similar to the fire effect on the left in Figure 6.48.

    c. In the **Content Browser** duplicate the **P_Fire_Ember** and rename the duplicate to **P_Fire_Ember_Smoke**.

    d. Open the other to **P_Fire_Ember_Smoke** in the Cascade Particle Editor.

    e. Add a **SpriteEmitter** to this particle system and make it spawn a material that looks like embers produced by the Fire. Your final Effect should look similar to the fire effect on the right in Figure 6.48.

7 Terrains and Landscapes in Unreal Engine

7.1 INTRODUCTION TO LANDSCAPES

So far we have played mostly indoors! In almost all tutorials in this book, we first set up a demo room with neat display items to showcase our creations and to develop a presentable set of displays. Now it's time to get outside and have some outdoors fun with Unreal Engine 4's brand new Landscapes!

In order to create vast expanses of outdoor levels with high quality visuals we need to fully utilize the power of landscapes in Unreal Engine 4. The good news is creating, manipulating, and developing fantastic looking outdoors scenes is quite easy with the landscape tools. Whether you want to create your landscape entirely in UE 4, or use third party terrain tools such as World Machine, Terragen, Mudbox, or ZBrush, to generate and import height maps and terrains into Unreal, the results will be quite impressive and the process fun.

In this chapter, much like all the other chapters, I have tried to confine our learning and exploration to Unreal Engine 4. As such, I tried to stay away from utilizing any other software as much as possible. To this end, we will work entirely in Unreal Engine for the scope of our adventures into landscapes. Once you go through this chapter and play with the Landscape editor in Unreal 4, and you would like to use third party tools to create your own terrains and import them into Unreal Engine, you will find the process quite straightforward.

So what exactly is a landscape? In Unreal Engine 4, a Landscape is pretty much the equivalent of a Terrain in UDK, Unreal Engine 3, or other 3D game engines. Much like terrains in UDK, a landscape in UE4 is an actor. It is used for the creation of vast outdoors environments based on a height map. This actor enables you to develop high mountains and deep valleys, cave openings, and even rivers and highways.

There is a significant advantage in using a landscape instead of a static mesh with the same number of vertices and polygons for terrains. Unreal Engine has the ability to utilize the landscape properties to automatically calculate the best LOD (Level of Details) based on the camera's distance from regions of the landscape that are being rendered. This will dramatically decrease the demand on both CPU and GPU operations to make vast terrains and landscapes render quite comfortably with real-time performance.

The geometry of a landscape is controlled from a map called a heightmap. A heightmap is a black and white bitmap in which the darker areas represent lower elevations, while brighter locations associate with higher elevations (see Figure 7.1).

The heightmap shown in Figure 7.1 corresponds to a raw landscape in Unreal Engine that looks like Figure 7.2. If the landscape looks bland and dull, it's because there aren't any landscape materials associated with it.

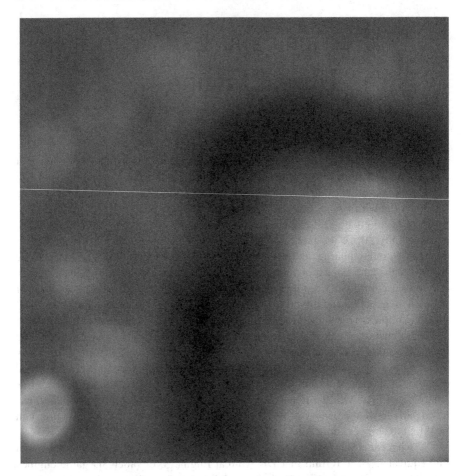

FIGURE 7.1: An Example of a Heightmap.

We will learn, in this chapter, how to create landscapes and make landscape materials to apply to our terrains. We will learn about how to blend different material networks to apply and to paint on our landscape for grassy areas, rocky mountains, and snow-capped mountains. We will also see how we can fill out landscapes with foliage actors, and a unique and newly introduced toolkit for creating landscape splines in our terrains.

7.2 LANDSCAPE SETUP

As I mention earlier, a landscape (or terrain) is an actor in Unreal Engine 4. Much like any other actor, you can create and place an instance of it in your level. Once a landscape is created and placed in a level, you will notice two actors in the Scene Outliner –a **Landscape Actor** and a **Landscape Gizmo Active Actor,** highlighted

FIGURE 7.2: A Landscape Created from Heightmap in Figure7.1.

in Figure 7.3(a).

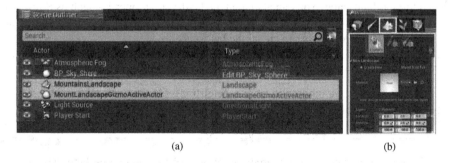

(a)   (b)

FIGURE 7.3: (a) Landscape Actor and Landscape Gizmo Actor. (b) Landscape Panel

7.2.1 CREATING A LANDSCAPE

Creating a landscape is a very easy process. The more time consuming process is to edit the landscape, to set up its materials and layers, and to make it look realistic and desirable.

To create a landscape, simply select the **Landscape Tool** of the **Modes** Panel (see Figure 7.3(b)). The Landscape tool looks like a Mountain icon. You can also open the Landscape tool by pressing `Shift + 3` on your keyboard. Under the Landscape Panel you will see three tabs. These are the modes of the landscape tool:

Manage: This tab has two main functionalities. The first is to create a landscape if there isn't one already created in your level. The second function is activated if you select a Landscape Actor, and allows you to manage the landscape by editing its components. We will see this function later in this chapter (the left tab in Figure 7.3(b)).

Sculpt: This tab is disabled if no landscape actor is present in your map. Once a landscape is created and selected in the map, this tab becomes active and gives you a host of tools to "sculpt" the landscape (the left middle in Figure 7.3(b)).

Paint: This tab is disabled if no landscape actor is present in your map. Once a landscape is created and selected in the map, this tab becomes active and allows you to paint landscape material on it (the right tab in Figure 7.3(b)).

There are two ways to create a landscape. The first is to create one from scratch. In creating a blank landscape from scratch you will need to click on the `Create New` radio button in the **Manage** section of the landscape panel. Before you create a new landscape, you may assign a landscape material to it, change its properties such as `Section Size`, `Overall Resolution`, etc. Once you are happy with its primitive properties either click on **Fill World** or **Create** buttons to create the landscape.

The second way to create a new landscape is to import one from a heightmap file. To do this, click on the `Import from File` radio button in the **Manage** section of the landscape button. This will take you to a rollout that allows you to browse and select a heightmap file, choose the heightmap resolution, and apply a landscape material to the landscape. You can also manage landscape properties such as `Section Size`, `Overall Resolution`, etc. Once you are ready to create the landscape, click on **Fit To Data** or **Import** to create the landscape.

NOTE

When importing a landscape from a heightmap file, pay attention to the file format. To avoid an unintended quality issues, make sure the height map is a 16-bit, gray scale, PNG file.

In both cases you will see a green wireframe of the impending landscape in the viewport. Once you create the landscape by either method, the **Sculpt** and **Paint** tabs will be activated and you can edit your landscape to create the outdoors look you wish to achieve.

7.2.2   THE LANDSCAPE MANAGE TAB (CREATION MODE)

As mentioned above, in the Landscape Manage Tab you can either create new landscapes or edit existing landscapes. Let's take a look at each property of the `New Landscape` mode of the manage tab [25]:

Create New: If selected, a new landscape will be created from scratch.

Import from File: If selected, a landscape will be created from a heightmap file.

Material: Allows you to assign a material to the landscape upon creation.

Location: The location in the world where the landscape will be created.

Rotation: The rotation of the landscape in the world.

Scale: The landscape scale in the world.

Section Size: Section size is used for landscape LOD (Level of Detail) and culling. Smaller sections make the landscape more aggressively utilize the LOD of sections at the cost of CPU calculations. Using larger sections will reduce the number of components, which in turn will result in less CPU cost.

Section per Component: This property in tandem with section size determines the landscape's LOD. Each section is the unit of the landscape LOD. So a 2×2 section gives 4 different LODs at once. Larger section sizes will allow for less CPU calculation time, but could result in too many draw calls on very large areas of landscape or on mobile devices [25].

Number of Components: Along with section size, this property sets the size of your landscape. It is highly recommended not to exceed component numbers of 32×32, as larger numbers could lead to performance issues.

Overall Resolution: Specifies the number of vertices in your landscape.

Fill World: Makes the landscape as big as possible – i.e., ignores the settings.

Create: Creates the landscape based on settings specified.

In Tutorial 7.1 you will create a landscape to get some experience with both methods of landscape creation. We will first create a blank landscape. Then we will very quickly modify it to create some elevation. After the landscape looks a bit less dull we will export its heightmap to a heightmap PNG file. Once we have set up the heightmap, we will delete our landscape and import it from the heightmap file.

TUTORIAL 7.1   Creating Your First Landscape

In this tutorial we will first create a new landscape. Then we will export its height map and recreate it from the heightmap.

CREATE A BLANK PROJECT

First, let's create an empty project. By now you should be familiar with creating a project, but if this is the first chapter you have picked up, follow these steps to create a blank project:

1. Open the Unreal Launcher and select the version of the engine you would like to work with.

FIGURE 7.4: Creating a Blank Project for Landscape Tutorials.

2. Once the Editor Opens, choose **New Project** (see Figure 7.4).
3. Select the **Blueprint** as your project type, and make sure that the **Blank** is selected.
4. Select your platform (Desktop/Console) and your graphics quality.
5. Make sure you include the starter content (see Figure 7.4).
6. Give your project a name and click **Create Project**.

CREATING A MAP AND ORGANIZING ASSETS:

You will notice that the **Advanced_Lighting** map is open. We would like to
create our own map as we will populate it through the tutorials in this chapter.
Take the following steps to organize your created maps and assets:

7. In the **Game** folder create a new folder. To do this select the **Game** folder. Then
   either `Right-Click` and select `New Folder` or simply click on **New** icon in the
   content browser and choose `New Folder`.
8. Name this folder something like `Maps`.
9. `Double-Click` on the `Maps` folder you just created to open it.
10. Click on the **New** asset icon and select **New Level** to create your new map.
11. Rename this level to `Outdoors`. You can do this by pressing the F2 key while
    having the map selected. (*Maps in the content browser are orange icons with the
    word **Level** on their thumbnail.*)
12. `Double-Click` on the level to open it up.

You will notice that your level is empty. Which means that it is *literally* empty – no lights, or sky sphere, or sounds. We will make some changes and populate the level to at least be able to see things. That means adding a **Directional Light** and a **Sky Sphere** blueprint to the level. To do this perform the following tasks:

FIGURE 7.5: Sky Sphere in the Level.

13. Under the **Modes** Panel (the upper left corner of the Unreal Editor) click on the `Search classes` and search **BP_Sky_Sphere** to look for the Sky Sphere class.
14. Drag the **BP_Sky_Sphere** class into the level to place an instance of this object into your level.
15. Click on the Sky Sphere Actor in the **Scene Outliner** (the upper right corner of the Unreal Editor). Press F2 to rename the actor to `LevelSkySphere`.
16. Move the Sky Sphere to (0,0,0) in the world by typing these numbers into its Location in the **Details** rollout (the lower right corner of the Unreal Editor).
17. Under the **Modes** Panel again click on the `Search classes` and search of **Directional_Light** to look for the Directional Light class.
18. Drag a copy of the **Directional_Light** and place it in the level.
19. Click on the light and press F2 to rename it to `LevelDirectionalLight`. Move it to (0,0,100) by typing these numbers in the **Location** section of the **Details** rollout.

20. Now we need to assign this light to the directional light of the **Sky_Sphere**. To do this, click on the **LevelSkySphere**, and open its `Directional Light Actor` drop-down box in its **Details** rollout.

21. In the drop-down, select the **LevelDirectionalLight** you just created.

22. Now we need to assign this light to the directional light of the **Sky_Sphere**. To do this, click on the **LevelSkySphere**, and open its `Directional Light Actor` drop-down box in its **Details** rollout.

23. In the drop-down, select the **LevelDirectionalLight** you just created.

24. Again under the **Modes** Panel click on the `Search classes` and search **Player Start** to look for the Directional Light class. Alternatively, you can click on **Basic** tab to access the **Player Start.**

25. Drag a copy of the **Player Start** and place it in the level.

26. Click on the Player Start icon and press **F2** to rename it to `LevelPlayerStart`. Move it to (0,0,200) by typing these numbers in the **Location** section of the **Details** rollout.

27. Save your level and progress so far. Your level should look like Figure 7.5.

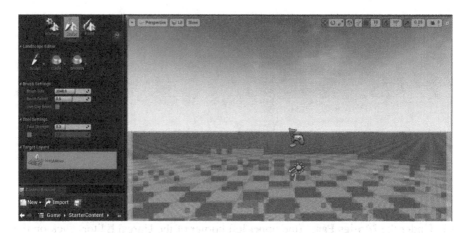

FIGURE 7.6: New Landscape Placed in the Level.

CREATE A LANDSCAPE:

Now with our Sky Sphere set up, and the directional light assigned, it's time to create a landscape.

28. In the **Modes** Panel, click on the **Landscape Tool** (The Mountain icon) to select the tool. You can alternatively press `Shift+3` on your keyboard to select the **Landscape Tool.**

29. In the Manage section of the Landscape tool make sure **Create New** radio button is selected. Use the following properties to create your landscape, and leave everything else as default.

Location: (0,0,-200)
Size Section: 15 × 15 Quads
Section Per Component: 2 × 2 Section
Number of Components: 4 × 4
Overall Resolution: 121 × 121

30. You will notice that the Landscape tool is now in **Sculpt** mode. Your Level should look like Figure 7.6.

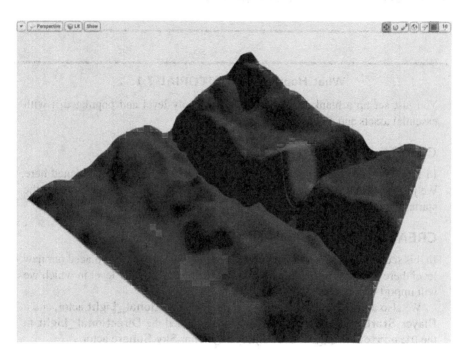

FIGURE 7.7: The View of a Sculpted Landscape from Afar.

SCULPT YOUR LANDSCAPE:

We will now make some very basic edits to our brand new landscape to create some hills and valleys.

31. Zoom out a little in your editor to get a good view of your landscape. *Note: Make sure you don't accidentally* Left-Click *on the landscape.*
32. Once you have a good view of your landscape from afar, you can start editing the landscape. The following actions will perform the minor edits we intend to do.
    Left-Click: Raises the landscape up to create hills.
    Shift + Left-Click: Lowers the landscape to create valleys.
33. Change the **Brush Size** to 2048.
34. Change the **Brush Falloff** to 0.5.

35. Change the **Tool Strength** to 0.3.
36. Now sculpt your landscape by left-clicking and dragging the mouse over the landscape to create hills, or by holding the `Shift` key and left-clicking while dragging the mouse over the landscape to create valleys.
37. Feel free to change your brush parameters such as its size, falloff, and strength.
38. Once you are satisfied with the look of your landscape you may build your lighting and save your level and progress.
39. My sculpted landscape looks like Figure 7.7.

What Happened in TUTORIAL 7.1...

You just set up a blank project, created an empty level and populated it with essential assets and a landscape.

CREATE A BLANK PROJECT

In this section you created an empty project. Nothing exciting happened here. We just made sure that our project is a Blueprint project and that it contains the starter contents.

CREATING A MAP AND ORGANIZING ASSETS:

In this section we just added a new folder to our Game folder and placed our new level there for organizational purposes. We will make another level in which we will import a landscape in the next tutorial.

We also added a **BP_Sky_Sphere** actor, a **Directional_Light** actor, and a **Player Start** actor into our level. We also assigned the **Directional_Light** to the `Directional Light Actor` property of our **Sky Sphere** actor.

CREATE A LANDSCAPE:

This section was actually the section in which we added the landscape to our level. Creating a new landscape was actually pretty easy. All we needed to do was to go to the **Landscape Tool** in the **Modes** Panel, enter some basic properties for our new landscape, and click on the **Create** button.

SCULPT YOUR LANDSCAPE:

Once the landscape was created, we made some sculpting edits to it to make it look pretty impressive. To sculpt our landscape we made some changes to our brush. Using `left-click` and `shift + left-click` of the mouse we raised and lowered the elevation of our landscape.

Finally, we built our level's lighting as the geometry of our level changed with the sculpting of the landscape.

Congratulations! You just created your first landscape in Unreal Engine 4. As you noticed, the creation of a landscape (even the simple sculpting we did) was fairly easy. Now let's export our landscape's heightmap to a PNG file. We will then duplicate our level, delete its terrain, and recreate it. Except this time, we will import the height map to create the landscape.

TUTORIAL 7.2   Creating a Landscape from Heightmap Files

If you haven't completed Tutorial 7.1, go to page 369 to create a Landscape. We will need this landscape to complete our work below.

EXPORTING THE HEIGHTMAP

In this section we will export the heightmap of our landscape.

1. Go to the **Landscape** Tool in the **Modes** Panel. To do this either click on the Mountain icon or press Shift+3 on your keyboard.
2. Since we already have a landscape in our level, you should be in the **Sculpt** mode of your landscape tool.

> **NOTE**
>
> If the sculpt mode is disabled, you probably don't have a terrain (landscape) in the level. Go to Tutorial 7.1 on page 369 to create one.

3. Right-Click on the Heightmap in the Sculpt mode and choose Export to File (see Figure 7.8).
4. When the Export Landscape Heightmap window pops open, navigate to a location where you can easily find the exported heightmap later.
5. Give your heightmap file a distinctive name, such as MyFirstHeightmap. *Note: I recommend not having spaces in the name.*

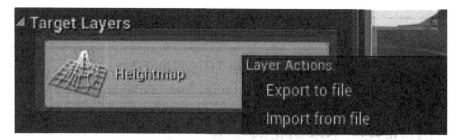

FIGURE 7.8: Exporting the Heightmap to File.

6. Before we proceed to duplicate our level, save everything.

DUPLICATING THE LEVEL AND IMPORT LANDSCAPE HEIGHTMAP

In this section we will duplicate our level, delete the Landscape actor, and create one by importing the heightmap.

7. In the Content Browser, double-click on the **Maps** folder you created in Tutorial 7.1 to open it.
8. You should see your **Outdoors** level (the orange thumbnail with the word "Level" on it).
9. Right-Click on the **Outdoors** Level, and choose Duplicate. Once Duplicated, UE4 will give it the name Outdoors2.
10. The duplicate level (**Outdoors2** will have a copy of all of our creations so far.
11. Select the level **Outdoors2** (Left-Click on it once) and save it by pressing Control+S on your keyboard.
12. In the Scene Outliner (upper right corner of the editor) find the **Landscape** actor. Select it by left-clicking on it once, and press the delete key on your keyboard to delete it. Once the Landscape is deleted, you should notice that the **Modes** Panel of the editor snaps back to the **Place** mode.
13. In the **Modes** Panel go back to the **Landscape** Tool (click on the Mountain icon, or press Shift+3).
14. This time, select the **Import from File** radio button.
15. Click on the "..." (or browse) button next to the Heightmap File and navigate to the folder to which you exported your heightmap in step 4.
16. Use the following properties for the landscape:
    Location: (0,0,–200)
    Size Section: 15 × 15 Quads
    Section Per Component: 2 × 2 Section
    Number of Components: 4 × 4
    Overall Resolution: 121 × 121
17. Click on the **Import** button to create your landscape.
18. Save your level.

What Happened in TUTORIAL 7.2...

You just exported the heightmap of your first landscape to used it to create another landscape.

EXPORTING THE HEIGHTMAP

In this section we exported our heightmap file to a PNG file. This is a great way to save your landscape heightmaps and reuse them in other projects and levels to save yourself a tremendous amount of time creating brand new landscapes from scratch.

DUPLICATING THE LEVEL AND IMPORTING THE LAND-SCAPE HEIGHTMAP

Creating a landscape from imported heightmap files was as easy as simply creating a new landscape actor. All you needed to do was to specify the heightmap, and choose the property of your landscape. Then you can just simply import the heightmap to create the landscape.

If you want to use the same landscape properties as the original landscape on which the heightmap is based, you can click the **Fit to Data** button. This will automatically fit the heightmap to the data.

Great! We have learned how to create landscapes with just the press of a button in two different ways. But as you can see the landscapes we have created so far (although sculpted) don't look nearly as nice as what you have imagined. That is because there's much more that goes into a landscape than just the heightmap.

You should have noticed that we left the landscape material empty when we created our landscapes in Tutorials 7.1 and 7.2.

In the following section we will discuss **Landscape Materials** [28] and Landscape specific **Material Expressions** [26]. A more comprehensive list and descriptions of functionalities may be found on the Unreal Engine documentation website.[1]

> ### CROSS-REFERENCE
>
> To learn more Unreal Engine 4's Materials and Material Editor check out Chapter 4 and Section 4.3 on page 127.

7.3 LANDSCAPE MATERIALS

Although you can use any material as a landscape material, Unreal Engine 4 allows for much more complex and specialized material systems to be used in tandem with landscapes. These specialized materials give you a tremendous amount of control and flexibility in texturing Landscapes in UE4. We will take a look at what is so special about Landscape Materials, learn how we can utilize them in our landscapes and how the rendering engine in UE4 provides specific functionalities to these materials.

7.3.1 HOW LANDSCAPE MATERIALS BLEND

In UE4, the rendering mechanism uses a weight blending approach in combining landscape materials, as opposed to alpha blending. The blending values for all of the layers involved with a landscape material at any given location will be normalized – i.e., they add up to 1.0.

---

[1]https://docs.unrealengine.com/latest/INT/Engine/Rendering/Materials/ExpressionReference/index.html

There are advantages and disadvantages to this approach. The advantage is that you will have the flexibility to paint any layer on any location in the landscape. As you add more and more of that layer, its weight increases while simultaneously decreasing the weights of the other layers.

This comes at a cost. If you have a layer at 100% weight – e.g., the first layer you paint, you may not be able to remove it. This is because when a layer is at 100% weight, normalization forces the weight of all the other layers to be 0. When attempting to remove this layer, UE4 will not have a mechanism to know which layer you want it to be replaced with.

7.3.2 LANDSCAPE MATERIAL EXPRESSIONS

Landscape material expressions are those expressions that allow you to design landscape specific functionalities for the materials to be used as a landscape material. The following list is adopted from the Unreal Engine 4 official online documentation [26].

CROSS-REFERENCE

A comprehensive list of Material Expressions may be found in Appendix A.

Landscape Layer Blend: This expression, shown in Figure 7.9, enables you to blend multiple textures or material networks together to be used as landscape layers. This expression uses an array of objects that store information about each layer. This information includes the layer's name, blend type, preview weight, layer input, and height input.
To add a layer to the array of layers, simply click on the + sign next to **Layers** in the **Details** rollout of this expression.
To remove a layer simply, click on the trash bin icon, and select the name of the layer to delete, or click on the triangle icon next to the name of the layer and choose delete.
- **Properties**
  Layers: The list of layers the node contains. Layers can be added by clicking in the + icon.
  Layer Name: The unique name to be used for the layer. The name corresponds to the layer name in the paint mode in the Landscape editing tool.
  Blend Type: The Blend Type of this expression specifies which of the LB_AlphaBlend, LB_HeightBlend or LB_WeightBlend to use for blending.
  Preview Weight: This is used as the weight for the layer to preview the blending in the material editor.
  Const Layer Input: This is for using a Const3Vector as the color to be used if you don't want to use a texture map. Useful for debugging purposes.

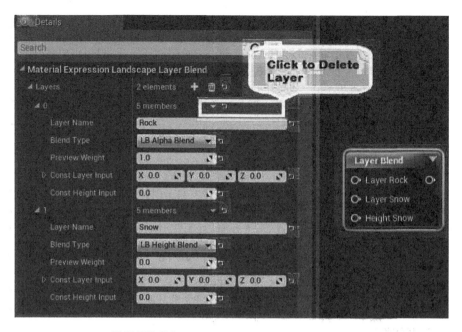

FIGURE 7.9: Landscape Layer Blend Expression.

Const Height Input: This is to be used as the value for the height if you don't want to use a texture for the height map.

- **Inputs**

  Layer *<LayerName>*: Each layer adds an input for the layer to blend together. These inputs will not be available until layers are added in the **Details** rollout of this expression.

  Height *<LayerName>*: This is where you supply a height map to blend with. *Note: This input will only be visible on layers that have their Blend Type property set to* `LB_HeightBlend`.

- **Outputs**

  Output: The result of the blended layers.

Example Usage: When you want to have the landscape materials blend together based on a heightmap of each layer, this can come from their alpha channel, for example), or their weight you will be able to utilize this expression to facilitate the functionality.

IMPORTANT NOTE

When using the `LB_HeightBlend` mode for all Landscape layers, there may be unpleasant artifacts such as black spots on the landscape. `LB_HeightBlend` works by modulating the blend factor,for the layer using the specified height value. This occurs when all the layers painted in a particular area simultaneously have a 0 height value. The situation is worse when you are blending a Normal map. If a blending normal map becomes (0,0,0) it will cause rendering problems, as it is an invalid normal. To avoid this problem use `LB_AlphaBlend` or `LB_WeightBlend` for one of the layers in your collection of layers [26].

IMPORTANT NOTE

If you are using `LB_AlphaBlend` for one of the layers in your collection of layer in the **Layer Blend** expression, make sure that its alpha channel is not zero, otherwise you might end up with black patches on your landscape.

IMPORTANT NOTE

If using `LB_AlphaBlend` or `LB_WeightBled` still didn't resolve the black pateches in the landscape where layers blend together, add small values such as 0.1 to the **Height** value being applied to the **Layer Blend** expression.

Landscape Layer Coords: This expression, shown in Figure 7.10, enables you to generate coordinates that will be used to map materials to the landscape terrain.

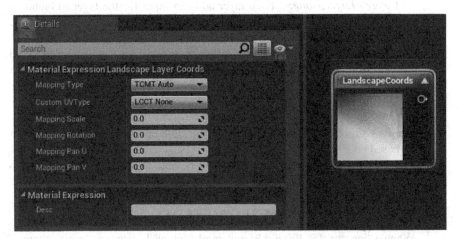

FIGURE 7.10: Landscape Coordinate Expression.

- **Properties**
    Mapping Type: Specifies the orientation to use when mapping the material or network to the landscape. Types include **Auto, XY Plane, XZ**

Plane, and **YZ Plane**. For example, **XZ** aligns the material to the XZ plane, while **Auto** allows the engine to use the best plane to map.

Custom UV Type: Specifies the UV coordinates to map on the landscape based on the given property values.

Mapping Scale: Specifies the uniform scaling to apply to the UV coordinates.

Mapping Rotation: The rotation (in degrees) to apply to the UV coordinates.

Mapping Pan U: The offset in U direction to apply to the UV coordinates.

Mapping Pan V: The offset in V direction to apply to the UV coordinates.

Output: Outputs the UV coordinates to apply to the texture samples for the landscape materials.

Landscape Layer Switch: When a particular material network does not contribute to a region of the landscape you can use this expression to exclude it from the calculations of the landscape material. This will be a mechanism to optimize your material by removing unnecessary calculations – i.e., when a particular layer's weight is 0.

- **Properties**
  Parameter Name: The unique name to be given to the parameter.
  Preview Used: If checked, will use a preview.
- **Inputs**
  Layer Used: The result to use when the layer specified in the expression's properties is in use by the region in the landscape.
  Layer Not Used: The result to use when the layer is not used by the current region of the landscape and has a weight of 0.
- **Outputs**
  Output: Outputs one of the Layer Used or Layer Not Used, depending on the contribution to the particular region of the landscape.

Landscape Layer Weight: This expression allows material networks to be blended based on the weight for the associated layer from the landscape on which the material is going to be applied.

- **Properties**
  Parameter Name: The unique name of the layer belonging to the landscape to be associated with this parameter. The weight for this layer is used as the alpha value for blending the two input networks.
  Preview Weight: The weight to use for previewing in the material editor.
  Const Base: A base color for the landscape.
- **Inputs**
  Base: The network to blend this layer with. This is generally the result of any previous layer blending, but can be empty if this is the first layer.
  Layer: The network to blend together to create this layer.

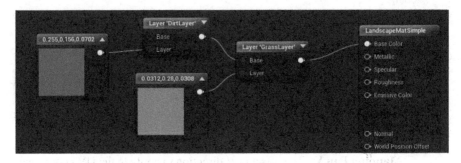

FIGURE 7.11: Landscape Layer Weight Expression.

- **Outputs**
  Output: Outputs the result of the blending between base and layer inputs
    based on the layer weight of the layers involved.
Example Usage: Suppose that you want to have two layers in your landscape
    material, the first layer to be a "Dirt" layer and the second layer to be a
    "Grass" layer. You will create the network for each of the materials, a net-
    work that creates a "Grass" and one that creates a "Dirt" material look. Make
    two **Layer Weight** expressions. Connect the output of your first network
    (e.g., the "Dirt") to the Layer of the first **Layer Weight** expression, leav-
    ing its Base input unconnected. You will then connect output of the first
    Layer Weight expression to the Base input of the second **Layer Weight**
    expression. Connect the network for your second layer's material (e.g., the
    "Grass") to the Layer input of the second **Layer Weight**. Connecting the
    output of the second expression to the appropriate channel (Base Color,
    Normal, etc.) of the material node will create this layered Landscape Mate-
    rial (see Figure 7.11).

Landscape Visibility Mask: To create holes in a landscape (e.g., creating cave
    openings), you can use this expression to remove the visibility of parts of the
    landscape.
- **Outputs**
  Output: Outputs the visibility mask properties.
To activate this expression, connect its sole output to the **Opacity Mask** channel
of the material node and choose the Blend Mode of your material (in its **Details**
rollout) to **Masked**.
Example Usage: Each Landscape actor allows you to assign a **Landscape Ma-
    terial** and a **Landscape Hole** material.

A Word on Tessellation and Displacement

You may use the UE4's **Tessellation** and **World Displacement** material channel
much like a standard material to add more details and deformations to your terrain.

Simply build the network you want and use the layer blending in tandem to create these effects.

> **NOTE**
>
> Like standard materials, the Tessellation and World Displacement in Landscape Materials are limited to use with DirectX11 enabled. If your hardware does not support DirectX 11, these effects will not be created and applied.

Creating and Working with Landscape Materials

Now that we have learned about the Landscape it is time to create some Landscape materials and use them in our landscape. In Tutorial 7.3 we will create a landscape material and apply it to our landscape. We will then use the **Paint** mode of the **Landscape** tool to paint this material onto our landscape to make it look better.

TUTORIAL 7.3 Creating a Simple Landscape Material

If you haven't completed Tutorial 7.1, go to page 369 to create a Landscape. We will need this landscape to complete our work below.

SETTING UP YOUR FIRST LANDSCAPE MATERIAL

In this section we will create a folder to organize our landscape materials. We will then create a very simple three layer material for our landscape to have sand, grass, and snow for us to paint on our landscape.

1. If you haven't created a landscape and this tutorial is your first in this chapter please follow the steps in Tutorial 7.1 to make a basic landscape to work with.
2. **Right-Click** in the **Content Browser**, on the Main **Game** folder and create a new folder. Name it **Landscape Materials**.
3. Double-click on this folder to open it.
4. **Right-Click** inside the **Landscape Materials** folder you just created and choose **New->Material** to create a new material.
5. Rename the new material **Mat_LScape_Simple**.
6. Double-click on the **Mat_LScape_Simple** to open it in the Material Editor.

We have created a material for our landscape. We will next edit it in the material editor to contain our landscape layers.

SETTING UP THE MATERIAL COLORS

Let's first start with the colors of our sand, grass, and snow materials. To keep the shader calculations simple, I will use Const4Vectors for Base Color of our material networks to feed to our layers.

7. In the graph editor in `Right-Click` somewhere to the far-left of the material node and create a Const3Vector. You can alternatively create this vector by pressing the key **3** on your keyboard and clicking somewhere on the graph editor.
8. Give this vector a brown color with **(R:0.25,G:0.15,B:0.05)** values.
9. In the description of this Vector, type in `Sand Color`.
10. Create another Const3Vector below the Sand Color.
11. Give this vector a green color with **(R:0.05,G:0.25,B:0.0)** values.
12. In the description of this Vector, type in `Grass Color`.
13. Create another Const3Vector below the Grass Color.
14. Give this vector a white color with **(R:0.75,G:0.75,B:0.75)** values.
15. In the description of this Vector, type in `Snow Color`.

CREATE MATERIAL LAYERS

Let's now set up our material layers. We will use **Landscape Layer Weight** expressions for this setup.

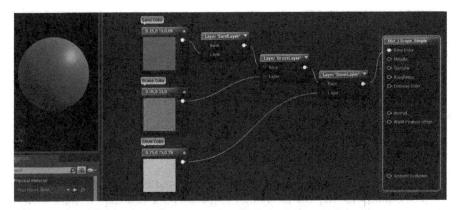

FIGURE 7.12: Simple Landscape Material Layer Setup.

16. In the graph editor `Right-Click` somewhere to the right of the **Sand Color** and search for `Landscape Layer Weight` expression.
17. Name this expression `SandLayer`. *Make sure the name is one word.*
18. In the **Details** rollout of this expression, type 1.0 in the `Preview Weight` section.
19. Connect the output channel of the **Sand Color** to the `Layer` input channel of the SandLayer **Layer Weight** expression.
20. Leave the `Base` input of this expression unconnect.
21. `Right-Click` to the right of the **SandLayer** expression and search for and place another **Layer Weight** expression.
22. Rename this expression to `Grasslayer`. *Make sure the name is one word.*
23. Connect the output channel of the **Grass Color** to the `Layer` input channel of the GrassLayer **Layer Weight** expression.

24. Connect the output channel of the `SandLayer` expression to the **Base** input of this expression.
25. `Right-Click` to the right of the **GrassLayer** expression and search for and place another **Layer Weight** expression.
26. Rename this expression to `SnowLayer`. *Make sure the name is one word.*
27. Connect the output channel of the **Snow Color** to the `Layer` input channel of the `SnowLayer` **Layer Weight** expression.
28. Connect the output channel of the `GrassLayer` expression to the **Base** input of this expression.
29. Your material setup should look like Figure 7.12 so far.
30. Compile and save your material.

This is great progress. We have just created a blending network for our first landscape material. Now is the time to get in our level and apply this material to our landscape.

APPLYING LANDSCAPE MATERIALS TO LANDSCAPE

To be able to paint our material layers onto our landscape, we need to associate the material to our Landscape actor. We will then need to create `Layer Info Assets` for each of the layers to be painted on the landscape.

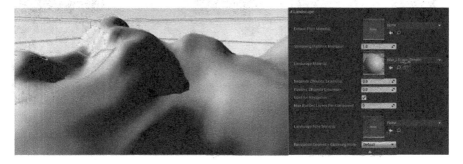

FIGURE 7.13: Landscape Material Applied to Landscape.

31. In the main editor click on the name of your Landscape Actor (NOT the Landscape Gizmo Actor) in the Scene Outliner to select it.
32. In the **Details** rollout of your landscape actor, find the `Landscape` section.
33. You will notice in the `Landscape` section there are two material slots. The `Landscape Material` slot is where your landscape material will have to go. If you have a landscape hole material to allow for the creation of openings (such as for caves) in the landscape it will go into the `Landscape Hole Material`.
34. With your landscape actor selected, navigate to your Materials folder you created earlier and find your `Mat_LandScape_Simple` material.
35. Drag the `Mat_Landscape_Simple` material into the **Landscape Material** section of your Landscape actor (see Figure 7.13).

36. This will apply the landscape material we created to your landscape. Notice that UE4 will immediately start compiling the shaders for this material.

37. At this stage your level editor should give you a warning about "Lighting Needs to Be Rebuilt". Click on the **Build** icon in the main editor toolbar to build your lighting. *If you don't have a Lightmass Importance Volume you may get a warning. To avoid the warning, create a Lightmass Importance Volume and make it fit your landscape.*

38. Compile and save your level.

Well, we're making great progress. We just created our first Landscape Material and applied it to our landscape. Let's now get into our **Landscape** Tool's **Paint** mode and start painting our material onto the terrain.

PAINTING MATERIAL LAYERS ON THE LANDSCAPE

Now let's paint some layers. To do this we will go to the **Paint** mode of our **Landscape** tool and select which layer to paint. We will then paint each layer and keep switching layers to paint. In this section, we will use a simple brush to paint the layers much like what we did in Tutorial 7.1 when we edited our landscape in the **Sculpt** mode.

FIGURE 7.14: Landscape Layer Info Missing Error.

39. In the **Landscape** tool in the **Modes** Panel select the **Paint** section.

40. Use the following values for your **Brush Settings** and **Tool Settings**:
    Brush Size: 512
    Brush Falloff: 0.5
    Tool Strength: 0.3

41. If you attempt to paint onto your landscape you will get an error message saying (see Figure 7.14):
    "This layer has no layer info assigned yet. You must create or assign a layer info before you can paint this layer".

42. This is because we just created landscape layers in our landscape material and haven't assigned to them a layer info asset for the engine to be able to apply appropriate blending to the layers. We will do that next.

43. Create Layer Infos for your SnowLayer, SandLayer, and GrassLayer:

FIGURE 7.15: Landscape Layers Painted.

  a. Select the **SandLayer** in the `Target Layers` Section of the **Paint** mode. Click on the + sign on the Sand Layer item to add a layer info for it (see Figure 7.14).
  b. From the pop up menu choose "`Weight Blended Layer (normal)`". This will allow for this layer to be blended with other layers painted on its position based on each layer's respective weight.
  c. Repeat the same process with the **GrassLayer** and the **SnowLayer** layers.
44. Now start painting your layers onto the landscape. Notice that the first layer (`SandLayer`) is already painted. But once you start painting, your editor will immediately start compiling shaders. You should keep adding layers and switch between Sand, Grass, and Snow to get the desired look.
45. I personally prefer to have the grass populate flat surfaces, Sand to be painted over steep areas, and snow to be located on the mountaintops.
46. Once you are satisfied with the look of your landscape and it looks something like Figure 7.15 you may stop.
47. Compile and save your level.

NOTE

When you first start painting your landscape the materials may disappear on the landscape and some black patches may appear. This issue occurs because for the first time around there is no paint layer data on your landscape. The solution to this issue is to paint over the landscape for some time, and as you continue to paint, the data will become available. To easily paint your base layer onto the landscape and to help facilitate with the first time data gathering, simply select a very large brush size (e.g., 8192) and brush all over the landscape.

What Happened in TUTORIAL 7.3...

You just created your first landscape material and applied its layers to your landscape. We will go over what we did in the tutorial step by step.

SETTING UP YOUR FIRST LANDSCAPE MATERIAL

In this section we just organized our assets. We created a folder to host our landscape materials and created a simple material in the folder as our first landscape material.

SETTING UP THE MATERIAL COLORS

Next, we set up the Base color network of our material. In this section, we created three Constant3Vectors for our Sand, Grass, and Snow material layers. We assigned a brown color to Sand, a green color to Grass, and a white color to the Snow Vectors.

CREATE MATERIAL LAYERS

This section was where most of the action takes place. We needed to create three layers for each material (Sand, Grass, and Snow) so that our rendered can combine and blend them together. So we created three Layers, a **SandLayer**, a **GrassLayer**, and a **SnowLayer**, using **Landscape Layer Weight** material expressions.

If you recall, these expressions have two inputs, a **Base** and a **Layer** input. The **Base** input takes in a material network to apply as the first (bottom) blend node. This layer will be the base of the combined calculations. The **Layer** input takes in the material network to apply as the second blend node. This layer will be applied on top of the base for the blend calculations.

We want the Sand to be the first layer, Grass the second, and Snow the last. This is because our landscape starts with a layer of sand (or rock). On top of the sand, we may have grass grow, and finally snow will go on top of the other two layers.

So for this reason, the **SandLayer** leaves the base input unconnected and takes the Sand Color as its **Layer** input network. Then **GrassLayer** took the output of the **SandLayer** as base and applied the Grass Color network as its **Layer** input. Finally, the **SnowLayer** took the result of the **GreenLayer** calculations as its **Base** input and the Snow Color network as the **Layer** input. The final output of this network was then applied to the **Base Color** channel of our material (see Figure 7.12).

APPLYING LANDSCAPE MATERIALS TO LANDSCAPE

Once our landscape material is created we can assign it to our landscape actor and start painting its layers. To assign a material (any material can be assigned to a landscape) all you need to do is to select the landscape actor in the Scene Outliner and drag the material from the **Content Browser** to the **Landscape Material** slot in its **Landscape** section in the **Details** rollout.

Next, we went to the **Paint** mode of the **Landscape** tool. In the paint mode you can select settings for your layer paintbrush, change the brush, and create and assign Layer Infos to your layers. Since we just created our layers, they didn't have any Layer Info assigned to them. We created one Layer Info for each of the SandLayer, GrassLayer, and SnowLayer.

With the Layer Infos created for our landscape layers, we selected appropriate settings for our paintbrush, selected one of the three layers and started painting our layers. We kept switching between layers until we got the appropriate look for our landscape.

Fantastic! Our landscape is starting to look better and better. But unless you were making a cartoon-like terrain we are'nt close enough to have finished our job. Now that being said, setting up simple materials and layers is a great way to get your level going and ready for the team programmers to work with. It is also a great way to debug the look and feel of your terrain without having to incur a lot of computational cost editing your level.

Before we move on to discussing other landscape features, we will create a nice looking material based on some real textures in Tutorial 7.4. Then we will create a relatively powerful blending network to have our layers blend with each other much more smoothly in Tutorial 7.6.

The first landscape material you created in Tutorial 7.3 was actually quite simple and didn't really have any interesting features. We will show you can build a much better and complex network for each of your material layer networks to make your landscape look more realistic.

TUTORIAL 7.4   Creating a Detailed Landscape Material

If you haven't completed Tutorial 7.1, go to page 369 to create a Landscape. We will need this landscape to complete our work below.

DUPLICATING LANDSCAPE MATERIAL

1. Go to the **Materials** folder you created in our earlier Tutorials.
2. **Right-Click** on the **Mat_LandScape_Simple** material we created in Tutorial 7.3 and duplicate it.
3. Rename the duplicated material to **Mat_LScape_Textured**.
4. Double-click the **Mat_LScape_Textured** material to open it in the material editor.

SETTING UP LAYER NETWORKS

With the new material opened in the Material Editor, let's go ahead and use some textures instead of the simple color 3Vectors for the **Sand** and **Grass**.

5. `Right-Click` to the left of the `Sand Color` vector and create a **Texture Sample** expression. Remember, you can alternatively create this expression by holding the T key and clicking on the graph editor.

6. In the **Details** rollout of this texture sample look for and apply the `T_Ground_Gravel_D` texture. To do this click on the drop-down box in front of the `Texture` section and search for this texture. This is one of the textures that comes with the UE4's `Starter Contents`.

7. Type `Gravel Texture` in the Description tag of this expression.

8. move the `Sand Color` vector out of the way and connect the RGBA channel of the `Gravel Texture` expression to the `Layer` input channel of the **SandLayer** expression.

9. `Right-Click` to the left of the `Grass Color` vector and create a **Texture Sample** expression. Remember, you can alternatively create this expression by holding the T key and clicking on the graph editor.

10. In the **Details** rollout of this texture sample look for and apply the `T_Ground_Grass_D` texture. To do this click on the drop-down box in front of the `Texture` section and search for this texture. This is one of the textures that comes with the UE4's `Starter Contents`.

11. Type `Grass Texture` in the Description tag of this expression.

12. Move the `Grass Color` vector out of the way and connect the RGBA channel of the `Grass Texture` expression to the `Layer` input channel of the **GrassLayer** expression.

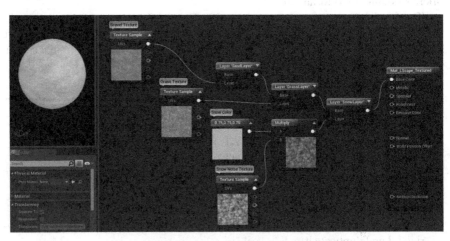

FIGURE 7.16: Landscape Material Texture Setup.

13. **Right-Click** below the **Snow Color** vector and create a **Texture Sample** expression. Remember, you can alternatively create this expression by holding the T key and clicking on the graph editor.

14. In the **Details** rollout of this texture sample look for and apply the **T_Perlin_Noise_M** texture. To do this click on the drop-down box in front of the **Texture** section and search for this texture. This is one of the textures that comes with the UE4's **Starter Contents**.

15. Type **Snow Noise Texture** in the Description tag of this expression.

16. **Right-Click** to the right of both the **Snow Noise Texture** and the **Snow Color** and place a **Multiply** expression.

17. Connect the output of the **Snow Color** to input **A** and the RGBA output of the **Snow Noise Texture** to input **B** of this **Multiply** expression.

18. Connect the output channel of the **Multiply** expression to the **Layer** input channel of the **SnowLayer** expression.

19. Make sure that the output channel of the **SnowLayer** is connected to the **Base Color** of our material node.

20. Delete the **Sand Color** and **Grass Color** expression.

21. Your network should look similar to Figure 7.16.

22. Save your material and close the material editor.

APPLYING THE MATERIAL

This material is already looking great! Let's apply it to our landscape and see how it looks. Applying the material to our landscape is easy, and you may remember the steps we took from Tutorial 7.3. But we will go through these steps one more time:

23. In the main editor click on the name of your Landscape Actor (NOT the Landscape Gizmo Actor) in the Scene Outliner to select it.

24. In the **Details** rollout of your landscape actor, find the **Landscape** section.

25. With your landscape actor selected, navigate to your Materials folder you created earlier and find your **Mat_LScape_Textured** material you just created.

26. Drag the **Mat_Landscape_Textured** material into the **Landscape Material** section of your Landscape actor.

27. This will apply the landscape material we created to your landscape. Notice that UE4 will immediately start compiling the shaders for this material.

28. At this stage your level editor should give you a warning about "**Lighting Needs to Be Rebuilt**". Click on the **Build** icon in the main editor toolbar to build your lighting.

29. Compile and save your level.

PAINTING MATERIAL LAYERS ON THE LANDSCAPE

Now let's paint our layers. To do this we will go to the **Paint** mode of our **Landscape** tool and select which layer to paint. We will then paint each layer and keep switching layers to paint.

FIGURE 7.17: Removing Old Landscape Layer Infos.

30. In the **Landscape** tool in the **Modes** Panel select the **Paint** section.
31. Use the following values for your **Brush Settings** and **Tool Settings**:
    Brush Size: 512
    Brush Falloff: 0.5
    Toll Strength: 0.3
32. We will first remove the old Layer Infos from our **Paint** mode. To do this simply click on the **X** icon next to the Obsolete Layer Infos (see Figure 7.17). These were the items we used in our previous tutorial.

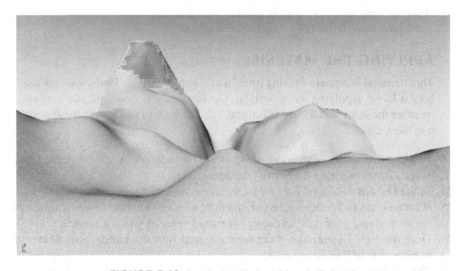

FIGURE 7.18: Landscape Textured Layers Painted.

33. Create new `Layer Infos` for your new SnowLayer, SandLayer, and GrassLayer:
    a. Select the **SandLayer** in the `Target Layers` Section of the **Paint** mode. Click on the **+** sign on the Sand Layer item to add a layer info for it (see Figure 7.14).
    b. From the pop up menu choose "`Weight Blended Layer (normal)`". This will allow for this layer to be blended with other layers painted on its position based on each layer's respective weight.
    c. Repeat the same process with the **GrassLayer** and the **SnowLayer** layers.

34. Now start painting your layers onto the landscape. Notice that the first layer (SandLayer) is already painted. But once you start painting, your editor will immediately start compiling shaders. You should keep adding layers and switch between Sand, Grass, and Snow to get the desired look.
35. I personally prefer to have the grass populate flat surfaces, Sand to be painted over steep areas, and snow to be located on the mountaintops.
36. Once you are satisfied with the look of your landscape and it looks something like Figure 7.18 you may stop.
37. Compile and save your level.

USING TEXTURE COORDINATES

If you look at our landscape so far, the materials look good from up close. But when you look into the distance, your see repeating patterns of UVs. This effect is pretty undesirable. We will next utilize a **Landscape Layer Coordinate** expression to fix this problem.

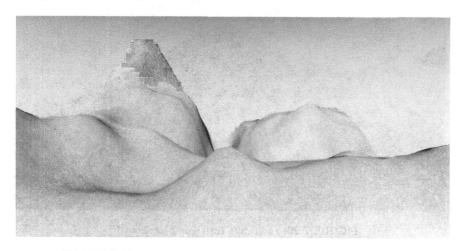

FIGURE 7.19: Landscape Textured Layers with Its Coordinates Scaled.

38. Navigate to your material folder and double-click on the UTTMat_LScape_Textured you created earlier to open it.
39. Right-Click to the left of all **Texture Sample** expressions and search for and place a **Landscape Layer Coord** expression on the graph editor.
40. Connect the output channel of the **Landscape Layer Coord** expression to the UVs input channels of the Gravel Texture, Grass Texture, and the Snow Noise Texture expressions.
41. In the **Details** rollout of the **Landscape Layer Coord** expression find the Mapping Scale and change it to a larger number such as 5.0 or 7.0.
42. Compile and Save your material.

43. Now if you go back to the main editor and let the UE4 finish compiling the shaders, you will notice those repetitive tiling patterns have disappeared. Your level should look similar to Figure 7.19.
44. Save everything in the **Content Browser** and your level.

SETTING UP THE NORMAL CHANNEL

Our landscape is now looking pretty impressive from afar! But there's still one problem left with this landscape. The problem is that everything on the landscape looks flat. The grass, gravel, even the snow doesn't really have any depth. This issue is most obvious if you look very closely at the terrain (see Figure 7.20).

Let's fix this problem now.

FIGURE 7.20: Landscape Textured Layers Look Flat.

45. Back in the **Content Browser** open up the Mat_LScape_Textured material by double-clicking it.
46. In the material editor hold the Control key on your keyboard and Left-Click on the following expressions to select them all.
    Gravel Texture
    Grass Texture
    SandLayer
    GrassLayer
    SnowLayer
47. Duplicate these expressions by pressing Control+W on your keyboard.
48. We will use these new **Layer Weight** expressions to create normal map layers for our material. To do this perform the following actions.
    a. Reorganize your duplicated **Texture Sample** and **Layer Weight** expressions.

b. Rename the duplicated **Texture Samples** as follows:
Rename Gravel Texture to Gravel Normal Texture
Rename Grass Texture to Grass Normal Texture

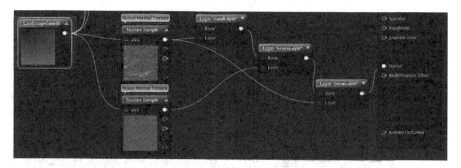

FIGURE 7.21: Network for Normal Map Layer Setup.

c. Connect the output of your **Landscape Layer Coord** expression to the UVs input of the `Sand Normal`, `Grass Normal`, and the `Snow Noise Normal` expressions.

d. In the **Details** rollout of the **Sand Normal Texture** expression look for and apply the `T_Ground_Gravel_N` texture. To do this click on the drop-down box in front of the `Texture` section and search for this texture. This is one of the textures that comes with the UE4's `Starter Contents`.

e. In the **Details** rollout of the **Grass Normal Texture** expression look for and apply the `T_Ground_Grass_N` texture. To do this click on the drop-down box in front of the `Texture` section and search for this texture. This is one of the textures that comes with the UE4's `Starter Contents`.

f. Connect the following output channels of your normal maps to the layer expressions (see Figure 7.21):
   - Connect the RGBA output of the `Sand Normal Texture` to the **Layer** input of the duplicate `SandLayer`.
   - Connect the output of the `SandLayer` to the **Base** input of the duplicate `GrassLayer`.
   - Connect the RGBA output of the `GrassNormal Texture` to the **Layer** input of the duplicate `GrassLayer`.
   - Connect the output of the `GrassLayer` to the **Base** input of the duplicate `SnowLayer`.
   - Connect the RGBA output of the `Sand Normal Texture` to the **Layer** input of the duplicate `SnowLayer`.
   - Connect the output of the `SnowLayer` to the **Normal** input of the material node.

g. Save and apply your material.

49. With the normal maps integrated into our layer blending system, the materials look great and with more realistic depth when viewed from up close in the landscape (see Figure 7.22).

FIGURE 7.22: Landscape Textured Layers Are Given Depth.

50. Now go ahead and work with your landscape a bit more, sculpt it and apply the three layers of Sand, Grass, and Snow to it.
51. When you are satisfied with the results, save your level and materials.

The level is looking pretty nice already. Before we move up to the next topic, let's tweak our materials a little to make the sand a bit darker and the grass a little more green. We will also set up a roughness channel for the material with its appropriate network to make the grass and snow a little less glossy.

FINAL TOUCHES TO THE LANDSCAPE MATERIAL

Now we will put the final touches on this material network to finish it up. First, let's make the materials' color a little more realistic.

52. Open up your `Mat_LScape_Textured` in the material editor by double-clicking on it in the **Content Browser**.
53. We first modify the Gravel Texture Color:
    a. Make some room between the **Gravel Texture** expression and the SandLayer expression.
    b. `Right-Click` above the `Gravel Texture` expression. Search for and place a **Vector Parameter** above the texture expression.
    c. In the **Parameter Name** and **Description** type in `Gravel Color`.
    d. Expand the **Gravel Color** Default Value and make the following changes:
    R: 0.61
    G: 0.32
    B: 0.12
    Alpha: 1.0

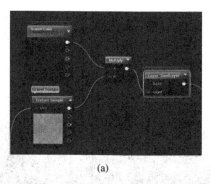

(a)

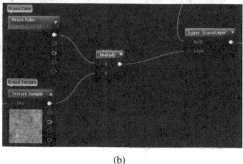

(b)

FIGURE 7.23: Landscape Textured Layers Are Given Depth.

  e. `Right-Click` to the right of the **Vector Parameter** and the **Gravel Tex-ture** and place a **Multiply** expression.
  f. Connect the RGBA channel of the **Gravel Color** to channel A, and the RGBA channel of the **Gravel Texture** to channel B of the **Multiply** expression.
  g. Connect the output channel of the **Multiply** expression to the input channel of the **SandLayer**.
  h. Your network should look similar to Figure 7.23(a).
54. If you save your material and apply it you will notice that the gravel areas on the landscape now look darker.
55. Now let's make the grass look a bit greener:
  a. Make some room between the `Grass Texture` expression and the `SandLayer` expression.
  b. `Right-Click` above the `Grass Texture` expression. Search for and place a **Vector Parameter** above the texture expression.
  c. In the **Parameter Name** and **Description** type in `Grass Color`.
  d. Expand the **Grass Color** Default Value and make the following changes:
  R: 0.2
  G: 0.3
  B: 0.1
  Alpha: 1.0

FIGURE 7.24: Landscape Texture Colors Modified.

    e. `Right-Click` to the right of the **Vector Parameter** and the **Grass Texture** and place a **Multiply** expression.

    f. Connect the `RGBA` channel of the **Gravel Color Offset** to channel A, and the `RGBA` channel of the **Grass Texture** to channel B of the **Multiply** expression.

    g. Connect the output channel of the **Multiply** expression to the input channel of the **GrassLayer**.

    h. Your network should look similar to Figure 7.23(b).

56. Save and apply your material.

57. Now if you go back to the main editor, after the shaders compilation is finished, your landscape should look more natural as shown in Figure 7.24.

58. Only one last thing is left before we finish up this Landscape Material. The material (especially on the sandy area looks too shiny!). Let's fix this issue next:

    a. Go back to your material (`Mat_LScape_Textured`) in the material editor.

    b. Duplicate the three **Layer Weight** expressions, the `SandLayer`, `GrassLayer`, and the `SnowLayer`. To do this, marquee select (or control-click) just the three **Landscape Layer Weight** expressions and then press `Control+W`.

    c. Move them close to the roughness channel of the material node. Feel free to rearrange your network if you need more room.

    d. Create two Constant expressions to the left of the duplicate **Layer Weight** expression.

    e. In the description of one of the Constant expressions type `Sand Grass Roughness` and change its R value to 1.0.

f. In the description of the second Constant expression type Snow Roughness and leave its R value at 0.25.

g. Connect the output of the **Sand Grass Roughness** to the Layer channel of both the **SandLayer** and the **GrassLayer**.

h. Connect the output of the **Snow Roughness** to the Layer channel of the **SnowLayer**.

i. Connect the output of the **SnowLayer** to the Roughness channel of your material node.

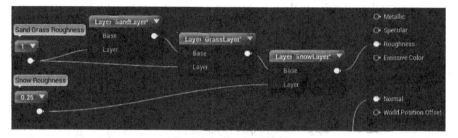

FIGURE 7.25: Landscape Texture Roughness Channel.

59. Now your snow should be glossy while sand and grass should look rough, just the way it's supposed to be.

60. Feel free to make modifications to your landscape as you wish to sculpt and paint your landscape more and see what the effect of our changes are on the look and feel of your landscape.

61. Save your level, materials, and all your progress so far.

What Happened in TUTORIAL 7.4...

You just created a more detailed landscape material and applied its layers to your landscape. We will go over what we did in the tutorial step by step.

DUPLICATING LANDSCAPE MATERIAL

In order to save ourselves some time, instead of re-creating a landscape material from scratch, we duplicated our previous landscape material. Remember, that material had three layers – i.e., the SandLayer, GrassLayer, and SnowLayer. Those layers were being fed by a simple network that was made up from simple Const3Vectors.

In our duplicate material, we will keep the layers. However, we will replace the Const3Vector Colors we used for the Sand, Grass, and Snow colors; we will use textures.

SETTING UP LAYER NETWORKS

In this step of the tutorial, we created three **Texture Sample** expressions to replace our Sand, Grass, and Snow layer material networks. The Starter Contents of the UE4 engine comes with a lot of useful textures.

We picked a `T_Ground_Gravel_D` texture (Figure 7.26(a)) for our sand (or gravel) and a `T_Ground_Grass_D` texture (Figure 7.26(b)) for our grass land. For the snowy areas we picked a `T_Perlin_Noise_M` texture (Figure 7.26(c)). Let's see how these textures were used.

Notice the `_D` at the end of the texture file name. It stands for the diffuse (or color) version of the texture. These textures also have an associated Normal Map which is signified by the prefix `_N` as we will see a little later.

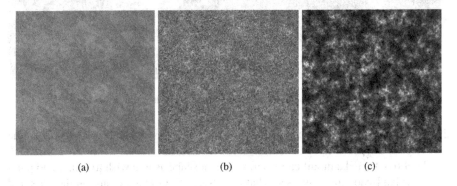

(a)   (b)   (c)

FIGURE 7.26: Texture Maps Used for the Landscape Material.

The network for the gravel and grass materials are fairly simple. All we needed to do was to connect the output of the gravel and grass texture sample expression to the **Layer** channel of their respective layer. We worked on the Snow layer a bit differently.

Notice in Figure 7.26(c) that the texture looks noisy, bright in some areas and dark in other. This texture works perfectly if we combine it with a white color to represent the uneven pattern of snowfall covering the ground. To achieve this effect, we multiplied the noise texture with the Snow Color (R:0.75,G:0.75,B:0.75) and used this result as the Snow texture.

APPLYING LANDSCAPE MATERIAL

After using the texture maps for the gravel and grass layers, and the combination of a noise texture and a snow color for the snow layer we applied the material to the **Landscape Material** of our Landscape actor. We then started painting the layers in the **Paint** mode of the **Landscape** tool. Just like the previous Tutorial, we had to create `Layer Info` assets to be able to paint the layer.

At this phase we noticed that the textures were too small for our vast outdoors environment. The tiling factors of our texture would make an enormous amount of repetitions and created undesirable wallflower-like patterns in the regions far from the viewer.

USING TEXTURE COORDINATES

The fix to the tiling artifacts on our landscape was fairly easy. It turns out that we could use a special Landscape Material Expression called **Landscape Layer Coord** to change the tiling scale of our textures. Applying a tiling scale of 5 or 7 would actually multiply our original texture UV coordinates by this larger number and would be suitable for this situation.

However, we are not done yet! Applying a tiling scale fixed the issue of the visual look of our landscape from far away. Looking closely at the landscape reveals another issue with our material that was yet to be addressed.

Looking closely, we noticed that the textures look like paint. There wasn't any depth to the materials on our landscape. It looks as if somebody just took a bucket of paint and painted those flat textures on the landscape. We fixed this issue with the use of Normal Maps.

SETTING UP NORMAL CHANNEL

The most important thing to keep in mind, when setting up our network for the normal channel of our landscape material, is to use a similar layer blending mechanism. For this reason, we duplicated the three **Layer Blend** expressions for the SandLayer, GrassLayer, and SnowLayer material layers to apply to our material's normal channel.

Once the duplicate **Layer Weight** expressions were created, we created two **Texture Sample** expressions to host our normal maps. The **Gravel Normal Texture** expression was given the T_Ground_Gravel_N and the **Grass Normal Texture** expression was filled with the T_Ground_Grass_N. Notice the prefix _N for these texture maps in the **Content Browser**. Although technically it doesn't do anything, the artists named the textures with _N to help us notice their functions.

Now let's take a look at the network setup. If you check out the normal channel's network in Figure 7.21 you will see that we applied the RGBA output of the **Gravel Normal Texture** to the Layer channels of both the **SandLayer** and the **SnowLayer**. By doing this, we basically applied the same depth (via normal maps) to the snow and gravel.

This will give us the option of having gravel (with the gravel color and depth patterns) or snow (with the snow color but with the gravel depth pattern). So for those areas that are snowy, it will look as though the snow is covering the gravel underneath. The case for the grass normal was easily done. We just applied the RGBA output channel of the grass normal map to the Layer input channel of its layer.

FINAL TOUCHES TO THE LANDSCAPE MATERIAL

So far our material looks pretty good, and has some depth to it when applied to the landscape. However, some parts of the landscape look too glossy for the type of material applied. For example, the grass and parts of the sand (gravel) look like plastic. The problem is that the roughness channel of our material is left unconnected.

FIGURE 7.27: The Final Look of Textured Landscape Material.

In UE4, the new material system is modeled after physically based materials. To represent different kinds of materials efficiently, UE4 materials make use of specialized channels such as **Metallic** and **Roughness**. The **Roughness** channel allows the material to have varying degrees of smoothness (or roughness) to them. Smooth material (e.g., plastic) reflect light back more perfectly than rough materials (e.g., cloth).

To this end, we want our gravel and grassy areas of the landscape to be more rough than those where there's snow on the ground. We achieved this look by duplicating our three **Layer Blend** expressions, and applying a value of 1 to the Sand and Grass layers and a value of 0.25 to the Snow Layer. The output of this network was then connected to the **Roughness** channel of our material.

Fantastic! Our landscape looks pretty great as we created a relatively professional looking landscape with little time and simple material networks. Next, we will take a look at a special expression called **Landscape Visibility Mask**. This expression allows us to mask the visibility of our landscape material when applied to certain locations to create things like cave openings and holes in our landscape.

NOTE

If you use the Visibility tool without having a Landscape Hole Material assigned, the Visibility tool will remove the Material layers applied to the selected sections, but will not create a hole in the Landscape itself[30].

TUTORIAL 7.5   Creating a Cave Opening

If you haven't completed Tutorial 7.1, go to page 369 to create a Landscape. We will need this landscape to complete our work below.

CREATING THE LANDSCAPE HOLE MATERIAL

In this section we will modify our material to allow for it to be used as a Landscape Hole Material.

1. Go back to the main editor and look for your material folder.
2. Double-click on the Mat_LScape_Textured you created before to open it in the material editor.
3. Click on the material node and look for **Blend Mode** in its **Details** rollout.
4. Set the material's **Blend Mode** to Masked.
5. Right-Click to the left of the material's now-activated Opacity Mask and place a Landscape Visibility Mask expression. Feel free to make arrangements to your other networks to make room if you need it.
6. Connect the output of the **Landscape Visibility Mask** Expression to the Opacity Mask of the material node.
7. Your material network should look similar to Figure 7.28(a).
8. Save your material.

Well, that was easy! Creating a Landscape Hole material is basically just one instruction, to mask the visibility of where it is applied, through an **Opacity Mask** channel. Next, we will need to apply this material to our landscape.

APPLYING THE LANDSCAPE HOLE MATERIAL TO ACTOR

Let's apply our newly created landscape hole material to the landscape actor. This process is similar to applying a regular landscape material to the landscape actor:

9. Go back to the main editor and select your Landscape actor by clicking on it in the Scene Outliner (the upper right corner of the main editor).
10. In the **Content Browser** find your **Mat_LScape_Textured** material.
11. Drag the **Mat_LScape_Textured** material to the **Landscape Hole Material** module of the Landscape section of your Landscape actor's **Details** rollout (see Figure 7.28(b)).

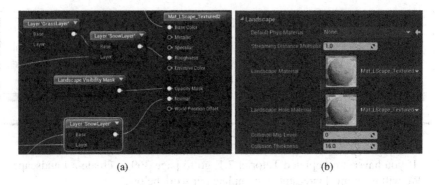

(a)   (b)

FIGURE 7.28: Creating and Applying Landscape Hole Material: (a) Landscape Material Hole Network. (b) Applying Landscape Material Hole to Landscape Actor.

12. That's it! Your landscape now has a visibility mask material (Or Landscape Hole Material) to use.
13. Save your progress so far.

MAKING HOLES IN THE LANDSCAPE

Let's apply our newly created landscape hole material to the landscape actor. This process is similar to applying a regular landscape material to the landscape actor:

14. Go to the **Landscape** tool in the **Modes** Panel in the main editor. Alternatively, you may click on the mountains icon in the **Modes** toolbar or press `Shift+3` on your keyboard.
15. To apply our Landscape Hole Material to create holes in the landscape we need to go to the **Sculpt** mode of the **Landscape Tool**. This is the difference between applying landscape hole materials and the landscape layers. We used the **Paint** mode to apply landscape layers.
16. In the **Sculpt** mode look for the **Landscape Editor** section. It is located immediately below the toolbar of the **Landscape Tool**.
17. Click on the left-most icon in the **Landscape Editor** section. It is called `Select Tool`.
18. From the drop-down menu click on the **Visibility Tool**. This tool allows you to paint your **Landscape Hole Material** to mask out visibility of portions of your landscape, with the following two options.
    Left-click adds Landscape holes to regions of the landscape.
    Shift+ left-click removes holes from regions of the landscape.
19. Use the above two options to add a cave opening to some location of your landscape. Take your time to work with the `Left-Click` and shift+left-click to get used to how this tool works. Feel free to change the **Brush Size** to make holes with different sizes.
20. Figure 7.29 shows the landscape after a cave opening is applied.

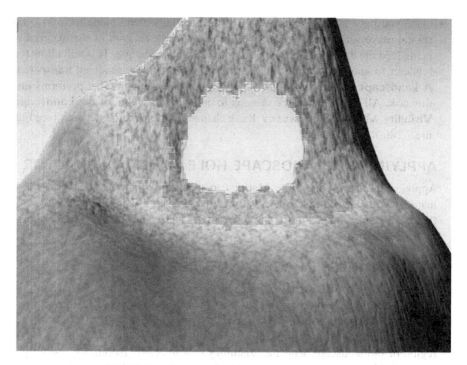

FIGURE 7.29: Cave Opening Created in Landscape.

21. Save your level and progress so far, when you feel satisfied with the look of your landscape.

What Happened in TUTORIAL 7.5...

You just created a cave opening in your landscape. It is important for you to remember that this opening is basically an opacity mask. If you want to use this as a cave opening, for example, you should place a Static Mesh and fit it to the opening; otherwise you will see seams in your level.

Let's take a look at how we created this opening:

CREATING THE LANDSCAPE HOLE MATERIAL

To make your material suitable for use as a **Landscape Hole Material** you need to do two things:

* First, you need to make sure that the **Blend Mode** of the material is set to Masked. This will allow your material to render completely transparent where you have an opacity mask.

- Once you have taken care of setting your material's blend mode to mask, you should make sure that you have the **Opacity Mask** channel of the material is being feed the data from the visibility masks of the landscape. This will allow the renderer to know which part of your landscape should be rendered transparent. A **Landscape Visibility Mask** expression is the expression that performs just this task. All that needs to be done is to connect the output of the **Landscape Visibility Mask** to the Opacity Mask channel of the material network (see Figure 7.28(a)).

APPLYING THE LANDSCAPE HOLE MATERIAL TO ACTOR

Applying the Landscape Hole Material to the actor is simple. Just drag the material with the **Landscape Visibility Mask** expression connected to its Opacity Mask channel into the respective Landscape Actor's Landscape Hole Material slot.

MAKING HOLES IN THE LANDSCAPE

To create holes in a landscape you need to use the **Sculpt** mode of your **Landscape Tool**. Just go to the Sculpt mode and open the Select Tool drop-down menu to choose the **Visibility** tool.

To apply the visibility mask and create holes, simply Left-Click on the region of the landscape with the **Visibility** tool selected. To remove visibility masks and holes from regions of the landscape, simply hold the **Shift** key on your keyboard and Left-Click on the landscape.

We are almost done with the landscape, we have three layers of materials, these materials look very realistic and have some depth to them, and we have holes and cave openings in our landscape. However, we can do even more!

There is one last, but supremely powerful Landscape Material expression we haven't discussed yet. It is called **Material Layer Blend**. I presented this material expression on page 378 and discussed its properties, inputs, and outputs. It is time now for us to see the power of this expression in action!

TUTORIAL 7.6   Creating Landscape Materials with Landscape Layer Blend

If you haven't completed Tutorial 7.1, go to page 369 to create a Landscape. We will need this landscape to complete our work below.

SETTING UP YOUR LANDSCAPE MATERIAL

In this section we will create a new material for our landscape utilizing **Landscape Layer Blend** expressions.

1. If you haven't created a landscape and this tutorial is your first in this chapter please follow the steps in Tutorial 7.1 to make a basic landscape to work with.

2. Right-Click inside the **Landscape Materials** folder you have created and choose **New->Material** to create a new material.
3. Rename the new material Mat_LScape_Complex.
4. Double-click on the **Mat_LScape_Complex** to open it in the Material Editor.

We have created a material for our landscape. We will next edit it in the material editor to contain work with our landscape layer blend expressions.

SETTING UP TEXTURE EXPRESSIONS

With the new material opened in the Material Editor, let's go ahead and use some textures. Much like the material we created in Tutorial 7.4 on page 389, we will create **Texture Sample** expressions with both diffuse and normal maps for a gravel texture and a grass texture. We will also create a **Texture Sample** expression with a noise texture map to use in our material.

Let's first create our Diffuse (Color) textures.

5. Right-Click to the left of the material node and create a **Texture Sample** expression. Remember, you can alternatively create this expression by holding the T key and clicking on the graph editor.
6. In the **Details** rollout of this texture sample apply the following changes:
   Texture: T_Ground_Gravel_D from the UE4's **Starter Contents**.
   Description: Gravel Texture.
7. Right-Click below the Gravel Texture expression and create a **Texture Sample** expression. Remember, you can alternatively create this expression by holding the T key and clicking on the graph editor.
8. In the **Details** rollout of this texture sample, apply the following changes:
   Texture: T_Ground_Grass_D from the UE4's **Starter Contents**.
   Description: Grass Texture.
9. Right-Click below the Grass Texture vector and create a **Texture Sample** expression. Remember, you can alternatively create this expression by holding the T key and clicking on the graph editor.
10. In the **Details** rollout of this texture sample apply the following changes:
    Texture: T_Perlin_Noise_M from the UE4's **Starter Contents**.
    Description: Snow Noise Texture.
11. Right-Click below the Snow Noise Texture and create a **VectorParameter** expression and make the following changes to its properties:
    Parameter Name: Snow Color.
    Default Value: (R:0.75,G:0.75,B:0.75, A:1.0).
    Description: Snow Color.
12. Right-Click to the right of both the Snow Noise Texture and the Snow Color and place a **Multiply** expression.
13. Connect the output of the Snow Color to input **A** and the RGBA output of the Snow Noise Texture to input **B** of this **Multiply** expression.
14. Your network should look like Figure 7.30(a) so far.

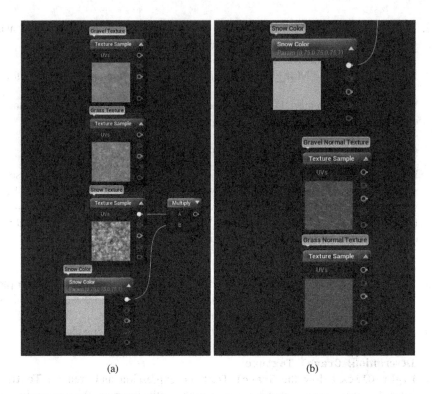

(a)   (b)

FIGURE 7.30: (a) Diffuse Textures Arrangement. (b) Normal Texture Arrangement.

With the diffuse (color) textures created we will now create the normal textures. In this case, I am going to use only normal maps from the gravel and grass and work them into the snow:

15. Right-Click to below the **Snow Color** expression and create a new **Texture Sample**. Remember, you can alternatively create this expression by holding the T key and clicking on the graph editor.
16. In the **Details** rollout of this texture sample apply the following changes:
    Texture: T_Ground_Gravel_N from the UE4's Starter Contents.
    Description: Gravel Normal Texture.
17. Right-Click below the Gravel Normal Texture expression and create a **Texture Sample** expression. Remember, you can alternatively create this expression by holding the T key and clicking on the graph editor.
18. In the **Details** rollout of this texture sample and apply the following changes:
    Texture: T_Ground_Grass_N from the UE4's Starter Contents.
    Description: Grass Normal Texture.
19. Your network should look like Figure 7.30(b) so far.

Now we will have to bring a **Landscape Layer Coord** expression to be able to scale the tiling of our final texture layers on the landscape:

20. **Right-Click** to the left of all of the **Texture Sample** and search for and place a **Landscape Layer Coord** on the graph editor.
21. In the **Details** rollout of the **Layer Coord** expression apply the following changes:
    Mapping Scale: 7.0
    Description: Landscape Texture Scaling.
22. Connect the output of the **Landscape Texture Scaling** to the UVs input of all of the **Texture Sample** expressions.

SETTING UP DIFFUSE LAYER

Now is the time to create our network of Landscape Layers for the Base Color. This time, instead of creating three **Layer Weight** expressions, we will combine the entire layer calculation into one **Layer Blend** expression. This will have the advantage of simplifying our network, while giving us the control over how we would like to blend our layers together.

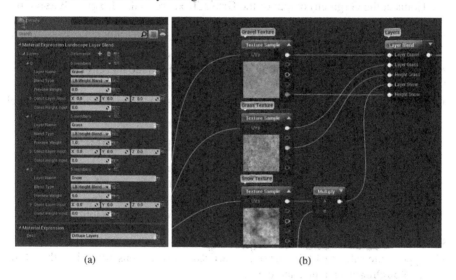

(a)   (b)

FIGURE 7.31: Diffuse Layers Network Setup: (a) Layer Blend Layers. (b) Network Connections.

23. **Right-Click** to the right of all of the Diffuse **Texture Sample** and search for and place a **Landscape Layer Blend** on the graph editor.
24. In the **Details** rollout of the **Layer Coord** expression apply the following changes (see Figure 7.31(a)):
    a. Name this expression:
       Description: Diffuse Layers.
    b. Click on the **+** Sign three times. This will create three layers for us to work with.

    c. Change the following properties of `Layer[0]`:
      Layer Name: `Gravel`
      Blend Type: `LB Weight Blend`
      Preview Weight: `1.0`
    d. Change the following properties of `Layer[1]`:
      Layer Name: `Grass`
      Blend Type: `LB Height Blend`
      Preview Weight: `0.0`
    e. Change the following properties of `Layer[2]`:
      Layer Name: `Snow`
      Blend Type: `LB Height Blend`
      Preview Weight: `0.0`

25. Connect the RGBA output of the **Gravel Texture** to the `Gravel` input of the **Diffuse Layers** expression.
26. Connect the RGBA output of the **Grass Texture** to the `Grass` input of the **Diffuse Layers** expression.
27. Connect the G (green) output of the **Grass Texture** to the `Height Grass` input of the **Diffuse Layers** expression.
28. Connect the output of the **Multiply** expression that multiplies the Noise Color and Noise Texture to the `Layer Snow` input of the **Diffuse Layers** expression.
29. Connect the Alpha channel of the **Gravel Texture** to the `Height Snow`.
30. Your network should look similar to Figure 7.31(b).
31. Connect the output of the **Diffuse Layers** expression to the **Base Color** channel of the material node.

SETTING UP SIMPLE METALLIC AND ROUGHNESS

Before we get to the Normal channel setup, let's make a couple of simple networks for our material's `Metallic` and `Roughness` channels. I want to make all layers non-metallic (so they wont reflect light). I want to also make all layers completely rough and non-glossy. To do this, let's complete the following tasks:

32. Hold the key 1 on your keyboard twice to create two **Constant** expressions.
33. Type in the value of 1.0 in one of the **Constant** expressions, move it to the left of the `Roughness` channel, and connect it.
34. Move the **Constant** expression with the value of 0.0 to the left of the `Metallic` channel and connect it.
35. Save the material.

SETTING UP THE NORMAL LAYERS

So far we have set up our diffuse color layer blending mechanism and assigned appropriate Roughness and Metallic values to our material. Next we will replicate the same network (or almost the same) for our Normal channel:

36. Duplicate the `Diffuse Layer` **Landscape Layer Blend** expression (by pressing `Control+W` when it is selected) to the right of the normal map expressions on the graph editor.

37. In the **Details** rollout of the `Layer Coord` expression apply the following changes:
    a. Name this expression:
       Description: `Normal Layers`
    b. Make sure the following properties of `Layer[0]` are as below:
       Layer Name: `Gravel`
       Blend Type: `LB Weight Blend`
       Preview Weight: `1.0`
    c. Make sure the following properties of `Layer[1]` are as below:
       Layer Name: `Grass`
       Blend Type: `LB Height Blend`
       Preview Weight: `0.0`
    d. Make sure the following properties of `Layer[2]` are as below:
       Layer Name: `Snow`
       Blend Type: `LB Height Blend`
       Preview Weight: `0.0`
38. Connect the RGBA output of the **Gravel Normal Texture** to the `Layer Gravel` input of the **Normal Layers** expression.
39. Connect the RGBA output of the **Grass Normal Texture** to the `Layer Grass` input of the **Normal Layers** expression.
40. Create a **Multiply** expression to the right of both **Grass Normal Texture** and **Gravel Normal Texture**.
41. Make the following connections for the **Multiply** expression:
    A → RGBA output of the **Gravel Normal Texture**.
    B → RGBA output of the **Grass Normal Texture**.
    Output → `Layer Snow` input of the **Normal Layers** expression.
42. Connect the G (green) output of the **Grass Texture** to the `Height Grass` input of the **Normal Layers** expression.
43. Connect the Alpha channel of the **Gravel Texture** to the `Height Snow` of the **Normal Layers** expression.
44. Connect the output of the **Normal Layers** expression to the **Normal** channel of the material node.

I have rearranged the network for your reference to check out your connections. The connections should look similar to Figure 7.32.

CREATING THE LANDSCAPE VISIBILITY MASK

Now, let's go ahead and create our Landscape Hole Material setup:

45. Click on the material node and look for `Blend Mode` in its **Details** rollout.
46. Set the material's **Blend Mode** to `Masked`.
47. `Right-Click` to the left of the material's now-activated `Opacity Mask` and place a `Landscape Visibility Mask` expression. Feel free to make arrangements to your other networks to make room if you need it.

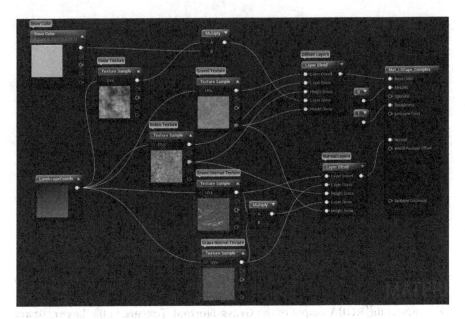

FIGURE 7.32: Landscape Layer Blend Diffuse and Normal Setup.

48. Connect the output of the **Landscape Visibility Mask** Expression to the `Opacity Mask` of the material node.
49. Save your material.

WARNING

There may be issues with crating holes in the landscape after applying your landscape visibility mask and landscape hole material. This issue may be caused due to having holes in the landscape from another landscape hole material. If you are not able to apply landscape holes, switch your landscape hole material back to the one you created in Tutorial 7.4 and remove all of the holes by holding the `Shift` key and `Left-Click`ing on the landscape where there are holes. Then switch your landscape hole material back to the material you created in this Tutorial.

ASSIGNING LANDSCAPE AND LANDSCAPE HOLE MATE-RIALS:

Now that our Landscape Material is ready, let's apply it to our landscape actor:

50. Go back to the main editor and select your Landscape actor by clicking on it in the Scene Outliner (the upper right corner of the main editor).
51. In the **Content Browser** find your **Mat_LScape_Complex** material.

52. Drag the **Mat_LScape_Complex** material to both the **Landscape Material** and the **Landscape Hole Material** module of the Landscape section of your Landscape actor's **Details** rollout.
53. That is it! Your landscape now has a material and a visibility mask material (or Landscape Hole Material) to use.
54. Save your progress so far.

EDITING AND PAINTING LAYERS

Well done! Now go to the main editor and select the **Paint** mode of the **Landscape Tool** and start painting your Gravel, Grass, and Snow layers. Feel free to change your brush settings to achieve a desirable look. We will discuss brush settings and properties later on in this chapter.

ADDING A LAYER TO THE BLEND EXPRESSIONS

Our last stop at Landscape Materials and Expressions incidentally will reveal another powerful aspect of the **Landscape Layer Blend** expression. If you are using this expression in creating blend layers in your landscape materials, you can simply add or remove a layer by clicking on the + sign or the trash bin in its **Details** rollout, respectively.

We will now add a layer to our Diffuse Layers and Normal Layer expressions to make a layer for stone walkways:

55. Open the **Mat_LScape_Complex** that you have been creating so far in the material editor.
56. Rearrange your network to allow for two more **Texture Sample** expressions to the left of both the Diffuse Layers and Normal Layers expressions.
57. Click on the **Diffuse Layers** expression and in its **Details** rollout click the + sign in front of the Layers section.
58. Make the following changes to the properties of **Layer[3]**:
    Layer Name: Stone
    Blend Type: LB Height Blend
    Preview Weight: 0.0
59. Click on the **Normal Layers** expression and in its **Details** rollout click the + sign in front of the Layers section.
60. Make the following changes to the properties of **Layer[3]**:
    Layer Name: Stone
    Blend Type: LB Height Blend
    Preview Weight: 0.0
61. Add a **Texture Sample** to the left of the **Diffuse Layers** expression.
62. Make the following changes to the **Texture Sample**:
    Texture: T_Brick_Hewn_Stone_D
    Description: Brick Texture
63. Make the following connections for the **Brick Texture**:
    RGBA → Layer Stone of the **Diffuse Layers** expression.

Alpha → Height Stone of the **Diffuse Layers** expression.

Alpha → Height Stone of the **Normal Layers** expression.

64. Add a **Texture Sample** to the left of the **Normal Layers** expression.

65. Make the following changes to this **Texture Sample**:
Texture: T_Brick_Hewn_Stone_N
Description: Brick Normal Texture

66. Make the following connections for the **Brick Normal Texture**:
RGBA → Layer Stone of the **Normal Layers** expression.

67. Save your material and apply it.

Yes, it is that simple to add new layers to the **Landscape Layer Blend** expressions. Simply add new layers in the Details rollout of the **Landscape Layer Blend** expression, change their properties, and connect textures to their respective input channels.

CREATING A LAYER INFO FOR THE NEW STONE LAYER

Now we need to create a layer info for our newly created Stone Layer so that we can paint stone pathways in the **Paint** mode of the **Landscape Tool**. To do this perform the following tasks:

68. Go back to your main Unreal Editor, and select the **Landscape Tool** (or simply press Shift+3).

69. Go to the **Paint** mode and scroll down to the **Target Layers** Section.

70. Find the **Stone** and click on the + sign to add a new layer info for it.

71. Choose the "Weight-Blended Layer (normal)" option.

72. Click "OK" to save the layer info in your Level's assets folder.

73. Save your level.

Now you should be able to go to your landscape, select the "Stone" layer and paint stone pathways into your level as you wish. Notice how well the snow, gravel, grass, and stone layers blend together as you keep adding them to the landscape (see Figure 7.33).

What Happened in TUTORIAL 7.6...

You just created your first landscape material and applied its layers to your landscape. We will go over what we did in the tutorial step by step.

SETTING UP YOUR LANDSCAPE MATERIAL

First we need to create a new material for our landscape. We named this material **Mat_LScape_Complex** to refer to it later on in the tutorial.

FIGURE 7.33: The Four Layers Blend Well.

SETTING UP TEXTURE EXPRESSIONS

In this section we created our texture samples and assigned appropriate textures to them. In particular we created diffuse textures for the gravel map, grass map and a noise texture for the snow map. We also created texture samples for the normal map of the grass and gravel. We will use the gravel normal map for the snow, much like what we did in Tutorial 7.4.

SETTING UP DIFFUSE AND NORMAL LAYER NETWORKS

In these two sections we first set up the diffuse normal layer blend network. The process was similar to setting up the base color network of the Tutorial 7.4, with one main difference. Here we used **Landscape Layer Blend** expression instead of **Landscape Layer Weight** expressions.

To set up the Diffuse network, we created a **Landscape Layer Blend** expression and created three layers for it, a Gravel, a Grass, and a Snow layer. We left the Gravel layer's Blend type to the regular `LB Weight Blend` type, but changed the blend type of the Grass and Snow layers to `LB Height Blend`. Doing so exposed two new input channels for those layers, i.e., their `Height` channel.

The `Height` input channel for these layers allow us to connect a heightmap (kind of like an alpha map) that ranges from black to white, with darker areas representing lower heights. With this channel we will be able to dictate how layers should blend with each other when they meet on the landscape.

For example, if you have an area with grass layer painted, and you start painting snow (over or close to the grass regions), the two layers will merge with each other based on their respective heights, so the snow (the newly painted layer) will start filling the grass from lower height to higher. We saw this feature more dominantly when we used a brick texture layer in the tutorial.

Now, let's discuss the connections. The `Gravel`, `Grass`, and `Snow` layer inputs of the **Layer Blend** expression were simply connected to their respective diffuse textures (and in the case of snow to the multiplication expression that makes up the final snow texture). Since the `Gravel` layer doesn't have a height blend, it doesn't need to be supplied a heightmap. However, the `Grass` and `Snow` layers do have a height pin available.

Figure 7.34(a) shows the alpha channel of the gravel texture. As you can see in the figure, the darker areas represent the lower locations of gravel. We use this texture to supply the heights of our Snow layer to use as a blending mechanism when it merges with other layers in our landscape.

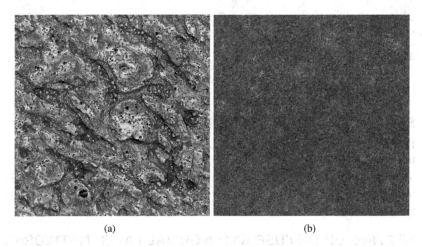

(a)   (b)

FIGURE 7.34: : (a) Gravel Texture Alpha Channel. (b) Grass Texture Green Channel.

Similarly, Figure 7.34(b) shows the green channel of the grass texture. As you can see in the figure, the brighter areas represent greener locations in the texture map. These locations coincide with where the grass is in the map. We use this texture to supply the heights of our Grass layer to use as a blending mechanism when it merges with other layers in our landscape.

To establish our Normal channel for the Landscape Material, we duplicated the **Layer Blend** expression we have named `Diffuse Layer`. This will ensure that the blend type and other properties of this expression would be similar to our `Diffuse Layer` blend expression. However, to make the snow normals to

To establish the layer blend for the normal map, we connected the RGBA channels **Gravel Normal Texture** and **Grass Normal Texture** to the Gravel and Grass layers of the blend expression, respectively. We also connected the alpha channel of the **Gravel Normal Texture** and the green channel of the **Grass Normal Texture** to the `Height` channels of the Snow and Grass, respectively.

FIGURE 7.35: The Three Layers Blended with the Layer Blend Expression.

For the Snow Layer, though, we multiplied the RGBA output channels of the `Gravel Normal Texture` and the `Grass Normal Texture` to achieve a smoother look on the snowy patches of the landscape. You can see the three regions in Figure 7.35.

CREATING VISIBILITY MASK AND APPLYING MATERIAL TO LANDSCAPE

The visibility mask creation is a fairly straightforward process, just like Tutorial 7.4. Just make the **Blend Mode** of your material `Masked` and connect a **Landscape Visibility Mask** expression to the now active `Opacity Mask` channel of your material node.

To apply your material to the landscape actor, simply drag the material from the **Content Browser** to the `Landscape Material` and `Landscape Hole Material` of your Landscape actor. This will make your material ready for use in painting on the landscape and creating holes into the landscape.

ADDING NEW LAYERS TO LAYER BLEND EXPRESSIONS

In this section we wanted to add a new layer so that we could paint brick pathways on the landscape as well. The process was actually fairly simple. First, we added new layers in both **Diffuse Layers** and **Normal Layers Landscape Layer Blend** expressions and made appropriate changes to the new layer's blend type.

Next, we created a diffuse texture sample and a normal texture sample expression. We then assigned a diffuse and a normal texture map associated with a brick texture to these texture samples. We connected RGBA channels of these texture samples to the `Layer Stone` of their respective Layer Blend expression.

We connected the alpha channel of the diffuse texture for the bricks to the `Height Stone` of the **Diffuse Layers** blend expression to act as a blending factor. If you look at the alpha channel you will see that it appropriately represents the crevices among the bricks with darker colors. This will allow the blending of other layers onto the Stone layer in the landscape to present nice blending features based on the heights of the bricks.

CREATING A LAYER INFO FOR THE NEW STONE LAYER

All that is left for us to do to be able to use our new stone layer is to create a layer info for it. We simply followed the same instructions we used for other layers – i.e., Clicking on the + sign and assigning a new layer info. We then saved our layer info in our level assets folder and started painting stone pathways onto our landscape.

7.4   EDITING LANDSCAPES

Now that we are quite proficient with utilizing **Landscape Material Expressions** to design realistic materials and layers for our landscapes, let's shift our focus to the other features in the **Landscape Tool** collections.

As you remember the **Landscape Tool** has three modes: `Manage`, `Sculpt`, and `Paint`.

We have already used all three modes, albeit modestly, to create our landscape, to sculpt and make hills and valleys, and to paint our landscape layers on it. In the following sections we will discuss the collections of tools available in both the **Sculpt** and **Paint** mode of the UE4's **Landscape Tool**.

7.4.1   LANDSCAPE SCULPT MODE

The process of sculpting a Landscape involves using one or more tools that modify the underlying heightmap [30]. The **Sculpt** mode of UE4 **Landscape Tool** will provide you with a range of items from, simple sculpting tool to much more complex mechanisms for erosion and hydro erosion effects on the landscapes.

The list, below, presents the current selection of tools in UE4's **Landscape Sculpt Mode** [30].

Sculpting Tool: This tool allows you to raise or lower regions within your landscape. In other words, this tool will simply increase or decrease the height of a particular region in the heightmap of the landscape.

To raise the heightmap, simply hold the `Left Mouse Button` and move your mouse over the region. To lower the heightmap, hold the `Shift` key while pressing the `Left Mouse Button` and move your mouse over the region.

- **Controls**

   Left Mouse Button: This raises the height of a region or selected layer's weight.

Shift + Left Mouse Button: This lowers the height of a region or selected layer's weight.
- **Options**
  Tool Strength: Controls the amount of changes this tool applies to the heightmap.

Smooth: This tool smooths the heightmap. In other words, it takes a region of the heightmap and tries to average out the height differences in the region.

To apply this tool simply `Left-Click` on the region in the landscape.
- **Options**
  Tool Strength: Controls the amount of smoothing this tool applies to the heightmap with each stroke.
  Filter Kernel Scale: This property sets the scale multiplier of the smoothing kernel. Larger values result in more smoothing.
  Detail Smooth: If this property is *True* (checked), preserves details while smoothing occurs. Larger value remove more details, while smaller values keep the details.

Flatten: This tool flattens the heightmap over a region in the landscape. In other words, it takes a region of the heightmap and tries makes all locations in the region share the same value as their heightmap elevation (Figure 7.36).

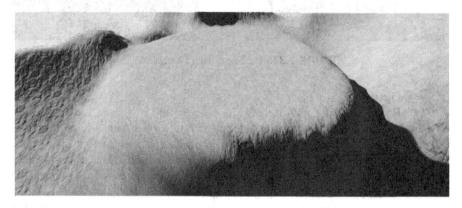

FIGURE 7.36: The Flatten Tool Example.

To apply this tool simply `Left-Click` on the region in the landscape.
- **Options**
  Tool Strength: Controls the amount of smoothing this tool applies to the heightmap with each stroke.
  Flatten Mode: This property determines whether the tool will raise or lower the elevation of the regions under the brush to flatten the landscape.

Use Slope Flatten: If *true* (checked), flattens the landscape along existing slope in the region, as opposed to flattening to a horizontal plane.

Pick Value Per Apply: If *true* (checked), constantly selects new values to flatten toward instead of using the first value when clicked.

Flatten Target: This property sets the target height towards which the tool flattens.

Ramp: This tool allows you to pick two points in your landscape and a fall-off region between which it creates a ramp. Figure 7.37 shows how this tool can be used to create ramps in the landscape.

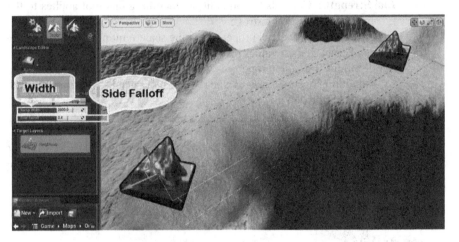

FIGURE 7.37: The Ramp Tool Example Usage.

- **Options**

  Ramp Width: Controls the width of the ramp.

  Side Falloff: Controls the amount of falloff on either side of the ramp where the ramp merges with the landscape. The amount of 0 means no falloff, making a sharp ramp transition into the landscape on either side. The amount of 1 makes a smooth transition between ramp and the surrounding landscape.

Usage: To create a ramp in the landscape between two points, perform the following actions:

1. Click on the first location (the start of ramp).
2. Click on the second location (the end of ramp).
3. In the **Tool Settings** make changes to the `Ramp Width` and the `Side Falloff`.
4. Click on `Add Ramp` button to add the ramp to the landscape. Pressing the `Reset` will reset the ramp tool back to step 1.

Erosion: This tools uses a thermal erosion simulation to adjust the height of the heightmap [30]. In other words, this simulates the transfer of soil from higher elevations to lower elevations. To allow for more natural appearances, the tool also provides a noise setting applied to the results of the erosion process.

- **Options**

    Tool Strength: Controls the amount of smoothing this tool applies to the heightmap with each stroke.

    Threshold: The minimum height difference necessary for the erosion to be applied. Smaller values will result in more erosion.

    Surface Thickness: The thickness of the surface for the layer weight erosion effect.

    Iterations: The number of iterations performed. Larger values result in more erosion.

    Noise Mode: Whether to apply noise to raise or lower the heightmap, or both.

    Noise Scale: The size of the noise filter used. The noise filter is related to position and scale.

Hydro Erosion: This tool uses a hydraulic erosion simulation to adjust the height of the heightmap [30]. In other words, this simulates the erosion that occurred due to water running down from higher elevations to lower elevations. To allow for more natural appearance, the tool also provides a noise setting applied to initial rainfall location.

- **Options**

    Tool Strength: Controls the amount of smoothing this tool applies to the heightmap with each stroke.

    Rain Amount: This is the amount of rain applied to the surface. Larger values result in more erosion.

    Sediment Cap: This is the amount of sediment that the washing rain can carry down the hills. Larger values result in more erosion.

    Iterations: The number of iterations performed. Larger values result in more erosion.

    Initial Rain Distributions: Sets whether the rain should be applied to the positive noise regions or the entire area.

    Rain Dist Scale: The scale of the noise filter to be applied to the initial rain on the surface.

    Detail Smooth: If *true* (checked), preserves details while smoothing during erosion time. Larger Detail Smoothing values remove more details, while smaller values preserved details while erosion occurs.

Noise: This tool applies a noise filter to the heightmap or layer weight [30]. In other words, it changes the elevation of the region under the brush by raising and lowering areas in a noisy pattern.

- **Options**
  Tool Strength: Controls the amount of smoothing this tool applies to the heightmap with each stroke.
  Use Target Value: This option if *true* (checked), will blend the values of the noise with the target value to apply changes to the region.
  Noise Mode: This option determines whether to apply the noise in an additive, subtractive, or both, manner. The additive adds the noise values to the heightmap, while the subtractive mode removes the noise values from the heightmap.

Retopologize: This tool re-topologizes the landscape vertices with an X/Y offset map to improve vertex density on cliffs and to reduce texture stretching [30]. *NOTE: Use this tool with caution and only if necessary, as it increases the computational complexity of rendering the landscape with the X/Y offset map.*

Visibility: This tool enables you to create holes in the landscape. Holding the `Left Mouse Button` while moving your mouse will apply the visibility mask and remove the visibility of portions of the landscape. Pressing `Shift` while holding the `Left Mouse Button` will replace the visibility back on the region.

> **IMPORTANT NOTE**
>
> While using the Visibility tool without a **Landscape Hole Material** assigned to the landscape actor removes material layers applied to the region but will not make holes in the landscape.

Region Selection: This tool selects regions of the Landscape using the current brush settings and tool strength to be used to fit a Landscape gizmo to a specific area or to act as a mask for copying data to, or pasting data from, a gizmo [30]. Holding the `Left Mouse Button` while moving your mouse will add the selected region. Pressing `Shift` while holding the `Left Mouse Button` will remove the selected region.

- **Options**
  Clear Region: Clears the currently selected region.
  Tool Strength: Controls the amount of smoothing this tool applies to the heightmap with each stroke.
  Use Region as Mask: This option when *true* (checked), makes the region selection act as a mask with the active area being comprised of the selected region.
  Negative Mask: This option when *true* (checked), makes the unselected area act as a mask. For this option to be active, the `Use Region as Mask` option must be checked.

Copy/Paste: This tool can be used to copy height data from one area of a Landscape to another through the use of Landscape gizmos. You can also import and export gizmo data [30].

7.4.2 LANDSCAPE PAINT MODE

The tools available in the **Paint** mode of the **Landscape Tool** in UE4 allow you to selectively apply material layers to your landscape [29]. The landscape painting tools are in many ways similar to the sculpting tool. The difference between the two is that, whereas you use the sculpting tools to manipulate the heightmap elevations, the painting tools are used to manipulate material layer weights.

The list below presents the current selection of tools in UE4's **Landscape Paint Mode** [29].

Painting Tool: This tool allows you to increase or decrease the weight of a particular material layer on the landscape.

To paint the selected material layer on a region in the landscape, simply hold the `Left Mouse Button` and move your mouse over the region. To remove the layer, hold the `Shift` key while pressing the `Left Mouse Button` and move your mouse over the region.

- **Options**

  Tool Strength: Controls the amount of smoothing this tool applies to the heightmap with each stroke.

  Use Region as Mask: This option when *true* (checked), makes the region selection act as a mask with the active area being comprised of the selected region.

  Negative Mask: This option when *true* (checked), makes the unselected area act as a mask. For this option to be active, the `Use Region as Mask` option must be checked.

  Use Target as Value: If *true* (checked), blends the value of the layer being applied to the target value.

Smooth: This tool smooths the layer weights. In other words, it takes a region of the landscape and tries to average out the layer height differences in the region. To apply this tool simply `Left-Click` on the region in the landscape.

- **Options**

  Tool Strength: Controls the amount of smoothing this tool applies to the heightmap with each stroke.

Use Region as Mask: This option when *true* (checked), makes the region selection act as a mask with the active area being comprised of the selected region.

Negative Mask: This option when *true* (checked), makes the unselected area act as a mask. For this option to be active, the `Use Region as Mask` option must be checked.

Filter Kernel Scale: Sets the scale of the smoothing kernel. Larger values result in more averaging of layer weights.

Detail Smooth: If *true* (checked), preserves details while smoothing. Larger values remove more details while smoothing layer weights, while smaller values keep more details.

Flatten: This tool flattens the weight of the selected material layer to the value of the `Tool Strength` slider in its settings.

To apply this tool simply `Left-Click` on the region in the landscape.

- **Options**

  Tool Strength: Controls the amount of smoothing this tool applies to the heightmap with each stroke.

  Use Region as Mask: This option when *true* (checked), makes the region selection act as a mask with the active area being comprised of the selected region.

  Negative Mask: This option when *true* (checked), makes the unselected area act as a mask. For this option to be active, the `Use Region as Mask` option must be checked.

  Flatten Mode: Determines whether the tool should increase or decrease the application of the selected layer's weight, or to do both.

Noise: This tool applies a noise filter to the layer weight [29]. In other words, it changes the weight of the selected material layer under the brush by raising and lowering according to a noise filter.

- **Options**

  Tool Strength: Controls the amount of smoothing this tool applies to the heightmap with each stroke.

  Use Region as Mask: This option when *true* (checked), makes the region selection act as a mask with the active area being comprised of the selected region.

  Negative Mask: This option when *true* (checked), makes the unselected area act as a mask. For this option to be active, the `Use Region as Mask` option must be checked.

  Noise Mode: Determines whether the apply noise effects result in increasing weights, those that result in decreasing weights, or all noise effects.

  Noise Scale: Determines the strength of the Perlin noise filter used.

Use Target Value: If *true* (checked), blends the values of the noise being applied toward a target value.

7.4.3 MANAGE MODE

You can perform several fundamental functions in the **Manage** mode of the **Landscape Tool**, such as creating landscapes, modifying existing landscape components, or adding splines to your landscape [27].

If there isn't any landscape in the level, when you click on the **Landscape Tool** in the **Modes** Panel, you will automatically be taken to the **Manage** mode in its `Landscape Creations` functionality. We have already seen how you can use this mode to create landscapes from scratch, or to import existing heightmaps from which you can create a landscape.

If there is more than one landscape in the level, the **Manage** mode will allow you to select which landscape you would like to manage. Simply click on the drop-down box under the `Landscape Editor` section and choose the landscape to edit.

Component Tools

This section will allow you to work with the building blocks of your landscape, called components. Components properties may also be managed in the main level editor under the **Details** rollout of the Landscape Actor.

The list below presents the current selection of tools in UE4's **Landscape Manage Mode** [27].

Selection Tool: This tool allows you to select landscape components, one at a time. The tool works like a toggle. To select a component simply `Left-Click` on it. To deselect a component `Left-Click` on it one more time. To deselect a component press the `Shift` key on the keyboard and `Left-click` on it.

To select multiple components, `Left-Click` one at a time. Each selected component will be highlighted red.
- **Options**
  Clear Component Selection: Clears the currently selected components.

Add: This tool allows you to add components to your landscape. The new component will be added to the location of the cursor. To apply this tool simply `Left-Click` on the region in the landscape.
- **Options**
  `Left-Click`: Adds a new component to the cursor location.

Delete: This tool allows you to delete a component from your landscape. To apply this tool simply `Left-Click` on the region in the landscape.

- **Options**

  `Left-Click:` Deletes selected components from the landscape. If there are no selected components, it will delete the highlighted component under the mask mouse cursor.

Move Level: This tool moves the selected components to the current streaming level. This is an optimization facility, allowing you to select parts of your landscape to a streaming level to stream the moved sections in and out of that level. After you have selected the options, click on the **Apply** button to apply the changes to the entire landscape.

Change Component Size: This tools makes it possible to change the size of the entire landscape.

- **Options**

  Section Per Size: This drop-down box gives you options for the number of quads in each landscape section.

  Section Per Component: This drop-down box gives you options for 1×1 or 2×2 sections per component. Controls LOD aggregation.

  Resize Mode: Specifies whether to expand or clip the current landscape to resize.

NOTE

The **Change Component Size** works on the entire landscape, not a selection of components.

Edit Splines: This tool allows you to create and edit splines in your landscape. Splines are powerful one-dimensional curves that can control certain features of the terrain by pushing or pulling its vertices to conform to a certain shape. For more information about these tools, please see Section 7.5.

7.5 LANDSCAPE SPLINES

You can create a **Spline Actor** in your landscape by using the `Edit Splines` tool in the **Manage** mode of the **Landscape Tool**. These powerful actors will be useful in creating features such as roads, rivers, or other items that in general follow a one-dimensional curved path through the terrain [31].

7.5.1 CREATING SPLINES

Creating **Landscape Splines** is fairly easy. To create a **Landscape Spline** you need to perform the following actions:

FIGURE 7.38: `Control+Click` on the Landscape to Add Spline Control Points.

1. Go to the **Manage** Mode of the **Landscape Tool**.
2. Find and click on the `Edit Splines` tool in the **Manage** mode.
3. On the currently selected landscape, while holding the **Control** key on the keyboard, `Left-Click` to create the first control point.
4. Repeat the above step for additional control points – i.e., while holding the **Control** key on the keyboard, `Left-Click` to create each additional control point (see Figure 7.38).

7.5.2 JOINING SPLINES

You can select to join two splines by selecting one and then pressing the `Control` key on the keyboard and `Left-clicking` on the second to merge the two.

7.5.3 SPLITTING SPLINES

To split a spline, press the `Control` key on the keyboard and `Left-Click` on a segment.

7.5.4 ASSIGNING STATIC MESH ACTORS TO SPLINES

One of the most widely used features of a **Landscape Spline** is the fact that you can assign a static mesh actor to the splines. Doing so will give you a tremendous amount of flexibility on customizing the visual look of the splines that run through your landscape.

The process of assigning static mesh actors to splines is easy. Perform the following steps and you can customize the look of your splines in no time (see Figure 7.39):

1. In the **Content Browser**, find and select a static mesh you wish to assign to your spline.

FIGURE 7.39: The Process of Assigning Static Mesh Actors to Landscape Splines.

2. In the editor window `Left-Click` on one of the control points of the spline to which you wish the actor to be assigned.

3. Find the `Landscape Spline` section of the **Details** rollout of the selected spline.

4. Click on **Segments** next to `Select all Connected:` section. This will ensure that the mesh will be applied to all of the segments of the spline you have selected.

5. Click on the **+** sign in the `Landscape Spline Meshes` section to add one mesh slot.

6. Expand the element of the `Splines Meshes` collection.

7. Press the `<-` button next to the `Mesh` slot to assign the selected mesh from the **Content Browser** to this spline. Alternatively, you can drag the mesh from the **Content Browser** into the `Mesh` slot, or click on the drop-down list and select a mesh from the opened list.

7.5.5 EDITING SPLINES

To edit a spline's shape and curvature, you need to select one of its control points. You may use the translation and rotation gizmos with spline in the usual way. Translation widget will move a control point along the X, Y, and Z axis, or a plane. The rotation widget will allow you to rotate the tangents of the control point.

Scaling the control points, allows you to interact with their tangents. This will make it possible to increase or decrease the curvature of a spline at a give control point.

7.5.6 APPLYING SPLINES TO A LANDSCAPE

To apply a spline to your landscape you can press **Apply Splines to Landscape**. This will modify the landscape's heightmap to make the spline conform with the landscape. This conformation of the spline and the landscape to each other follows the information provided within the properties sections of the spline at the time of its creation.

Spline Properties and Interfaces

Below is a list of spline control points or segments properties [31].

Control Point Properties: The following properties govern various aspects of a spline's control point [31].
- **Property**

    Location: Position of the control point relative to the Landscape it is attached to.

    Rotation: Rotation of the control point, controls the direction of the tangent of any attached spline segments at this point.

    Width: Width of the spline at this point. Shown as solid lines. Affects all connected segments.

    Side Falloff: The width of the cosine-blended falloff region on either side of the spline at this point. Shown as dotted lines.

    End Falloff: Only relevant at the end of a spline (a control point with only one attached segment), the length of the cosine-blended falloff region that smoothly ends the spline segment.

    Layer Name: Name of the blend mask layer to paint to when the spline is applied to the Landscape.

    Raise Terrain: Raises the Landscape to match spline when the spline is applied to the Landscape. Good for roads on embankments.

    Lower Terrain: Lowers the Landscape to match spline when the spline is applied to the Landscape. This is good for rivers and ditches.

Spline Segment Properties: The following properties control various aspects of a spline's segment [31].
- **Landscape Spline Segment**

    Connections: Settings specific to the two control points this segment is attached to. The Connections sub-properties are as follows:

    Tangent Len: Scale of the tangent at this point, controls how curved the segment is. Negative tangents cause the segment to connect to the back of the control point.

    Socket Name: Socket on the control point this segment end is connected to.

    Layer Name: Name of the blend mask layer to paint to when the spline is applied to the Landscape.

    Raise Terrain: Raises the Landscape to match spline when the spline is applied to the Landscape. Good for roads on embankments.

    Lower Terrain: Lowers the Landscape to match spline when the spline is applied to the Landscape. Good for rivers and ditches.
- **Landscape Spline Meshes**

    Spline Meshes: The meshes to apply to the spline. Multiple meshes will be applied in random order controlled by the random seed. The items below are the Spline Meshes sub-properties (on a per-mesh basis):

Mesh: The Static Mesh to use.

Material Overrides: Overrides the Static Mesh's assigned Material with a different Material for the spline.

Center H: Whether to horizontally center the mesh on the spline or use the mesh's origin.

Offset: Offsets the mesh from the spline (units in unscaled mesh-space).

Scale to Width: Whether to scale the mesh to fit the spline width or to use the mesh unchanged.

Scale: Multiplier to the size of the mesh. If Scale to Width is enabled, the Scale specified here is relative to the spline width; otherwise, it is relative to the mesh's natural size.

Forward Axis: Chooses the Forward axis of the `Spline Mesh`.

Up Axis: Chooses the Up axis of the `Spline Mesh`.

Random Seed: Controls the order in which multiple spline meshes are applied.

Enable Collision: Enables collision of spline meshes.

Cast Shadow: Enables the casting of shadows by the mesh.

Manipulating Control Points/ Segments: The following list presents an overview of control-point manipulation shortcuts [31].

Left-Click: Selects a control point or segment.

Shift + Left-Click: Selects multiple control points or segments.

Control+A: Selects all control points connected to the currently selected point and/or all segments connected to the currently selected segment.

Control + Left-Click: On landscape, adds a new control point, connected to any selected control point.

Control + Left-Click: With a control point selected, will create a segment joining any selected control points to the new control point.

Control + Left-Click: With a segment selected, splits the segment at that point and inserts a new control point.

Del: Deletes the selected control points or segments.

R: Automatically calculate rotation for selected spline control points.

T: Automatically flip the tangents for selected control points or segments.

F: Flips selected spline segments (only affects meshes on the spline).

End: Snaps the selected control point to the landscape below.

TUTORIAL 7.7   Creating Landscape Splines: A Cobblestone Walkway

With our landscape built and painted, it is time for us to populate it with meshes and objects. Let's imagine that the level we have been building so far is to be a part of a mountain range with a shrine nestled somewhere high up. It would be great to be able to place a walkway for our visitors to walk up to reach the shrine.

This scenario brings us to a place where we can see the power of a unique and newly introduced tool in UE4 – the **Landscape Splines**.

If you haven't completed Tutorial 7.1, go to page 369 to create a Landscape. We will need this landscape to complete our work below.

It would be great if you also have finished one of the Tutorials 7.3, Tutorial 7.4, or Tutorial 7.6. In these tutorials you set up materials and layers for your landscapes so that your work would look like the figures shown in this tutorial.

CREATING THE WALKWAY MESH AND MATERIAL

Before we get to play with UE4 **Landscape Splines**, let's first set up a mesh which we will later use as a walkway. I wanted the walkway to be made of some cobblestone pathways. As such, I will go ahead and reuse a box mesh and cobblestone materials already provided in the starter contents. We will modify these items to suit our use and then jump into working with **Landscape Splines**.

Let's first create a folder to organize our meshes:

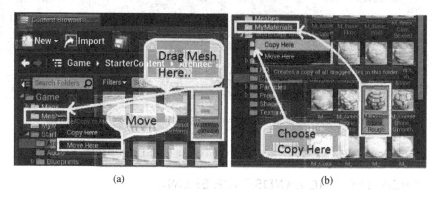

(a) (b)

FIGURE 7.40: (a) Moving the Walkway Mesh to Our Meshes Folder. (b) Copying the Cobblestone Materials.

1. **Right-Click** in the **Content Browser** to create a new folder in your main **Game Folder**.
2. Rename this folder **Meshes**.
3. Again in the **Content Browser**, find the **Starter Content** folder and **Double-Click** on the **Architecture** folder to open it up.
4. In the **Architecture** folder, find a mesh called **Floor_400×400**.
5. **Right-Click** on **Floor_400×400** and choose **Duplicate**. This will make a copy of this mesh in the **Architecture** folder of the **Starter Content**.
6. Rename the duplicated mesh to **Walkway_400×400**.
7. Drag the **Walkway_400×400** mesh into your newly created folder **Meshes** and choose the **Move Here** option (see Figure 7.40(a)).
8. Again in the **Content Browser**, find the **Materials** folder and **Double-Click** on the **Materials** folder to open it up.

9. In the `Materials` folder, find a material called `M_CobbleStone_Rough`.

10. Drag the `M_CobbleStone_Rough` material into your materials folder you created earlier and then choose the `Copy Here` option (see Figure 7.40(b)).

11. Go to your materials folder and rename the copy of the material to `M_Walkway_CobbleStone`.

12. The final step here is to apply the `M_Walkway_CobbleStone` material to our `Walkway_400×400` mesh. To do so, `Double-Click` on the `Walkway_400×400` mesh to open it up in the UE4's **Static Mesh Editor**.

13. Drag the `M_Walkway_CobbleStone` material to the `Element 0` section of the `Walkway_400×400` mesh in its **LOD0** section in the **Details** rollout of the **Static Mesh Editor** (see Figure 7.41).

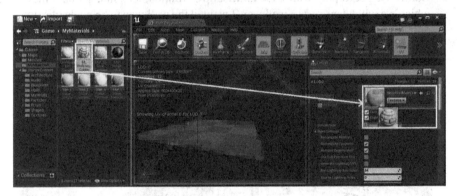

FIGURE 7.41: Assigning the Cobblestone Material to Walkway Mesh.

14. Save your `Walkway_400×400` mesh and close the **Static Mesh Editor**.

CREATING THE LANDSCAPE SPLINE

Now that our mesh and its material are set up and ready, let's create our first landscape spline.

15. In the main editor **Modes** Panel go to the **Landscape Tool** (`Shift+3`).

16. Click on the **Manage** mode.

17. In the **Manage** mode, click on the `Selection Tool` icon under the **Landscape Editor** section and from the drop-down menu choose **Edit Splines** tool. *Note: If these tools are not activated, you don't have a spline actor in the level. Go to Tutorial 7.1 on page 369 to create one.*

18. Hold the `Control` key on your keyboard and `Left-Click` somewhere on the landscape to create your splines' first `Control Point`.

19. While still holding the `Control` key on your keyboard click on another location on your landscape to create the second `Control Point`.

20. After your second `Control Point` is created you should see the two points and the segment connecting them on your landscape (see Figure 7.42).

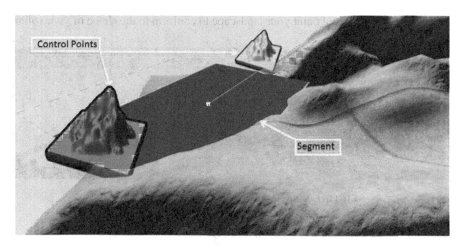

FIGURE 7.42: The Spline's First Two Control Points.

21. Keep adding more **Control Points** to your spline by `Control+Left-clicking` on your landscape.

22. After you have added some **Control Points**, click on the `Control Points` button in the `Landscape Spline` section of the **Details** rollout of the editor (see Figure 7.43). This will select all of your control points. We will make some modifications to the points.

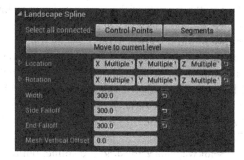

FIGURE 7.43: Selecting All of Spline's Control Points and Adjusting Control Points Properties.

23. With all of the **Control Points** selected, find the `Landscape Spline Control Point` section of the **Details** rollout.

24. Make the following changes to the **Control Points** properties (see Figure 7.43):
    Width: 300
    Side Falloff: 300
    End Falloff: 300

25. `Left-Click` on the **All Splines** button in the **Tool Settings** of the **Manage** mode of the **Landscape Tool** a few times (see Figure 7.44).

26. This will deform and paint your landscape to conform to the shape of your spline.

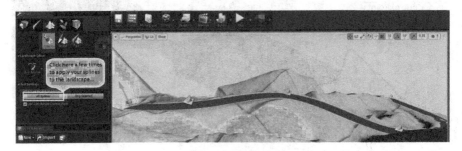

FIGURE 7.44: Applying the Spline to the Landscape.

27. We will next apply our mesh to this spline.

APPLYING STATIC MESHES TO SPLINES

Now that our spline is placed in the level, and fits snugly on top of the landscape, we can go ahead and apply the brick walkway mesh to it to customize its look.

28. If you have switched from the **Manage** mode to another mode in the**Landscape Editor**, go back to the **Manage** mode.
29. Make sure you have selected the `Edit Splines` tool in the **Manage** mode.
30. `Left-Click` on one of the spline's control points.
31. In the **Details** rollout find the `Landscape Spline` section and click on the **Segments** button. This will select all of the segments in the spline and allows us to make the changes we are about to make to all segments.
32. Find the `Landscape Meshes` section in the **Details** rollout.
33. In the **Landscape Spline Meshes** section, `Left-Click` on the + sign, next to the `Spline Meshes` section once to add one(1) mesh slot to the segments.
34. In the **Content Browser**, `Double-Click` on the `Meshes` folder you created earlier in the tutorial and find the **Walkway_400×400** mesh.
35. Drag the **Walkway_400×400** mesh into the `Mesh` slot of the spline's **Details** rollout (Figure 7.45).
36. After applying the walkway static mesh to the spline, build your level's lighting and check it out.

ADJUSTING THE SPLINE AND FINAL TOUCHES

After assigning our landscape static mesh and building the level's lighting, you might notice that some parts of the spline seem to have been buried under the landscape. There is also another minor issue with our mesh. The cobblestones don't seem to be aligned with the direction of the walkway. The stones look like they are placed sideways. We will fix these and a couple of other minor issues next.

37. Let's first fix the portions of our spline being buried in the landscape:

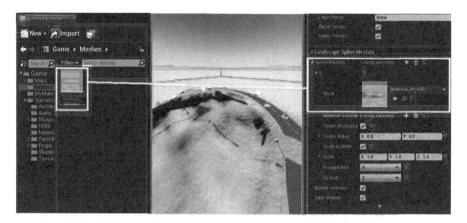

FIGURE 7.45: Assigning a Static Mesh to the Spline.

   a. To do this, just `Left-Click` on each of the control points for the buried sections.

   b. With each control point selected, press W on your keyboard to activate the translation gizmo. Drag the blue Z axis of the control point up just a few units. This will bring the segment up along the Z axis.

   c. Repeat this process for any other segment that is partially covered under the landscape.

38. Now that our spline is all above the landscape, let's change its forward axis. This will effectively align the walkway mesh with the forward direction of the spline:

   a. In the `Landscape Spline` section of the **Details** rollout, click on **Segments** button to select all of the spline segments.

   b. Find the `Forward Axis` in the `Landscape Spline Meshes` section and change it to Y. This will take care of aligning the static mesh with our spline.

39. The final modification left to do on our static mesh is to adjust its materials UV scales. This will change the size of each stone on the walkway:

   a. In the **Content Browser**, find the material folder in which you stored the copy of the walkway cobblestone material.

   b. `Double-Click` on the `M_Walkway_CobbleStone` to open it in the material editor.

   c. Once in the material editor, pan the event graph to the left to find the **TexCoord** (texture coordinate) expression.

   d. `Left-Click` on the **TexCoord** expression and change both the UTiling and VTiling to 0.5.

   e. Save and apply the material.

40. With these changes applied to your spline mesh, the walkway should look similar to Figure 7.46.

41. Save all your progress and your level.

FIGURE 7.46: Final Adjustments Made to the Spline.

ADDING A JUNCTION

Before wrapping up our work with the walkway, let's make a junction (or a fork) in the road. The UE4's Spline Editor has a very easy process to add sections to the currently existing splines. We will use this to add a new road that forks out of the walkway.

42. Go to the **Spline Editor** tool if you have exited it. Expand the `Select Tool` drop-down in the **Manage** mode and choose `Edit Splines`.
43. `Left-Click` on one of the control points in the existing spline.
44. With one of the control points selected, hold the `Control` key on your keyboard and `Left-Click` on the landscape away from the current road. This will add a new control point and a segment that forks out of the currently existing road.
45. Note that since you already have a mesh assigned to this spline, the UE4 will automatically use the mesh for the additional segments you add to this spline.
46. While still holding the `Control` key, `Left-Click` a few times to add some more segments.
47. Your map should look similar to Figure 7.47.
48. As you see in Figure 7.47, the new segments cut through the landscape. Let's fix this problem now:
    a. `Left-Click` on the first segment of the newly added section in your spline (at the junction with the existing spline) to select it.
    b. Hold the `Shift` key on your keyboard and `Left-Click` on the second segment of the newly added spline. This will add the new segment to your selection.
    c. With the `Shift` key still pressed, `Left-Click` on the rest of the segments of the newly added spline to add them to your selection.
    d. When you have selected all of the newly added segments, in the **Tool Settings** `Left-Click` on the **Only Selected** button to deform the landscape

FIGURE 7.47: Adding More Segments to the Spline.

to the selected segment.

e. This will make the landscape conform to the new portion of our spline. Since the previous portion was already conforming to the landscape, there isn't any need to make the deformation for all of the splines.

f. If the new segments of the spline get a little covered under the landscape, you can simply `Left-Click` on the individual control points and move them up a little to fix the issue.

g. Take your time working with the new segments of your spline until you are satisfied with the results.

49. My landscape and the walkway splines are shown in Figure 7.48.

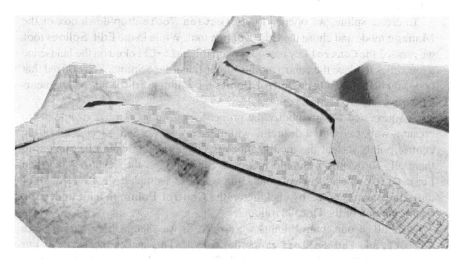

FIGURE 7.48: Fixing the Issues with Newly Added Segments to the Spline.

50. Save your progress and the level.

What Happened in TUTORIAL 7.7...

You just set up your first **Landscape Spline** in UE4. The newly introduced **Landscape Splines** are a powerful tool for developing linear features in your landscape that conform to the heightmap, and even have the ability to change the heightmap to conform to their path.

CREATING THE WALKWAY MESH AND MATERIAL

In this section, we simply created a folder to host the mesh we will use later to visualize our **Landscape Spline**. The process should not be new to you at this point. We simply duplicated a planar mesh from the starter content, and moved it to our own `Meshes` folder. We then made a copy of an already built material in the starter content called `M_CobbleStone_Rough` into our own `My Materials` folder. Next, we applied the `M_CobbleStone_Rough` to the mesh we will use in our spline actor later.

CREATING THE LANDSCAPE SPLINE

After creating (or rather modifying) our walkway mesh, it was time to actually create our spline. The first step in creating the spline is to go to the **Manage** mode of the **Landscape Tool**. If there you have at least one landscape actor in the level, the **Manage** mode will allow you to select and modify one of the landscapes. We only have one landscape actor in the level, so it was automatically selected.

To create spline, we opened the `Selection Tools` drop-down box of the **Manage** mode and chose the **Edit Splines** tool. While in the **Edit Splines** tool, we pressed the `Control` key on your keyboard, `Left-Clicked` on the landscape a few times to place the control points of our Landscape Spline. You noticed that once you had at least two **Control Points** the **Splines Editor** placed Segments between each two control points.

The next step was to modify the properties of our spline's control points to create a walkway with a desirable width. To do so, we first selected all of the control points so that the modifications we were making would be applied to them all. To do this we could press the **Shift** key on the keyboard and then `Left-Click` on each control point. But we chose a simpler way to select all of the control points – i.e., by clicking on the **Control Points** in the **Landscape Spline** section of the **Details** rollout.

Once all of our control points were selected we changed the `Width`, `Side Falloff`, and `End Falloff` properties to 300. This makes the width of our spline to be 300 unreal units and the falloff on either side or ends of our spline to be also 300 unreal units. After applying our spline to the landscape, these values will make it fit snugly into the landscape.

The last step that is left to do is to apply our spline to the landscape. To do so, we clicked a few times on the **All Splines** button under the `Tool Settings` of our **Spline Editor** in the **Manage** mode. This deformed the terrain (raised some parts and lowered others) to conform to the shape of our spline.

APPLYING STATIC MESHES TO SPLINES

After creating and applying our spline to the landscape, it was time to customize its look. We have already created a static mesh and a material for our spline(by duplicating one of the architectural meshes and one of the materials from the Starter Contents).

To apply the Walkway static mesh to the spline, we first selected all of its segments by clicking on the **Segments** button in the `Landscape Spline` section of the **Details** rollout. We then added one mesh slot (element) to the `Spline Meshes` section and assigned the walkway mesh to this element. Now our spline has a renderable static mesh that looks like a walkway made of cobblestones.

ADJUSTING THE SPLINE AND FINAL TOUCHES

After applying our static mesh, we found a couple of issues in our spline that needed final touches to finish it up. The first issue was with some portions of our spline being buried under the landscape. This issue is caused when we adjust the landscape to conform to the shape of our spline; some areas will be raised while some will be lowered. Doing so might make parts of the spline intersect the landscape.

This fix for the issue of portions of the spline being covered in the landscape is easy. We just need to select the control points at either end of the spline segments being covered under the landscape and raise them a little along the `Z` (blue) axis.

The next issue is due to the fact that when we applied the mesh to our spline segments, the `X` axis of the mesh was automatically aligned with the `Forward Axis` of our spline. We wanted the `Y` axis of the mesh to align with the `Forward Axis` of the spline. The fix for this issue is also rather easy. In the **Landscape Spline Meshes** section of a spline's detail rollout, there is a property called `Forward Axis`. We simply need to choose the axis from the original mesh (e.g., the `Y` axis) to assign to the **Forward Axis** here.

Finally, we adjusted the UV tilings of the **TexCoord** material expression in the **M_Walkway_CobbleStone** material to make the bricks look a little bigger on the walkway. We used the value of 0.5 for both `UTiling` and `VTiling` in the material editor.

ADDING A JUNCTION

In the final portion of our tutorial we added a junction to our walkway. The process involves two very easy steps. In the first, we will have to select one control point (or segment) from which we would like to fork the road. Once the location for the junction is selected we can add new segments to our road by simply pressing the `Control` key and `Left-clicking` on the landscape.

In the second step, we will `Shift+Left-click` on each newly added segment to select it. We then press the **Only Selected** button under the `Deform`

Landscape to Splines to make the landscape conform only to the newly added segments of our spline. We will then go through another clean-up process if some portions of the newly added segments get buried under the landscape.

Looks like our humble landscape is shaping up nicely. There are just a couple more things we need to do to complete our journey outdoors. It would be great if we could add a river to the bottom of the valley in the landscape.

It would also be great if we could add some props, like tree trunks, stones, and bushes to the landscape to make it look more rich. We will make these additions next. Let's start by learning how to add instanced meshes to our landscape.

7.6 FOLIAGE AND FOLIAGE EDITOR

Unreal Engine 4 allows you to easily add static mesh instances to your level with its **Foliage System** [14]. The process of adding instances of static meshes on a landscape is very much like painting landscape layers. However, there's another significant benefit to using the foliage system to add meshes to your landscape.

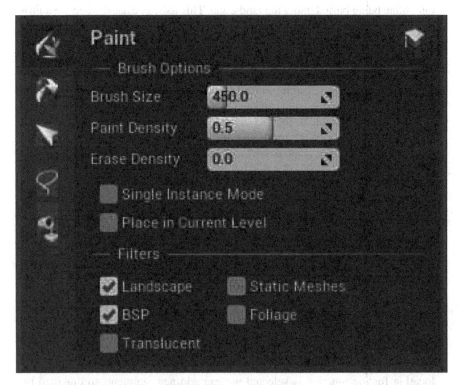

FIGURE 7.49: The Foliage Tool.

When you add instanced meshes with the use of the foliage system, the meshes will be grouped together into clusters that are rendered by means of instancing. In other words, instead of having to make one draw call for each individual mesh, a single call will render all of the instances within a cluster at once.

To add instanced meshes to your landscape or to other meshes, you should use the **Foliage Tool** – shown in Figure 7.49. The **Foliage Tool** can be accessed in the **Modes** panel by clicking on the branch icon or by pressing Shift+4 on your keyboard. Once in the **Foliage Tool** you will be given access to five (5) modes: Paint, Reapply, Select, Lasso, and Fill modes.

You will notice that the Meshes section of the **Foliage Tool** will be empty (see Figure 7.49). Before you can paint static mesh instances using the **Foliage Tool** you must add some static meshes to this list. To assign static meshes to the **Foliage Tool** to draw on your landscape, simply drag a static mesh from the **Content Browser** onto the Meshes section of the **Foliage Tool**.

NOTE

To add your first mesh to the list of meshes in the **Foliage Tool** you must drag it from the **Content Browser** onto the black bar that reads "Drag static meshes from content browser into this area". Once you have added your first static mesh, you may add additional meshes by dragging them from the **Content Browser** on top of the existing ones in the Meshes section.

Each static mesh in the Meshes list of the **Foliage Tool** will have three modes:

Hide Details: This mode will hide all of the mesh settings and parameters. Once you have made the necessary adjustments to each mesh's parameters in the list, you can click on this mode to easily select (or deselect) the meshes you would like to paint or modify in the viewport.

Painting Tab: This mode shows the parameters that control how the instances of the mesh will be placed in the level.

Instance Settings Tab: This mode shows the parameters that affect the instance already placed in the level.

To select a mesh in the Meshes list of the **Foliage Tool** simply Left-Click on the checkbox next to its name. Each selected mesh will be highlighted with an orange color. To deselect a mesh, Left-Click on its checkbox again.

It is important to note that only selected meshes will be affected in the editor. For example, suppose you have some rocks and some trees in the level editor, and want to erase only the trees while leaving the rocks. Simply deselect the rock mesh in the Meshes list and select the tree mesh (Figure 7.50(a)). Pressing the Shift key and Left-clicking on the level will only remove the trees (since the tree mesh is the only mesh selected in the Meshes list of the **Foliage Tool**).

The properties that control the currently selected tool are displayed above the Meshes list (e.g., Figure 7.50(b) shows Paint Tool properties). The following list presents a description of each property:

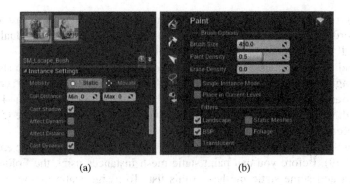

(a)   (b)

FIGURE 7.50: (a) Selecting and Deselecting Meshes in the Foliage Tool. (b) Brush Settings.

Brush Size: This setting controls the size of the brush in Unreal Units.

Paint Density: This setting controls the target density you wish to achieve by `Control+Click` to add mesh instances. The value for brush density ranges between 0 and 1. A value of 1 will paint mesh instances at the maximum density listed in the `Mesh Properties` for each mesh [14]. If the density is already higher than this value, no additional mesh instances will be added.

Erase Density: This setting controls target density you wish to achieve when erasing instances by `Control+Shift+Click`. The value ranges between 0 and 1. If the current density is already lower than this value, no more meshes will be removed.

Filter: This setting controls the type of objects that you wish the mesh instances to be painted on. For example, if you only want to place foliage mesh instances to the landscape and not any other object type, deselect all but the landscape in the `Filter` section.

7.6.1 FOLIAGE TOOLS

As of Unreal Engine 4.6 release, there are five tools (modes) available in the **Foliage Tool**. Each of these tools allows you to perform a specific action designed to work with foliage and static mesh instances. The following descriptions are adopted from Unreal Engine's Official Documentation [14].

Painting Settings

The `Painting Settings` affect the way the **Foliage** system places/removes mesh instances to/from the level.

Paint Tool: This tool allows you to add/remove mesh instances to/from the world. To add instances to the brush area hold the `Control` key on the keyboard and `Left-Click` on the target area. To remove foliage from the level, hold `Control+Shift` and `Left-Click` on a target area. *Note: Only selected meshes in the **Foliage Tool** will be added/removed.*

- Paint Settings

  Density /1Kuu^2: The number of instances placed for this mesh for each 1000×1000 Unreal Unit area.

  Radius: This is the minimum distance between mesh instances for this mesh.

  Align to Normal: This setting if *true* (checked), orients mesh instances to orient with the direction of the normal to the surface at which they will be placed.

  Max Angle: This setting specifies the maximum angle to allow when aligning a mesh instance with surface normals.

  Random Yaw: This setting if *true* (checked), rotates each instance of the placed mesh randomly along its Z axis.

  Uniform Scale: This setting if *true* (checked), makes the instances of the mesh scale uniform. Uncheck if you wish to have instances scale on X, Y, and Z axes independently.

  Scale Min/Max: Each mesh instance will be randomly scaled between the Min and Max values, when placed.

  Random Pitch $\pm$: Adds values up to the specified value to the orientation of each instance.

  Ground Slope: If non-zero, will place foliage instances if the slope is less than this value. Will ignore surfaces steeper than this value for adding instances. If the value is negative, will add foliage instances to surfaces steeper than the specified value.

  Height Min/Max: Will not place any instances outside of this range.

  Landscape Layer: If this value is specified, the instances will be painted with a density proportional to the weight of this landscape layer.

Reapply Tool: This tool allows you to change the parameters of instance that are already placed in the level. In this tool you may check the appropriate setting(s)' check box and make modifications. When you brush over the existing instances the changes will be applied. Most of the settings in this tool are similar to those of the **Pain Tool**, but there are few differences:

- Reapply Settings

  Density Adjust: This setting is a density multiplier for existing instances. For example, setting the value to 2.0, will double the number of instances in a particular, while a value of 0.5 will leave only half of the instances remaining after painting.

  Ground Slope: This setting will remove instances that do not satisfy the ground slope criteria. No new instances will be added.

  Height Min/Max: This setting will remove instances that do not satisfy the height criteria. No new instances will be added.

  Landscape Layer: This setting will remove instances in proportion to the specified layer. No new instances will be added.

Selection Tool: This tool allows you to select individual instances for moving, removing, editing, etc.

- Actions per Selected Instance

    Translate: Translate (move) a selected instance (group of instances) by dragging the translation widget axes. You can activate the translate widget by pressing W or clicking on the translation button in the editor viewport.

    Rotate: Rotate a selected instance (group of instances) by dragging the rotation widget axes. You can activate the rotation widget by pressing E or clicking on the rotation button in the editor viewport.

    Scale: Scale a selected instance (group of instances) by dragging the scale widget axes. You can activate translate widget by pressing R or clicking on the scale button in the editor viewport.

    Duplicate: Duplicate a selected instance (group of instances) by holding Alt key and dragging the widget axes.

    Delete: Press the Del key to delete a selected instance (group of instances).

    Snap To Floor: Press the End key to attempt to snap a selected instance (group of instances) to the floor.

Lasso Tool: This tool allows you to use a paintbrush to select instances simultaneously in the level. You may use the Filter settings or select/deselect meshes from the Meshes list to further customize this tool.

- Available Actions

    Left-Click: Will select the instances that fall under the brush.

    Shift+Left-Click: Will remove instances from the selection.

Fill Tool: This tool determines the number of mesh instances to place with the paint tool. After setting the density and other properties of the mesh instances, you can use this tool to fill an entire actor with the instances of foliage meshes in your level.

Instance Settings

You can use this mode to modify the instances of meshes already placed in the level.

Instance Count: This setting shows the number of instances of this mesh currently placed in the level (currently streaming level).

Cluster Count: This setting shows the number of clusters used to render instances of this mesh in the level.

- Clustering:

Max Instance Per Cluster: This setting specifies the maximum number of instances used in a cluster. A good idea is to set this value to use the number of polygons per mesh. Since each cluster will be rendered in a single draw call, using very large numbers for this setting, if the poly count of each mesh is high, it might result in performance issues. Setting very low values for this setting will eliminate clustering effectiveness.

Max Cluster Radius: This setting specifies the maximum size to which a cluster could grow before allocating new instances to new clusters. Reducing this value will increase the number of clusters, but improve occlusion.

- Culling:

Start Cull Distance: This setting specifies the distance (in world units) from which instances start to fade. This value needs to be set up in the material.

End Cull Distance: This setting specifies the distance (in world units) from which instances will be completely culled. If the material is not set up to support fading of individual instances, the entire cluster will disappear (reappear) as the player gets farther from (closer to) at least one instance within the cluster.

7.6.2 CULLING INSTANCES

As I discussed earlier, one of the most important advantages of the **Foliage** system in UE4 is its efficiency in utilizing clustering to increase the rendering performance of large numbers of static meshes on vast outdoor environments. To further increase performance, the foliage system uses a mechanism called **Culling**.

Culling allows the engine to determine when a cluster of instances is far enough from the player that ignoring it to be rendered will not be detrimental to the player's experience. We discussed the two parameters in the `Instance Settings` that controlled how the engine should determine the distances from which to start the culling process and to completely cull a cluster from being rendered.

To use the culling mechanism of the foliage system, we should set a `Start Cull Distance` and an `End Cull Distance`. Since foliage instances are rendered on a per-cluster basis, setting the cull distances will result in an entire cluster of instances to disappear if their cluster surpasses the `End Cull Distance`. This, if noticeable, could have negative effects on the player's experience.

Figure 7.51(a) shows a view of a landscape with some Rock and Bush instances without culling parameters set up. An `End Cull Distance` has been set for the Rock in Figure 7.51(b), resulting in all of the rock instances disappearing if viewed from farther than the `End Cull Distance`.

In order for the culling mechanism to work properly, the material on the mesh instances must be set up properly. If the culling distances are not supported in the mesh's material, culled instances will suddenly disappear from the view. Setting up the materials to support culling is actually quite easy and straightforward.

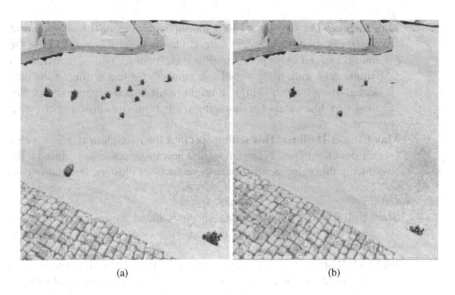

(a)   (b)

FIGURE 7.51: (a) Culling Distances Are Not Set. (b) An Entire Cluster Disappears Due to Culling.

Unreal Engine 4 has a material expression called **Per Instance Fade Amount**. This expression returns a value between 0 and 1, based on the output of the cull distance calculations. If the instance of a mesh with the material is closer than the `Start Cull Distance`, the value for **Per Instance Cull Amount** will be 1. If the instance of the mesh is farther than the `End Cull Distance`, the value for this expression will be 0.

To set up a material to support culling properly, simply integrate the output of the **Per Instance Fade Amount** into an Opacity (or Opacity Mask) network. Doing so will allow for the material to render opaque if the instances are close, and start to fade away as instances get farther away from the `Start Cull Distance`. Once the instances reach the `End Cull Distance` they will become transparent and culling them would not be noticeable by the player.

Figure 7.52(a) shows a material network that supports proper per instance culling. To achieve this effect, we use a **Per Instance Fade Amount** and Multiply its output with the output of a network that makes some parts of the mesh transparent as they fade away. The result of the fade amount calculation is then supplied to the **Opacity Mask** channel of the material node. As a result, when instances of the rock object get farther and farther from the player, parts of the instances start to be masked until the entire mesh instance is culled from view (see Figure 7.52(b)).

Now it's time to populate our level with some props. In Tutorial 7.8 we will set up a couple of Foliage Mesh Instances and populate our level with these props to make the landscape look less empty.

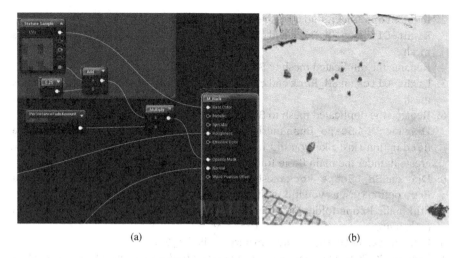

(a) (b)

FIGURE 7.52: (a) A Network to Support Proper Per Instance Culling. (b) A View of the Same Level Shown in Figure 7.51(b) with Materials Supporting Culling. Notice how the closer rocks still persist in the level as the ones that are farther away start to fade.

TUTORIAL 7.8 Populating the Landscape with Foliage Mesh Instances

It is time for us to populate our landscape with some objects. We will use the UE4's **Foliage Tool** to paint instances of a rock static mesh and a bush static mesh on the landscape.

NOTE

If you haven't completed Tutorial 7.1, go to page 369 to create a Landscape. We will need this landscape to complete our work below.

NOTE

It would be great if you also have finished one of the Tutorials 7.3, Tutorial 7.4, or Tutorial 7.6.

ORGANIZING ASSETS

Much like the other tutorials in this book, let's first organize the assets which we will use to create our foliage instances. We will use two static meshes from the Starter Content and their materials. We will copy these assets into our `Meshes` and `MyMaterials` folders.

1. Find the `Starter Content` folder in the `Content Browser`, and `Double-Click` on the `Props` folder to open it up.

2. In the **Props** folder, find a mesh called **SM_Bush**.

3. **Right-Click** on **SM_Bush** and choose **Duplicate**. This will make a copy of this mesh.

4. Rename the duplicated mesh to **SM_LScape_Bush**.

5. **Right-Click** on **SM_Rock** and choose **Duplicate**. This will make a copy of this mesh.

6. Rename the duplicated mesh to **SM_LScape_Rock**.

7. Drag the **SM_LScape_Bush** mesh into your **Meshes** folder and choose the **Move Here** option (just like you did in Figure 7.40(a)). If you don't have this folder, create it under the main **Game** folder.

8. Drag the **SM_LScape_Rock** mesh into your **Meshes** folder and choose the **Move Here** option (just as you did in Figure 7.40(a)).

9. Still in the **Props** folder, find the **Materials** folder and **Double-Click** on it to open it up.

10. In the **Materials** folder, find a material called **M_Bush**.

11. Drag the **M_Bush** material into your materials folder you created earlier (I called my folder **MyMaterials**) and choose the **Copy Here** option (like Figure 7.40(b)).

12. Still in the **Materials** folder of the **Props** folder, find a material called **M_Rock**.

13. Drag the **M_Rock** material into your materials folder you created earlier (I called my folder **MyMaterials**) and choose the **Copy Here** option (like Figure 7.40(b)).

14. Go to your materials folder and rename the copy of the **M_Bush** material to **M_LScape_Bush**.

15. Still in your materials folder, rename the copy of the **M_Rock** material to **M_LScape_Rock**.

16. The final step here is to apply the **M_LScape_Bush** and **M_LScape_Rock** materials to our **SM_LScape_Bush** and **SM_LSCape_Rock** static meshes, respectively. To do so perform the following tasks:

    a. Go to your own **Meshes** folder that you have created under the **Game** folder.

    b. **Double-Click** on the **SM_LScape_Bush** mesh to open it up in the UE4's **Static Mesh Editor**.

    c. Drag the **M_LScape_Bush** material to the **Element 0** section of the **SM_LScape_Bush** mesh in its **LOD0** section in the **Details** rollout of the **Static Mesh Editor** (just like Figure 7.41).

    d. **Double-Click** on the **SM_LScape_Rock** mesh to open it up in the UE4's **Static Mesh Editor**.

    e. Drag the **M_LScape_Rock** material to the **Element 0** section of the **SM_LScape_Rock** mesh in its **LOD0** section in the **Details** rollout of the **Static Mesh Editor** (just like Figure 7.41).

17. Save your **SM_LScape_Rock** and **SM_LScape_Bush** meshes and close the **Static Mesh Editor**.

ADDING FOLIAGE MESHES

So far, we have organized our assets. We now have a copy of a Rock and a Bush static mesh in our own **Meshes** folder. We also have a copy of their respective materials in our own materials folder. With the assets ready, let's go ahead and apply them to our **Foliage Tool**:

18. Open the **Foliage Tool** by pressing `Shift+4`, or by clicking on the branch icon in the **Modes** Panel.

19. In the **Content Browser**, `Double-Click` on the `Meshes` folder to open it up. This is the folder where we just placed copies of our duplicate Rock and Bush static meshes.

20. Drag the `SM_LScape_Rock` into the black area that reads "`Drag Foliage Here`". You will have to place the static mesh directly into the thin area, and not into the gray area beneath it. This will add the `SM_LScape_Rock` to the **Foliage System** of which you can place instances into the level.

21. Drag the `SM_LScape_Bush` on top of the Rock mesh you placed in the **Foliage System**.

SETTING FOLIAGE MESH PROPERTIES

Now that we have added the foliage instance static meshes, let's set up their properties so that they will be placed neatly in the level.

22. Change the following settings for the `SM_LScape_Rock`:
Density/1Kuu^2: 5.0
Scale Min: 0.2
Scale Max: 0.8
Z-Offset Min: -15
Z-Offset Max: 0
Random Pitch $\pm$: 45

23. Change the following settings for the `SM_LScape_Bush`:
Density/1Kuu^2: 3.0
Scale Min: 0.5
Scale Max: 1.5

PAINTING FOLIAGE MESHES

With the Foliage settings established, it is now time to start painting the foliage instances into our level. But first, we want to ensure that we have the right brush size. We would also like to exclude static mesh actors from the list of potential locations on which our foliage instances will be placed. This is because we don't want the foliage instances to be placed on the road we created earlier (the road is a static mesh).

24. Change the `Brush Size` in the **Foliage Tool** to a small brush, e.g., 450.

25. In the `Filter` section of the **Foliage Tool**, uncheck the `Static Meshes`. This will ensure that our instanced foliage meshes will not be placed on static meshes. We don't want any brush or rocks to be placed on the walkway mesh we used in the Spline Editor.

26. With these settings now established, `Left-Click` while moving your mouse on your landscape to place some foliage instance on the landscape (see Figure 7.53).

FIGURE 7.53: Foliage Instance Added to the Landscape.

SETTING THE CULLING AND FADING SUPPORT

We are almost done! The last item of business is to set up our culling support for the landscape foliage mesh instances. I am going to intentionally do this process in three steps.

In the first step, I will set up a `Start Cull Distance` and an `End Cull Distance` for both the Bush and the Rock instances. Doing so will perfectly demonstrate the cluster instancing done in UE4's **Foliage System**, and you will see that entire clusters of foliage instances will disappear when they are farther away from the camera than the `End Cull Distance`.

In the second step, I will show you how to set up the fading support in the Bush's material. We will do this for the Bush material first, since it already has an opacity mask network and modifying this network to support Per Instance Fading will be really easy.

Finally, we will set up a network to support Per Instance Fading for the Rock material. This task is also pretty easy: we will simply change the material **Blend Mode** to support masking, and then build the `Opacity Mask` network to incorporate **Per Instance Fading Amount**.

27. Go to the **Foliage System** in the **Modes** Panel (by pressing `Shift+4`).
28. It shouldn't matter which mode you are in the **Foliage System**. Navigate to the `Instance Settings` of the **SM_LScape_Rock** mesh.
29. In the `Instance Settings` section of the SM_LScape_Rock static mesh, make the following changes to the properties:
    Min Cull Distance: 2000

Max Cull Distance: 4000
Cast Dynamic Shadow: Unchecked

30. In the `Instance Settings` section of the `SM_LScape_Bush` static mesh, make the following changes to the properties:
Start Cull Distance: 2000
End Cull Distance: 4000
Cast Dynamic Shadow: Unchecked

(a)   (b)

FIGURE 7.54: (a) Clusters in the Landscape. (b) Far Away Clusters Are Culled.

31. After applying the above values, you will notice two prominent changes:
    a. The values for `Instance Count` and `Cluster Count` have changed for both the **SM_LSCape_Rock** and **SM_LScape_Bush**. This is because we now have smaller clusters in our level.
    b. If you zoom out in the level editor, you should notice that entire groups of Rock and Bush instances will suddenly disappear (see Figure 7.54(b)).
32. Walk around in the editor viewport and check out your landscape.

PER INSTANCE FADING FOR BUSH MATERIALS

So the good news is our cluster culling works. When we are away from a cluster by more than the **End Cull Distance** the renderer culls the cluster. The bad news is entire clusters of foliage instances suddenly disappear (see Figure 7.54(a) vs. Figure 7.54(b)). Of course if we had a huge landscape, and the clusters were really really far away, the sudden disappearance of foliage instances wouldn't have been a terribly negative experience. But we can notice this negative effect and should fix it.

The really good news is there is a very easy fix to the problem of cluster disappearance. It is called **Per Instance Fading** and Unreal Engine 4's Material Editor support is through a material expression called **Per Instance Fade**

Amount. We will next use this expression to make our Bush instances fade away as we walk away from them.

33. In the **Content Browser**, go to your materials folder in which you placed copies of the Bush and Rock materials.
34. **Double-Click** on the **M_LScape_Bush** material to open it in the Material Editor. We will now modify this material to support **Per Instance Fading**.
35. **Right-Click** on the graph editor, below the **Texture Sample** with the leaves texture to search for and place a **Per Instance Fade Amount** expression.
36. Place a **Multiply** expression to the right of both the **Texture Sample** and the **Per Instance Fade Amount** expressions and make the following connections (Figure 7.55):
    Multiply A → Alpha output of leaves **Texture Sample**
    Multiply B → Output of **Per Instance Fade Amount**
    Multiply output → `Opacity Mask` channel of material node

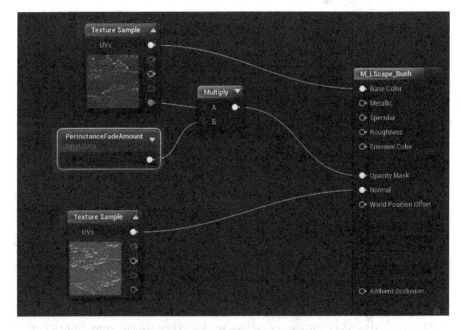

FIGURE 7.55: Bush Material Fading Support.

37. Save and apply your material.
38. Now in the editor viewport, move around in the landscape and see how this effect makes each bush instance fade, before it is completely culled, to make for a smooth transition.

PER INSTANCE FADING FOR ROCK MATERIALS

Great! With our **Per Instance Fading** set up for the Bush materials, when we move around in the level, bushes appear to fade away. What's more, they will fade away individually instead of as a whole cluster.

Let's establish the same network for our Rock foliage instanced meshes as well:

39. In the **Content Browser**, go to your materials folder in which you placed copies of the Bush and Rock materials.

40. **Double-Click** on the **M_LScape_Rock** material to open it in the Material Editor. We will now modify this material to support **Per Instance Fading**.

41. The first difference that you should notice in your Rock Material is that its **Opacity Mask** Channel is disabled. This is because this material has its **Blend Mode** set to opaque. To allow for the **Per Instance Fading** support we need to be able to use the opacity mask channel.

42. Click on the material node in the graph editor.

43. With the material node selected, look for the **Blend Mode** in the **Details** rollout.

44. Open the **Blend Mode** drop-down and select **Masked** (Figure 7.56(a)). This will activate the **Opacity Mask** channel of your material.

45. **Right-Click** on the graph editor, to the left of now-activated **Opacity Mask** channel and place a **Per Instance Fade Amount** expression.

46. Connect the output channel of the **Per Instance Fade Amount** expression to the **Opacity Mask** channel of your material (Figure 7.56(b)).

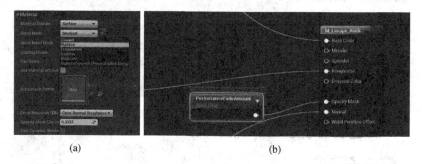

(a)   (b)

FIGURE 7.56: (a) Setting Up Masked Blend Mode. (b) Simple Fading Network.

47. Save and apply your material.

48. Now go back to the level editor and move around in the landscape to see the effect your changes made to the visibility of Rock instances.

After moving around in the landscape you should notice that the Rock foliage instances now disappear from view individually, instead of as a whole cluster. Although this look is much more desirable than what we were getting before setting up the **Opacity Mask** network, the rock instances still disappear. We need a network a little bit more complicated than what we have set up so far to achieve the desired look. Let's do that next:

49. Open the **SM_LScape_Rock** material in the material editor, if you have closed it.

50. Move the **Per Instance Fade Amount** expression below the **Texture Sample** expression that has Rock Base Color texture (Figure 7.57).
51. Place an **Add** expression to the right of the Rock texture's **Texture Sample**.
52. Connect the Alpha channel of the Rock Base Color **Texture Sample** to the **A** channel of the **Add** expression.
53. Place a **Constant** expression (by holding the 1 key and left-clicking) to the left of the **Add** expression.
54. Type the value of 0.25 in the **R** value of the **Constant** expression and connect its output to the **B** channel of the **Add** expression.
55. Place a **Multiply** expression to the right of both the **Add** and the **Per Instance Fade Amount** expressions.
56. Place a **Clamp** expression to the right of the **Multiply** expression and make the following connections (Figure 7.57):

    Multiply A → output of **Add**

    Multiply B → Output of **Per Instance Fade Amount**

    Multiply output → Input of **Clamp** expression

    Clamp output → `Opacity Mask` channel of material node

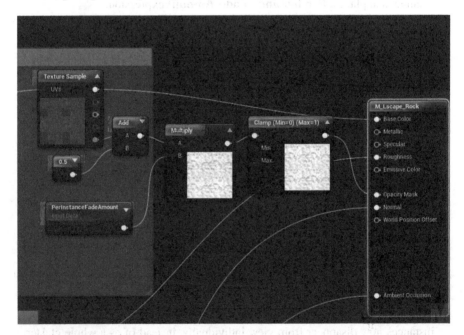

FIGURE 7.57: Setting Up the Complete Fading Network for Rock Materials.

57. Save and apply your material.
58. Now in the editor viewport, move around in the landscape and see how this effect makes each rock instance fade before it is completely culled, to make for a smooth transition.

What Happened in TUTORIAL 7.8...

Congratulations! You just learned how to populate your landscape with lots of static mesh instances, also known as foliage instances. As we discussed, using the **Foliage System** in UE4 has two primary benefits. The first advantage is in regards to speeding up the process of populating your vast outdoors levels with lots of props, since the process is basically like painting on the landscape.

However, the second and most important advantage of using the **Foliage System** is in its efficiency in rendering instanced static meshes, by means of cluster instancing. We learned, in this chapter, that UE4 utilizes the cluster instancing to render all of the instanced static meshes in a cluster with one single draw call. Moreover, foliage instances may also be set up to be culled. That is, when a cluster of foliage instances is far enough, it may be set up to be ignored by the rendering pipeline. However, for the culling to work efficiently, one must make sure that the material for such instances is set up to support fading of the instances from view before they are completely culled.

In this tutorial I emphasized both of the aforementioned advantages. We learned how to first set up our instance meshes in the **Foliage System** and how to paint them on our landscape. We also learned how to set up the materials applied to our foliage static meshes properly to support fading and culling by the **Foliage System**.

ORGANIZING ASSETS

First, and before we delved into our foliage setup, we organized our assets to be used in this tutorial. We were going to use two static meshes for our foliage instances, a Bush static mesh and a Rock static mesh. Luckily, the Starter Content comes equipped with these two meshes. In order to preserve the original meshes, we made a copy of each of these static meshes into our own `Meshes` folder.

These static meshes have a material applied to them. We were going to make changes to the materials later in the tutorial to support fading and culling. In order to preserve the original materials in the Starter Contents, we made copies of the static mesh materials for both the Rock mesh and the Bush mesh into our own `My Materials` folder. Once we had the copies of these materials, we applied them to the copies of their respective meshes.

ADDING FOLIAGE MESHES

Now with our static mesh copies ready and proper material copies applied, it was time to set them up in the **Foliage System**. We added our copy of the Rock and Bush static meshes to the **Foliage System**.

SETTING FOLIAGE MESH PROPERTIES

We wanted to give some random look to the placement of the rocks as they are being painted. Therefore, we set up the `Random Pitch` to allow for up to 45°. Next, we made the Z offset to allow for -15 units of placement, making some of the rock instances look partially buried. To make the size of instances vary, we also allowed `Foliage Paint Tool` to scale the instances between 20% and 80% of the actual mesh size. Finally, for a sparse placement we used a value of 5/Kuu^2 for the density of the rock instanced meshes.

We only changed two of the settings for the Bush instanced foliage meshes. We set the density of the Bush instances at 3/Kuu^2 and their scale to vary between 50% and 150% of the original Bush static mesh size.

PAINTING FOLIAGE MESHES

As you noticed, placement of the foliage instanced meshes in the landscape was pretty straightforward. All we needed to do was to set up our brush size and then paint the instances onto the landscape by holding **Control** and `Left-Clicking` on the landscape. To remove instances, we pressed the `Shift` key and `Left-Clicked` on the landscape.

I wanted to avoid placing any rock or bushes onto the road mesh we placed in the landscape in Tutorial 7.7. This was a fairly easy task to do by using the `Filter` in **Foliage System**. All we needed to do was to uncheck the `Static Mesh` in the **Paint Mode**. This will avoid painting foliage instances if the brush covers static meshes in the level.

SETTING THE CULLING MECHANISM

The first task to perform to enable culling in the **Foliage System** is to set the start and end cull distances. But before setting our cull distances, we made two minor changes to our cluster sizes for the Rock and Bush static meshes. By default the **Cluster Radius** is set to 10,000 world units. Our landscape is relatively small, and I wanted us to see the culling effect better over the course of the next few steps. So we simply reduced the **Cluster Radius** for both of our meshes to 2000 world units to make smaller clusters of foliage instances in the landscape.

Our next order of business was to go to the `Show Instance Setting` section of each foliage static mesh, and set the `Start Cull Distance` and the `End Cull Distance` properties. We set the `Start Cull Distance` to 2000 and the `End Cull Distance` to 4000 for both the **SM_LScape_Rock** and **SM_LScape_Bush** meshes.

Setting the start and end cull distance will trigger the engine to perform two tasks. When each cluster reaches the **Start Cull Distance** the engine will start calculating the fading per instance process. This is a value that is calculated for each instance in the cluster and supplied to the Unreal Engine's Material Editor via a **Per Instance Fade Amount** material expression. When a cluster reaches the **End Cull Distance**, the rendered will cull it, in its entirety, from the view.

So far in our progress, we saw the second effect – i.e., after zooming out in the editor viewport, clusters disappeared (Figure 7.54(b)). But what happened to the instance fading? Well, the materials for neither Bush nor Rock instances support fading, yet. That's why foliage instances in the landscape suddenly disappeared once you walked away from them. We set up the fading support in the materials next.

PER INSTANCE FADING FOR BUSH MATERIALS

As it turns out, supporting per instance fading is relatively easy to set up in the material editor. We first supported fading for the bush material, since it already had an Opacity Mask network.

The Bush material is made of a texture sample that represents leaves' colors and texture. However, upon close inspection, you will notice that this texture also has an Alpha channel that is fed to the Opacity Mask channel of the material. When applied to the Bush Static Mesh, this material will make only the leaves and branches of the mesh visible and masks the rest of the mesh as completely transparent.

Well, this is perfect for our use in the fading support network. We created a **Per Instance Fade Amount** expression in the material editor. The output of this expression is a value between 0 and 1, for each instance of the mesh on which the material is applied. The value is calculated as a ratio between the Start and End Cull Distances set up in the **Foliage System**.

If the instance is closer to the camera than the `Start Cull Distance` the value for the **Per Instance Fade Amount** will be 1. If the instance is farther than the `End Cull Distance` the value for the **Per Instance Fade Amount** will be 0. The value ranges from 1 to 0 as the instance goes from the `Start Cull Distance` to `End Cull Distance`.

If we multiply the output of the **Per Instance Fade Amount** with the Alpha channel of our **Texture Sample** (as shown in Figure 7.55) and supply the result to the opacity mask of our material node, the bush instances will fade away as they get farther and farther from the camera.

PER INSTANCE FADING FOR BUSH MATERIALS

Finally, we are ready to wrap up our foliage work by making the Rock instances fade away as did the Bush instances. But we noticed that the Rock material was opaque and didn't allow for Opacity Masking.

So we first changed the blend mode of our rock material to **Masked**. This exposes the `Opacity Mask` channel of our rock material to be programmed. We first make our opacity masking simple, i.e., we just connected the output of the **Per Instance Fade Amount** to the `Opacity Mask` channel of our material node.

Playing in the level revealed that now our rock instances don't disappear as whole clusters, but rather individually, as we walk away from them. This seems to be an odd behavior, considering that we connected the output channel of the **Per Instance Fade Amount** to the `Opacity Mask` channel.

If you remember from the discussion we had about material node channels in Chapter 4, the `Opacity Mask` is a binary channel. That is, it only accepts binary values, either 0 or 1. Connecting the **Per Instance Fade Amount** to the `Opacity Mask` channel will make the material fully opaque for as long as the value is non-zero. And suddenly makes it transparent when the **Per Instance Fade Amount** becomes 0 (i.e., at the `End Cull Distance`).

Although we could have stopped here and allowed the rock instance to disappear, I wanted to show you how to simulate the fading behavior by working with the alpha channel of our Rock material's texture. If you inspect the Texture of the Rock material you will notice that its alpha channel (shown in Figure 7.58) is a bitmap with dark and bright values.

Bingo! If I use this alpha map (with values ranging from 0 to 1) and work it into my `Opacity Mask` channel with the **Per Instance Fade Amount** (which also ranges from 0 to 1) I can make parts of my rock material disappear before its entire mesh is culled. This will simulate the fading effect I am looking for.

FIGURE 7.58: The Alpha Channel of the Rock Texture.

To achieve this, I first added a value such as (0.25) to my Rock texture's alpha channel. Then I multiplied the result by the output of my **Per Instance Fade Amount**. I clamped the result of this multiplication to make it still fall between 0 and 1. Finally, I connected the output of the clamp expression to the `Opacity`

Mask channel of my Rock Material.

That was it; our **Foliage System** is ready and our landscape is filled with a lot of rocks and bushes. Our instances even support fading per instance and culling from view when we are far away from them.

7.7 WATER IN THE LANDSCAPE

Our landscape is coming along very nicely. We now have a foliage system set up to literally paint static mesh instances into our landscape. We used this system to add some rocks and bushes to the landscape. We even modified the rock and bush materials to make the instances gradually fade away as our camera moves away from them.

But our landscape is not quite complete without water! In our final Tutorial, we will add a river to the landscape to fill the valley full of water. We will make our water reflect the environment with the help of a **Reflection Capture** actor. We will also make our water look murky and blur our vision when we go under water with the help of a **Post Process** volume.

TUTORIAL 7.9 Finishing Up the Landscape: Adding a River

Let's get started adding a deep river to our landscape.

> **NOTE**
>
> If you haven't completed Tutorial 7.1, go to page 369 to create a Landscape. We will need this landscape to complete our work below.

> **NOTE**
>
> It would be great if you also have finished one of the Tutorials 7.3, Tutorial 7.4, or Tutorial 7.6.

ORGANIZING ASSETS

Much like the other tutorials in this book, let's first organize the assets which we will use to create our river and its water effects. We will use a plane static mesh and a water material already made from the Starter Content. We will copy these assets into our **Meshes** and **MyMaterials** folders.

1. Find the **Starter Content** folder in the **Content Browser**, and **Double-Click** on the Shapes folder to open it up.
2. In the **Shapes** folder, find a mesh called **SM_Plane**.

3. **Right-Click** on `Shape_Plane` and choose **Duplicate**. This will make a copy of this mesh.
4. Rename the duplicated mesh to `Shape_LScape_WaterPlane`.
5. Drag the `SM_LScape_WaterPlane` mesh into your `Meshes` folder and choose the **Move Here** option (just like you did in Figure 7.40(a)). If you don't have this folder, create it under the main `Game` folder.
6. Open the **Materials** folder of the **Starter Content**.
7. Drag the `M_Water_Lake` material into your materials folder you created earlier (I called my folder `MyMaterials`) and choose the **Copy Here** option (like Figure 7.40(b)).
8. Go to your materials folder and rename the copy of the `M_Water_Lake` material to `M_LScape_Water`.
9. The final step here is to apply the `M_LScape_Water` material to our `Shape_LScape_WaterPlane` static meshes. To do so perform the following tasks (see Figure 7.59):
   a. Go to your own `Meshes` folder that you have created under the `Game` folder.
   b. **Double-Click** on the `Shape_LScape_WaterPlane` mesh to open it up in the UE4's **Static Mesh Editor**.
   c. In the Static Mesh Editor, uncheck both **Cast Shadow** and **Enable Collision** settings of the `Element[0]`.
   d. Drag the `M_LScape_Water` material to the `Element 0` section of the `Shape_LScape_WaterPlane` mesh in its **LOD0** section in the **Details** roll-out of the **Static Mesh Editor** (just like Figure 7.41).
10. Now our Water surface is set up to be placed in the level.
11. Save your `Shape_LScape_WaterPlane` mesh and close the **Static Mesh Editor**.

PLACING WATER IN THE LANDSCAPE AND SETTING UP REFLECTION

With our Water Plane static mesh ready, we can now add it to the landscape.

12. Go to your `Meshes` folder and drag a copy of the `Shape_LScape_WaterPlane` mesh into the level.
13. Make the following changes to the properties of the `Shape_LScape_WaterPlane` mesh actor in the level (*Note: These values may differ for your level, as your landscape size and location may be different.*):
    Location: R:0, G:0, B:0
    Scale: R:120, G:120, B:1
    Collision Presets: No Collision
14. Your Water Surface should look similar to Figure 7.60 and should fill up the valley in the landscape.

MODIFYING WATER WAVES

The level looks good with the water surface added, if viewed from far away. However, if you look closely at the water surface, you will realize that there

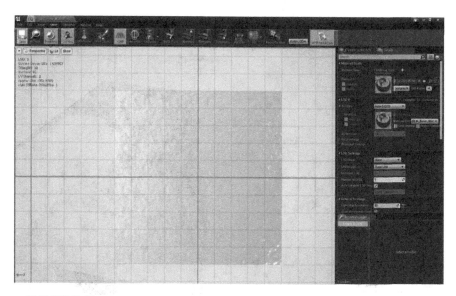

FIGURE 7.59: The Static Mesh of the Water Surface with the Water Material Applied.

are a couple of issues. For starters, the ripples and waves on the surface are not quite visible. Moreover, the water doesn't reflect light (as it should) and it is completely opaque.

Some of these issues can be fixed in the Water material (e.g., M_LScape_Water), but for completely setting up reflection we will need to have a **Reflection Capture** actor in the scene. Let's fix the water material problems first:

Let's adjust the waves on our water surface to be much more visible when the surface is viewed from a close distance:

15. Go to your MyMaterials folder that we created earlier in the main **Game** folder and Double-Click on the M_LScape_Water material to open it in the Material Editor.

16. Scroll to the left of the graph editor until you locate the section called "Micro Normal". This section is responsible for creating the waves on the water surface when viewed closely on the surface. In this section we will see four (4) **TexCoord** expressions. These expressions and their respective **Panner** expressions make the waves and move them on the water surface. From the top, the **TexCoord**'s U and V tilings are 1.0, 0.5, 0.3, and 0.25. These values are quite small for our level. We will modify these by multiplying them with a large number, next:

   a. Place a **Multiply** expression to the right of each of the **TexCoord** expressions in the "Micro Normal" section.

   b. Connect the output channel of each of the **TexCoord** expressions to the A channel of the **Multiply** expression you placed to its right.

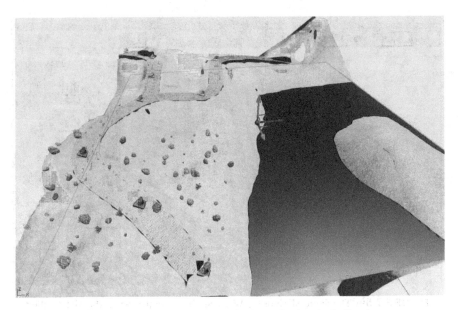

FIGURE 7.60: The Static Mesh of the Water Surface in the Landscape.

   c. Place a **Constant** expression to the far left of the four **TexCoord** expressions. *Note: Holding the 1 key and left-clicking will place a constant expression on the graph editor.*

   d. Type a value of 8 in the **Value** section of the **Constant** expression.

   e. Connect the output of the **Constant** to the input B of the four **Multiply** expressions.

   f. Connect the output of each **Multiply** expression the **Coordinate** input channel of its respective **Panner** expressions (see Figure 7.61).

17. This will adjust the Normals of the water surface for the large scales we will need to use in our landscape.

18. Save and apply your material.

19. If you look closely at your Water Surface in the editor viewport, it should look similar to Figure 7.63(a) and the waves should be visible when you are close to the surface.

   Now let's adjust the waves on the water surface to be more visible when viewed from a distance:

20. If you look closely at your Water Surface in the editor viewport, it should look similar to Figure 7.63(a) and the waves should be visible when you are close to the surface.

21. Open up the **M_LScape_Water** material again in the Material Editor, if you have closed it.

22. Scroll to the bottom of the graph editor until you locate the section called "**Macro Normal**". This section is responsible for creating waves on the water surface when

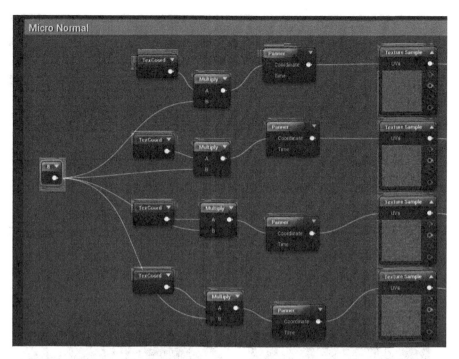

FIGURE 7.61: Adjusting the Coordinate Tiling of Micro Normals for the Water Surface.

viewed from a distance. In this section we will see two (2) **TexCoord** expressions. These expressions and their respective **Panner** expressions make the waves and move them on the water surface. From the top, the **TexCoord**'s U and V tilings are 0.1 and (0.08, 0.04). These values are quite small for our level. We will modify these by multiplying them with a large number, next:

    a. Place a **Multiply** expression to the right of each of the **TexCoord** expressions in the "Macro Normal" section.

    b. Place a **Constant** expression between the two **TexCoord** expressions in the "Macro Normal" section.

    c. Connect the output channel of each of the **TexCoord** expressions to the A channel of the **Multiply** expression you placed to its right.

    d. Type a value of 24 in the Value section of the **Constant** expression.

    e. Connect the output of the **Constant** to the input B of the four **Multiply** expressions.

    f. Connect the output of each **Multiply** expression the Coordinate input channel of its respective **Panner** expressions (see Figure 7.62).

23. This will adjust the Normals of the water surface for the large scales we will need to use in our landscape.

24. Save and apply your material.

25. If you look closely at your Water Surface in the editor viewport, it should look similar to Figure 7.63(b) and the waves should be visible when viewed from a distance.

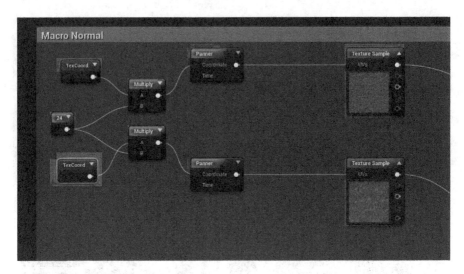

FIGURE 7.62: Adjusting the Coordinate Tiling of Macro Normals for the Water Surface.

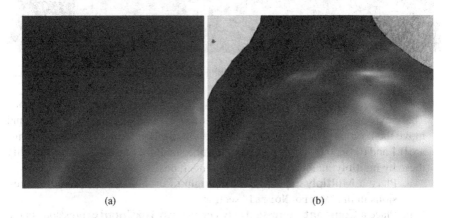

(a)   (b)

FIGURE 7.63: (a) Closeup View of Waves on the Water Surface. (b) Distant View of Waves on the Water Surface.

SETTING UP REFLECTION AND TRANSPARENCY

With the adjustment we made to the texture coordinates, we now have our water waves looking pretty good. But the water looks more like crude oil. It's quite opaque and dark. Moreover, it doesn't really reflect anything. Let's fix the reflection problem first:

26. Go to the main editor, and in the `Search Classes` bar in the **Models Panel** type `Reflection`. This will look up the **Reflection Capture** classes for you.
27. Drag a **Sphere Reflection Capture** into the level.
28. Make the following changes to the property of the `Sphere Reflection Capture Actor` in the **Details** rollout:

    Location: R:1000, G:1000, B:200 (*Note: These values may be different in your level. Place the Reflection Capture Actor just above the river surface in your level.*)

    Influence Radius: 5000
29. This will place a Reflection Capture actor in the level. This actor will then capture the reflection to be rendered onto the surfaces with low **Roughness** values. For this to work on our water surface, we will need to modify its **Roughness** value:
30. Open the `M_LScape_Water` material again in the Material Editor, if you have closed it.
31. In the material editor find the **Constant** expression connected to the `Roughness` channel of the material node and change its value to 0.
32. After making this change to your level and material, your water surface should look very reflective, similar to Figure 7.66(a).

With our water surface reflection set up, now let's make the water surface a bit transparent. We will perform three tasks to achieve this effect.

First, we will have to set up our material's **Blend Mode** to become transparent. Secondly, we will need to create a network for the material's transparency. Finally, we will need to make a network for our material's emissive color to give it a shiny look.

So let's get started:

33. Select the material node, and look for **Blend Mode** in its **Details** rollout.
34. Make the following changes. You may need to expand the Translucency section of the Details Panel.

    Blend Mode: Translucent

    Mobile Separate Translucency: Checked

    Responsive AA: Checked

    Translucency Lighting Mode: Surface Translucency Volume
35. This makes our material translucent, but you notice if the material is compiled, we will lose much of the detail. This is because we have'nt set up the Opacity and Emissive Colors of our now-translucent material. So let's first set up the Opacity network:

    a. Place a **Fresnel** expression to the right of the **Lerp** expression that is connected to the `Normal` channel of the material. *Note: If you need more room, move the material node to the right a little.*

    b. Connect a wire from the output channel of this **Lerp** expression to the `Normal` input of the **Fresnel** expression.

    c. Place a **Lerp** expression to the right of the **Fresnel** expression and connect the output of the **Fresnel** to the `Alpha` input of this **Lerp** expression.

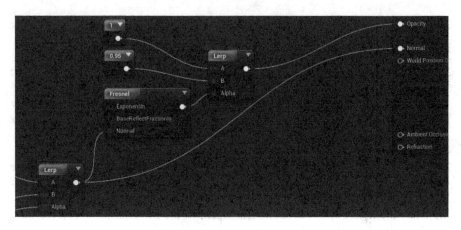

FIGURE 7.64: Water Material Opacity Network.

    d. Place two **Constant** expressions to above the **Fresnel** expression.

    e. Type a value of 1 into the top **Constant** expression, and a value of 0.95 into the bottom one.

    f. Connect the 1 constant to the **A** input of the **Lerp** expression.

    g. Connect the 0.95 constant to the **A** input of the **Lerp** expression.

    h. Connect the output of the **Lerp** expression to the `Opacity` channel of the material node.

36. This makes our material look translucent, and the amount of translucency will increase as the viewer angle increases. It is a pretty close simulation of actual water surfaces – when you look straight on they look translucent, but viewed from an angle the surface become opaque.

37. Now, let's finish up our material by setting up its `Emissive Color` channel:

    a. Place a **Constant** expression below the `Color` parameter and give it a value of 0.05.

    b. Place a **Multiply** expression to the right of this 0.05 constant expression and make the following connections:

        RGBA (white) channel of Color Parameter → **A** channel of the **Multiply** expression

        Output of 0.05 Constant Expression → **B** channel of the **Multiply** expression

        Output of Multiply Expression → `Emissive Color` channel of Material Node.

38. This will set up the `Emissive Color` of our water material, so as to not look too dark. Notice that we used the material color to supply the network for the `Emissive Color` Channel.

39. Now save and apply your material. The input channel networks of your material node should look similar to Figure 7.65.

40. Take a test drive in your level and test your now completed water material. Your material should now look similar to Figure 7.66(b).

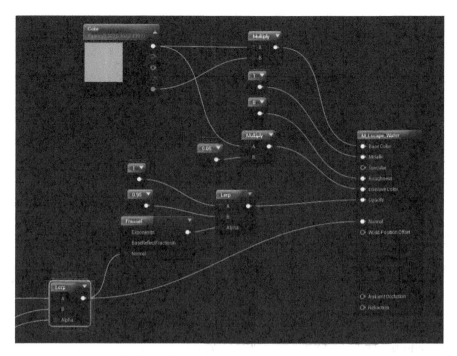

FIGURE 7.65: Water Material Complete Network.

UNDERWATER BLUR EFFECT

Our last stop in completing our landscape is to establish a blur effect for the underwater area. If you've tested the locations under water (in the valley) you notice that the view is too clear to accurately represent underwater scenes. We will fix this issue now to complete our landscape level:

41. Go to the main editor, and in the `Search Classes` bar in the **Modes Panel** type `Post Process`. This will look up the **Post Process Volume** class for you.
42. Drag a **Post Processes Volume** into the level.
43. Make the following changes to the properties of the `Post Process Volume` **Actor** in the **Details** rollout:
    - `Brush Settings`
    Brush Shape: Box
    X 12000
    Y 12000
    Z 3000
    - `Mobile Tonemeter`
    Tint Checkbox: Checked
    Tint: R:0.2, G: 0.4, B: 0.95, A:1.0
    - `Dept of Field (Lens Section)`
    Method: Checked and set to `Gaussian`

(a)   (b)

FIGURE 7.66: (a) Water Surface Is Now Reflective but Opaque. (b) Water Surface Is Reflective and Translucent.

Near Transition Region: Checked and set to 3000
Far Transition Region: Checked and set to 5000

44. Now select the **Post Process Volume** and place it in such a way that it is centered in the landscape, and slightly below the surface of water. *Hint: You might find using the* Top, Side, *and* front *viewports much more helpful in adjusting the location of the* **Post Process Volume Actor** *in the scene.*
45. Save your level and move around in the viewport to test out our new underwater effect.
46. The underwater effect should now look similar to Figure 7.67.

FIGURE 7.67: The Postprocess Volume Creates a Nice Underwater Effect.

What Happened in TUTORIAL 7.9...

You just set up a river to run through our landscape. This was actually a multistep task. We first organized our assets for the surface of the river comprising a plane mesh and a water material.

After placing our mesh with the water material applied, we modified the material in a number of steps to have realistic water-like qualities. This included reflection, transparency, and waves. To achieve reflection we needed the help of a special actor class called **Reflection Capture**.

After we achieved the look on the water material, we placed a **Post Process Volume** to create the underwater tint and blur effect.

ORGANIZING ASSETS

Again, much like our other tutorials, we organized our assets in our own folders. To have a fully customized river in our level we needed two items, a plane mesh and a material to simulate the effects of water surfaces. Thankfully, the Starter Content gives us both of these items. But we do need to make a few adjustments to make them work with our landscape.

PLACING WATER IN THE LANDSCAPE

The first task after we made our own copies of the plane static mesh and the water material was to apply the material to the mesh, modify the mesh collisions so that it won't block actors, and create a static mesh actor based on the plane static mesh in our level.

The plane mesh is quite small with respect to the size of our landscape. So the next task was to modify its scale so that it fits well into our landscape. We also translated the plane so that it covers the valleys in our landscape.

MODIFYING WATER WAVES

After placing our water surface plane into the landscape, we realized that it didn't nearly looked like water. Well, there wasn't anything really wrong with the water material. But there were a few things that needed adjustment before this water would work with our landscape.

For starters, upon a close inspection of the water material networks in the material editor, you would notice that there are two main networks responsible for creating waves on the surface of the water. These networks modify the normals of the surface on which the water material is applied. The first wave network (`Micro Normal`) is responsible for the look of ripples on the water surface when viewed closely, while the second network (`Macro Normals`) creates the ripple look (or waves) when the surface is viewed from a distance.

Let's first break the `Micro Normal` (shown in Figure 7.68) network down. There are four **TexCoord** expressions, each connected to a **Panner** expression. The **Panner** expressions are then connected to the **UVs** input of **Texture Sample** expressions. All four **Texture Sample** expressions have the same normal map – i.e., `T_Water_N`. The U and V Tiling values for the top two **TexCoord**

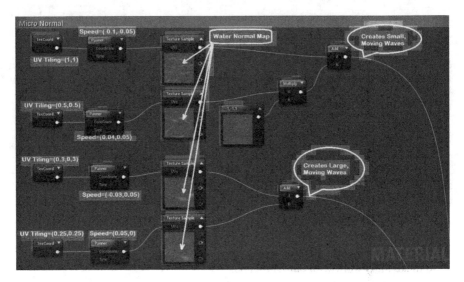

FIGURE 7.68: The Original Network Responsible for Creation of Waves When Water is Viewed Up Close.

expressions make the Normal map tile smaller (more repetitions on a surface), while the U and V Tiling values for the bottom two **TexCoord** expressions make their normal maps have larger tile sizes (less repetition on a surface). This, effectively, creates four waves –two small-size and two large-size wave patterns.

The **Panner** expressions have different speeds in the X and Y directions. This makes each of the four ripples created move at a different speed, giving the overall look of the combined waves some degree of randomness.

Now that we have our small-scale and large-scale waves, we can combine them based on the surface distance from the camera. The network in Figure 7.69 shows the process in detail. First, pixel depths (distance from camera) are used in an equation to return values between 0 and 1. First we subtract the depth of each pixel from 100, then divide the result by 400, and finally clamp the result between 0 and 1. The results of our calculation based on pixel depth are shown in Table 7.1.

TABLE 7.1

Linear Interpolate for Micro Normal. The Resolution is $1/400 = 0.0025$.

Pixel Depth=x	Value of Divide Expression=d(x)	Value of Clamp=C(d)
$x < 100$	$d(x) < 0$	$C(d) = 0$
$100 \leq x \leq 500$	$0 \leq d(x) \leq 1$	$0 \leq C(d) \leq 1$
$500 < x$	$1 < d(x)$	$C(d) = 1$

If a pixel is closer than 100 world units to the camera, this calculation will return a negative number which will be clamped at 0. If a pixel is farther than

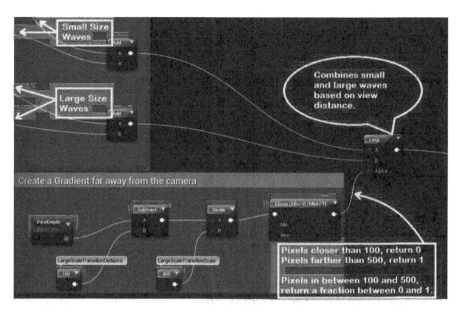

FIGURE 7.69: The Micro Waves Are Combined Based on Distance from the Camera with a Linear Interpolation Expression.

500 units from the camera, the result will be a number greater than 1, which will be clamped at 1. Any pixel between 100 to 500 units from the camera will have a value between 0 and 1 with a resolution of $\frac{1}{400} = 0.0025$. With this network we can choose up to 400 combinations of small-scale waves and large-scale waves for closeup views of the water surface. In other words, if you are too close to the water surface, you'll only see small waves, and as you walk away from the surface you will be able to see small waves start to fade, while larger waves start to appear.

A similar network is set up for distances that are farther than 500 units from the camera. To check it out, take a look at the `Macro Normal` network and see if you can figure out the wave scales, speeds, and tiling values. Try to find out the pixel-depth calculations and see if you can figure out the values for the clamp distances and Linear Interpolation resolutions (one of the exercises at the end of this chapter asks you to specify these values).

As I mentioned earlier, before we got into the details of wave and ripple calculations, for a large surface (such as our landscape river) the tiling values in both the `Macro Normal` and `Micro Normal` expressions were far too small. To fix this issue and to make our water ripples (waves) more visible I multiplied the outputs of the four **TexCoord** expressions in the `Micro Normal` section by 8, and those of the `Macro Normal` section by 24 (see Figure 7.61 and Figure 7.62).

SETTING UP REFLECTION AND TRANSPARENCY

Now that our water waves look much more suitable for the grand scale of our landscape, it's time to work on making the water look like water. That is, to make our water more reflective and a bit more translucent. We tackle the simpler task first –making the water reflective.

There are two tasks to perform to allow our water surface to show reflections of its surroundings. The first task was to create a **Reflection Capture** actor in the level. The **Reflection Capture** actor will receive indirect and static lighting from the scene and create a cubemap for the reflections to be projected onto parts of the scene that receive reflection (i.e., parts of the scene that are within the actor's area of influence). We placed a **Sphere Reflection Capture** actor close to the surface of a river and made its area of influence large enough to affect the entire river.

Once the Reflection Capture actor was set up in the scene, we changed the roughness of our water material to 0. This change makes the water material very reflective. The material is already set up to be fully metallic, so the specularity of our material is taken care of.

The next step was to make the water surface a little translucent. To do so, we first changed our material's **Blend Mode** to be `Translucent`. With the **Blend Mode** set to Translucent, two changes become apparent. First, the **Opacity** channel of the material node will become active to receive opacity values. Second, you will be able to set up your material's Translucency properties.

We changed the `Translucency Lighting Mode` of our material to **TLM Surface**. This is the preferred Translucency Lighting Mode for water and glass surfaces. We established our material's `Opacity` channel. We could have simply created a constant value (e.g., 0.95) and plugged it directly into the `Opacity` channel of our material node. However, I wanted to achieve a more profound water-like look.

In our level we have a very large area of water (i.e., the river flowing through a valley). As such when you look at the river surface, there are some areas where your view angle is large (i.e., close to where you are located), while within the same view there are water areas where your view angle is small (i.e., at the horizon). When you look at a water surface dead-on, it looks more transparent, while looking at it from an angle makes it look more opaque.

To achieve this effect, I used a **Fresnel** expression whose normal value is being supplied from the normal of our water surface. This expression gives us a value ranging from 0 to 1 based on the angle at which we are viewing the surface. I used the output of the **Fresnel** expression to interpolate between an opacity value of 0.95 (slightly transparent) to 1 (completely opaque), depending on whether we are looking at the water straight-on or at an angle, respectively. I finally connected a fraction of the water Base Color to the `Emissive Color` channel of the water material to make it look a bit shiny.

UNDERWATER BLUR EFFECT

The final effect to add to our landscape was to simulate the blurriness of the under-water areas. This effect can be achieved by placing a **Post Process Volume** into our level, aligning it with the water surface, and modifying its properties to create a murky blue tint and to simulate the depth of field.

Post Process Volume actors are processes in the fragment shader, and as such they will not really receive information or interact with the geometry of the level. In other words, these volumes work by modifying the final look of the pixels at render time. As such, they are powerful tools to create after-effects, such as Auto Exposure, Lens Flare, Bloom, Motion Blur, Depth of Field, etc.

In our level, we needed two of these features, a `Tint` to make the underwater area have a blue tint, and a `Depth of Field` to make underwater scenes fuzzy. To achieve this effect, we gave the **Post Process Volume** a tint with a color value of (R:0.2, G:0.4, B:0.95, A:1). For the `Depth of Field` values, I used `Gaussian` as the filtering method with `Near Transition Region` of 3000, and `Far Transition Region` of 5000. This will make the areas start to become blurry from a few thousand world units in front of the camera.

7.8 SUMMARY

In this chapter we worked with a newly introduced system in Unreal Engine 4, called Landscape. Landscapes are the equivalent of Terrains in other 3D game engines and are quite useful in efficiently designing and rendering outdoors environments.

Much like in other chapters in this book, we first learned about the features and functionalities of the engine component –in this case landscape tools. We then went through a series of Tutorials to help us learn how to work with landscapes in Unreal Engine 4 in a progressive manner.

In particular, we learned about all of the tools and modes that **Landscape Tool** affords us and about their usage and functionalities. We also looked at two important tools in UE4 that work well in tandem with landscapes, the Landscape Spline Tool and the Foliage System.

We learned how to add, edit, and manage splines in our landscapes to create linear features that conform to the shape of the terrain, such as roads, river banks, etc. We also worked with the Foliage System in UE4 and learned how to fully utilize this system to populate our level with static mesh instances.

We discovered the benefits of utilizing foliage instanced meshes in efficiently rendering large numbers of such instances by means of clustering and culling. We also learned about setting up culling and fading support in the materials of our instance meshes.

The chapter concluded with a complete coverage of creating and integrating massive reflective and translucent materials such as river, lake, or ocean surfaces into a landscape. We discussed the use of Texture Coordinate systems for tiling, panning, and combining dynamic looks for our water surfaces. We also learned about properly setting up reflections and translucency for water surfaces. We finished our outdoors journey by creating a Post Process Volume to create an underwater effect for underwater areas in our landscape.

7.9 EXERCISES

Exercise 1. The Grand Canyon:

    a) Use the **Landscape Tool** to create a rendition of the Grand Canyon. Search for an areal view of the Grand Canyon for your reference. For this exercise our goal is the geometry of the canyon, so don't worry about setting up materials or any effect. You may find a few web addresses where you may be able to find suitable areal photos:

        • http://www.nps.gov/grca/photosmultimedia/
        • https://www.flickr.com/photos/grand_canyon_nps/

    b) Use the techniques you learned in this chapter to set up Landscape Materials, create a material for the view of the Grand Canyon you created in **Exercise 1.a)** and apply your materials to the landscape.

    c) It usually doesn't snow in the Grand Canyon. However, to make your canyon "unreal," add a snow layer to the landscape material you created in **Exercise 1.b)** and apply some of the snow to the high elevations in the canyon.

    d) Either create a few static meshes that you should usually find in the Grand Canyon, or use some of the already created meshes within different UE4 content projects to populate your landscape.

    e) Edit materials used for the foliage instanced meshes from **Exercise 1.d)** to create Culling and Fading support when used in the landscape.

    f) Create a highway that passes through the canyon.

Exercise 2. Water Materials:

    a) In Tutorial 7.9 we used a copy of the M_Water_Lake material from the starter contents. Can you modify this material so that it doesn't use Metallic channels, but is still perfectly reflective?

    b) In the Linear Interpolation network for the Macro Normal section of the water material in Tutorial 7.9 can you find out what is the minimum view distance that starts the blending of the Macro Normals?

    c) In the Linear Interpolation network for the Macro Normal section of the water material in Tutorial 7.9 can you find out what is the resolution of the blending of the two normal channels?

Exercise 3. Underwater Scenes:

    a) We used a Post Process Volume for the underwater effects in Tutorial 7.9. Use this volume to create lens effects.

b) Create the so-called **God Rays** with the help of a post process volume.

c) Add a volume (you will have to find out what kind) to create the effect of buoyancy – i.e., when the player submerges in the water, the water should create a push to float the player.

Section III

Example Games: Advanced Game Development Concepts

Section III

8 Advanced Blueprint Concepts

8.1 INTRODUCTION

In this chapter, we will be going over advanced blueprint concepts to further your understanding of the blueprint system. We will cover communicating between multiple blueprints, creating custom HUDs, as well as saving and loading data. This will require the use of different blueprint types such as Save Game blueprints and HUD blueprints. We will also be using event dispatchers, object references, and polymorphism to achieve our goals for this project.

Just as the previous blueprint chapter, we will be creating projects and building upon them throughout the chapter. It is important to complete each tutorial before continuing on to the next one. Throughout this chapter, we will be creating a sort of item collecting game. We will be picking up balls that are randomly spawning throughout a level that we will be creating. This will require communication between multiple blueprints in order to spawn/destroy actors, as well as display information to the player about remaining time, score, and high score. We will be building on this project throughout the chapter until we have a complete game.

8.2 COMMUNICATION BETWEEN BLUEPRINTS

When you are working with a Blueprint, you may sometimes find that you want to access the Functions, Events, or Variables that are contained in another Blueprint. There are several approaches that you can use to access and communicate between multiple Blueprints depending upon your needs. In the following, we will present several approaches to blueprint communications based on the official UE4 documentation pages [3].

8.2.1 DIRECT BLUEPRINT COMMUNICATION

This is the most common approach of communications between blueprints. You can use this method when you wish to have two blueprint actors to talk to each other at a certain point.

This type of blueprint communication is always one-on-one – i.e., only one blueprint can request to access to another one. The simplest way to implement this method is to reference the target blueprint through a publicly exposed object variable and then specify which instance of, or object within, that blueprint you wish to access [3].

8.2.2 BLUEPRINT CASTING

The Direct Blueprint Communication method above works well for communicating with two Actors placed inside your level, as you can select the instance in the level that will be the Target Blueprint. However, this technique will fail when one of the actors is not actively represented or when it is not easily accessible within the level.

For example suppose you wish to communicate between an actor within the level and one of the player characters. Let's think of a scenario in which we wish the player to take damage when they walk into flowing toxic material. In this scenario, we want to apply damage to the player. Therefore, the player character Blueprint would be the Target Blueprint that we want to access. The problem is, however we cannot specify it as the "target" since it is not a publicly exposed object variable and it does not exist in the world until we start the game.

In this situation we could use Blueprint Casting to take the playable character and Cast To our **Target Blueprint** (Character Blueprint) [3]. This will give us access to our Character class functions, variables, and events. For example, suppose that we want to count how many times a player has entered/or exited a trigger box for a door. Figure 8.1 shows an example of how this scenario may be implemented using Blueprint Casting.

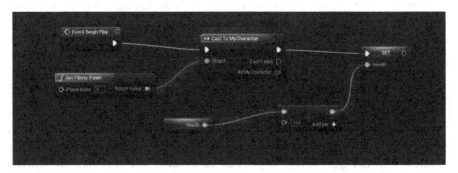

FIGURE 8.1: Blueprint Casting.

8.2.3   EVENT DISPATCHERS

By binding one or more Events to an Event Dispatcher, you can cause all of Events that are bound to the dispatcher to fire once the Event Dispatcher is called. The following scenario is adapted from the UE4 official documentations page for you to consider [3].

For example, suppose that you want to spawn an enemy in a random location in the level whenever the player presses a key. To do this, create an **Event Dispatcher** called "SpawnEnemy" inside the player character Blueprint. Inside your level you place several spawn points from which an enemy can spawn. Bind the SpawnEnemy Event Dispatcher from the character Blueprint with an Event in the Level Blueprint called "ExecuteSpawn" that randomly chooses a spawn location and spawns an enemy. Whenever the player presses the key, the Event Dispatcher is called and since it is bound to the "ExecuteSpawn" Event in the Level Blueprint, that Event is also called resulting in an enemy being spawned.

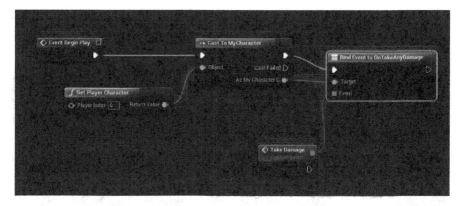

FIGURE 8.2: Binding Events to Event Dispatchers.

Figure 8.2 shows an example of using event dispatchers to perform an action to bind an event on a player when a certain situation happens, in this case, binding a custom take damage event to the character.

8.2.4   BLUEPRINT INTERFACES

Blueprint Interfaces allow for a common method of interacting with multiple types of objects that all share some specific functionality. This means you can have completely different types of objects, such as a car and a tree, that share one specific thing; they can both be shot by weapon fire and take damage. By creating a Blueprint Interface that contains an "OnTakeWeaponFire" function and having both the car and the tree implement that Blueprint Interface, you can treat the car and the tree as the same and simply call the "OnTakeWeaponFire" function when either of them is shot and have them respond differently [3].

8.3   CHAPTER SYNOPSIS

In this section, we will create projects with multiple blueprint systems that interact with each other to create a game. Communication between different systems in our game is an essential part of game programming and the blueprint system makes it easy to map out large intricate systems in a visual way. The first thing we need to do for our project is create our level.

To find updates to this tutorial and updated instructions about its implementation on other UE4 versions please visit the book's companion website at: http://www.RVRLAB.com/UE4Book/

TUTORIAL 8.1   Creating a Project and Including Starter Contents

FIGURE 8.3: Creating a Blank Project.

CREATING A FIRST PERSON PROJECT

We will use the **First Person Blueprint Template** to create this game so that
we can focus on our gameplay.

1. Open the Unreal Launcher and select the version of the engine you would like to
   work with.
2. Once the Editor Opens, choose **New Project** (see Figure 8.3).
3. Select the **Blueprint** as your project type, and make sure that the **First Person** is
   selected.
4. Select your platform (Desktop/Console) and your graphics quality.
5. Make sure you include the starter content (see Figure 8.3).
6. Give your project a name and click **Create Project**.

SETTING UP THE MAPS

When you click Create Project, the Editor will open to the default **Exam-
ple_Map**. We will go ahead and use this map to save time in creating our
game.

7. Find "Save As.." under **File** and save this map again with the name Level01. We will do this so as to not lose the original level (just in case you want to look at it for something later).

8. Once this is done, you will be editing the new level and it should display Level01 on the tab in the top left.

9. It might also be beneficial to you to set the default map/startup map to Level01 as well. To do this perform the following tasks:

   a. Go to **Project Settings**.

   b. Left-Click on the Maps & Modes tab on the left.

   c. Associate the Level01 to editor startup map. the This way, if you close the project and reopen later, you won't have to relocate Level01.

10. The next thing we need to do is delete all the boxes within the four outer walls of the level including the two large gray boxes extruding from the walls themselves.

11. Once you are done, you should be left with a small open area with four walls and a Player Start (see Figure 8.4).

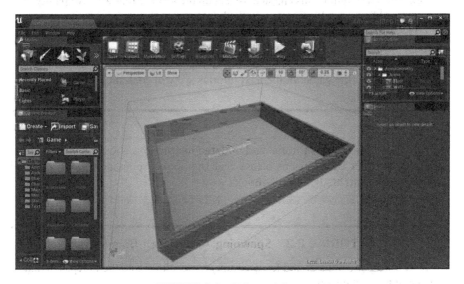

FIGURE 8.4: FPS Level Setup.

MODIFYING THE CHARACTER BLUEPRINT

Next, we will make some modifications to the Character blueprint so that the character fits in with our gameplay.

12. Open the FirstPersonCharacter blueprint.

13. Find the InputAction Fire event at the bottom.

14. Simply disconnect this event by holding the Alt key and clicking the Pressed pin, or by Right-clicking and breaking the link.

15. Now the default weapon will no longer fire.

16. Lastly, we can hide the visibility of the character mesh as it's not relevant to our game anymore. To do this perform the following tasks:
    a. Go to the **Components** tab of the `FirstPersonCharacter` blueprint.
    b. Select `Mesh2P` and `FP_Gun` meshes in the components list.
    c. Scroll down to the **Rendering** section of the Details window.
    d. Check `Hidden in Game` to temporally hide the mesh.
17. When you compile and save, the arms will be visible in the editor but when the game is played, they will be hidden.

What Happened in TUTORIAL 8.1...

At this point, we have completed our initial setup of the main project we will be working on throughout this chapter. We set up the level so that we have plenty of room to add our own blueprints into the level.

The `MyCharacter` blueprint is now set up to function as a first person controller, without the weapon asset. We removed it because we don't need the weapon in the game we are making but if you would like to add it back in, it shouldn't affect the game. In the next tutorial, we will continue on to create our ball spawner.

To find updates to this tutorial and updated instructions about its implementation on other UE4 versions please visit the book's companion website at: `http://www.RVRLAB.com/UE4Book/`

TUTORIAL 8.2   Spawning Actors with Blueprints

Now with our character and level set up, we need to create the blueprints that we will be working on.

CREATING THE BALL AND BALL SPAWNER BLUEPRINTS

1. Navigate to the **Blueprints** folder in the **Content Browser**.
2. Create a new **Actor** blueprint.
3. Give it the name `Ball` and leave it alone for now. We will create our object using this particular class blueprint later.
4. Next, create another **Actor** blueprint.
5. Give the second blueprint the name `BallSpawner`.
6. `Double-Click` on the `BallSpawner` blueprint to open it.

ADDING COMPONENTS TO BALLSPAWNER

The purpose of the `BallSpawner` is to be able to spawn our `Ball` blueprint at the location of the spawner itself. When we have this blueprint placed in-game, the user will not be able to see it (unless we have it visible for debugging purposes). This will let us have the illusion of spawning at random locations on the board, when in reality it is going to be tightly controlled.

For level design and debugging purposes only, we will place a mesh in the components section, so that we can see where our spawners are in the level.

7. Go to the **Components** tab of the `Ball Spawner` blueprint.
8. `Left-Click` on the `Add Component`, and place a `Capsule Collision` in the blueprint. This will be our visual representation of the spawner so that we can easily move them around and know where they are located.
9. Rename the capsule to `Spawner`.
10. Locate the Details window and scroll down to the **Rendering** section.
11. Uncheck `Hidden in Game` so that it will be visible for the time being.
12. Once this is done you can compile and save.
13. Your blueprint components tab should look similar to Figure 8.5.

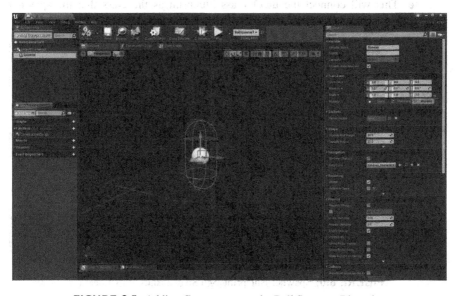

FIGURE 8.5: Adding Components to the Ball Spawner Blueprint.

ADDING FUNCTIONALITY TO THE BALL SPAWNER

14. Move to the event graph of our `BallSpawner` blueprint so we can add the functionality we need. To do this, `Left-Click` on the **Graph** tab on the upper right corner of the blueprint editor. The script in this particular blueprint will need to

handle the spawning of the ball as well as telling the ball when to be destroyed and informing other blueprints that this has happened. We will be building up to this so that we can learn what each piece of the puzzle is doing as we go.

15. We need to create a custom event that will fire when it is called upon by either the level blueprint or another class blueprint. To create a custom event, perform the following tasks:

    a. Right-Click on the event graph.

    b. Type Add Custom Event in the search box.

    c. Place a Custom Event in the graph.

    d. Once placed, give the Custom Event the name Spawn Ball.

16. To place an actor in the game, we will use a function called SpawnActor. To do this perform the following tasks:

    a. Branch off a wire from the Spawn Ball custom event we just created.

    b. Search for a function called Spawn Actor from Class by typing the Spawn Actor from Class in the search bar.

    c. The class we will be using is our Ball class that we made at the beginning of the tutorial.

    d. Left-Click on the arrow next to the Class pin of the Spawn Actor from Class and search for the Ball blueprint.

    e. This will connect the Ball class blueprint as the class that the spawner should spawn.

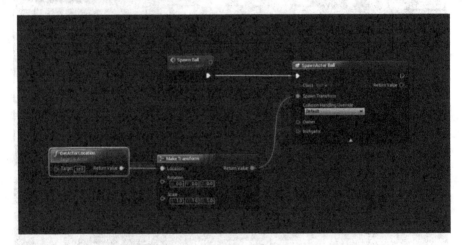

FIGURE 8.6: Spawner Blueprint Will Spawn Balls at Its Location.

17. Now we will give the spawned objects a Transform so that the function knows the orientation, location, and scale of the object it will be placing in the level. To quickly make a transform, perform the following actions:

    a. Drag off a wire from the Spawn Transform pin of the Spawn Actor function to the left and search for Make Transform.

b. For our purposes, we need to feed the location of our blueprint into the transform location. This will ensure that the ball will spawn at the origin of our spawner, as well as have the default scale and rotation.

c. Drag off a wire from the `Location` pin and search for `Get Actor Location`.

d. When you place the `Get Actor Location` in the event graph, the `Target` should be **self** which is the current blueprint we are working in.

18. Your network should look similar to Figure 8.6.

19. Compile and save the blueprint. If you get a compiler error, double check that you have the class set to `Ball` in the `SpawnActor` Class function and that you have your `Make Transform` hooked up correctly (see Figure 8.6 for reference).

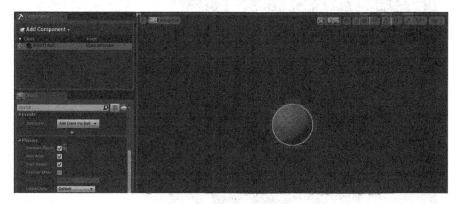

FIGURE 8.7: Ball Blueprint with Physics Activated.

MODIFYING THE BALL BLUEPRINT

Next, we will add a mesh to the Ball blueprint we created earlier.

20. Open the `Ball` blueprint.

21. Navigate to the `Components` tab.

22. `Left-Click` on `Add Component`, add a `Static Mesh` to the components list.

23. Rename the static mesh to `Ball`.

24. Find the **Static Mesh** section in the Details rollout.

25. `Left-Click` on the drop-down menu and find a mesh called `MaterialSphere`. This mesh is a part of the starter content.

26. Lastly, we need to enable physics for the ball. Find the **Physics** section in the Details rollout and check `Simulate Physics`.

27. As always remember to compile and save the blueprint.

28. The `Ball` blueprint should look similar to Figure 8.7.

TESTING OUT THE LEVEL

Now that we have the ball and spawner done, we should quickly test out our newly created blueprints.

29. Place a **BallSpawner** in the level by dragging it onto the screen.
30. With the **BallSpawner** still selected, open the level blueprint (by clicking blueprints at the top of the editor and selecting Open Level Blueprint).
31. Create an **Event Begin Play** event and attach it to a **Spawn Ball** function. This will create the event call and automatically add a reference to our **BallSpawner**, which we have placed in the level, as the target (see Figure 8.8(a)).

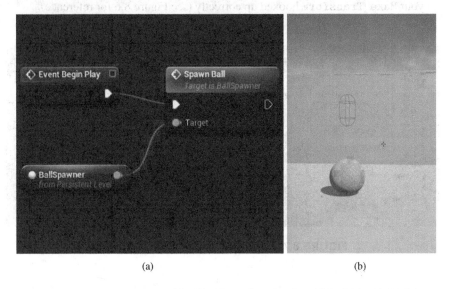

(a)   (b)

FIGURE 8.8: Testing the Ball Spawner Blueprint: (a) Level Blueprint. (b) One of the Ball Spawners Placed in the Level.

32. What this is going to do is spawn a ball at the location of our BallSpawner that we have placed in the level.
33. This ball will spawn one time as soon as you press play. If your spawner is floating above the ground a bit as is shown in Figure 8.8(b), the ball should immediately simulate physics and fall to the floor. If you walk up to the ball, your character's collision box should push the ball as well.

What Happened in TUTORIAL 8.2...

We have successfully created a system to be able to spawn an object using a custom event. This will set us up for the next tutorial where we will create a system to spawn a single ball in a random location in our game field. Keep in mind that we only spawned a ball from a single ball spawner using the event begin play node. We will be expanding on this functionality to spawn a single ball from a group of ball spawners based on how much time has passed. The ball class won't have much more to it than what we already have in place. Additional functionality of the ball class will be given to it by the ball spawner class instead. In the next tutorial, we will begin to create our ball spawning system so the ball will appear in different parts of the map instead of at the single ball spawner we just created.

To find updates to this tutorial and updated instructions about its implementation on other UE4 versions please visit the book's companion website at: http://www.RVRLAB.com/UE4Book/

TUTORIAL 8.3   Spawning Actors with Blueprints

The next thing we will do is to create the logic to spawn balls in various locations on the map. We need to place multiple **BallSpawners** throughout the level and call upon only one at a time. We also want to call upon a random **BallSpawner** so that the location of the next ball is unpredictable by the player.

BALLSPAWNERS PLACEMENT

First we will place eight **BallSpawners** throughout the level. They don't need to be exactly how they are in the image, but give them plenty of space for the ball to be able to spawn properly. If a spawner is too close to the floor or a wall, the ball will not spawn. Also, once you have the spawners placed, you can place them all into a folder in the **Scene Outliner** window so that they can be found easily.

1. Make 7 more copies of the **BallSpawner** actor you have in the level and place them in random locations throughout the level. Give your BallSpawners plenty of space above, below, and to the sides, so that the ball will be able to spawn properly.
2. Create a new folder in the **Scene Outliner** and rename it to **BallSpawners**.
3. Select the 8 **BallSpawner** actors, **Right-Click** and choose **Move To Folder** ▶ **BallSpawners** to move the actors to the folder.
4. Your level should look similar to Figure 8.9(a).
5. Save your level.

PROGRAMMING THE SPAWNING LOGIC

Because the logic we are going to write is unique to our level, we will place it in the level blueprint.

6. Go ahead and open up the Level Blueprint to view the event graph for our level. We currently have a bit of test logic in here that we need to delete for now.

7. Marquee select the three nodes we created in the previous tutorial to spawn a ball at the start of the game and remove them. Once you have deleted the test logic, there should be nothing in the Event Graph.

8. Next, we need to create an array variable to hold our `BallSpawner` objects. To do this perform the following tasks:

    a. On the left side of the event graph, in the `My Blueprint` pane, `Left-Click` on the **Variable** (V^+) button to add a new variable to the list.

    b. Name this variable `BallSpawners`.

    c. In the Details rollout of the `BallSpawners` variable, change the variable type to **Actor** either by searching for it or looking under `Object Reference` and selecting it.

    d. The blue icon just to the right of the variable type will toggle whether or not the variable is a single object or an array of objects.

    e. Select it once to change it to an array. The icon should look like a 9×9 grid of light blue squares (see Figure 8.9(b)).

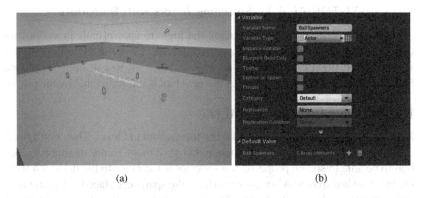

(a)   (b)

FIGURE 8.9: Placing Spawners in the Level and Making an Array.

9. We want the array to be set immediately when the level starts.

    a. Place an `Even Begin Play` event in the graph by right clicking and searching for it.

    b. Now when the level begins, this event will be called and we can set up the array before anything else happens.

10. We need to create the array by feeding in references to our Ball Spawner objects. To do this perform the following tasks:

    a. First, hold the `Alt` button and `Left-Click` -and-drag the `BallSpawners` array variable onto the Event Graph to place a **Set** function. *Note: You can also do this by just dragging the variable and selecting **Set** but using the `Alt` key is a bit of a shortcut.*

    b. Once you have the **Set** function placed, drag to the left from the `BallSpawners` array pin.

    c. Search for **Make Array** and place it in the event graph. This will let us feed all of our ball spawner objects into the array that we have created.

    d. **Left-Click** on the **Add Pin** until you have eight (8) pins (or one for each ball spawner object). Note that Arrays are zero-based indexed so you will have pins zero through seven for a total of eight.

11. Next, you need to add references to all eight of the **BallSpawner** objects themselves. To do this quickly and easily do the following:

    a. Return to the level editor and find the Scene Outliner window.

    b. Select all eight of the **BallSpawner** objects in the list.

    c. With all of the **BallSpawner** objects selected bring up the level blueprint again.

    d. **Right-Click** on the left side of the **Make Array** node and select **Create References to 8 selected Actors**. This will place references to each one in your event graph.

    e. Finally, wire each one of them up to an individual input on the **Make Array** node.

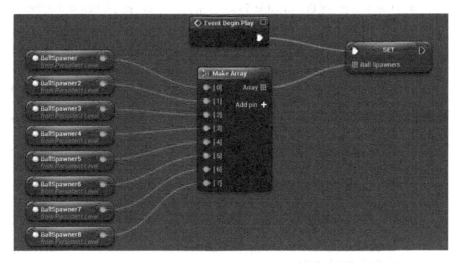

FIGURE 8.10: Initializing Arrays of BallSpawners.

12. The result of your network should look like Figure 8.10.

13. Compile and save the blueprint.

RANDOMIZED SPAWNING

For now, the desired effect that we want is to randomly choose a single spawn point every few seconds or so. To do this, we need a timer.

14. Start by creating a variable called **Timer** in the Level Blueprint. Press the **Variable(V^+)** button to add a variable.

15. Change the variable type to `Float`. This variable will be a single variable (NOT an array) and holds a number with a decimal point.
16. By default, this will be initialized to 0.0 which is perfect for what we need.
17. Compile and Save the blueprint.
18. Now that we have our variable, we need to use it in the game loop. To do this perform the following task:
19. Place an `Event Tick` event in the Event Graph. This event will fire on every iteration of the main game loop and gives us a double variable called `Delta Seconds`.
20. Delta Seconds will tell us how much time has passed between iterations of `Event Tick` because each tick is never going to take the exact same amount of time. Our logic for the timer will be driven by the `Event Tick`. We need to add `Delta Seconds` to our `Timer` on every `Event Tick` and check if it is greater than or equal to the number of seconds we wish between each spawn of the balls. If it is, then we can move on and spawn a ball. This will guarantee that a certain amount of time has passed in-between the balls being spawned. To do this perform the following tasks:
    a. Drag a copy of the variable `Timer` onto the event graph below the `Event Tick` node.
    b. Select **Get**.
    c. Drag a wire off the `Delta Seconds` and place a `float+float` node.
    d. Connect the output of the `Timer` getter to the second input of the + node.
    e. Select the `Timer` variable from the `My Blueprint` pane, and `Alt+drag` it to the right of the + node.
    f. Drag a wire from the output pin of the + node and connect it to the `Timer` input pin of the `Set` node.
    g. Connect the exec (white) output of the `Event Tick` to the exec (white) pin of the `Set`.
    h. Drag a wire off the output pin of the `Timer` getter you placed in step 20b.
    i. Type in > in the search box to place a `float>float` node.
    j. Type in a value of 5.0 in the second input of the > expression.
    k. Drag from the output (red) pin of the > node and place a `Branch` node.
    l. Connect the exec (white) output of the `Set` function to the exec (white) input of the `Branch` node.
21. Your event graph should look like Figure 8.11.
22. What we need to do next is immediately set the `Timer` back to zero, after 5 seconds has passed. If we don't, the timer will increase indefinitely and the branch will always return True after five seconds. To do this perform the following tasks:
    a. Duplicate the `Set` function of the `Timer` variable. *Note: you can do this by selecting the Set and pressing* `Control+W`.
    b. Bring in the duplicate `Set` function for the Timer variable to the right of the `Branch` node.
    c. Attach the `True` output of the `Branch` to the exec(white) input of the `Set` function.
    d. Make sure that the Timer value of the `Set` function is set at 0.0.

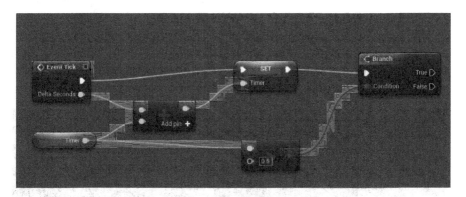

FIGURE 8.11: Testing for Time Between Spawns.

23. Next, we need to get a random ball spawner from our array that we created. To do this perform the following tasks:
    a. Select the `BallSpawners` array from the `My Blueprint` pane.
    b. Drag the `BallSpawners` array to the event graph.
    c. Select the `Get` option to place a Get function for the array. This will get the array as a whole, but we want to get only one object from the array.
    d. Drag off a wire from the array we just placed, you can search for a `Get` utility. This function is under the `Utility` section. The purpose of this function is to take a single object at a specific index from an array.
    e. Drag off a wire from the bottom input pin of the `GET` array function.
    f. Type `Random Integer` in the search bar, and place a `Random Integer` function. This will be connected to the index pin of the `GET` function.
    g. Type `8` in the `Max` input pin of the `Random Integer` function.
24. Your script should be the same as in Figure 8.12.

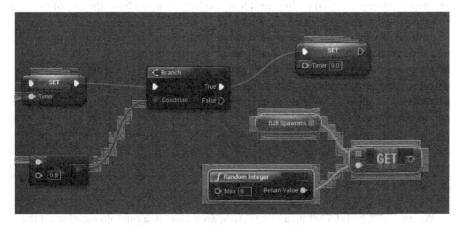

FIGURE 8.12: Getting a Randomized Index from Arrays.

CASTING OBJECTS TO SPAWN BALLS

The next thing we need to do is downcast our array object to a `BallSpawner` object. Remember earlier in the chapter we discussed blueprint communication modes. Our array is designed to hold any type of `Object` which all blueprints extend from so the data is cast to a general `Object` container.

FIGURE 8.13: Spawning from Randomized Spawner.

You could say that a `BallSpawner` is an Object but an Object is not always a `BallSpawner`. If you are familiar with the concept of polymorphism in programming, this is exactly the same concept. So, since our `BallSpawner` data is currently stored in a superclass container, we need to cast it back to a `BallSpawner` container so we can access the event we created within it.

25. Drag a wire from the `GET` array utility function.
26. Search by typing `Cast To BallSpawner` to place the `Cast to BallSpawner` function.
27. Connect the exec (white) output of the cast function to the `Set` function.
28. The last thing we need to do is to spawn the ball. Drag off from the end of the cast function and search for `Spawn Ball`. If you can't find it, you might need to drag off from the `As Ball Spawner` pin instead so that the context sensitive search functionality is able to locate the `Spawn Ball` event.
29. Your script should look like Figure 8.13.
30. Once the script is complete, compile, save, and return to the main level editor.
31. When you press play, a ball should be appearing at a random spawner every five seconds.

What Happened in TUTORIAL 8.3...

We have successfully set up a system to spawn a ball at a random location on the map. We used an event tick to set up a time interval between spawns and used polymorphism to store our data in an object array.

If you are not familiar with basic programming, then arrays might be a little confusing at first. A normal variable is designed to reference a particular type of data, such as an integer or an object reference. An array however is designed to store more than one instance of a particular type of data. The data is stored in order from zero to n number of array elements.

We created an array that stored eight objects under one variable. We can access each object by calling the number where the particular array element is stored, which is what we did with the **Array Get** function. For instance, if the random number turns out to be three, then we would get the object stored at array element three (which would be the fourth ball spawner in our case because we start counting at zero).

Another programming fundamental that we utilized is polymorphism. All the blueprints available to us are subclasses of the **Object** class. In object oriented programming, this means that all blueprints are technically objects. Because of this, we can store the data from any blueprint into an **Object** variable. This is useful when we want to store many types of blueprints into a single list of a common type. The problem with this is that in order to access the contents of the blueprint, we must have the data stored in a variable of the correct type. This is why we downcast the object variable to a BallSpawner variable. The cast allows us to use the **BallSpawner** variable to access the data inside that object.

Now we will have our character interact with the balls that are placed in the level. We also need to keep track of the amount of balls that we have collected, so we can calculate a score to display on our HUD, which we will create later on in this chapter. This task will require simple modifications to the current blueprint.

To find updates to this tutorial and updated instructions about its implementation on other UE4 versions please visit the book's companion website at: http://www.RVRLAB.com/UE4Book/

TUTORIAL 8.4   Destroying Actors

What we want to do here is give the player the ability to "pickup" the ball when they walk up to it. To do this, we will be using a special function to bind an event to the balls as they are spawned. Otherwise, we would have to reference the **Ball** object itself and because it doesn't exist in the level yet, we are unable to do this.

If you remember from earlier on in this chapter, we discussed the use of event dispatchers specifically for this kind of communication between blueprints. Since the ball objects don't exist in the level, before they are spawned, we cannot directly make a reference to them in our player's blueprint to detect whether they overlapped.

To accommodate this, we will create a custom event, and bind it to one of the functions that our Ball blueprints have –e.g., the **Begin Overlap**. This binding will expose our actor's overlap event to a custom event which will be called when an overlap occurs.

EVENT DISPATCHER AND BINDING EVENTS

1. Open up the **BallSpawner** blueprint. This is where the ball blueprints are actually spawned into the level.
2. Once inside the event graph, locate the **SpawnActor Ball** function and use the **Return Value** pin to add a function called **Assign On Actor Begin Overlap**.
3. This will automatically create the function as well as a custom event. Rename the custom event **OverlapBall**.
4. Please note that you must drag from the **Return Value** pin. Otherwise it will assign the target to self and you will be unable to change it to the correct object.
5. Basically we take a custom event and send it to the Ball blueprint itself as it is being created in the level. This custom event is assigned to the **Actor Begin Overlap** event that already exists for every actor. Basically, this custom event is fired when something overlaps each **Ball** actor that has just spawned in the level.
6. This binding mechanism is what we discussed earlier in the Blueprint Communications Section of this chapter.
7. Your event graph should look similar to Figure 8.14.

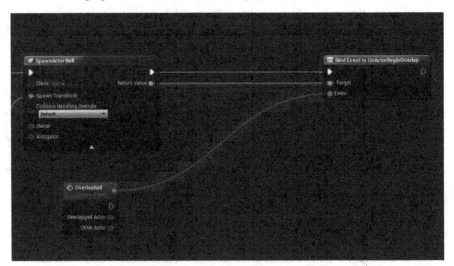

FIGURE 8.14: Binding Actor Overlap Event to a Custom Function.

8. Next, we simply treat this custom event as if it were inside the **Ball** blueprint itself. We want to destroy the actor when the player walks up to it, so we need to first check that the object that overlapped the actor is indeed the player. To do this, perform the following tasks:

a. Drag off from the custom event's exec (white) arrow and add a **Branch** statement.

b. Drag off from the **Other Actor** pin and search for and place **==** (equals equals) utility function.

c. Drag from the second input pin of the **==** function and search for and place a **Get Player Pawn** function.

d. This checks to see if the player pawn is equal to the actor that intersected the Ball.

e. The result of this network is shown in Figure 8.15.

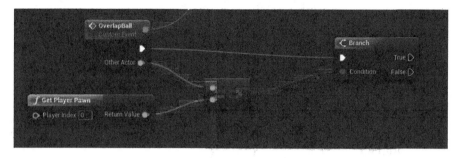

FIGURE 8.15: Checking to See if Player Overlaps the Ball.

SPAWNING ONLY ONE BALL AT A TIME

Another thing we need to do is to disable spawning of a new ball if one already exists from that particular **BallSpawner**.

9. Open up the **BallSpawner** blueprint if you have closed it.
10. In the **MyBlueprint** pane, add a **Boolean** variable.
11. Name this boolean variable **Is Spawn Active**.
12. Next, in-between the **Spawn Ball** event and the **SpawnActor** function, add a **Branch** statement that will check the state of our variable and only move forward if the value is false. To do this perform the following steps:

a. Disconnect the **SpawnBall** event from the **SpawnActor Ball**. Hold the **Alt** key and **Left-Click** on either end of the connection.

b. Drag the **SpawnBall** event to the left.

c. Place a **Get** function for the **Is Spawn Active** variable below the **SpawnBall** event. You can do this by pressing the **Control** key and dragging the variable onto the event graph.

d. Drag a wire off of the **Is Spawn Active** and place a **Branch** node.

e. Connect the exec (white) output of the **Spawn Ball** event to the exec (white) input pin of the **Branch**.

f. Connect the **false** output of the **Branch** to the exec (white) **SpawnActor Ball** function.

g. Your network should look similar to Figure 8.16.

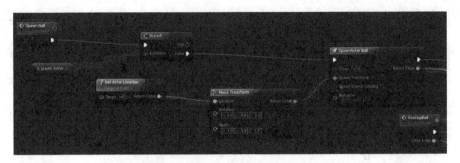

FIGURE 8.16: Spawn Only if Spawn Is Active.

13. We will set our **Is Spawn Active** variable to true after we call the event dispatcher that we create in step 7. To do this quickly perform the following tasks:

   a. Hold the **Alt** key and drag the **Is Spawn Active** variable to the right of the **Assign On Actor Begin Overlap** event dispatcher and connect them together.

   b. Make sure you check the box on the Set function to set the Boolean value to true.

14. The last thing we need to do in this blueprint is to destroy the actor and set the active state back to false. To do this perform the following tasks:

   a. Find the **Branch** statement coming from the **OverlapBall** event.

   b. Drag off a wire from the **True** pin.

   c. Search for **Destroy Actor** and place it in the graph.

   d. The target in this case is going to be our **Ball**, so connect the **Target** to the **Return Value** pin on the **SpawnActor Ball** function.

   e. Lastly duplicate the **Set** function of the **Is Spawn Active** variable and Connect it to the **Destroy Actor** function.

   f. This time, make sure the box is left unchecked.

   g. Your complete network should look similar to Figure 8.17.

15. Compile and save your Blueprint.

SETTING UP OVERLAP VOLUMES FOR THE BALL

If we were to play the game at this point, the balls would spawn as they did before, except we are still not able to pick them up. The reason for this is because we are not technically overlapping them when we walk near them. We must add a box volume component to our ball so that walking near the ball is enough to destroy the actor.

16. Open the **Ball** blueprint and find the components section.

17. Add a **Box** component and name it **Intersect Volume**.

18. You will need to increase its size using the Scale Tool. Bring up the scale tool by pressing the R key on your keyboard.

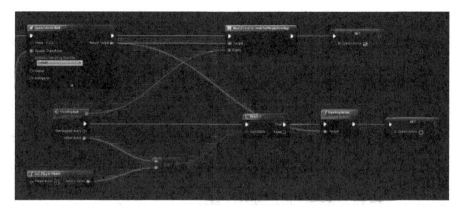

FIGURE 8.17: Destroying Balls on Overlap.

19. Increase the size of the box so that it is about three times the width and height of the ball. Alternatively, you can manually type the scale values if you prefer. The magic number used in the image is 4×4×4.
20. Keep in mind that this box is invisible to the player. If we wanted to make it visible in game for debugging purposes, we could simply enable it in the Detail window.
21. Compile and save the blueprint.
22. Return to the main level editor and play the game. When a ball spawns, walk up to it to destroy it.

What Happened in TUTORIAL 8.4...

We successfully added the destroy functionality to the existing blueprints. We used a delegate to pass an event into a blueprint. This event contained functionality that we implemented in a completely different blueprint.

We had to do it this way because the `Ball` blueprint doesn't exist when the game starts. We created our own event and assigned it to an existing event in the ball blueprint. Even though we did not implement any events ourselves in the Ball blueprint, there are still events that are a part of the parent class (Actor in this case) that are inherited by our custom blueprint.

The `OverlapBall` event we created is bound to the `On Actor Begin Overlap` event inside the `Ball` blueprint. When `On Actor Begin Overlap` is fired from the `Ball` blueprint, all events that are bound to it will also fire.

Now that we can spawn balls and our player can pick them up, we will pass data between blueprints and create a custom HUD from scratch using the existing HUD as reference.

8.4 CREATING THE HUD

In the previous section, we set up a system to spawn balls on a timer and destroy them as the player approaches. For this section, we will be expanding upon that functionality. The first person template provides us with a HUD blueprint or Heads Up Display that, at this time, only contains a crosshair in the middle of the screen.

We will be creating a custom HUD to display the remaining time, high-score, and current score. Almost all video games these days have some sort of persistent HUD to display score, time, kills, enemies, maps, items, and many other things. Using blueprints to create a HUD is a fairly simple process while still being quite power-ful. Just as in the case of other blueprint classes, HUDs can be made entirely using blueprints.

> To find updates to this tutorial and updated instructions about its implemen-tation on other UE4 versions please visit the book's companion website at:
> http://www.RVRLAB.com/UE4Book/

TUTORIAL 8.5   Creating the MyHUD Blueprint

The first person template gives us a HUD by default; however, if we needed to create one from scratch it would be beneficial to learn how.

CREATING THE HUD

First we will have to create the HUD blueprint. To do this:

1. Navigate to the Blueprints folder in the **Content Browser**.
2. Create a new blueprint.
3. When you pick a parent class, you will need to search for **HUD** at the bottom as the HUD class contains specific functions just for drawing the HUD on the screen.
4. Once you have found the parent class, name your blueprint MyNewHUD and save the project.
5. Open the new blueprint and go to the blank event graph.
6. The main event that we will be using is called **Event Receive Draw HUD**, which will constantly update the HUD and draw the information we want.
7. In this case, we are just going to place the crosshair back on the screen.
8. Using the exec (white) pin, attach a function called **Draw Texture**. As you can see from this function, we are given quite a lot of options.
9. To position the crosshair in the center of the screen, we need to get the halfway point for the width and height of the screen. We can do this by taking the Size X and Size Y pins and dividing them in half with a math function.
10. Drag a wire from Size X and place a divide function.
11. Make the function divide by 2.
12. Drag a wire from Size Y and place a divide function.
13. Make the function divide by 2.

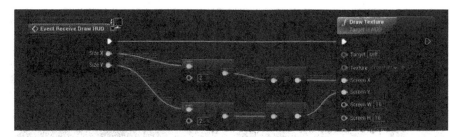

FIGURE 8.18: Calculating the Crosshair HUD Location.

14. These two variables are exact integers because they match the resolution of the play window. However, the position of our texture on the screen can be placed with a higher level of precision.

15. If you drag from the divide functions over to the Screen X and Screen Y tabs of the **Draw Texture** node, an extra function is automatically placed in-between to convert the Integer into Float values (see Figure 8.18).

16. Next, go to the **Texture** pin and **Left-Click** on the drop-down menu.

17. Find the **Crosshair** texture and select it. This is a texture that has been designed specifically for use with the HUD.

18. At this point, the HUD should be set up to draw the texture in the middle of the screen.

19. But, let's first add a **Tint Color** just as they have done in the default MyHUD blueprint. To do this perform the following tasks:

    a. Click the colored square to the right of **Tint Color**.

    b. Select the color you want or you can drag off from the pin and add a **Make LinearColor** node to accomplish the same thing.

    c. In the original MyHUD blueprint, a value of "1" is used for the RGB values as well as the alpha channel for a completely opaque texture that is not colored in any way.

    d. Play with these values by changing them from zero to one as you see fit.

    e. Make sure you give the alpha a value of 1 so that it is not transparent.

20. Next, we need to give the texture a **Width** and **Height** in pixels, just as is done in the MyHUD blueprint. If you increase this value, it will increase the size of the crosshair.

    a. In our case, give the **Screen W** and **Screen H** pins the value 32.

    b. This will draw the crosshair twice the size of the original.

    c. The last values we need to change are the **Texture UWidth** and the **Texture VHeight**.

    d. If we give these both the value of 1 it will fill the allotted space with the texture only one time in the X and Y directions.

21. The result should look like Figure 8.19.

22. Compile and save the blueprint.

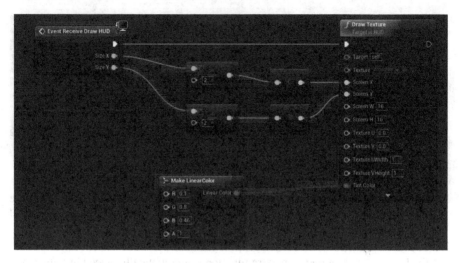

FIGURE 8.19: Crosshair in the HUD Completed.

ESTABLISHING THE NEW HUD

When you compile and save, the new HUD we created still won't be shown on the screen. The HUD to be drawn on the screen is actually a variable inside the main GameMode blueprint. In this case, it is called MyGame. This blueprint was generated automatically when we used the First Person Template.

23. Open the FirstPersonGameMode blueprint from the **Content Browser**.
24. Alternatively, you can edit its settings by going to the project settings:
    a. Left-Click on Maps and Modes
    b. Look under the Default Modes tab.
25. For now, simply open the MyFirstPersonGameModeGame blueprint and change the HUD Class value to MyNewHUD.
26. Compile and save the blueprint before closing it.
27. Now at this point, when you play the game, you will be seeing your own custom crosshair from the HUD blueprint we just created. You should notice it is a different color and is twice as large as it was before (see Figure 8.20).

What Happened in TUTORIAL 8.5...

In the previous tutorial, we learned how to build a HUD from scratch and have it appear in our game. Drawing a texture on the screen is simple but it could take some time to get it positioned exactly where you want it. It is a good idea to plan out how you want the HUD to look before you start trying to work it out in the

FIGURE 8.20: Your New HUD in Game.

engine. In the next tutorial, we will continue building on this HUD by adding a timer to the screen.

To find updates to this tutorial and updated instructions about its implementation on other UE4 versions please visit the book's companion website at: http://www.RVRLAB.com/UE4Book/

TUTORIAL 8.6   Adding the Score

Our HUD so far only uses a texture to draw out a crosshair in the middle of the screen. We want the HUD to also show some vital statistics to the player as well, such as a timer, number of pickups, etc.

IMPORTING FONTS

The first thing we will be doing is migrating a font into our game's folder from the Content folder in the engine itself. We will use the Unreal Engine's Engine Fonts.

> **NOTE**
>
> By default, the Unreal Engine will be located in **ProgramFiles** or **ProgramFiles(x86)** folder. The folder structure of Unreal Engine 4 is similar to the structure when you view the projects in Windows.

1. Open up a window explorer window.
2. Navigate to the main **Unreal Engine** folder.
3. Go to Unreal **Version Number** folder.
4. Go to **Engine** folder.
5. Go to **Content** folder.

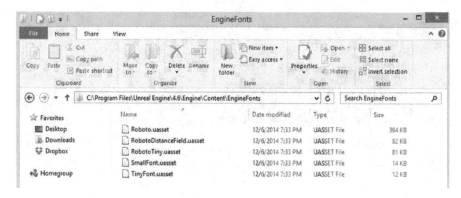

FIGURE 8.21: Engine Fonts Location.

6. Go to `EngineFonts` folder.
7. You should be in a location such as the one shown in Figure 8.21.
8. The `.uasset` file we will be using is called `RobotoDistanceField.uasset`.
9. Copy and paste this file into your project's `Content` ▸ `Texture` folder (see Figure 8.22).

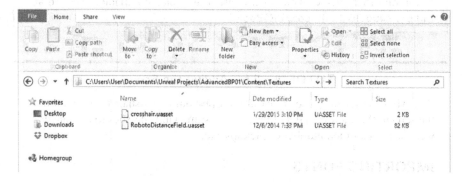

FIGURE 8.22: Importing Fonts into Your Game.

10. Your project folder will be located wherever you originally saved it.
11. Now you can locate it in the content browser.
12. If you still have your project open in UE4, the font should appear in the **Content Browser** under the `Textures` folder. The folder structure in Unreal Engine 4 folder structure is similar to Windows.

USING THE FONT IN BLUEPRINT

Now that the font is loaded into the **Content Browser**, we can use it in our `MyNewHUD` blueprint. This will keep us from having to create our own Font.

13. Open up the `MyNewHUD` blueprint.

14. Make sure you are in the event graph that we worked on in the previous tutorial.
15. The first thing we need to do here is to add a Sequence flow control node in-between the `Receive Draw HUD` event and the `Draw Texture` function. To do this perform the following tasks (see Figure 8.23):
    a. Disconnect the `Receive Draw HUD` event from the `Draw Texture` by `Alt`+Clicking on either end of the connection.
    b. Drag a wire off from the exec (white) output of the `Receive Draw HUD` event and search for and place a `Sequence` node.
    c. Connect the `Then 0` output pin of the `Sequence` node to the input exec (white) pin of the `Draw Texture` function.
16. This will allow us to run a list of tasks one after another every time the `Receive Draw HUD` event is called. This is necessary when drawing multiple things on the HUD.
17. Comment the existing cluster of nodes (the network that is responsible for drawing the crosshair texture) to avoid confusion in the future. It is recommended that you always comment your blueprints this way.

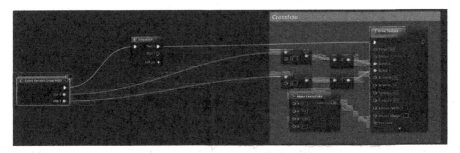

FIGURE 8.23: Using a Sequence Node in Flow Control.

18. The `Sequence` flow control node will run everything branching off of it one at a time until it reaches the end of the list. To add more pins to the `Sequence` node, just click the `Add pin +` at the bottom of the node.
19. Now, drag off a wire from the `Then 1` pin underneath the crosshair code.
20. Add a `Draw Text` function. Type the name in the search box and select `Draw Text`.
21. For `Screen X` and `Screen Y` we will take the `Size X` and `Size Y` pins of the `Receive Draw HUD` divide by 8:
    a. Drag a wire off of the `Size X` of the `Receive Draw HUD` event.
    b. Search for and place a `Divide` node.
    c. Type a value of 8 in the second input of the `Divide` node.
    d. Drag a wire off of the `Size Y` of the `Receive Draw HUD` event.
    e. Search for and place a `Divide` node.
    f. Type a value of 8 in the second input of the `Divide` node.
22. The above steps place the text to be drawn closer to the top left corner.
23. Type the word `Text` in the `Text` (pink) input of the `Draw Text` function. We will add an actual string to be shown in the HUD later.

24. **Left-Click** on the drop-down list under Font pin, use the drop-down menu to find the font that we brought into our project called **RobotoDistanceField**.
25. Lastly, change the scale to a value of 3.
26. Your network to draw text on the HUD should look like Figure 8.24.

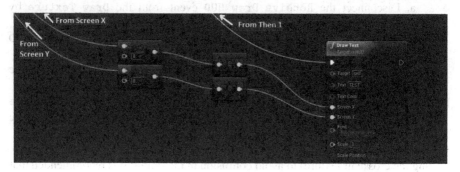

FIGURE 8.24: Drawing Text on the HUD.

27. Compile and Save the Blueprint. Also, save all your progress so far.
28. At this point, you should be able to press play and see the word **TEST** in the upper left portion of the screen.

CREATING AN EVENT DISPATCHER TO UPDATE SCORE

Fantastic, we can play the game and see a generic text shown in the upper left corner of the screen. The actual text we want to display at this time is the amount of balls that we have collected. In order to get this number, we need to create an **Event Dispatcher** in the **MyCharacter** blueprint. This custom event will be fired when it is called inside our **BallSpawner** blueprint.

29. Navigate to the **Blueprints** folder.
30. Open the **FirstPersonCharacter** blueprint and go to Event Graph.
31. Add a new **Event Dispatcher** by clicking its button at the top of the **My Blueprint** pane.
32. Please note, if you do not see it, click the **»** icon to reveal more options. The pane may be too narrow to show the **Create Event Dispatcher** button.
33. Once the **Event Dispatcher** is created, give it the name **UpdateScore**.
34. Next, drag the event dispatcher into the Event Graph.
35. **Left-Click** the **Event** option when the menu appears. This will create the event that will be fired off from another class.
36. For debugging purposes, attach a **Print String** function to this event and give it the text **UpdateScore Fired!**.
37. Compile and save the blueprint.
38. Your graph should look similar to Figure 8.25.

FIGURE 8.25: Update Score Event Dispatcher.

With our Event Dispatcher created we must call the event from the **BallSpawner** blueprint to check if it is working properly. Because we are updating the score after the Ball actor is being destroyed, we will put this event call at the end of the Set function following the Destroy Actor function. First, we need to tell the function which object we are calling the function with. In this case, we want to use the **Player Character**.

39. Open the **BallSpawner** blueprint and go to its event graph.
40. **Right-Click** on the Event Graph just below the **Set Is Spawn Active** next to the **Destroy Actor** function.
41. Search for and place a **Get Player Character** function.
42. From the **Return Value** output pin of the **Get Player Character** drag off a wire and attach a **Cast To MyCharacter** node. This will give us access to the blueprint class functions and events.
43. Connect the exec (white) output pin of the **Set Is Spawn Active** node to the exec (white) input pin of the **Cast To MyCharacter**.
44. Drag a wire off from the **As MyCharacter** output pin of the **Cast To MyCharacter** and search for the **Update Score Event** call.
45. Calling this function will fire the event in the **MyCharacter** class.
46. Your network should look similar to Figure 8.26.
47. Compile and save your blueprint and progress so far.
48. After you compile and save the project, play the game to make sure the event is being executed properly. It should execute as soon as you pick up one of the balls and display the text **Update Score Fired!** in the upper left corner. The text sounds indicate that we haven't implemented the update score functionality yet, but the event itself is working properly.

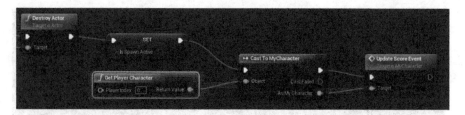

FIGURE 8.26: Calling Even Dispatchers from Other Blueprints.

UPDATING THE SCORE

Now that we have the `Event Dispatcher` set up and working properly, we can add the functionality we need to update the player's current score.

49. Return to the `MyCharacter` blueprint. If you have already closed the `MyCharacter` blueprint open it up.
50. Add an `Integer` variable called `Score` in the `MyBlueprint` window. You can `Left-Click` on the V^+ button and change the variable type and name from the Details rollout.
51. This variable will store the current score, which we will send to the HUD in the same way that the `UpdateScore` event is being called.
52. Delete the `Print String` function, as we won't need this log anymore.
53. Attach a `Set` function for the `Score` variable to the `UpdateScore_Event` and increment the score (see Figure 8.27). To do this perform the following tasks:
    a. Drag a `Get` for the `Score` variable just below the `UpdateScore_Event`. *NOTE: You can Alt+Drag the variable to place a getter function.*
    b. Drag a wire off of the `Get` and place a + function.
    c. Type a value of 1 into the unconnected pin of the + function.
    d. Drag a `Set` for the `Score` variable to the right of the `UpdateScore_Event` and the + function. *NOTE: You can Alt+Drag the variable to place a setter function.*
    e. Connect the exec (white) output pin of the `UpdateScore_Event` to the input exec (white) pin of the `Set Score`.
54. Compile and save your blueprint.

CREATING THE HUD EVENT DISPATCHER

Great! Now we have the functionality in our player character's blueprint to detect when he/she collects the balls and to update the score accordingly. The next thing we need to do is jump into the `MyNewHUD` blueprint to add an event dispatcher to show the updated score on the HUD.

55. Open up the `MyNewHUD` blueprint and go to its event graph.
56. Create an `Event Dispatcher` in the `My Blueprint` pane of the `MyNewHUD` (see Figure 8.28(a)).

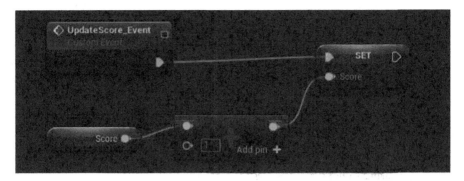

FIGURE 8.27: Updating Score.

57. Once you have the event dispatcher created, give it the name `UpdateScore_HUD` so it can't be confused with the event from the `MyCharacter` class.
58. `Left-Click` on the event dispatcher
59. With the event dispatcher selected, go to the Details rollout.
60. Add an `Integer` input called `Score` (see Figure 8.28(b)). This will allow us to send the score value to the HUD using this event.

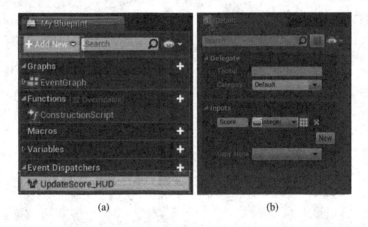

(a)   (b)

FIGURE 8.28: Adding an Event Dispatcher and Creating a Parameter.

61. Create a new variable of type `String` by pressing the V^+ button and name it `Score`.
62. Make sure that the type of this variable is String (pink).
63. This variable will store the score in string format so that we can show it as text. We will use a string instead of an integer because the `Draw Text` function takes in a string to be drawn on the screen.
64. To create the event which will read the integer score and convert it to string, perform the following steps:

a. **Left-Click** on the **UpdateScore_HUD** event dispatcher and drag it onto the event graph.

b. Select **Event** from the menu.

c. Next, drag a **Set** function for the **Score** string to the right of the **UpdateScore_HUD**. *Note: You can do this by* **Alt+***dragging the variable on the event graph.*

d. Connect the exec (white) output of the **UpdateScore_HUD** to the exec (white) input of the **Set**.

e. Connect the integer **Score** of the **UpdateScore_HUD** to the String **Score** of the **Set**. This will automatically place a function to cast the integer value to a string value.

65. Lastly, place a **Get** function for the **Score** String variable to the left of the **Draw Text** function. *Note: You can do this by* **Control+***dragging the variable onto the event graph.*

66. Attach the **Get** to the **Text** pin on the Draw Text function.

67. The result and your network should look similar to shown in Figure 8.29.

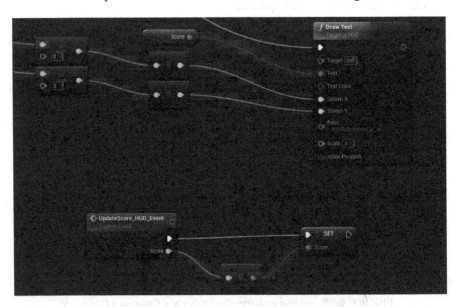

FIGURE 8.29: Updating Score in the MyNewHUD Blueprint.

68. Compile and Save the **MyNewHUD** blueprint.

UPDATING THE SCORE IN HUD

69. Return to the **MyCharacter** blueprint. If this blueprint is already closed, open it up.

70. After the **Set Score** function, add a **Cast to MyNewHUD** function. To do this perform the following tasks:

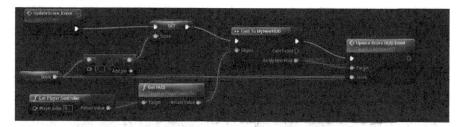

FIGURE 8.30: Calling MyNewHUD Event Dispatcher from Character Blueprint.

    a. `Right-Click` on the event graph just below the `Score` getter and the + function.

    b. Search for and place a `Get Player Controller` function in order to get a reference to the current HUD being used.

    c. Drag off a wire from the `Return Value`, search for and place a `Get HUD` function.

    d. Once this function is in place, pull a wire from the `Return Value` and search for the `Cast To MyNewHUD` function.

71. Next, pull from the `As My New HUD` output pin of the `Cast To MyNewHUD` function and search for the `Update Score HUD Event` function.

72. Once the `Update Score HUD Function` is placed, connect its exec (white) input pin to the cast function's exec (white) output pin to the update function.

73. Attach the `Score` variable getter to the `Score` pin on the `Update Score HUD Event` function.

74. Your network should look similar to Figure 8.30.

75. Once you have your event set up properly, compile and save the game.

76. Return to the main level editor and press play to see your HUD in action (see Figure 8.31).

What Happened in TUTORIAL 8.6...

We successfully created a system to keep the HUD up to date with the latest score. From here, we will add more values to the HUD to provide users with more information about the game they are playing. We will be modifying the spawn system and reusing the timer in order to give the player a time limit to collect as many balls as possible.

Before we do this, it would be wise to add comments to avoid confusion when we have a lot of wires and nodes all over the place. In the `MyCharacter` blueprint for example, add a comment for the new script.

I also added comments in the `MyNewHUD` blueprint to keep things organized. Another thing you can do to keep your blueprints clean and organized is utilize

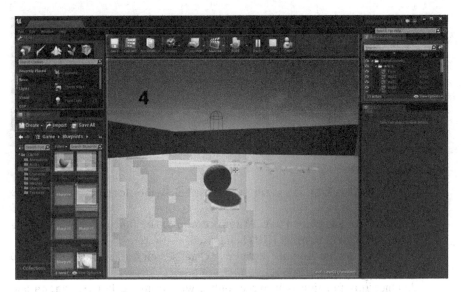

FIGURE 8.31: HUD Updating Scores Properly.

Reroute Nodes. A reroute node allows you to run the wire in a more optimal path from node to node, to avoid the wires running across other nodes. In the case of the MyNewHUD blueprint, I added a reroute node between the Sequence node and the Draw Text node. To do this quickly, drag from the pin you want to add the Reroute Node to and search for Reroute Node to add one.

Before adding this node, the wire flowed through the crosshair comment box and appeared to be a bit sloppy. Now, this does not happen. In future projects, you could have dozens of nodes all over the event graph and following the flow of logic can be quite difficult without reroute nodes.

In the next tutorial, we will be modifying the timer logic to display a time remaining on the HUD. We will also be changing the way the balls are spawned. They will no longer spawn on a time interval, but instead, a new ball will spawn every time an old ball has been destroyed.

> To find updates to this tutorial and updated instructions about its implementation on other UE4 versions please visit the book's companion website at: http://www.RVRLAB.com/UE4Book/

TUTORIAL 8.7   Adding the Score

Now that we have our blueprints communicating with each other to enable our character to pickup balls and update the score, and we also have a basic HUD system in place, let's make the game a bit more challenging. We will establish

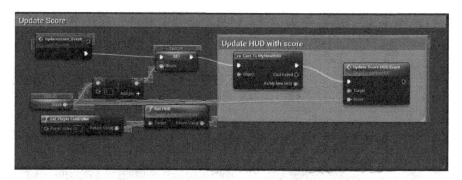

FIGURE 8.32: Commenting Updating Scores HUD.

a time limit for our player to pick up the spawned objects.

ADDING A GAME TIMER

To start off, we need to modify our Timer logic in the level blueprint. We will add a time limit so the player can attempt to collect as many balls as possible before the time runs out.

1. Open up the Level Blueprint.
2. Find the timer logic.
3. Add a variable called `GameTimer` that we will use to calculate the remaining time that the player has left.
4. Make the type of the `GameTimer` a float type.
5. Also, change the existing `Timer` variable to `SpawnTimer` so we won't get the two confused (see Figure 8.34).
6. We will be using `Event Tick` to calculate both timers and separating out the logic will be a good idea. To do this hold the `Alt` key and `Left-Click` on the connection.
7. Place a `Sequence` node in-between the two nodes you just disconnected.
8. Connect the exec (white) input of the `Set` function to the `Then 1` output pin of the `Sequence` node so that it will run after we create our `GameTimer` logic (see Figure 8.35).
9. The `GameTimer` will work similar to the existing timer, except it will count down from a value of thirty seconds.
10. Change the default value of the `GameTimer` variable to 30 in the Details window.
11. We will take this value and subtract the `Delta Seconds` value from it using a `float - float`, or `Subtract` Math function. We will use this value as the time remaining to show on the HUD. Therefore, we want to show the number if it is positive and once we count down to a negative number we want to show 0. Perform the following tasks to do this:
    a. Drag in the `GameTimer` variable and select `Get`. *Note: You can do this by `Control`+drag the variable onto the graph editor.*

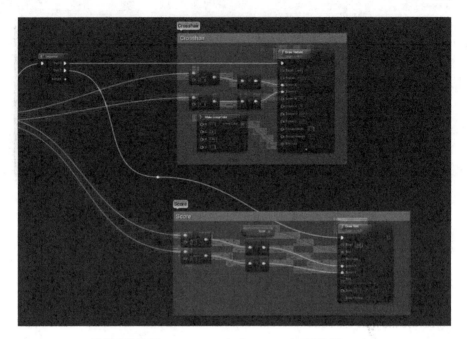

FIGURE 8.33: Reroute Node Comments in HUD Blueprint.

   b. Drag a wire off from **Game Timer Get** function and place a **Subtract** node.

   c. Connect the **Delta Seconds** from the **Event Tick** to the second input of the **float - float** node.

   d. Drag a wire off from the output pin of the **float - float** node and place a **Max** node.

   e. Drag the **GameTimer** variable from the **MyBlueprint** onto the event graph on the right of the **Max** node and choose **Set**.

   f. Connect the **Then** 0 output pin of the **Sequence** node to the exec (white) input pin of the **Set**.

12. This way, if the **GameTimer** drops below zero, we can simply return the value of zero.

13. Your network should look similar to Figure 8.36.

14. Take your time to make sure everything is connected properly. At this point, the timer should be counting down, but the player cannot see it. We need to pass the timer's value to the HUD to be displayed to the player.

PASSING TIMER TO UPDATE HUD

With our game timer created and counting down, it's now time for us to pass it to the HUD to show how much time is left to the player.

15. Open up the **MyNewHUD** blueprint.

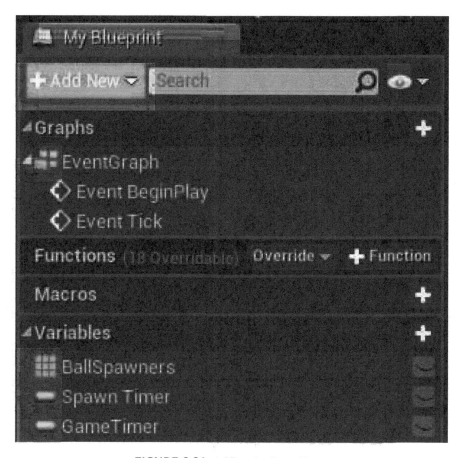

FIGURE 8.34: Adding the Game Timer.

16. Add an **Event Dispatcher** called **UpdateTimer_HUD**.
17. Add a **Float** input to the event dispatcher called **Timer** in its Details window. This will allow us to pass the value of the timer through the event call.
18. We also need to add a **String** variable called **Timer** to store the value of the Timer in text format to be drawn on the screen.
19. Once you have this variable added, drag the **UpdateTimer_HUD** event dispatcher into the graph and select **Event**.
20. Attach this event to a **Timer** set function by performing the following steps:
    a. Drag a wire off from the **Timer** output of the **UpdateTimer_HUD_Event**.
    b. Place an **FCeil** function by typing **FCeil** in the search box.
    c. Drag the **Timer** variable onto the event graph and select a **Set** function. *Note: You can do this by **Alt**+dragging the **Timer** string variable.*
    d. Connect the output of the **FCeil** to the **Timer** (pink) input of the **Set** function.

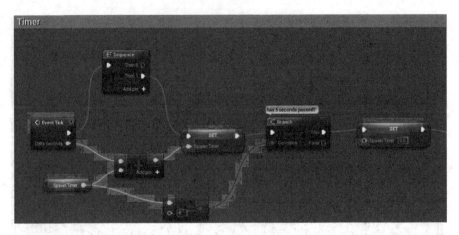

FIGURE 8.35: A Sequence Added to the Network.

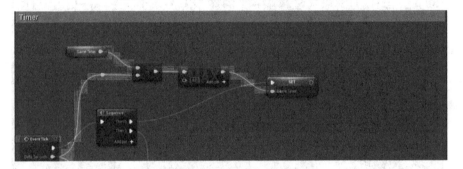

FIGURE 8.36: Game Timer Network.

    e. Connect the exec (white) output of the **Update_Timer_HUD_Event** to the exec (white) input of the **Set** function

21. Comment this network as **Update Timer** (see Figure 8.37).

DRAW THE TIME ON THE HUD

Now that this is complete, we need to display the timer on the HUD. We will add a new pin to the Sequence function and attach a new Draw Text function to it. It will be set up in a similar way to the Score logic so you can use this as reference.

22. Add another pin to the **Sequence** function.
23. Drag a wire off of this pin and attach a new **Draw Text** function to it.
24. We will divide the **Size X** pin value by 8 and **Size Y** value by 16 so that the timer is placed just above the existing score and connect them to our **Draw Text** node. To do this, perform the following tasks (see Figure 8.38):

    a. Drag a wire off of the **Size X** pin of the **Receive Draw HUD** event.

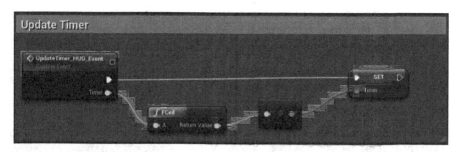

FIGURE 8.37: Convert and Update Timer String.

    b. Search for and place a `Divide` node.

    c. Type a value of 8 in the second input of the `Divide` node.

    d. Drag a wire off of the `Size Y` pin of the `Receive Draw HUD` event.

    e. Search for and place a `Divide` node.

    f. Type a value of 16 in the second input of the `Divide` node.

    g. Connect the results of the division operation for `X` to the `Screen X`.

    h. Connect the results of the division for `Y` to the `Screen Y`.

25. Compile and save your blueprint.

APPENDING STRINGS

When we attach the string value to the `Draw Text`, we will use a string function called `Append`. This will allow us to append two string values into a single string. This way, we can give meaning to the numbers we are displaying on the screen. For the `Timer` we append a string value of `Time:` (with a space at the end) to the beginning of the `Timer value`. For the existing `Score` string, we will also append a string such as `Score:` (with a space at the end) to the beginning of the `Score` value. The HUD will then read `Time: 25` and `Score: 3` instead of just showing the numbers. To do this, perform the following tasks:

26. Drag the `Time` variable and select `Get` to place a `Get` function for the `Time` string variable to the left of the `Draw Text` for the Timer. *Note: You can Control+drag the variable to place a getter.*

27. `Right-Click` to the right of `Get` for the `Timer` variable, type `String Append` in the search bar and place an `Append` function.

28. Connect the output of the `Get` for the time variable to the `B` input of the `Append`.

29. Type `Time:` (with the space at the end) in the `A` input of the `Append`.

30. Connect the `Append` output pin to the `Text` input pin of the `Draw Text` for time.

31. Disconnect the `Score` variable and `Draw Text` by `Alt+clicking` on their connection.

32. `Right-Click` between the `Score` variable and `Draw Text`, type `String Append` in the search bar and place an `Append` function.

33. Connect the `Score` to the `B` input of this `Append`.

34. Type `Score:` (with the space at the end) in the `A` input of the `Append`.

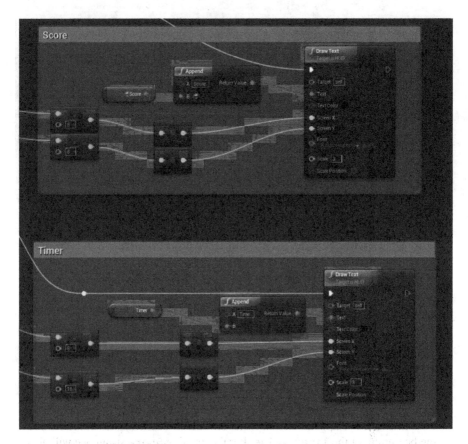

FIGURE 8.38: Showing the Time and Score on the HUD.

35. Connect the second **Append** output pin to the **Text** input pin of the **Draw Text** for score.
36. Your network for showing the score and time on the HUD should look similar to Figure 8.38.

IMPLEMENTING THE EVENT DISPATCHER CALL FOR GAME TIMER

We need to call the **UpdateTimer_HUD** event and give it the GameTimer value.

37. Return to the level blueprint.
38. Look for the script we recently created to update the **GameTimer** off of **Event Tick**.
39. Add a **Get Player Controller** function below the **Max** function.
40. Drag a wire off of the **Get Player Controller** node's **Return Value** and type **Get HUD**. This will attach a **Get HUD** function to our **Get Player Controller**.

41. Drag a wire off of the **Return Value** of the **Get HUD** function and place a **Cast To MyNewHUD** function.
42. Attach the exec (white) input of the cast function to the exec (white) output of the set function so we can cast our HUD reference to the correct blueprint type.
43. Finally, drag a wire off the **As My New HUD** pin.
44. Add the **Update Timer HUD Event** function call.
45. Drag a **Get** for the **GameTimer** variable to the left of the **Update Timer HUD Event**. *Note: You can do this by control+dragging the **GameTimer** variable from the **MyBlueprint** pane.*
46. Connect the output of the **GameTimer** variable to the **Timer** input of the **Update Timer HUD** function.
47. Your network should look similar to Figure 8.39.
48. Compile and save your blueprint.

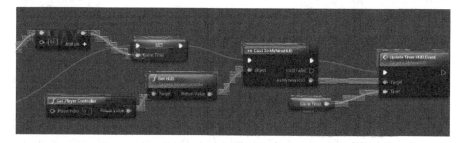

FIGURE 8.39: Calling the HUD Update Timer Event.

49. After this is done, return to the main editor.
50. Play the game. You should see the **Timer** value and **Score** value on the screen and the numbers should be updating (see Figure 8.40).

What Happened in TUTORIAL 8.7...

We have successfully updated our HUD to include the current timer value, as well as updated the score value to correctly label our information. The information the player sees is an important part of the player experience with the game. The player would not know what was happening behind the scenes if it weren't for a well-designed HUD providing quick and current data.

8.5 SAVING AND LOADING GAME DATA

Most current games of this day and age have some kind of saving/loading system built in, so you can keep you game progress, high scores, game settings, items, and so on. This option can be given to the user so they can save their progress manually,

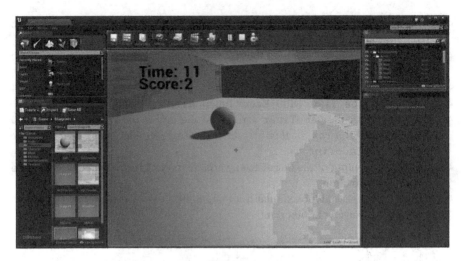

FIGURE 8.40: HUD Updates the Time and Score.

or it can be done automatically by the game when you cross a checkpoint or enter a new area in the game.

For our game, we want to keep a record of the player's high score in the game. This high score will be saved automatically when the timer has run out, and it will load on the startup of the level to be displayed to the player even after the game has been closed and reopened. Once again, blueprints will make this task very easy to visualize and script out in a fast and efficient manner.

To find updates to this tutorial and updated instructions about its implementation on other UE4 versions please visit the book's companion website at: http://www.RVRLAB.com/UE4Book/

TUTORIAL 8.8 Adding the Score

In this tutorial we will establish our game start/end conditions. We will also implement a save/load mechanism to allow for the game to retain the highest score by the player.

ESTABLISHING ACTIVE GAME STATE

The first thing we need to do is setup our game to start and end based on the **Game Timer** we created in the previous tutorial. Once this is done, we will be able to check if the current high score has been surpassed at the end of the game, and update it if necessary. When the game is loaded up for the first time, we will check if a save file exists, and load the data from this file to be displayed on the HUD.

1. First, open up the level blueprint.
2. We need to add a `Boolean` variable that we will use to determine if the game is currently active or not. To do this perform the following tasks:
   a. Create this variable and give it the name `IsGameActive`.
   b. With the `IsGameActive` selected go to its Details window, set its default value to `True` by checking the box.
3. For our purposes, we will define an active game state to be any state where the `Game Timer` is not equal to zero. We simply need to check the `GameTimer` variable to see if it is equal to zero, then act accordingly. Perform the following tasks:
   a. Find the `Timer Logic` network that we created in the previous tutorial.
   b. Drag a wire off from the `Update Timer HUD Event` function call, and add a `Branch` statement.
   c. Pull a wire off from the `Game Timer` variable and search for a `==` (two equal signs).
   d. Connect the output of the `==` to the `Condition` input of the `Branch` variable. This will check if this variable is equal to the value 0.0.
   e. Drag a `Set` for the `IsGameActive` variable to the right of the `Branch` statement.
   f. Connect the `True` output of the `Branch` to the exec (white) input of the `Set` for the `IsGameActive` variable. Make sure that the checkbox next to the `IsGameActive` is unchecked. This will set our `IsGameActive` to False.

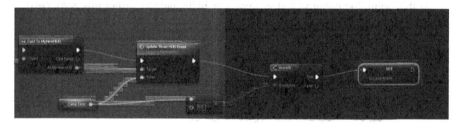

FIGURE 8.41: Establishing Game Active State.

ENABLING SPAWN BEHAVIOR ON ACTIVE GAME STATE

Now that we have our Active Game State set up, we need to add a Branch statement to the spawn logic to prevent new balls from spawning once the game has ended.

4. Inside the Timer logic, find the `Then 1` pin on the Sequence function that we connected to `Set` function for updating the spawn timer.
5. Disconnect the `Then 1` from the `Set Spawn Timer` by `Alt+clicking` on either end of the connection.
6. Add a `Branch` in the now-open area between the `Then 1` from the `Set Spawn Timer`.

7. Also, add a `Get` for the `IsGameActive` variable by `Control+Dragging` the `IsGameActive` variable to the left of the `Branch` node that you just added.
8. Connect the `IsGameActive` getter to the `Condition` of the `Branch`.
9. Connect the `True` output of the `Branch` to the exec (white) input of the `Set` node. This will make sure that the ball will only spawn if the game is currently active.
10. Your network should look similar to Figure 8.42.

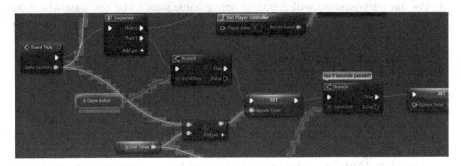

FIGURE 8.42: Spawning Network for when the Game Is Active.

ESTABLISHING INACTIVE GAME STATE

At this point, the game will stop spawning balls once the timer hits zero. Next, we have to tell the `BallSpawner` class that the game has become inactive. If we don't do this, the player will be able to continue to score points after the time has expired by picking up balls that already existed before the timer ran out.

11. First, go to the `BallSpawner` class and open it up.
12. We will now create a variable and an event which will set this variable as the state of the game. To do this perform the following tasks:
   a. `Right-Click` on the event graph to add a custom event called `GameState`.
   b. With the `GameState` custom event selected look in the Details rollout and create a Boolean input called Is `Game Active`. We will use this to pass in a Boolean so that the `BallSpawner` is aware of the current game state.
   c. Create a variable called `IsGameActive` in the `BallSpawner` class and attach it to the event.
   d. Drag the `IsGameActive` variable and place a `Set` for it to the right of the `GameState`. *Note: You can place a setter by Alt+Dragging the variable onto the event graph.*
   e. Connect the output `IsGameActive` of the `GameState` event to the `IsGameActive` input of the `Set`.
13. Your network should look similar to Figure 8.43.
14. Next, we need to make a condition to only update the character's score if the game is active. To do this perform the following tasks:
   a. Disconnect the `Destroy Actor` from the `Set` for the Is `Spawn Active` variable.

FIGURE 8.43: Setting Game State in the Ball Spawner Event.

b. Add a **Branch** statement between the **Destroy Actor** function and before the **Update Score Event**.
c. Place a **Get** for the new Boolean **IsGameActive** below the **Destroy Actor** and to the left of the **Branch**.
d. Connect this getter to the **Condition** for the branch statement.
e. Connect the **true** output of the **Branch** to the exec (white) input of the **Set Is Spawn Active** that you just disconnected.

15. Your network should look similar to Figure 8.44.

FIGURE 8.44: Only Update Score if Active Ball Spawner Event.

16. Now, if the player continues to collect balls after the time has expired, the game simply won't add them to the score.
17. Compile and save your blueprint.
18. Next, we will need to make sure that each **Ball Spawner** keeps track of the game state. To do this we will communicate this information from the level blueprint by calling each spawner's **GameState** event. To do this perform the following tasks:
    a. Return to the level blueprint. Open it up if it is closed.
    b. Find the **Set** function for the **GameIsActive** variable.
    c. Drag a wire off from this **Set** function.
    d. Search for and place a **For Each Loop**.
    e. Drag a **Get** for the array of **BallSpawners** to the left of the **For Each Loop**. *Note: You can Control+Drag the BallSpawners array from the MyBlueprint to place a getter for it.*
    f. Connect the output of the **BallSpawners** to the **Array** input of the **For Each Loop**.
    g. Drag a wire from the **Array Element** and place a **Cast To BallSpawner** function.

     h. Make sure that the exec (white) output of the **For Each Loop** is also connected to the input exec (white) pin of the **Cast to BallSpawner** function.

     i. Drag a wire off from the **As Ball Spawner** output pin of the cast function and place a **Game State** function call.

     j. Make sure that the **IsGameActive** checkbox is unchecked.

19. Your network should look similar to Figure 8.45.

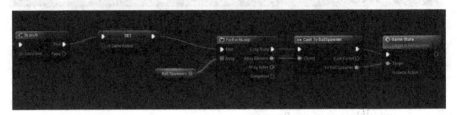

FIGURE 8.45: Update BallSpawners Game Active Variable.

20. This makes sure that when the for each loop is called, we will tell each **BallSpawner** in our level that the game has ended and we don't want to add any more points to our score.

21. Compile and save the blueprint.

22. Give your game a try to make sure that the logic is implemented properly and that when the game ends, no more objects are spawned, and the player's score no longer updates.

ESTABLISHING THE GAME SAVE/LOAD FUNCTIONALITY

With our game state working, we can set up our saving and loading system. We will create a blueprint based on the **SaveGame** class. A **SaveGame** blueprint is a special blueprint used only for saving and loading game data.

23. Navigate to the **Content Browser** and go to the **Blueprints** folder.

24. Create a new blueprint.

25. The parent class we will be using this time is the **SaveGame** class. Search for this at the bottom and hit select.

26. Give your new blueprint the name **MySaveGame** and open it.

As you can see, you cannot put physical components into this blueprint. This blueprint should only contain data that you want to have saved and loaded in your game. In our case, the only piece of data we will be saving is the player's high score.

27. Create an **Integer** variable called **High Score**.

28. In the **My Blueprint** pane, there should be an icon that looks like a closed eye next to the variable.

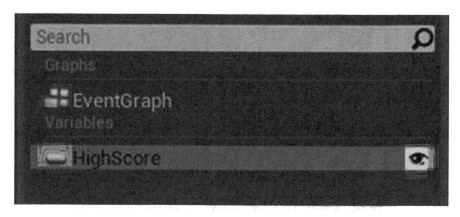

FIGURE 8.46: Creating the High Score Variable.

29. **Left-Click** on this icon so that it looks like an open eye. This will make the variable public so we can access it using get and set functions. Note that if the eye is yellow, it warns you that there is no Tooltip included for this variable.
30. Go to the Details rollout and add a Tooltip that reads **High Score for the game**. This will get rid of the warning and the eye will have a green background.
31. Compile, save, and close the **MySaveGame** blueprint.
32. That is all we need to do to set up the **MySaveGame** blueprint at this point.
33. Now we need to save and load the game data in the Level Blueprint.
    a. Open up the level blueprint.
    b. Locate the **Setup Array** logic (this is where we included each individual **Ball Spawner** into the **BallSpawners** Array).
    c. We will need to use the **Event Begin Play** to load the game on startup.
    d. Create a **Sequence** node above the **Setup Array** network.
    e. Disconnect the **Event Begin Play** from the **Set** of the BallSpawners by **Alt**+Clicking on either end of the connection.
    f. Connect the exec (white) output of the **Event Begin Play** function to the exec (white) input of the **Sequence** node.
    g. Attach the **Then 1** pin to the existing **Set Ball Spawners** function.
    h. Your network should look similar to Figure 8.47 so far.
34. To make things easier, we can create a variable to store the name of the save file, to make sure we don't accidently name it incorrectly in another location.
    a. Create a String variable called **SaveName**.
    b. Set the default value of this variable to **Level01SaveFile** in its Details rollout.
    c. We will also need a variable to temporarily store a reference to our save game data.
    d. Create a variable called **SaveGameLocal** and set its variable type to **Save Game**.
    e. Lastly, we need to store our current high score in a variable as well.

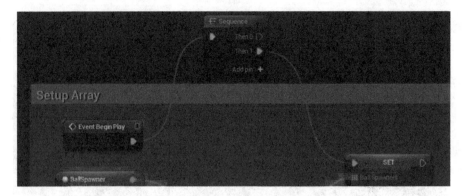

FIGURE 8.47: Placing the Sequence for the Game Load/Save.

      f. Create an integer variable and name it `CurrentHighScore`.

      g. The default value for this variable should be left at zero.

35. The first thing we need to check is if the `Save Game` file exists in the default save location.

      a. Drag a wire off from the `Then 0` and place function called `Does Save Game Exist` to the Then 0 pin on the `Sequence` node.

      b. Place a `Get` for the `Save Name` variable we created earlier to the left of this function. *Note: You can* `Control+Drag` *the* `SaveName` *variable to place a getter.*

      c. Connect the `Slot Name` pin to the `SaveName` variable we just created. This will check for a save file called `Level01SaveFile` and return true or false on its `Return Value` pin depending on whether or not it exists.

      d. Your network should look similar to Figure 8.48.

FIGURE 8.48: Check Whether the Save File Exists.

36. Now we will create two networks for either case, if the save file exists or if it doesn't exist. If the save game file does not exist, we must create it using a `Create Save Game Object` function by performing the following steps:

      a. Drag a wire off from the `Return Value` of the `Does Save Game Exist` node and place a `Branch` statement.

b. Make sure that the input of the Branch and the Does Save File Exist are connected.

c. Drag a wire from the False output of the Branch and place a Create Save Game Object.

d. For the Save Game Class of the Create Save Game Object select the drop-down menu.

e. From the menu choose My Save Game.

f. Place a Set for the SaveGameLocal variable to the right of the CreateSaveGameObject function. You may Alt+drag the variable to place a setter function.

g. Connect both the exec (white) and object (blue) pins of the Set and the CreateSaveGameObject.

h. Drag a getter function for the SaveGameLocal below the Set function. You may Control+Drag the variable to place a getter.

i. Drag a wire off from the Get SaveGameLocal, search for and place a Cast To MySaveGame function.

j. Connect the SaveGameLocal to the Object of the Cast To node, if it is not already connected.

k. Drag a wire off from the Cast To function, search for and place a SaveGametoSlot function.

l. Make sure that the As My Save Game is connected to the SaveGameObject.

m. Drag a getter function for the SaveName and connect it to the Slot Name of the SaveGametoSlot function.

n. Your network should look similar to Figure 8.49.

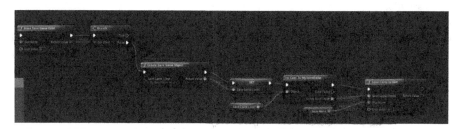

FIGURE 8.49: Save Game into File and Store Name if It Doesn't Exist.

37. This will create our save file if one does not already exist. Next, we need to add the logic, to handle the save file if it already exists:

a. Drag a wire off from the True pin of the Branch node.

b. Add a Load Game from Slot function.

c. Again, create a Get for the Save Name variable and place it to the left of the Slot Name.

d. Connect the Get to the Save Name pin of the Load Game from Slot function. Leave the user index at zero.

e. Next, place a Set function for the Save Game Local variable and connect its input pin to the Return Value of the load function.

    f. Connect the exec (white) output pin of the `Load Game from Slot` to the input exec (white) pin of the `Set`.

    g. Place a `Get` for the `SaveGameLocal` variable below the `Set`,

    h. Drag a wire off from this `Get` to add another `Cast To MySaveGame` function to cast it to a `MySaveGame` variable.

    i. Drag from the `As My Save Game` and place a `Get High Score`.

    j. Add a `Set` function for the `CurrentHighScore` variable to the right of this network and feed it the `High Score` variable.

38. Your network should look similar to Figure 8.50.

FIGURE 8.50: Load if Save Game File Exists.

ADDING THE HIGH SCORE SAVE FUNCTIONALITY

Now that we are loading our data properly, we need to save the current high score. We will add this logic to the `FirstPersonCharacter` where the score is stored.

39. Open up the `FirstPersonCharacter` blueprint.

40. Add a variable called `HighScore` so we can compare it to the current `Score` variable.

41. Make sure the type of the `HighScore` variable is integer.

42. Add another event dispatcher and call it `CheckForNewHighScore`. This event will be called once the game has ended to check if we need to change the value of the high score. This event needs to take in a string, an integer, and a Save Game variable to communicate (see Figure 8.51).

    a. Select the `CheckForNewHighScore` event dispatcher.

    b. In the Details rollout create a string input and call it `Save Slot Name`.

    c. Create an integer input called `Current High Score` so we can compare the high score with the current score.

    d. Lastly, create a `Save Game` input and call it `Save Game` to take in our Save Game variable so we don't need to re-create it in the `MyCharacter` blueprint.

    e. Once this event dispatcher is created, drag it into the event graph and select `Event`.

43. Now we have everything we need to save the game.

    a. Drag a wire off from the exec (white) output pin of the `CheckForNewHighScore` event to add a `Branch` statement.

    b. Drag a wire off from the `Current High Score` variable and place a < (less-than) expression.

    c. Bring a `get` for the `Score` variable and connect it to the second input of the < (less-than) expression.

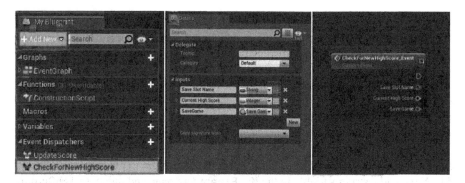

FIGURE 8.51: Event Dispatcher for the Check High Score.

    d. Connect the output of the < (less-than) expression to the `Condition` input of the `Branch` expression.

    e. Drag a wire off from the `Save Game` pin of the `CheckForNewHighScore` event and add a `Cast To MySaveGame` function to the right of the `Branch` expression.

    f. Connect the `True` pin of the `Branch` to the exec (white) input pin of the `Cast To MySaveGame`.

    g. Place another get function for the `Score` below the `cast To MySaveGame`.

    h. Drag a wire off from the `As MySaveGame`, search for, and place a `Set High Score` function.

    i. Connect the `Score` to the `High Score` input of the `Set`.

    j. Lastly, drag a wire from the `As MySaveGame` and place a `Save Game to Slot` function to the right of the `Set` function.

    k. Connect the exec (white) output of the `Set` function to the exec (white) input of the `Save Game to Slot`

    l. Connect the `Save Slot Name` output pin of the `CheckForNewHighScore` event to the `Slot Name` of this `Save Game to Slot` function.

    m. Remember to use reroute nodes to clean up the wires.

44. Once you created the network, it should look similar to Figure 8.52.
45. Compile and save your blueprint.

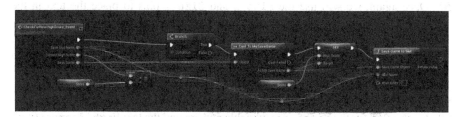

FIGURE 8.52: Event Dispatcher for the Check High Score Network.

DISPLAYING HIGH SCORE ON HUD

At this point, we should be saving and loading the data properly. However, our current HUD isn't set up to display the high score.

46. Open up the MyNewHUD blueprint.
47. Add another event dispatcher to the MyNewHUD.
48. Give this event dispatcher the name UpdateHighScore_HUD.
49. Add an integer input to the event dispatcher in its Details rollout named HighScore.
50. Drag this event dispatcher in the graph and select **Event** to place it.
51. Next, add a string variable in the **My Blueprint** pane and name it HighScore.
52. Drag a Set function for this variable and attach it to the UpdateHighScore_HUD event.
53. Connect the High Score pin of the UpdateHighScore_HUD to the High Score (pink) input of the Set. This should place a cast from integer to string, automatically.
54. Your network should look similar to Figure 8.53.

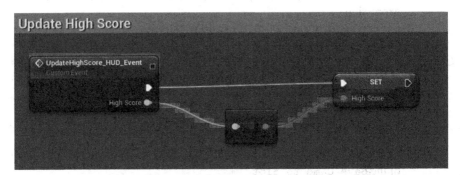

FIGURE 8.53: Setting the High Score In HUD Event Dispatcher.

55. Next, locate the Sequence node and add another pin to it.
56. Drag a wire from the new output pin of the Sequence node and and attach a new Draw Text function.
57. Once again, we will use the Size X and Size Y pins to place the text in the correct spot.
    a. Divide the Size X value by 8.
    b. This time we will leave the Screen Y value at 0.0 to place the High Score text just above the existing score.
58. The Font should be set to RobotoDistanceField.
59. The Scale should be set to 3 just like the other Draw Text functions.
60. Place a Get for the HighScore variable and append the text High Score: (with a space at the end) to the front of the string.
61. Connect the result of the Append to the Text input of Draw Text function.
62. Your network should look similar to Figure 8.54.

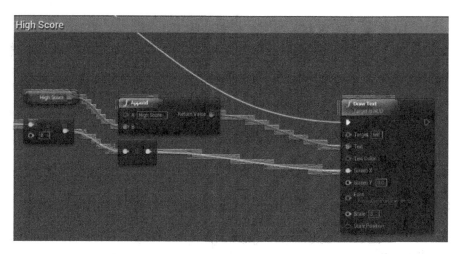

FIGURE 8.54: Drawing the High Score Value on HUD.

63. Our HUD is now set up to display the high score on the screen. We need to update the HUD in two different places and call the event dispatchers. First we will make this call in the `FirstPersonCharacter` blueprint. Later we will make the needed function calls in the `Level Blueprint`.

    a. First, go back to the `FirstPersonCharacter` blueprint.

    b. Place a `Get Player Controller` function below the `Save Game to Slot` function we placed a few steps ago.

    c. Drag a wire from the `Get Player Controller` and place a `Get HUD` function.

    d. Drag a wire from the `Return Value` of the `Get HUD`, add a `Cast To MyNewHUD` function.

    e. Place a `Get` for the `Score` variable below this `Cast To MyNewHUD` node.

    f. Drag a wire from the `As MyNewHUD` output pin of the cast function and place an `Update High Score HUD Event` function call.

    g. Connect the `Score` variable to the `High Score` pin as it will be the new high score value.

64. Your network should look similar to Figure 8.55.

65. Compile and save your blueprint.

WRAPPING EVERYTHING UP IN THE LEVEL BLUEPRINT

Now we will go back to the level blueprint and make the final function calls to wrap the level up.

66. Return to the Level Blueprint and find the Load game logic we created earlier.

67. Place a `Get Player Controller` just below the `Set` function for the `Current High Score` variable.

68. Drag a wire from the `Get Player Controller` function, and place a `Get HUD` function.

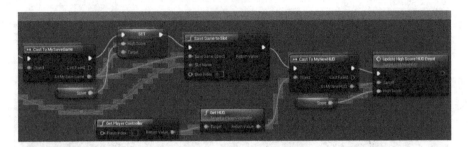

FIGURE 8.55: Call Update High Score of the HUD from Character Blueprint.

69. Drag a wire from the **Return Value** of the **Get HUD** to place a **Cast To MyNewHUD** function.

70. Place a **Get** for the **Current High Score** variable just below the **Cast to MyNewHUD**.

71. Drag a wire from the **As MyNewHUD** output pin and place an **Update High Score HUD Event** function just as we did in the **FirstPersonCharacter** blueprint.

72. Connect the **Current High Score** variable to the **High Score** pin on the **Update High Score HUD Event** function.

73. Your network should look similar to Figure 8.56.

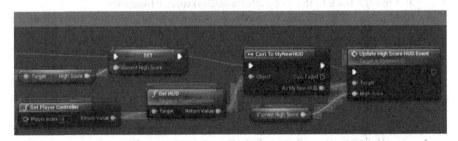

FIGURE 8.56: Call Update High Score of the HUD from Level Blueprint.

74. Lastly, we need to call the **Check for New High Score Event** function from the game over logic in the level blueprint.

   a. Locate the **Game State** function call.

   b. Add a **Get Player Character** function just below the **GameState**.

   c. Drag a wire off from the **Return Value** of the **Get Player Controller** and place a **Cast To FirstPersonCharacter** function.

   d. Connect the exec (white) input of the cast function to the exec (white) output of the **Game State** function.

   e. Drag a wire off from the **As My Character** pin to add a **Check for New High Score Event** function.

   f. Place **Get** functions for the **SaveName**, **CurentHighScore**, and **SaveGameLocal** variables to the left of the **Check for New High Score Event** function.

g. Connect the the `SaveName`, `CurentHighScore`, and `SaveGameLocal` variables to their respective input pins on the `Check for New High Score Event` function.

75. Your network should look similar to Figure 8.57.

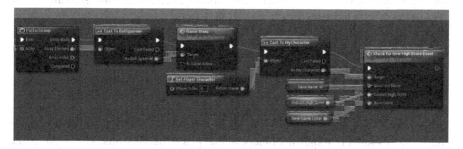

FIGURE 8.57: Call New High Score of the Character from Level Blueprint.

76. Compile and save all the blueprints if you haven't already done so.
77. At this point, when you run the game, the `High Score` value will be zero. The save file did not previously exist so it has been created for you.
78. Once the Timer hits zero, the `High Score` will be updated.
79. Stop the gameplay and restart the game.
80. This time when the game starts, the save game file will be loaded and the previous high score will persist.
81. Try to get a larger high score, stop the game, and start it once again.

What Happened in TUTORIAL 8.8...

We successfully implemented a system to save and load our high score automatically. Saving and loading data is extremely important for every game, even if you are not keeping any type of score at all. Save Game blueprints can be used to save and load game settings such as key bindings, graphics properties, login names, and anything else you can think of.

In more complex games, it might be a good idea to have separated save game blueprints, to keep the settings separated from the actual game data. The Unreal Engine 4's blueprint system is quite powerful helping you design almost all aspects of your game purely in the blueprint visual scripting system. Once again, the blueprint system offers the same features that you would get using code.

At this point, we have completed all the tutorials for this chapter, but this does not mean you should abandon the project. Try adding your own functionalities to the game or perhaps adding your own materials or sounds. Set a goal, even if you have no idea how to get there, and work your way step by step. Use the Unreal Engine 4 documentation and forums if you are stuck and don't get discouraged.

The more you use Unreal Engine 4 blueprints, the more you will understand and you will move forward to larger and larger projects. Also, understand that the blueprint system is basically visual programming. Having an understanding of object oriented programming practices will be a huge benefit when creating systems with blueprints and blueprints should not be used as a complete substitution for programming on large projects.

8.6 SUMMARY

In this chapter, we went over advanced blueprint topics to help you understand how blueprints communicate with each other, how to create a HUD, and how to save data. We created a BallSpawner blueprint that placed another blueprint in our game world, and passed it a delegate function to tell it when to destroy itself. We created a HUD from scratch to look the same as the default HUD. We expanded greatly on this HUD to display the high score, the remaining time, and the current score. We used a SaveGame blueprint to store our high score value and load it back into the game.

9 A Top-Down Game with Blueprints

W HEN looking back at the history of gaming, some of the most iconic games are top-down shooters such as: Asteroids, Centipede, and the more modern Geometry Wars. With the power of Unreal 4 we can now explore the steps necessary to create our own action packed top-down shooter that has an old school arcade feel but with a modern presentation.

9.1 SYNOPSIS

One of the most fundamental things you must tackle when creating a game is making the most intuitive control scheme possible so the player doesn't feel like they are fighting against the hordes of enemies you will create along with the controls. To avoid this, our game will use the popular WASD setup for movement and use the mouse to aim our character. The character should rotate to face the direction our mouse is so it just "feels" natural.

A game like this wouldn't be challenging without enemies. Our game will have enemies spawning from the corners of the map that will relentlessly chase down our player. Not only will the player have to worry about shooting enemies, but he/she also has to dodge them as they come from multiple directions. This is a good example of why a solid control scheme is such a necessity.

We will put together our own top-down shooter template and build our game based on this model. Below is a short overview of the tasks and concepts covered in this chapter to set up this functional Top-Down Shooter Game:

1. Level Setup
   - Using Content Examples
   - Building the Map
2. Player, Controller, and Game Mode Setup
   - Character Setup
   - Player Controller Setup
   - Game Mode Setup
3. Character Movement and Interaction
   - Axis Mapping
   - Action Mapping
4. Projectile Class Setup
   - Projectile Blueprints
   - Firing Mechanism
   - Projectiles Damage Implementation
5. Damage Functionality

- Enemy Damage
- Player Damage

6. Game Over!!!!
   - A Simple Gameover Cinematic
   - When the Player Dies
7. AI and Enemy Spawning
   - Spawning Enemies Implementation
   - AI and Navigation
8. Visual Effects
   - Death Particle Effects
   - Hi Effects and Material Swapping

9.2   SETTING UP THE LEVEL

In this section we will be setting up the initial level and creating our character controller as well as the appropriate user inputs to control the character.

TUTORIAL 9.1   Setting Up the Level

The first thing to do in making any kind of game is to set its level(s) up. So we will create an area for our players in this tutorial. Our levels will be quite simple. We will have an area with four walls and a floor.

SETTING UP THE LEVEL

In the next few steps we will create a blank project. We could choose the top-down template, but we are going to start off from a blank project to build our interactions, game mode, and player controller to learn about the behind the scenes of creating the basic gameplay mechanics.

1. Start by creating a blank New Project. (Make sure the "Include Starter Content" is selected/enabled as we will be using some of these in our project.)
2. When the Engine loads click **file->New Level->Default**.
3. You can name your project something like "TopDownShooter".
4. You may want to delete the maps that already exist in the **Starter Content** folder.
5. Make sure to leave your created level available.
6. With your level now open, delete anything in the level except for any light source that may be in your level. (It should be there by default.)
7. We want to now create a floor by selecting Geometry in the Modes box and selecting the Box object.
8. Open the materials folder in the content browser.
9. Find a material that you would like to use as your floor. For this example we will use the "**M_Tech_Hex_Tile**".
10. With the material selected, drag a box object onto the level. In the details portion of the editor change the brush settings to

> **X: 3000**
> **Y: 3000**
> **Z: 100**

11. The area will now be more appropriate as the floor for our small level.
12. Use the same box tool to add walls around the level using the XYZ values of 300, 50, 200, respectively. (You can hold ALT while dragging the gizmo on your brush to duplicate walls.)
13. Place the same material on the walls as the floor.
14. Go ahead and build the project. Save your progress so far.

What Happened in TUTORIAL 9.1...

In this tutorial we created a blank project with the starter content conveniently imported for our future use.

LEVEL CREATION

We created our own level to work and removed the imported starter levels. We created a plane and walls for our battle arena using box brushes. We applied a simple material to the floor and walls to make it more aesthetically pleasing.

9.3 CHARACTER, CONTROLLER, AND GAME MODE BLUEPRINTS

In this section we will set up our character blueprint, player controller blueprint, and game mode blueprint. These are the blueprint classes that define the main gameplay functionality of our game.

TUTORIAL 9.2   Setting Up Classes

Since our project is built on a blank template, we will need to create the foundations of our gameplay by implementing our game mode, character, and player controller. In this tutorial we will implement these three classes, which will be used later on to develop our topdown game.

CREATING CHARACTER CONTROLLERS

Now that we have our level available, we will create controllers for our player.

1. Click **Blueprints** at the top of the editor and select **New Class Blueprint**.
2. When the pick parent class dialog box opens select **PlayerController**. We will name this blueprint `RotationController`.

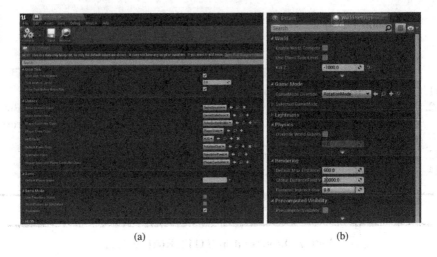

          (a)   (b)

FIGURE 9.1: (a) Setting Up the Game Mode. (b) Establishing Game Mode Override.

3. Create another class blueprint of the type **Character**. We will name this one RotationChar.
4. Finally create another class blueprint of the type **Game Mode** and name it RotationMode.
5. Inside the **RotationMode** blueprint, click the **Defaults** tab (the leftmost tab on the top-right corner of the editor).
6. In the **Defaults** tab do the following:
    a. Under the default pawn class select the arrow to drop-down a selection box and choose your RotationChar that you just created.
    b. Now in the player controller class field select the RotationController that you just created.
    c. Compile and save this blueprint (see Figure 9.1(a)).
7. In the main editor click the world setting button and under the **GameMode Override** field select the RotationMode you just created (see Figure 9.1(b)). If the world setting window is not open, click on the **Window** tab and check the World Setting item.
8. Save your level.

SETTING UP CHARACTER COMPONENTS

Now that our basics are done, we will set up the look of our character in the character's blueprint.

9. Open the blueprint for the RotationChar.
10. Make sure you are in the viewport.
11. We want to add a shape for our character to use. To do so, we will take the following steps:

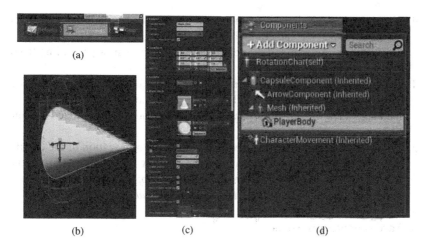

FIGURE 9.2: (a) Blueprint Components Tab. (b) Adding Items to Components List. (c) Setting Up Static Mesh Properties. (d) Parenting the Player's Body Static Mesh.

    a. Open up the shapes folder in the content browser. It is normally found in the starter content folder.

    b. Drag the shape **Shape_Cone** into the **Components** section of the RotationChar blueprint details (see Figure 9.2(c).

    c. Rename the shape you added to the character's blueprint to PlayerBody. To do this, click in the **Variable Name** in the **Variable** section of the **Details** Panel.

    d. Attach the newly added shape to the Mesh component in the **component** section of the RotationChar blueprint (see Figure 9.2(d)).

12. Rotate the cone 90 degrees so that the tip of the wedge faces the same direction as the arrow component (the light blue arrow).

13. Move the cone so the collision capsule is entirely enclosed inside the cone when viewed from above. *We will worry about getting better collision detection later on.*

14. Save and compile the blueprint.

15. Your player should now look like Figure 9.2(b).

SETTING UP THE CAMERA

In this stage of the process, we should be ready to establish our camera. The game we are aiming for is a top-down game. As such, the camera is located above the player and looking down. We will establish this camera system by taking the following steps:

16. With the RotationChar blueprint still open perform the following tasks:

    a. Click the down arrow in the **Add Component** box and search for **Camera**.

    b. Select camera to add it to the components section of the blueprint.

    c. Now search for the component **Spring Arm** and add it to the blueprint.

d. Next, you have to drag the camera onto the spring arm in the components section to attach the camera to the spring arm.

e. Select the spring arm and rotate it 90 degrees so it is now protruding from the top of the cone object.

f. In the details panel with the spring arm still selected, change the value of the **Target Arm Length** to 1000. Basically, the value controls the distance of the camera from where the character is located and can be changed to your liking.

g. With the spring arm still selected under the transform section of the details box, click on **rotation** and change its value to world or absolute rotation. *NOTE: If your camera is not attached at the end of the spring arm you may need to move the camera manually towards the end of the spring arm.*

h. Compile the blueprint.

i. Save your progress so far.

SETTING UP THE PLAYER CONTROLLER

We will now need to set up our character controllers.

17. With the player's blueprint still open perform the following tasks – if you have closed the blueprint, open it from the content browser:

a. Click the **Defaults** tab next to the **Components** tab.

b. In the search box type in `auto possess`.

c. Change the value from disabled to Player 0.

d. Compile and save.

18. Open the `RotationController` blueprint:

a. Check the boxes next to **Show Mouse Cursor** and **Enable Click Events**.

b. Change the default mouse cursor to **crosshairs**.

c. Compile and save the blueprint.

SETTING UP PLAYER CONTROLLER'S FUNCTIONALITIES

19. With the `RotationController`'s blueprint still open perform the following tasks – if you have closed the blueprint, open it from the content browser:

20. Click the **Graph** tab to the right of the **Components** tab.

21. In the event graph we need to add an **event tick** node. To do this, right-click somewhere on the **EventGraph** canvas, and type `Even Tick` in the context-sensitive search box. Click and place the **Event Tick** in the event graph (Figure 9.3(a)).

22. Right-click to the left of the **Event Tick** node and search for `Get Controlled Pawn` to place a getter function to your player pawn (Figure 9.3(a)).

23. From the return value of get controlled pawn drag off and search for `Get Actor Location` (Figure 9.3(b)). *You may need to uncheck context sensitivity.*

24. Right-click below the **Get Actor Location** node and search for `Convert Mouse Location to World Space` (Figure 9.3(c)).

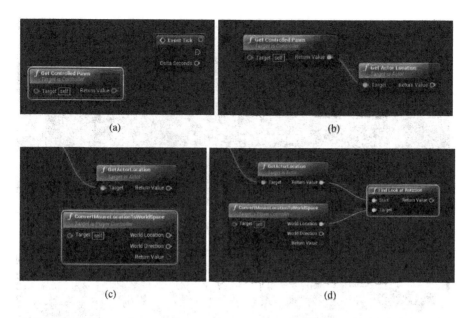

FIGURE 9.3: (a) Placing a Get Controlled Pawn Node. (b) Getting the Pawn's Location. (c) Converting Local Coordinate to Global/World Coordinate. (d) Establishing the LookAt Vector.

25. Drag a wire from the **Return Value** of the **Get Actor Location** and from the context-sensitive menu search for and place a `Find Look At Rotation` node (Figure 9.3(d)).

26. Connect the **World Location** output of the **Convert Mouse Location to World Space** to the **Target** input of the **Find Look At Rotation** (Figure 9.3(d)).

27. Drag a wire from the **Return Value** of the **Find Look At Rotation** and type in the context-sensitive search `Break Rotator`. This will place a Break Rotator node to convert the orientation values to rotation values needed to control the actor's rotation (bottom of Figure 9.4).

28. Drag a wire from the **Yaw** output of the **Brake Rot** node and type in the context-sensitive search `Make Rotator`. Make sure that only the **Yaw** output of the **Break Rotator** is connected to the **Yaw** input of the **Make Rotator** and the Pitch and Roll values of the **Make Rotator** are 0 (bottom of Figure 9.4).

29. Drag a wire from the **Return Value** of the **Make Rotator** and type `Set Actor Rotation` in the context-sensitive search box. This will place a **Set Actor Rotation** node and feed its input rotation from the output of the **Make Rotator** node (right of Figure 9.4).

30. Connect the **Return Value** of the **Get Controlled Pawn** to the **Target** input of the **Set Actor Rotation** (top-left of Figure 9.4).

31. Connect the **exec** output of the **Event Tick** (the white triangle) to the **exec** input of the **Set Actor Rotation** (top of Figure 9.4).

32. Compile and save.

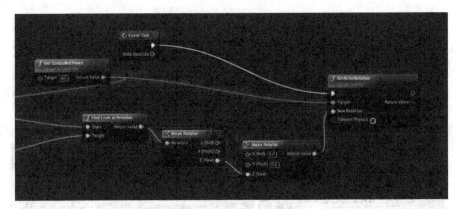

FIGURE 9.4: Setting Up the Actor Rotation.

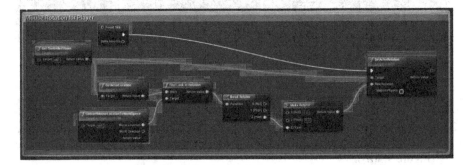

FIGURE 9.5: Commenting the Network.

COMMENTING IN THE EVENT GRAPH

Commenting your blueprint graphs is a great way to keep your code organized, as well as to remember what the big-picture functionality of each of the graphs.

33. To highlight all the nodes we have created thus far, marquee drag around the graphs. Press C key (on your keyboard) while the nodes are highlighted to comment the highlighted section of your code.

34. Name the comments `Mouse Rotation for Player` or something that will help you easily remember its function (Figure 9.5). *You can also organize your blueprint nodes by moving them around in the graph editor so they are easier to follow and read before commenting them.*

What Happened in TUTORIAL 9.2...

In this tutorial we set up our controller, player, and game mode classes.

SETTING UP CHARACTER CONTROLLER AND GAME MODE

In this section of our work, we created 3 important blueprint classes that are necessary for our game to work.

The `Rotation Controller` is essentially a class that inherits from the **Player Controller** blueprint. We use this blueprint class to create the controls for the player character. This class will house the mouse rotation and keyboard input mechanics.

We also created a `RotationChar` blueprint. This is our main player's character and is inherited from a **Player** base class.

Finally we created the `RotatingMode`. This is a blueprint that inherits from the **Game Mode** base class. The `RotationMode` blueprint tells the engine to have the camera rotate around the `RotationChar` – i.e., our player, now set as the default pawn class.

SETTING UP CHARACTER COMPONENTS

To customize the visual look of our player character we assigned a simple shape to its mesh. If you have an artist friend who can create a nice looking mesh for your character, you can easily plug that mesh instead of the generic **Cone** mesh we used here.

SETTING UP THE CAMERA SYSTEM

To wrap things up, we attached a spring arm camera to the pawn. This camera will follow the player's character until the game ends or the player is killed. (More on this later.)

SETTING UP CONTROLLER FUNCTIONALITIES

In this section, we used the graph editor of the `RotationController` (our Player Controller class) to allow our player to move by rotating towards the location of the mouse in the level. To get this functionality, we first created an instance of our player pawn and set its rotation to the rotation calculated from the world location of the mouse (Figure 9.4).

9.4 CHARACTER MOVEMENT AND USER INPUT

With our character, game mode, and player controller classes implemented and ready to develop we need to establish the input interfaces for our player character. Unreal Engine 4 allows you to perform two types of mappings to establish you input interfaces.

Axis mapping is the mechanism by which you can bin events to continuous inputs such as movements of your mouse, or controlling the character's direction. For example, to control the camera orientation we can map it to the X and Y movements of the mouse. Action mapping, on the other hand, allows you to map discrete actions and bind them to their respective events. For example, we can bind a key press on the keyboard to an event that makes the character jump up.

TUTORIAL 9.3   Establishing Movements

Now that we have our player controller configured to give us the basic functionalities needed for controlling our character, we need a way for the engine to communicate user inputs to the game. This is done through a process called Axis and Action Mappings.

SETTING UP ACTION AND AXIS MAPPINGS

Action and Axis Mapping is made incredibly simple in Unreal Engine 4. Basically, these processes are now hosted within the project setting. We will set up Axis Maps for our project at this point.

1. In the main editor window go to **Edit->Project Settings**.
2. Under the **Engine** section click on **Input**. You will see both Action Mapping and Axis Mapping options in the **Input** section.
3. Now we will add our Axis Mappings. To do so perform the following tasks:
    a. Click the plus sign next to **Axis Mapping** located under the **Bindings** section. This will add an Axis Mapping to our user W-S input functionalities.
    b. Name this axis mapping "Move up" and click the small arrow to the left of the name.
    c. In the drop box that is created click keyboard and search for the **W** key.
    d. Leave the scale for this Axis Mapping (W) at 1.0.
    e. This time click the plus sign next to the Move up binding you created and search for the **S** key. Set the scale of the binding for the **S** key to –1.0.
    f. Click the plus sign next to **Axis Mapping** again. This will add another Axis Mapping to our user A-D input functionalities.
    g. Name this axis mapping "Move right" and click the small arrow to the left of the name.
    h. In the drop box that is created click keyboard and search for the **D** key.
    i. Leave the scale for this Axis Mapping (D) at 1.0.
    j. This time click the plus sign next to the Move right binding you created and search for the **A** key. Set the scale of the binding for the **A** key to –1.0.
4. Save your progress so far.

PROGRAMMING CHARACTER MOVEMENTS

Now we will program the Axis Mappings we created in the Engine Input into our player controller class.

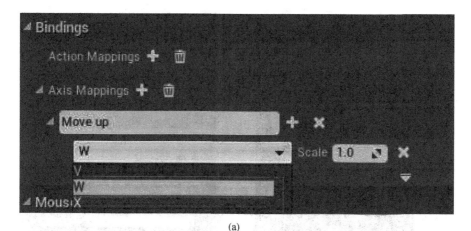

FIGURE 9.6: (a) Setting Up MoveUp Axis Mapping. (b) Setting Up MoveRight Axis Mapping.

5. Open the event graph of the `RotationController` blueprint you created earlier if it is closed.
6. Click on the **Graph** tab on the toolbar to open the controller's event graph.
7. Right-click on the event graph (away from the commented sections we have created so far) and in the context-sensitive section search for the following modules:
   a. Place an **InputAxis Move up** Event in the event graph. *You should choose the **Move up** node from the **Axis Events** and not the **Axis Values** in the context-sensitive search window.*
   b. Place a **Get Controlled Pawn** below the **InputAxis MoveUP**.
   c. Place an **InputAxis Move right** below the **Get Controlled Pawn**. *You should choose the **Move right** node from the **Axis Events** and not the **Axis Values** in the context-sensitive search window.*
8. Right-click to the right of the above three nodes, and search for and add the fol-

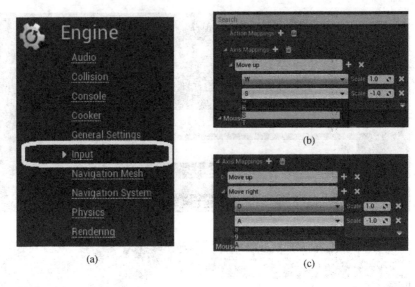

FIGURE 9.7: (a) Input Section of the `Project Settings`. (b) Setting Up MoveUp (reverse). (c) Setting Up Move Right (reverse).

lowing modules:

  a. Drag a wire out of the Return Value of the **Get Controlled Pawn**, search for and place an **Add Movement Input** in the event graph to the right of the **InputAxis Move UP** node.
  b. Place another **Add Movement Input** in the event graph to the right of the **InputAxis Move Right** node.

9. Connect the **Axis Value** output channels of the **InputAxis MoveUP** module to the **Scale** input of the top **Add Movement Input**.

10. In the `World Direction` of this **Add Movement Input** change the X value to 1.0.

11. Connect the **Axis Value** output channels of the **InputAxis MoveRight** module to the **Scale** input of the bottom **Add Movement Input**.

12. For the second **Add Movement Input** change the Y value to 1.0 in the `World Direction` channel.

13. Select all of the nodes, by marquee-dragging around them. Press the C key (on your keyboard) to comment this section of the blueprint. Give the commented section a name, such as `Keyboard Movement for Player`, to remember its functionality easily in the future.

14. Your graph should look like Figure 9.8.

15. Save your progress so far.

ADJUSTING THE CHARACTER COMPONENTS

16. Open the `RotationChar` blueprint you created earlier if it is closed.

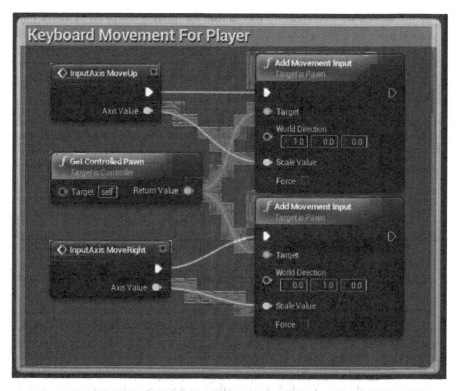

FIGURE 9.8: Player Keyboard Movements.

17. Head to the components section and click on the **PlayerBody** under the Mesh – remember we changed the name of the mesh to be more representative of its function.

18. In the Details rollout change the transform scale XYZ to 0.5, 0.5, and 0.75, respectively.

19. Move your character mesh so that is is inside the capsule component.

20. Now select **Character Movement** in the **Components** section of the **RotationChar** blueprint.

21. In the Detail rollout find the section titled **Character Movement**. There you will find a value for **Max Walk Speed**; change this value to 1500.

22. In the **Shape** section of the Details rollout of the **RotationChar** blueprint change the capsule half height to 40.

23. Compile and save the **RotationChar** blueprint.

What Happened in TUTORIAL 9.3...

In this tutorial we also created a mechanism for rotating our pawn to follow our mouse movement as well as to accept keyboard inputs to move in the 4 cardinal directions – WASD movement. We also adjusted the pawn's movement speed, size, and collision capsule size.

SETTING UP AXIS MAPPING

In Unreal Engine 4, the mechanism by which the movement of a player character is acquired from the user input is integrated within the input parameters of the engine. This makes setting up interactions relatively easy. There are a number of ways that interaction can be established between human players and playable character, or any object that allows for user interactions. Axis and Action Mappings are two of the most used and basic interaction mechanisms. As the name "Mapping" suggests, both of these mechanisms take the user input and map it into the interaction models.

The difference between Axis and Action mapping is in the nature of inter-action mapping they set up. Axis mapping takes user input (e.g., keyboard key presses, mouse buttons, etc.) and maps the input into Axes (i.e., a real-valued number, called **Axis Scale**). Action mapping, on the other hand, maps user inputs to discrete values, called actions. This is useful if we wanted to set up an interaction such as jumping, associated with pressing of the Left Mouse Button.

You can think of axis mapping as taking user input (such as pressing the key "W" and associating to it a weight for how much the character speed should be moving forward). We achieved this effect by mapping the key W to positive value on the Move UP axis. Similarly we map the key S to a negative value on the same axis as the key W to make the character move backwards on the press of S on the keyboard. To make our character move right or left we mapped keys D and A to positive and negative values, respectively, on the Move Right axis.

ADJUSTING THE PLAYER CHARACTER

Finally, we adjusted our character's scale and speed and ensured that the character's mesh is completely enclosed within the collision capsule. We also resized the collision capsule's height so that it fits our character more snugly.

9.5 PROJECTILE CLASS BLUEPRINT AND FUNCTIONALITY

Now that we have setup our character blueprint, the controller and game mode blueprints, and established a mechanism to control the movement of our character, it's time to think about setting up and programming our projectile classes for the character's armament.

TUTORIAL 9.4   Setting Up Projectiles

In this tutorial we will create our projectiles class so that our player can shoot at the enemies.

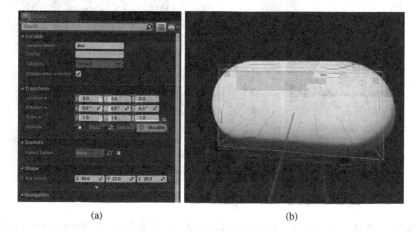

(a)   (b)

FIGURE 9.9: (a) Projectile Collision Box Details Rollout. (b) Collision Box Shape Mesh.

1. Go to your folder where you created the past blueprints and create a new blueprint of the type Actor. Name this blueprint `Projectile`.
2. Inside the components section of the blueprint, add a box component and name it `CollisionBox`.
3. Within the Content Browser drag the shape called **Shape_NarrowCapsule** from the starter content into the **Components** section of the blueprint and rename it `BulletMesh`.
4. Rotate the object and drag it down to fit inside the collision box.
5. You can resize the collision box from the **Shape** rollout of the `CollisionBox` component to better fit your capsule. Try to set XYZ values of 40, 23, 20, respectively (see Figure 9.9(a)). *Note: You may need to play around with the size of the collision box and move the capsule to achieve the best fit.*
6. Your projectile should look like Figure 9.9(b).
7. Click the **Add Component** button in the Components tab and type `Projectile Movement` in the search box. Add the **Projectile Movement** component to the components of your projectile blueprint.
8. Rename the **Projectile Movement** you just added to `Projectile Movement` if its name is different.
9. Save your progress so far.

SETTING UP PROJECTILE MATERIAL

Now we will create a fairly simple, and shiny, material for our projectiles.

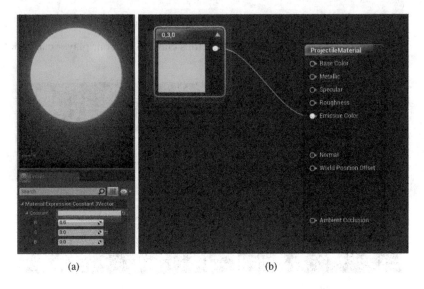

                                (a)   (b)

FIGURE 9.10: (a) Projectile Color Preview and Details Rollout. (b) Projectile Color Network.

10. Back in the main editor inside the starter content folder you will find the materials folder. Double-click on it to go inside the folder.

11. Click on the **New** icon in the content browser and choose **Material** to create a new material.

12. Rename the newly created material to `ProjectileMaterial` and open the materials editor.

13. Create a Vector3 color value for the emissive color of your material by taking the following actions:

   a. Add a Vector3 expression to the left of the `ProjectileMaterial` node in the material editor. You can do this by either; right-clicking on the canvas and searching for `Constant3Vector` or by holding the key 3 on the keyboard and left-clicking in the canvas.

   b. With the `Constant3Vector` node selected expand the **Constant** value in the **Details** rollout and change the RGB values to 0.0, 3.0, 0.0, respectively (Figure 9.10(a)).

   c. Drag a wire from the output channel of the `3Vector` node to the **Emissive** channel of the `ProjectileMaterial` (Figure 9.10(a)).

14. Save your material and close the Unreal Material Editor.

15. Head back into the Projectile blueprint's components section.

16. Select the `BulletMesh` we created earlier and in the **Details** rollout find the **Materials** section.

17. Click the plus sign next to **Materials** and click the drop-down arrow next to the empty material element.

18. Find our projectile material we just created to assign it to the `BulletMesh`.

19. Save the blueprint.

FINAL TOUCHES ON THE PROJECTILE

20. Select the `ProjectileMovement` component and under the **Projectile** section change the value of **Projectile Gravity Scale** to 0.0.
21. Change the value of both the **Initial Speed** and **Maximum Speed** to 1000.

What Happened in TUTORIAL 9.4...

In this tutorial we created a projectile for our character to shoot.

SETTING UP PROJECTILE CLASS BLUEPRINT

In order for our character to be able to shoot at enemies, we need to create a class blueprint for it to use as its ammo. We created this class based on the **Actor** class. To customize this actor class to use movements of a projectile-like nature, we added a movement component called projectile movement. This will enable our actor to receive physics properties and follow projectile motions.

We further customized the look of this projectile by adding a capsule-looking mesh to its components and adjusted the transform parameters of this mesh and the collision capsule.

SETTING UP PROJECTILE MATERIALS

To further customize the look of our mesh, we created a shiny material. This material is very simple. It is only composed of a **Constant3Vector** with the values of $(r = 0.0, g = 3.0, b = 0.0)$, deriving its **Emissive Color** channel. This will give the material a bright green glow.

Remember from our chapter on Materials in Unreal, that the Emissive Channel simulates a material that is shining with a color that derives this channel. However, it is important to note that this shininess is not an actual light and does not cast shadows.

9.5.1 FIRING MECHANISM

Now that we have the projectiles class created, we will need to program the firing functionalities. Basically, our firing mechanism will use the `Fire` event to spawn the projectiles. We will use the character's location and forward direction to design the projectiles' trajectories.

TUTORIAL 9.5   Setting Up Projectile Firing Mechanism

In this tutorial we will establish a mechanism by which our character will be able to fire at enemies.

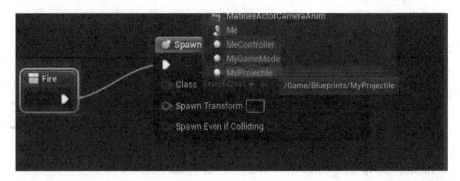

FIGURE 9.11: Spawning Projectile on Fire Event.

SETTING UP THE FIRING MECHANISM

1. Open up the `RotationChar` class blueprint you created earlier and open up the **Graph Editor**.
2. Here create a new function and call it `Fire`.
3. Inside this new function drag off a new node from the `Fire` execution channel and search for `Spawn Actor from Class`.
4. In the drop-down box next to class in the **Spawn Actor from Class** node look for our projectile class we created earlier (See Figure 9.11).
5. Now we will build the network that will derive the location of the fired projectiles from the actor location. This will be a combination of the player actor's forward vector and location (assuming that the actor holds the weapon from which the projectiles fire aiming forward). To do this follow these steps to establish the required network:
   a. From the **Spawn Transform** channel of the **Spawn Actor from Class** node drag off a node and search for `Make Transform`. We will create this transformation to feed the transform channel of the Spawning node.
   b. We need to add the rotation and location of our character actor.
   c. Right-click on the canvas, far to the left of the **Make Transform** node and search for a node called `Get Actor Rotation`.
   d. Drag off its return value to the **Rotation** channel of the **Make transform** node (See Figure 9.12(a)).
   e. Next we will combine this rotation value with the player's location value to find the actual spawn location for the projectiles. To do so drag off a new node from the return value of the **Get Actor Rotation** and search for `Get Forward Vector`.
   f. From **Return Value** of the **Get Forward Vector** drag off a new node and search for `Multiply Vector Float`. Enter a value of 70 in the float field of the **Multiply Vector Float**.
   g. Right-click above the **Get Forward Vector** node and search for `Get Actor Location` to place the node on the canvas.
   h. Drag a node from the **Return Value** of the **Get Actor Location** and place

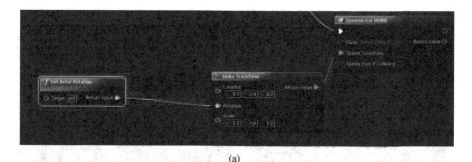

FIGURE 9.12: (a) Projectile Rotation. (b) Projectile Firing Location Calculation.

  an Add Vector + Vector node.
  i. Connect the **Output** pin of the **Multiply Vector Float** to the second **Input** pin of the **Add Vector + Vector** node.
  j. Finally connect the output pin of the **Add Vector + Vector** to the **Loca-tion** channel of the **Make Transform** node.
  k. In the scale channel of the **Make Transform** node change the XYZ values to 0.3, 0.3, 0.3, respectively.
  l. Your network should look like Figure 9.12(b).
6. Save your progress so far.

SETTING UP THE ACTION MAPPING

Now that our projectile class blueprint is created and setup, we will establish an action mapping to enable the player to fire the projectiles. Remember that we have set up the Firing function triggers earlier.

7. Go back to the main editor and open the project settings again.
8. Go to the input section and create a new **Action Mapping**. Rename it to `FireProjectile`.
9. Set this action to the left click mouse button. You can close project settings after setting this action (See Figure 9.13).

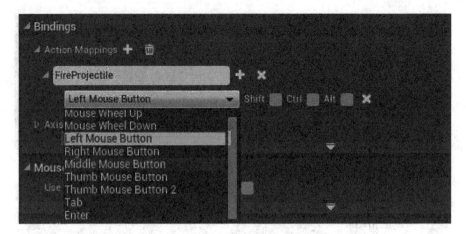

FIGURE 9.13: Firing Action Mapping.

SETTING UP EVENT BEGIN PLAY AND CASTING OUR CHARACTER

Now we will establish the mechanism by which we can pick the player character in our character controller class blueprint. Remember that we called this blueprint `RotationController`.

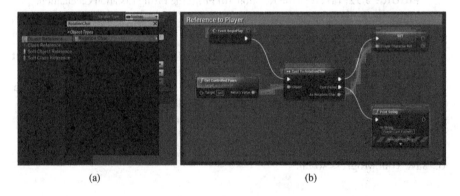

(a)   (b)

FIGURE 9.14: (a) Creating a Reference to the Player. (b) Startup Game Network.

10. Open up the `RotationController` blueprint and head to the event graph portion of the graph editing mode.
    a. Create a new Variable of the object type `RotationChar` and name it `PlayerCharacter Reference`.
    b. To do this, click on the ^{+}V sign for new variable.
    c. In the **Details** rollout of this variable, click on the drop-down list next to **Variable Type** and search for `RotationChar` (See Figure 9.14(a)). *Note:*

*If your character blueprint has a different name, your object type will be the name you gave your character blueprint. Hint: The type is under the **Object** section of the **Variable Type**.*

    d. Search for new nodes titled: **Event Begin Play** and **Get Controlled Pawn** by right-clicking in the canvas and typing their names in the context-sensitive search box, respectively.

    e. From the return value of **Get Controlled Pawn** drag off a node and search for `Cast to RotationChar`.

    f. Connect the output of the **Event Begin Play** into the new casting node.

    g. From the Variable list, drag off your created variable (the one we called `PlayerCharacter Reference` in step 10a above) onto the canvas to the right of the **Cast to RotationChar** node and select **SET**.

    h. Connect the exec (white) output of the **Cast to RotationChar** node to the exec (white) input channel of the **SET** node.

    i. Connect the output to the input of the **SET** node.

    j. From the **Cast Failed** channel drag off a new node and search for `Print String`.

    k. In the string box type in `Player Cast Failed!!!`. *This will allow us to troubleshoot later on if our fire projectile function malfunctions.*

    l. Comment this section as `Reference to Player`.

11. Compile and save your work.

12. Your Network should look like Figure 9.14(b) so far.

PLACING PLAYER REFERENCES

Before we proceed with setting up the firing mechanism, there is one task we need to perform so that we will not end up with null references to the player character when he dies.

13. Make sure you are still in the `RotationController` blueprint.

14. Now we will have to place the player reference instead of the two **Get Controlled Pawn** nodes in the `Keyboard Movement for Player` section and in the `Mouse Rotation for Player` sections. This will prevent the game from creating Null references when the player is killed.

15. Drag a copy of the **PlayerCharRef** variable onto the canvas below the **Get Controlled Pawn** in the `Mouse Rotation For Player` and select **GET**.

16. Connect the output of the **PlayerCharRef** to each input channel where the **Get Controlled Pawn** is connected to. When done, delete the **Get Controlled Pawn** node (see Figure 9.15(a)).

17. Drag a copy of the **PlayerCharRef** variable onto the canvas below the **Get Controlled Pawn** in the `Keyboard Movement for Player` and choose **GET**.

18. Connect the output of the **PlayerCharRef** to each input channel where the **Get Controlled Pawn** is connected to. When done, delete the **Get Controlled Pawn** node (see Figure 9.15(b)).

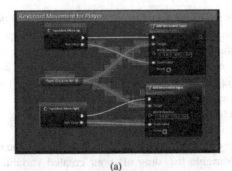

(a)

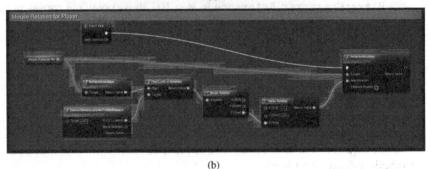

(b)

FIGURE 9.15: (a) Player Reference in Keyboard Movement Network. (b) Player Reference in Mouse Movement Network.

SETTING UP THE FIRING PROCESS

We will now set up the firing functionality in our character controller. What we want to do is create an event that fires when the player presses and releases the Left Mouse Button. We will achieve this by means of action mapping. We will then use this event to open and close an execution path within our program that calls a function that spawns our projectiles.

19. Right-click on the canvas to the right of the **Set Actor Rotation**.
20. Type Input Action to search for Input Action. You should see our FireProjectile that we created earlier in step 8 available for use.
21. Place the FireProjectiles event on the Event Graph.
22. Right-click to the right of the **InputAction FireProjectile** and type Gate.
23. Place the Gate expression to the right of the InputAction Fire Projectiles.
24. Connect the **Pressed** and **Released** channels of the **InputAction FireProjectile** to the **Open** and **Closed** channels of **Gate** node, respectively (see Figure 9.16).
25. Connect the **exec** (white) channel of the **Set Actor Rotation** to the **Enter** of the **Gate** node.
26. Drag from the **Exit** channel of the **Gate** and type Delay to place a **Delay** node. Set its value to 0.1.

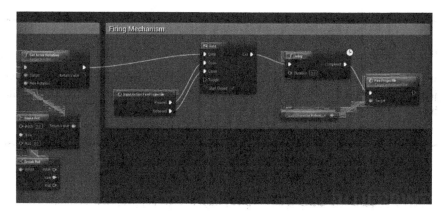

FIGURE 9.16: Projectile Firing Mechanism Network.

27. Drag from the **Completed** channel of the **Delay** node and type `FireProjectile`.
28. Drag the `PlayerCharacter Reference` variable we created earlier onto the canvas below the **Delay** node and choose **GET**.
29. Drag the output of this `PlayerCharacter Reference` to the **Target** of the **Fire-Projectile** event you created in the above steps.
30. Your Network should look like Figure 9.16.
31. Compile and save your blueprint.

What Happened in TUTORIAL 9.5...

In this tutorial we established our firing mechanism. There were several tasks we needed to perform to be able to create a way for our player to shoot at the enemy.

First, we created a function to call when the player fires at the enemy. Once this function is called, we will spawn objects from our projectiles class. We used the player's location and orientation to calculate the location at which the projectiles should be spawned. To calculate the projectiles' trajectories we used the same information (i.e., player's location and orientation).

Next, we created an action mapping to bind the `Left-Click` to the firing event. This will enable the player to press the `Left-Mouse-Button` to fire at the enemy while moving the mouse to rotate around.

To allow for a steady firing process, we listened to the `Left-Click` press and release events, and used a **Gate** expression to toggle the call to the **Fire** function of the player character. The **Gate** expression has two input patterns that activate (e.g., open) or deactivate (e.g., close) the gate and the program flow through. We issued the `Open` command on the **Gate** on the press of the `Left-Mouse-Button` and issued a `close` command on the **Gate** on the release of the `Left-Mouse-Button`.

9.5.2 SETTING UP COLLISIONS

In the next tutorial we will set up the collision mechanisms for our player and projectiles. This way we will be able to detect when a player, an enemy, or a projectile hit one another.

TUTORIAL 9.6   Setting Up Projectile and Player Collisions

In this tutorial we will set up the bullet's and player's collision system and proper mechanisms for the collision system to affect appropriate actors.

SETTING UP BULLET'S COLLISIONS

1. Go into the **Projectile** blueprint you created and under its **Components** mode and in the BulletMesh's detail rollout search for **Collision** in the search box. Set the **Collision Preset** to No Collision.
2. To set up the projectiles' collisions perform the following tasks:

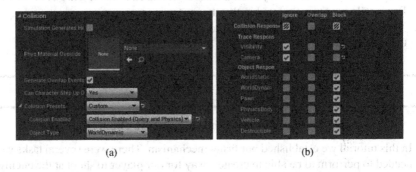

(a)   (b)

FIGURE 9.17: (a) Making Custom Collision Presets. (b) Custom Collision Presets.

     a. Click the **[ROOT] Collision Box** in the **Components** rollout and set the **Collision Preset** to Custom (see Figure 9.17(a)).

     b. Click on the dropbox for the **Collision Enabled** to Collision Enabled to enable the collision (see Figure 9.17(a)).

     c. Make sure the **Object Type** is set to World Dynamic (see Figure 9.17(a)).

     d. For now set all the check boxes to Block except the **Visibility** and **Camera**.

     e. Set the **Visibility** and **Camera** checkboxes to ignore. We will be changing some of these later (Figure 9.17(b)) .

3. Click on the triangle pointing down below these collision checkboxes (Figure 9.18(a)) and check the box labled "Use CCD" (Figure 9.18(c)).

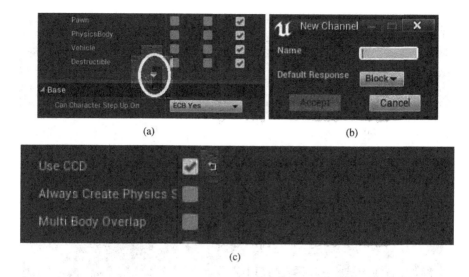

FIGURE 9.18: (a) Expand the Collision Rollout. (b) Leaving Default Response. (c) Set Up CCD.

CREATING DEFAULT COLLISIONS

4. To make things easier for ourselves we will create our own custom collision presets like the default ones shown in Figure 9.17(a).

   a. To do this go back to the main editor window and go to **Edit -> Project Settings**.

   b. In the **Project Settings** window select the **Collision** under the **Engine** section from the left-hand column.

   c. We want to create three (3) new **Object Channels**: Player, PlayerProjectile, and Enemy.

   d. When creating each collision channel, leave the **Default Response** in the **New Channel** to Block (see Figure 9.18(b)). *Note: We won't be using the enemy channel until a later tutorial.*

   e. Close the Project Settings window.

5. Now go back into the **Components Editor** of the **Projectile** blueprint.

6. Change the **Collision Object Type** from World Dynamic to the newly created **PlayerProjectile** (See Figure 9.19(a)).

7. In the **Collision Responses** check the **Ignore** box for the Player and Player Projectile so that bullets do not collide with either the player or other bullets (See Figure 9.19(b)).

8. Compile and save the **Projectiles** blueprint.

SETTING UP PLAYER'S COLLISION

9. If the **RotationChar** blueprint is closed, open it up.

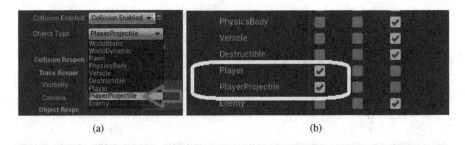

(a)   (b)

FIGURE 9.19: (a) Change Collision Type to Our Own Type. (b) Ignore Collision between Bullets and Player – you don't want the player to be affected by his/her own projectiles.

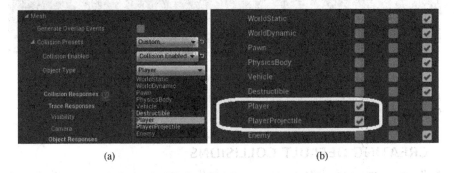

(a)   (b)

FIGURE 9.20: (a) Set Player Collision Type. (b) Disable Collision between Player and Projectiles.

10. Go into the **Defaults** tab of the **RotationChar** blueprint and change the **Collision Preset** under the mesh to `Custom`.

11. Change the **Object Type** to the newly created **Player** from the drop-down box (see Figure 9.20(a)).

12. Also set everything to `Block` except for **Visibility**, **Player**, and **PlayerProjectile**.

13. Set **Visibility**, **Player**, and **PlayerProjectile** to `Ignore` (See Figure 9.20(b)).

14. Go to the components mode of the **RotationChar** and change the collision preset of its **[ROOT]Capsule Component**, as below:

    a. Change the **Collision** to `Custom` (see Figure 9.21(a)).

    b. Set the **Object Type** to `Player`.

    c. Set the **Object Responses** as before; `Block` for everything except for **Player** and **Player Projectile**.

    d. Set the **Object Responses** for the **Player** and **Player Projectile** to `Ignore` (See Figure 9.21(b)).

15. Compile and save the blueprint.

FINISHING UP THE PROJECTILES

16. Set a lifetime for the **Projectiles**. To do so perform the following actions:

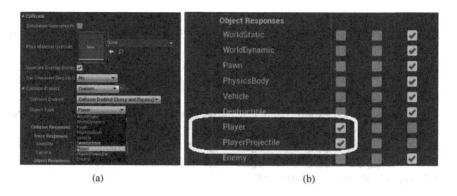

(a)   (b)

FIGURE 9.21: (a) Select Object Type. (b) Set Collision to Ignore between Player and Projectile Actors.

a. Go into the **Defaults** tab in the **Projectile** blueprint. Open the blueprint if you have closed it.
b. Set the initial life span to 3.0 (see Figure 9.22(a)). This will ensure that bullets will automatically be destroyed after 3 seconds to prevent memory consumption. Three seconds is enough time for each projectile to go from one side of the map to the other before being destroyed.

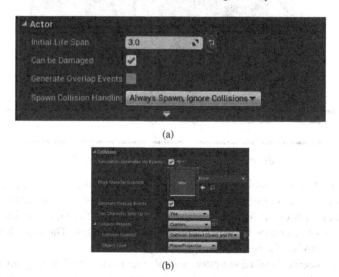

(a)

(b)

FIGURE 9.22: (a) Setting Projectile Lifespan. (b) Projectiles Generate Hit Event.

17. Go back to the **Components** tab of the **Projectiles** blueprint.
18. Check box that says **Simulation Generates Hit Events** in the **Collision** section of the Details rollout (see Figure 9.22(b)). This will allow us to make things

happen when hit events occur with the projectiles.

19. We will now demonstrate this by having the bullets destroy themselves when they collide with another object.

    a. Go into the **Event Graph** in the **Projectile** blueprint.

    b. Add a new **Event Hit** node. To this, Right-click on the canvas and search for the **Event Hit**.

    c. From the execution channel (white) drag off a new node and search for **Destroy Actor** (see Figure 9.23).

    d. The **Target** is conveniently already set to `self` to destroy the projectile itself. This works since this is being called within the **Projectile** blueprint.

20. Compile and save your blueprint.

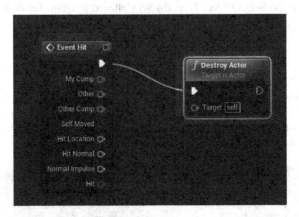

FIGURE 9.23: Destroy Projectile on Event Hit.

What Happened in TUTORIAL 9.6...

In this tutorial we established our collision system. This is a very important part since the collision system will create a mechanism for us to be able to detect when hit events occur. We will use these hit events for the player to detect when he is hit by the enemy to activate a damage functionality. The same logic goes for the enemy's collision events.

The projectiles' collision system will also let us detect when they hit a wall or an enemy. We will use these events to decide to cast damage on the enemy and to destroy the projectiles, when they hit an object.

We first established three collision object channels in the `Collision` category of our `Project Settings`. This will help later on to assign these channels as presets when we wish to establish collisions in our class blueprints, and to streamline the process.

After setting our collision system up for the player and the projectile class, we performed one last modification to the projectile class. This modification allows the projectile objects to simulate hit events. We use these hit events to damage the enemy and to destroy the projectile when it hits an enemy or a wall.

9.6 CREATING THE ENEMY CLASS AND IMPLEMENTING DAMAGE

Now that our player interactions and the projectiles are created, it's time to shift our focus to another equally important aspect of the game – the enemy. In the next few sets of tutorials we will go over the enemy class and populate it with the needed functionality, both in terms of taking damage from being hit and casting damage to the player.

TUTORIAL 9.7   The Enemy Class and Damage Implementation

In this tutorial we will create the enemy class, assign its basic components, and establish its collision system.

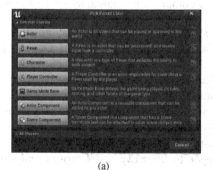

(a)

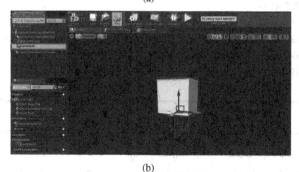

(b)

FIGURE 9.24: (a) The Enemy Class Is Based on Character Class. (b) Adding Enemy Components.

CREATING THE ENEMY CLASS BLUEPRINT

1. Create a new **Class Blueprint** based on the **Character** type (see Figure 9.24(a)).
2. Name this blueprint **Enemy**.
3. Drag the **Shape_Cube** shape from the **Shapes** folder of the content browser into the component area of the newly created **Enemy** blueprint.
4. Rename the cube mesh **EnemyMesh** (Figure 9.24(b)).
5. Add a material of your choice to your enemy.
   - a. Remember to do this, click on the **EnemyBox** mesh you just added to the **Components** of your **Enemy** blueprint.
   - b. Go to the **Materials** section in the **Details** rollout.
   - c. Click the + sign next to the **Materials**.
   - d. Either drag a material from the content browser into the **Materials[0]** or Click on the search icon (the magnifying glass) and look up a suitable material to apply to this mesh.
6. Still in the **Components** tab of the **Enemy** blueprint, click on the [Root]CapsuleComponent. Change its **Capsule Half Height** to 40 and **Radius** to 20.

ENEMY COLLISIONS

Now with our enemy components created, let's establish its collision system.

7. We will now change the **Collision** properties of our enemy.
   - a. Still in the **Details** rollout of the **[Root] CapsuleComponent**, go to the **Collision** section.
   - b. Change the **Collision Presets** to Custom.
   - c. If the **Collision Presets** is closed, click on the triangle icon to expand it.
   - d. Make sure that **Collision Enabled** is set to No Physics Collision.
   - e. Change the **Object Type** to Enemy (Figure 9.25(a)).
   - f. Leave all **Responses** as Blocked.
   - g. Now set **Player** to Overlap and **Camera** and **Enemy** to Ignore (Figure 9.25(b)).
   - h. Set the collision presets to the root capsule component of the enemy to the same configuration, except on the collision enabled field, change to no physics collision.
8. Compile and save your progress.

What Happened in TUTORIAL 9.7...

In this tutorial we implemented our enemy class. The enemy class is based on the Character parent class. This will give the enemy the ability to be controlled in the level by an AI controller when we create our AI system later on in this chapter.

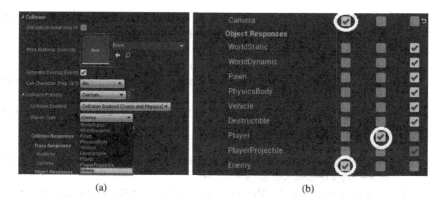

(a)   (b)

FIGURE 9.25: (a) Collision Object Type, (b) Setting Up Appropriate Collision Responses.

We added a few components in the **Components** tab of our enemy blueprint. The enemy's body is simple a box mesh, and its collision module is a capsule component. In order for our enemy to interact with the player and the projectile objects in-game, we established its collision system as well.

Since we already have created a collision object channel for the enemy in the `Project Setting` we used it as a preset, and made the collision channel overlap the player and camera, but ignore the enemy and camera classes. We left the projectiles collision on the enemy class to `Block` so as to not let the projectiles go through the enemies when they collide.

9.6.1 ENEMY DAMAGE IMPLEMENTATION

Now that our enemy has a body, a collision box, and is capable of detecting collision events with the player and the projectile class, it is the time to program its collision functionality. In the next tutorial we will set up the needed system to implement the enemy damage.

TUTORIAL 9.8 The Enemy Class and Damage Implementation

In this tutorial we will actually get to implement the enemy class and its damage mechanism.

ENEMY DAMAGE AND DESTRUCTION

The first item we will establish is the functionality for the enemy to take damage and to destruct.

1. Go to the **Event Graph** of the `Enemy` blueprint.
2. Create 2 new public variables of the type **Float**.

    a. To do this click on the ^+V or right-click in the gray area on **MyBlueprint** rollout and choose **Add New->Variable** from the popup menu.

    b. To make these variables public and editable either click on the closed eye icon to the right of the variable name in the **My Blueprint** rollout to make it look like an open eye, or check the box next to **Editable** in the **Details** rollout of the variable.

    c. To change the variable to float, select `float` from the **Variable Type** in the **Details** rollout.

    d. Name one of the variables `Hitpoints` and the other `EnemyDamage`.

    e. Compile the blueprint to make the **Default Value** of these variables available in the **Details** rollout.

    f. Set the default value for `Hitpoints` to 3.0 and for `EnemyDamage` to 1.0.

3. Right-click in the canvas to create a new node called **Event any Damage**.

4. Drag a **GET** node and a **SET** node for **Hitpoints** variable on the graph. (Hint: To do this drag the variable onto the canvas, and choose **GET** and **SET** from the popup menu, respectively.)

5. Move the **SET** node to the right of the **Event Any Damage** node.

6. Connect the execution channel of the **Event Any Damage** to the execution channel of the **SET** node.

7. Move the **GET** node below the **Event Any Damage**.

8. Drag a node out from the **Hitpoints** output of the **GET** node and search `float-float` to place a subtraction node on the canvas.

9. Connect the **Damage** output of the **Event Any Damage** to the bottom input of the subtraction node.

10. Connect the output of the subtraction node to the **Hitpoints** channel of the **SET** node.

11. Your graph should look like Figure 9.26.

12. Now we need to test if the enemy's died. To do this we will test whether `Hitpoints` falls to or below 0. If that happens then we have destroyed the enemy. To do this perform the following tasks:

    a. Drag a new **GET** from the variable **Hitpoints** onto the graph and place it below the subtraction node.

    b. From this new **GET** node drag off a wire and place a **float <= float** node.

    c. From the output (red) channel of **<=** condition node drag off a wire and place a **Branch**.

    d. Connect the execution channel of the **SET** node to the execution channel of the **Branch** node.

    e. From the true slot of the **Branch** drag off a wire and place a **Destroy Actor** node. *We will come back after the particle effects tutorial to add some nice effects here.*

    f. Your full enemy damage network should look like Figure 9.27.

13. Feel free to comment this section like **Damage taken from player with visual feedback**.

14. Compile and save your progress.

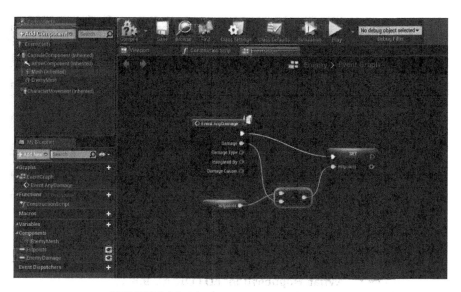

FIGURE 9.26: The Enemy Damage Functionality.

CAUSING DAMAGE TO PLAYER

Now that our enemy can calculate the damage and be destroyed if it's health falls to 0, it is time to implement the functionality to allow the enemy to cast damage on the player as well.

15. Right-click on the canvas to add a new node by searching for **Event Actor Begin Overlap**. This will be the damage causing event when the enemy overlaps with another object.
16. From the execution channel of the **Event Actor Begin Overlap** drag off a new node by searching for **Apply Damage**.
17. Drag the **EnemyDamage** variable you created earlier onto the canvas below the **Event Actor Begin Overlap** node and select a **GET**.
18. Right-click below the **EnemyDamage** node you just created and search for **self** to add a node that is a reference to self.
19. Connect the **Other Actor** channel of the **Event Actor Begin Overlap** node to the **Damaged Actor** channel of the **Apply Damage** node.
20. Then connect the **EnemyDamage** to the **Base Damage** channel of the **Apply Damage** node.
21. Finally connect the self-reference node to the **Damage Causer** channel of the **Apply Damage** node.
22. You can comment this as `Enemy Damages Player` (see Figure 9.28).
23. Compile and save the blueprint and your progress so far.

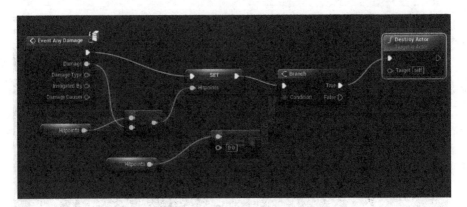

FIGURE 9.27: The Complete Enemy Damage Network.

What Happened in TUTORIAL 9.8...

In this tutorial we programmed our enemy class to conduct two kinds of damage logic, i.e., to take damage when it is hit, and to cast damage when it overlaps with the player object. We first created two variables for our enemy class to hold its health (hitpoint) and the amount of damage it can cast on the player.

We use an **Event Any Damage** event to detect when the enemy is damaged (i.e., receives damage from another actor, and in this game the projectile objects). Once we receive this event, we subtract the value of the damage cast on the enemy from its hitpoint and update its health. We will then perform a test to see if the enemy's health has reached zero. If the enemy's health has reached zero, we will call a function to destroy the enemy actor.

We use the enemy's collision capsule to determine whether the enemy has overlapped with the player. If so, we use the value of the **Enemy Damage** variable to apply that amount of damage to the player.

9.6.2 IMPLEMENTING THE PLAYER DAMAGE

Fantastic! So far our Enemy Class is coming along pretty well. It is capable of detecting when it is hit, and has become damaged (even destroyed). It is also capable of casting damage on the player character.

In the next tutorial we will implement the player damage functionalities.

TUTORIAL 9.9 The Player Damage Implementation

In this tutorial we will implement the player damage functionality. We will calculate the amount of damage caused to the player and apply the damage. We will also implement the projectile damage functionality in this tutorial.

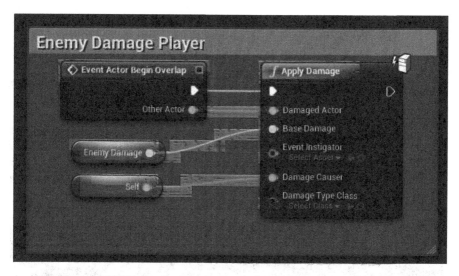

FIGURE 9.28: The Network to Enable Enemy to Cast Damage on the Player.

CALCULATING DAMAGE TO PLAYER

First, let's calculate the damage caused to the player character.

1. Go to the **RotationChar** blueprint. Open it if you have already closed the blueprint.
2. Click on the **Graph** tab to go to its **Event Graph**.
3. Create a **Public** float variable and call it `Player HP`. *See the previous tutorial to see how to make a variable public.*
4. Compile the blueprint to make the default value of the `Player HP` variable available.
5. Set the default value of the `Player HP` to 3.0.
6. Next we need to calculate the damage done to the player and destroy it when the health is less than or equal to zero. To do this perform the following tasks:
   a. Right-click in the canvas to create a new node called **Event any Damage**.
   b. Drag a **GET** node and a **SET** node for **Player HP** variable on the graph. (Hint: To do this drag the variable onto the canvas, and choose **GET** and **SET** from the popup menu, respectively.)
   c. Move the **SET** node to the right of the **Event Any Damage** node.
   d. Connect the execution channel of the **Event Any Damage** to the execution channel of the **SET** node.
   e. Move the **GET** node below the **Event Any Damage**.
   f. Drag a node out from the **Player HP** output of the **GET** node and search `float-float` to place a subtraction node on the canvas.
   g. Connect the **Damage** output of the **Event Any Damage** to the bottom input of the subtraction node.

h. Connect the output of the subtraction node to the **Player HP** channel of the **SET** node.

i. Drag a new **GET** from the variable **Player HP** onto the graph and place it below the subtraction node.

j. From this new **GET** node drag off a wire and place a **float <= float** node.

k. From the output (red) channel of **<=** condition node drag off a wire and place a **Branch**.

l. Connect the execution channel of the **SET** node to the execution channel of the **Branch** node.

m. From the true slot of the **Branch** drag off a wire and place a **Destroy Actor** node. *We will come back after the particle effects tutorial to add some nice effects here.*

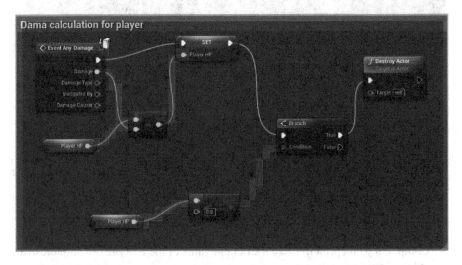

FIGURE 9.29: The Full Network for Player Damage Calculation and Destruction.

n. Your full enemy damage network should look like Figure 9.29.

o. Feel free to comment this section like **Damage calculation for the player**.

p. Compile and save your progress.

IMPLEMENTING PROJECTILES DAMAGE

Our next order of business is now to implement damage functionalities on our projectiles class.

7. Open the **Projectiles** blueprint if you have closed it.

8. Go to the **Event Graph** of the blueprint.

9. Now we need to create a public float variable in the **Projectile** blueprint. *See the previous tutorials to see how to make a variable public.*

10. Rename this variable to Damage.

11. Compile the blueprint to make the default value of this variable accessible and set the default value to 1.0.

12. Drag a damage GET node onto the event graph on top of the **Event Hit** node.

13. Right-click above the **Damage GET** node and add a **Reference to Self** node.

14. Break the current connection between the **Event Hit** and the **Destroy Actor** node. To do this `Alt+Click` on either end of the connection.

15. Move the **Destroy Actor** node to the right to make some room.

16. Right-click in the space between the **Destroy Actor** and the **Event Hit** nodes that you just disconnected, and search for a new node called **Apply Damage**.

17. Connect the output of **Damage** node to the `Base Damage` channel of the **Apply Damage** node.

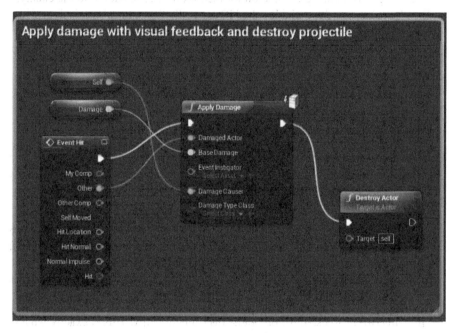

FIGURE 9.30: The Network Responsible for Casting Damage and Destroying the Projectile when Hit.

18. Connect the `Other` from the **Event Hit** to the `Damaged Actor` of the **Apply Damage** node.

19. Connect the `self-reference` node to the `Damage Causer` channel of the **Apply Damage** node.

20. Your networks should look like Figure 9.30. *We will be adding particle effects to this in a later tutorial.*

21. Feel free to comment this network to something like `Apply damage with visual feedback and destroy projectile`.

22. Compile and save your progress so far.

What Happened in TUTORIAL 9.9...

In this tutorial we created the damage functionality for our player and projectiles. The player will be damaged when it is hit by an enemy. Much like an enemy, when the player's health reaches zero, he will die. For the projectiles, we implemented a functionality for them to be able to cause damage when they hit an enemy object. We also made the projectiles to be destroyed when such a hit event occurs.

The logic for damage calculation for the player is quite similar to the enemy. The player has a health variable called `Player HP`. When the player is damaged by overlapping with an enemy actor (see the previous tutorial) we subtract the amount of damage caused from its current health and update the health. If the health falls to zero, we will destroy the player.

The logic for the projectiles' damage causing functionality was also similar to the enemy's damage causing functionality. There is one difference, however, in that the projectiles will apply damage upon a `Hit` event. We make the projectiles apply the amount of damage we defined in their `Damage` variable to the actor they hit and then to self destruct!

9.7 IMPLEMENTING GAME OVER!!!

Well, now our enemy, player, and projectiles can cause damage to one another, take damage from one another and get destroyed. We will need to implement a mechanism in our game to be able to end the gameplay when the player is destroyed. We will first implement the game over functionality, wait a few seconds and restart the level.

TUTORIAL 9.10   Game Over Cinematic Implementation

It is time for us to establish our game over functionality. This is exactly what we will be doing over the next few steps.

SETTING UP THE GAME OVER SCENE

In order for us to convey to the players that they have been hit and destroyed, we will set up a kind of a cut-scene. First we will set up the game over camera.

1. Go back into the main editor and drag a new camera onto the level and rename it `GameOver Camera`.
2. Rotate it so that it is pointing down at the ground of your level (see Figure 9.31).
3. In the **Details** rollout of the **GameOver Camera** change the **Aspect Ratio** to 1.0.
4. Drag the camera high into the air until it has a bird's eye view of the entire map (You can see its view on the small preview window.)

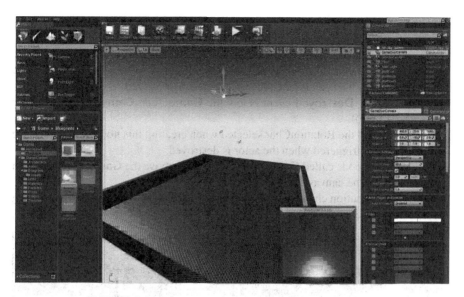

FIGURE 9.31: Placing a Camera for Game Over Cinematics.

5. With that camera still selected; open up the level blueprint (see Figure 9.32(a)).

6. Right-click somewhere on the **Event Graph** canvas of the Level Blueprint and search for `Create reference to ...` to place a `Reference to GameOver Camera` node. We will use this reference to set up a bird's eye view of the scene to see the player explosion effect on a player's death.

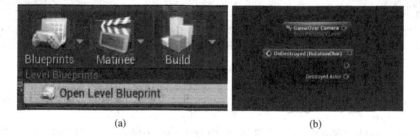

(a)   (b)

FIGURE 9.32: (a) Level Blueprint. (b) When Character Is Destroyed by Means of On Destroyed Event.

IMPLEMENTING PLAYER'S DEATH SEQUENCE

Now we are ready to implement our cut-scene. I didn't want to have to go through setting up a matinee sequence for this project. Instead, we will switch our camera upon the player's destruction event and play a particle system for a few seconds.

7. Go back to the the main editor.

8. Drag your **RotationChar** character you created onto the level.
9. Select your **RotationChar** in the level by clicking on it.
10. With the **RotationChar** still selected, go back to the **Level Blueprint**. Right-click on the canvas of the **Event Graph** and search for a new node called On Destroyed. This is an Event node, and therefore looks red.
11. Place the **On Destroyed** event below the **GameOver Camera** reference (see Figure 9.32(b)).
12. Since you had the RotationChar selected when creating this node, you will notice that it is now triggered when the actor is destroyed.
13. Create a new node called **Get Player Controller** above the **GameOver Camera** reference on the canvas.
14. From the execution channel of the **On Destroyed** node drag off an **Print String** node and have it output Game Over!!!.

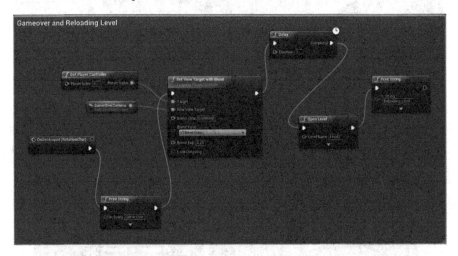

FIGURE 9.33: The Game Over Cut-scene Network.

15. From this node drag off a new one called **Set View Target With Blend**. *Note that you may have to turn context sensitivity off to find this node.*
16. Connect the return value of the **Get Player Controller** to the Target of the **Set View Target with Blend**.
17. Connect the return value of the **GameOver Camera** reference to the New View Target.
18. Change the Blend Func to VTBlend Cubic and set the blend time to 0.25.
19. From the set view target with blend drag off a delay node with a duration of 5.0.
20. From that **Delay** node drag off a **Open Level** node and type in your level name in the Level Name box.
21. Finally from the **Open Level** node drag off another **Print String** node that outputs Reloading level....
22. You can comment all these as Gameover and Reloading Level (see Figure 9.33).

23. Compile and save your blueprint.

What Happened in TUTORIAL 9.10...

With the logic for our player, enemy, and projectile's damage implemented, we need to have a mechanism to declare game over. We will also need to visually convey the end game to the player's attention through a cut-scene.

In this tutorial we implemented the end game and game over cinematic. We first created a second camera to change our view from the top-down view of the player to the game over view. This view will have a wider angle and looks at the player in a wider area of the level. Later on, when we implement the visual effects for the player's death sequence with fires and smoke, this view will be pretty interesting.

To cut to the new camera, we looked for an event on the player character's class called onDestroyed. When a player's health reaches zero, from the damage logic we had called a Destroy Actor function to destroy the player. Once this happens, the onDestroyed event will fire. When the event fires, we will cut to the game over camera, stay there for 5 minutes and restart the level.

9.8 AI AND ENEMY SPAWNING

We have been making great progress so far in establishing our level, designing our character, projectiles, and enemy classes and implementing the damage functionalities. However, our game is nowhere close to being playable. For one thing, our enemies are going to be quite static if we place them in the game.

This is because we don't have a mechanism in place for our enemy to play the game. That requires Artificial Intelligence (AI). The AI we will establish in this level is going to be quite simple. In fact, it will be so simple that only one behavior could describe it. That behavior is the seeking behavior. We will implement this behavior in such a way the our enemy instances could detect the player and try to chase him.

The nice thing about implementing the chasing behavior is that it is simple enough for us to be able to program it quickly, which fits well with the limited number of pages we have to describe its implementation. However, the chasing behavior is visually complicated enough to give us a nice competitive enemy class to play against.

But before we get into the details about implementation of our AI, we first need to be able to spawn enemies inside our level. This is what we will tackle in the next tutorial.

9.8.1 SPAWNING ENEMIES

The first item for us to implement to pin the player and enemies against each other is to spawn the enemy in the level.

TUTORIAL 9.11   Spawning Enemies

In this tutorial we will implement the spawning functionalities in our game in such a way that one enemy will be spawned at a certain interval from a randomly selected spawn base.

FIGURE 9.34: Placing Enemy Spawn Bases in the Level.

PLACING ENEMY BASES

To spawn the enemies in the level, we will first establish certain locations in our map (e.g., each corner) as a spawn point. We will, first, place a spawn base (a static mesh to visualize it) in each corner of the level.

1. We want to drag 4 prop objects from the starter content into the 4 corners of our map as enemy bases. Our enemies are going to spawn off of these bases.
2. From the content browser, open the **Props** folder and place 4 of the **SM_MatPreviewMesh_02** into the 4 corners of our map.
3. Rotate the bases so they're facing the center of the map.
4. Rename those objects `TopLeft`, `TopRight`, `BottomLeft`, and `BottomRight`.
5. Your map should look like Figure 9.34.

FIGURE 9.35: Creating a Variable for the Enemy to Spawn.

6. This is primarily to keep track of them in the level blueprint as we will be making references to them shortly.

SETTING UP SPAWN INTERVALS

Next, we will need to establish a mechanism for our spawning functionality to take place at a certain interval. This is the task we will tackle next.

7. Open the **Level Blueprint**.
8. Create a new public variable called **EnemyToSpawn**. This variable is going to be of type **Class** and must be searched for manually.
9. To assign the variable type, use the drop-down box of the **Variable Type** and in the search box type Enemy (or any name you gave to your enemy class) that is color coded PURPLE.
10. Compile the blueprint and then in the **Default Value** section of the **Details** roll-out use the drop-down box to select Enemy (see Figure 9.35).
11. Now create a new **Event Begin Play** node in the Event Graph of the Level Blueprint.
12. Right-click below the **Event Begin Play** node and create a **Custom Event**. NOTE: You may need to make sure that the Context Sensitive checkbox is checked.
13. Rename the **Custom Event** to Spawn Enemies.
14. Right-click to the right of **Event Begin Play** and search for and add a **Set Time by Event** node.
15. Connect execution channels from both the **Event Begin Play** and Spawn Enemies **Custom Event** nodes to the input execution channel of the **Timer Delegate** node.
16. Then connect the red output channel of the **Spawn Enemies** custom event into the Delegate channel of the **Set Timer Delegate** node.

17. Set the `Time Value` to 3.0.

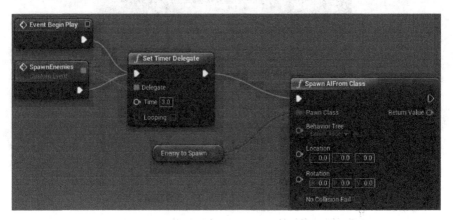

FIGURE 9.36: Creating the Set Timer Delegate.

18. Your network should look like the left portion of Figure 9.36 so far.
19. From the execution channel of the **Set Timer Delegate** output channel drag off and search for **Spawn AI from Class** node.
20. Drag the **EnemyToSpawn** variable you created earlier and drop it into the `Pawn Class` channel of the **Spawn AI from Class** node (see Figure 9.36).

SPAWNING ENEMIES FINAL IMPLEMENTATION

Now that we have our basic requisites set up for our functionality to spawn the enemies, we need to calculate the spawn locations at which each enemy will be spawned. The next few steps will guide us through creating this mechanism.

21. Go into the main editor and drag a reference to the `TopLeft` actor from the **Scene Outliner** into the event graph of the **Level Blueprint**.
22. Drag a wire from the output channel of this reference off and search for `Get Actor Location`. *NOTE: You may need to turn context sensitivity off.*
23. Drag another wire from the output channel of the actor reference and search for `Get Actor Forward Vector` node and place it below the **Get Actor Location**.
24. Right-click to the right of the **Get Actor Forward Vector** node and place a `Vector*Float` node and put the value of 250 into the float box of this node.
25. From the **Get Actor Location** channel drag off a `Vector + Vector` node and place it above and to the right of the `Vector*Float`.
26. Connect the output of the multiplication node into the B (bottom) channel of the addition node (see top portion of Figure 9.37).
27. We essentially need to repeat this process 3 more times for a total of 4 corners spawning enemies. The only difference is instead of the top left reference we need the corresponding actor on the map for each respective corner (see Figure 9.37).
28. Now that all of our spawn locations are set up, we will establish a mechanism to randomly pick one of these spawn locations to spawn the enemies from. Perform

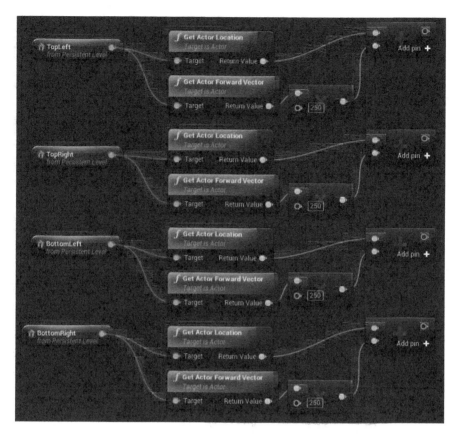

FIGURE 9.37: Calculating the Spawn Locations Based on the Location and Direction of Each Base.

the following tasks to do this randomized spawning:

a. Right-click on the canvas and make sure the **Context Sensitive** check box is checked.

b. Search for `Make Array` node and place it to the right of the four(4) Addition nodes.

c. Click on the `Add Pin` (the + icon) of the **Make Arrow** node three (3) times to make it have 4 (four) entries. These four entries are indexed [0] to [3].

d. Connect the output channel of the **Addition** nodes to the entries by connecting the topmost addition to the entry indexed [0], the second top to [1] and so forth (see bottom left of Figure 9.38).

e. Right-click below the **Make Array** node and search for `Random Integer In Range`. Type 0 and 3 in the top and bottom input channels of this node, respectively.

f. From the output channel of the **Make Array** drag a wire and type GET to place a **Get** node.

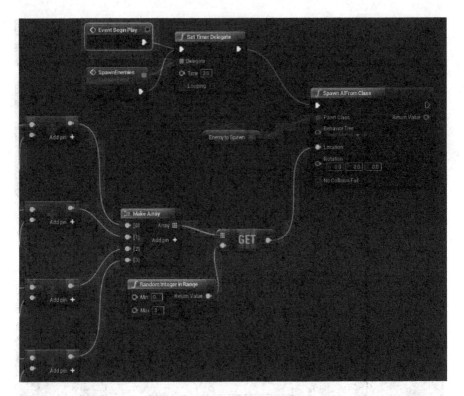

FIGURE 9.38: The Network Responsible for Randomly Picking from the Four Enemy Bases to Spawn Enemies.

  g. Connect the output of the **Random Integer In Range** to the Index channel of the **GET** node.
  h. Finally connect the output of the **GET** array node to the Location channel of the **Spawn AI from Class** node (see Figure 9.38).
29. You may rearrange the network to make it look more organized and comment it as Spawning Enemies.
30. Compile and save the level blueprint.
31. If you like, you can test the level. You should be able to run around the level and see enemies being spawned in front of the bases at random.

What Happened in TUTORIAL 9.11...

In this tutorial we implemented the part of our program that is responsible for spawning enemy actors into the level. To do this, we placed four static meshes inside the level (in each corner of the arena) as the enemy base locations. We used the location of these four bases to populate an array of spawn locations.

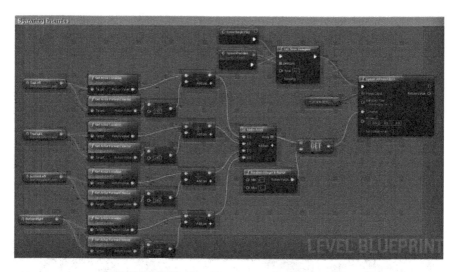

FIGURE 9.39: The Complete Spawning Network.

Once the spawn location array was established, we used a random number generator to generate an integer between 0 and 3 at a regular time period. The random number is then used as the index to the location arrays to pick one out of the four possible enemy base locations to spawn an enemy actor. Once we have determined which location to have the enemy spawn, we called the spawn actor function to spawn an enemy.

We used a **Timer Delegate** to call a custom event we created called **Spawn Enemy**, in order to call the spawn enemy function on regular intervals. We set the timing of this delegate to 3 seconds and associated the delegate at the **Event Begin Play** (i.e., the start of the gameplay). This will make the **Spawn Enemy** event fire every three seconds from the beginning of the game.

9.8.2 SETTING UP ENEMY ARTIFICIAL INTELLIGENCE

Fantastic! Now that we have our spawn bases created and are able to spawn enemies randomly from each base, it is time to tackle the Artificial Intelligence (AI) component of our spawned enemies. This will enable each spawned enemy to seek the player and try to collide with him to cause damage and destroy the player.

TUTORIAL 9.12   Setting Up Enemy AI and Behaviors

In this tutorial we will create our Enemy's Artificial Intelligence and behaviors. The first order of business is to create a behavior tree for our enemies. We will then create a controller for them to be able to program their behaviors.

This enemy controller will be pretty much like the player controller in nature, but instead of getting input from the player through keyboard or mouse clicks, it will get its input from the AI behavior tree and settings. For this purpose, the parent class of our enemy controller class will be an AI Controller.

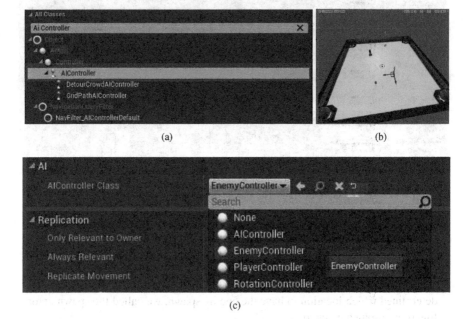

(a)   (b)

(c)

FIGURE 9.40: (a) AI Controller as the Parent Class for Enemy Controller. (b) Placing a Navigation Mesh in the Level for Pathfinding Used in the AI Class. (c). Assigning the Enemy Controller to AI.

CREATING THE AI CONTROLLER

The first item we need to create is the AI Controller and a behavior tree for our enemy characters.

1. In the folder you have been creating your new blueprints, create a new folder and call it **AI**.
2. Double-click on the AI folder you just created to go into it.
3. Inside this new folder we need to create a new **Behavior Tree** and a new **Blackboard**. To do this perform the following tasks:
   a. Right-click in the AI folder and choose
      `New->Artificial Intelligence->Behavior Tree`.
   b. Right-click in the AI folder again and select
      `New->Artificial Intelligence->Blackboard`.
   c. Name your **Behavior Tree** EnemyBT and your **Blackboard** EnemyBB.

4. Now we need to create a new blueprint for the Enemy Controller. Perform the following tasks:
    a. When creating this blueprint, click `All Classes`.
    b. In the search are search for `AI Controller` and select it as the base-class (see Figure 9.40(a)).
    c. Name this class blueprint `EnemyController`.
5. Now go back to the main editor and search for `Nav Mesh Bounds Volume` in the search are under the **Modes** tab.
6. Drag the **Nav Mesh Bounds Volume** onto the scene.
7. Change the scale of the volume to be roughly the same size as our arena. Remember that the size of our arena was X: 3000, Y: 3000, Z:200. I suggest using values like X:3200, Y:3200, and Z:300 for the size of your **Nav Mesh Bounds Volume**.
8. Press the P key to see the **Nav Mesh** coverage on the scene. It will show up as a green area.
9. Align the **Nav Mesh Bounds Volume** so it covers the entire ground of the level (see Figure 9.40(b)). *NOTE: It's okay if it goes through walls a bit as the enemies will collide with the wall anyway.*
10. Now open up the behavior tree we created earlier by double-clicking it.
11. Make sure that in the **Details** rollout of the behavior tree the `Blackboard Asset` is set to the **EnemyBB** we created earlier in step (3c).
12. Go into the event graph of the **Enemy Controller** we just created in step 4.
13. Create a new `Event Begin Play` node.
14. Drag a wire off of the **Event Begin Play** and place a `Run Behavior Tree` node.
15. Set the `BTAsset` channel of the **Run Behavior Tree** to our created **EnemyBT** behavior tree in step (3a). You can click on the drop-down section and search for the behavior tree.
16. Compile and save your **Enemy Controller** blueprint.
17. Now we will setup the AI controller of our Enemy class. Perform the following tasks:
    a. Open the **Enemy** blueprint.
    b. Click on the **Defaults** mode of the Enemy blueprint.
    c. Scroll down to the Pawn section and change the **AIController** class to our created **Enemy Controller** (see Figure 9.40(c)).
18. Compile and save the Enemy blueprint.

IMPLEMENTING THE BEHAVIOR TREE

Now that we have our AI controller and Behavior Tree, it's time to program the Behavior Tree to control our enemy characters.

19. Open the **EnemyBT** behavior tree and select the **Blackboard** mode. This is the right-most tab on the toolbar (see Figure 9.41(a)).
20. Click the **New Key** button and create a new Vector. Call it `PlayerPosition` (see Figure 9.41(b)).

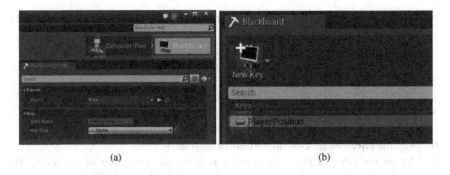

(a)   (b)

FIGURE 9.41: (a) Blackboard for Programming the AI Behavior Tree. (b) Adding a New Key in Blackboard.

21. Click on the **Behavior Tree** mode and create a **New Task**.
22. With the **Event Graph** of the New Task open, go back to the main editor.
23. Go into your AI folder in the **Content Browser** you created in step (1).
24. You will see that this new task has been created and named for you in the content browser. Rename it something like SetPlayerPosition.
25. Inside the event graph of this new blueprint create a new public variable called Position.
26. Change the type of this variable to **Blackboard Key Selector**. There are two easy ways to change this variable type. You can do either one of the following:
    a. Click on the drop-down menu next to **Variable Type** and expand **Structure** section (see Figure 9.42).
    b. Click on the drop-down menu next to **Variable Type** and search for BlackboardKeySelector.
27. Right-click on the canvas and search for Event Receive Execute to place this node in the Event Graph.
28. Right-click to the left and below the **Event Receive Execute** node and create a **Get Player Pawn**.
29. Drag a wire from the **Get Player Pawn** and place a **Cast to RotationChar** node to its right.
30. Connect the execution channel of the **Event Receive Execute** to the execution channel of the **Cast to RotationChar**.
31. From the the execution channel of the **Cast to RotationChar** drag off a wire and search for Set Blackboard Value as Vector.
32. From the **Set Blackboard Value as Vector** node drag a wire and search for Finish Execute, place the node and check the Success checkbox.
33. Drop the **Position** variable we created in step (25) into the Key channel of the **Set Blackboard Value as Vector**.
34. Drag a wire out of the As RotationChar C channel of the **Cast to Rotation-Char** node and create a **Get Actor Location**. *NOTE: You may have to turn context sensitivity off.*

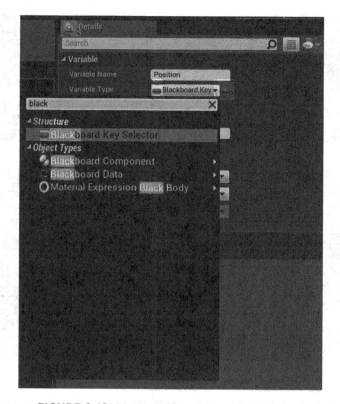

FIGURE 9.42: Blackboard Key Selector Variable Type.

35. Connect the **Return Value** channel from the **Get Actor Location** to the **Value** input channel of the **Set Blackboard Value as Vector** node (see Figure 9.43(a)).

36. Go back into the behavior tree and create yet another task. *You can choose the BTTask_BlueprintBase.*

37. We will need to go back into the content browser and rename this task to **ChasePlayer**.

38. Open the event graph of the **ChasePlayer**.

39. Create a new public variable called **TargetPosition**.

40. Make the variable type also **Blackboard Key Selector** (see step 26).

41. Right-click on the canvas and search for a new node called **Event Receive Execute** to place it on the event graph.

42. From the **Owner Actor** channel drag off a new node called **Cast to AIController**. *NOTE: You may need context sensitivity turned off for these nodes.*

43. Make sure that the execution channel of the event node is connected to the cast to **AI controller**.

44. From the casting node's **As AIController** channel drag off a **Move to Location** node.

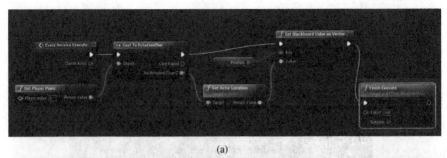

(a)

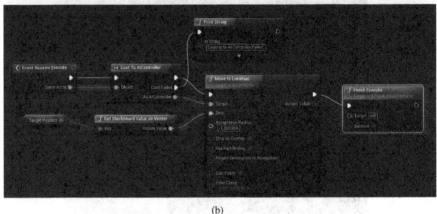

(b)

FIGURE 9.43: (a) Send Player Position to Blackboard. (b) Chase the Player Network.

45. Control-Drag the **TargetPosition** variable created earlier onto the graph below the **Event Receive Execute**. This will create a **GET** node for the variable.

46. Drag a wire from **TargetPosition** you just created to place a **Get Blackboard Value as Vector** node.

47. Connect the `Return Value` channel of the **Get Blackboard Value as Vector** node to the `Destination` channel of the **Move to Location** node.

48. From the `Cast Failed` channel of the casting node drag off a **Print String** node that outputs `Casting to AI Controller Failed`. This could prove useful for troubleshooting if necessary.

49. Finally drag off the execution channel of the **Move to Location** node a **Finish Execute Node**.

50. As always check the `Success` checkbox (see Figure 9.43(b)).

51. Go back into the **Behavior Tree** and drag off a sequence from the `Root` (see Figure 9.44(a)).

52. From the sequence drag off two new nodes; one of them a **SetPlayerPosition** and the other a **ChasePlayer** – you may type these names in the search bar, or expand the **Tasks** section when you drag off off the **Sequence** (see Figure 9.44(b)).

53. Compile and save your blueprint.

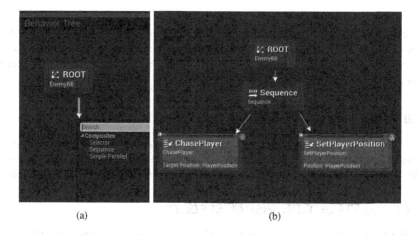

(a)   (b)

FIGURE 9.44: (a) Drag a Wire from Root to Place Sequence. (b) Create the Chase Player and the Set Player Position Behaviors.

54. Test drive your level and see how the AI behaves. Make any tweaks necessary to make the Enemies chase the player and try to catch up with him.

What Happened in TUTORIAL 9.12...

In this tutorial we gave our enemy actors an Artificial Intelligence behavior to enable them to seek and chase the player. In order to establish this behavior, we will have to create a behavior tree and a blackboard for programming our sequences. We will also need to create an AI controller to communicate with the enemy class to make them dynamic.

Before programming our AI, we first need to have a tool called a Navigation Mesh (or Nav Mesh for short) in our level. A Nav Mesh enables our AI characters to perform pathfinding and to be able to autonomously navigate inside of the level geometry. Once the Nav Mesh is placed in the level, the areas which can be navigated and traversed by the AI controlled actors will be highlighted with a green color. To see the Nav Mesh area you can press the P key on your keyboard to toggle the view on and off.

Our next step in establishing our AI is to create the behavior tree and a blackboard for programming our AI behavior. Once you create your behavior tree, you will be able to assign tasks. We created two tasks, one for the AI to update the position based on where the player is located, and one to enable the AI actors to chase the player's position.

These two tasks were then, in turn, programmed in the sequence of behaviors in the behavior tree. This will make our AI characters able to perceive the location of the player and actively attempt to seek the player.

The game is really coming along well. If you play the game now, your AI enemy characters should spawn and chase the player. Each enemy should take damage and get destroyed when the player projectiles hit it. The player projectiles should also destruct when they hit an enemy or a wall. And the player should die if it is hit multiple times by an enemy.

9.9   PARTICLE SYSTEMS AND VISUAL EFFECTS

So far we have implemented a great deal of functionality into our game, but the destruction of the enemy, player, and bullets are kind of anit-climactic! We will fix this issue by implementing a couple of particle effects in the next set of tutorials.

9.9.1   DESTRUCTION VISUAL EFFECTS

In the next tutorial we will implement the visual effects for when the player and the enemy are destroyed. This will involve spawning a particle system actor at the location where the destruction happens.

TUTORIAL 9.13   Destruction Visual Effects

In this tutorial we will implement a visual effect for when our enemy and player are destroyed.

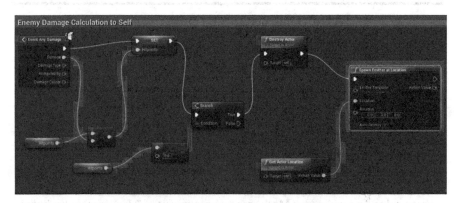

FIGURE 9.45: The Network for Enemy Death Particle Effect.

SETTING ENEMY DEATH VISUAL EFFECTS

To establish a visual effect for the enemy destruction event, we will spawn a fire particle system at the location where the enemy is destroyed.

1. Go to the **Enemy** blueprint's **Event Graph**
2. Drag node off the **Destroy Actor** node.

3. Search and place the **Spawn Emitter at Location**.
4. Set the `Emitter Template` to **P_Explosion**.
5. Right-click to the left of the **Spawn Emitter at Location** and add a **Get Actor Location**.
6. Connect return value of the **Get Actor Location** to the `Location` channel of the **Spawn Emitter at Location** (See Figure 9.45).

SETTING THE PLAYER DEATH VISUAL EFFECTS

We will perform a similar activity for when the player is destroyed. However, we will also spawn an explosion particle system for the player to make the player's destruction sequence a little more dramatic.

7. Now go into the **RotationChar** `Event Graph`.
8. Drag node off the **Destroy Actor** node.

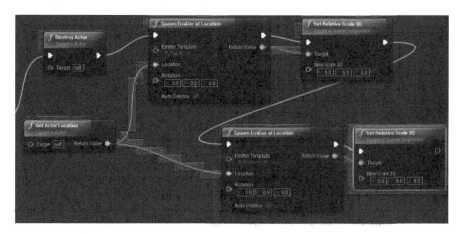

FIGURE 9.46: Player's Destruction Sequence Particle System Network.

9. Now add a new **Spawn Emitter at Location** to connect it to the **Destroy Actor**.
10. Set the `Emitter Template` to **P_Fire**.
11. Right-click to the left of the **Spawn Emitter at Location** and add a **Get Actor Location**.
12. Connect return value of the **Get Actor Location** to the `Location` channel of the **Spawn Emitter at Location**
13. From the **Spawn Emitter at Location** node drag off a new **Set Relative Scale 3D** node. *NOTE: You may have to uncheck the Context Sensitive option to be able to search for this node.*
14. Set the `Return Value` of the **P_Fire Spawn Emitter at Location** node to the target of the **Set Relative Scale 3D** node.
15. Enter the `New Scale` 3D values of 5.0, 5.0, 5.0, for X, Y, and Z, respectively.
16. From the **Set Relative Scale 3D** node drag off another **Spawn Emitter at Location** node.

17. Set the `Emitter Template` of the second emitter to **P_Explosion**. Also, be sure to set the location input of this node. You can use the same getter we created earlier.

18. Add another **Relative Scale 3D** to the right of the second explosion emitter we just created.

19. Set the `Return Value` of the **P_Explosion Spawn Emitter at Location** node to the target of the second **Set Relative Scale 3D** node. *NOTE: You may have to uncheck the Context Sensitive option to be able to search for this node.*

20. Enter the second `New Scale` 3D values to 5.0, 5.0, 5.0, for X, Y, and Z, respectively (see Figure 9.46).

21. Compile and save your blueprints and your progress so far.

22. You can test drive and see how the player explodes and catches on fire after its destruction.

What Happened in TUTORIAL 9.13...

In this tutorial we set up a mechanism to spawn a particle system whenever the player and the enemy die. This will give us a better visual effect to convey to the player, visually, when an enemy actor is destroyed or when the player actor is destroyed.

We chose a particle system from the `Starter Content` that simulates the effects of an explosion. We used the destroyed actors location as the spawning location for our visual effect. We also need to modify the scale of the particle system to represent the appropriate sizes of the player and the enemy actors and the explosion they should create when they are destroyed.

9.9.2 HIT VISUAL EFFECTS

Let's implement some visual effects to enhance our game. We want to have the bullets burst some sparks when they hit an enemy or the walls. To do this we will set up a mechanism to a spawn sparks particle system when a hit event occurs. We will also make the player and enemy flash with a bright material when they are hit to visualize the effect of taking damage.

TUTORIAL 9.14   Projectiles' Hit Visual Effects

In this tutorial we will establish a particle system for when a projectile hits a wall or an enemy to create a spark effect.

SETTING PROJECTILES' HIT VISUAL EFFECTS

We will first make minor modifications to our Spark Emitter in the Cascade Particle Editor.

1. Go into the main editor and in the content browser look through the starter content until you find the particle effect called **P_Sparks**.
2. Right-click this and duplicate it. Name this duplicate `ImpactSparks`. *NOTE: we will be duplicating the* `ImpactSparks` *later on after we edit its values.*
3. Double-click the **ImpactSparks** to open it up.
4. In the CASCADE particle editor, click on the `Smoke` emitter to select it and press `delete` on your keyboard to remove it.
5. At this stage you should have two emitters **Sparks** and **Spark burst** (see Figure 9.47(a)).

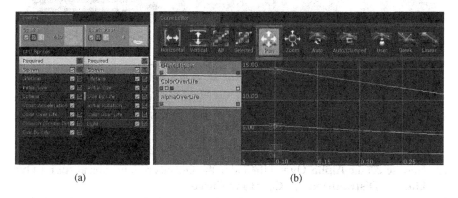

(a)   (b)

FIGURE 9.47: (a) The Spark Emitter and Its Modules. (b) The Sparks' Color Over Life Graph.

6. On the Sparks emitter click on the small graph icon next to **Color over Life**. This will open up the graph of this parameter in the `Curve Editor` just below the Emitters section.
7. In the `Curve Editor` click on the small yellow boxes on the **LifeMultiplier** channel and **AlphaOverLife** to hide their values from the curve editor (see Figure 9.47(b)).

WORKING WITH SPARKS

Let's make some changes to the **Color Over Life** and **Alpha Over Life** distribution to make them suitable for our purpose.

8. Make sure **Color Over Life** is still selected and in the **Details** rollout expand **Color Over Life -> Distribution -> Constant Curve**.
9. Make sure you have 2 `elements` for **Points** attributed for the Constant Curve (see Figure 9.48(a)).
10. Expand **Points -> 0** and **Points -> 1**.
11. To make the sparks shine with a color similar to the color of our projectile, in the **Points[0]** and **Points[1]**, make the following changes (see Figure 9.48(b)):

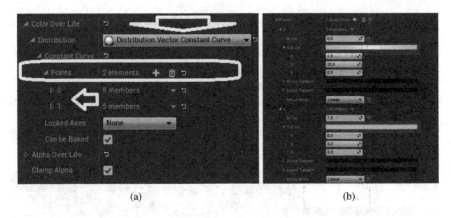

FIGURE 9.48: (a) Color Over Life Distribution. (b) Color Over Life Values.

Points->[0]				Points->[1]			
In Val	0.0			**In Val**	1.0		
Out Val	R 1.0	G 20.0	B 0.0	**Out Val**	R 0.0	G 3.0	B 0.0

12. Now Select the **Alpha Over Life** and in the **Details** rollout expand **Alpha Over Life -> Distribution -> Constant Curve**.
13. Make sure you have **2 elements** for **Points** attributed for the Constant Curve (see Figure 9.49(a)).
14. Expand **Points -> 0** and **Points -> 1**.
15. To make the sparks disappear much more quickly, in the **Points[0]** and **Points[1]**, make the following changes (see Figure 9.49(b)):

Points->[0]		Points->[1]	
In Val	0.0	**In Val**	0.3
Out Val	1.0	**Out Val**	0.0

16. Select the **Spark Burst** emitter. This is the component of the effect that looks like a fire burst on the point of impact.
17. In the **Details** rollout, expand the **Color Over Life** and from there expand **Distribution** and then expand **Constant**.
18. Change the **XYZ** constant values to 1, 20, 1, respectively, to make it glow green.

A BIG BURST OF SPARKS

Now we need to make this effect to be more like a burst of sparks, rather than a constant spawning of sparks.

19. To do this select **Spawn** module in the **Sparks** emitter.
20. Expand **Rate -> Distribution** and change the value for constant to 0.
21. In the **Burst** section we want to add an element to the burst list. Click on the + sign to add an element. This will be called [0].

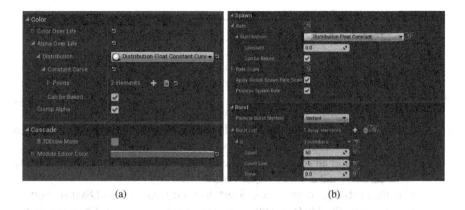

FIGURE 9.49: (a) Alpha Over Life Distribution. (b) Alpha Over Life Values.

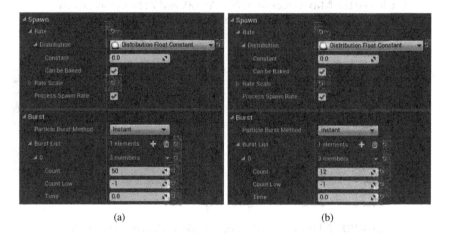

(a)   (b)

FIGURE 9.50: (a) Spawning Section of Sparks. (b) Spawning Section of Sparks Burst.

22. Change the **Count** value to 50 (See Figure 9.50(a)).
23. Now we want to do the exact same thing under the spawning of the spark burst **except** make the count in the burst list element 12 instead of 50 (see Figure 9.50(b)).
24. Now we will have to make the emitter only burst once per hit. To do this perform the following tasks:
    a. Select the **Required** module of the **Sparks** emitter.
    b. Change the **Emitter Loops** to 1 in the **Duration** section of the **Details** rollout. This will make the emitter create the particles once.
    c. Select the **Required** module of the **Spark Burst** emitter.
    d. Change the **Emitter Loops** to 1 in the **Duration** section of the **Details** rollout. This will make the emitter create these particles once.

SETTING UP SPARKS' VELOCITY

Now that our spark's burst is set up, let's make some modifications to the velocity of our sparks.

25. Go into the **Sphere** module of the **Sparks** emitter.
26. In the **Details** rollout, expand **Velocity Scale** and then its **Distribution**. Change the **Constant** value to 200 (see Figure 9.51(a)).
27. Now we want to make our effect a single burst that looks like an explosion when our projectiles will collide. To do this, perform the following tasks:
    a. Right-click in an empty area in the **Sparks** emitter below the **Size By Life** module and add a **Velocity -> Initial Velocity** module.
    b. In the **Details** rollout expand **Start Velocity** and then its **Distribution**.
    c. Make sure the **Distribution** is Distribution Vector Uniform. If not select it from the drop-down menu.
    d. Change the **Max** values to X:200, Y:200, and Z:200, respectively.
    e. Change the **Min** values to X:-200, Y:-200, and Z:-200, respectively.
    f. The value should represent something like Figure 9.51(b).

(a)   (b)

FIGURE 9.51: (a) Sparks' Velocity Scale. (b) Velocity Distribution.

28. Save your **ImpactSparks** particle effect.

PROGRAMMING THE HIT VISUAL EFFECTS

Now that our particle effects are ready, we can go ahead and program the visual effect.

29. Head back into the event graph of our **Projectile** blueprint. If you open the blueprint, the event graph should open up. If not, click on the Graph tab on the top right corner.
30. Look up the **Destroy Actor** node and from it drag off a **Spawn Emitter at Location**.
31. Set our **ImpactSparks** we created earlier as the Emitter Template.
32. Connect the HitLocation of the **Event Hit** node to the Location channel of the **Spawn Emitter at Location** node.

33. Drag off a wire from the **Spawn Emitter at Location** node and search for and place a **Set relative Scale 3D** (context sensitivity may have to be off).
34. Connect the `Return Value` of the **Spawn Emitter at Location** node to the `Target` of the **Scale 3D** node.
35. Set the XYZ Values to 2, 2, 2, respectively (see Figure 9.52).

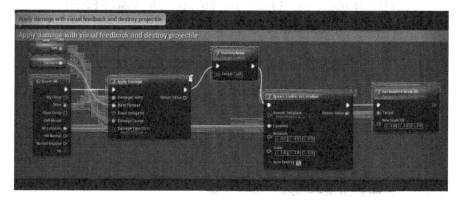

FIGURE 9.52: Spawning Sparks when Bullets Hit.

36. Compile and save your blueprint.

What Happened in TUTORIAL 9.14...

In this tutorial we implemented the visual effects for when our projectiles hit an object. We want to create a spark-like effect to show that the projectiles hit the object at a high speed and created the spark.

To achieve this effect, we cannot directly use any of the particle systems that come with the `Starter Content`. However, the `Starter Content` comes with a spark effect that we can modify to suit our needs.

We first duplicated the P_Sparks effects from the `Starter Content` in order to keep the original spark particle system intact. We then opened the duplicated sparks particle system in the **Cascade Particle Editor** and made the modifications we needed. These modifications included the changes to the `Color` and `Color Over Life` modules' distributions of the two emitter components in the particle system to give them a fiery look. We also made modifications to the `Spawn` and `Burst Rate` of these two emitter modules.

Our game is almost complete! The only remaining item is to create an effect on the player and enemy materials to flash with a bright color for a fraction of a second to give them the effect of being hit and sustaining some damage.

In the next tutorial we will implement the hit flash effect by using material interfaces. The material interface objects give us the ability to communicate from our blueprint with the Unreal Engine to change the object's material at runtime.

TUTORIAL 9.15   Player and Enemy's Hit Visual Effects

In this tutorial we will add some visual feedback for when the player or an enemy is hit. To achieve this we will set up a network to make some changes to the materials in such a way that it flashes when the object is hit.

SETTING UP THE MATERIALS

Let's first create a material with an ember color and a relatively high emissive property. This will be the material we will use as a flash.

1. Go to the main editor and create a new material. You may create a new folder to hold this material or create it in the Materials folder of the starter content.
2. Call this material HitFlash.
3. Double-click the **HitFlash** material to open up the **Material Editor**.
4. Inside the material editor create two **Constant3Vector** nodes and one **Constant** node. To create the **Constant3Vector**, you may hold key "3" on your keyboard and left-click somewhere on the canvas or right-click and search for Constant3Vector. Similarly, holding the "1" key on the keyboard and left-clicking will place a **Constant** node.
5. Select the **Constant** node you created, and type 1.0 in its **Value** in the Details rollout.
6. Connect the **Constant** to the Roughness channel of the **HitFlash** material.
7. Select the **Constant3Vector Node**.
8. Type the values of 1.0, 0.384, 0.0 into the R, G, B components of the **Constant3Vector** in its Details rollout.
9. Connect the **Constant3Vector** to the Base Color of the **HitFlash** material.
10. Finally, create another **Constant3Vector** and change its values to R:10.0, G:3.8, B:0.0, respectively.
11. Connect this last node to the Emissive Color channel of the **HitFlash** material.
12. Your material should look like Figure 9.53.
13. Save the material.
14. Close the material editor.

IMPLEMENTING HIT FLASH ON ENEMY

Now we will set up the network in blueprints responsible for showing a flash on an enemy's body when player projectiles hit it.

15. Open up the **Enemy** blueprint.
16. Create a new variable called MeshMat in the **Enemy** event graph.

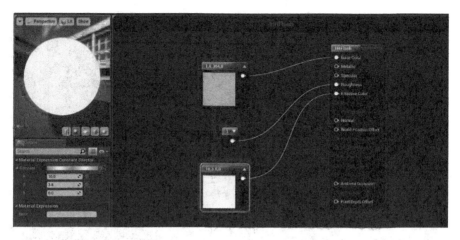

FIGURE 9.53: Damage Material Network.

17. Change the type of this new variable to **Material Interface**. To do this, you can either click on the drop-down box next to the **Variable Type** and search for **Material Interface** in the search bar, or open the **Object Reference** tab and scroll down to **Material Interface** (see Figure 9.54(a)).

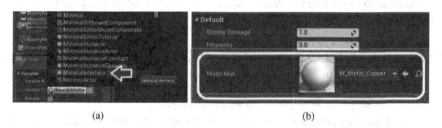

(a)   (b)

FIGURE 9.54: (a) Adding a Material Interface Variable. (b) Assigning Non-Flash (Regular) Material.

18. Click on the **Defaults** section of the **Enemy** blueprint.
19. Scroll down to the **Default** rollout.
20. Click on the material selector next to the **Mesh Mat**.
21. From the drop-down menu select and apply the same material our **Enemy** class has (see Figure 9.54(b)). If you don't remember the material, perform the following tasks:
    a. Go to the **Components** tab.
    b. Click on the **Enemy Mesh**.
    c. In the **Details** rollout, scroll down and find the **Materials** section.
    d. Expand the **Materials** item and see the material we applied to the element **[0]**.
    e. Go back to the **Defaults** tab by clicking on it from the top toolbar.

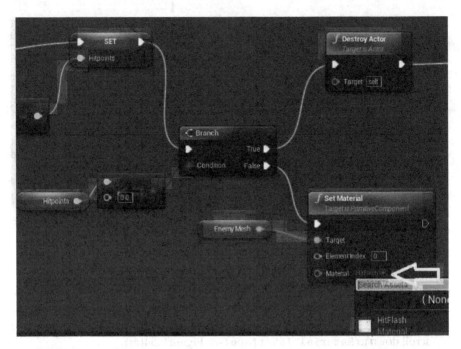

FIGURE 9.55: Switching the Mesh's Material when Hit to Flash Material and Back to Normal.

    f. Go to step (21) and find and apply the material.

22. Now we will implement the network to make the Enemy shine with the Hit Flash when hit, and turn back to its original material after a while (say a quarter of a second).

    a. Go to the event graph of the **Enemy** blueprint.

    b. Find the network we created for the `Enemy Damage Calculation...` in step (12c) on page 567.

    c. Find the **Branch** node. Its `True` channel should be already connected to a **Destroy Actor** node. This is because the branch tests for the Hitpoint of the enemy and if it is 0 or less, it destroys the Enemy.

    d. We will use the `False` channel to perform our `HitFlash` material swap.

    e. Drag a wire from the `False` channel of the **Branch** node and place a **Set Material** node (*you have to turn off the context sensitivity*).

    f. Drop a copy of the **EnemyMesh** variable into the `Target` channel of the **Set Material** node.

    g. Click on the drop-down menu on the `Material` channel of the **Set Material** node and select the **HitFlash** material we created earlier in step 12.

    h. Your network should look like Figure 9.55.

    i. Drag a wire off of the execution channel of the **Set Material** node and search for and place a `Delay` node. Change the `Duration` to 0.25.

    j. Drag a wire off of the execution channel of the **Delay** node and search for and place another `Set Material` on the canvas.

k. Drag the **EnemyMesh** variable onto the `Target` channel and the **MeshMat** variable onto the `Material` channel of the **Set Material** node.

l. Compile and save the **Enemy** blueprint.

m. Your complete enemy damage network with the hit flash material swap should look similar to Figure 9.56.

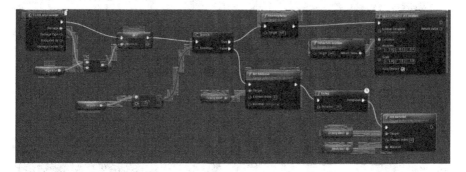

FIGURE 9.56: Complete Enemy's Material Hit Flash Blueprint Network.

IMPLEMENTING HIT FLASH ON PLAYER

Now we will set up the network in blueprints responsible for showing a flash when player is hit by the enemy.

23. Open up the **RotationChar** blueprint.

24. Create a new variable called `PlayerMat` in the **RotationChar** event graph.

25. Change the type of this new variable to `Material Interface`. To do this, you can either click on the drop-down box next to the **Variable Type** and search for `Material Interface` in the search bar, or open the **Object Reference** tab and scroll down to `Material Interface` (see Figure 9.54(a)).

(a)   (b)

FIGURE 9.57: (a) Adding a Material Interface Variable. (b) Assigning Non-Flash (Regular) Material.

26. Click on the **Defaults** section of the **RotationChar** blueprint.

27. Scroll down to the `Default` rollout.

28. Click on the material selector next to the **PlayerMat**.

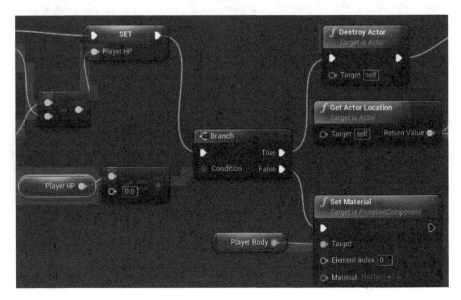

FIGURE 9.58: Switching the Mesh's Material when Hit to Flash Material and Back to Normal.

29. From the drop-down menu select and apply the same material our **RotationChar** class has (see Figure 9.54(b)).
30. Now we will implement the network to make the Player shine with the Hit Flash when hit by enemies, and turn back to its original material after a while (say, a quarter of a second).
    a. Go to the event graph of the **RotationChar** blueprint.
    b. Find the network we created for the Damage Calculation for Player in step (6) on page 570.
    c. Find the **Branch** node. Its **True** channel should be already connected to a **Destroy Actor** node. This is because the branch tests for the Hitpoint of the player and if it is 0 or less, it destroys the Player Character.
    d. We will use the **False** channel to perform our **HitFlash** material swap.
    e. Drag a wire from the **False** channel of the **Branch** node and place a **Set Material** node (*you have to turn off the context sensitivity*).
    f. Drop a copy of the **PlayerBody** variable into the **Target** channel of the **Set Material** node.
    g. Click on the drop-down menu on the **Material** channel of the **Set Material** node and select the **HitFlash** material we created earlier in step 12.
    h. Your network so far should look like Figure 9.58.
    i. Drag a wire off of the execution channel of the **Set Material** node and search for and place a **Delay** node. Change the **Duration** to 0.25.
    j. Drag a wire off of the execution channel of the **Delay** node and search for and place another **Set Material** on the canvas.

k. Drag the **PlayerBody** variable (or the mesh name you created for the body of the player) onto the `Target` channel and the **PlayerMat** variable onto the `Material` channel of the **Set Material** node.

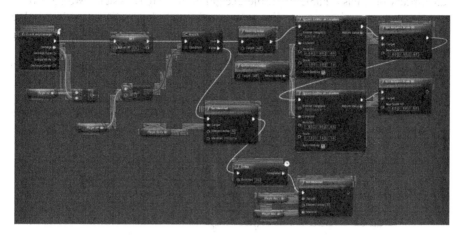

FIGURE 9.59: Complete Player Material Hit Flash Blueprint Network.

31. Compile and save the **RotationChar** blueprint.
32. Your complete player damage network with the hit flash material swap should look similar to Figure 9.59.

What Happened in TUTORIAL 9.15...

This was the last in our series of tutorials to create a top-down space shooter game from scratch. In this tutorial we implemented the final visual effects in which the material of our enemy and player actors would switch to a glowing ember color for a fraction of a second before changing back to the original materials, when the player is hit by the enemy and when the enemy is hit by the projectiles. This will give our actors the look that they are being hit and taking damage.

To achieve this, we utilized material interfaces. A material interface is an object that can contain a material parameter and is exposed in-game at runtime to our blueprint program. We can use these material interfaces to make changes to the materials of a static mesh or any other geometry we reference in the blueprint event graph.

In our player and enemy blueprints we added the change of material logic by setting the materials of our enemy and the player to `Hit Flash` materials when they are hit. We switched the materials back to the normal materials after about a quarter of a second. This creates the bright flashing glow on our player and enemy actors when they are hit and take damage before going back to normal.

9.10 SUMMARY

In this chapter we created a top-down game from scratch. We implemented almost all aspects of a basic game, with the exception of a HUD system. We started by creating our own player controller, game mode, and player character classes. We then implemented our own projectile class for the ammunition our player will use to hit enemies.

We implemented our game over logic and the functionality for our player, projectiles, and enemies to cast and receive damage. We also got experience with setting up a basic AI for our enemy to be able to chase the player in the level.

Finally, we brushed the visual looks of our level by implementing some particle systems based on damage, destruction, and hit events to give nicer visual feedback to the player about the state of the game.

A Material Expressions in Unreal Engine 4

$\mathbf{T}$HIS appendix presents a reference to all material expression nodes available in Unreal Engine 4 [36].

A.1 INTRODUCTION

Material Expressions are the building blocks of materials in Unreal Engine 4. They are the mathematical terms that either provide values or perform certain operations needed in the calculation of the light-material interactions.

A.2 ATMOSPHERE EXPRESSIONS

This category includes expressions that interact with the atmospheric effects at the post-process stage of the pipeline [1].

ATMOSPHERIC FOG COLOR

This Material Expression allows you to query the current color of the level's **Atmospheric Fog**, at any position in World Space. If no World Position is fed into it, then the world position of the pixel in question is used. This is useful when you need Materials to appear to fade into a distant fog color.

In the example below, The Base Color is being set using an Atmospheric Fog node, with the World Position receiving a simple network that queries the location that is always 50,000 units behind the object, relative to the position of the camera.

A.3 COLOR

This category of expressions includes those that interact with the color of input channels by performing certain mapping on them. As of Unreal Engine 4.6, the only expression in this category includes **Desaturation** [5].

DESATURATION

The **Desaturation** expression desaturates its input, or converts the colors of its input into shades of gray, based a certain percentage.

As an example, if the desaturation color input vector is $\mathbf{D}$, the input color is $\mathbf{I}$ and the luminance factor is L, then the output value will be calculated according to the following equations:

$$\mathbf{O} = (1 - \alpha) \times (\mathbf{D} \cdot \mathbf{I}) + \alpha \times \mathbf{I} \tag{A.1}$$

where **O** is the output color vector, · is the dot product, and α is the percentage parameter of the **Desaturation** expression.

- **Properties**
  Luminance Factor: Specifies the amount that each channel contributes to the desaturated color. This is what controls that green is brighter than red which is brighter than blue when desaturated.
  Fraction: Specifies the amount of desaturation to apply to the input. Percent can range from 0.0 (fully desaturated) to 1.0 (full original color, no desaturation).

A.4 CONSTANT EXPRESSIONS

The items in this category represent material expressions whose values don't generally change once set in the editor or when the play begins [7]. These expression includes the following items:

CONSTANT

The Constant expression outputs a single float value. It is one of the most commonly used expressions and can be connected to any input, regardless of the number of channels the input expects. For instance, if you connect a Constant to an input expecting a 3 Vector, the constant value will be used for all 3 elements. When supplying a single number, it can be useful to collapse the node using the small triangle icon in the description area.

- **Properties**
  R: Specifies the float value of the expression output.

Shortcut: To place this expression you may hold the key 1 on your keyboard and left-click in the graph editor.
Example: 0.7, −10, 2.35

CONSTANT2VECTOR

The Constant2Vector expression outputs a two-channel vector value, in other words, two constant numbers.

- **Properties**
  R: Specifies the first float value of the expression output.
  G: Specifies the second float value of the expression output.

Shortcut: To place this expression you may hold the key 2 on your keyboard and left-click in the graph editor.
Example: (0.7, −10) or (2.35, 247)
Usage Example: You may use this expression to modify texture coordinates, since the texture coordinates are 2-dimensional.

CONSTANT3VECTOR

The Constant3Vector expression outputs a three-channel vector value, in other words, three constant numbers. An RGB color can be thought of as a Constant3Vector, where each channel is assigned to a color (red, green, blue).

- **Properties**
  R: Specifies the first float value of the expression output.
  G: Specifies the second float value of the expression output.
  B: Specifies the third float value of the expression output.

Shortcut: To place this expression you may hold the key 3 on your keyboard and left-click in the graph editor.
Example: (0.35, 0.75, 0.75), (0.7, −10, 2.0) or (150, 235, 247)

Constant4Vector

The Constant4Vector expression outputs a four-channel vector value, in other words, four constant numbers. An RGBA color can be thought of as a Constant4Vector, where each channel is assigned to a color (red, green, blue, alpha).

- **Properties**
  R: Specifies the first float value of the expression output.
  G: Specifies the second float value of the expression output.
  B: Specifies the third float value of the expression output.
  A: Specifies the fourth float value of the expression output.

Shortcut: To place this expression you may hold the key 4 on your keyboard and left-click in the graph editor.
Example: (0.35, 0.75, 0.75,0.0), (0.7, −10, 2.0,0.76) or (150, 235, 247, 100)

DISTANCE CULL FADE

The **Distance Cull Fade** expression outputs a scalar value that fades from black to white and can be used to fade an object in once it comes within the cull distance. It should be noted that it does not fade the object out. This expression is quite useful if applied to the **Opacity** channel of the material nodes to make them fade in and out of view when the camera comes within the Cull distance (instead of popping in and out).

Per Instance Fade Amount

The **PerInstance Fade Amount** expression outputs a float value associated with the amount of fade applied to an instanced Static Mesh, such as foliage. It is constant, but can be a different number for each individual instance of a mesh.

Note: This expression works only when it is applied to an InstancedStaticMesh Actor or other Actors that utilize InstanceStaticMeshComponents.

Per Instance Random

The **PerInstance Random** expression outputs a different random float value per Static Mesh instance to which the material is applied. Instanced Static Mesh Component sets a random float for instance, which is exposed so that it can be used for whatever is desired (e.g., random light level behind a window). It is constant, but different, for each instance of the mesh.

The output value will be a whole number between 0 and RAND_MAX for the target platform.

Note: This expression work only when it is applied to an Instanced Static Mesh Actor or other Actors that utilize Instance Static Mesh Components.

TIME

The **Time** expression is used to add the passage of time to a material, such as by applying it to a **Panner**, **Cosine**, or other time-dependent expressions and operations.

- **Properties**
  Ignore Pause: If set to true, this expression will continue to march on even if the game is paused.

Usage Example: You may connect the output channel of the **Time** expression to the input of a **Sine** expression to create dynamic values that range between -1.0 to $+1.0$ in value.

TWO SIDED SIGN

The **Two Sided Sign** expression is useful for flipping the normal on backfaces of two sided custom lighting materials to match the functionality of the Phong shading models. Use the value of $+1$ for frontfaces, -1 for backfaces of a two sided material.

VERTEX COLOR

The **Vertex Color** expression is the access point for the material to the outputs of color modules affecting sprite particle emitters.

- **Properties**
  RGB: Specifies the RGB (3-channel) value of the expression output.
  R: Specifies the red color value of the expression output.
  G: Specifies the green color value of the expression output.
  B: Specifies the blue color value of the expression output.
  A: Specifies the alpha value of the expression output.

Usage Example: Use the RGB and Alpha output channels of this expression to multiply by the RGB and Alpha channels of a **TextureSample** expression to create sprite colors for a particle system.

A.5 COORDINATE EXPRESSIONS

These expressions utilize the 2D or 3D coordinate systems in the World Space or Texture Coordinates to enable interactions between these coordinate spaces and certain aspects of the materials [9].

ACTOR POSITION WS

The **Actor Position WS** expression outputs a 3vector (RGB) data representing the location, in world space, of the object on which this material is applied.

Usage Example: This expression can be used to change the color of a mesh as it moves across the world, or to apply the same material to different parts of the level geometry and have the engine change the color of each part according to its location –i.e., geographically color-coding objects.

CAMERA POSITION WS

The **Camera World Position** expression outputs a three-channel vector value representing the camera's position in world space.

Usage Example: This expression can be used in a network to make the mesh on which the material is applied change color depending on the direction viewed by the camera.

LIGHTMAP UVS

The **Lightmap UVs** expression outputs the lightmap UV texture coordinates in the forum of a two-channel vector value. If lightmap UVs are unavailable, it will output a two-channel vector value of (0,0).

OBJECT ORIENTATION

The **Object Orientation** expression outputs the world-space up vector of the object. In other words, this is the direction the local positive Z-axis of the object, on which the material is applied, is pointing.

Usage Example: This expression can be connected to the color input channels of a material node to change the color of a mesh as it rotates, or to apply the same material to different parts of the level geometry and have the engine change the color of each part according to its up vector (orientation).

OBJECT POSITION WS

The **Object Position WS** expression outputs the world-space center position of the object's bounds. This is useful for creating spherical lighting for foliage, for example.

Usage Example: This expression can be used to change the color of a mesh as it moves across the world, or to apply the same material to different parts of the level geometry and have the engine change the color of each part according to its location –i.e., geographically color-coding objects.

OBJECT RADIUS

The **Object Radius** generates an output value equal to the radius of a given object in Unreal units. Scaling is taken into account and the results can be unique for each individual object.

Usage Example: Connecting a network based on this object to the **Emissive** channel of a material node will make the mesh on which the material is applied brighten up and glow as the mesh gets bigger in size.

PANNER

The **Panner** expression outputs UV texture coordinates that can be used to create panning, or moving, textures. This expression generates UVs that change according to its Time input. The Coordinate input can be used to manipulate (e.g., offset) the UVs of a **Texture Sample** expression.

- **Properties**
  SpeedX: Specifies the speed to pan in the U coordinate direction.
  SpeedY: Specifies the speed to pan in the V coordinate direction.
  Coordinate: Takes the base UV texture coordinates to modify by the expression.
  Time: Takes in the value used to determine the current rotation position.

Usage Example: To move the texture on a surface you usually connect the output of a **Time** expression or a network based on the **Time** Expression to the Time channel of the **Panner** expression. However, you may use a parameter for this input and dynamically control the value of the parameter through Matinee or Blueprint sequences. You then connect the output of this expression to the UVs input channel of a **Texture Sample** expression to move the texture across the surface on which the material will be applied.

PARTICLE POSITION WS

The **Particle Position WS** expression outputs the 3Vector (RGB) data representing each individual particle's position in world space.

PIXEL NORMAL WS

The **Pixel Normal WS** expression outputs vector data representing the direction that pixels are facing based on the current normal.

ROTATOR

This expression creates UV coordinates that are rotated by the speed. The **Rotator** has two input channels: Coordinate and Time, and three properties as described below:

- **Properties**
  CenterX: Specifies the U coordinate to use as the center of rotation.
  CenterY: Specifies the V coordinate to use as the center of rotation.
  Speed: Specifies the speed to rotate the coordinate. Positive values are clockwise and negative values are counter clockwise.
  Coordinate: Takes the base UV texture coordinates to modify by the expression.
  Time: Takes in the value used to determine the current rotation position.

Usage Example: To rotate the texture on a surface you usually connect the output of a **Time** expression or a network based on the **Time** Expression to the Time channel of the **Rotator** expression. However, you may use a parameter for this input and dynamically control the value of the parameter through Matinee or Blueprint sequences. You then connect the output of this expression to the UVs input channel of a **Texture Sample** expression to rotate the texture.

SCREEN TEXEL SIZE

The **Scene Texel Size** expression allows you to offset by texel sizes, as you would when using the **Scene Color** and **Scene Depth** expressions. This is useful for edge detection in multi-resolution systems, because without this calculation you would be forced to use a small static value, resulting in inconsistent results at lower resolutions.

SCREEN POSITION

The **Screen Position** expression outputs the screen-space position of the pixel currently being rendered via its 2-channel vector output.

Usage Example: If you connect the output of this expression to the UVs inputs channel of a **Texture Sample** expression, it will use the screen coordinates of pixels on the mesh to pick the texture values. The resulting imagery is the effect of having the texture fixed, and if the mesh moves, it will move across the texture.

TEXTURE COORDINATE

The **TextureCoordinate** expression outputs the UV texture coordinates in the form of a two-channel vector value. This allows materials to use different UV channels, specify tiling, and otherwise operate on the UVs of a mesh.

- **Properties**
  Coordinate Index: Specifies the UV channel use.
  UTiling: Specifies the amount of tiling in U direction.

VTiling: Specifies the amount of tiling in V direction.

Un-Mirror U: If True, undo the mirroring in the U direction.

Un-Mirror V: If True, undo the mirroring in the V direction.

Usage Example: To access the second UV channel of a mesh, create a **Texture Co-ordinate** expression, set its CoordinateIndex to 1 (0 - first channel, 1 - second channel, etc.), and connect it to the UVs input of a **Texture Sample** expression.

VERTEX NORMAL WS

The **Vertex Normal WS** expression outputs the world space vertex normal. It can only be used in material inputs that are executed in the vertex shader. An example of such material is one that is using its **World Position Offset** channel.

Usage Example: This expression is useful for making a mesh grow or shrink. Simply connect the output of this expression to a **Multiply** expression and feed the results into the **World Position Offset** channel of a material node. *Note that offsetting position along the normal will cause the geometry to split apart along UV seams.*

VIEW SIZE

The **View Size** expression outputs a 2D vector giving the size of the current view in pixels. This is useful for causing various changes in your materials based on the current resolution of the screen.

WORLD POSITION

The **World Position** expression outputs the position of the current pixel in world space. Common uses for this expression are to find the radial distance of a pixel from the camera (as opposed to the orthogonal distance from PixelDepth). To visualize the values of this expression simply plug its output channel into the **Emissive Color** channel of a material node.

Usage Example: World Position expression may be used as a texture coordinate and have unrelated meshes using the texture coordinate match up when they are near each other.

A.6   DEPTH EXPRESSIONS

These expressions utilize the frame buffer to calculate the depth [12]. This depth is then used to create seamless transitions within the scene.

DEPTH FADE

This expression can be used to remove the artifacts that appear as objects intersect each other, especially when translucent objects intersect with opaque objects.

- **Properties**

  Fade Distance Property: World Space distance over which the fade should take place. This is used if the FadeDistance Input is not connected.

  Opacity Input: Takes in the existing opacity for the object prior to the depth fade.

  Fade Distance Input: World Space distance over which the fade should take place.

PIXEL DEPTH

This expression generates as output the distance of each pixel from camera at render-time. This is very useful in generating special effects such as murkiness in the water as the depth increases.

Example Usage: Scene depth can be used in a network if connected to the alpha channel of a **Lerp** expression to interpolate between two colors based on the distance of pixels on the object from the camera to darken long hallways.

SCENE DEPTH

This expression generates as output the existing scene depth. This is similar to **PixelDepth**, except that **PixelDepth** can sample the depth only at the pixel currently being drawn, whereas **SceneDepth** can sample depth at any location.

- **Properties**

  UVs Input: Takes in the UV texture coordinates used to determine how to sample the depth texture.

Example Usage: Scene depth can be used in a network if connected to the alpha channel of a **Lerp** expression to interpolate between two colors based on the distance of all locations in the scene. *Note: Only translucent materials may utilize the **Scene Depth** expression.*

A.7   FONT EXPRESSIONS

The Font category of Material Expressions deals with creating font materials to be displayed using a TextRender component within Unreal Engine 4 [15].

FONT SAMPLE

This expression allows you to sample font textures from a font resource into a two-dimensional texture. The Alpha channel of the font should contain the font outline value. Only valid Font pages are allowed to be specified. This expression has two properties: Font and Font Texture Page:

- **Properties**
    Font: Holds the default font asset (from the Content Browser) to be held within the expression.
    Font Texture Page: The current font texture page to be used as a part of the texture.

FONT SAMPLE PARAMETER

This expression provides a way to create a font-based parameter using a material instance constant. This allows easy switching between different fonts without having to use many different font materials. This expression has four properties:

- **Properties**
    Parameter Name: Specified the name used to identify the parameter in the material instance through code or blueprint sequence.
    Group: Provides a way to organize parameter names into groups, or categories, within a Material Instance Constant. All parameters within a material that have the same Group property name will be listed underneath that category in the instance.
    Font: Hold the default font asset (from the content browser) to be held within the expression.
    Font Texture Page: The current font texture page to be used as a part of the texture.

A.8   FUNCTION

The following material expressions are specifically designed to be used with material functions.

FUNCTION INPUT

This expression can only be placed in a material function, where it defines one of the function's inputs.

- **Properties**
    Input Name: The input's name, which will be displayed on Material Function Call expressions that use the material function containing the input.
    Description: A description of the input, which will be displayed as a tooltip when the connector for this output on a Material Function Call expression is hovered over with the mouse.

Input Type: The type of data this input expects. Data passed to this input will be cast to this type, throwing a compiler error if the cast fails because the data is not compatible.

Preview Value: The value to use as a preview for this input when editing the material function containing it.

Use Preview Value As Default: If enabled, the Preview Value will be used as the default value for this input if no data is passed in.

Set Priority: Specifies the priority for this output to use when determining the order of the outputs to be displayed on a Material Function Call expression.

FUNCTION OUTPUT

This expression can only be placed in a material function, where it defines one of the function's outputs.

- **Properties**
  Output Name: The output's name, which will be displayed on Material Function Call expressions that use the material function containing the output.

  Description: A description of the output, which will be displayed as a tooltip when the connector for this output on a Material Function Call expression is hovered over with the mouse.

  Set Priority: Specifies the priority for this output to use when determining the order of the outputs to be displayed on a Material Function Call expression.

MATERIAL FUNCTION CALL

This expression allows you to use an external **Material Function** from another material or function. The external function's input and output nodes become inputs and outputs of the function call node. If a **Material Function** is selected in the Content Browser when placing one of these expressions, it will automatically be assigned.

- **Properties**
  Material Function: Specifies the Material Function to be used.

Shortcut: To place this expression in the graph editor, hold the F key on your keyboard and left-click on the graph editor.

STATIC BOOL

This expression is used to provide a default bool value for a static bool function input within a function. This node does not switch between anything, so it must be used in conjunction with a StaticSwitch node.

- **Properties**
  Value: The value of the bool, True (checked) or False.

STATIC SWITCH

This expression works like a StaticSwitchParameter, except that it only implements the switch and does not create a parameter.

* **Properties**
  Default Value: The default boolean value of the parameter that determines which input is active, True (checked) or False.
* **Inputs**
  Ture: The input that is used when the Value of the switch is `True`.
  False: The input that is used when the Value of the switch is `False`.
  Value: Takes in a **bool** value that determines which input is active.

TEXTURE OBJECT

This expression is used to provide a default texture for a texture function input within a function. This node does not actually sample the texture, so it must be used in conjunction with a **Texture Sample** expression.

* **Properties**
  Texture: The texture from the Content Browser that will be applied to this node.
  Sampler Type: The type of data that will be output from the node.

A.9 MATERIAL ATTRIBUTES EXPRESSIONS

Material Attribute expressions are ideal for use in Layered Materials [34]. There are two such expressions as of the release of Unreal Engine 4.18: The **Break Material Attributes** and the **Make Material Attributes** expressions.

BREAK MATERIAL ATTRIBUTES

The **Break Material Attributes** expression is ideal when using a Layered Material – a feature of the Material Functions system. When using a Material Layer Function within a Material, you may want to use only one aspect of the layer. For example, you may have a Material Layer that defines a nice looking generic Material, such as steel.

You may want to use only the Roughness and Base Color attributes from that layer in your final Material, rather than using the whole thing. In such cases, you can use a Break Material Attributes node to split up all of the incoming attributes of the Material Layer, and then just plug in the ones you want. This also allows for complex blending of various Material Attributes.

MAKE MATERIAL ATTRIBUTES

The **Make Material Attributes** node does exactly the opposite of the Break Material Attributes node. Instead of splitting attributes apart, this brings them together. This is useful when creating your own Material Layer functions, as you will have access to all of the standard attributes for your output. This can also be used for complex Material setups in which you want to define more than one type of Material and blend them together, all within one Material.

NOTE

In order to have access to a `Material Attributes` channel of a material to connect to a **Make Material Attributes** expression, make sure that the **Use Material Attributes** checkbox is set to *true* in the **Details** rollout of the Material.

A.10 MATH EXPRESSION

Mathematical expressions in Unreal Engine's materials allow us to combine values from other expressions, variables, and objects in the game and create values that are useful for our calculations of all aspects of a material. These expressions are basically mathematical functions – they take some input values and combine these inputs to generate resulting values.

ABS:

This expression takes a value (positive or negative) and drops the sign and returns the absolute value of the input it receives. In mathematical terms, the absolute value of a number x is calculated according to the following equation:

$$\text{ABS}(x) = |x| = \begin{cases} x & x \geq 0 \\ -x & x < 0 \end{cases} \tag{A.2}$$

Examples: **Abs** of –3.4 is 3.4 and **Abs** of 4.32 is 4.32. We write this mathematically as $|-3.4| = 3.4$ and $|4.32| = 4.32$, respectively.

Example Usage: The **Abs** expression is commonly used on the result of a **Dot Product** to take the sign of the value out and use the actual number, regardless of whether it is positive or negative.

ADD:

This expression takes its two input values (A and B) and returns the summation of the two values. The addition operation is performed on a per-channel basis. In other words, if you add to Constant3Vectors, the result will be a Constant3Vector in which the R, G, and B components are the sum of the two input R, G, and B channels, respectively.

Mathematically speaking, Let **X** and **Y** be two N-channel vectors. Then the **Add** expression of these two values will be:

$$\text{ADD}(\mathbf{X}, \mathbf{Y}) = \mathbf{X} + \mathbf{Y} = [x_1 + y_1, x_2 + y_2, \cdots, x_N + y_N] \tag{A.3}$$

• **Properties**

Const A: Take the value to add to. Only used if the A input channel is not connected.

Const B: Take the value to be added to. Only used if the B input channel is not connected.

- **Inputs**

  A: Take the value to add to.

  B: Take the value to be added to.

Example Usage: You can connect the output channels of two **Texture Sample** expressions to the A and B inputs of an **Add** expression to create a combination of the two textures. *Note: If the result of the Add expression on two Texture Samples is used as base color it brightens the material.*

APPEND VECTOR:

This operation, as the name suggests, takes in two inputs and creates a vector from these two inputs by appending the B input channel value to the end of the A input channel value. For example, if you use two Constant expressions c_1 and c_2 and connect them to the A and B input channels of the **Append Vector** expression, the output will be a 2-channel vector with c_1 being the first component, and c_2 being the second component.

- **Inputs**

  A: Take the value to be appended to.

  B: Take the value to be appended.

Example Usage: To create an RGB color from three Constant values r, g, and b you may use two **Append Vector** expressions, connect the r and g to the A, and B, channel of the first expression. Then connect the result of the first expression to the A channel, and the value b to the B channel of the second expression (see Figure 4.49).

CEIL:

This operation, as the name suggests, takes in one input and returns its ceiling value, i.e., rounds the input up to the next integer number. If the input to this expression is a vector, then the expression outputs the ceiling on a per-channel basis.

Example: The ceiling of 3.4 is 4, and the ceiling of 3.9 is also 4.

CLAMP:

This expression takes one input channel and MIN input and one MAX input, and returns a clamped output from the input value. If the input value is less than MIN, the output will return MIN. If the input value is greater than MAX, the output returns MAX. Otherwise, the expression returns the input value unchanged.

Mathematically, let x be the input value, and MAX and MIN be the maximum and minimum clamp input values, the output o will be calculated according to the following equation:

$$\text{CLAMP}(x, MIN, MAX) = \begin{cases} MAX & x \geq MAX \\ x & MIN < x < MAX \\ MIN & x \leq MIN \end{cases} \quad (A.4)$$

- **Properties**

  Clamp Mode: Selects the type of clamp. `CMODE_Clamp` will clamp both ends of the range. `CMODE_ClampMin` and `CMODE_ClampMax` will only clamp their respective ends of the range.

  Min Default: Takes in the value to use as the minimum when clamping. Only used when the Min input is unused.

  Max Default: Takes in the value to use as the maximum when clamping. Only used when the Max input is unused.

- **Inputs**

  Min: Takes in the value to use as the minimum when clamping.

  Max: Takes in the value to use as the maximum when clamping.

Example Usage: When you want to ensure that the result of a calculation never falls outside of a certain range, you can use the minimum and maximum values of the range to ensure your output will always be in range.

COMPONENT MASK:

This expression allows you to select a specific subset of channels (R, G, B, and/or A) from the expression's input to pass through to the expression's outputs. The current channels selected to be passed through are displayed in the title bar of the expression. In case of the expressions that are more than one-dimensional, if the channel is not available an error will occur if you check that channel to be passed through. A description of the properties of a Constant expression are listed below:

- **Properties**

  R: If checked, the Red (or first) component of the vector will be masked and available to pass through from input to output.

  G: If checked, the Green (or second) component of the vector will be masked and available to pass through from input to output.

  B: If checked, the Blue (or third) component of the vector will be masked and available to pass through from input to output.

  A: If checked, the Alpha (or fourth) component of the vector will be masked and available to pass through from input to output.

Example: If you have an RGB Constant3Vector of (1.2, 3.2, 5.3, 1.0) as the input to this expression and check the R, and A boxes, the output will be (1.2, 1.0).

COSINE:

This expression calculates and returns the cosine of its input value. Note that the input value is always in radians (and not in degrees). By connecting the output channel of a **Time** expression to this expression you will be able to create a waveform that oscillates between -1.0 and $+1.0$ over time.

- **Properties**
  Period: Specifies the period of the resulting wave form. Larger values result in slower oscillations while smaller values result in faster oscillations.

Example Usage: To create a pulsating material, connect the **Time** expression to the input of a **Cosine** expression and plug the output channel of the cosine to the `Emissive Color` channel of the material node.

CROSS PRODUCT:

This expression takes two vectors as input and returns a vector that is equal to the cross product of the two input vectors. Mathematically speaking, the cross product will create a vector that is perpendicular to the two input vectors and whose length is proportional to the Sine of the angle between the two input vectors.

Let **X** and **Y** be two vectors. The cross product of these two vectors is calculated according to the following equation:

$$\mathbf{X} \otimes \mathbf{Y} = |\mathbf{X}| \cdot |\mathbf{Y}| \cdot \sin(\theta) \cdot \mathbf{n} \qquad (A.5)$$

where θ is the angle between vectors **X** and **Y**, and **n** be the normal to the plane composed of the two vectors.

- **Inputs**
  A: Takes in a 3-channel vector value as the first vector.
  B: Takes in a 3-channel vector value as the second vector.

Example Usage: Use the cross product of two vectors to find the normal to their plane. In other words, to find a vector that is perpendicular to both.

DIVIDE:

This expression takes its two input values (A and B) and returns the division of the first value by the second value. The division operation is performed on a per-channel basis. In other words, if you add to Constant3Vectors, the result will be a Constant3Vector in which the R, G, and B components are the division of the two input R, G, and B channels, respectively.

Mathematically speaking, Let **X** and **Y** be two N-channel vectors. Then the **Add** expression of these two values will be:

$$\text{DIVIDE}(\mathbf{X}, \mathbf{Y}) = \frac{\mathbf{X}}{\mathbf{Y}} = \left[\frac{x_1}{y_1}, \frac{x_2}{y_2}, \cdots, \frac{x_N}{y_N} \right] \qquad (A.6)$$

- **Properties**
    Const A: Take the value to be divided. Only used if the A input channel is not connected.
    Const B: Take the value to divide by. Only used if the B input channel is not connected.
- **Inputs**
    A: Take the value to be divided, the dividend.
    B: Take the value to divide by, the divisor.

Example Usage: You can connect the output channels of one **Texture Sample** expression to the A and a Constant value to the B input of an **Divide** expression to make the texture look dimmer. *Note: The constant value must be greater than 1.0 to make the texture dimmer. If the constant value is less than 1.0, the texture will look brighter.*

DOT PRODUCT:

This expression takes two vectors as input and returns a scalar value that is equal to the dot product of the two input vectors. Mathematically speaking, the dot product will create a scalar that is proportional Cosine of the angle between the two input vectors.

Let **X** and **Y** be two vectors. The dot product of these two vectors is calculated according to the following equation:

$$\mathbf{X} \odot \mathbf{Y} = |\mathbf{X}| \cdot |\mathbf{Y}| \cdot \cos(\theta) \tag{A.7}$$

where θ is the angle between vectors **X** and **Y**.

- **Inputs**
    A: Takes in a value or vector of any length as the first vector.
    B: Takes in a value or vector of any length as the second vector.

Example Usage: Use the cross product of two vectors to find the angle between them. If the vectors are parallel the value will be close to +1 or −1. If the vectors are perpendicular the value will be 0. Otherwise the value will range between −1 and +1.

FLOOR:

This operation, as the name suggests, takes in one input and returns its floor value, i.e., rounds the input down to the previous integer number. If the input to this expression is a vector, then the expression outputs the floor value on a per-channel basis.

Example: The floor of 3.4 is 3, and the floor of 3.9 is also 3.

Example Usage: You can multiply a vector or constant by some constant K, then take the ceiling of the result and divide it by the same constant K to create bands with varying colors. Similar to what we did for the Ceiling expression on page 184.

FMOD:

This operation, takes in two inputs and returns the floating point reminder of their division. If the input to this expression is a vector, then the expression outputs the floor value on a per-channel basis.

Example: The FMod of 3.4 by 2.3 is 1.1.

FRAC:

This operation, as the name suggests, takes in one input and returns its decimal part, i.e., removes the integer part of the input value. If the input to this expression is a vector, then the expression outputs the floor value on a per-channel basis.

Example: The ceiling of 3.4 is .4, and the ceiling of (3.9, 1.27) is (0.9, 0.27).

IF:

This expression, compares two scalar floating point input values, and three condition values. Then it passes through one of the three values from its input condition channels based on which condition is true on the two input scalar values.

- **Inputs**
  A: Takes in a scalar floating point value as the first input.
  B: Takes in a scalar floating point value as the second input.
  A<B: Takes in a value to output if the A is less than B.
  A=B: Takes in a value to output if the A is equal to B.
  A>B: Takes in a value to output if the A is greater than B.

Example Usage: You can connect a Texture Sample to the A input and a scalar value Th (as the threshold) to the B channel, then connect three different Constant3Vectors to the A<B, A=B, and A>B to create a tri-color map based on the input texture and the threshold value (see Figure 4.51).

LINEAR INTERPOLATE (LERP):

This expression blends between two input value(s) based on a third input value used as a mask. This can be thought of as a mask to define transitions between two textures, like a layer mask in Photoshop.

The intensity of the mask Alpha channel determines the ratio of color to take from the two input values. If Alpha is 0.0/white, the first input is used. If Alpha is 1.0/black, the second input is used. If Alpha is grey (somewhere between 0.0 and 1.0), the output is a blend between the two inputs.

Mathematically speaking, let A be the first input, B be the second input, and $0 \leq \alpha \leq 1$ be the mask input. The output O will be calculated according to the following equation:

$$O = (1 - \alpha) \times A + \alpha \times B \qquad (A.8)$$

Keep in mind that the blend happens per channel. So, if Alpha is an RGB color, Alpha's red channel value defines the blend between A and B's red channels independently of Alpha's green channel, which defines the blend between A and B's green channels.

- **Properties**
  Const A: The value mapped to black (0.0). Only used if the A input is unconnected.
  Const B: The value mapped to white (1.0). Only used if the A input is unconnected.
  Const Alpha: Takes in the value to use as the mask alpha. Only used if the Alpha input is unconnected.
- **Inputs**
  A: Takes in the value(s) mapped to black (0.0).
  B: Takes in the value(s) mapped to white (1.0).
  Alpha: Takes in the value to use as the mask alpha.

Example Usage: You can connect two Constant3Vector RGB colors to the inputs A and B and the alpha channel of a Texture Sample to the Alpha input channel of the Lerp expression to Interpolate the values between two colors. Connecting the output channel of the Lerp to the Base color channel of a material node will have the result shown in color (see Figure 4.52).

MAX:

This expression takes in two inputs and returns the maximum of the two as output.

- **Properties**
  Const A: The first value taken as input. Only used if the A input is unconnected.
  Const B: The second value taken as input. Only used if the A input is unconnected.
- **Inputs**
  A: The first value taken as input.
  B: The second value taken as input.

MIN:

This expression takes in two inputs and returns the maximum of the two as output.

- **Properties**
  Const A: The first value taken as input. Only used if the A input is unconnected.
  Const B: The second value taken as input. Only used if the A input is unconnected.
- **Inputs**
  A: The first value taken as input.
  B: The second value taken as input.

MULTIPLY:

This expression takes its two input values (A and B) and returns the multiplication of the first value by the second value. The multiply operation is performed on a per-channel basis. In other words, if you add to Constant3Vectors, the result will be a Constant3Vector in which the R, G, and B components are the multiplication of the two input R, G, and B channels, respectively.

Mathematically speaking, Let **X** and **Y** be two N-channel vectors. Then the **Multiply** expression of these two values will be:

$$\text{MULTIPLY}(\mathbf{X}, \mathbf{Y}) = [x_1 \times y_1, x_2 \times y_2, \cdots, x_N \times y_N] \tag{A.9}$$

- **Properties**
  Const A: Take the value to be multiplied. Only used if the A input channel is not connected.
  Const B: Take the value to multiply to. Only used if the B input channel is not connected.
- **Inputs**
  A: Take the first value to multiply, multiplicand.
  B: Take the second value to multiply, the multiplier.

Example Usage: You can connect the output channels of two **Texture Sample** expressions to the A and B inputs of a **Multiply** expression to make the texture affect each other. *Note: If the input texture RGB values are less than one, the resulting texture will look much dimmer. You may need to multiply the result by a constant value greater than 1 to compensate.*

NORMALIZE:

This expression performs a very important operation on vectors called normalization. The Normalize expression takes in a vector as input and normalizes it and returns the normalized vector. Mathematically speaking, the normalization operation will make the length of the vector to be equal to unit length (i.e., 1).

Unreal Engine uses L-2 lengths– the square root of the sum of squares of each element in the vector.

Let $\mathbf{X} = [x_1, x_2, \cdots, x_N]$ be an N-dimensional vector, the L-2 norm (or length) of **X** is calculated according to the following equations:

$$|\mathbf{X}| = \sqrt{\sum_{i=1}^{N} x_i^2} \tag{A.10}$$

Then the normalized vector $\hat{\mathbf{X}}$ is calculated by dividing **X** by its L-2 norm:

$$\hat{\mathbf{X}} = \frac{\mathbf{X}}{|\mathbf{X}|} \tag{A.11}$$

Notice that after normalization the length (L-2 norm) of the normalized vector will be equal to 1.

Example Usage: When using the **Cross Product** expression to find the perpendicular vector to a plane of two input vectors, you can normalize the result to get a unit vector. This may be helpful in deciding to apply a World Position Offset with exact measurements.

ONE MINUS

This expression, as the name suggests, takes an input and returns an output value that is exactly equal to 1 minus the input value. Like other basic arithmetic expressions in Unreal Engine 4, this expression performs its operation on a per-channel basis. For example if the input is a 3Vector with R, G, and B values, the output of the **One Minus** will be a 3Vector with values of 1-R, 1-G, and 1-B.

Mathematically, let $\mathbf{X} = [x_1, x_2, \cdots, x_N]$ be an N-dimensional vector. The result of the **One Minus** expression on $\mathbf{X}$ will be:

$$\text{ONEMINUS}(\mathbf{X}) = \mathbf{1} - \mathbf{X} = [1 - x_1, 1 - x_2, \cdots, 1 - x_N] \qquad (A.12)$$

Example: OneMinus value of 0.1 is 0.9 and OneMinus value of (1.3,0.4,–0.7) is (–0.3,0.6,1.7).

Example Usage: You can use this expression to invert the colors of a texture map, much like negative photography (see Figure 4.54).

POWER:

This expression takes two input values, the Base and the Exp. The output will be equal to the Base raised to the Exp power. This operation multiplies the value of Base, Exp times, by itself.

Mathematically, let $\mathbf{X} = [x_1, x_2, \cdots, x_N]$ be an N-dimensional vector and p be a constant. The result of the **Power** expression on $\mathbf{X}$ as Base and p as Exp will be:

$$\text{POWER}(\mathbf{X}, p) = \left[x_1^p, x_2^p, \cdots, x_N^p\right] \qquad (A.13)$$

- **Properties**
  Const Exponent: Takes in the exponent value. Used only if the Exp input is unused.
- **Inputs**
  Base: Takes in the base value.
  Exp: Takes in the exponent value.

Example: Power of 0.1 as base and 2 as exp is 0.01 and Power of (0.9,0.5,0.1) as base and 3 as exp is (0.729,0.125,0.001).

Example Usage: You can use this expression as a kind of contrast adjuster. Looking at the example above, notice that raising 0.9 to the power of 3 still gives a relatively high value of 0.729, while raising a small value of 0.1 to the same power makes it much smaller (0.001). If you feed a black and white texture map as base of the Power expression and an exponent greater than 1, the result will have more contrast (see Figure 4.55). We usually use a Multiply expression after the power to brighten up the texture map.

SINE:

This expression calculates and returns the sine of its input value. Note that the input value is always in radians (and not in degrees). By connecting the output channel of a **Time** expression to this expression you will be able to create a waveform that oscillates between −1.0 and +1.0 over time.

- **Properties**
  Period: Specifies the period of the resulting wave form. Larger values result in slower oscillations while smaller values result in faster oscillations.

Example Usage: To create a pulsating material, connect the **Time** expression to the input of a **Sine** expression and plug the output channel of the Sine to the Emissive Color channel of the material node.

SQUARE ROOT:

This expression takes in one input value and returns the square root of its input value.

SUBTRACT:

This expression takes its two input values (A and B), subtracts the second input (B) from the first input (A) and returns the subtraction value. The Subtract operation is performed on a per-channel basis. In other words, if you Subtract two Constant3Vectors, the result will be a Constant3Vector in which the R, G, and B components are the subtraction of the two input R, G, and B channels, respectively.

Mathematically speaking, Let **X** and **Y** be two N-channel vectors. Then the **Subtract** expression of these two values will be:

$$\text{SUBTRACT}(\mathbf{X}, \mathbf{Y}) = \mathbf{X} - \mathbf{Y} = [x_1 - y_1, x_2 - y_2, \cdots, x_N - y_N] \qquad (A.14)$$

- **Properties**
  Const A: Take the value to subtract from. Only used if the A input channel is not connected.
  Const B: Take the value to be subtracted. Only used if the B input channel is not connected.
- **Inputs**
  A: Take the value to subtract from.
  B: Take the value to be subtracted.

Example Usage: You can connect the output channels of two **Texture Sample** expressions to the A and B inputs of a **Subtract** expression to create a combination of the two textures. *Note: If the result of the Subtract expression on two Texture Samples is used as base color it darkens the material* (see Figure 4.56).

A.11   PARAMETERS EXPRESSIONS

This section presents an overview of Parameter Expressions. These are expressions that can be referenced in Materials, Textures, Blueprints, etc. You can think of these expressions as variables in a programming language. Much like variables, you may use the name of these parameters to reference them and make modifications to their values [42].

COLLECTION PARAMETERS:

This expression is used to act as a reference to access a Parameter Collection Asset. These will be a group of assets that may be reused by many different assets such as materials, blueprints, etc.

You can think of these collections as a generic or bundling of scalar and vector parameters that can be referenced in any material. These collections may be used to get global data and apply them to many materials at once. Moreover, these collections are very handy in driving per-level effects via blueprints, such as moisture amount, damage amount, etc.

DYNAMIC PARAMETER:

This expression gives you a mechanism to pass up to four values in a material used for a particle system. Cascade particle editor will give access to this parameter via the **Parameter Dynamic** module to use these values in an manner in the particle system.

- **Properties**
  Param Names: An array of names to be used as parameters. These values will determine the text on the output of the expression in the Material Editor and will be used to interact with the **Parameter Dynamic** module in the Cascade Particle Editor.
- **Inputs**
  Param1: Outputs the value of the first parameter in the Param Names property. Based on the value in Param Names property the value of this output can change.
  Param2: Outputs the value of the second parameter in the Param Names property. Based on the value in Param Names property the value of this output can change.
  Param3: Outputs the value of the third parameter in the Param Names property. Based on the value in Param Names property the value of this output can change.
  Param4: Outputs the value of the fourth parameter in the Param Names property. Based on the value in Param Names property the value of this output can change.

FONT SAMPLER PARAMETER:

This expression provides a way to expose a font-based parameter in a material instance constant, making it easy to use different fonts in different instances. The alpha channel of the font will contain the font outline value. Only valid font pages are allowed to be specified.

- **Properties**
  Parameter Name: Specifies the name used to identify the parameter in instance of the material and through code.
  Group: Provides a way to organize parameter names into groups, or categories, within a **Material Instance Constant**. All parameters within a material that have the same Group property name will be listed underneath that category in the instance.
  Font: Holds the default font asset (from the Content Browser) to be held within the expression.
  Font Texture Page: The current font texture page to be used as a part of the texture.

SCALAR PARAMETER:

This parameter expression is equivalent to a Constant expression in that it stores a single float value and returns this value. However, like all other parameters in Unreal Engine, it can be referenced and its values changed in an instance of the material at run-time, by level designers, or by the other engine components such as Cascade and Matinee.

- **Properties**
  Parameter Name: Specifies the name used to identify the parameter in instance of the material and through code.
  Group: Provides a way to organize parameter names into groups, or categories, within a `Material Instance Constant`. All parameters within a material that have the same Group property name will be listed underneath that category in the instance.
  Default Value: Specifies the initial value that the parameter takes on.

VECTOR PARAMETER:

This parameter expression is equivalent to a Constant4Vector expression in that it stores a four values (RGBA) and returns these values. However, like all other parameters in Unreal Engine, it can be referenced and its values changed in an instance of the material at run-time, by level designers, or by the other engine components such as Cascade and Matinee.

- **Properties**

Parameter Name: Specifies the name used to identify the parameter in instance of the material and through code.

Group: Provides a way to organize parameter names into groups, or categories, within a `Material Instance Constant`. All parameters within a material that have the same Group property name will be listed underneath that category in the instance.

Default Value R: Specifies the initial value of the first, or red, channel that the parameter takes on.

Default Value G: Specifies the initial value of the second, or green, channel that the parameter takes on.

Default Value B: Specifies the initial value of the third, or blue, channel that the parameter takes on.

Default Value A: Specifies the initial value of the fourth, or alpha, channel that the parameter takes on.

TEXTURE SAMPLE PARAMETER2D:

This parameter expression is equivalent to a Texture Sample expression in that it stores a texture map and returns these values. However, like all other parameters in Unreal Engine, it can be referenced and its values changed in an instance of the material at run-time, by level designers, or by the other engine components such as Cascade and Matinee.

- **Properties**

  Parameter Name: Specifies the name used to identify the parameter in instance of the material and through code.

  Group: Provides a way to organize parameter names into groups, or categories, within a `Material Instance Constant`. All parameters within a material that have the same Group property name will be listed underneath that category in the instance.

  Texture: Specifies the texture sampled by the expression.

  Sampler Type: The type of data that will be sampled and output from the node.

  Mip Value Mode: Applies a noise value to the texture that affects the look and performance.

- **Inputs**

  UVs: Takes in UV texture coordinates to use for the texture. If no values are input to the UVs, the texture coordinates of the mesh the material is applied to are used.

- **Outputs**

  RGB: Outputs the three-channel RGB vector value of the color.

  R: Outputs the red channel value of the color.

  G: Outputs the green channel value of the color.

  B: Outputs the blue channel value of the color.

  A: Outputs the alpha channel vector value of the color.

TEXTURE SAMPLE PARAMETER SUB UV:

This parameter expression is equivalent to a Texture Sample expression in that it stores a texture map and returns these values. However, like all other parameters in Unreal Engine, it can be referenced and its values changed in an instance of the material at run-time, by level designers, or by the other engine components such as Cascade and Matinee.

- **Properties**

  Parameter Name: Specifies the name used to identify the parameter in instance of the material and through code.

  Group: Provides a way to organize parameter names into groups, or categories, within a `Material Instance Constant`. All parameters within a material that have the same Group property name will be listed underneath that category in the instance.

  Blend: Blends together each frame of the SubUV sprite layout, rather than instantly "popping" from one frame to the next.

  Texture: Specifies the texture sampled by the expression.

  Sampler Type: The type of data that will be sampled and output from the node.

  Mip Value Mode: Applies a noise value to the texture that affects the look and performance.

- **Inputs**

  UVs: Takes in UV texture coordinates to use for the texture. If no values are input to the UVs, the texture coordinates of the mesh the material is applied to are used.

- **Outputs**

  RGB: Outputs the three-channel RGB vector value of the color.

  R: Outputs the red channel value of the color.

  G: Outputs the green channel value of the color.

  B: Outputs the blue channel value of the color.

  A: Outputs the alpha channel vector value of the color.

TEXTURE SAMPLE PARAMETER CUBE:

This parameter expression is equivalent to a Texture Sample expression in that it stores a texture map and returns these values except that it only accepts cubemaps. Moreover, like all other parameters in Unreal Engine, it can be referenced and its values changed in an instance of the material at run-time, by level designers, or by the other engine components such as Cascade and Matinee.

- **Properties**

  Parameter Name: Specifies the name used to identify the parameter in instance of the material and through code.

  Group: Provides a way to organize parameter names into groups, or categories, within a `Material Instance Constant`. All parameters within a material that have the same Group property name will be listed underneath that category in the instance.

Blend: Blends together each frame of the SubUV sprite layout, rather than instantly "popping" from one frame to the next.

Texture: Specifies the texture sampled by the expression.

Sampler Type: The type of data that will be sampled and output from the node.

Mip Value Mode: Applies a noise value to the texture that affects the look and performance.

- **Inputs**

  UVs: Takes in UV texture coordinates to use for the texture. If no values are input to the UVs, the texture coordinates of the mesh the material is applied to are used.

- **Outputs**

  RGB: Outputs the three-channel RGB vector value of the color.

  R: Outputs the red channel value of the color.

  G: Outputs the green channel value of the color.

  B: Outputs the blue channel value of the color.

  A: Outputs the alpha channel vector value of the color.

TEXTURE SAMPLE PARAMETER MOVIE:

This parameter expression is equivalent to a Texture Sample expression in that it stores a texture map and returns these values except that it only accepts movie textures. The movie textures must be Bink movies. Moreover, like all other parameters in Unreal Engine, it can be referenced and its values changed in an instance of the material at run-time, by level designers, or by the other engine components such as Cascade and Matinee.

- **Properties**

  Parameter Name: Specifies the name used to identify the parameter in instance of the material and through code.

  Group: Provides a way to organize parameter names into groups, or categories, within a Material Instance Constant. All parameters within a material that have the same Group property name will be listed underneath that category in the instance.

  Blend: Blends together each frame of the SubUV sprite layout, rather than instantly "popping" from one frame to the next.

  Texture: Specifies the texture sampled by the expression.

  Sampler Type: The type of data that will be sampled and output from the node.

  Mip Value Mode: Applies a noise value to the texture that affects the look and performance.

- **Inputs**

  UVs: Takes in UV texture coordinates to use for the texture. If no values are input to the UVs, the texture coordinates of the mesh the material is applied to are used.

- **Outputs**

  RGB: Outputs the three-channel RGB vector value of the color.

R: Outputs the red channel value of the color.
G: Outputs the green channel value of the color.
B: Outputs the blue channel value of the color.
A: Outputs the alpha channel vector value of the color.

A.12 PARTICLES

These expressions act as a bridge between the Material Editor and Cascade Particle System Editor. This link allows for a dynamic interaction between material components and those of per-particle based particle systems. Expressions in this category include Particle Color, Particle Direction, Particle Radius, Particle Size, Dynamic Parameter, Particle MacroUV, and so on [43].

PARTICLE COLOR:

This expression must be a part of the network that is plugged into the appropriate channel (e.g., Emissive Color). The expression creates a link between the Unreal renderer and the particle systems and makes it possible to control any per-particle data within Cascade.

- **Outputs**
  RGBA: Outputs the RGBA vector data.
  R: Outputs the red channel data.
  G: Outputs the green channel data.
  B: Outputs the blue channel data.
  A: Outputs the alpha channel data.

Example Usage: Connecting the RGBA output channel of this expression to the Emissive Color and a network driving from its alpha channel to the opacity channel of a material will expose the color of the material to the particle system. You can then manipulate the color, alpha, color over life, and alpha over life of each particle in an emitter from **Initial Color** and **Color Over Life** modules in the cascade editor (see Figure 5.3).

PARTICLE DIRECTION:

This expression creates a link between the Unreal renderer and the particle systems and makes it possible to control the color of any per-particle data from the location of each particle in the world. This expression must be a part of the network that is plugged into the appropriate material channel (e.g., Emissive Color).

Example Usage: Connecting the RGBA output channel of this expression through a network to the Emissive Color channel of a material will expose the rotation of each particle to the emissive color of the material. You can then manipulate the orientation of each particle in an emitter to change the emissive color of its material (see Figure 5.4).

A.12.1 PARTICLE MACRO UV:

This expression outputs UV texture coordinates that can be used to map any 2D texture onto the entire particle system in a continuous way. This will make the texture appear seamless across particles. The UVs will be centered around the `MacroUVPosition` with the `MacroUVRadius`. The `MacroUVPosition` and the `MacroUVRadius` can be found under the **Macro UV** section of the **Details** rollout of the **Required** emitter module.

The **Particle Macro UV** expression is useful for mapping continuous noise onto particles to break up the pattern introduced by mapping a texture onto each particle with normal texture coordinates. *Note: As of Unreal Engine 4.5, this expression is not compatible with GPU particle systems.*

Example Usage: Create a **Particle Macro UV** expression and connect its output channel to the UVs input channel of a **Texture Sample** expression. Set the texture of this **Texture Sample** expression to the texture you would like to map as the backdrop of your particle effect. Connecting the RGBA output channel of the **Texture Sample** expression to the Emissive Color channel of the material will create the effect shown in Figure 5.5.

PARTICLE MOTION BLUR FADE:

This expression outputs the value of the amount of fade to be applied on a particle (on a per-particle basis) as a result of motion blue. Higher values represent less blur.

PARTICLE WORLD POSITION WS:

This expression exposes each particle's position in the world space coordinate to the material. You may use the output of this expression in a network to drive various aspects of particles' material. *Note: This expression works on a per-particle basis.*

Example Usage: Create a **Particle World Position** expression and connect its output channel to a network that creates a 3Vector representing a color based on the position of each particle in the world space. Connecting the result of this network to the Emissive Color channel of a material node will create particles whose color will change based on their position in the world space as shown in Figure 5.6.

One important note to keep in mind, is that this expression will return the actual world space position of each particle in the material editor. As a result if the emitter is moved in the world, this will impact the position of spawned particles. This should be compensated for in a network within the material editor to avoid undesirable effects.

PARTICLE RADIUS:

This expression exposes each particle's radius to the material. You may use the output of this expression in a network to drive various aspects of particles' material. *Note: This expression works on a per-particle basis.*

Example Usage: Create a **Particle Radius** expression and connect its output channel to an **If** expression to pick between two colors based on the radius of each particle. Connecting the result of this network to the Emissive Color channel of a material node will create particles whose color will change based on their radius as shown in Figure 5.7.

PARTICLE RELATIVE TIME:

This expression exposes each particle's relative time (i.e., a particle's age as a number between 0 and 1) to the material. You may use the output of this expression in a network to drive various aspects of particles' material. *Note: This expression works on a per-particle basis.*

Example Usage: Create a **Particle Relative Time** expression and connect its output channel to the alpha channel of a **Lerp** expression to pick between two colors based on the relative age of each particle. Connecting the result of this network to the Emissive Color channel of a material node will create particles whose color will change as they age (see Figure 5.8).

PARTICLE SIZE:

This expression exposes each particle's X and Y size (i.e., a particle's height and width) to the material. You may use the output of this expression in a network to drive various aspects of particles' material. *Note: This expression works on a per-particle basis.*

Example Usage: Create a **Particle Size** expression and multiply its output channel with an opacity texture and the emissive color network of the material. Connecting the result of this network to the Emissive and Opacity channels of a material node will create particles that will fade as their sizes shrink or get more opaque as well as glow more as their sizes increase (see Figure 5.9).

PARTICLE SPEED:

This expression exposes each particle's speed to the material. You may use the output of this expression in a network to drive various aspects of particles' material. *Note: This expression works on a per-particle basis.*

Example Usage: Use the output channel of a **Particle Speed** to drive the opacity texture or the emissive color networks of a material. Connecting the result of these networks to the Emissive or Opacity channels of a material node will create particles that will fade as they slow down, or get more opaque and glow more as their speeds increase (see Figure 5.10).

SPHERICAL PARTICLE OPACITY:

This expression provides a less expensive mechanism to create opacity masks that would allow a particle to appear spherical.

Example Usage: Use the output channel of a **Particle Speed** to drive the opacity texture or the emissive color networks of a material. Connecting the result of these networks to the Emissive or Opacity channels of a material node will create particles that will fade as they slow down, or get more opaque and glow more as their speeds increase (see Figure 5.10).

- **Inputs**
  Density: A value ranging between 0 and 1 that controls the density of the sphere map. Default value is 1, which results in more opaque particles.

PARTICLE SUB UV:

This expression can be used to render sub-images of a texture map to use in particle systems. Similar to flipbook (one of sprite editing features of the Unreal Engine 4) in that it allows for texture animation manipulation, but it exposes the textures to the Cascade Particle System editor.

- **Properties**
  Blend: Blends together each frame of the SUb UV sprite layout, rather than instantly "popping" from one frame to another.
  Texture: Specifies the texture sampled by the expression.
  Sampler Type: The type of data that will be sampled and output from the node.
  Mip Value Mode: Applies a noise value to the texture that affects the look and performance.
- **Inputs**
  UVs: Takes in UV texture coordinates to use for the texture. If no values are input to the UVs, the texture coordinates of the mesh the material is applied to are used.
- **Outputs**
  RGB: Outputs the three-channel RGB vector value of the color.
  R: Outputs the red channel value of the color.
  G: Outputs the green channel value of the color.
  B: Outputs the blue channel value of the color.
  A: Outputs the alpha channel vector value of the color.

Example Usage: Set the Texture of a **Particle SubUVs** to a texture map with Sub UVs. Use the output channel of this expression to drive the opacity texture or the emissive color networks of a material. Connecting the result of these networks to the Emissive and Opacity channels of a material node will create particles that will use the Sub UVs of the input texture (see Figure 5.11).

A.13   LANDSCAPE

Landscape material expressions are those expressions that allow you to design landscape specific functionalities for the materials to be used as a landscape material. The following list is adapted from the Unreal Engine 4 official online documentation [26].

LANDSCAPE LAYER BLEND:

This expression enables you to blend multiple textures or material networks together to be used as landscape layers. This expression uses an array of objects that store information about each layer. This information includes the layer's name, blend type, preview weight, layer input, and height input.

To add a layer to the array of layers, simply click on the + sign next to **Layers** in the **Details** rollout of this expression.

- **Properties**
  Layers: The list of layers the node contains. Layers can be added by clicking in the + icon.
  Layer Name: The unique name to be used for the layer. The name corresponds to the layer name in the paint mode in the Landscape editing tool.
  Blend Type: The Blend Type of this expression. Specifies which of the `LB_AlphaBlend`, `LB_HeightBlend` or `LB_WeightBlend` to use for blending.
  Preview Weight: This is used as the weight for the layer to preview the blending in the material editor.
  Const Layer Input: This is for using a Const3Vector as the color to be used if you don't want to use a texture map. Useful for debugging purposes.
  Const Height Input: This is to be used as the value for the height if you don't want to use a texture for the heightmap.
- **Inputs**
  Layer <*LayerName*>: Each layer adds an input for the layer to blend together. These inputs will not be available until layers are added in the **Details** rollout of this expression.
  Height <*LayerName*>: This is where you supply a heightmap to blend with. *Note: This input will only be visible on layers that have their Blend Type property set to LB_HeightBlend.*
- **Outputs**
  Output: The result of the blended layers.

NOTE: When using the `LB_HeightBlend` mode for all Landscape layers, there may be unpleasant artifacts such as black spots on the landscape. `LB_HeightBlend` works by modulating the blend factor, for the layer using the specified height value. This occurs when all the layers painted in a particular area simultaneously have a 0 height value. The situation is worse when you are blending a Normal map. If a blending normal map becomes (0,0,0) it will cause rendering problems, as it is an invalid normal. To avoid this problem use `LB_AlphaBlend` for one of the layers in your collection of layers.

LANDSCAPE LAYER COORDS:

This expression enables you to generate coordinates that will be used to map materials to the landscape terrain.

- **Properties**
  Mapping Type: Specifies the orientation to use when mapping the material or network to the landscape.
  Custom UV Type: Specifies the UV coordinates to map on the landscape based on the given property values.
  Mapping Scale: Specifies the uniform scaling to apply to the UV coordinates.
  Mapping Rotation: The rotation (in degrees) to apply to the UV coordinates.
  Mapping Pan U: The offset in U direction to apply to the UV coordinates.
  Mapping Pan V: The offset in V direction to apply to the UV coordinates.
  Output: Outputs the UV coordinates to apply to the texture samples for the landscape materials.

LANDSCAPE LAYER SWITCH:

When a particular material network does not contribute to a region of the landscape you can use this expression to exclude it from the calculations of the landscape material. This will be a mechanism to optimize your material by removing unnecessary calculations – i.e., when a particular layer's weight is negligible.

- **Properties**
  Parameter Name: The unique name to be given to the parameter.
  Preview Used: If checked, will use a preview.
- **Inputs**
  Layer Used: The result to use when the layer specified in the expression's properties is in use by the region in the landscape.
  Layer Not Used: The result to use when the layer is not used by the current region of the landscape and has a weight of 0.
- **Outputs**
  Output: Outputs either Layer Used or Layer Not Used, depending on the contribution to the particular region of the landscape.

LANDSCAPE LAYER WEIGHT:

This expression allows material networks to be blended based on the weight for the associated layer from the landscape on which the material is going to be applied.

- **Properties**
  Parameter Name: The unique name of the layer belonging to the landscape to be associated to this parameter. The weight for this layer is used as the alpha value for blending the two input networks.
  Preview Weight: The weight to use for previewing in the material editor.

Const Base: A base color for the landscape.
- **Inputs**
  Base: The network to blend this layer with. This is generally the result of any previous layer blending, but can be empty if this is the first layer.
  Layer: The network to blend together to create this layer.
- **Outputs**
  Output: Outputs the result of the blending between base and layer inputs based on the layer weight of the layers involved.

LANDSCAPE VISIBILITY MASK:

To create wholes in a landscape (e.g., creating cave openings), you can use this expression to remove the visibility of parts of the landscape.

- **Outputs**
  Output: Outputs the visibility mask properties.

To activate this expression, connect its sole output to the **Opacity Mask** channel of the material node and choose the Blend Mode of your material (in its **Details** rollout) to **Masked**.

A.14   TEXTURE

These expressions allow you to read a texture map or other bitmaps and use their values according to UV texture coordinates to wrap the material on a 3D piece of geometry [48].

FONT SAMPLE:

This expression allows you to sample the texture pages from a font resource as regular 2D textures. The alpha channel of the font will contain the font outline value. Only valid font pages are allowed to be specified.

- **Properties**
  Font: This property holds the font asset from the **Content Browser**.
  Font Texture Page: This property holds the current font texture page to be used as a part of the texture.

FONT SAMPLER PARAMETER:

This expression provides a way to expose a font-based parameter in a material instance constant, making it easy to use different fonts in different instances. The alpha channel of the font will contain the font outline value. Only valid font pages are allowed to be specified.

- **Properties**

Parameter Name: Specifies the name used to identify the parameter in instance of the material and through code.

Group: Provides a way to organize parameter names into groups, or categories, within a **Material Instance Constant**. All parameters within a material that have the same Group property name will be listed underneath that category in the instance.

Font: Holds the default font asset (from the Content Browser) to be held within the expression.

Font Texture Page: The current font texture page to be used as a part of the texture.

SCENE COLOR:

This expression outputs the existing scene color.

- **Inputs**
  Offset Fraction: This input takes a 2D vector to offset the scene color in screen space.

SPRITE TEXTURE SAMPLE:

This expression automatically pipes a rendered sprite's texture into a Texture Parameter called `Sprite Texture` in the material. Useful for working with sprites in Paper 2D. Sprite instances pass their color as a vertex color.

- **Properties**
  Texture: Specifies the texture sampled by the expression.
  Sampler Type: This is the type of data to be sampled from the node.
  Mip Value Mode: Applies a noise value to the texture.
- **Inputs**
  UVs: This input takes a UV Texture Coordinate to use for the texture.
- **Outputs**
  RGB: Outputs the three-channel RGB vector value of the color.
  R: Outputs the red channel of the color.
  G: Outputs the green channel of the color.
  B: Outputs the blue channel of the color.
  A: Outputs the Alpha channel of the color.

TEXTURE OBJECT:

This expression is used to provide a default texture for a texture function input within a function. This node does not actually sample the texture, so it must be used in conjunction with a **Texture Sample** expression.

- **Properties**
  Texture: Specifies the texture sampled by the expression.
  Sampler Type: This is the type of data to be sampled from the node.

TEXTURE SAMPLE:

This expression outputs the color value(s) from a texture. This texture can be a regular Texture2D (including normal maps), a cubemap, or a movie texture.

- **Properties**
  Texture: Specifies the texture sampled by the expression. To select a texture, you might first **Left-Click** on it in the **Content Browser**. When the texture is selected in the **Content Browser**, click on the **Left Arrow** in the **Details** rollout of this expression in the **Material Editor** to apply the texture.
  Sampler Type: This is the type of data to be sampled from the expression.
  Mip Value Mode: Applies a noise value to the texture.
- **Inputs**
  UVs: This input takes a UV Texture Coordinate to use for the texture.
- **Outputs**
  RGB: Outputs the three-channel RGB vector value of the color.
  R: Outputs the red channel of the color.
  G: Outputs the green channel of the color.
  B: Outputs the blue channel of the color.
  A: Outputs the Alpha channel of the color.

A.15 UTILITY

These expressions allow you to perform some utility functions in Unreal Engine in support of material and rendering functionalities. The following is adapted based on a comprehensive list of these functions, found online at Unreal Engine Documentation Pages [51].

BLACK BODY:

This expression simulates the effects of black body radiation in a material. The user may provide input parameter temperature in Kelvin and connect the resulting outputs to the **Base Color** and **Emissive Color** channels of the material node for physically accurate results.

Example Usage: You can connect the **Temp** input channel of this expression to a network that statically or dynamically derives the temperature in kelvin of a material (such as lava, stars, etc.). Feed the output result of this expression to the **Base Color** and the **Emissive Color** channels of the material to achieve physically realistic results. Figure 4.74 shows a network that moves noise texture coordinates, while the noise texture samples temperatures range between 500°K (cold) and 5000°K (hot) on a surface of a radiating object.

BUMP OFFSET:

This expression is the Unreal Engine 4 term for what is commonly known as parallax mapping. The **Bump Offset** expression allows a material to give the illusion of depth without the need for additional geometry. Materials with bump offset use a grayscale heightmap to give depth information. The brighter the value in the heightmap, the more popped out the material will be; these areas will parallax (shift) as a camera moves across the surface. Darker areas in the heightmap are further away and will shift the least.

- **Properties**

   Height Ratio: Multiplier for the depth taken from the `heightmap`. The larger the value, the more extreme the depth will be. Typical values range from 0.02 to 0.1.

   Reference Plane: This value specifies the approximate height in texture space to apply the effect. A value of 0 will appear to distort the texture completely off the surface, whereas a value of 0.5 (the default) means that some of the surface will pop off while some areas will be sunken in.

- **Inputs**

   Coordinates: This input takes in base texture coordinates to be modified by the expression.

   Height: This input takes in the texture (or a value) to be used as the heightmap.

   Height Ratio Input: This input is the multiplier for the depth taken from the heightmap. The larger the value, the more extreme the depth will be. Typical values range from 0.02 to 0.1. If used, this input supersedes any value in the Height Ratio property.

CONSTANT BIAS SCALE:

This expression takes an input value, adds a bias value to it, and then multiplies it by a scaling factor outputting the result. So for example, to convert input data from [−1,1] to [0,1] you would use a bias of 1.0 and a scale of 0.5.

- **Properties**

   Bias: This value specifies the bias to be added to the input.

   Scale: This value specifies the multiplier for the bias result.

DDX AND DDY:

The DDX expression exposes DDX derivative calculation, a GPU hardware feature used in pixel shader calculation.

   The DDY expression exposes DDY derivative calculation, a GPU hardware feature used in pixel shader calculation.

DEPTH FADE:

This expression is used to hide unsightly seams that appear when translucent objects intersect with opaque ones.

- **Properties**
  Fade Distance: This value is the world space distance over which the fade should take place. This is used if the **Fade Distance** input is unconnected.
- **Inputs**
  Opacity: This input takes in the existing opacity for the object prior to the depth fade.
  Fade Distance: This input takes in the world space distance over which the fade should take place.

DEPTH OF FIELD FUNCTION:

This expression is designed to give artists control over what happens to a Material when it is being blurred by Depth of Field. It outputs a value between 0 and 1 such that 0 represents "in focus" and 1 represents "completely blurred." This is useful for interpolating between sharp and blurry versions of a texture, for instance. The Depth input allows for the existing results from the scene's Depth of Field calculations to be overridden by other calculations.

DESATURATION:

This expression converts the colors of its input to softer shades based on a certain percentage. Let X be the original color, L be the Luminance Factor and f be the Fraction value, then the desaturated color D will be calculated according to the following equation:

$$D = (1 - f) \times (X \odot L) + f \times X \qquad (A.15)$$

- **Properties**
  Luminance Factors: This property specifies the amount of each channel's contribution to the desaturated color.
- **Inputs**
  Fraction: This input value specifies the amount of desaturation to apply to the input color, or texture. An amount of 0 is used for no desaturation (full original color), or an amount of 1 is used for full desaturation (no colors, only grayscale).

Example Usage: Use this expression to soften the colors of high contrast colored textures. You can control how much of the red, green, or blue colors of the original texture to keep based on the Luminance Factor you can specify. Figure 4.76(a) shows an original texture applied to the Base Color and the Emissive Color channels of a material. Figure 4.76(b) shows the same texture applied to the Base Color and Emissive Color channels after being desaturated with the Luminance Factor of (R:0.33, G:0.51, B:0.11) and 20% Fraction.

DISTANCE:

This expression calculates the Euclidean distance between two vectors. These vectors could represent colors, positions, etc. The expression can take on vectors with any number of dimensions.

- **Inputs**
  A: The first input vector of any dimension.
  B: The second input vector of any dimension.

FEATURE LEVEL SWITCH:

This expression is useful to allow you to create different networks with varying levels of complexity to target for different platforms. For example, you might create a material with complex mathematics and many textures to target for high-end consoles, but simpler texture and math to target mobile devices.

- **Inputs**
  Default: The default feature level.
  ES2: Feature Level defined for core capabilities of OpenGL ES2.
  ES3.1: Feature Level defined for core capabilities of Metal-Level devices (OpenGL ES3.1).
  SM4: Feature Level defined for core capabilities of DirectX 10 Shader Model 4.
  SM5: Feature Level defined for core capabilities of DirectX 11 Shader Model 5.

FRESNEL:

This expression calculates the amount of fall off based on the dot product of the surface normal and the viewer vector. In other words, if the viewer is directly looking at a surface the output value is 0. When the viewer is looking at the surface perpendicularly, the Fresnel will output a value of 1. The result of this expression is clamped to [0,1]. Mathematically, let $\mathbf{N}$ be the surface normal, $\mathbf{V}$ be the camera vector, and p be the exponent value, the **Fresnel** output is calculated according to the following equation:

$$\text{FRES}(\mathbf{N}, \mathbf{V}, p) = (1 - \mathbf{N} \odot \mathbf{V})^p \tag{A.16}$$

In UE4, the **Fresnel** expression also takes into account a `Base Reflection Fraction` value, b. This value augments the result of the Normal and Camera vector dot product to account for the fraction of the light specular reflection on the surface. A value of 0 for b is equivalent to the above equation, while a value of 1 for `Base Reflection Fraction` disables the **Fresnel**. The complete equation for the **Fresnel** expression is as follows:

$$\text{FRES}(\mathbf{N}, \mathbf{V}, p, b) = [1 - ((1 - b) \times (\mathbf{N} \odot \mathbf{V}))]^p \tag{A.17}$$

- **Properties**

Exponent: This property specifies how quickly the results fall off. The value p in equations (A.16) and (A.17). Larger values make the result fall off more quickly and have tighter boundaries.

Base Reflection Fraction: This property specifies the amount of specular reflection if viewed straight on. A value of 1 disables the **Fresnel** expression.

- **Inputs**
  Exponent In: This input specifies the fall of values. It will replace the `Exponent` property if connected.

  Base Reflection Fraction: This input specifies the fraction of specular reflection if viewed straight on. It will replace the `Base Reflection Fraction` property if connected.

  Normal: This input takes in a 3-D vector as the Surface Normal. If you have used a normal map in the material, you can connect this input to a **Vertex Normal WS** expression to account for the normal map of the object. If this input is not connected, the engine will use the Tangent normal of the mesh.

Example Usage: Use this expression to simulate proper and physically accurate reflection/refraction of reflective and translucent objects. This expression is widely used to simulate water, glass, and other reflective and refractive surfaces. Figure 4.77(a) and Figure 4.77(b) show two materials with a Fresnel expression with exponent values of 1 and 5, respectively, controlling the `Emissive Color` and `Opacity` channels. Figure 4.77(c) shows the network.

GI REPLACE

This expression allows artists to specify a different, usually simpler, expression chain when the material is being used for Global Illumination.

- **Inputs**
  Default: The default GI.
  Static Indirect: This input is used for baked indirect lighting.
  Dynamic Indirect: This input is used for dynamic indirect lighting.

LIGHTMASS REPLACE

This expression simply passes through the Realtime input when compiling the material for normal rendering purposes, and passes through the Lightmass input when exporting the material to Lightmass for global illumination. This is useful to workaround material expressions that the exported version cannot handle correctly, for example `World Position`.

- **Inputs**
  Realtime: This input takes in the value(s) to pass through for normal rendering.
  Lightmass: This input takes in the value(s) to pass through when exporting the material to Lightmass.

NOISE:

This expression creates a procedural noise field. With the many properties of this expression you can control how the noise field is generated to suit your application.

- **Properties**
  Scale: This property controls the overall size of the noise cells. Lower numbers make the noise larger.
  Quality: This property controls the tradeoff between quality and performance. A value of 0 is fast, but with lower quality.
  Function: This property controls the type of noise. There are three options: `Simplex`, `Perlin`, and `Gradient`.
  Turbulence: This property controls whether to calculate multiple levels of noise in iterations.
  Levels: This property specifies the different levels of noise to combine. Used when Turbulence is checked.
  Output Min: The minimum value of noise output.
  Output Max: The maximum value of noise output.
  Level Scale: This property controls the scale of individual levels when Turbulence is active and checked.
- **Inputs**
  Position: This input controls the adjustment of the texture size with a 3D vector.
  Filter Width: This input controls how much blur to be applied to the noise texture.

Example Usage: You can connect this expression to a texture or color to add some randomness to the look of your material (see Figure 4.78).

QUALITY SWITCH:

This expression allows you to control the quality of the material based on the engine quality settings. You can connect different expression networks when working with different quality levels.

- **Inputs**
  Default: This input is used with the material networks designed for the default visual quality.
  Low: This input is used with the material networks designed for the lower visual quality.
  High: This input is used with the material networks designed for the higher visual quality.

Example Usage: You can connect this expression to a texture or color to add some randomness to the look of your material (see Figure 4.78).

ROTATE ABOUT AXIS:

This expression rotates a three-channel vector input about a given rotation axis and a pivot point. It is very helpful for animating objects using the **World Position Offset** channel of the material node.

- **Inputs**
  Normalized Rotation Axis: This input is the normalized rotation vector about which to rotate the object.
  Rotation Angle: This input is the angle of rotation. 1 equals full 360° rotation.
  Pivot Point: This is the three channel vector used as the pivot point for rotation.
  Position: This is a 3D vector representing the position of the object. The **Absolute World Position** expression is automatically created to be connected to this expression to calculate the location of the object to be rotated.

Example Usage: You can connect this expression to the `World Position Offset` channel of the material node to rotate the object on which the material is applied.

SPHERE MASK:

This expression outputs a mask value based on a distance calculation. If one input is the position of a point and the other input is the center of a sphere with some radius, the mask value is 0 outside and 1 inside with some transition area. This works on one, two, three, and four component vectors.

- **Properties**
  Attenuation Radius: This value specifies the radius for the distance calculation.
  Hardness Percent: This value specifies the transition area size.
- **Inputs**
  A: This input takes in the position of the point to check.
  B: This input takes in the center of the sphere.

Example Usage: You can connect this expression to control the opacity channel of a material, when the object becomes farther than a certain distance from the camera, it will fade away and finally disappear (see Figure 4.79).

ANTIALIASED TEXTURE MASK:

This expression allows you to create a material using a soft (anti-aliased) transition mask. The mask can be used to blend between two complex material properties or to fade out alpha blended materials (works well with SoftMasked). This expression is a parameter, allowing the Texture property to be overridden by child `Material Instances`.

- **Properties**
  Threshold: This value specifies the cutoff point: values less than threshold become black, and those larger than threshold become white.

Channel: This value specifies the texture channel to use as mask.

Texture: This value specifies the texture mask to use.

- **Inputs**

  UVs: This input takes in the texture coordinates to apply to the texture mask.

A.16 VECTOR OPERATIONS

These expressions perform certain operations on vectors [52]. We have already covered most of these expressions in the above sections. Below is a list of the vector expressions we haven't covered so far.

TRANSFORM:

This expression converts a three-channel vector value from one reference coordinate system to another.

By default, all shader calculations in a material are done in tangent space. The vector constants, camera vector, light vector, etc., are all transformed to tangent space before being used in a material. The Transform expression allows these vectors to be transformed from tangent space to world-space, local-space, or view-space coordinate systems. In addition, it allows world-space and local-space vectors to be transformed to any of the other reference coordinate systems.

- **Properties**

  Source: This value specifies the current coordinate system to transform the vector from.

  Destination: This value specifies the coordinate system to transform the vector to.

The Transform node accounts for mirrored UVs, thus allowing, for example, highlights that only affect the right edge of a character.

Example Usage: The **Transform** expression is useful for generating world space normals for sampling a cubemap. A normal map can be transformed to world space and then supplied to the UVs coordinate inputs of a cubemap.

A.17 VECTOR EXPRESSIONS

These expressions are all in the form of Vectors (multidimensional entities in Unreal Engine 4). We have covered some of these expressions above.

The **Vector** expressions not covered so far include the following:

CAMERA VECTOR:

This expression outputs a three-channel vector value representing the direction of the camera with respect to the surface, in other words, the direction from the pixel to the camera. We can think of this vector as the Viewer vector as well.

Example Usage: Camera Vector is often used to fake environment maps by connecting the **Camera Vector** to a **Component Mask** and use the x and y channels of the **Camera Vector** as texture coordinates.

OBJECT BOUNDS:

This expression outputs the size of the object in each axis.

Example Usage: You can use the X, Y, and Z values of this expression as the R, G, and B colors of an object to change its color based on its size and shape.

REFLECTION VECTOR:

This expression outputs a three-channel vector value representing the direction of the reflection with respect to the surface.

Example Usage: Much like **Camera Vector**, the **Reflection Vector** is often used to fake environment maps by connecting the **Camera Vector** to a **Component Mask** and uses the x and y channels of the **Reflection Vector** as texture coordinates.

B Distributions in Unreal Engine 4

THE contents of this appendix are adapted from the Unreal Engine 4's official documentations [13].

B.1 INTRODUCTION

In Unreal Engine, a distribution is a group of data types that allow you to create several numerical objects such as constants, random numbers, interpolated values, etc. There are several distribution types that can be assigned to a component that support a distribution. For example, most particle properties such as `Particle Color, Color Over Life`, etc., employ `Float` or `Vector` distribution types. Each distribution type gives you a number of options to control the details of its values.

B.2 FLOAT DISTRIBUTIONS

These distributions are used when you need a scalar value property. For example, you may use a float distribution to control the lifetime of a particle. The Float Distributions may be further selected to be one of the following types:

B.2.1 DISTRIBUTIONFLOATCONSTANT

This type of distribution creates only one float value as the property and keeps it constant. For example the value of 3.1415 would be the value that may be contained in a `DistributionFloatConstant` type. This type has the following properties that can be edited from the Details Panel [13].

- **Property**
  Constant: This is a static constant number assigned to the property.

B.2.2 DISTRIBUTIONFLOATUNIFORM

This type of distribution creates a value randomly selected from a range between a minimum value and a maximum value. This type has the following properties that can be edited from the Details Panel [13].

- **Property**
  Min: The minimum value for the random number
  Max: The maximum value for the random number

B.2.3   DISTRIBUTIONFLOATCONSTANTCURVE

This type of distribution creates a value that may change over time. The changes in the value of this type may be defined and controlled within the **Curve Editor**. This type has the following properties that can be edited from the Details Panel [13].

- **Property**
  Points: This is an array property that contains all the points in your curve. You may create points here using the `Add Point` button ▛. However, it will generally be easier and more intuitive to add points in the graph editor.
- **Points Properties**
  In Val: This is the location of the point along the graph's horizontal axis, generally calculated as time.
  Out Val: This is the location of the point along the graph's vertical axis, generally calculated as property value.
  Arrive Tangent: Provides the angle of the incoming tangent for the point. Useful values range from about −150 to 150.
  Leave Tangent: Provides the angle of the outgoing tangent for the point. Useful values range from about −150 to 150.
  InterpMode: Allows the user to choose between a variety of interpolation modes for the curve.

B.2.4   DISTRIBUTIONFLOATUNIFORMCURVE

This type of distribution creates a value that may change over time and that is generated from two curves, a min curve and a max curve. As such, this distribution type takes in a min curve and a max curve, both similar to a `DistributionFloatConstantCurve`. The value is then selected along the timeline of the distribution from values between the minimum and maximum curves. This type has the following properties that can be edited from the Details Panel [13].

- **Property**
  Points: This is an array property that contains all the points in your curve. You may create points here using the `Add Point` button ▛. However, it will generally be easier and more intuitive to add points in the graph editor.
- **Points Properties**
  In Val: This is the location of the point along the graph's horizontal axis, generally calculated as time.
  Out Val: This is the location of the point along the graph's vertical axis, generally calculated as property value. In the case of a **Uniform Curve**, this property will contain an **X** and a **Y** value representing the `Min` and `Max` of the output, respectively.
  Arrive Tangent: Provides the angle of the incoming tangent for the point. Useful values range from about −150 to 150.

Leave Tangent: Provides the angle of the outgoing tangent for the point. Useful values range from about −150 to 150.

InterpMode: Allows the user to choose between a variety of interpolation modes for the curve.

B.2.5   DISTRIBUTIONFLOATPARTICLEPARAM

This type is used to allow for simple game-code setting of parameters for emitters, so that they can be manipulated via code, Blueprints, or Matinee. It provides the ability to map input values from one range to another, allowing for tweaking of the parameter in Cascade-space without requiring game-play code to be updated. Once an established Input range is determined by the game-play coder, the artist is free to adjust the property through the Output mapping [13].

- **Properties**

    Parameter Name: This is the name by which the parameter will be referenced in code or in Blueprints scripting.

    Min Input: This is the minimum value that can be passed into the distribution, typically via game code.

    Max Input: This is the maximum value that can be passed into the distribution, typically via game code.

    Min Output: This is the minimum value that can be output into Cascade, as mapped from the range of inputs.

    Max Output: This is the maximum value that can be output into Cascade, as mapped from the range of inputs.

    ParamMode: This controls how the input values will be used. See the Param Mode Flag table below.

    Constant: This provides a default value for the system in the absence of any inputs.

- **ParamMode Flag**

    DPM_Normal: Leave the input value alone.

    DPM_Abs: Use the absolute value of the input before remapping.

    DPM_Direct: Use the input value directly without remapping.

B.3   VECTOR DISTRIBUTIONS

These distributions are used when you need a vector value property. For example, you may use a vector distribution to control the velocity or color of a particle. The Vector Distributions may be further selected to be one of the following types:

B.3.1 DISTRIBUTIONVECTORCONSTANT

This type of the vector distribution is used to generate a constant vector. This type has the following properties that can be edited from the Details Panel [13].

- **Property**
  Constant: This is the static number (in vector domain) that is generated. The vector will contain an **X**, a **Y**, and a **Z** value.
  Locked Axes: This locks one of the three axes to another one.
- **Locked Axes Flags**
  EDVLF_None: No axes are locked.
  EDVLF_XY: The Y-axis is locked to the X-axis value.
  EDVLF_XZ: The Z-axis is locked to the X-axis value.
  EDVLF_YZ: The Z-axis is locked to the Y-axis value.
  EDVLF_XYZ: The Y-axis and Z-axis are locked to the X-axis value.

B.3.2   DISTRIBUTIONVECTORUNIFORM

These distributions are used when you need a vector value property to be selected randomly from a minimum and maximum range. This type has the following properties that can be edited from the Details Panel [13].

- **Property**

  Min: The minimum value for the random calculation. In the case of a Vector Uniform, this will contain values for X, Y, and Z.

  Max: The maximum value for the random calculation. In the case of a Vector Uniform, this will contain values for X, Y, and Z.

  Use Extremes: Indicates that the values for Min and Max should be used as well, rather than just the values between them.
- **Locked Axes Flags**

  EDVLF_None: No axes are locked.

  EDVLF_XY: The Y-axis is locked to the X-axis value.

  EDVLF_XZ: The Z-axis is locked to the X-axis value.

  EDVLF_YZ: The Z-axis is locked to the Y-axis value.

  EDVLF_XYZ: The Y-axis and Z-axis are locked to the X-axis value.
- MirrorFlags

  EDVMF_None: Use the Max value for Min as well.

  EDVMF_Different: Use each value as set.

  EDVMF_Mirror: The Min value will be the inverse of the Max (Max * −1).

B.3.3   DISTRIBUTIONVECTORCONSTANTCURVE

These distributions are used when you need the vector value property to follow a timeline. This type has the following properties that can be edited from the Details Panel [13].

- **Property**

  Points: This is an array property that contains all the points in your curve. You may create points here using the **Add Point** button ▣. However, it will generally be easier and more intuitive to add points in the graph editor.
- **Points Properties**

  In Val: This is the location of the point along the graph's horizontal axis, generally calculated as time.

  Out Val: This is the location of the point along the graph's vertical axis, generally calculated as property value.

  Arrive Tangent: Provides the angle of the incoming tangent for the point. Useful values range from about −150 to 150.

  Leave Tangent: Provides the angle of the outgoing tangent for the point. Useful values range from about -s-150 to 150.

    InterpMode: Allows the user to choose between a variety of interpolation modes for the curve.
- **Locked Axes Flags**
    EDVLF_None: No axes are locked.
    EDVLF_XY: The Y-axis is locked to the X-axis value.
    EDVLF_XZ: The Z-axis is locked to the X-axis value.
    EDVLF_YZ: The Z-axis is locked to the Y-axis value.
    EDVLF_XYZ: The Y-axis and Z-axis are locked to the X-axis value.

B.3.4   DISTRIBUTIONVECTORUNIFORMCURVE

This type of distribution creates a vector that may change over time and that is generated from two curves, a min curve and a max curve. As such, this distribution type takes in a min vector curve and a max vector curve, both similar to a `DistributionVectorConstantCurve`. The vector is then selected along the timeline of the distribution from values between the minimum and maximum curves. This type has the following properties that can be edited from the Details Panel [13].

- **Property**
    Points: This is an array property that contains all the points in your curve. You may create points here using the **Add Point** button ⊞. However, it will generally be easier and more intuitive to add points in the graph editor.
- **Points Properties**
    In Val: This is the location of the point along the graph's horizontal axis, generally calculated as time.
    Out Val: This is the location of the point along the graph's vertical axis, generally calculated as property value. In the case of a **Vector Uniform Curve**, this property will contain a **V1** and **V2** value representing the **Min** and **Max** of the output, respectively. Each of those values will contain values for the X, Y, and Z axes.
    Arrive Tangent: Provides the angle of the outgoing tangent for the points for both X and Y (min and max). Useful values range from about −150 to 150. In the case of a **Vector Uniform Curve**, this property will contain a **V1** and **V2** value representing the Min and Max of the output, respectively. Each of those values will contain values for the X, Y, and Z axes.
    Leave Tangent: Provides the angle of the outgoing tangent for the point. Useful values range from about −150 to 150.
    InterpMode: Allows the user to choose between a variety of interpolation modes for the curve.
    Use Extremes: Indicates that the values for Min and Max should be used as well, rather than just the values between them.
- **Locked Axes Flags**
    EDVLF_None: No axes are locked.

EDVLF_XY: The Y-axis is locked to the X-axis value.
EDVLF_XZ: The Z-axis is locked to the X-axis value.
EDVLF_YZ: The Z-axis is locked to the Y-axis value.
EDVLF_XYZ: The Y-axis and Z-axis are locked to the X-axis value.

B.3.5   DISTRIBUTIONVECTORPARTICLEPARAM

This type is the vector equivalent of the **FloatParticleParam** type discussed above. It allows a value to be manipulated via code, Blueprints, or Matinee [13].

- **Properties**
    Parameter Name: This is the name by which the parameter will be referenced in code or in Blueprints scripting.
    Min Input: This is the minimum value that can be passed into the distribution, typically via game code.
    Max Input: This is the maximum value that can be passed into the distribution, typically via game code.
    Min Output: This is the minimum value that can be output into Cascade, as mapped from the range of inputs.
    Max Output: This is the maximum value that can be output into Cascade, as mapped from the range of inputs.
    ParamMode: This controls how the input values will be used. See the Param Mode Flag table below.
    Constant: This provides a default value for the system in the absence of any inputs.
- **Locked Axes Flags**
    EDVLF_None: No axes are locked.
    EDVLF_XY: The Y-axis is locked to the X-axis value.
    EDVLF_XZ: The Z-axis is locked to the X-axis value.
    EDVLF_YZ: The Z-axis is locked to the Y-axis value.
    EDVLF_XYZ: The Y-axis and Z-axis are locked to the X-axis value.
- **ParamMode Flag**
    DPM_Normal: Leave the input value alone.
    DPM_Abs: Use the absolute value of the input before remapping.
    DPM_Direct: Use the input value directly without remapping.

C The Curve Editor in Unreal Engine 4

THE contents of this appendix are adapted from the Unreal Engine 4's official documentations [10].

C.1 INTRODUCTION

The curve editor in Unreal Engine controls how properties change over time, such as distribution curves. The curve editor is heavily used in the **Cascade** particle editor and the **Matinee**.

C.2 CURVE EDITOR LAYOUT

You will see three sections in the Curve Editor. The top section is called the toolbar and contains tools useful in creating keyframes, in controlling the interpolation modes for each key and in panning and zooming of the curve along its vertical and horizontal axes.

The left section of the Curve Editor is called the Track list. The active tracks and curves in the editor are listed here. Float curves will have one small red square, while vector curves will have three small red, green, and blue squares indicating their type. You may click on each square to toggle the curve's visibility within the curve editor.

The right section of the Curve Editor is the graph. It is a graphical representation of the curve with time (input value) along the horizontal axis and the property value (output value) along the vertical axis. Keys along the curve are displayed as points which can be selected and manipulated to visually edit the curve. You may control the shape of the curve by dragging each keyframe and its tangents on the graph.

C.3 CURVE EDITOR CONTROLS

The following list gives you a tabular overview of the controls used in the Unreal Curve Editor [10]:

C.3.1 MOUSE CONTROLS

- **In Pan/Edit Mode**
  Left-Click +**Drag:** Pans the view
  Mouse Scroll: Zooms in and out
  Left-Click **on Key:** Selects point
  Control+Left-Click **on point:** Toggles selection of point

Control+Left-Click **on curve:** Adds new key at location
Control+Left-Click+**Drag:** Moves current selection
Control+Alt+Left-Click+**Drag:** Box selection
Control+Alt+Shift+Left-Click+**Drag:** Adds to current box selection

- **In Zoom Mode**
Left-Click+**Drag:** Zoom Y-axis
Right-Click+**Drag:** Zoom X-axis
Right-Click+Left-Click+**Drag:** Zoom X- and Y- axes

C.3.2   KEYBOARD CONTROLS

- **In Pan/Edit Mode**
Del: Deletes selected points
Z: Puts you into the zoom mode while held

C.3.3   SHORTCUTS

- **Hot Keys**
Control+Z: Undo
Control+Y: Redo

C.4   INTERPOLATION MODES

The interpolation mode buttons control the method each point on the curve will use to reach the next point. If you are using one of the curve modes (Auto, User, or Break), you will see white handles that you can click and drag to give you more control over the curve between points. If you select a key that is in Auto curve mode and adjust its tangents using the white handles, it will automatically convert to User curve mode [10].

Below are the available interpolation modes:

C.4.1   AUTO

This mode sets the curve keyframe to Bezier. However, it will make the incoming and outgoing tangents of the keyframe to be automatically calculated to result in a smooth Curve.

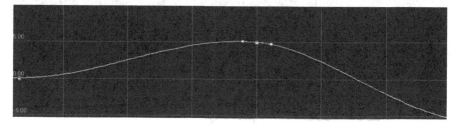

FIGURE C.1: Auto Keys.

C.4.2   AUTO CLAMPED

This mode sets the curve keyframe to Bezier. However, it will make the incoming and outgoing tangents of the keyframe to be automatically horizontal.

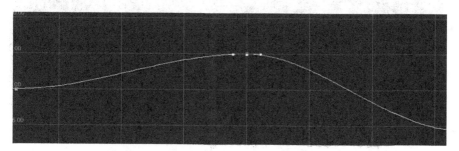

FIGURE C.2: Auto Clamped Keys.

C.4.3   USER

This mode sets the curve keyframe to Bezier. It will give the user the control over changing the incoming and outgoing tangents of the keyframe. However, the changes in one tangent will also change the other tangent to result in a smooth curve.

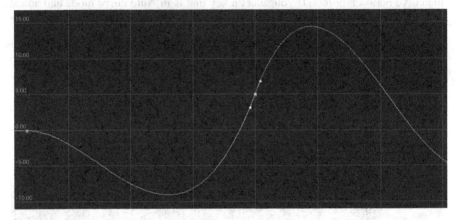

FIGURE C.3: User Keys.

C.4.4   BREAK

This mode sets the curve keyframe to Bezier-corner. It will give the user the control over changing the incoming and outgoing tangents of the keyframe. The user will be able to change the incoming and outgoing tangents of the keyframe independently.

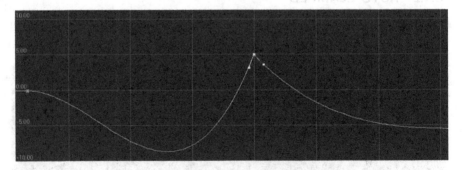

FIGURE C.4: Break Keys.

C.4.5   LINEAR

This mode sets the curve keyframe to Linear. The curve will become a line between this keyframe and the next keyframe.

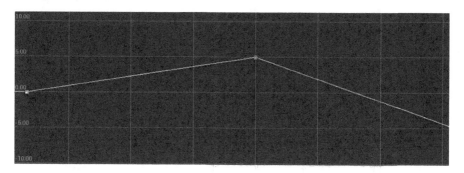

FIGURE C.5: Linear Keys.

C.4.6   CONSTANT

This mode sets the curve keyframe to Step. The curve will become a step between this keyframe and the next keyframe.

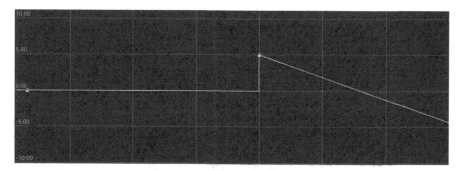

FIGURE C.6: Constant Keys.

References

1. Epic Games Inc.   Atmospheric Expressions: `https://docs.unrealengine.com/latest/INT/Engine/Rendering/Materials/ExpressionReference/Atmosphere/index.html`.

2. Epic Games Inc. Beam Type Data Reference: `https://docs.unrealengine.com/latest/INT/Engine/Rendering/ParticleSystems/Reference/TypeData/Beam/index.html`.

3. Epic Games Inc. Blueprint Communication Usage: `https://docs.unrealengine.com/latest/INT/Engine/Blueprints/UserGuide/BlueprintCommsUsage/index.html`.

4. Epic Games Inc. Blueprint Types: `https://docs.unrealengine.com/latest/INT/Engine/Blueprints/UserGuide/Types/index.html`.

5. Epic Games Inc. Color Expressions: `https://docs.unrealengine.com/latest/INT/Engine/Rendering/Materials/ExpressionReference/Color/index.html`.

6. Epic   Games   Inc.   Components   Mode   and   Components   List: `https://docs.unrealengine.com/latest/INT/Engine/Blueprints/UserGuide/Components/index.html`.

7. Epic   Games   Inc.   Constant   Expressions: `https://docs.unrealengine.com/latest/INT/Engine/Rendering/Materials/ExpressionReference/Constant/index.html`.

8. Epic Games Inc. Construction Script: `https://docs.unrealengine.com/latest/INT/Engine/Blueprints/UserGuide/UserConstructionScript/index.html`.

9. Epic   Games   Inc.   Coordinate   Expressions: `https://docs.unrealengine.com/latest/INT/Engine/Rendering/Materials/ExpressionReference/Coordinates/index.html`.

10. Epic Games Inc. Curve Editor in Unreal Engine 4: `https://docs.unrealengine.com/latest/INT/Engine/UI/CurveEditor/index.html`.

11. Epic   Games   Inc.   Decals: `https://docs.unrealengine.com/latest/INT/Resources/ContentExamples/Decals/index.html`.

12. Epic Games Inc. Depth Expressions: `https://docs.unrealengine.com/latest/INT/Engine/Rendering/Materials/ExpressionReference/Depth/index.html`.

13. Epic Games Inc. Distributiosn in Unreal Engine 4: `https://docs.unrealengine.com/latest/INT/Engine/Basics/Distributions/index.html`.

14. Epic Games Inc. Foliage System: `https://docs.unrealengine.com/latest/INT/Engine/Foliage/index.html`.

15. Epic Games Inc. Font Expressions: `https://docs.unrealengine.com/latest/INT/Engine/Rendering/Materials/ExpressionReference/Font/index.html`.

16. Epic Games Inc. Geometry Brush Refrence: `https://docs.unrealengine.com/latest/INT/Engine/Actors/Brushes/index.html`.

17. Epic Games Inc. GPU Type Data Motion: `https://docs.unrealengine.com/latest/INT/Engine/Rendering/ParticleSystems/Reference/TypeData/GPUSprites/index.html#motion`.

18. Epic Games Inc. GPU Type Data Performance: `https://docs.unrealengine.com/latest/INT/Engine/Rendering/ParticleSystems/Reference/TypeData/GPUSprites/index.html#performance`.

19. Epic Games Inc. GPU Type Data Reference: `https://docs.unrealengine.com/latest/INT/Engine/Rendering/ParticleSystems/Reference/TypeData/GPUSprites/index.html`.

20. Epic Games Inc. GPU Type Data Supported Attributes: `https://docs.unrealengine.com/latest/INT/Engine/Rendering/ParticleSystems/Reference/TypeData/GPUSprites/index.html#supportedattributes`.

21. Epic Games Inc. GPU Type Data Vector Fields: `https://docs.unrealengine.com/latest/INT/Engine/Rendering/ParticleSystems/Reference/TypeData/GPUSprites/index.html#vectorfields`.

22. Epic Games Inc. Graph Editor: `https://docs.unrealengine.com/latest/INT/Engine/Blueprints/Editor/UIComponents/GraphEditor/index.html`.

23. Epic Games Inc. Input Action & Axis Mapping in UE4: `https://www.unrealengine.com/blog/input-action-and-axis-mappings-in-ue4`.

24. Epic Games Inc. Input: `https://docs.unrealengine.com/latest/INT/Gameplay/Input/index.html`.

25. Epic Games Inc. Landscape Creation: `https://docs.unrealengine.com/latest/INT/Engine/Landscape/Creation/index.html`.

26. Epic Games Inc. Landscape Expressions: `https://docs.unrealengine.com/latest/INT/Engine/Rendering/Materials/ExpressionReference/index.html`.

27. Epic Games Inc. Landscape Manage Mode: `https://docs.unrealengine.com/latest/INT/Engine/Landscape/Editing/ManageMode/index.html`.

28. Epic Games Inc. Landscape Materials: `https://docs.unrealengine.com/latest/INT/Engine/Landscape/Materials/index.html`.

29. Epic Games Inc. Landscape Paint Mode: `https://docs.unrealengine.com/latest/INT/Engine/Landscape/Editing/PaintMode/index.html`.

30. Epic Games Inc. Landscape Sculpt Mode: `https://docs.unrealengine.com/latest/INT/Engine/Landscape/Materials/index.html`.

31. Epic Games Inc. Landscape Splines: `https://docs.unrealengine.com/latest/INT/Engine/Landscape/Editing/Splines/index.html`.

32. Epic Games Inc. Layered Materials: `https://docs.unrealengine.com/latest/INT/Engine/Rendering/Materials/LayeredMaterials/index.html`.

33. Epic Games Inc. Level Blueprint: `https://docs.unrealengine.com/latest/INT/Engine/Blueprints/UserGuide/Types/LevelBlueprint/index.html`.

34. Epic Games Inc. Material Attribute Expressions: `https://docs.unrealengine.com/latest/INT/Engine/Rendering/Materials/ExpressionReference/MaterialAttributes/index.html`.

35. Epic Games Inc. Material Blend Modes in Unreal Engine 4: `https://docs.unrealengine.com/latest/INT/Engine/Rendering/Materials/MaterialProperties/BlendModes/index.html`.

36. Epic Games Inc. Material Expressions Reference: `https://docs.unrealengine.com/latest/INT/Engine/Rendering/Materials/ExpressionReference/index.html`.

37. Epic Games Inc. Material Function Expressions: `https://docs.unrealengine.com/latest/INT/Engine/Rendering/Materials/ExpressionReference/`

Functions/index.html.

38. Epic Games Inc. Material Functions: `https://docs.unrealengine.com/latest/INT/Engine/Rendering/Materials/Functions/index.html`.

39. Epic Games Inc. Material Propeties: `https://docs.unrealengine.com/latest/INT/Engine/Rendering/Materials/MaterialProperties/index.html`.

40. Epic Games Inc. Math Expressions: `https://docs.unrealengine.com/latest/INT/Engine/Rendering/Materials/ExpressionReference/Math/index.html`.

41. Epic Games Inc. Mesh Type Data Reference: `https://docs.unrealengine.com/latest/INT/Engine/Rendering/ParticleSystems/Reference/TypeData/Mesh/index.html`.

42. Epic Games Inc. Parameter Expressions: `https://docs.unrealengine.com/latest/INT/Engine/Rendering/Materials/ExpressionReference/Parameters/index.html`.

43. Epic Games Inc. Particle Expressions: `https://docs.unrealengine.com/latest/INT/Engine/Rendering/Materials/ExpressionReference/Particles/index.html`.

44. Epic Games Inc. Particle System Reference: `https://docs.unrealengine.com/latest/INT/Engine/Rendering/ParticleSystems/Reference/index.html`.

45. Epic Games Inc. Particle Systems Overview: `https://docs.unrealengine.com/latest/INT/Engine/Rendering/ParticleSystems/Overview/index.html`.

46. Epic Games Inc. Physically Based Materials: `https://docs.unrealengine.com/latest/INT/Engine/Rendering/Materials/PhysicallyBased/index.html#karis`.

47. Epic Games Inc. Ribbon Type Data Reference: `https://docs.unrealengine.com/latest/INT/Engine/Rendering/ParticleSystems/Reference/TypeData/Ribbon/index.html`.

48. Epic Games Inc. Texture Expressions: `https://docs.unrealengine.com/latest/INT/Engine/Rendering/Materials/ExpressionReference/Textures/index.html`.

49. Epic Games Inc. Unreal Engine 4 Shading Models: `https://docs.unrealengine.com/latest/INT/Engine/Rendering/Materials/MaterialProperties/LightingModels/index.html`.

50. Epic Games Inc. Unreal Engine 4 Supsurface Profile Shading Models: `https://docs.unrealengine.com/latest/INT/Engine/Rendering/Materials/LightingModels/SubSurfaceProfile/index.html`.

51. Epic Games Inc. Utility Expressions: `https://docs.unrealengine.com/latest/INT/Engine/Rendering/Materials/ExpressionReference/Utility/index.html`.

52. Epic Games Inc. Vector Operation Expressions: `https://docs.unrealengine.com/latest/INT/Engine/Rendering/Materials/ExpressionReference/VectorOps/index.html`.

53. Jorge Jimenez, Timothy Scully, Nuno Barbosa, Craig Donner, Xenxo Alvarez, Teresa Vieira, Paul Matts, Verónica Orvalho, Diego Gutierrez, and Tim Weyrich. A practical appearance model for dynamic facial color. *ACM Transactions on Graphics (Proc. SIGGRAPH Asia)*, 29(6):141:1–141:10, 2010.

54. Brian Karis. Real shading in Unreal Engine 4. In *SIGGRAPH 2013 Course: Physically Based Shading in Theory and Practice*, 2013. Available from `http://blog.selfshadow.com/publications/s2013-shading-course/`

karis/s2013_pbs_epic_notes_v2.pdf.

55. SIGGRAPH.   Physically Based Shading Model in Theory and Prac-
    tice: `http://s2013.siggraph.org/attendees/courses/session/`
    `physically-based-shading-theory-and-practice`.

Index